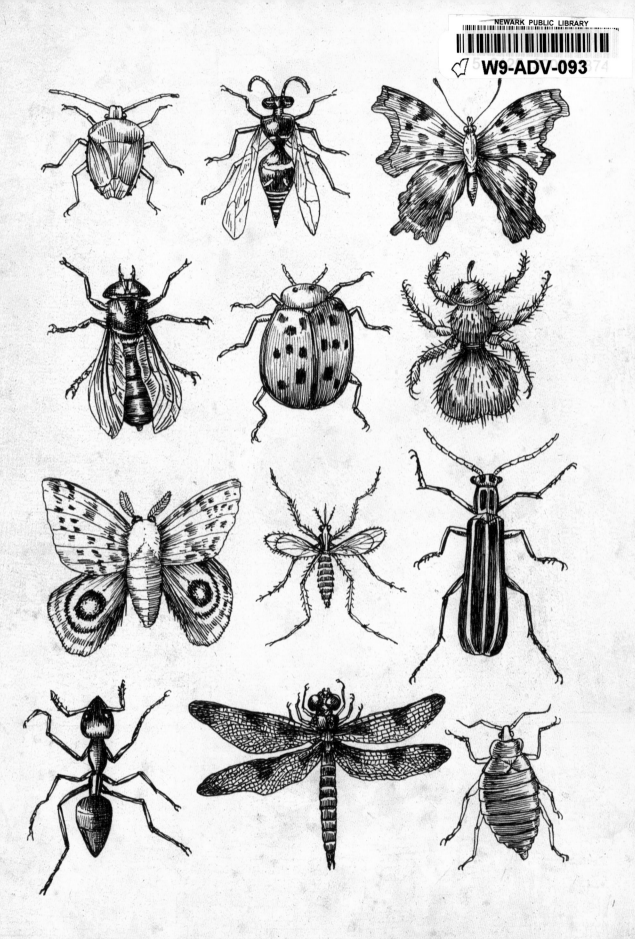

Dedicated to
pollinators everywhere.

First published 2015
by SelfMadeHero
139-141 Pancras Road
London NW1 1UN
www.selfmadehero.com

© 2015 SelfMadeHero

Written and Illustrated by: Peter Kuper
Edited by: Dan Lockwood

Publishing Assistant: Guillaume Rater
Sales & Marketing Manager: Sam Humphrey
UK Publicist: Paul Smith
US Publicist: Maya Bradford
Publishing Director: Emma Hayley
Designer: Kate McLauchlan

Author photo © Holly Kuper 2014
Cover art and book design by Peter Kuper
© Peter Kuper 2015
www.peterkuper.com

A CIP record for this book is available from the British Library

ISBN: 978-1-906838-98-0

10 9 8 7 6 5 4 3 2 1

Printed and bound in China

RUINS

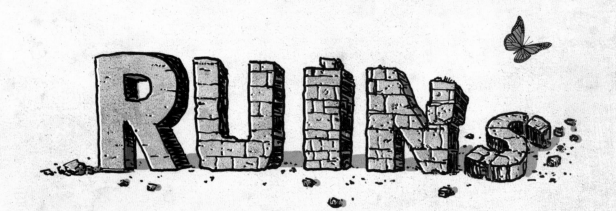

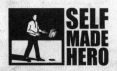

SELF MADE HERO

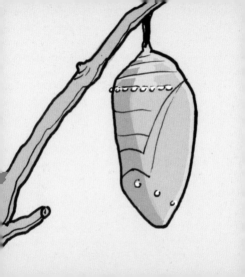

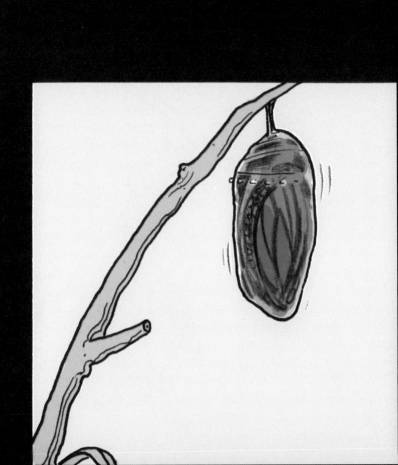

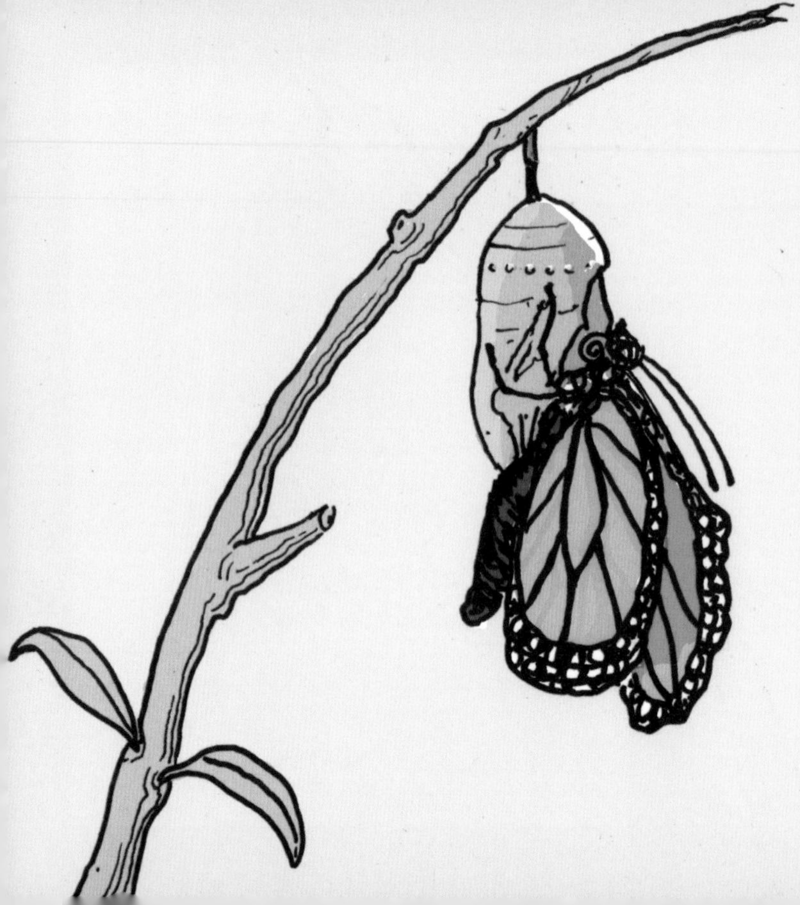

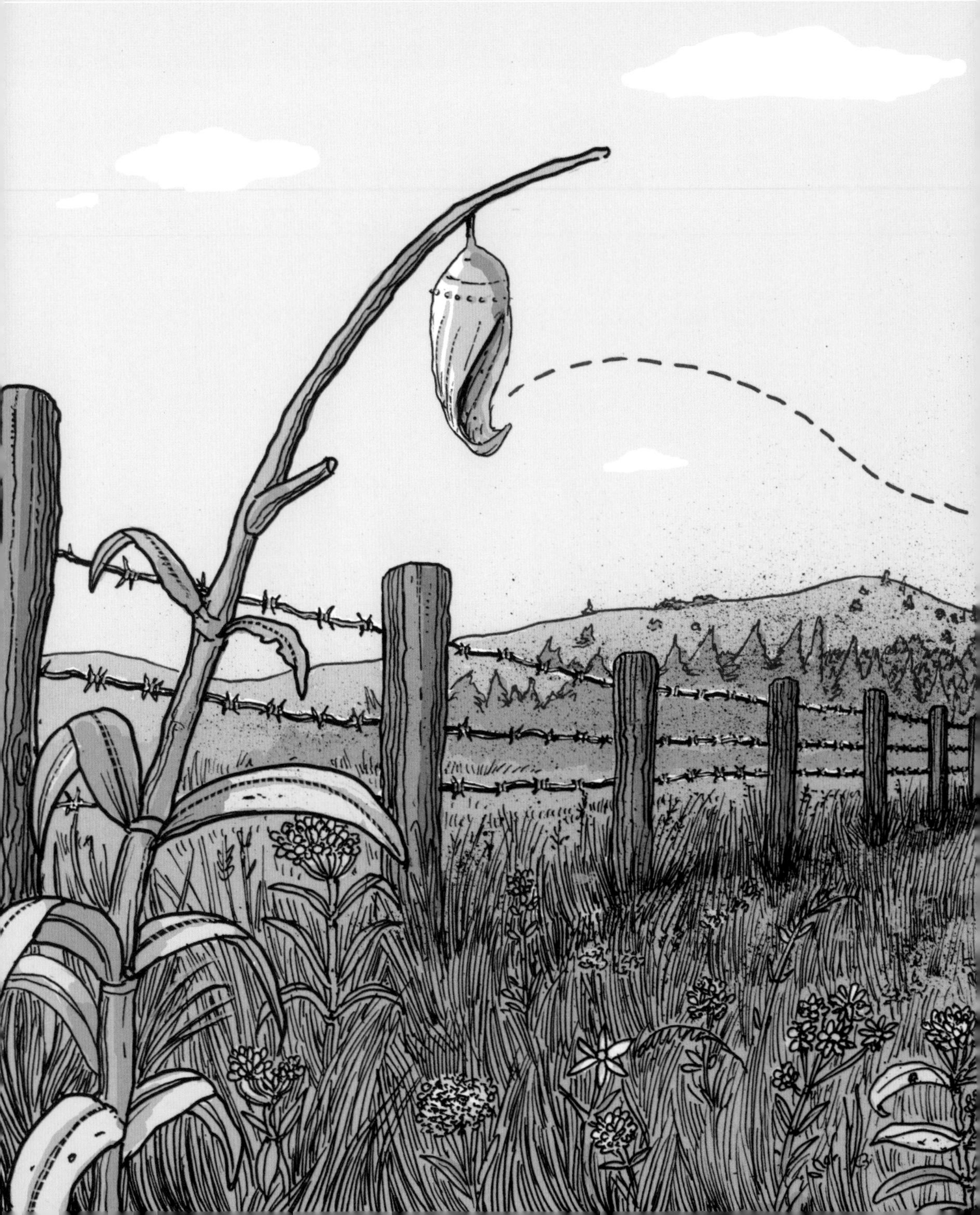

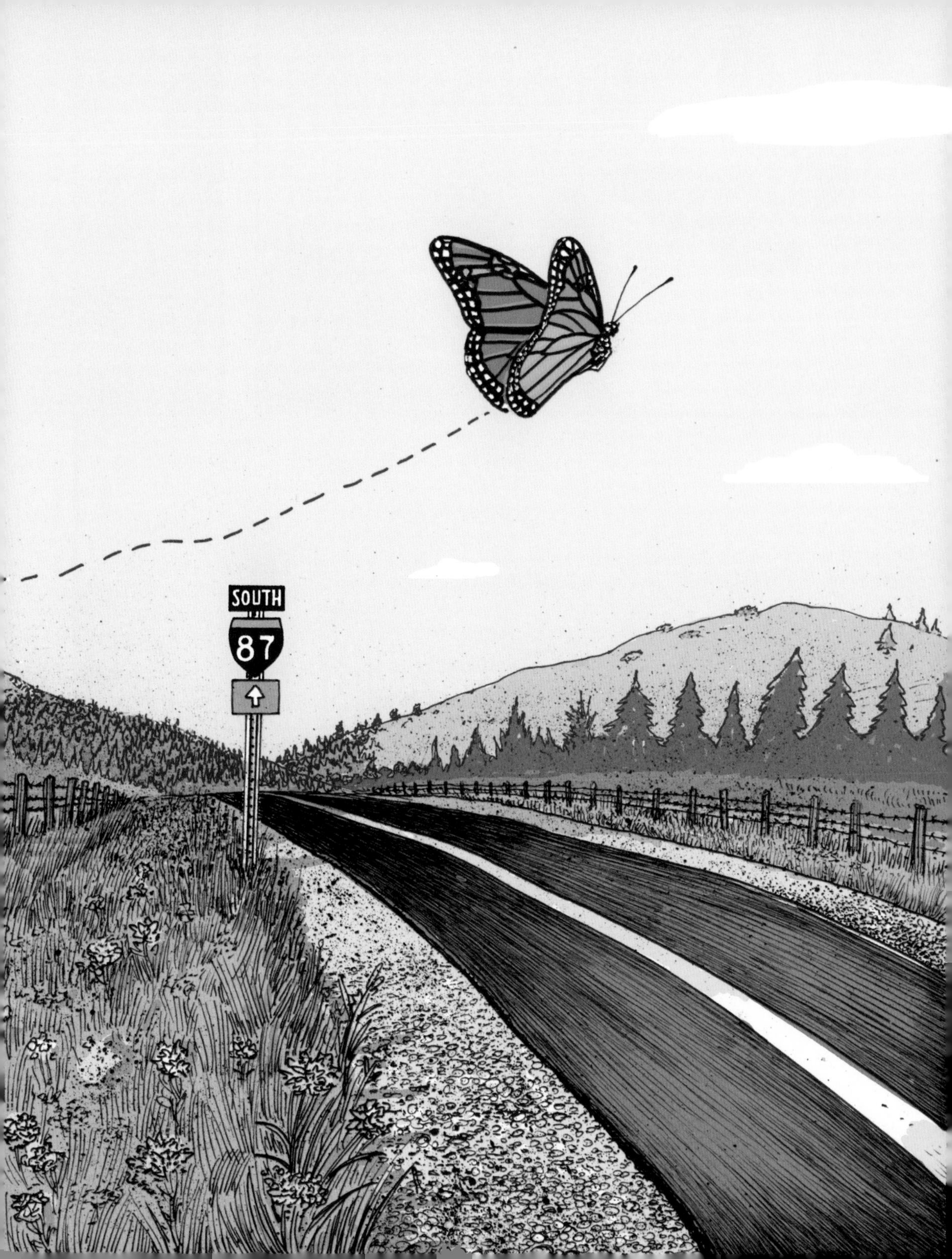
SOUTH
87

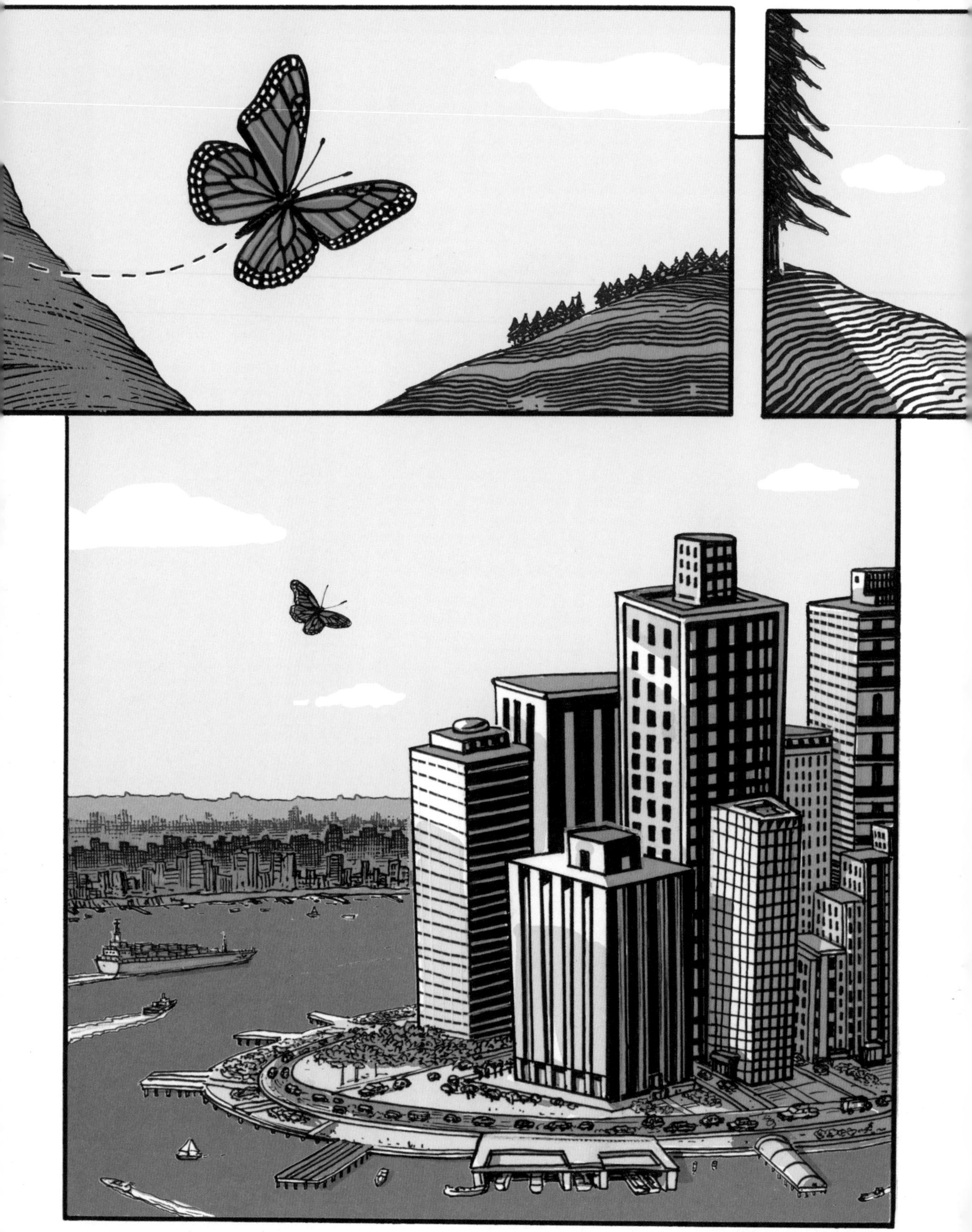

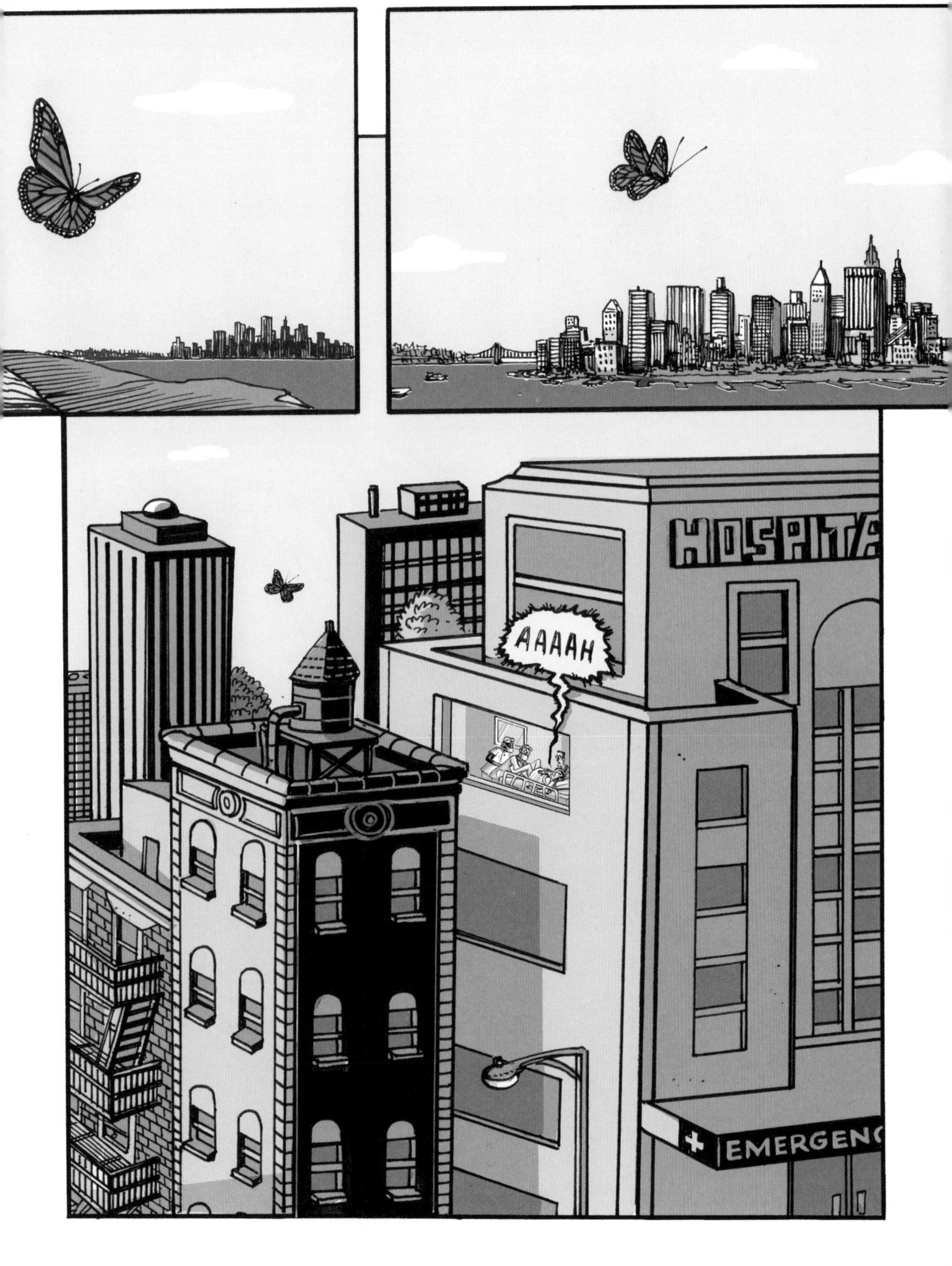
HOSPITA
AAAAH
EMERGENC

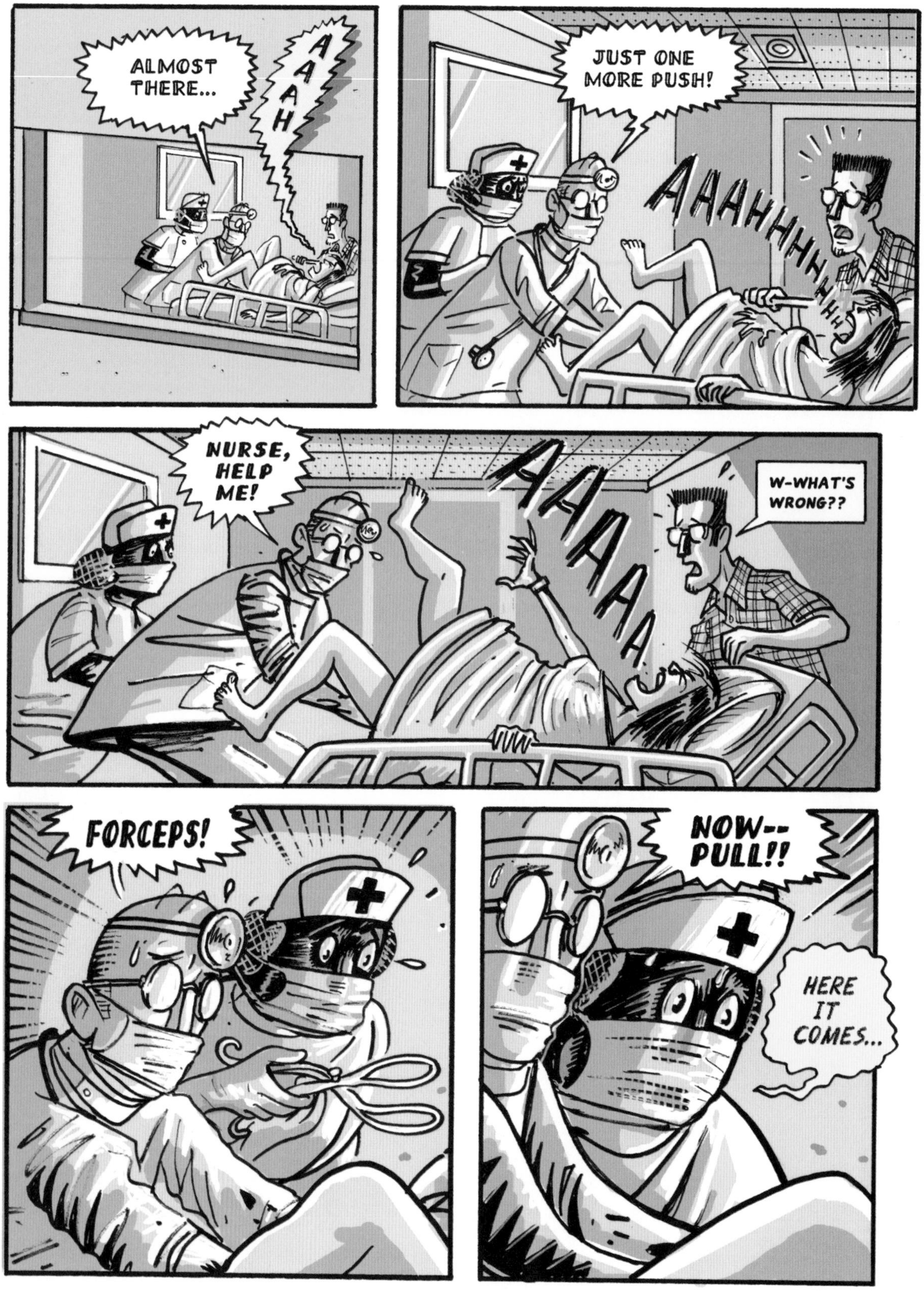
ALMOST THERE...
AAAH
JUST ONE MORE PUSH!
AAAHHHHHHHH
NURSE, HELP ME!
AAAAAAA
W-WHAT'S WRONG??
FORCEPS!
NOW-- PULL!!
HERE IT COMES...

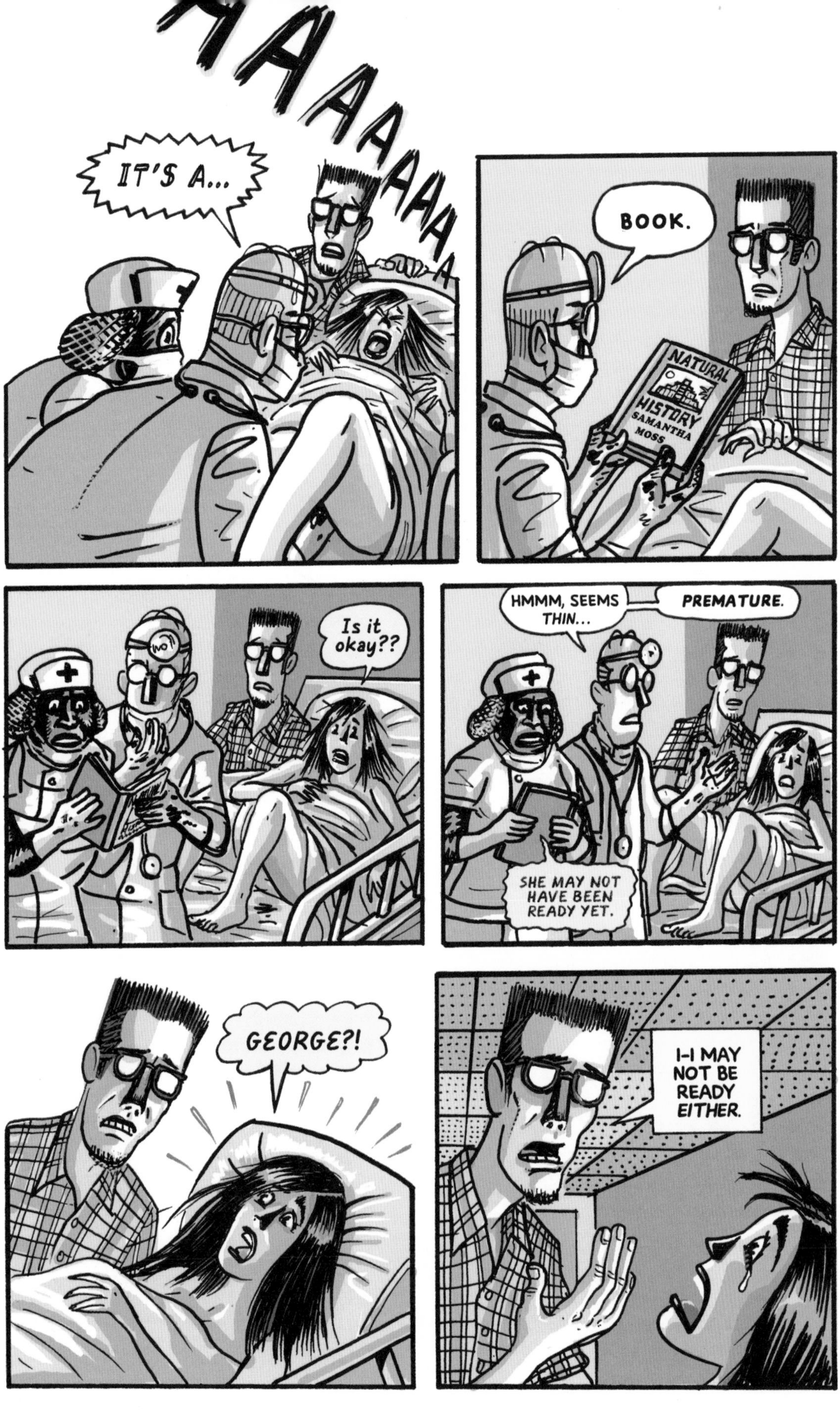
AAAAAAAAA
IT'S A...
BOOK.
NATURAL HISTORY
SAMANTHA MOSS
Is it okay??
HMMM, SEEMS THIN...
PREMATURE.
SHE MAY NOT HAVE BEEN READY YET.
GEORGE?!
I-I MAY NOT BE READY EITHER.

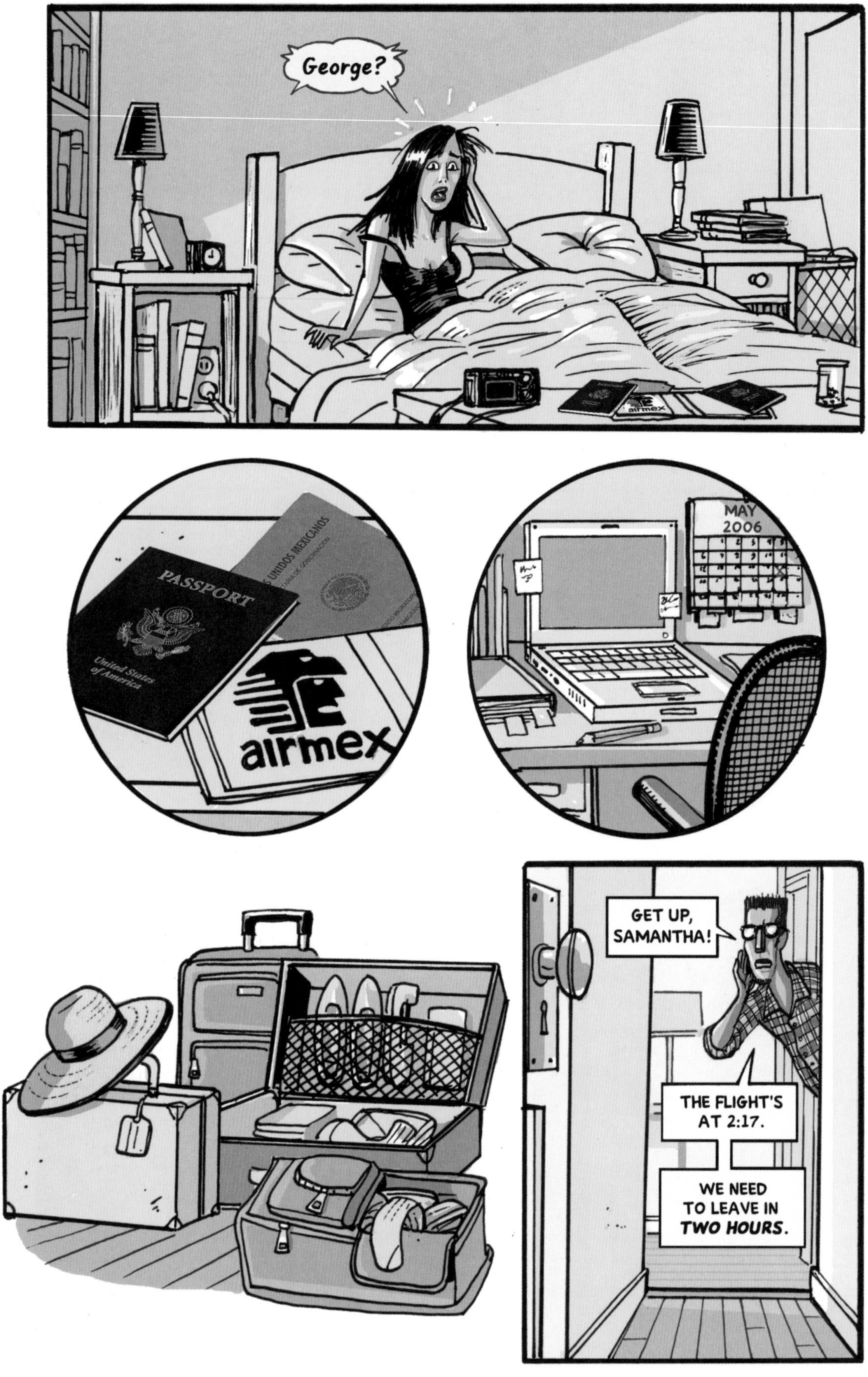
George?
PASSPORT
United States of America
S UNIDOS MEXICANOS
airmex
MAY 2006
GET UP, SAMANTHA!
THE FLIGHT'S AT 2:17.
WE NEED TO LEAVE IN *TWO HOURS*.

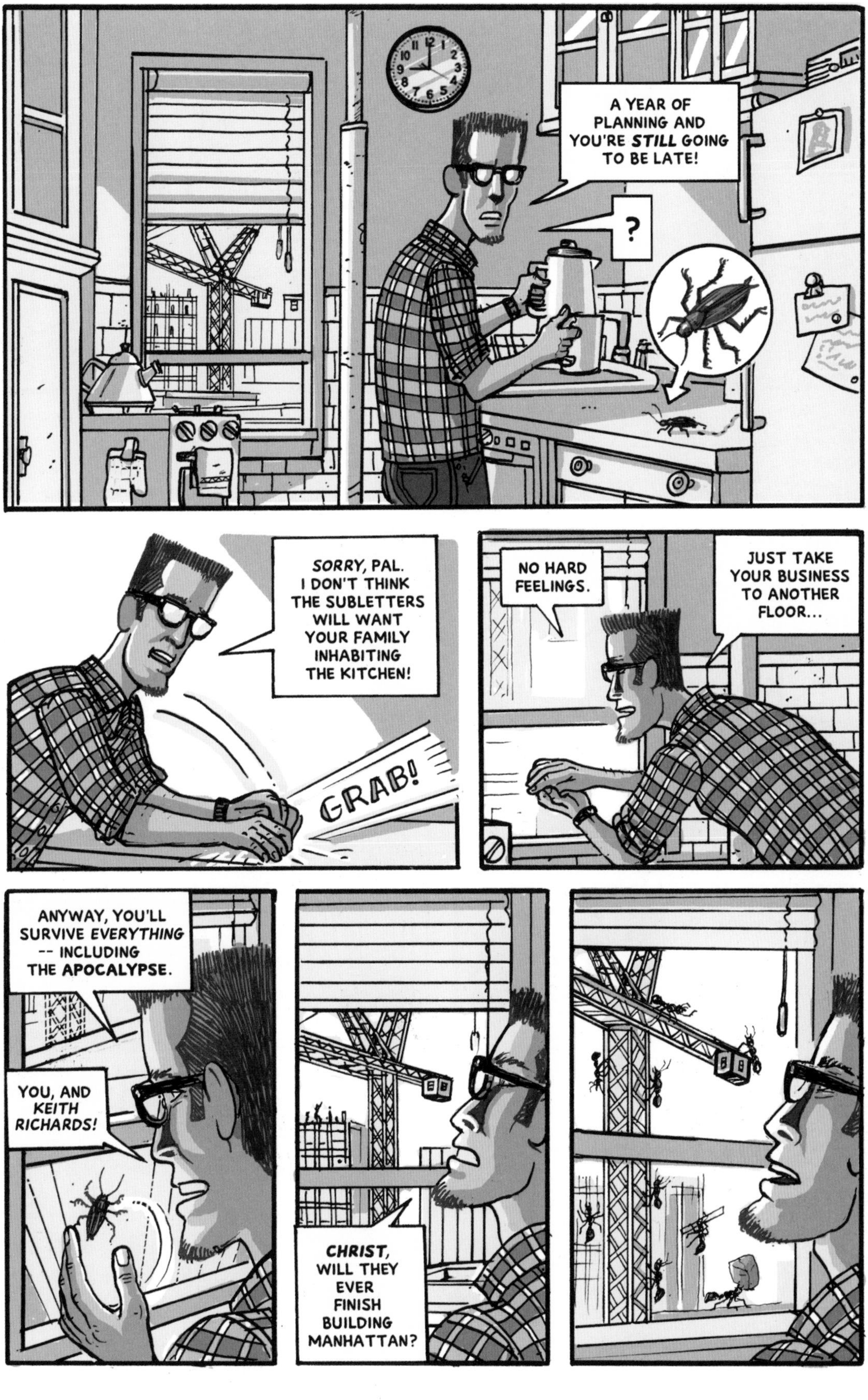
A YEAR OF PLANNING AND YOU'RE *STILL* GOING TO BE LATE!
?
SORRY, PAL. I DON'T THINK THE SUBLETTERS WILL WANT YOUR FAMILY INHABITING THE KITCHEN!
GRAB!
NO HARD FEELINGS.
JUST TAKE YOUR BUSINESS TO ANOTHER FLOOR...
ANYWAY, YOU'LL SURVIVE *EVERYTHING* -- INCLUDING THE **APOCALYPSE**.
YOU, AND *KEITH RICHARDS!*
CHRIST, WILL THEY EVER FINISH BUILDING MANHATTAN?

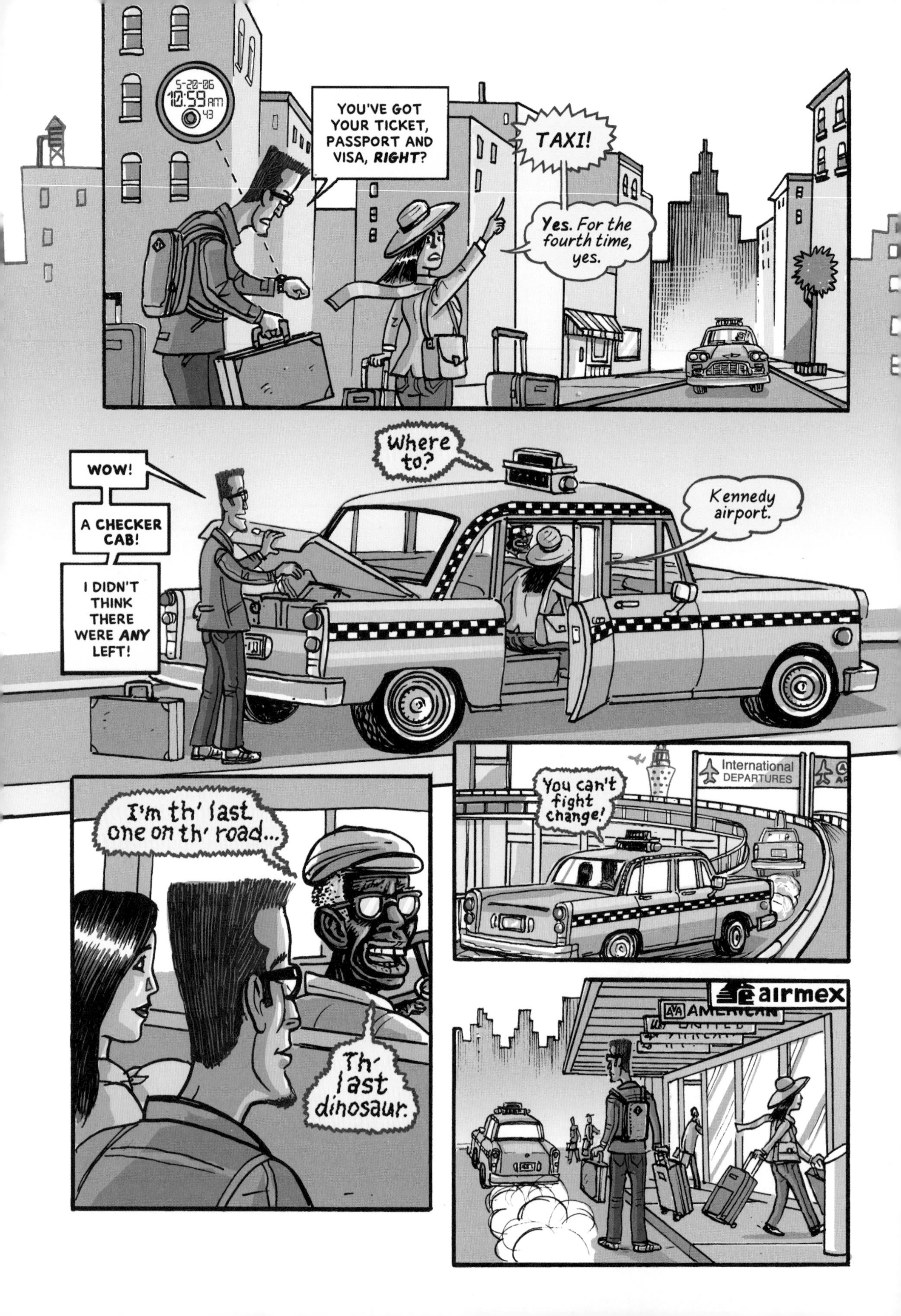
5-20-06
10:59 AM
43
YOU'VE GOT YOUR TICKET, PASSPORT AND VISA, *RIGHT*?
TAXI!
Yes. For the fourth time, yes.
WOW!
A CHECKER CAB!
I DIDN'T THINK THERE WERE *ANY* LEFT!
Where to?
Kennedy airport.
I'm th' last one on th' road...
Th' last dinosaur.
International DEPARTURES
You can't fight change!
airmex
AMERICAN

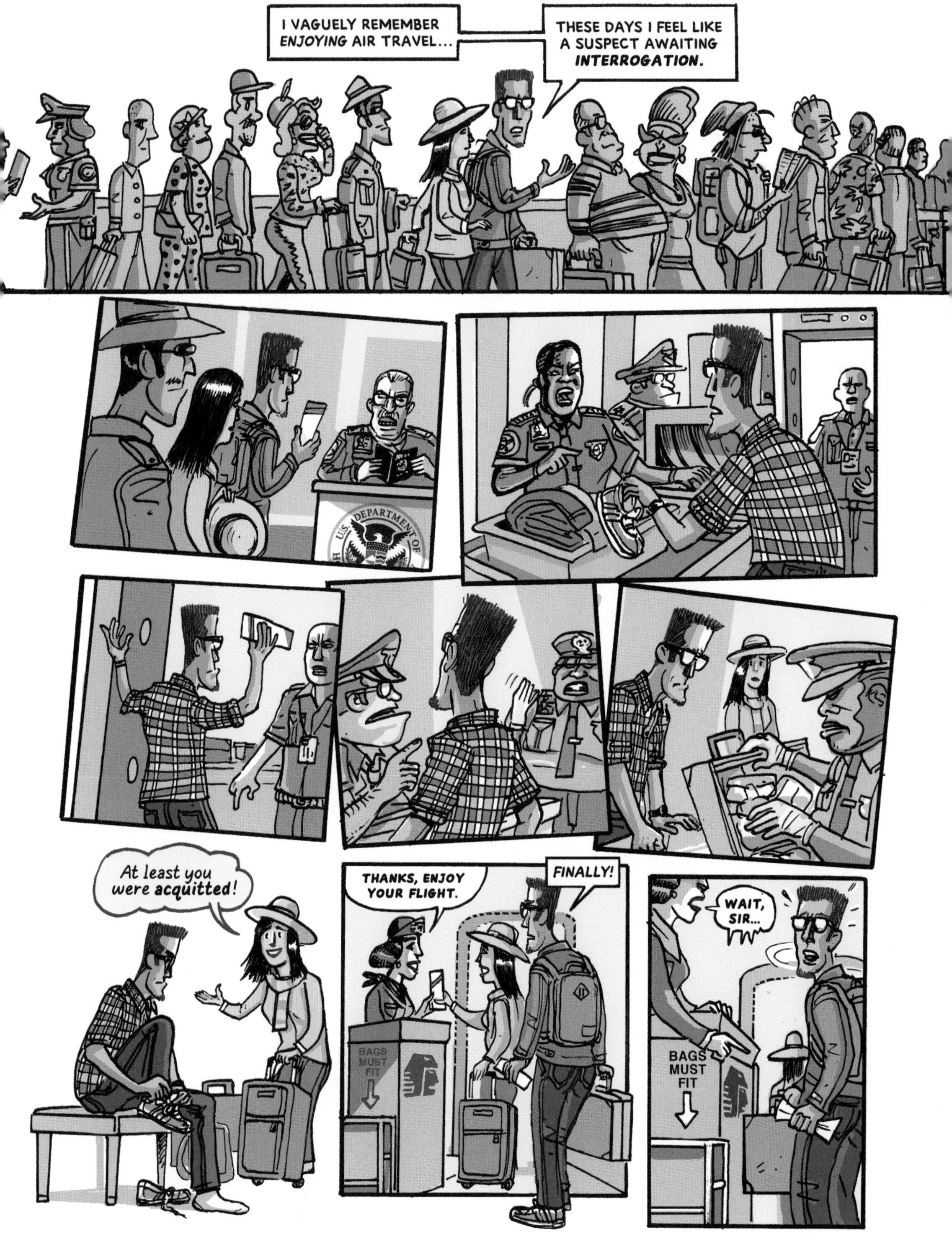
I VAGUELY REMEMBER ENJOYING AIR TRAVEL...
THESE DAYS I FEEL LIKE A SUSPECT AWAITING INTERROGATION.
At least you were acquitted!
THANKS, ENJOY YOUR FLIGHT.
BAGS MUST FIT
FINALLY!
WAIT, SIR...
BAGS MUST FIT

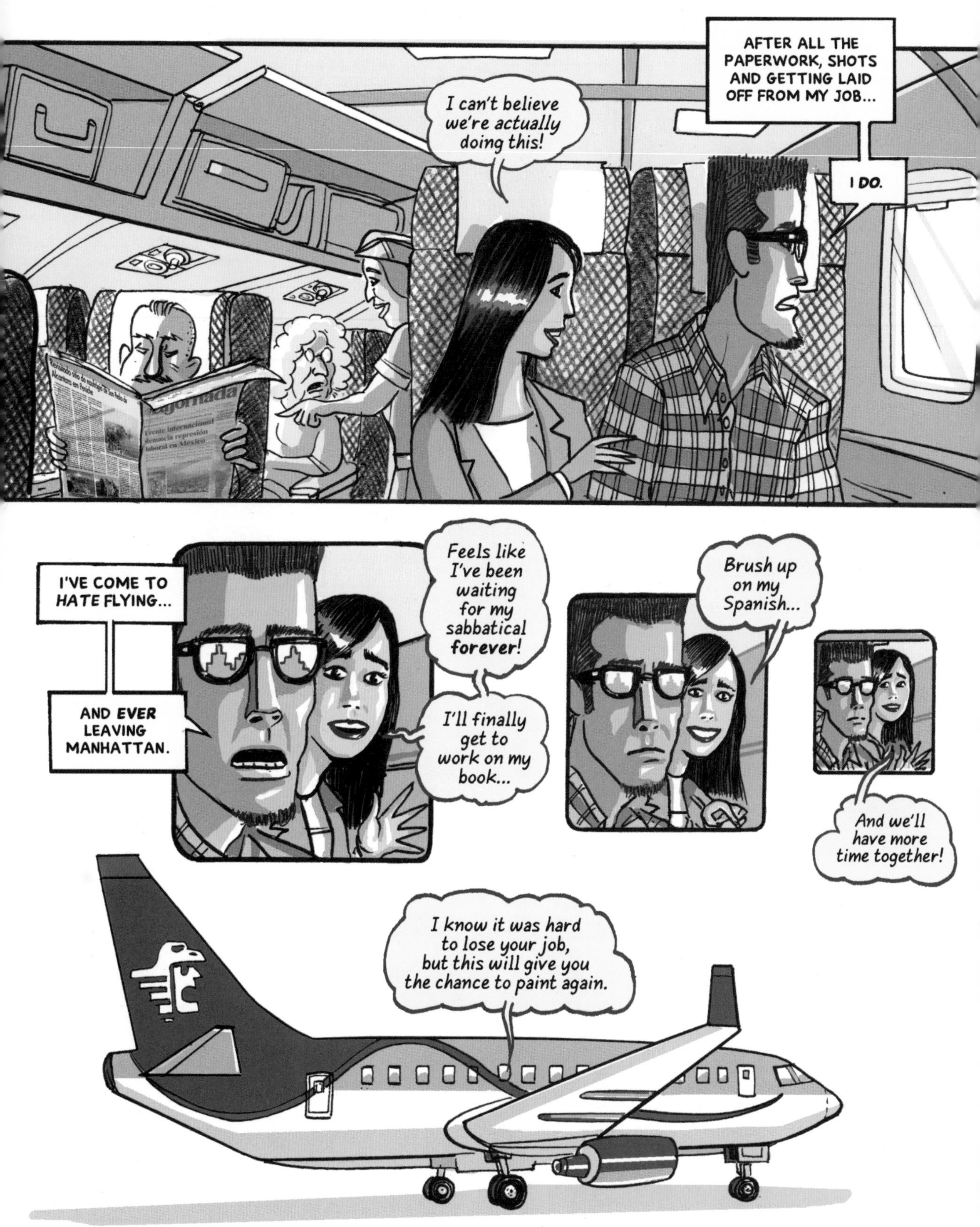
AFTER ALL THE PAPERWORK, SHOTS AND GETTING LAID OFF FROM MY JOB...
I can't believe we're actually doing this!
I DO.
Frente internacional denuncia represión laboral en México
I'VE COME TO HATE FLYING...
AND EVER LEAVING MANHATTAN.
Feels like I've been waiting for my sabbatical forever!
I'll finally get to work on my book...
Brush up on my Spanish...
And we'll have more time together!
I know it was hard to lose your job, but this will give you the chance to paint again.

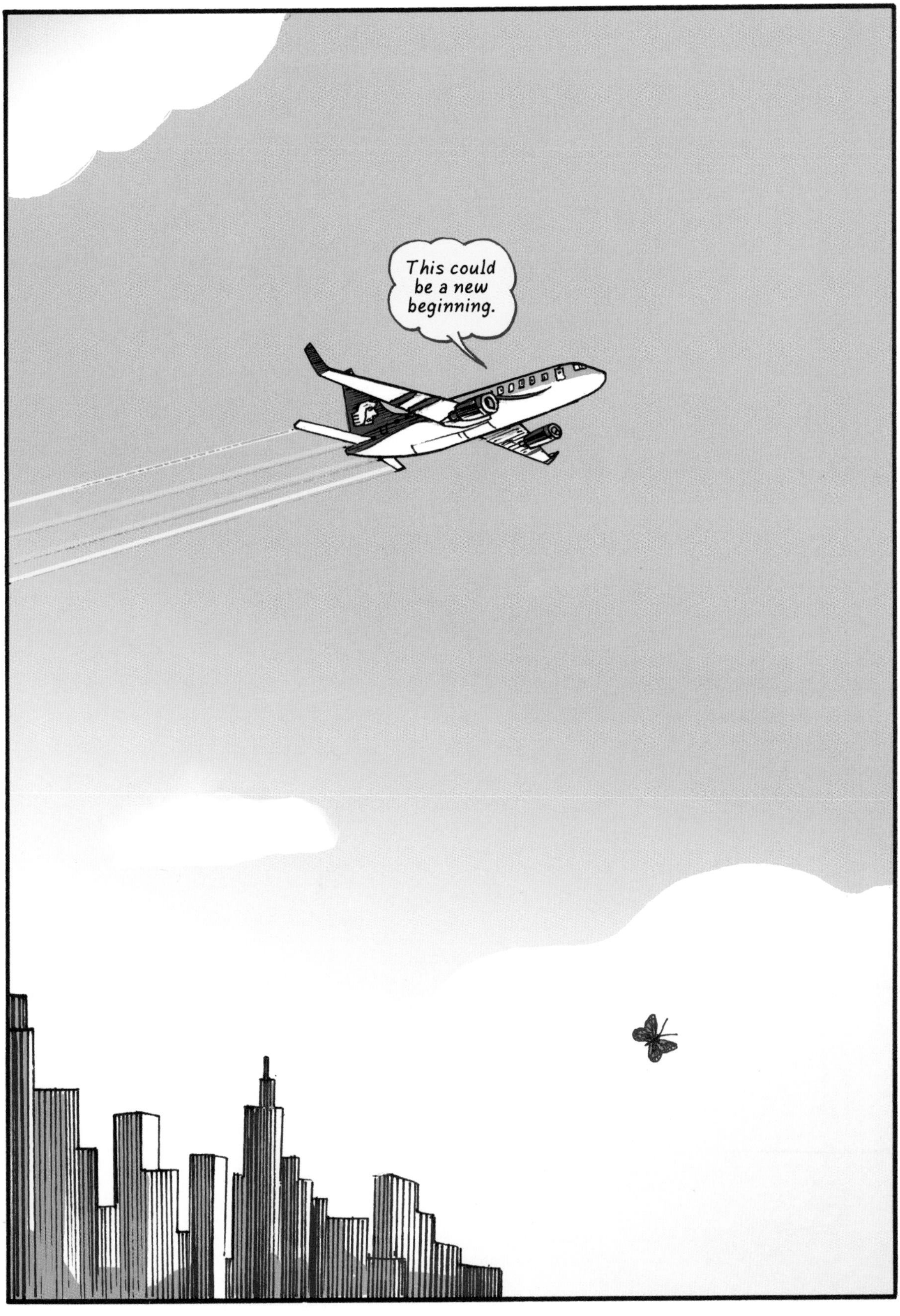
This could be a new beginning.

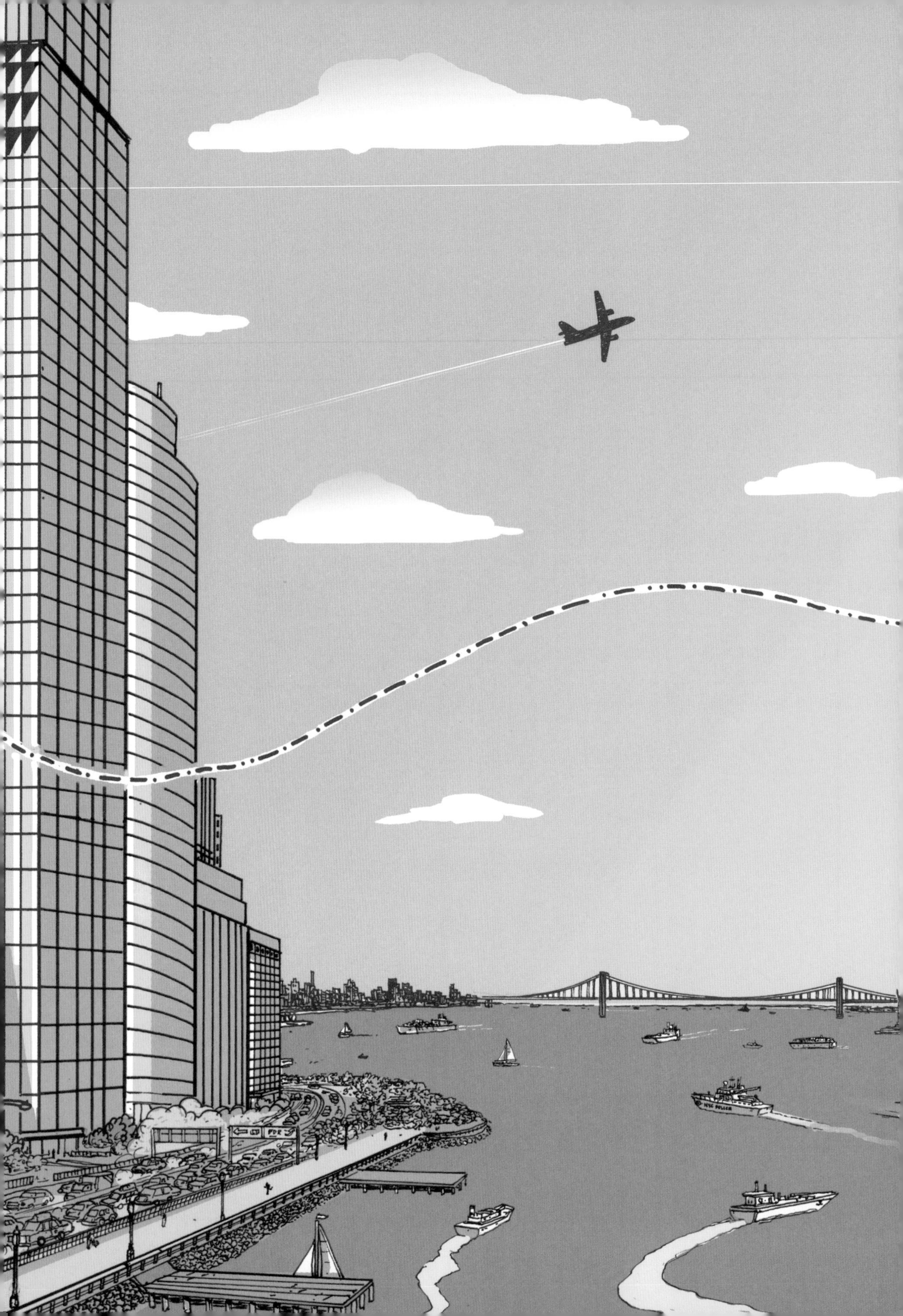

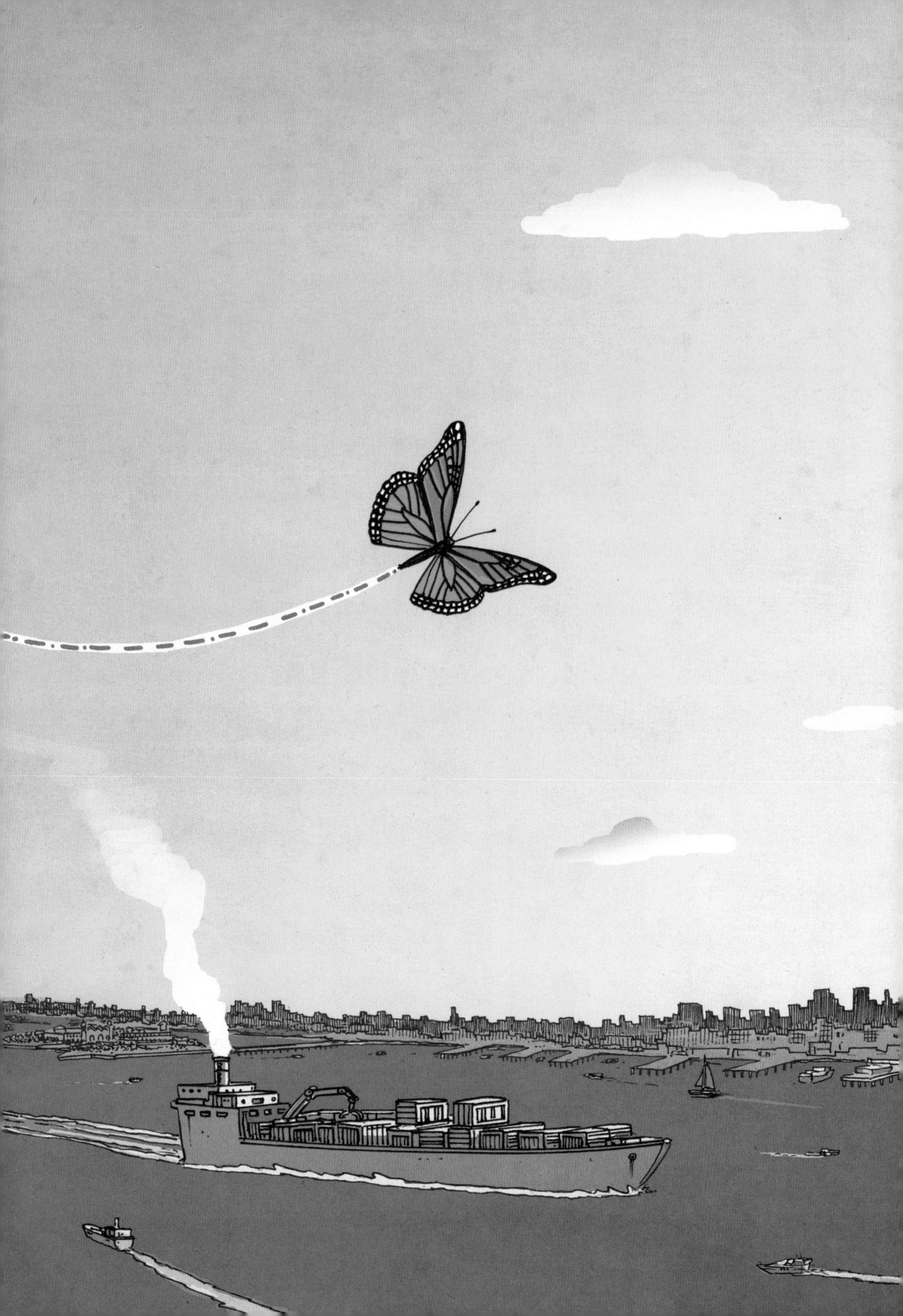

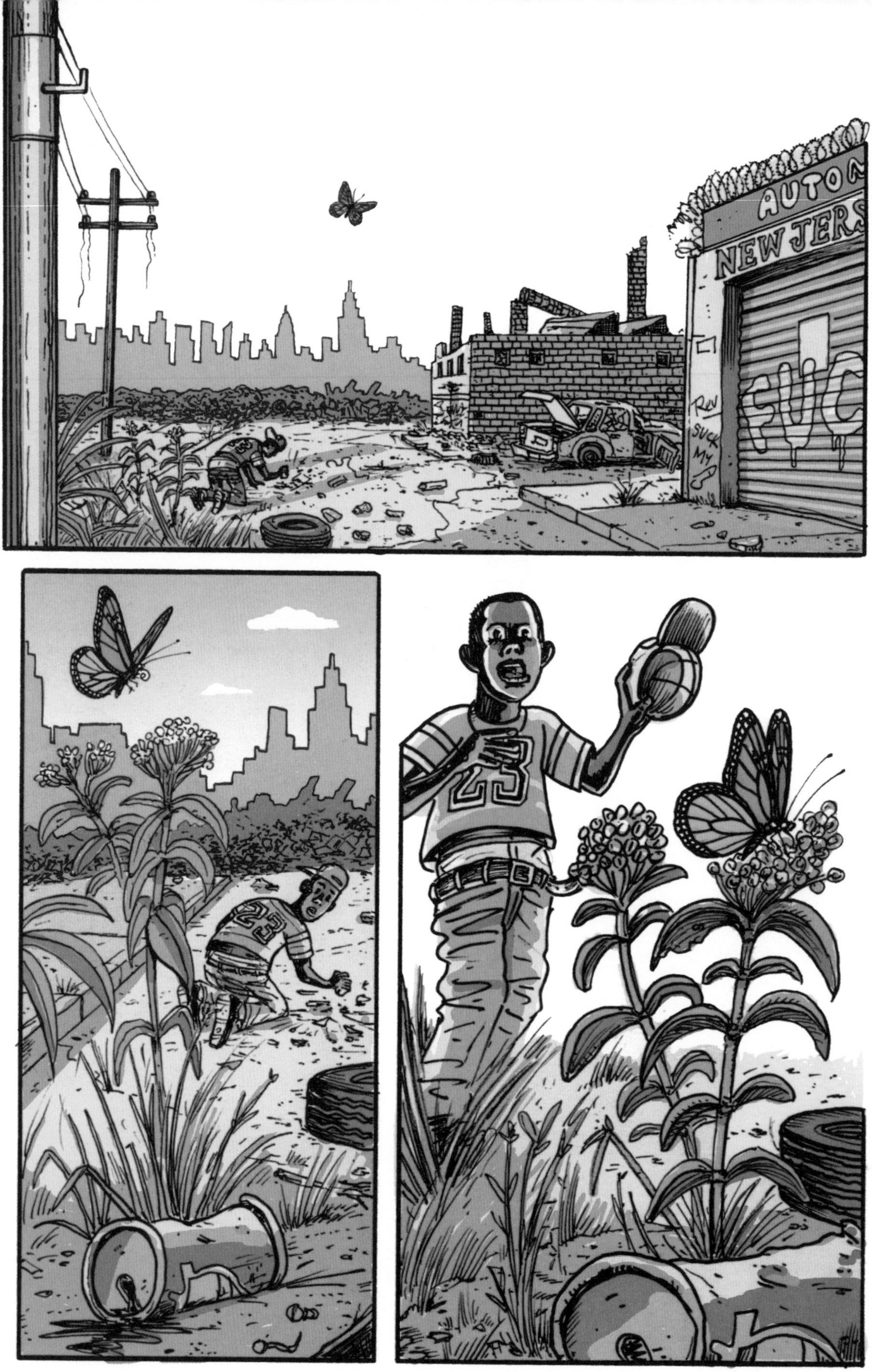
AUTO
NEW JERS
REV
SUCK
MY

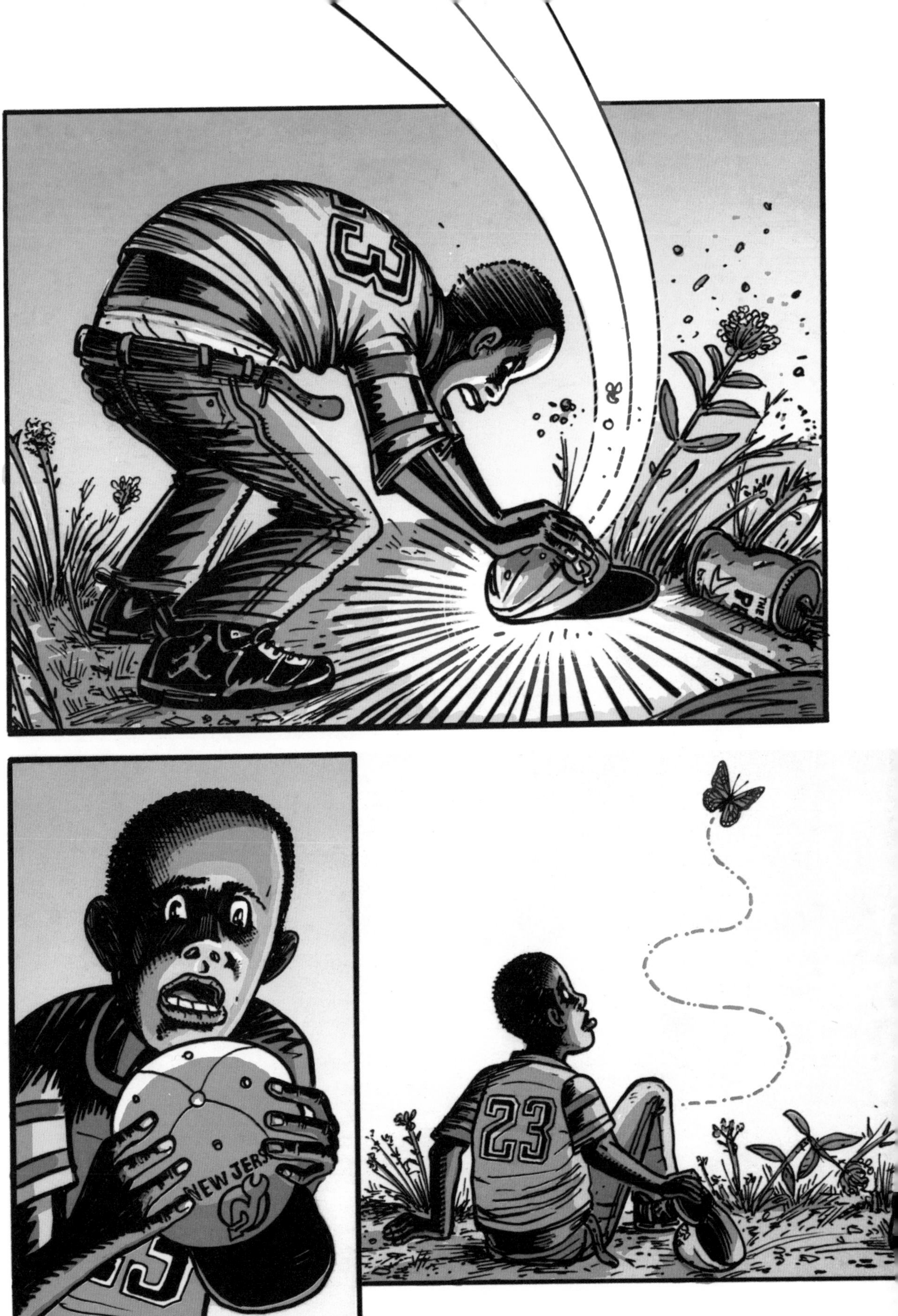
NEW JERS
23

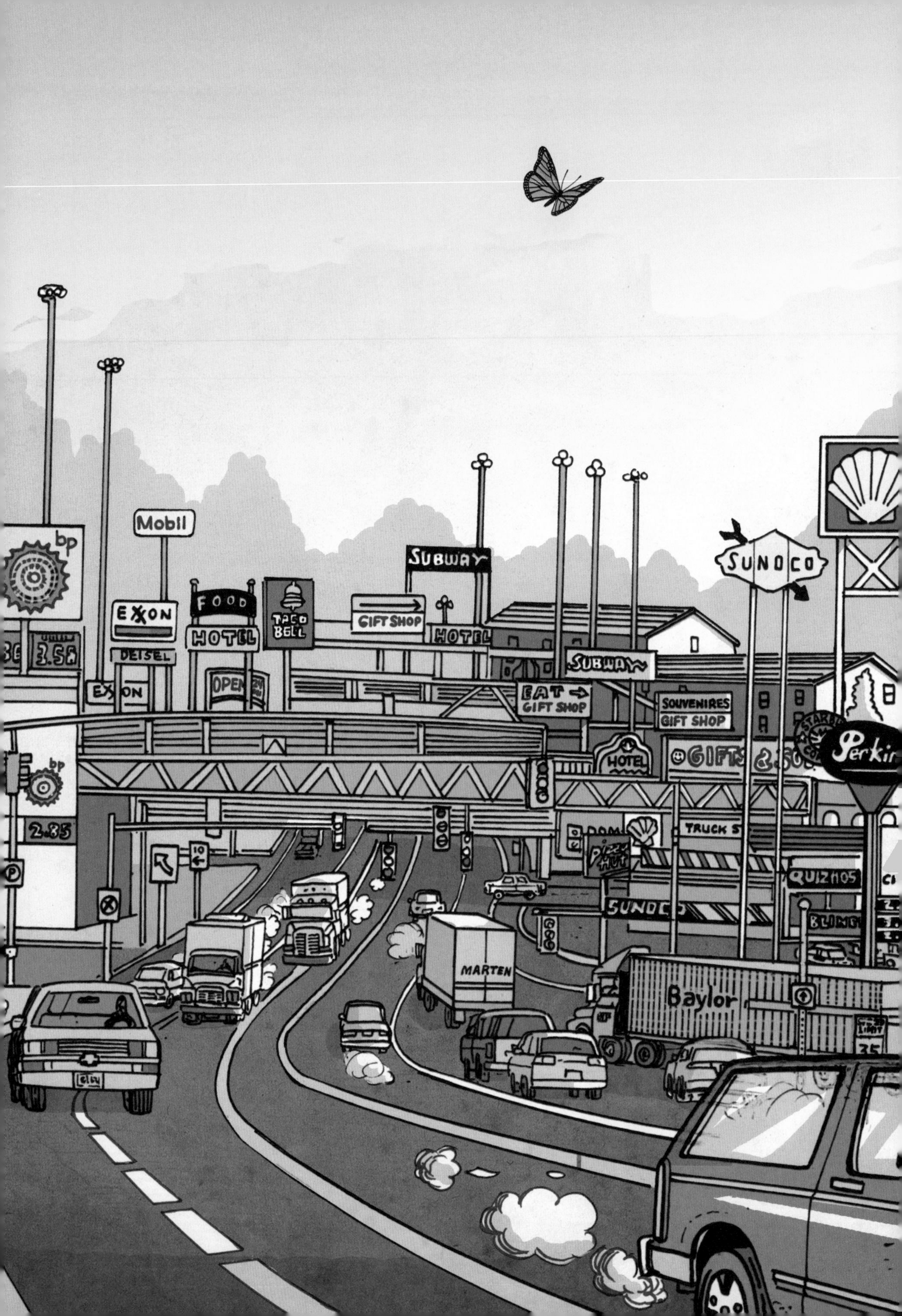

bp
Mobil
EXXON
3.58
DEISEL
EXXON
FOOD
HOTEL
TACO BELL
OPEN
SUBWAY
GIFT SHOP
HOTEL
SUBWAY
EAT
GIFT SHOP
SOUVENIRES
GIFT SHOP
HOTEL
SUNOCO
bp
2.85
QUIZNOS
MARTEN
Baylor
35

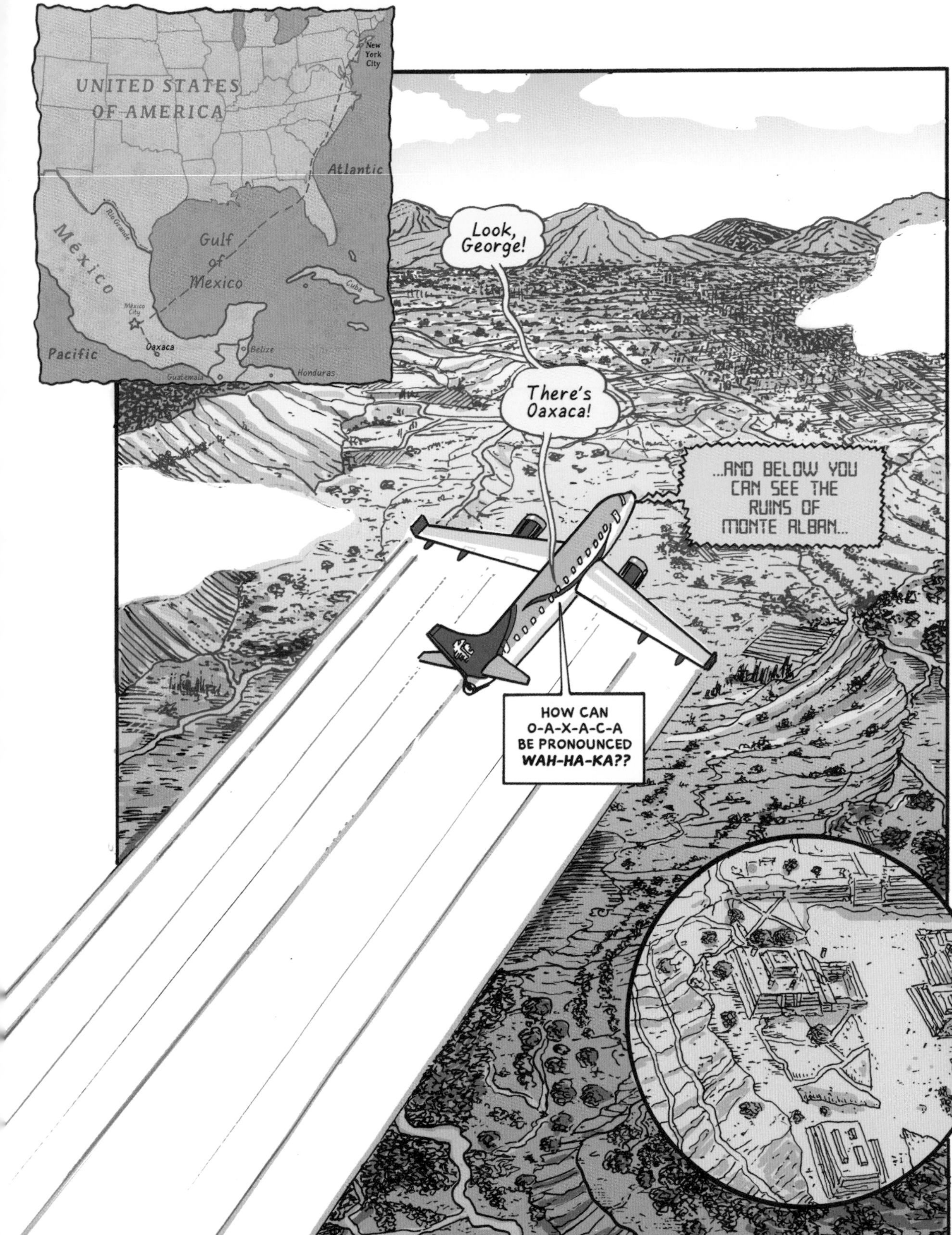
New York City
UNITED STATES OF AMERICA
Atlantic
México
Rio Grande
Gulf of Mexico
Cuba
México City
Oaxaca
Belize
Pacific
Guatemala
Honduras
Look, George!
There's Oaxaca!
...AND BELOW YOU CAN SEE THE RUINS OF MONTE ALBAN...
HOW CAN O-A-X-A-C-A BE PRONOUNCED **WAH-HA-KA??**

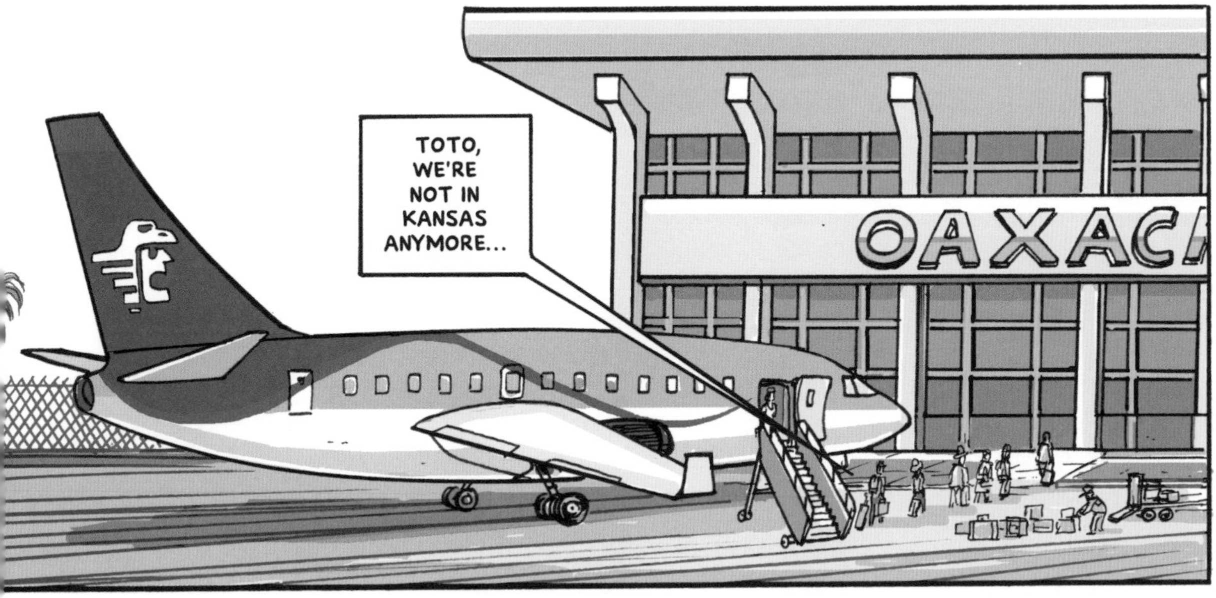
TOTO, WE'RE NOT IN KANSAS ANYMORE...
OAXACA

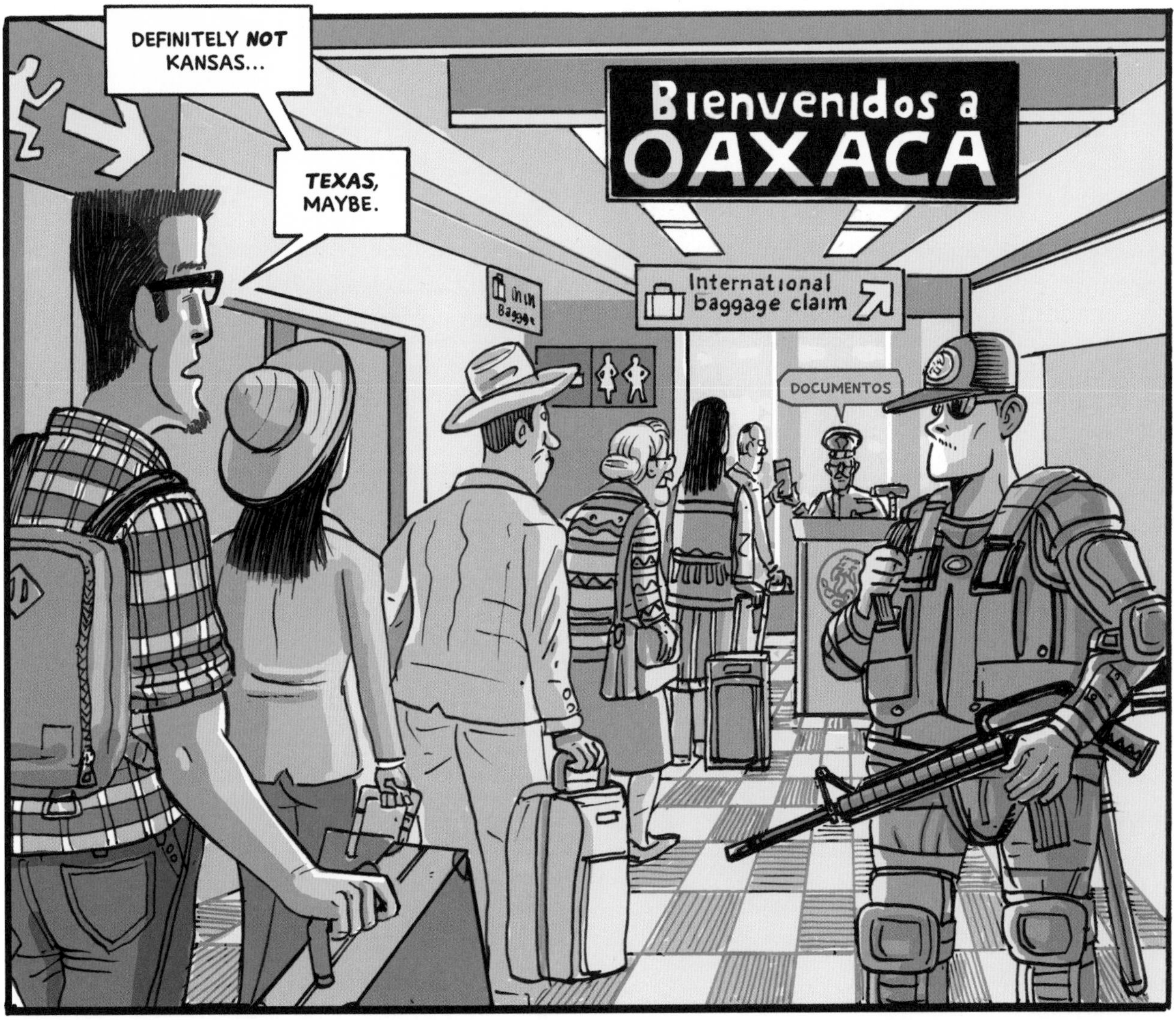
DEFINITELY **NOT** KANSAS...
TEXAS, MAYBE.
Bienvenidos a OAXACA
International baggage claim
DOCUMENTOS

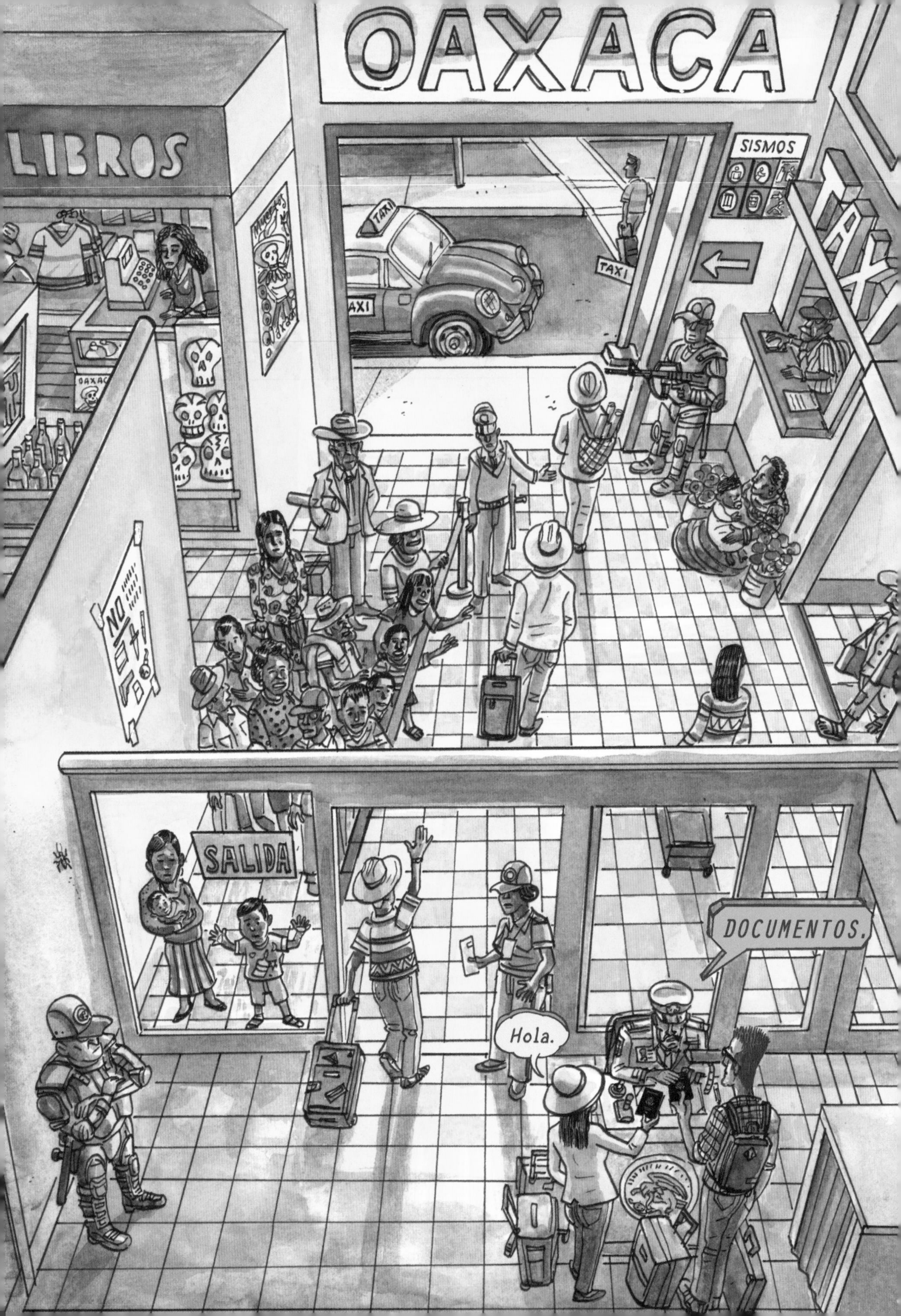
OAXACA
LIBROS
SISMOS
TAXI
TAXI
NO
SALIDA
DOCUMENTOS.
Hola.

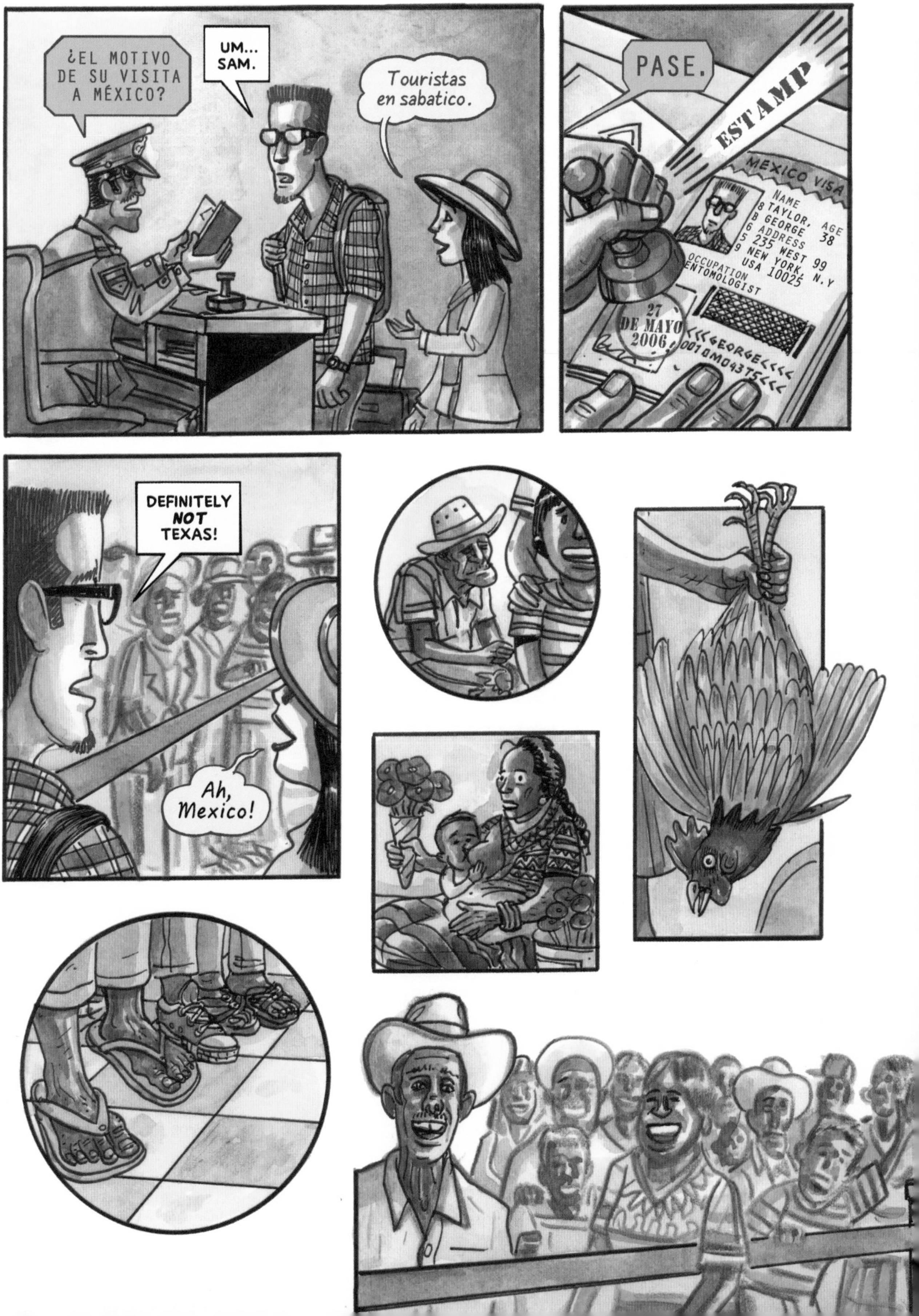

¿EL MOTIVO DE SU VISITA A MÉXICO?
UM... SAM.
Touristas en sabatico.
PASE.
ESTAMP
MEXICO VISA
NAME TAYLOR, GEORGE
AGE 38
ADDRESS 235 WEST 99 NEW YORK, N.Y USA 10025
OCCUPATION ENTOMOLOGIST
27 DE MAYO 2006
DEFINITELY NOT TEXAS!
Ah, Mexico!

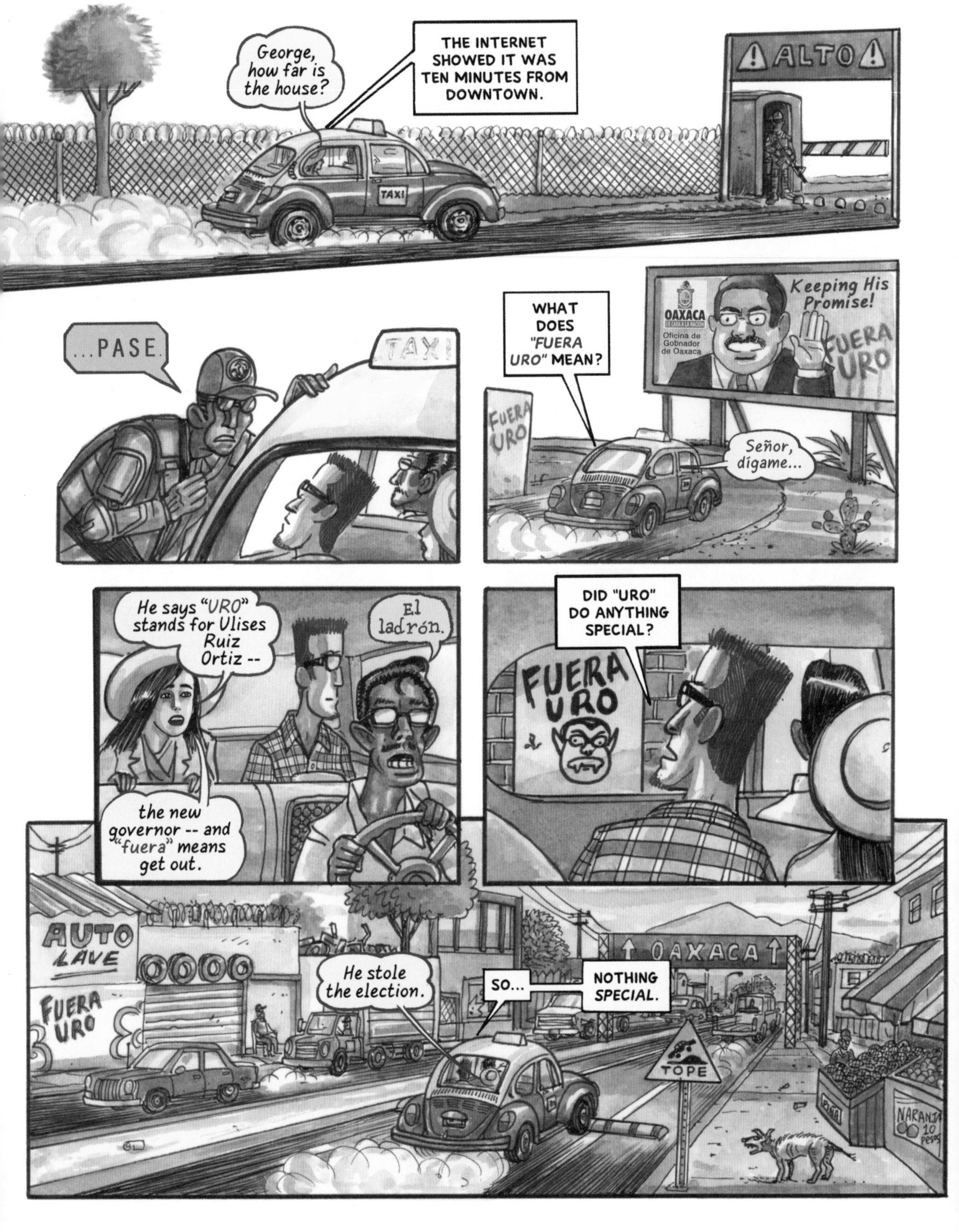

George, how far is the house?
THE INTERNET SHOWED IT WAS TEN MINUTES FROM DOWNTOWN.
ALTO
TAXI
...PASE.
TAXI
OAXACA
Oficina de Gobnador de Oaxaca
Keeping His Promise!
FUERA URO
WHAT DOES "FUERA URO" MEAN?
FUERA URO
Señor, dígame...
He says "URO" stands for Ulises Ruiz Ortiz --
El ladrón.
the new governor -- and "fuera" means get out.
DID "URO" DO ANYTHING SPECIAL?
FUERA URO
AUTO LAVE
FUERA URO
OAXACA
He stole the election.
SO...
NOTHING SPECIAL.
TOPE
NARANJA 10 pesos

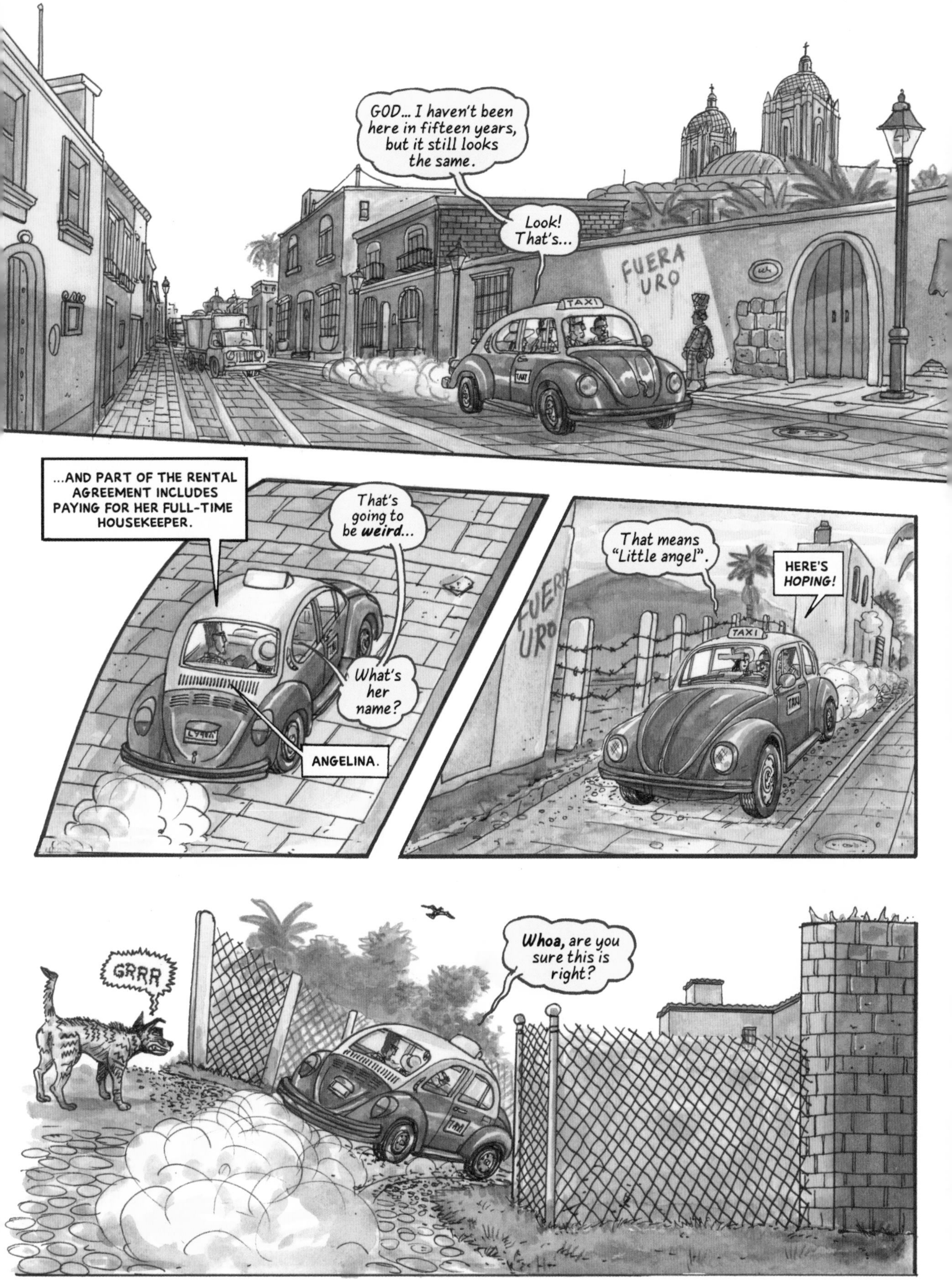
GOD... I haven't been here in fifteen years, but it still looks the same.
Look! That's...
FUERA URO
TAXI
...AND PART OF THE RENTAL AGREEMENT INCLUDES PAYING FOR HER FULL-TIME HOUSEKEEPER.
That's going to be *weird*...
What's her name?
ANGELINA.
That means "Little angel".
HERE'S HOPING!
FUERA URO
TAXI
GRRR
Whoa, are you sure this is right?

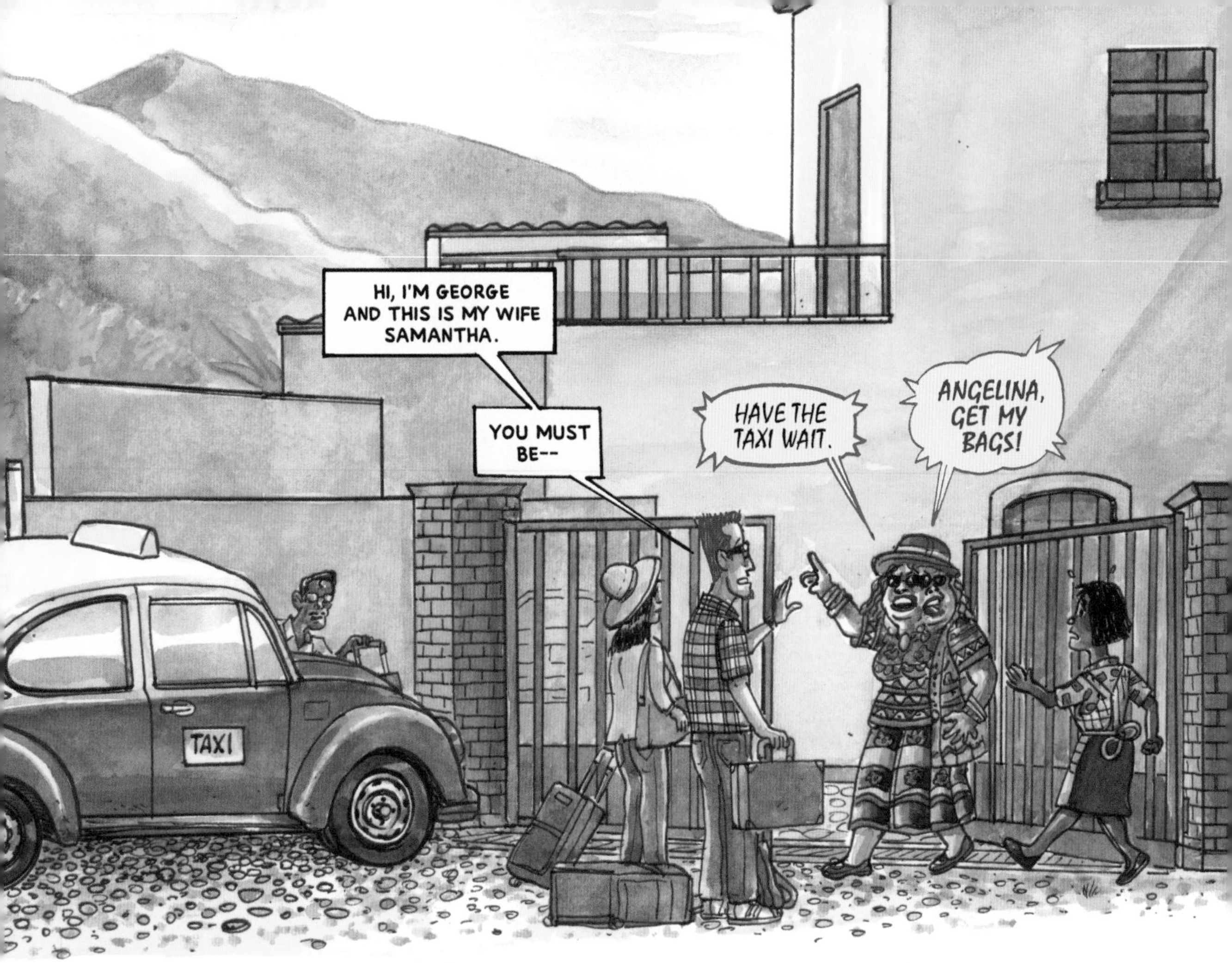
HI, I'M GEORGE AND THIS IS MY WIFE SAMANTHA.
YOU MUST BE--
HAVE THE TAXI WAIT.
ANGELINA, GET MY BAGS!
TAXI

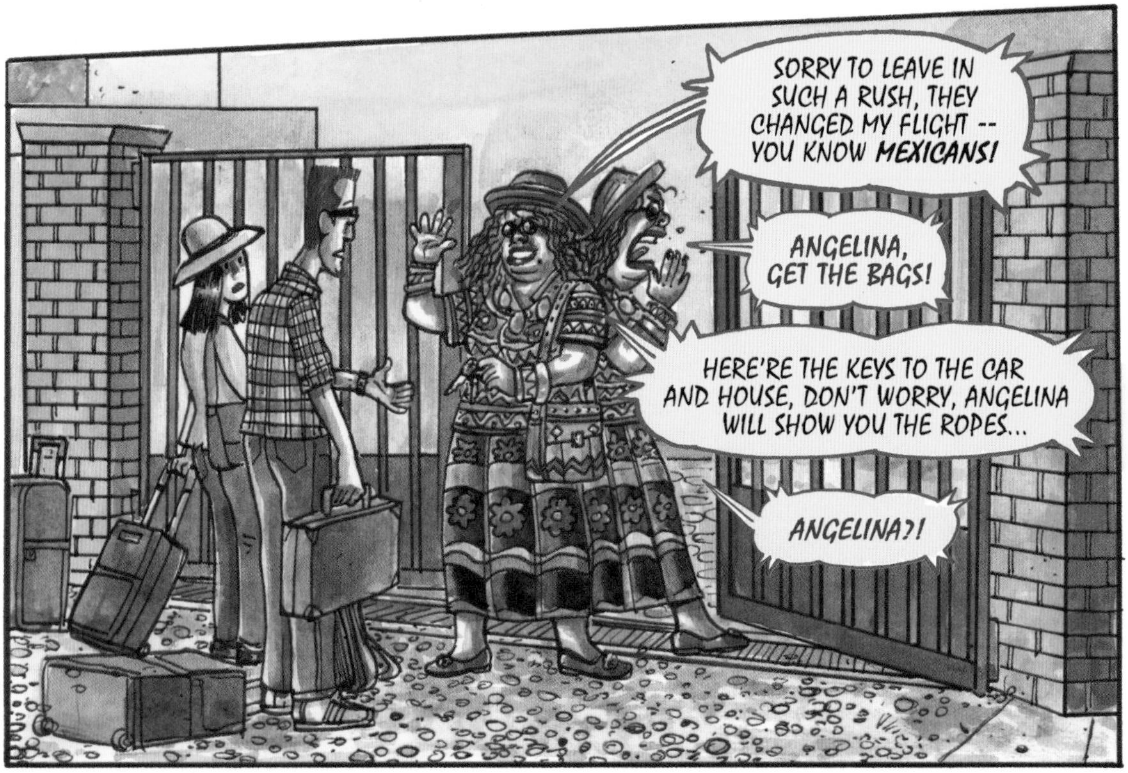
SORRY TO LEAVE IN SUCH A RUSH, THEY CHANGED MY FLIGHT -- YOU KNOW ***MEXICANS!***
ANGELINA, GET THE BAGS!
HERE'RE THE KEYS TO THE CAR AND HOUSE, DON'T WORRY, ANGELINA WILL SHOW YOU THE ROPES...
ANGELINA?!

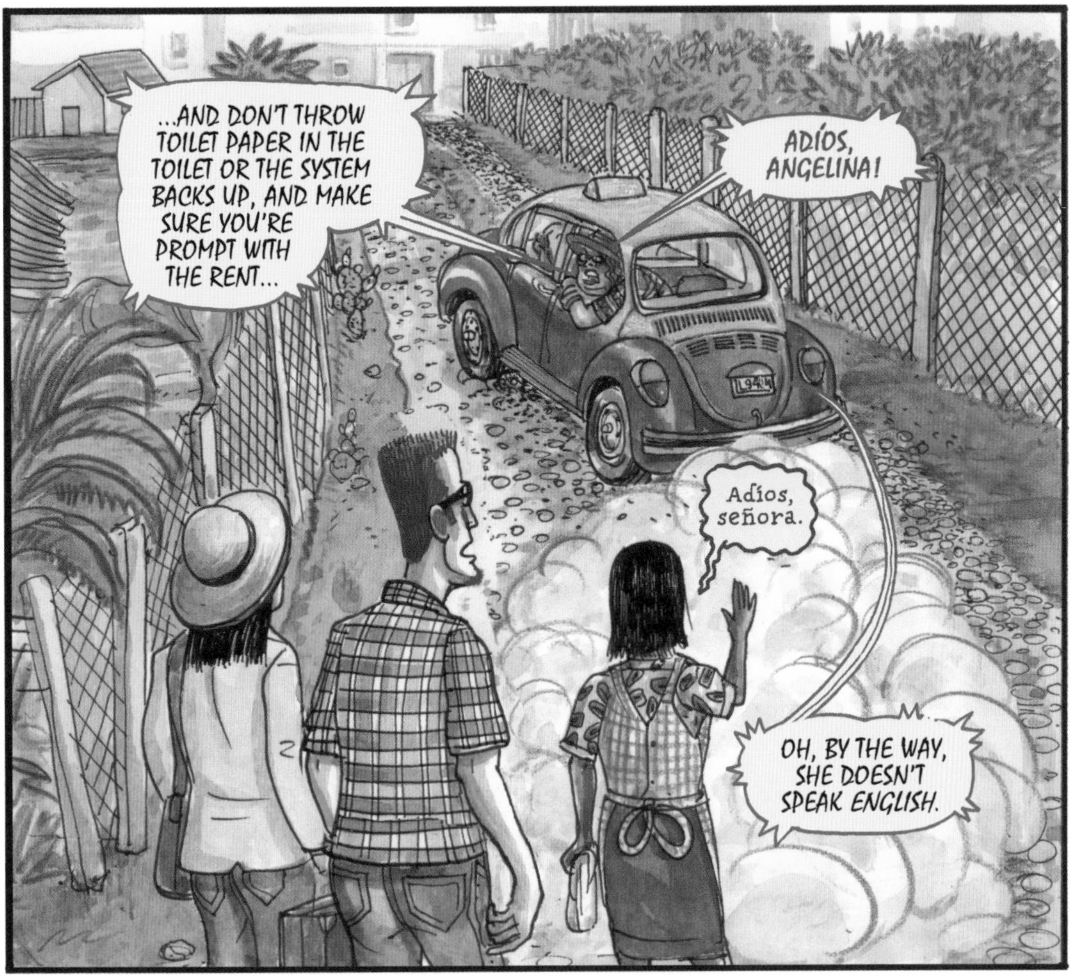
...AND DON'T THROW TOILET PAPER IN THE TOILET OR THE SYSTEM BACKS UP, AND MAKE SURE YOU'RE PROMPT WITH THE RENT...
ADÍOS, ANGELINA!
Adíos, señora.
OH, BY THE WAY, SHE DOESN'T SPEAK ENGLISH.

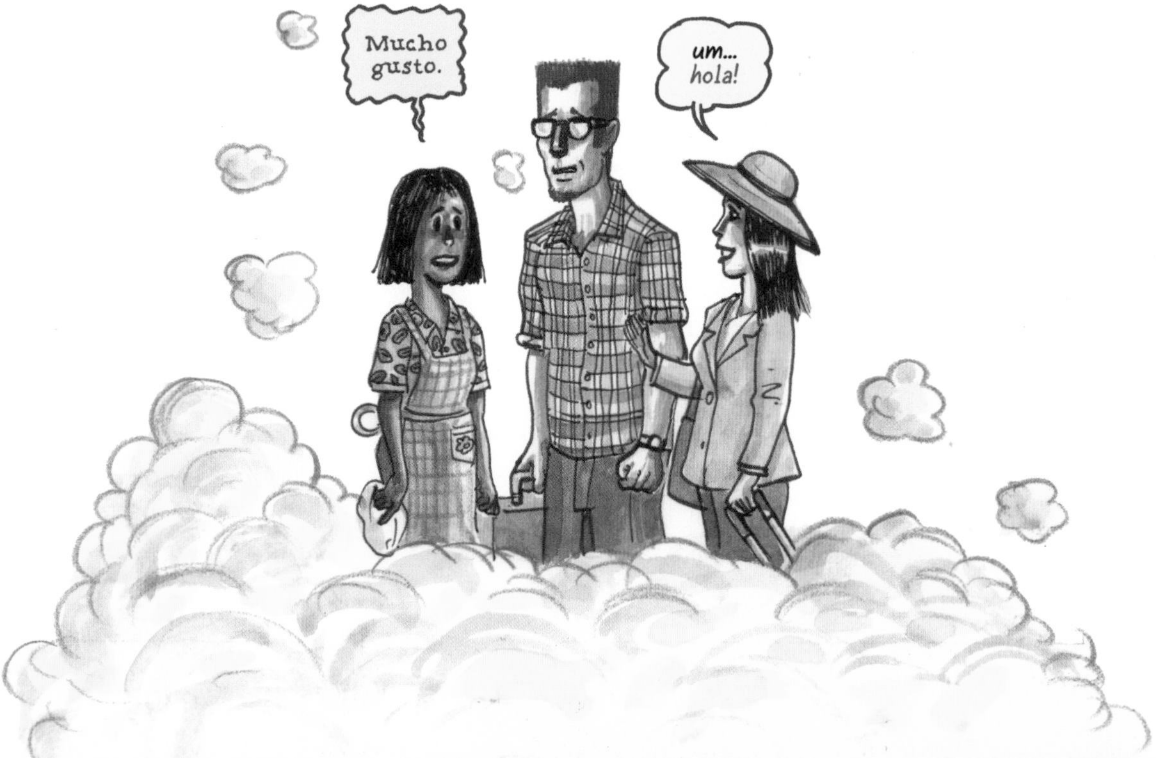
Mucho gusto.
um... hola!

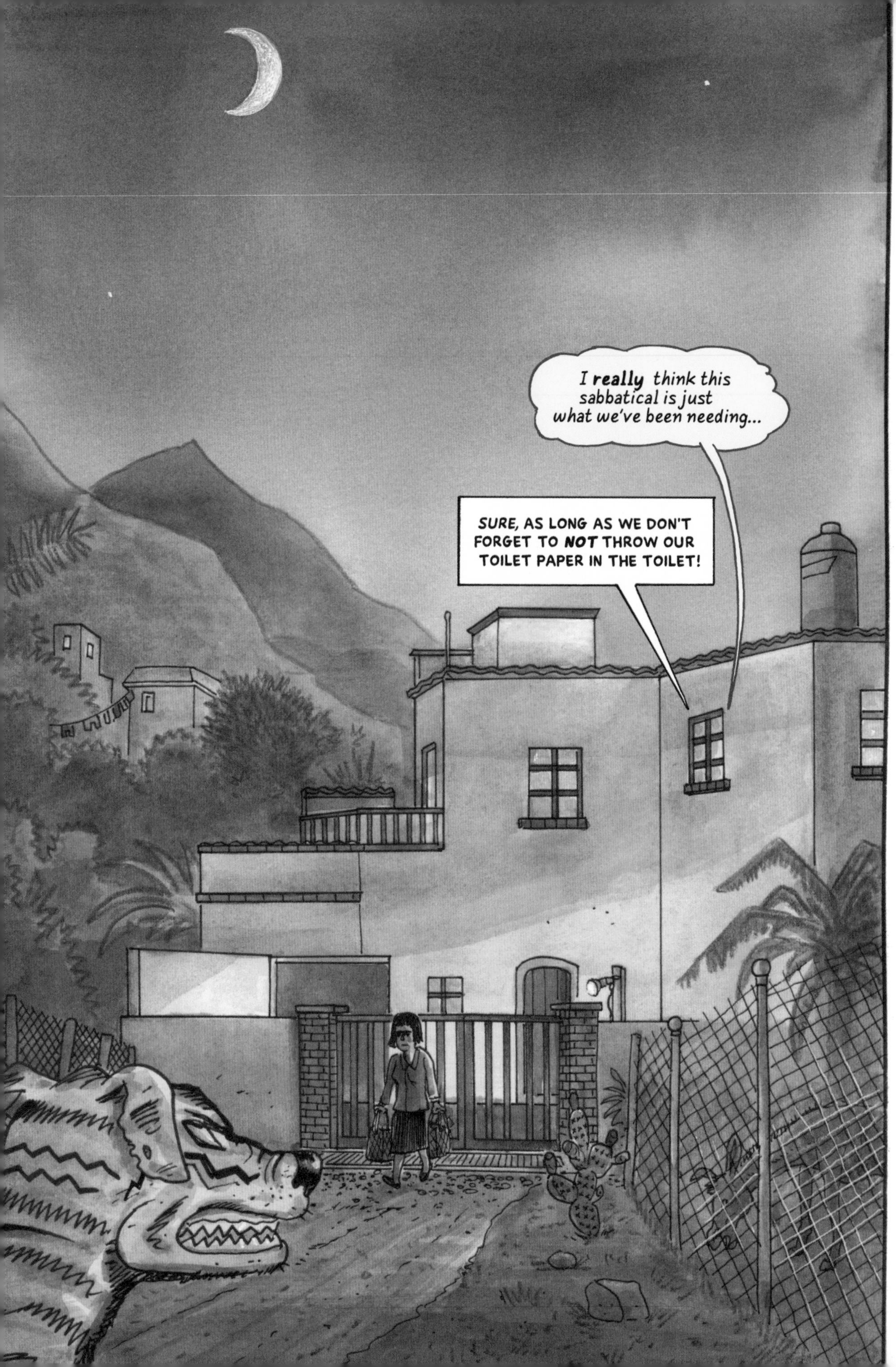
I really think this sabbatical is just what we've been needing...
SURE, AS LONG AS WE DON'T FORGET TO NOT THROW OUR TOILET PAPER IN THE TOILET!

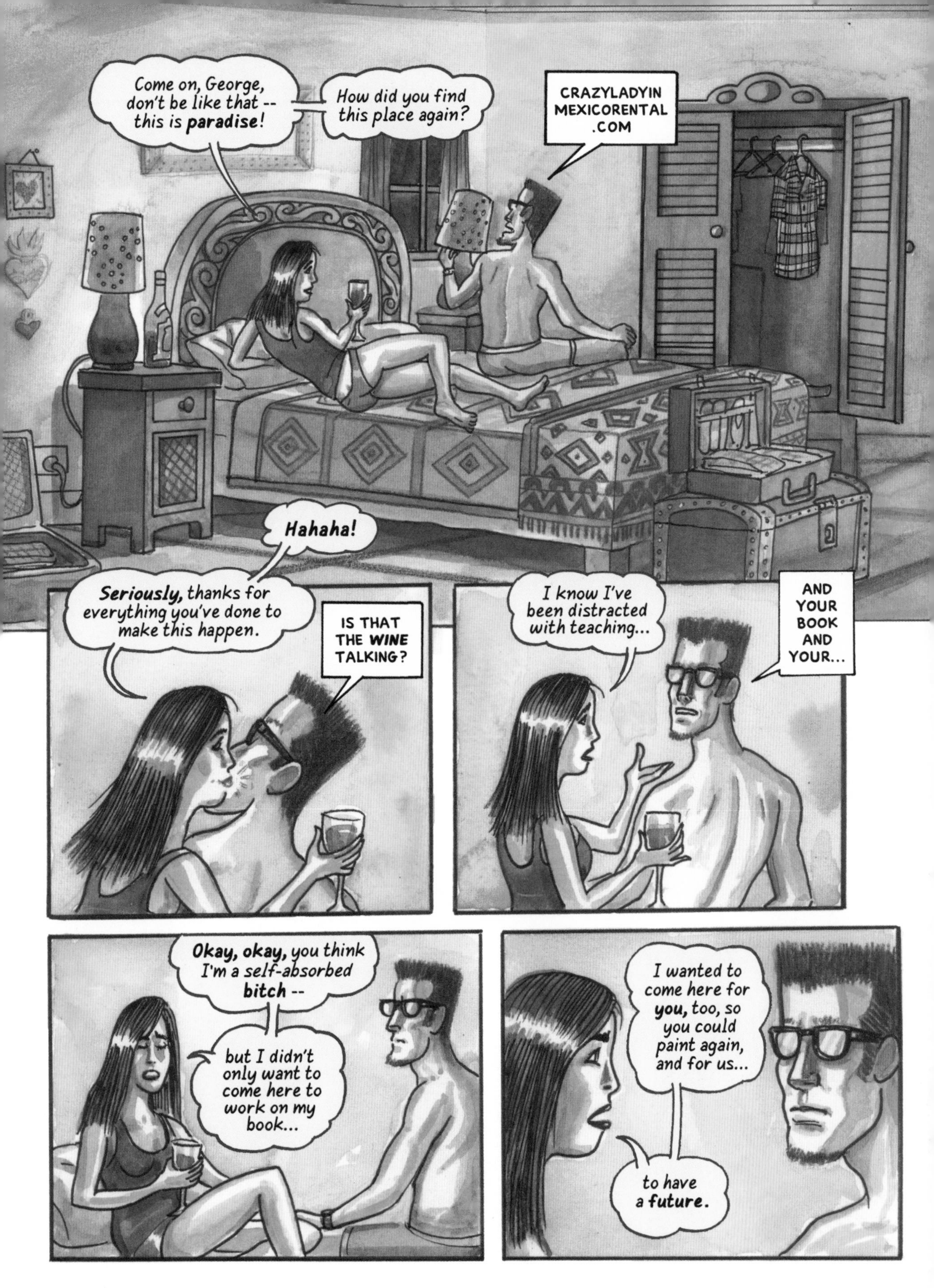
Come on, George, don't be like that -- this is **paradise**!
How did you find this place again?
CRAZYLADYIN MEXICORENTAL .COM
Hahaha!
Seriously, thanks for everything you've done to make this happen.
IS THAT THE **WINE** TALKING?
I know I've been distracted with teaching...
AND YOUR BOOK AND YOUR...
Okay, okay, you think I'm a self-absorbed **bitch** --
but I didn't only want to come here to work on my book...
I wanted to come here for **you,** too, so you could paint again, and for us...
to have a **future**.

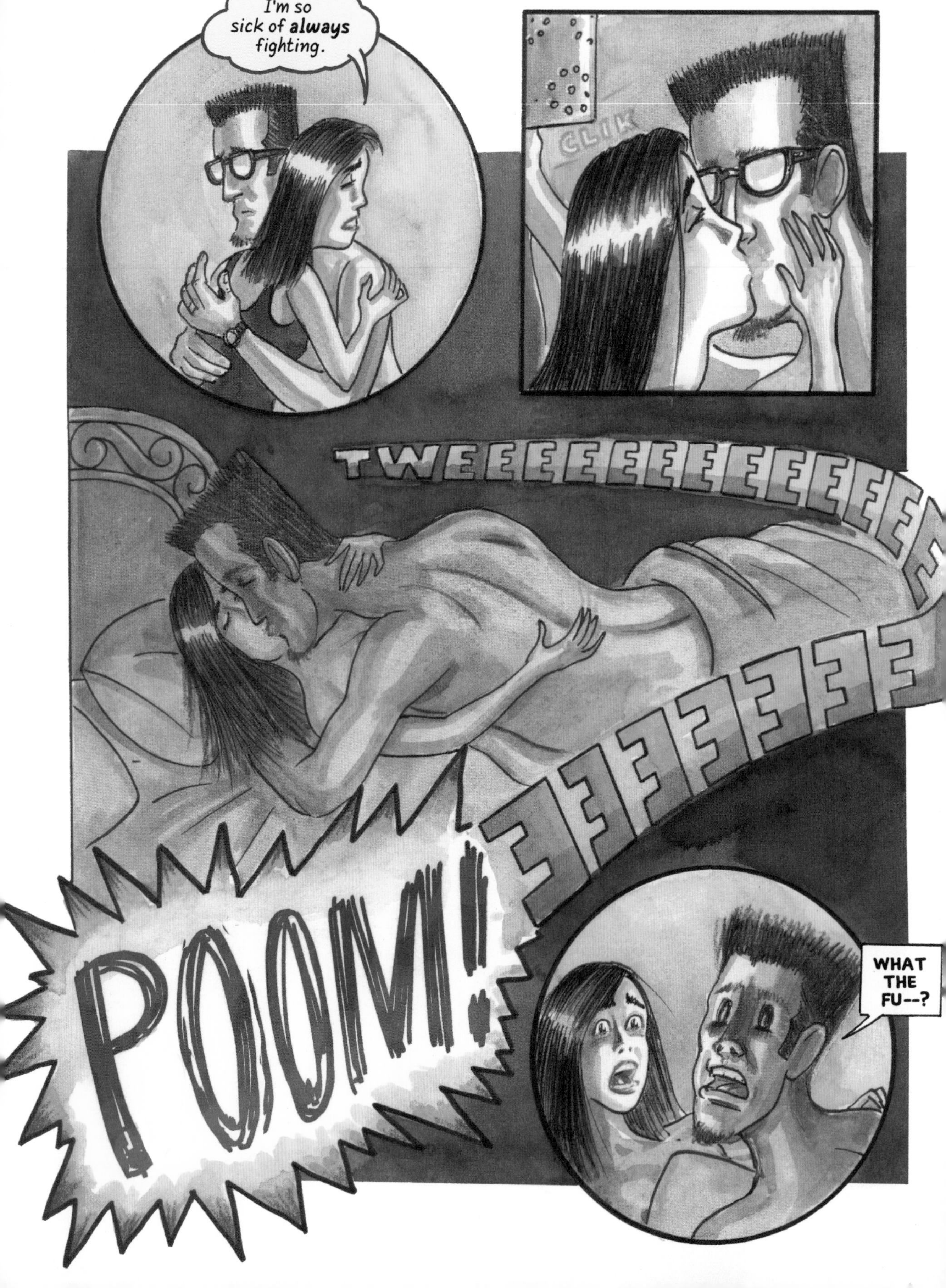
I'm so sick of always fighting.
CLIK
TWEEEEEEEEEEEEEEEEEEEEEEEEE
POOM!
WHAT THE FU--?

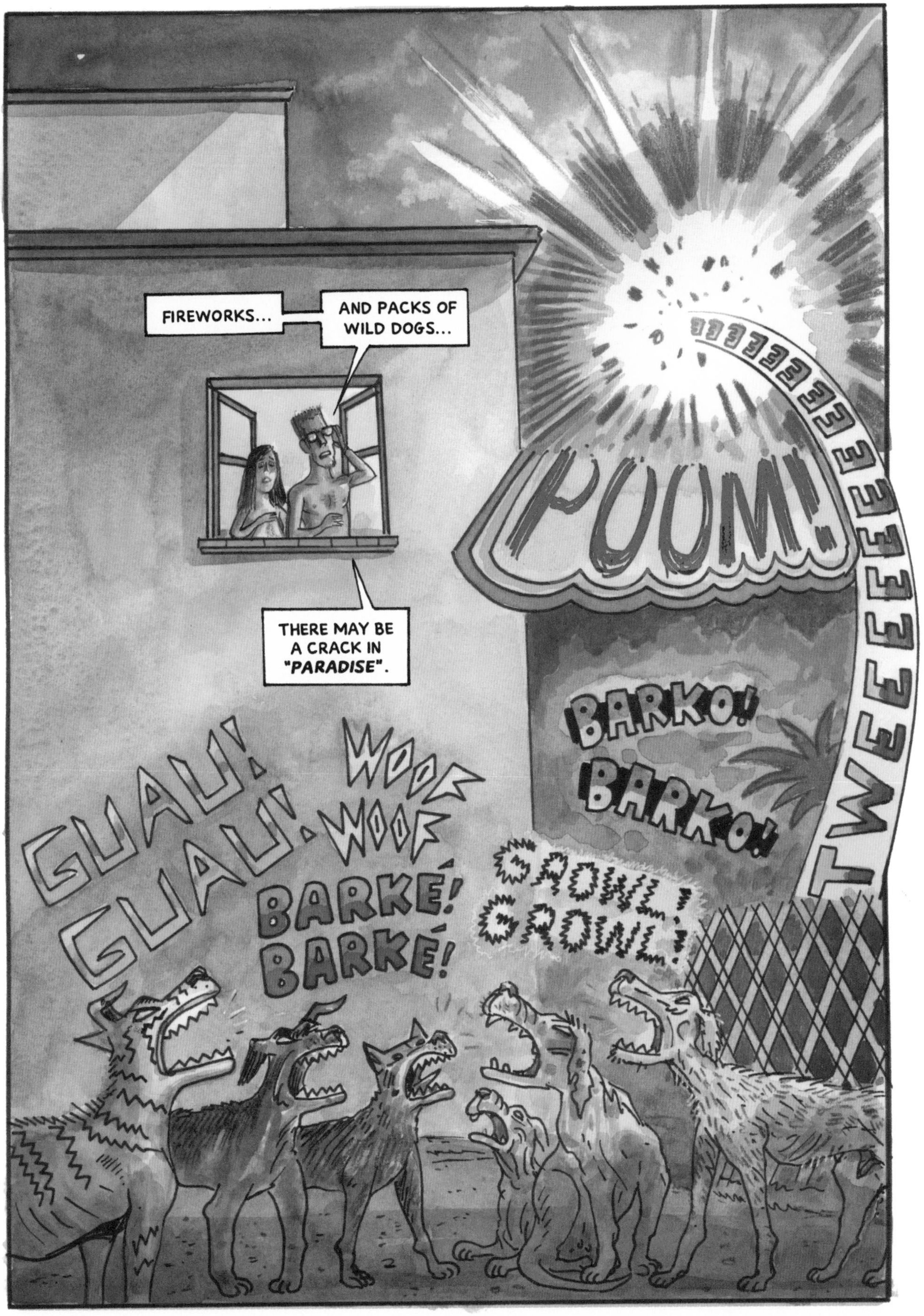
FIREWORKS...
AND PACKS OF WILD DOGS...
THERE MAY BE A CRACK IN "*PARADISE*".
POOM!
TWEEEEEEEEEEEEEE
BARKO! BARKO!
GUAU! GUAU!
WOOF WOOF
BARKÉ! BARKÉ!
GROWL! GROWL!

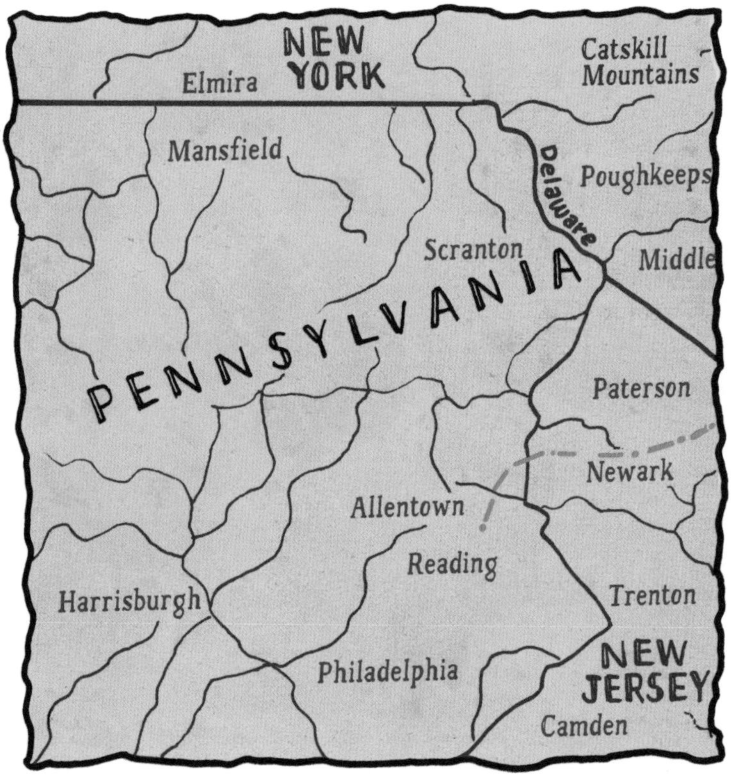
NEW YORK
Elmira
Catskill Mountains
Mansfield
Delaware
Poughkeeps
Scranton
Middle
PENNSYLVANIA
Paterson
Newark
Allentown
Reading
Harrisburgh
Trenton
Philadelphia
NEW JERSEY
Camden

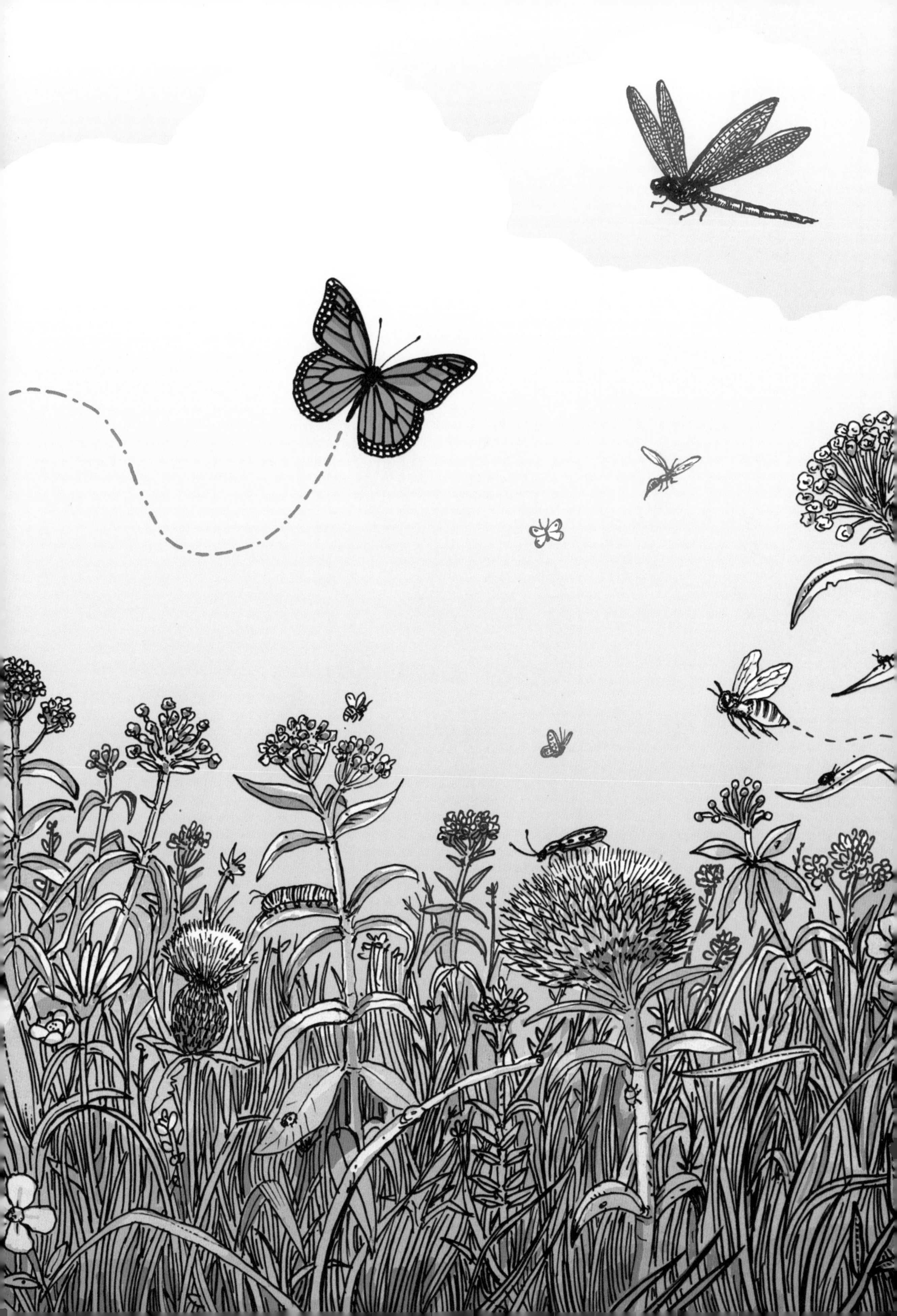

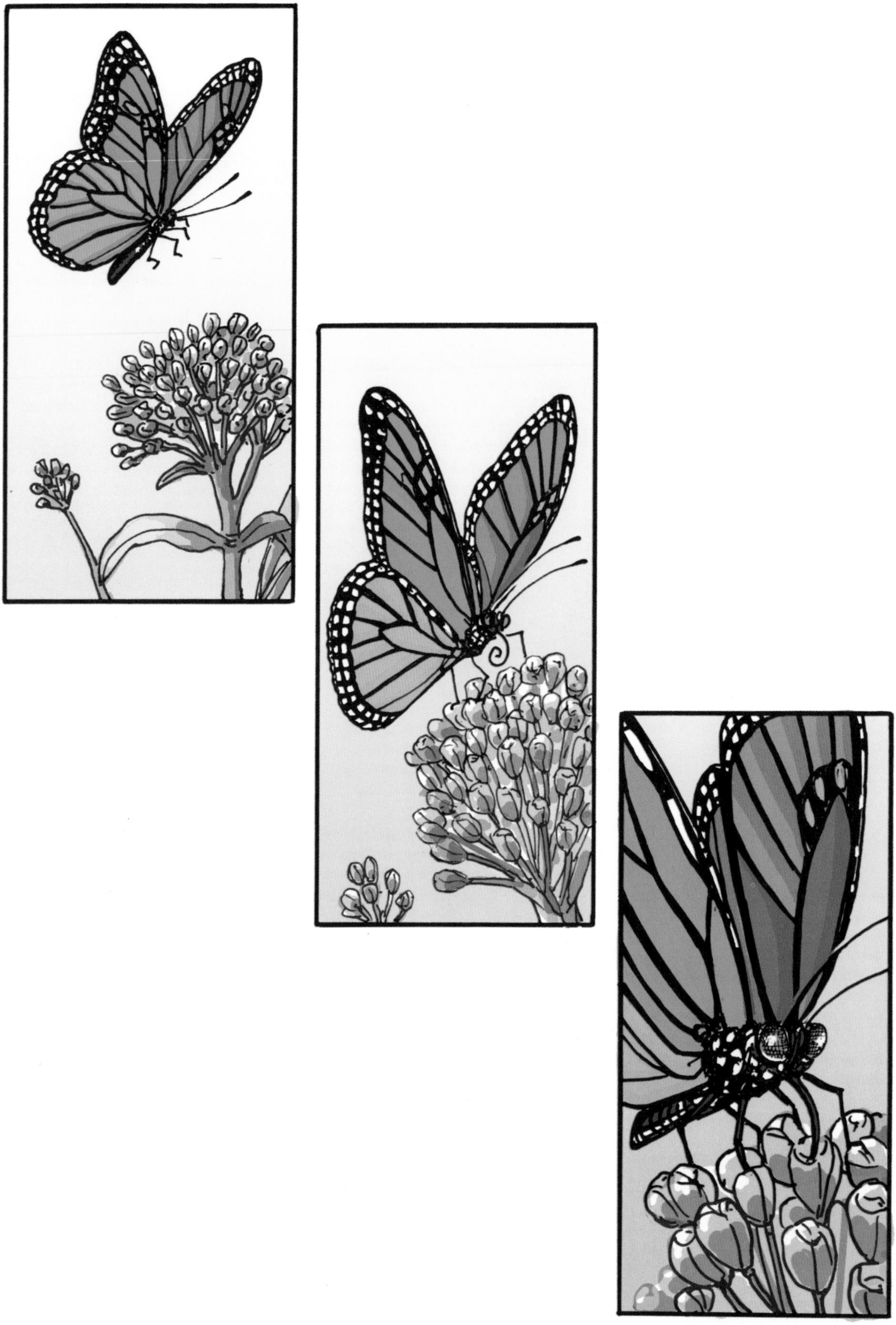

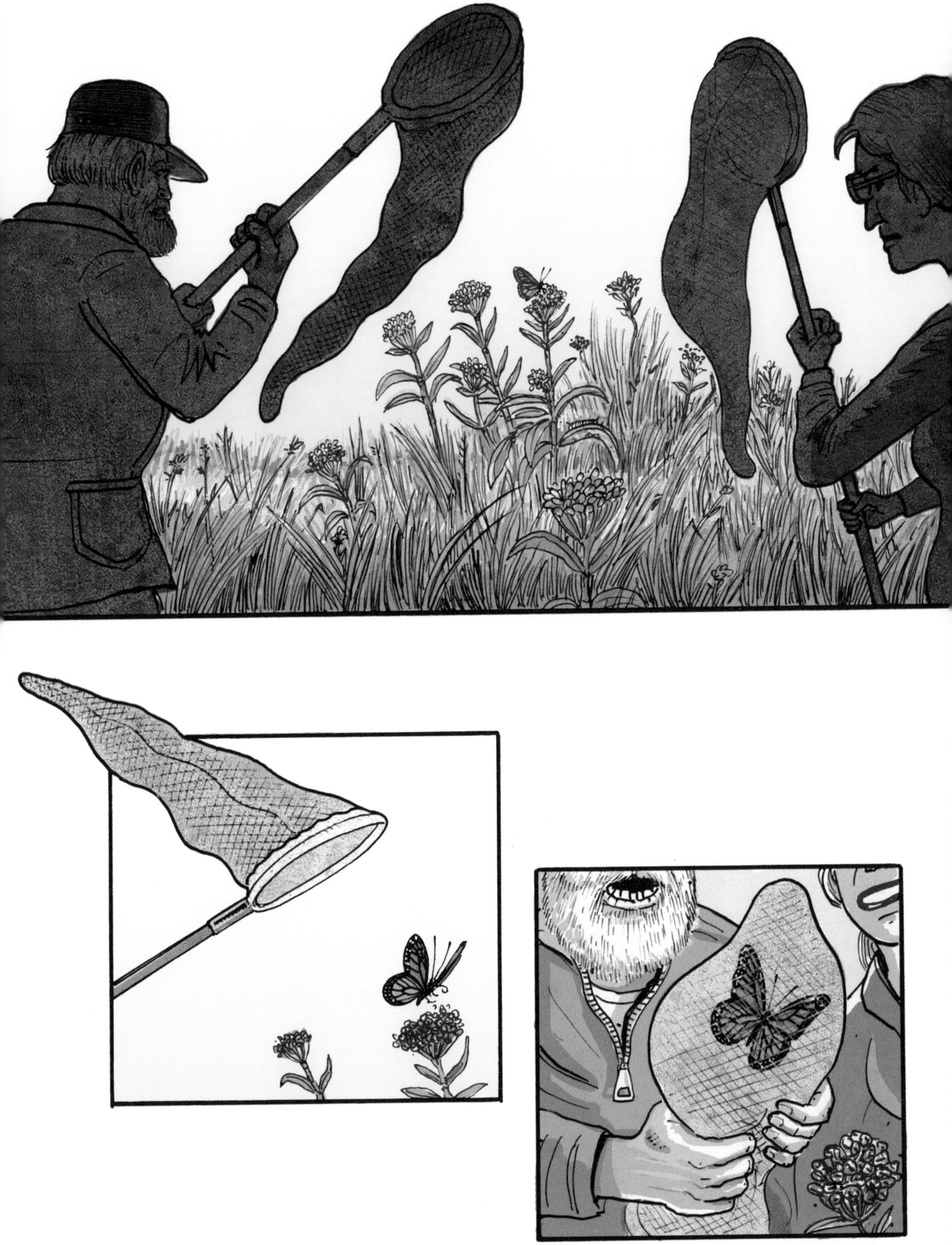

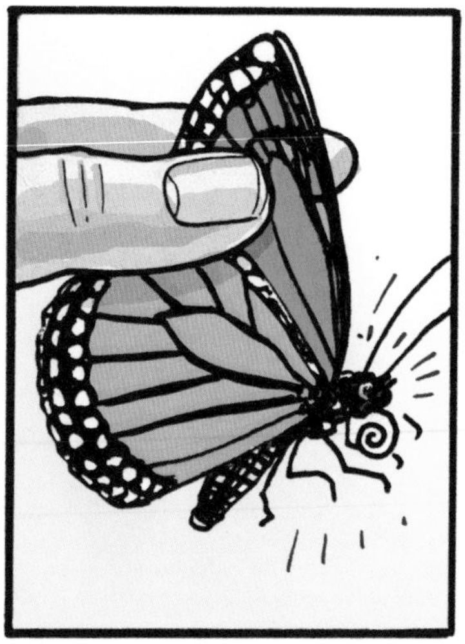

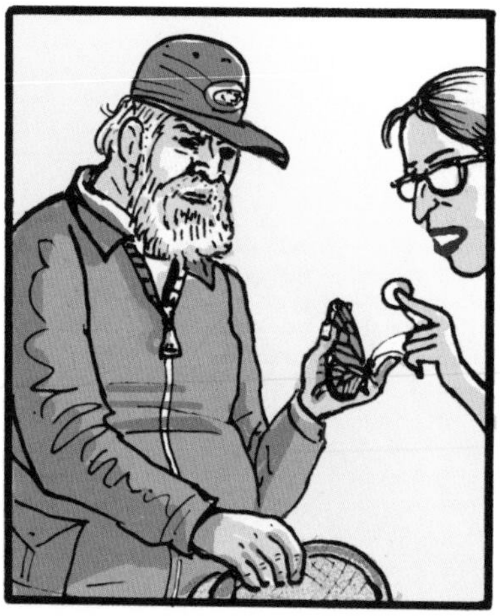

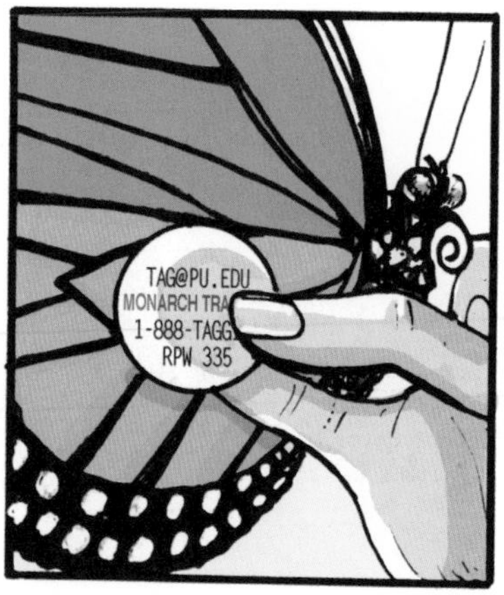
TAG@PU.EDU
1-888-TAGG
RPW 335

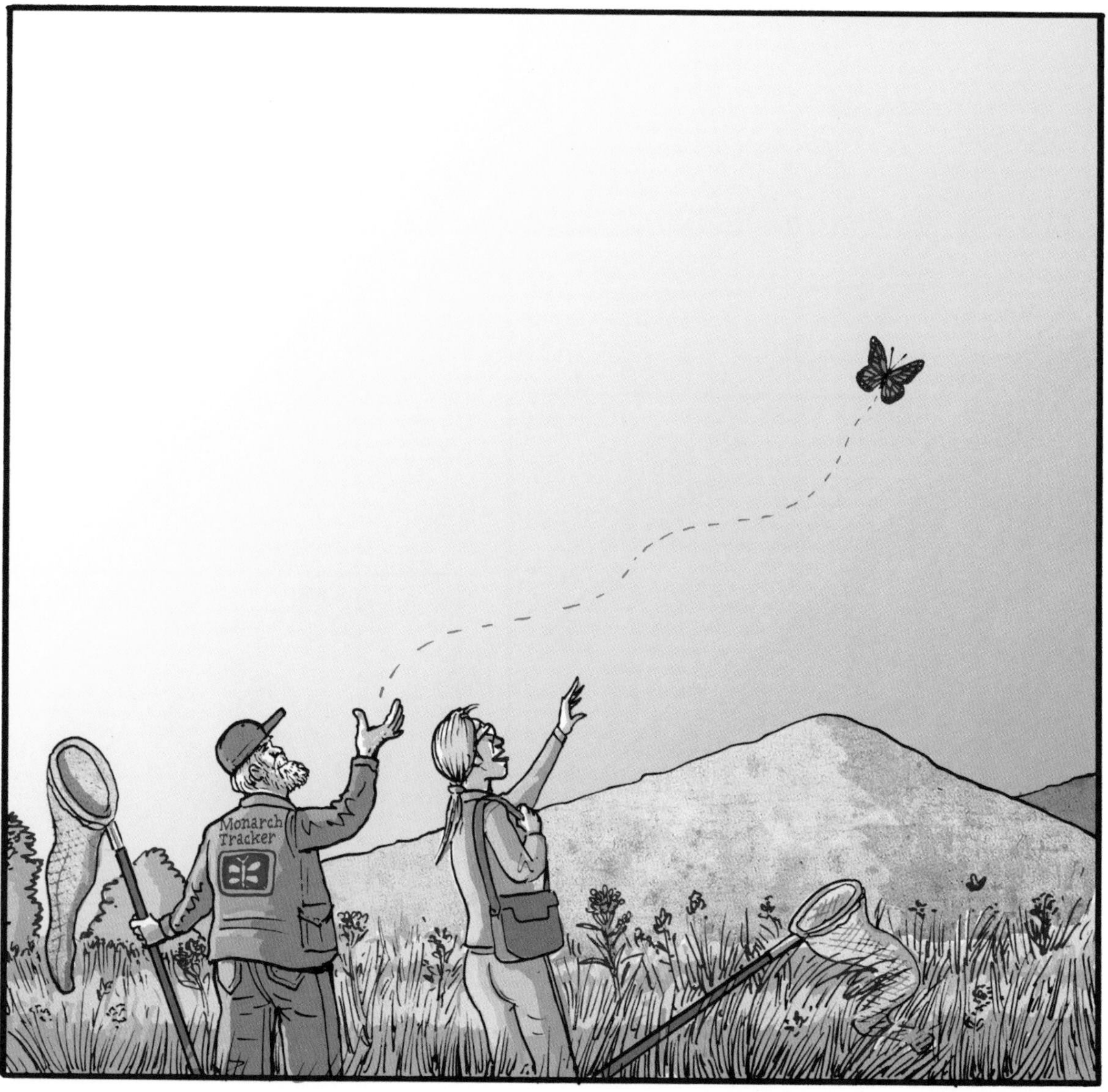
Monarch
Tracker

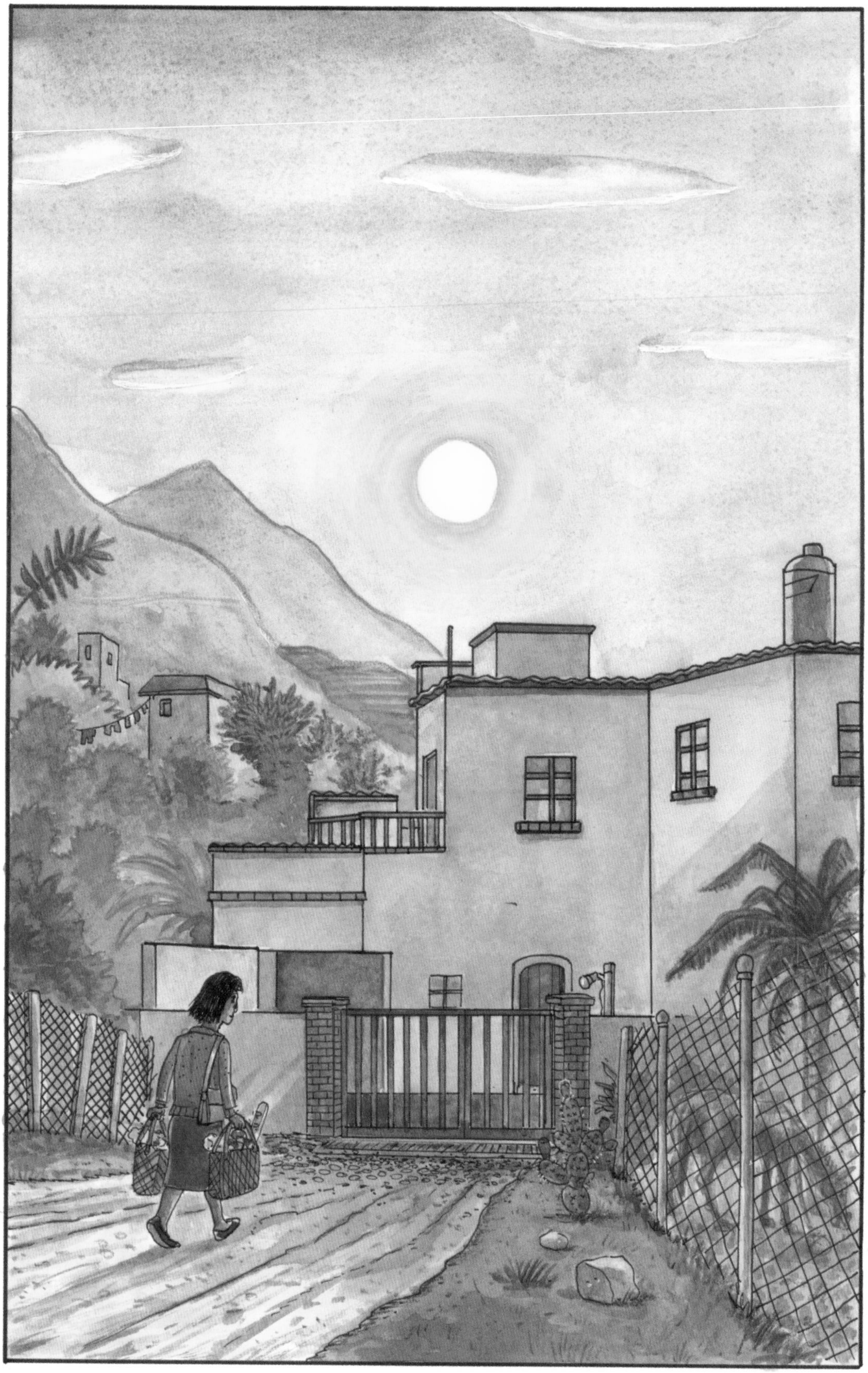

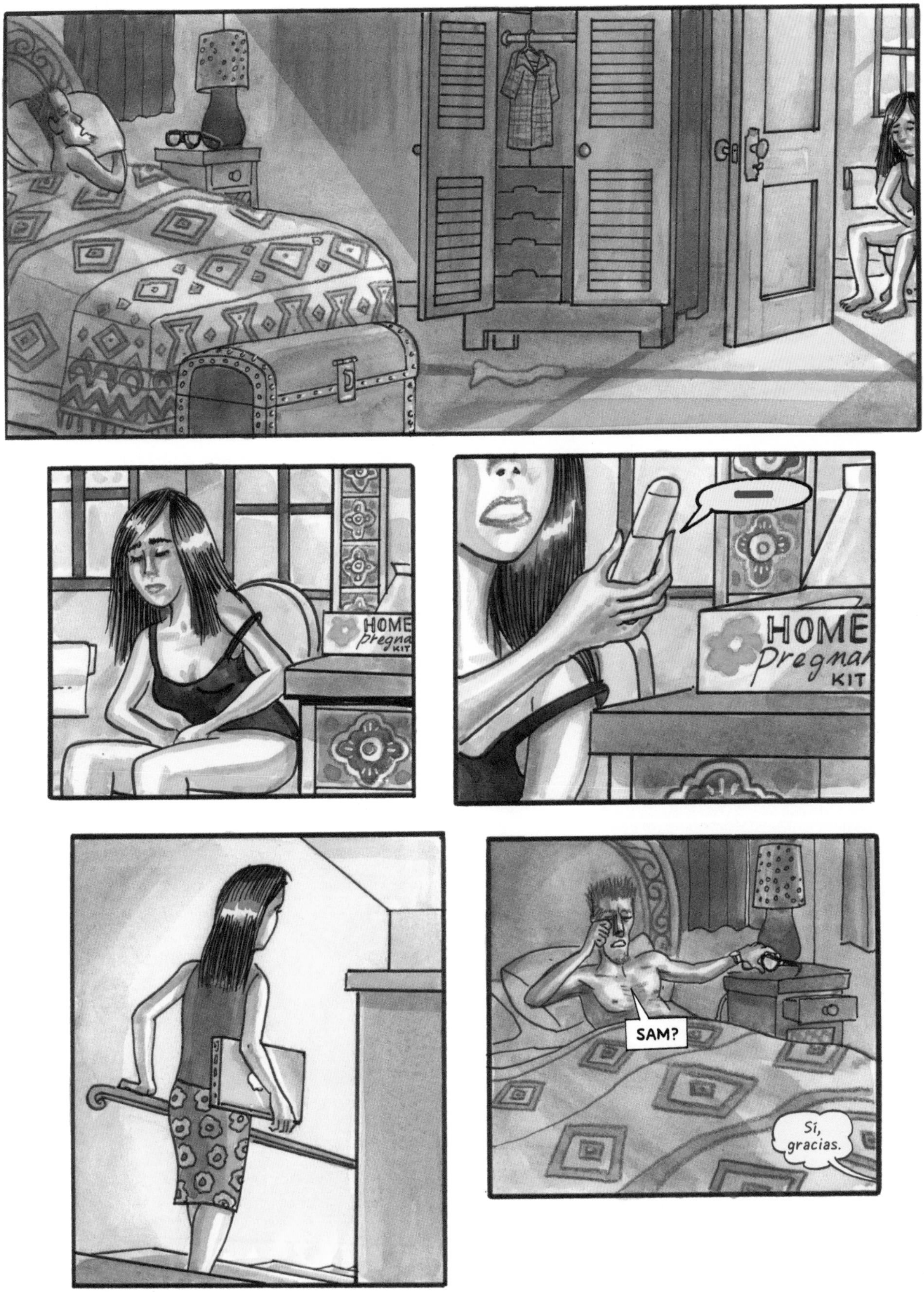
HOME
pregna
KIT
HOME
pregna
KIT
SAM?
Sí, gracias.

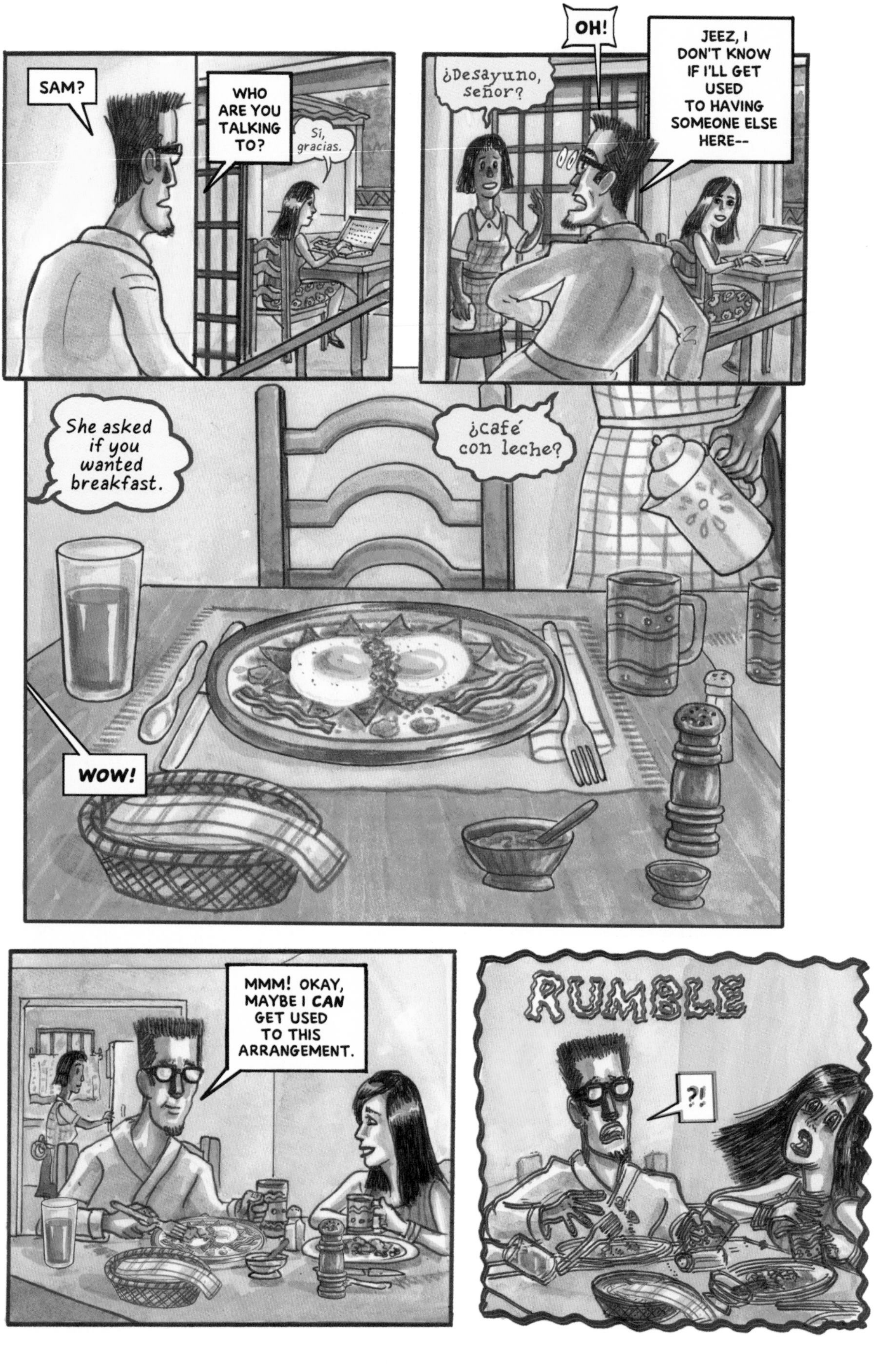
SAM?
WHO ARE YOU TALKING TO?
Sí, gracias.
¿Desayuno, señor?
OH!
JEEZ, I DON'T KNOW IF I'LL GET USED TO HAVING SOMEONE ELSE HERE--
She asked if you wanted breakfast.
¿café con leche?
WOW!
MMM! OKAY, MAYBE I CAN GET USED TO THIS ARRANGEMENT.
RUMBLE
?!

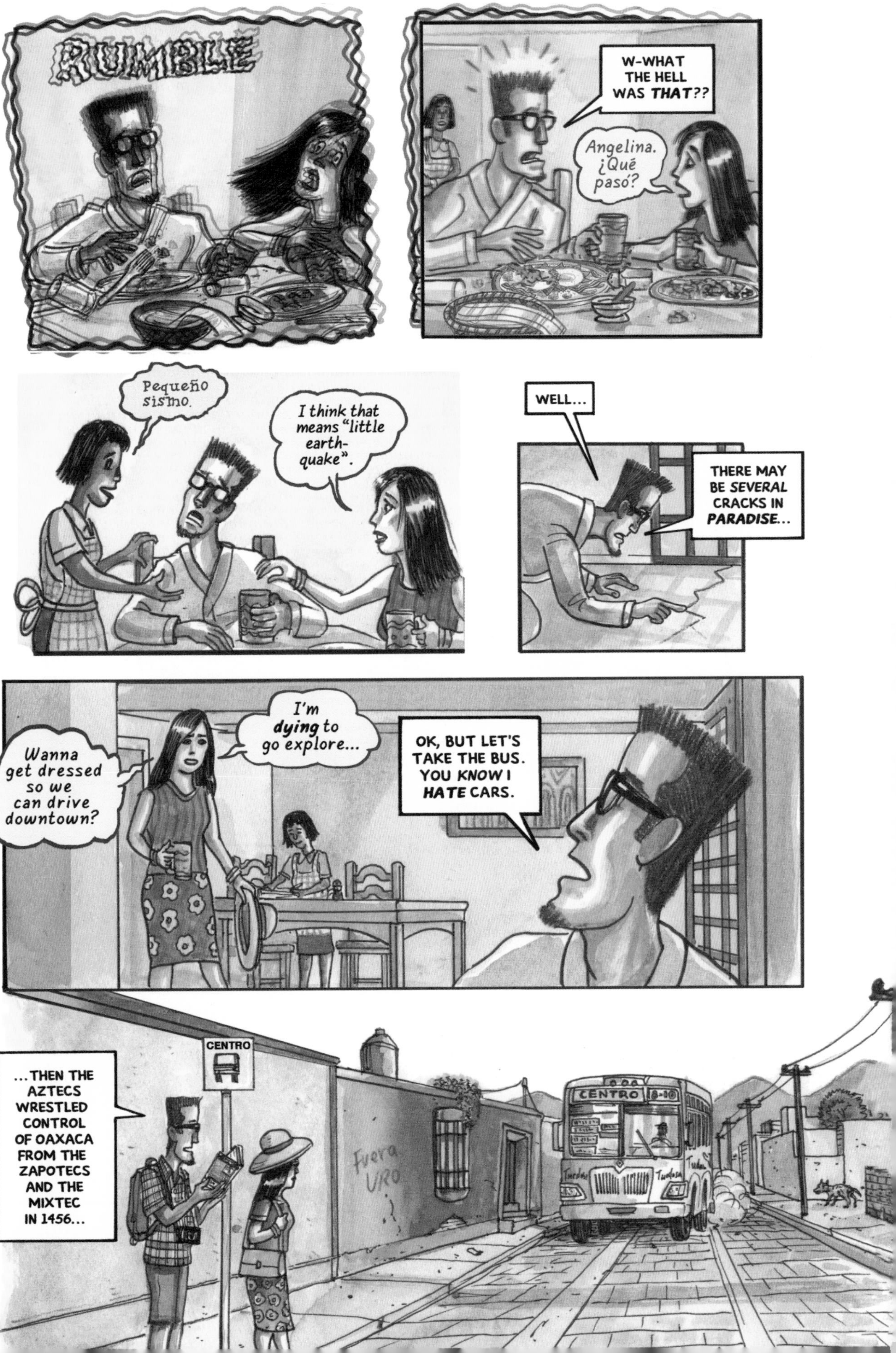
RUMBLE
W-WHAT THE HELL WAS *THAT*??
Angelina. ¿Qué pasó?
Pequeño sismo.
I think that means "little earth-quake".
WELL...
THERE MAY BE *SEVERAL* CRACKS IN *PARADISE*...
Wanna get dressed so we can drive downtown?
I'm *dying* to go explore...
OK, BUT LET'S TAKE THE BUS. YOU *KNOW* I *HATE* CARS.
CENTRO
...THEN THE AZTECS WRESTLED CONTROL OF OAXACA FROM THE ZAPOTECS AND THE MIXTEC IN 1456...
Fuera URO
CENTRO

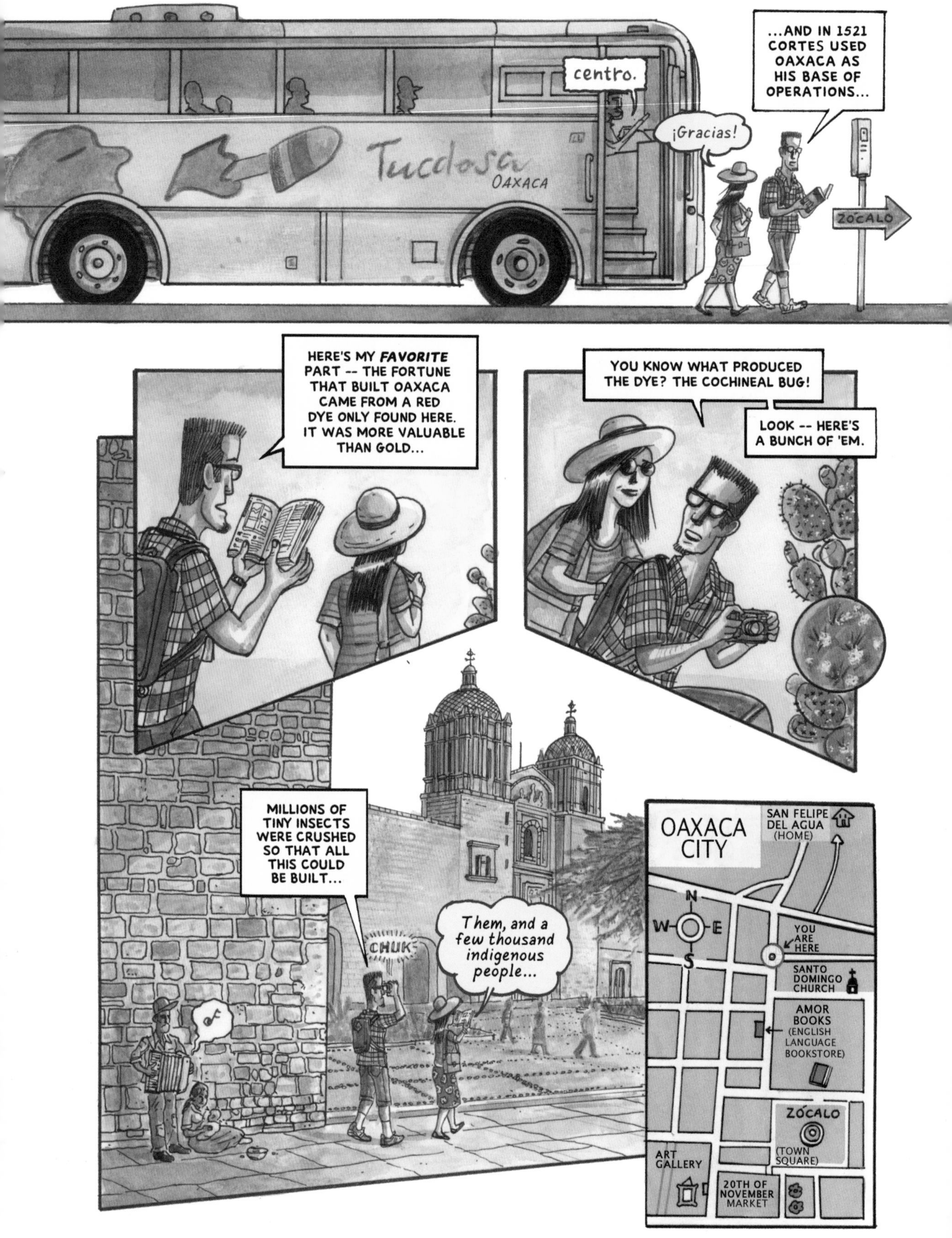
centro.
¡Gracias!
...AND IN 1521 CORTES USED OAXACA AS HIS BASE OF OPERATIONS...
ZÓCALO
HERE'S MY *FAVORITE* PART -- THE FORTUNE THAT BUILT OAXACA CAME FROM A RED DYE ONLY FOUND HERE. IT WAS MORE VALUABLE THAN GOLD...
YOU KNOW WHAT PRODUCED THE DYE? THE COCHINEAL BUG!
LOOK -- HERE'S A BUNCH OF 'EM.
MILLIONS OF TINY INSECTS WERE CRUSHED SO THAT ALL THIS COULD BE BUILT...
CHUK
Them, and a few thousand indigenous people...
OAXACA CITY
SAN FELIPE DEL AGUA (HOME)
N
W
E
S
YOU ARE HERE
SANTO DOMINGO CHURCH
AMOR BOOKS (ENGLISH LANGUAGE BOOKSTORE)
ZÓCALO (TOWN SQUARE)
ART GALLERY
20TH OF NOVEMBER MARKET

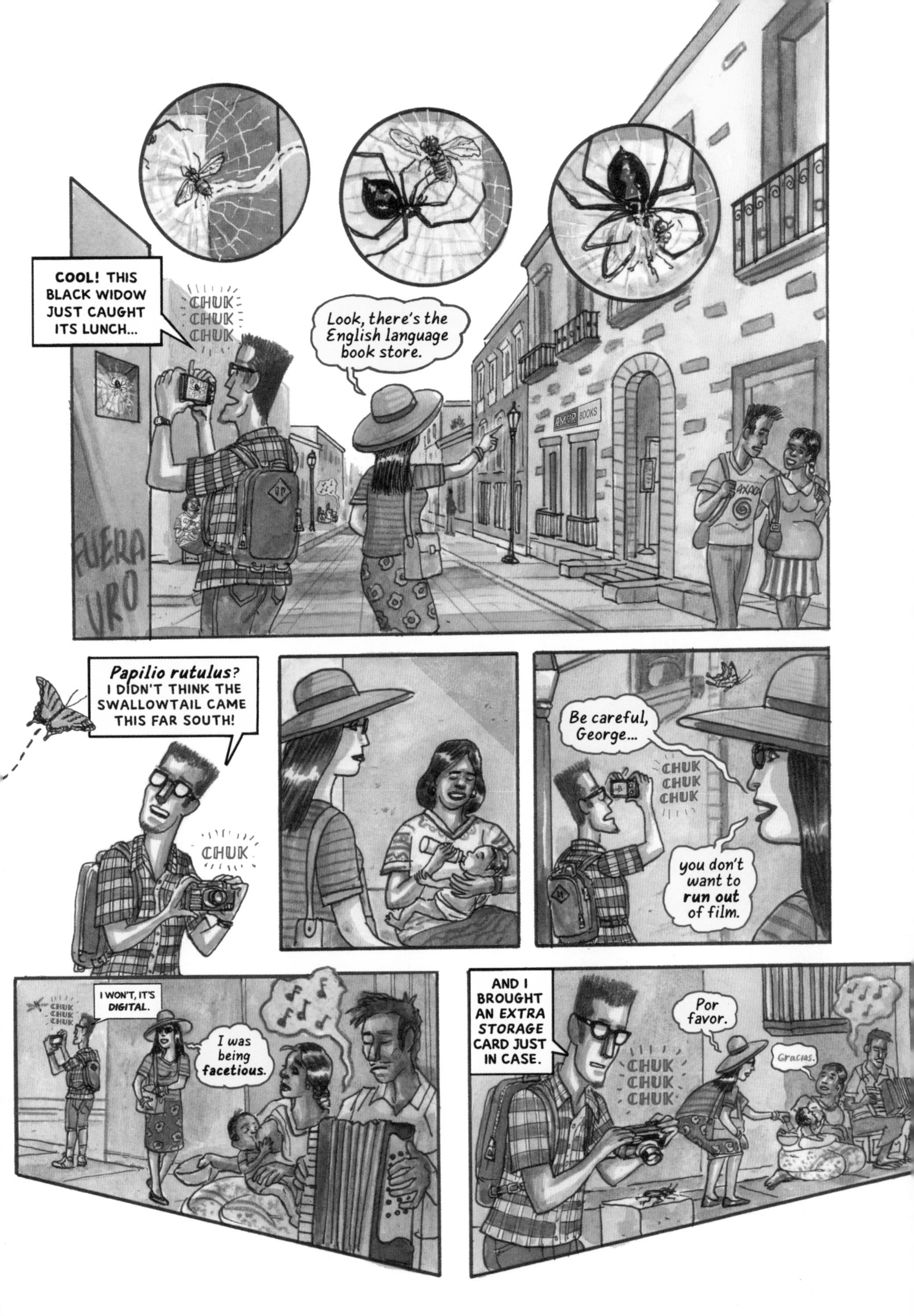
COOL! THIS BLACK WIDOW JUST CAUGHT ITS LUNCH...
CHUK CHUK CHUK
Look, there's the English language book store.
AMOR BOOKS
FUERA URO
Papilio rutulus? I DIDN'T THINK THE SWALLOWTAIL CAME THIS FAR SOUTH!
CHUK
Be careful, George...
CHUK CHUK CHUK
you don't want to **run out** of film.
CHUK CHUK CHUK
I WON'T, IT'S **DIGITAL**.
I was being **facetious**.
AND I BROUGHT AN *EXTRA* STORAGE CARD JUST IN CASE.
CHUK CHUK CHUK
Por favor.
Gracias.

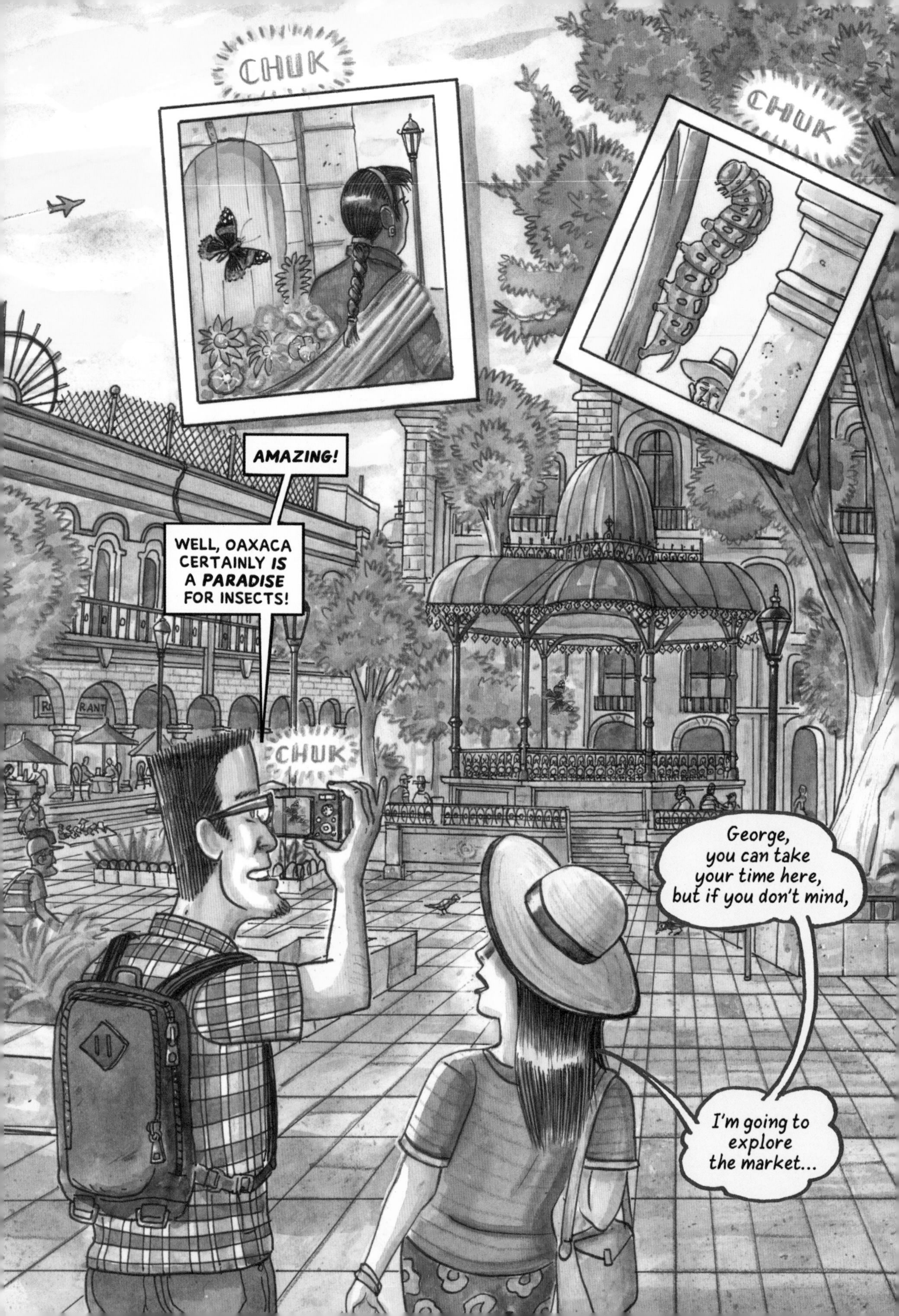
CHUK
CHUK
AMAZING!
WELL, OAXACA CERTAINLY IS A PARADISE FOR INSECTS!
CHUK
George, you can take your time here, but if you don't mind,
I'm going to explore the market...

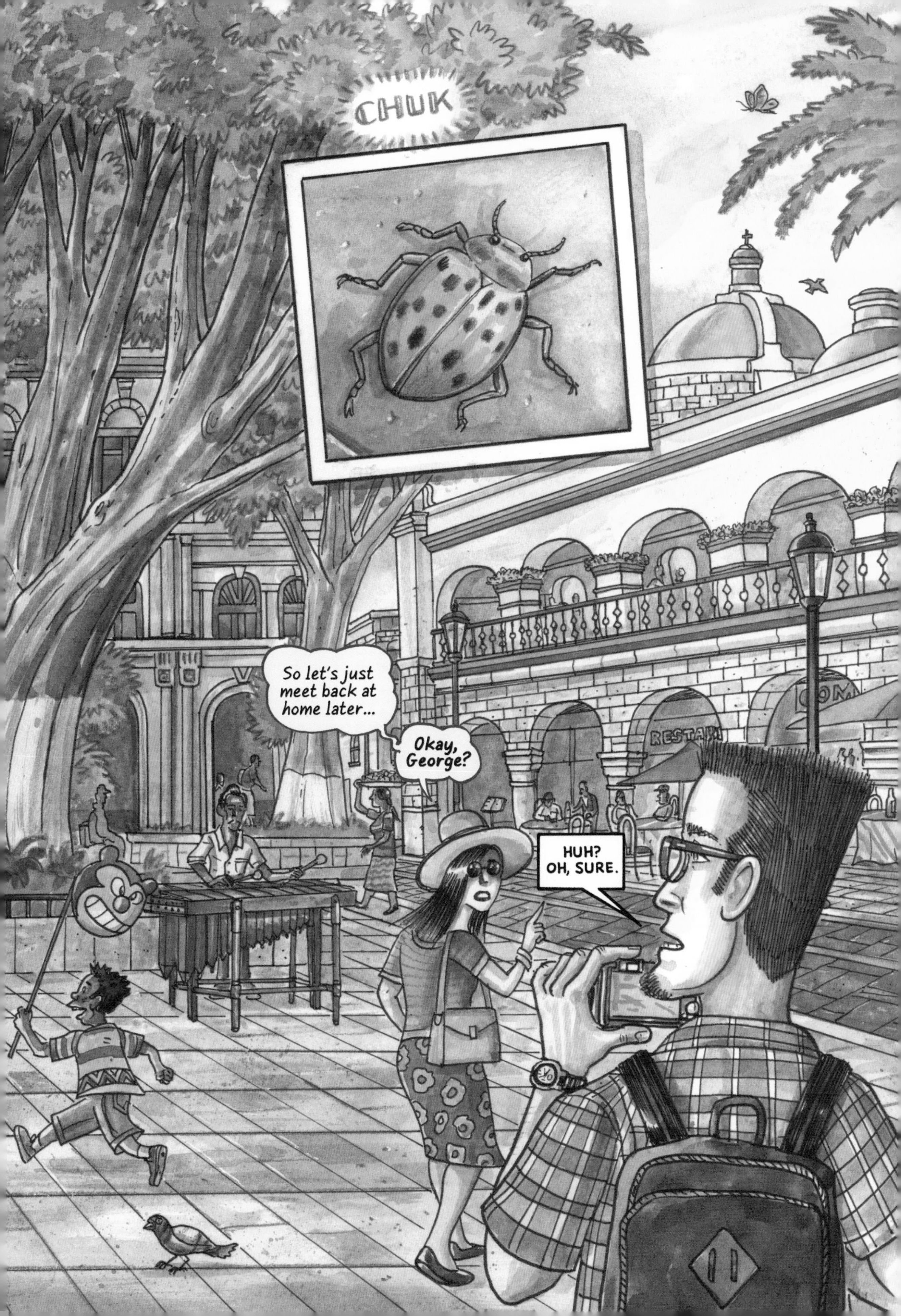
CHUK
So let's just meet back at home later...
Okay, George?
HUH? OH, SURE.

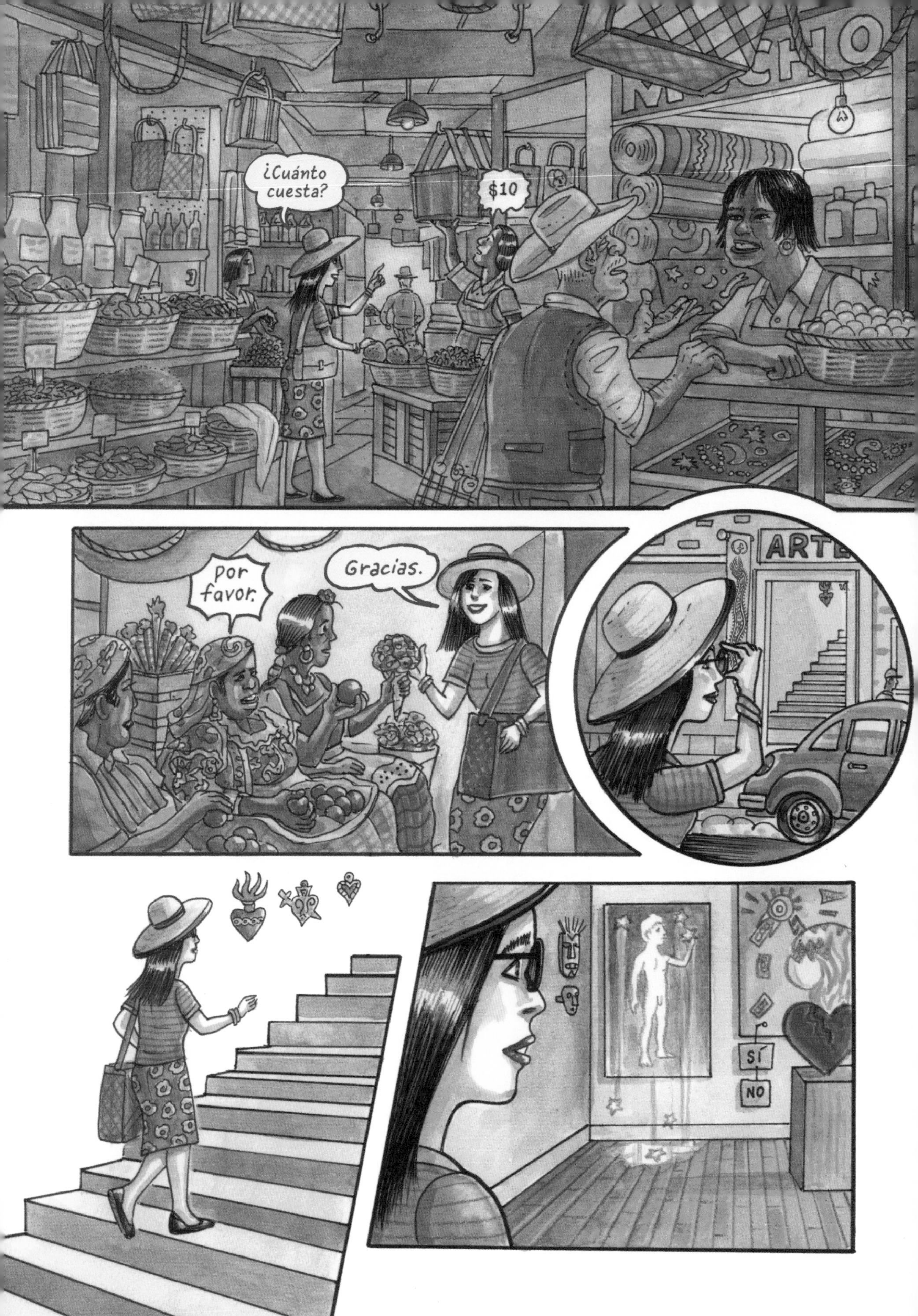

¿Cuánto cuesta?
$10
Por favor.
Gracias.
ARTE
SÍ
NO

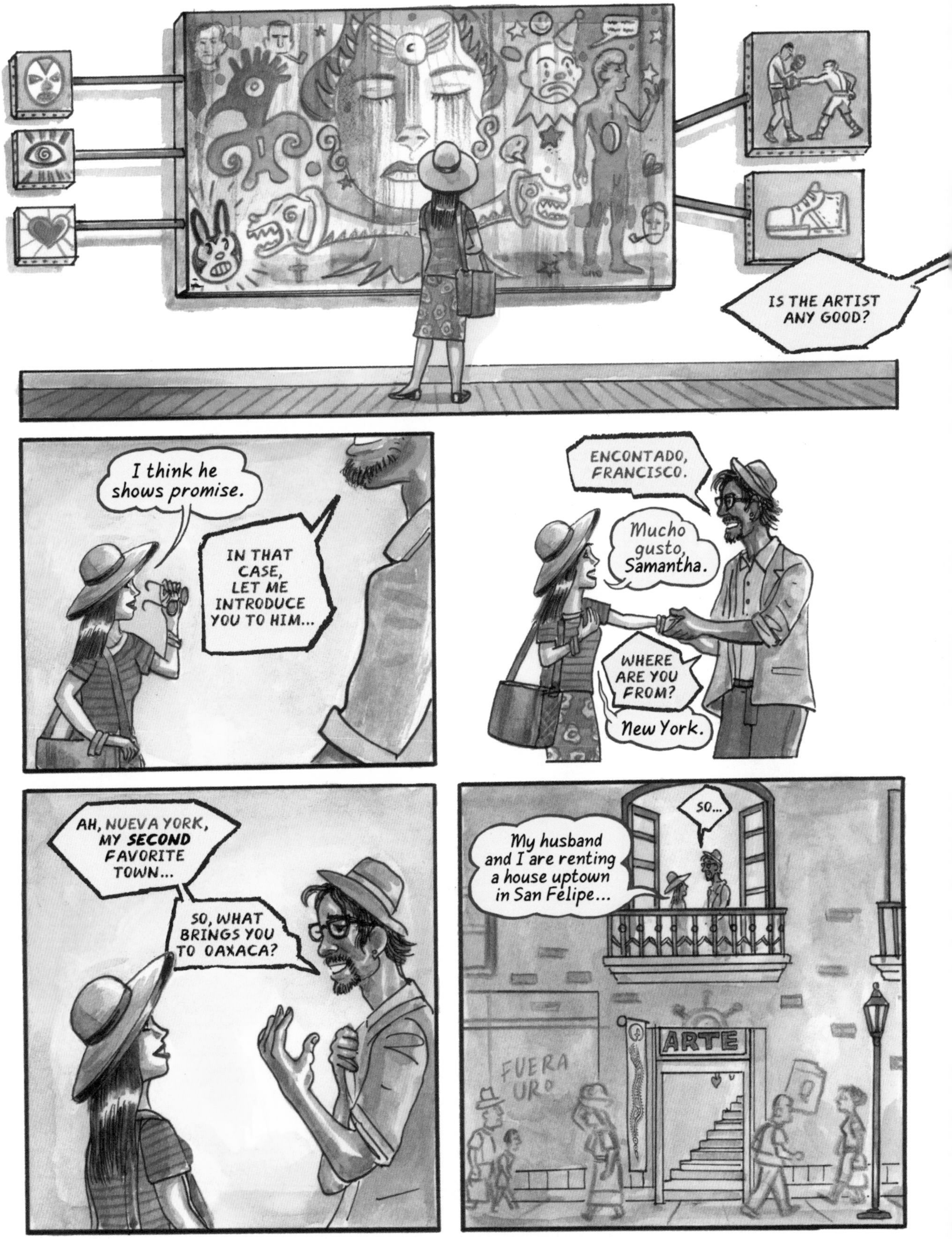
IS THE ARTIST ANY GOOD?
I think he shows promise.
IN THAT CASE, LET ME INTRODUCE YOU TO HIM...
ENCONTADO, FRANCISCO.
Mucho gusto, Samantha.
WHERE ARE YOU FROM?
New York.
AH, NUEVA YORK, MY **SECOND** FAVORITE TOWN...
SO, WHAT BRINGS YOU TO OAXACA?
SO...
My husband and I are renting a house uptown in San Felipe...
FUERA URO
ARTE

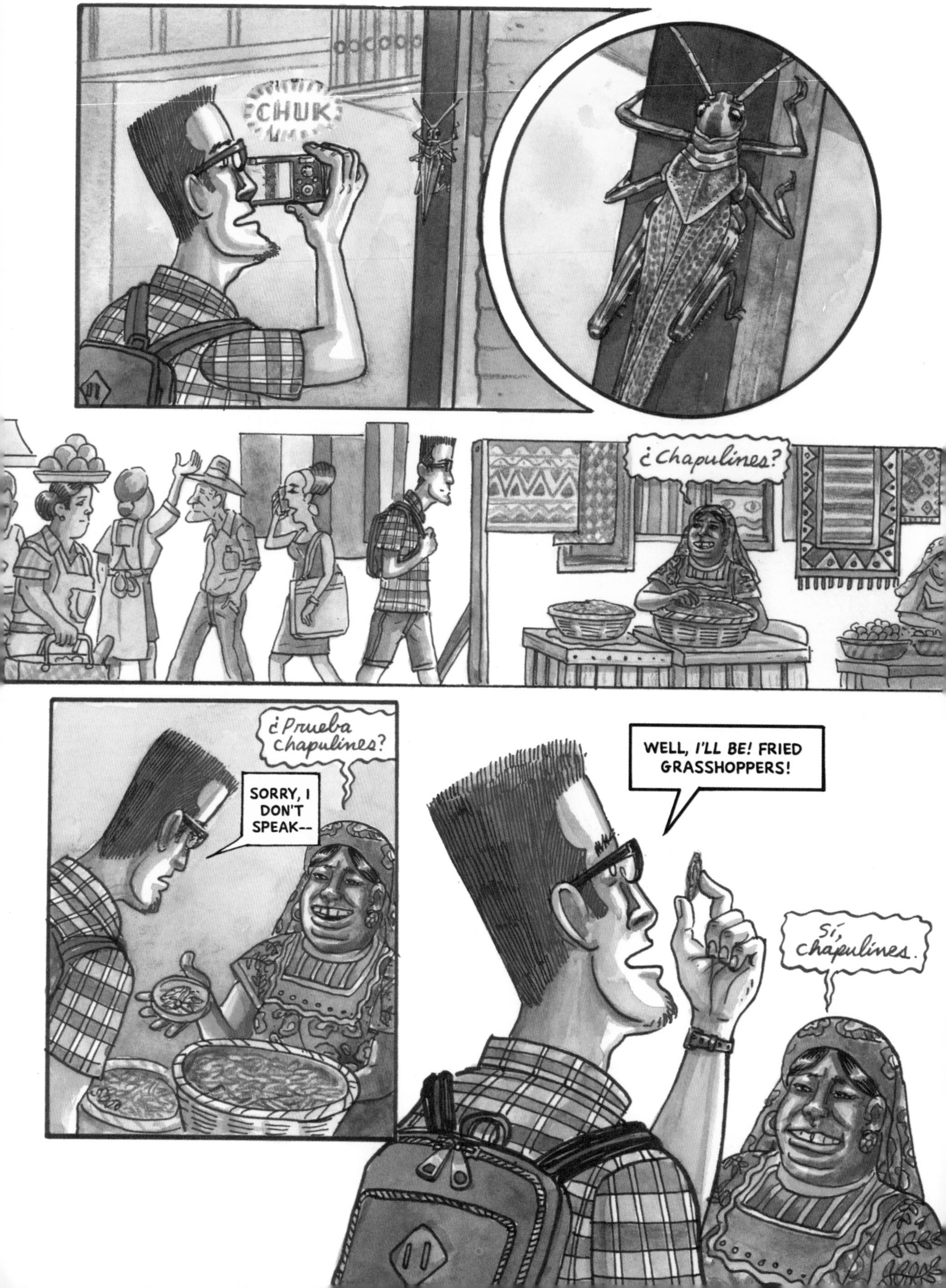
CHUK
¿Chapulines?
¿Prueba chapulines?
SORRY, I DON'T SPEAK--
WELL, I'LL BE! FRIED GRASSHOPPERS!
Sí, chapulines.

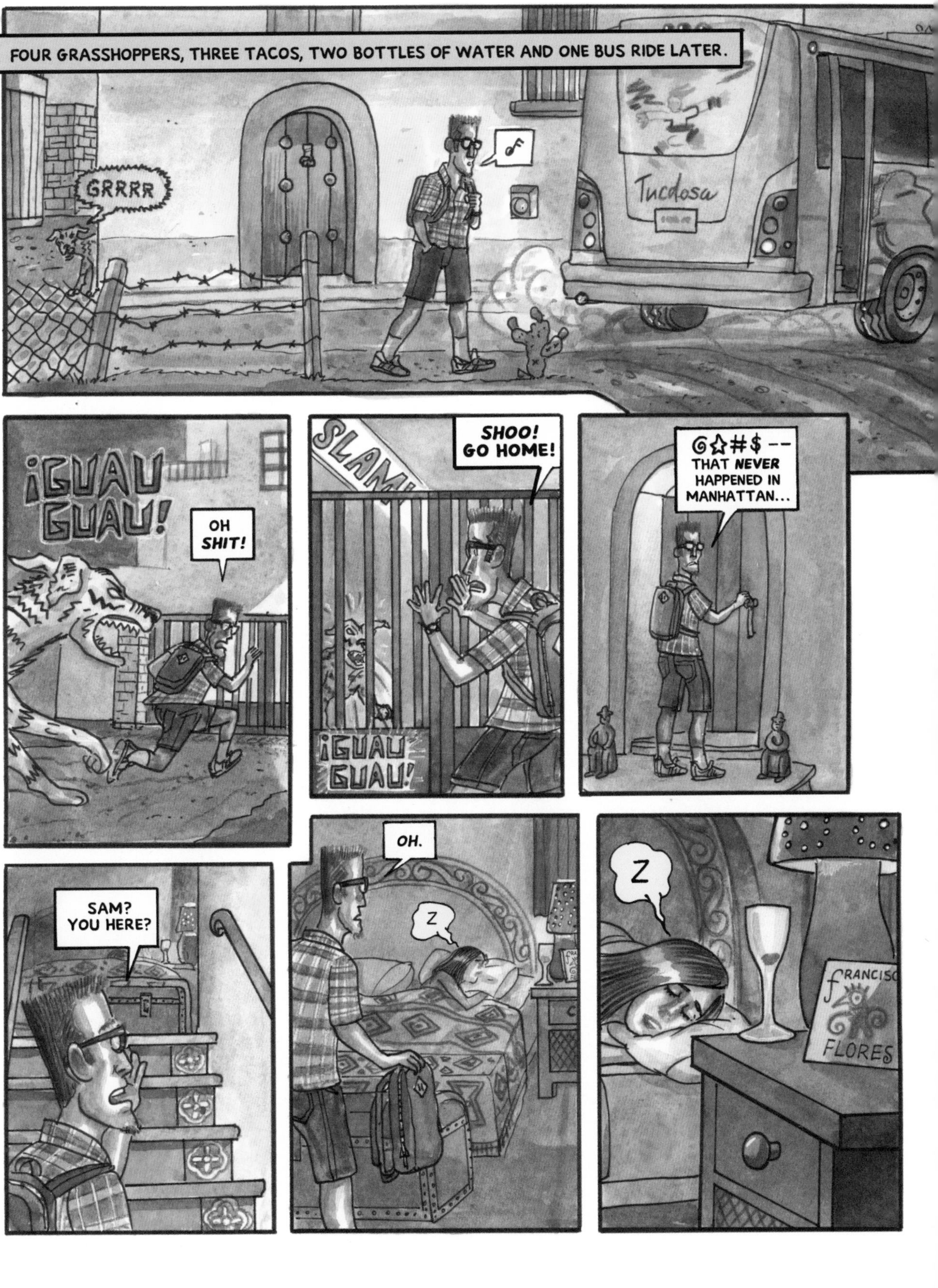
FOUR GRASSHOPPERS, THREE TACOS, TWO BOTTLES OF WATER AND ONE BUS RIDE LATER.
GRRRR
Tucdosa
¡GUAU GUAU!
OH SHIT!
SLAM!
SHOO! GO HOME!
¡GUAU GUAU!
@☆#$ -- THAT NEVER HAPPENED IN MANHATTAN...
SAM? YOU HERE?
OH.
Z
Z
FRANCISCO FLORES

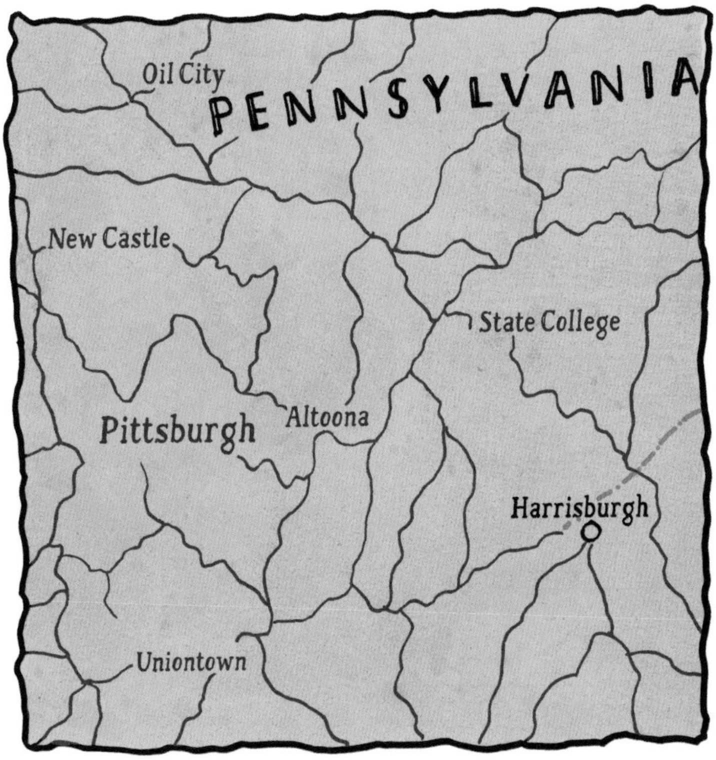
Oil City
PENNSYLVANIA
New Castle
State College
Pittsburgh
Altoona
Harrisburgh
Uniontown

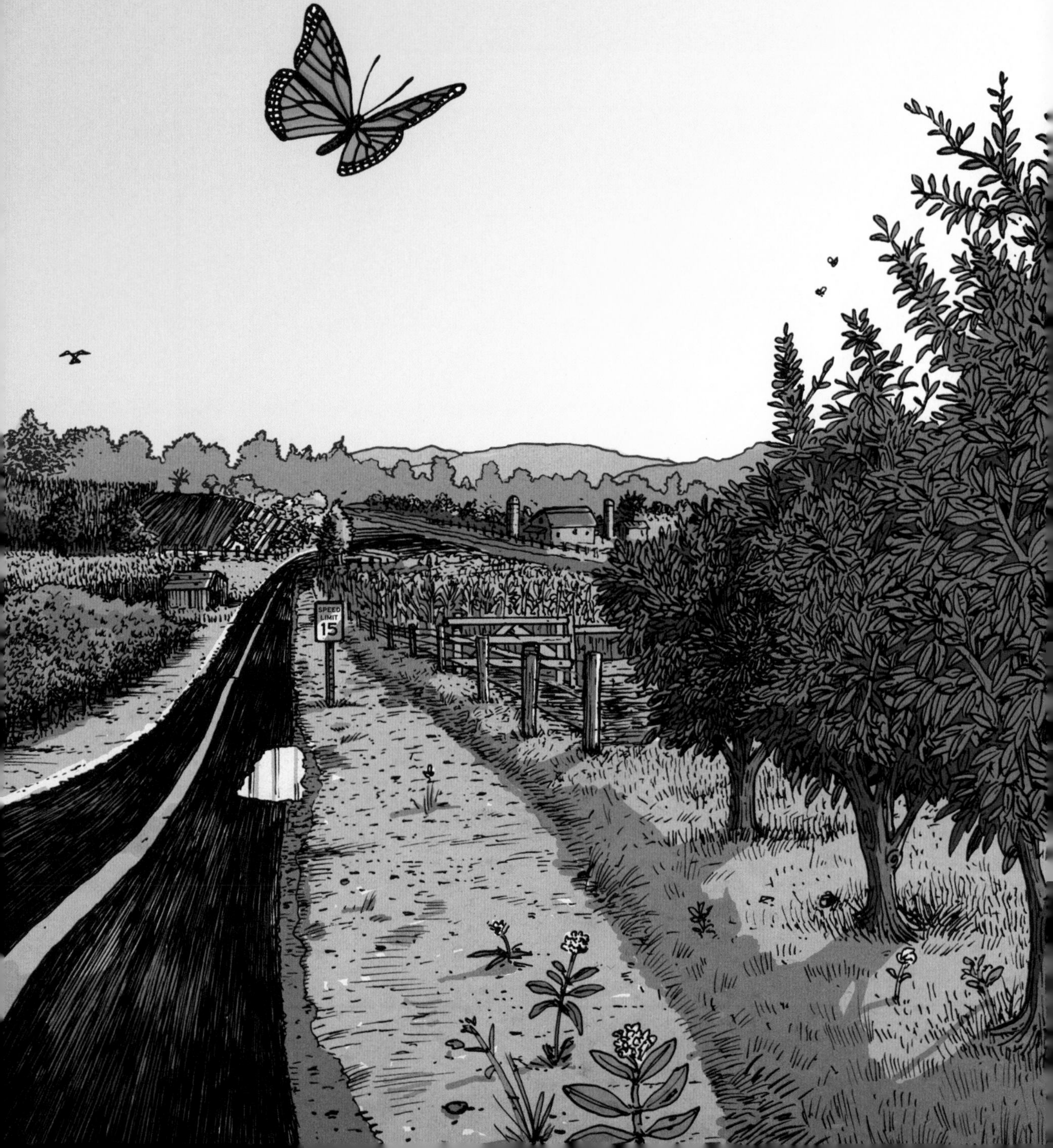
SPEED LIMIT
15

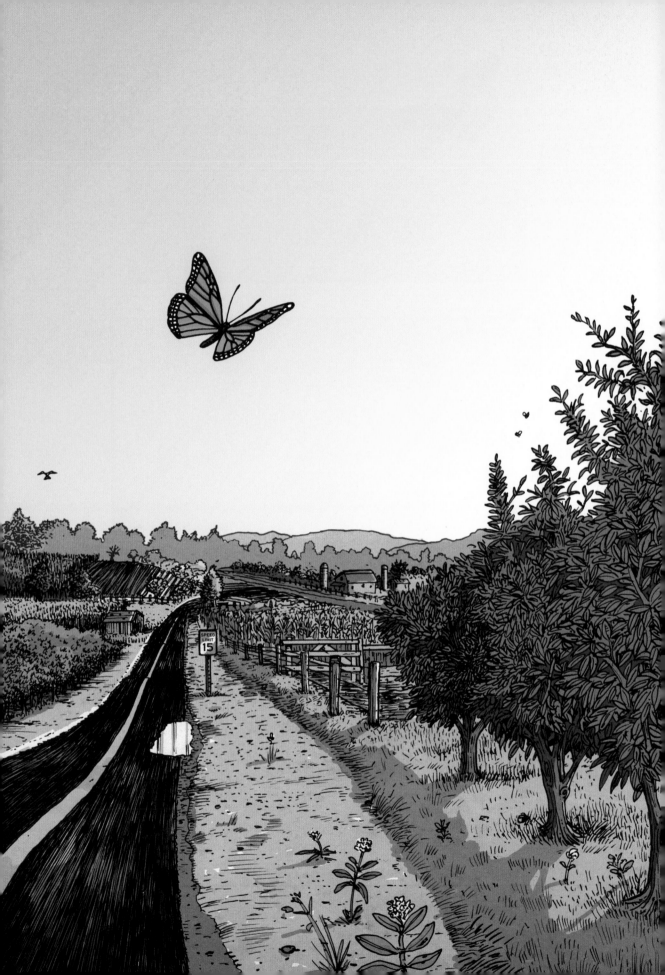

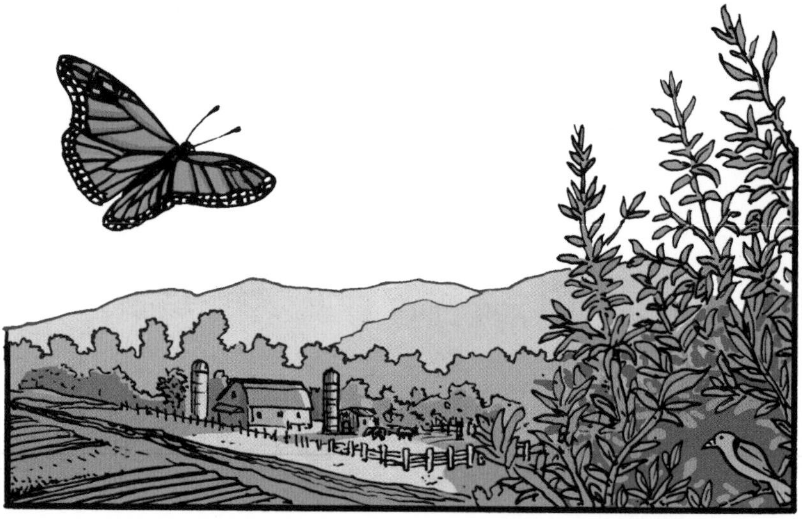
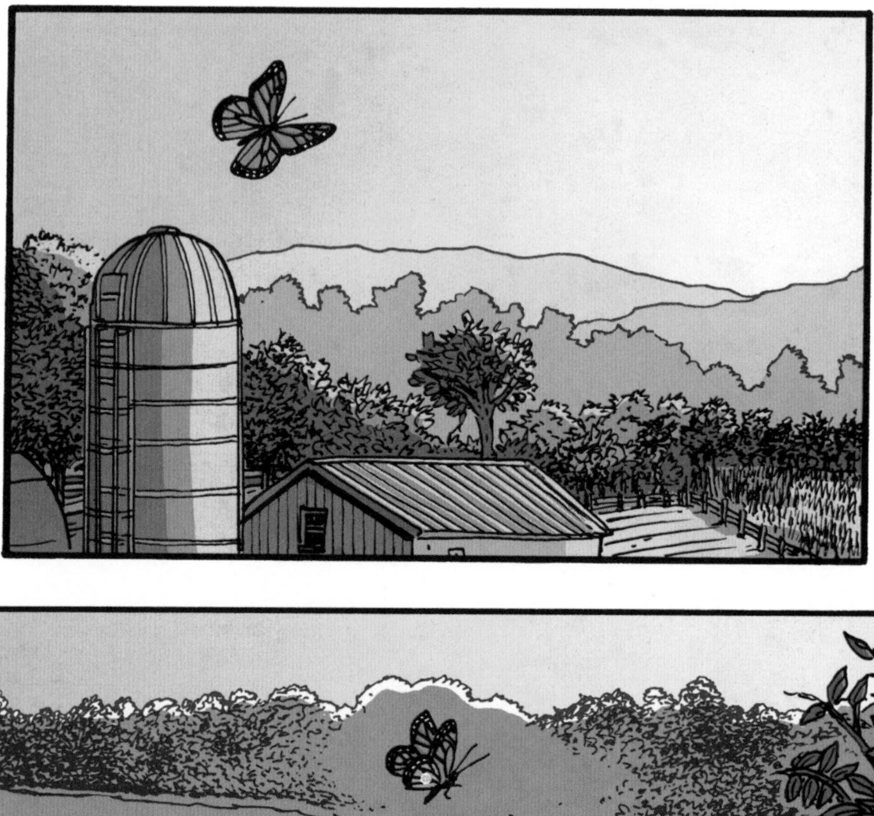
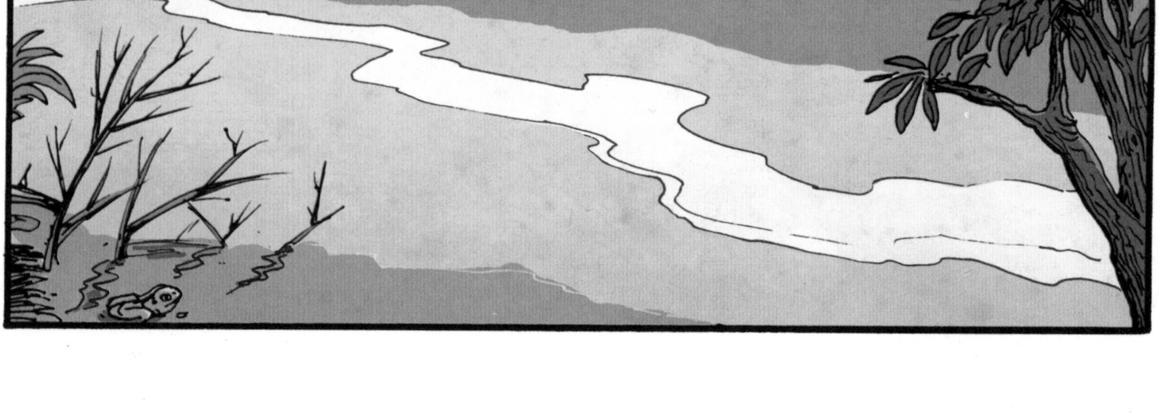

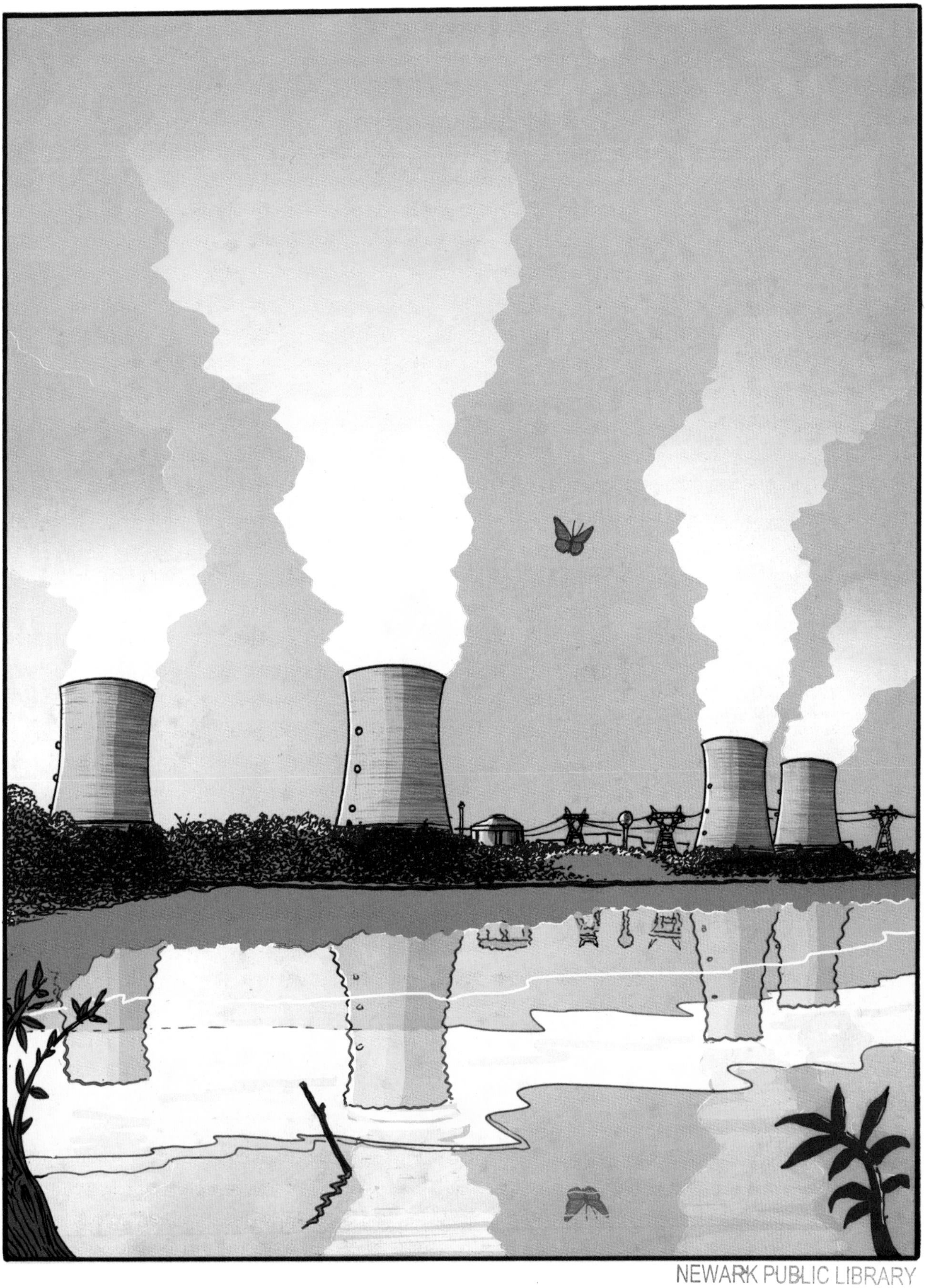

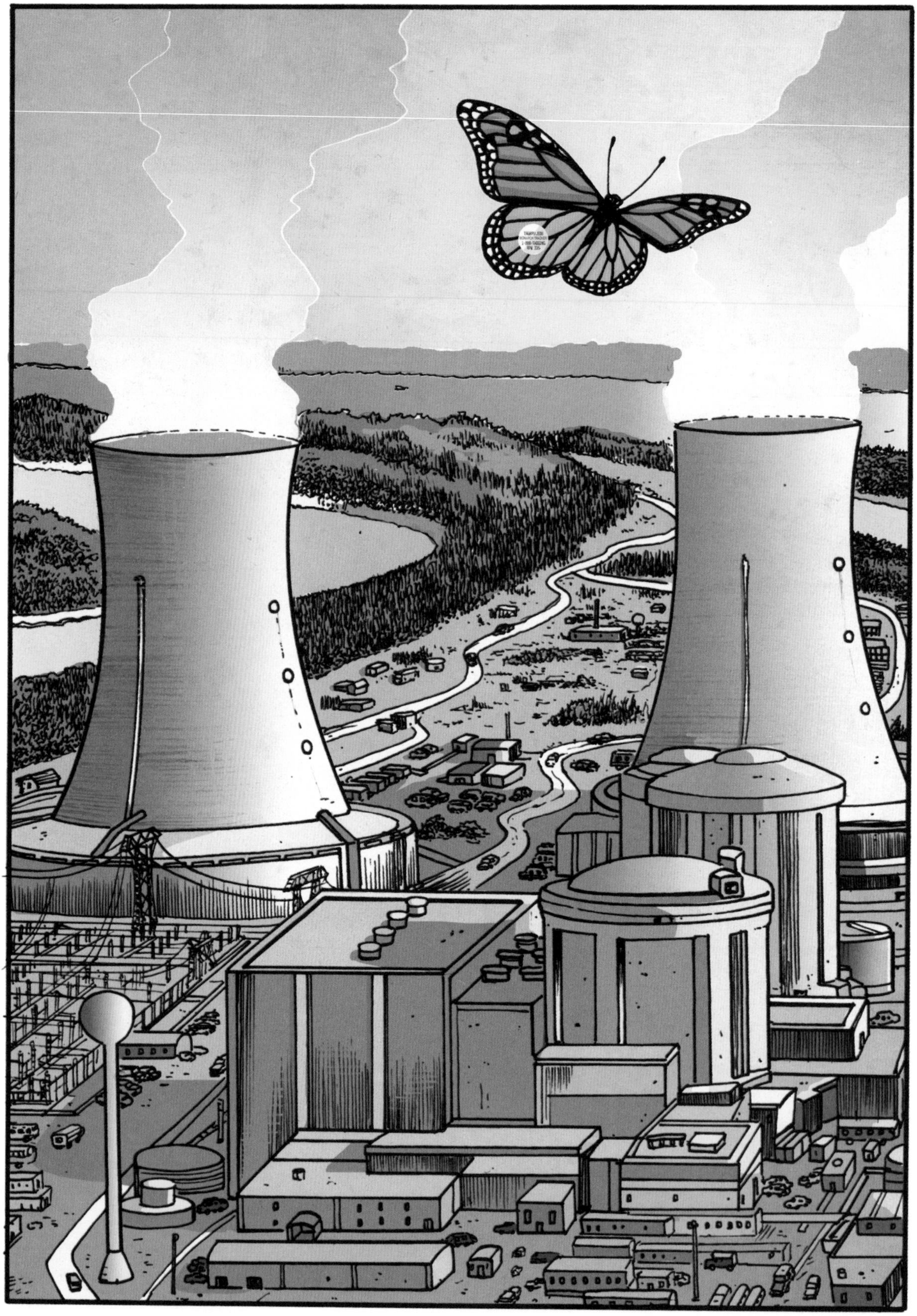

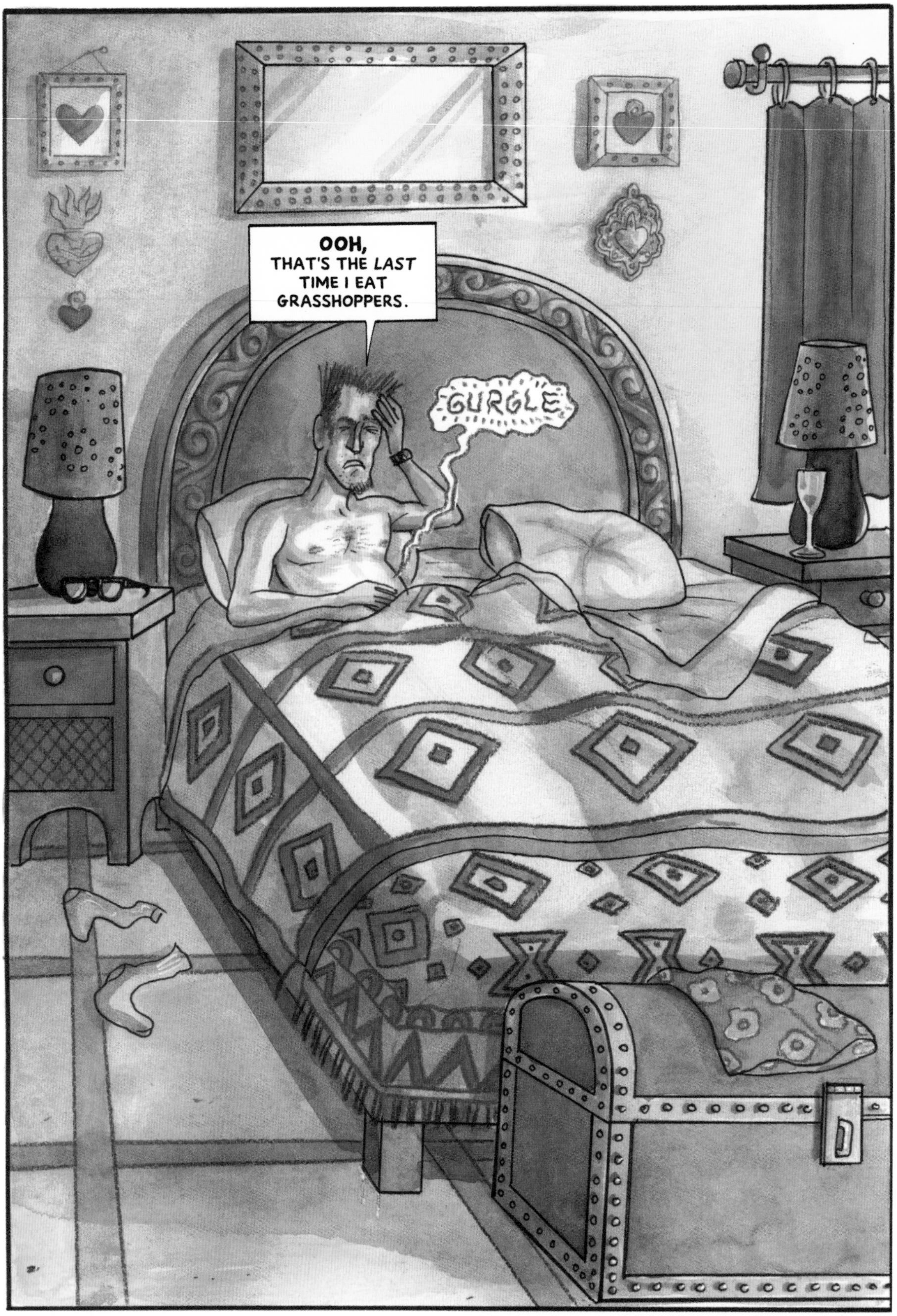
OOH, THAT'S THE *LAST* TIME I EAT GRASSHOPPERS.
GURGLE

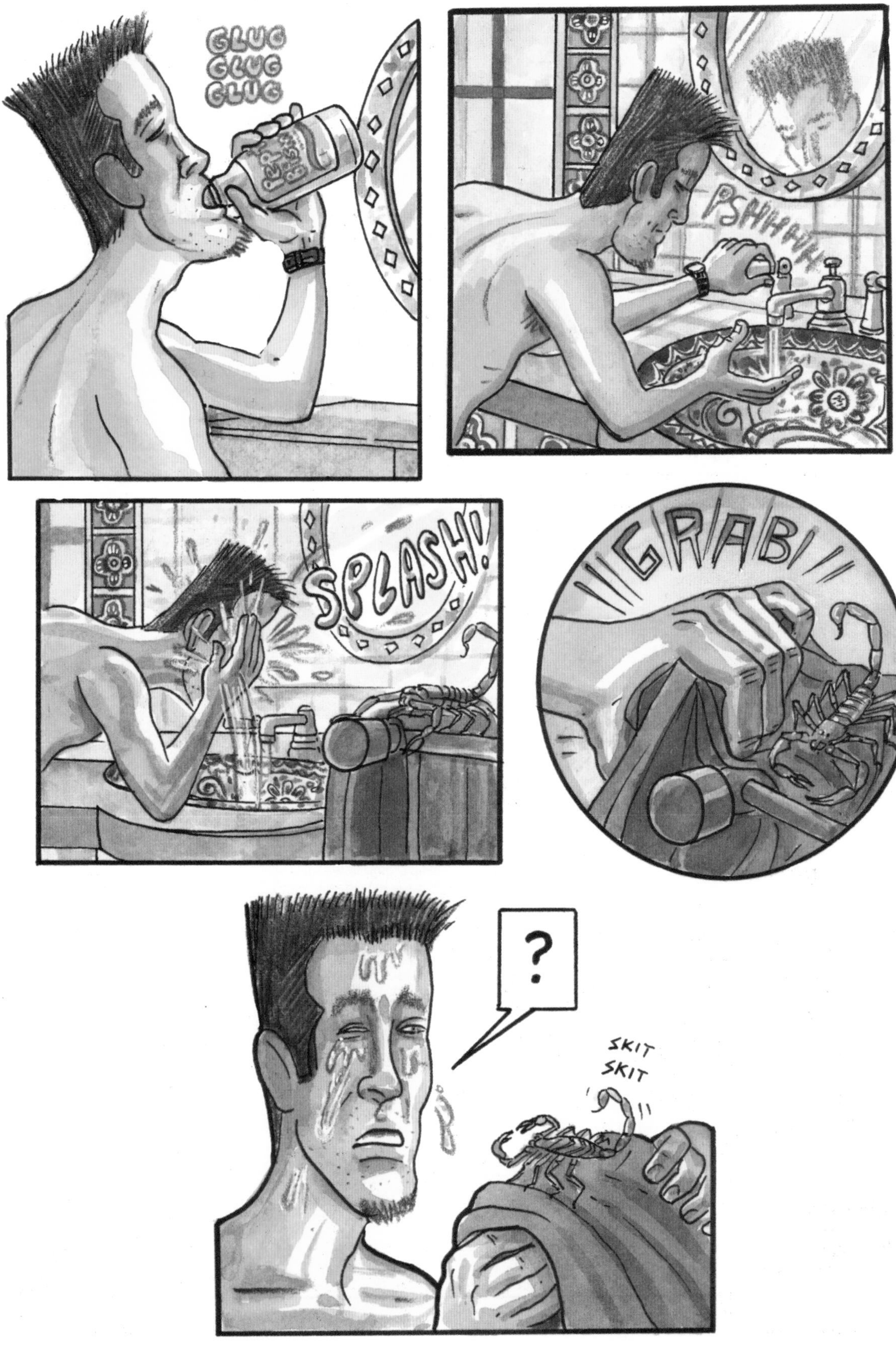
GLUG
GLUG
GLUG
PSHHHHH
SPLASH!
GRAB!
?
SKIT
SKIT

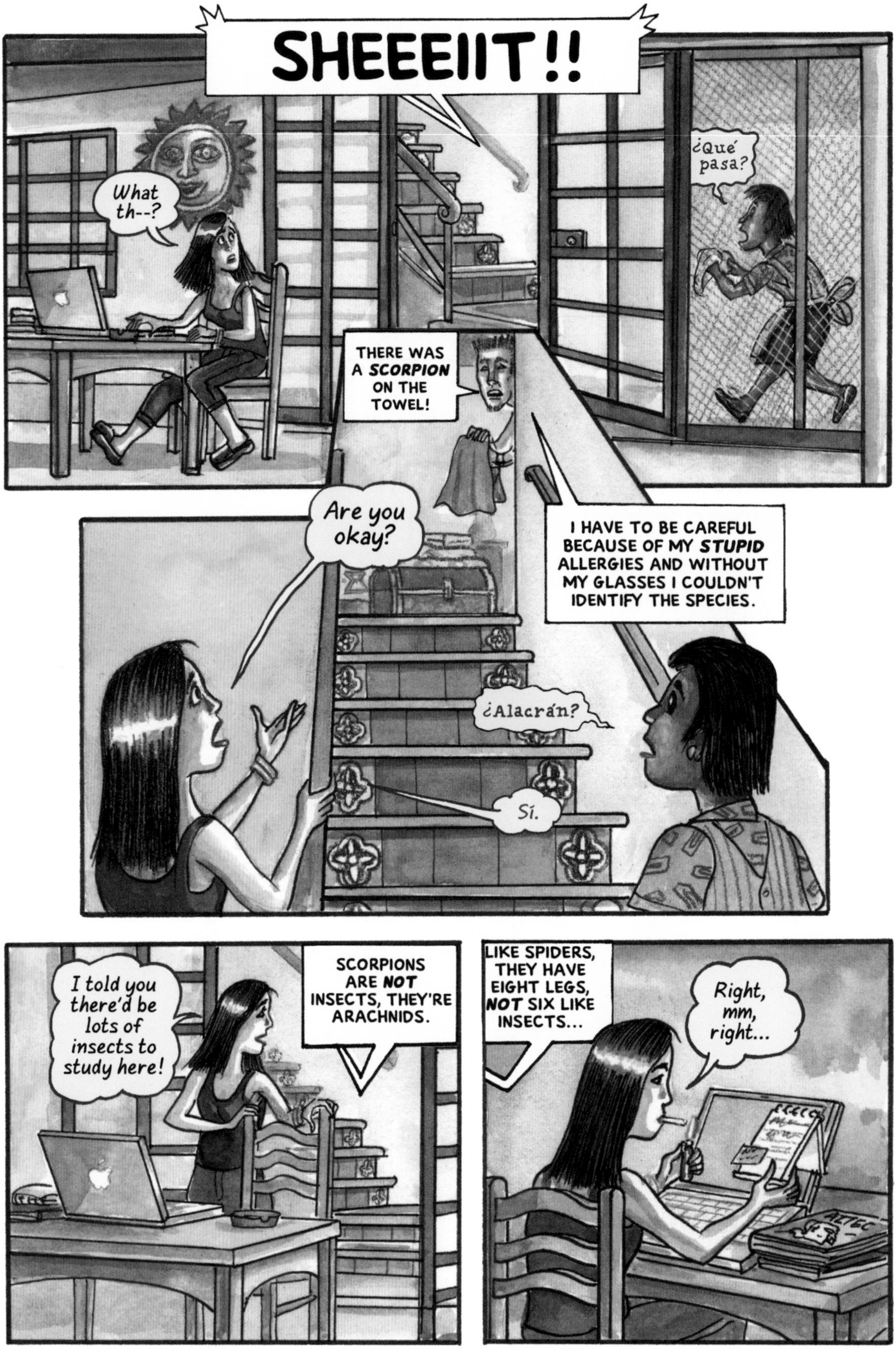

SHEEEIIT!!
What th--?
¿Qué pasa?
THERE WAS A SCORPION ON THE TOWEL!
Are you okay?
I HAVE TO BE CAREFUL BECAUSE OF MY STUPID ALLERGIES AND WITHOUT MY GLASSES I COULDN'T IDENTIFY THE SPECIES.
¿Alacrán?
Sí.
I told you there'd be lots of insects to study here!
SCORPIONS ARE NOT INSECTS, THEY'RE ARACHNIDS.
LIKE SPIDERS, THEY HAVE EIGHT LEGS, NOT SIX LIKE INSECTS...
Right, mm, right...

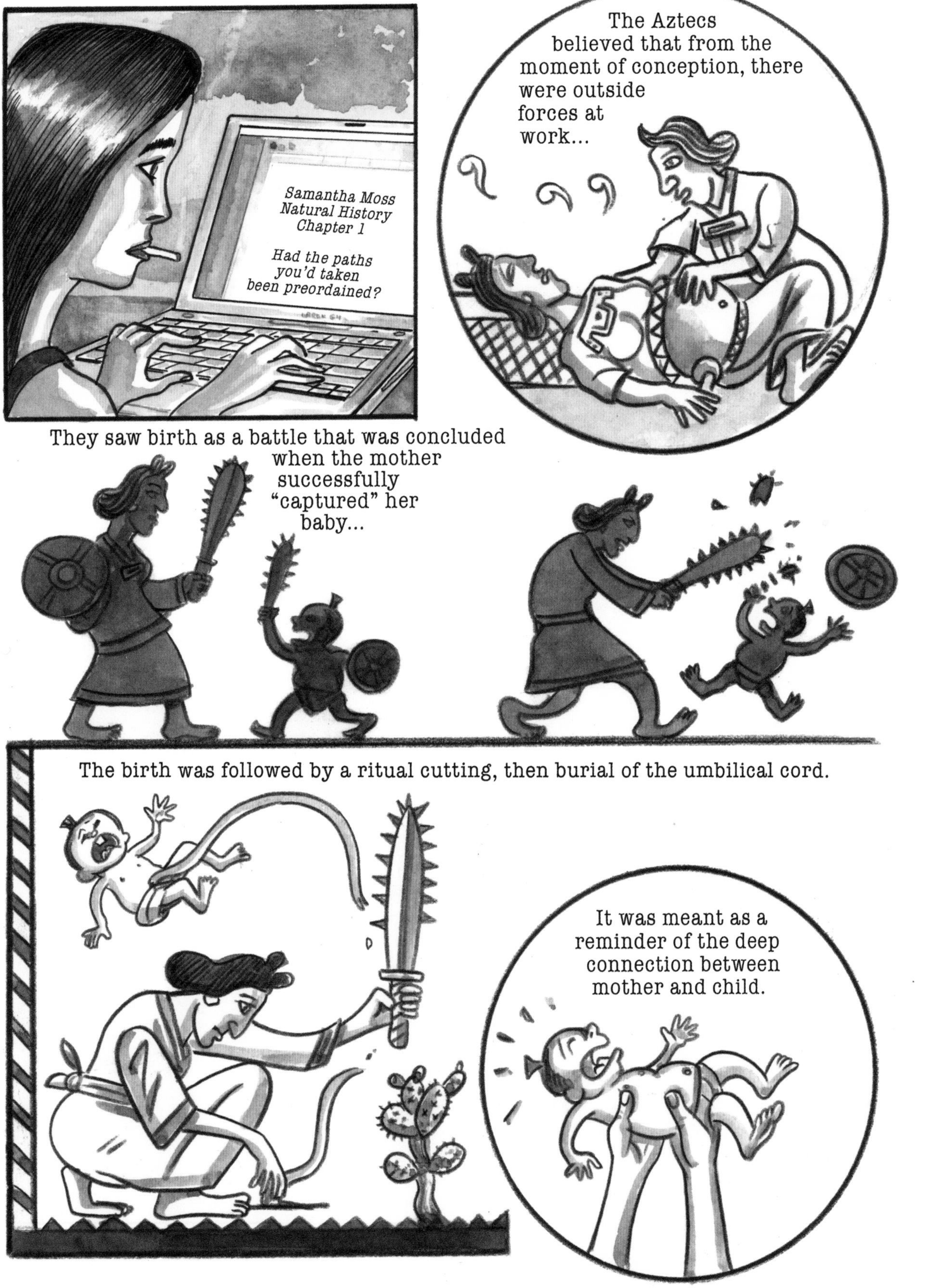
Samantha Moss
Natural History
Chapter 1
Had the paths
you'd taken
been preordained?
The Aztecs believed that from the moment of conception, there were outside forces at work...
They saw birth as a battle that was concluded when the mother successfully "captured" her baby...
The birth was followed by a ritual cutting, then burial of the umbilical cord.
It was meant as a reminder of the deep connection between mother and child.

This sequence, from conception forward, was overseen by a series of deities with names like Centeotl, Xochipilli, Xochiquetzal and Macuilxochitl...

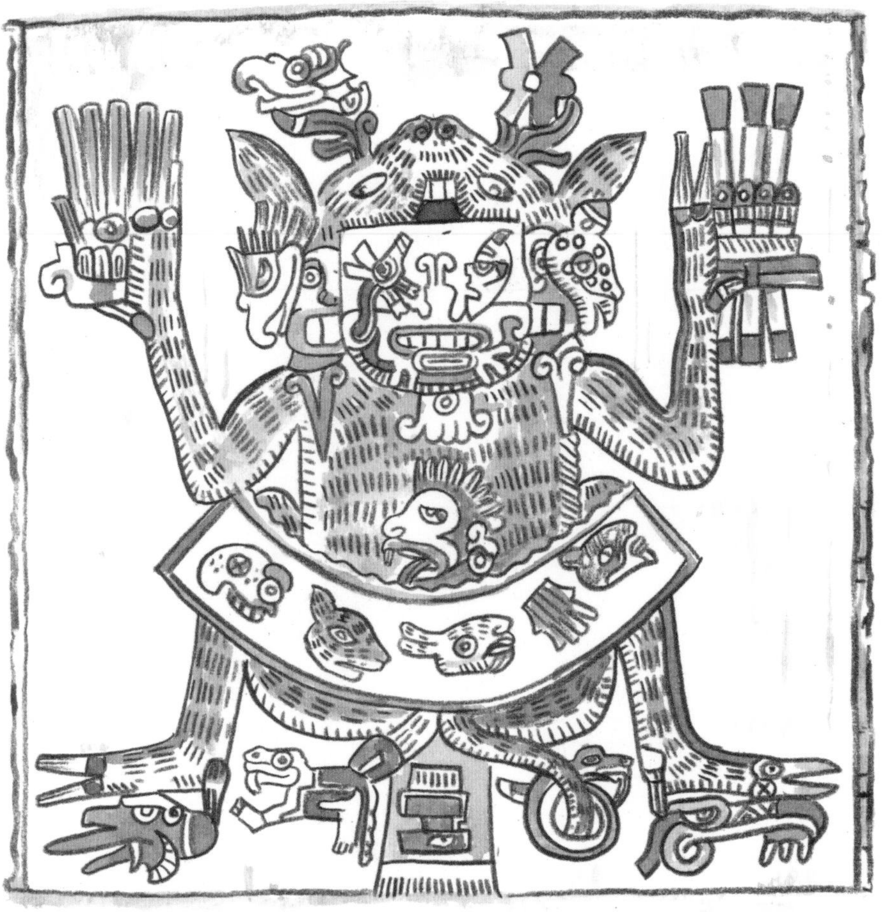

These ancient cultures also believed your date of birth was associated with specific day signs. Some days were connected to powerful positive characters...

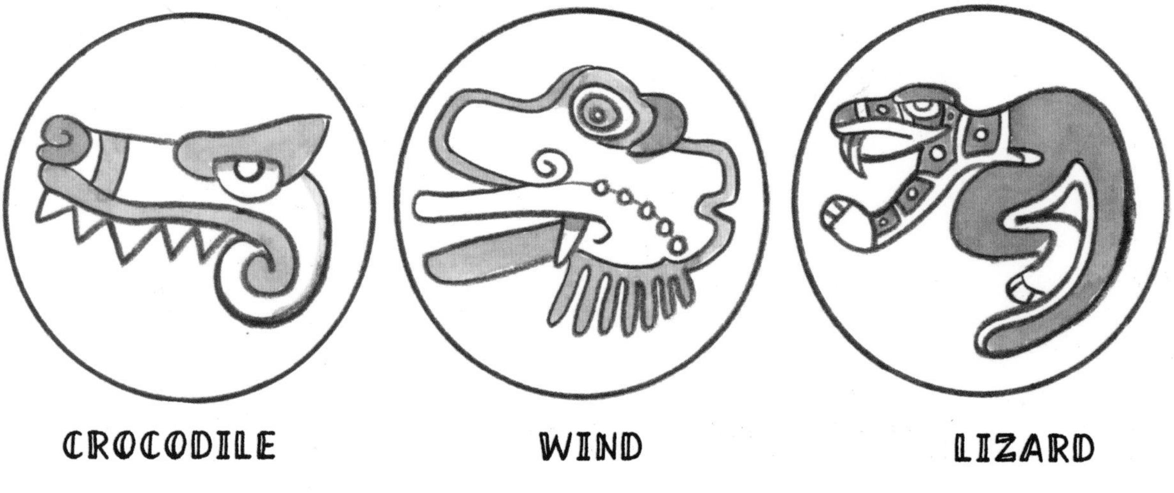
CROCODILE
WIND
LIZARD

Yet other birth dates foretold a troubled and difficult future.

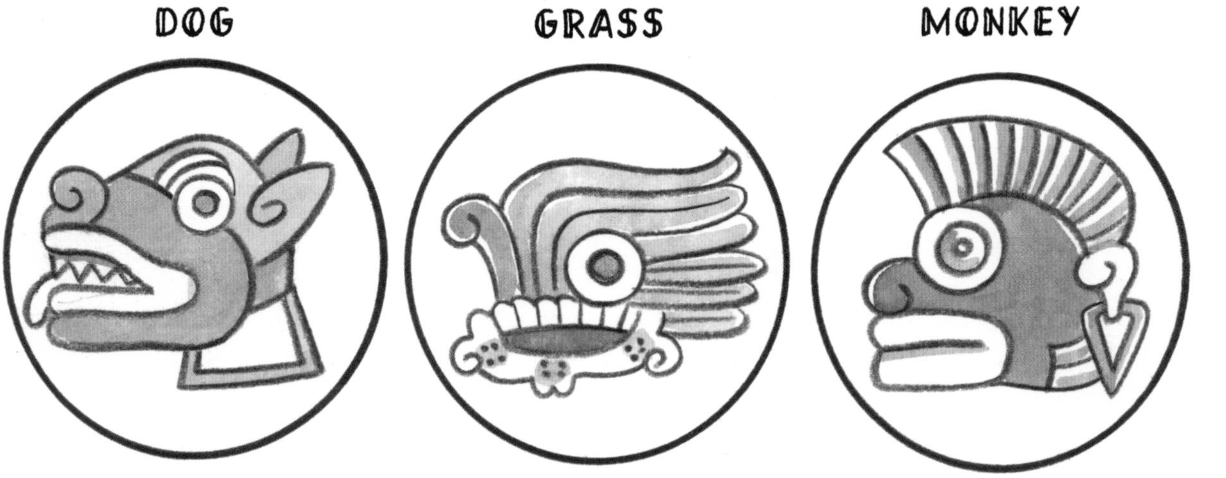
DOG
GRASS
MONKEY

These signs were associated with sacrifice, failure and death. A person born under any of these could expect trouble. So, what day sign were you born under? October 27th -- that was *Water*. And according to those ancient astrologers...

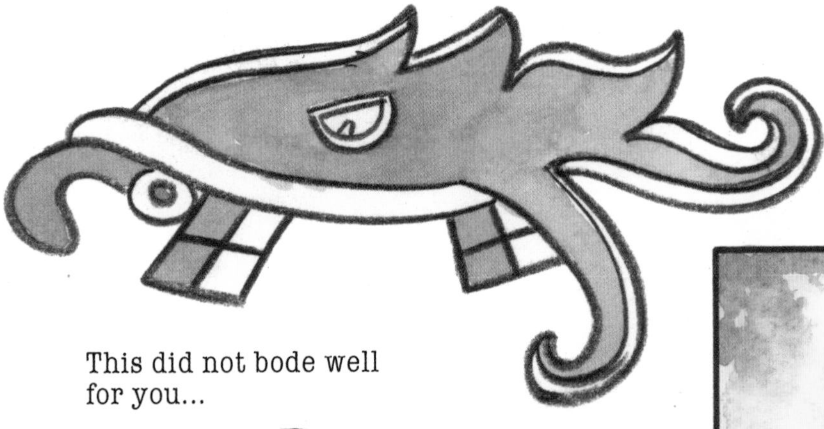

This did not bode well for you...

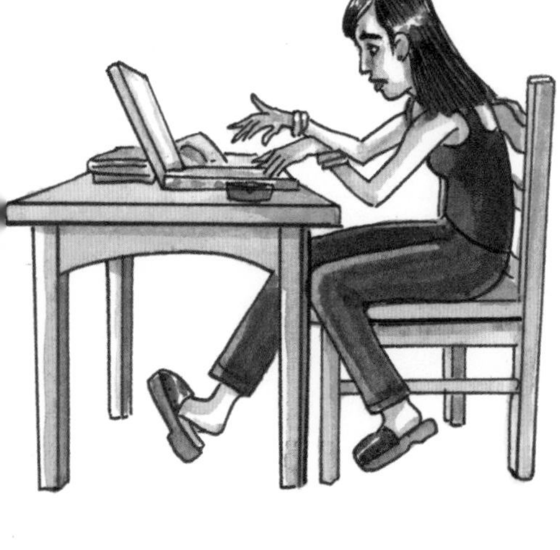

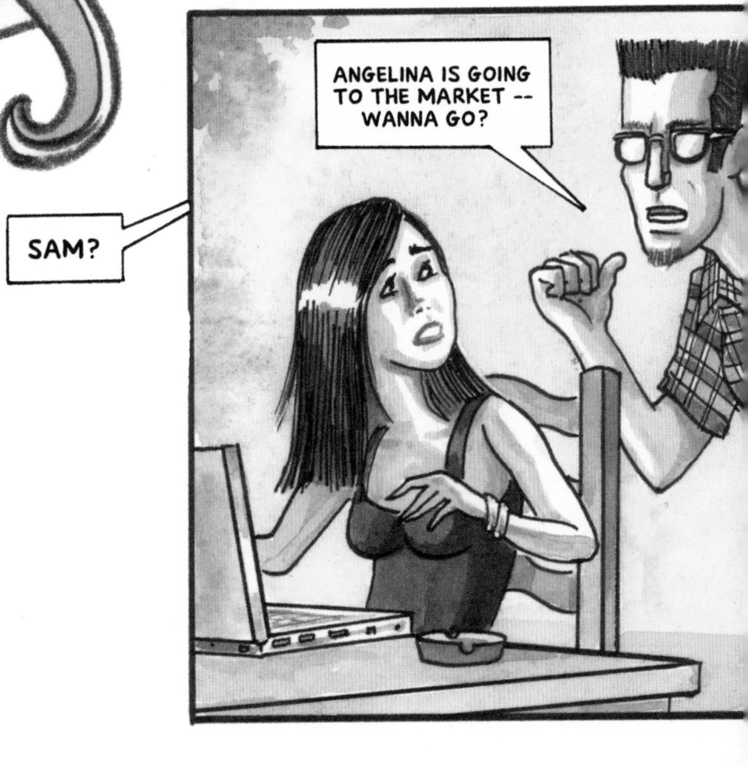
SAM?
ANGELINA IS GOING TO THE MARKET -- WANNA GO?

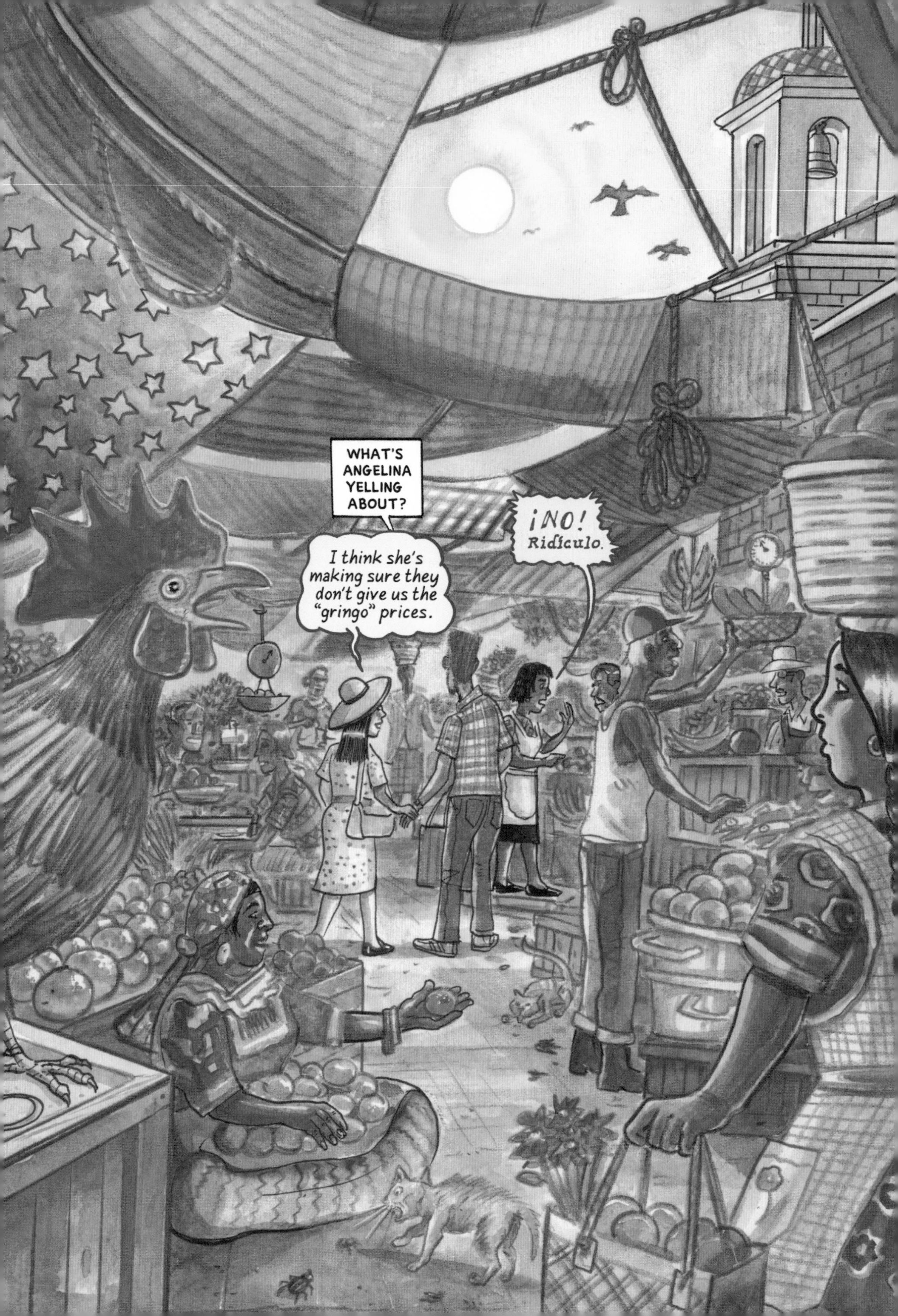
WHAT'S ANGELINA YELLING ABOUT?
I think she's making sure they don't give us the "gringo" prices.
¡NO! Ridículo.

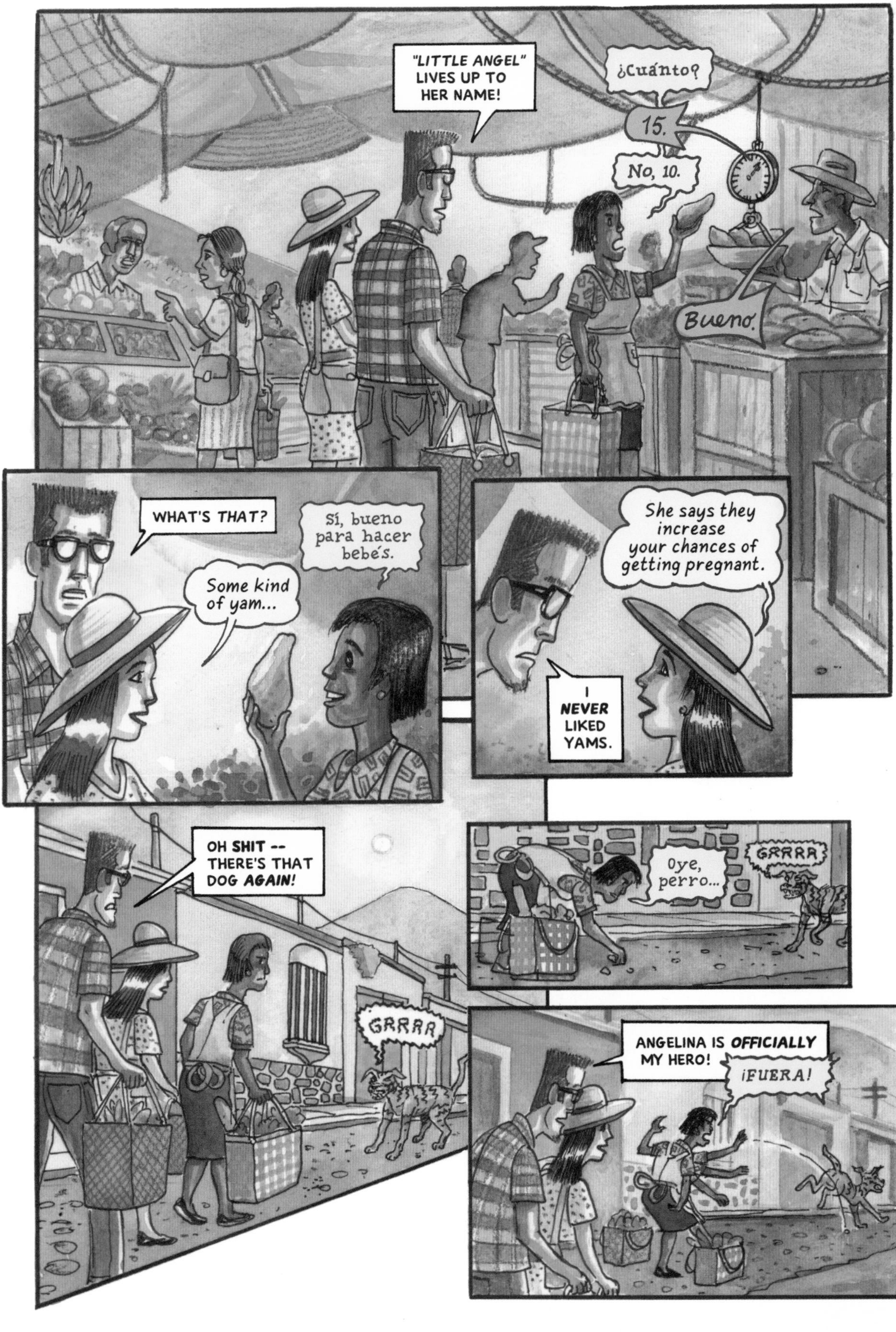
"LITTLE ANGEL" LIVES UP TO HER NAME!
¿Cuánto?
15.
No, 10.
Bueno.
WHAT'S THAT?
Sí, bueno para hacer bebés.
Some kind of yam...
She says they increase your chances of getting pregnant.
I **NEVER** LIKED YAMS.
OH **SHIT** -- THERE'S THAT DOG **AGAIN**!
GRRRR
Oye, perro...
GRRRR
ANGELINA IS **OFFICIALLY** MY HERO!
¡FUERA!

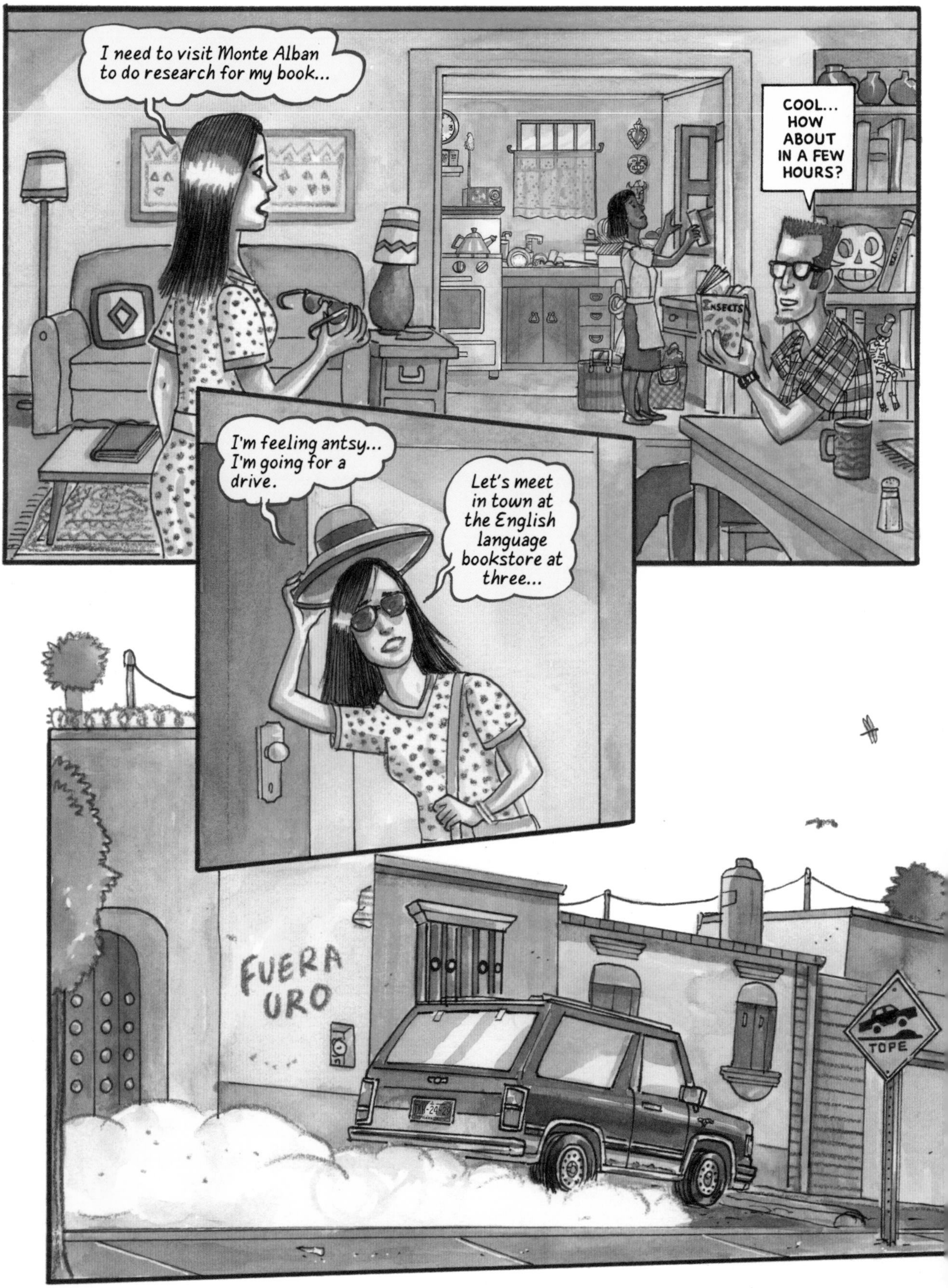
I need to visit Monte Alban to do research for my book...
COOL... HOW ABOUT IN A FEW HOURS?
INSECTS
I'm feeling antsy... I'm going for a drive.
Let's meet in town at the English language bookstore at three...
FUERA URO
TOPE

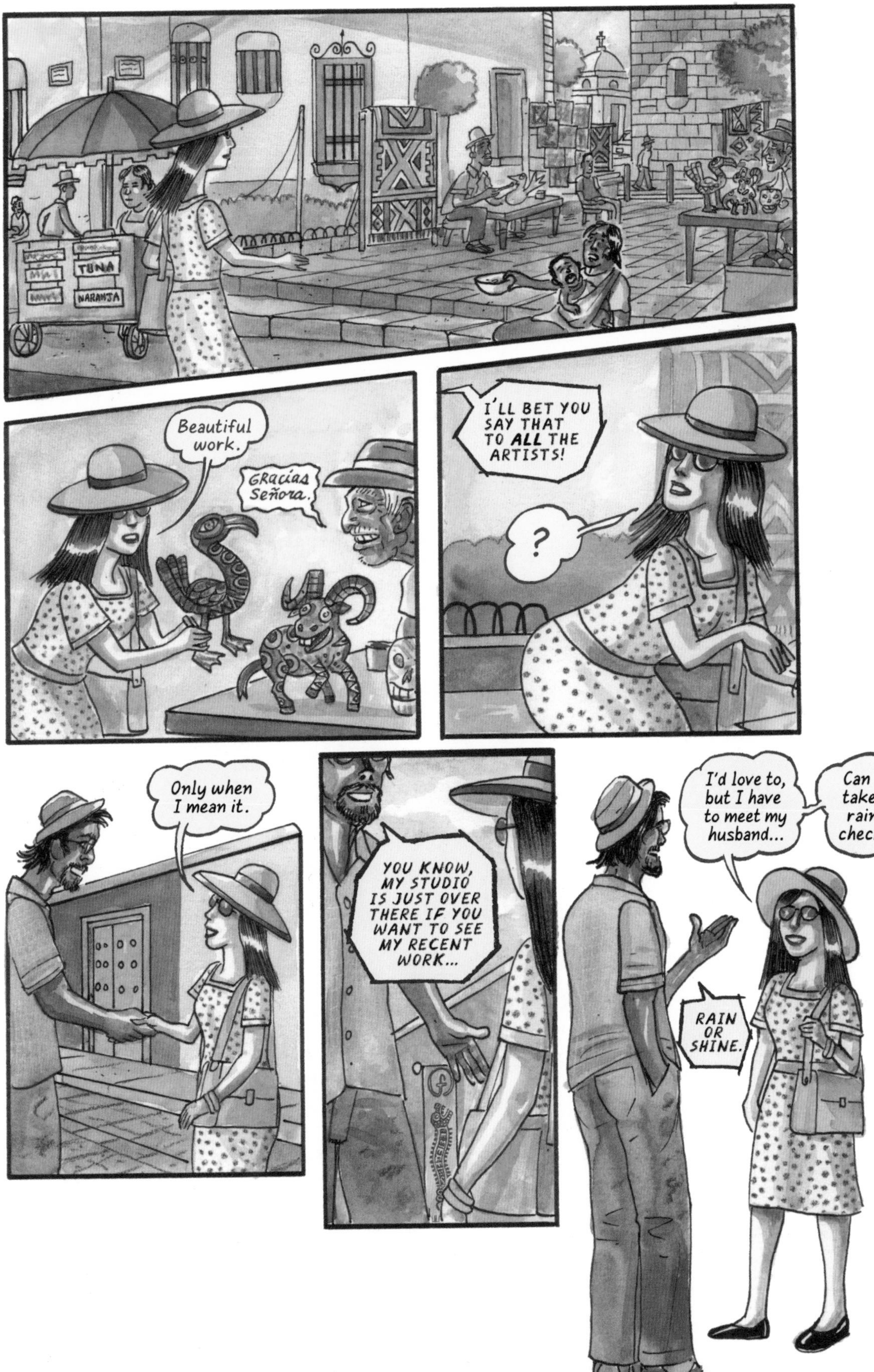
TUNA
NARANJA
Beautiful work.
Gracias Señora.
I'LL BET YOU SAY THAT TO ALL THE ARTISTS!
?
Only when I mean it.
YOU KNOW, MY STUDIO IS JUST OVER THERE IF YOU WANT TO SEE MY RECENT WORK...
I'd love to, but I have to meet my husband...
Can I take a rain-check?
RAIN OR SHINE.

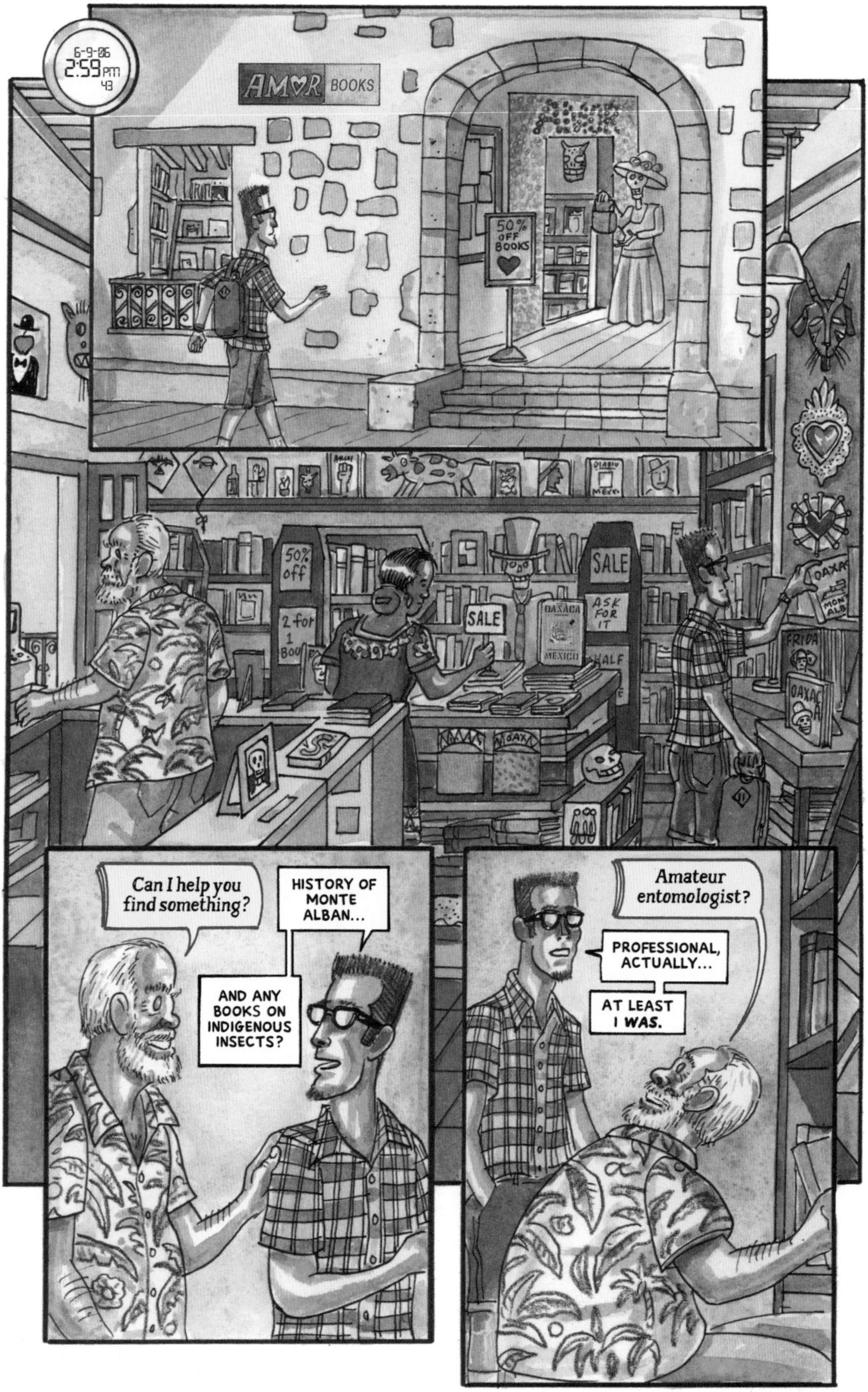
6-9-06
2:59pm
43
AMOR BOOKS
50% OFF BOOKS
50% off
2 for 1
SALE
SALE
ASK FOR IT
OAXACA
MEXICO
FRIDA
Can I help you find something?
HISTORY OF MONTE ALBAN...
AND ANY BOOKS ON INDIGENOUS INSECTS?
Amateur entomologist?
PROFESSIONAL, ACTUALLY...
AT LEAST I *WAS.*

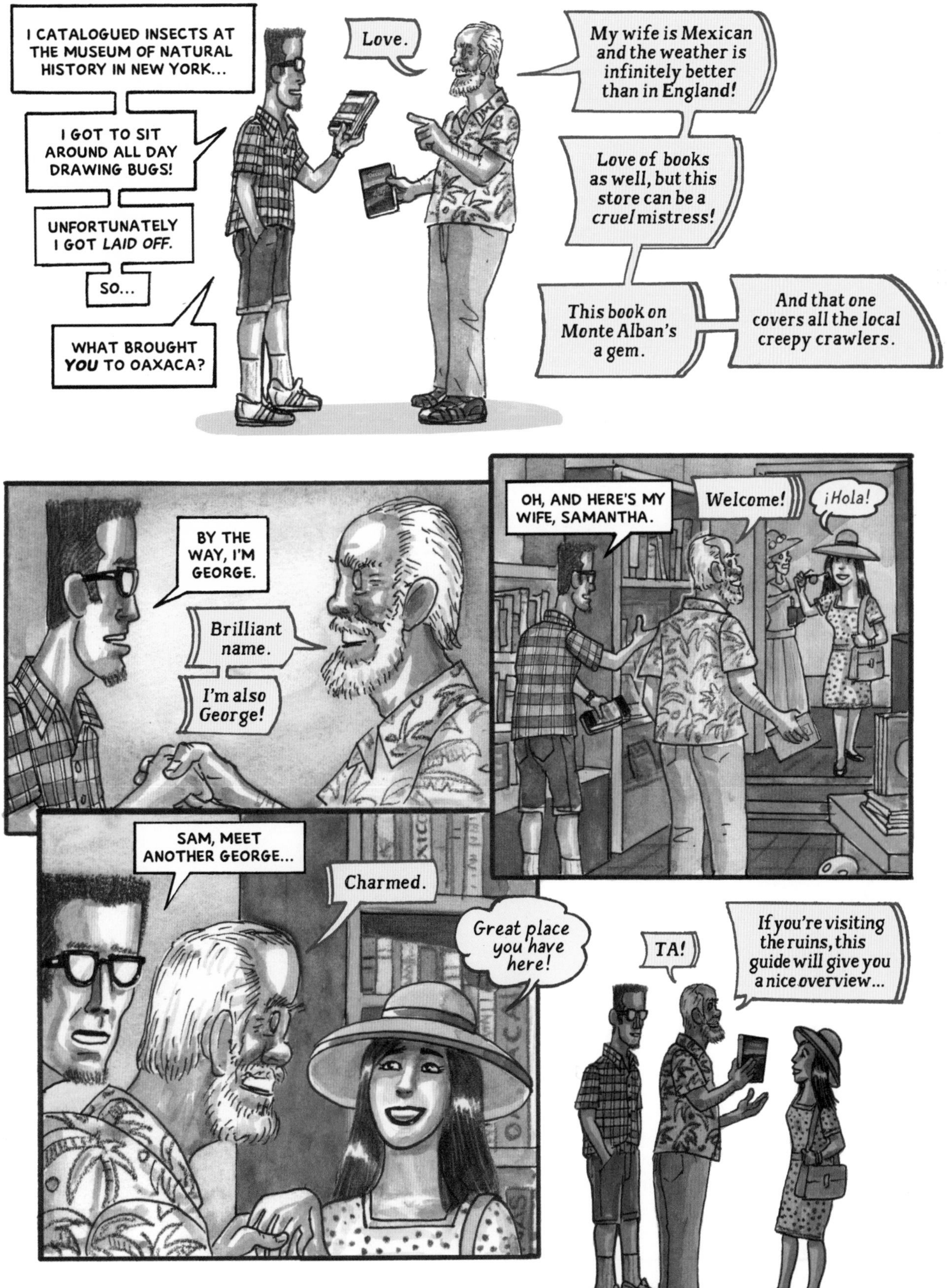

I CATALOGUED INSECTS AT THE MUSEUM OF NATURAL HISTORY IN NEW YORK...
I GOT TO SIT AROUND ALL DAY DRAWING BUGS!
UNFORTUNATELY I GOT *LAID OFF*.
SO...
WHAT BROUGHT ***YOU*** TO OAXACA?
Love.
My wife is Mexican and the weather is infinitely better than in England!
Love of books as well, but this store can be a *cruel* mistress!
This book on Monte Alban's a gem.
And that one covers all the local creepy crawlers.
BY THE WAY, I'M GEORGE.
Brilliant name.
I'm also George!
OH, AND HERE'S MY WIFE, SAMANTHA.
Welcome!
¡Hola!
SAM, MEET ANOTHER GEORGE...
Charmed.
Great place you have here!
TA!
If you're visiting the ruins, this guide will give you a nice overview...

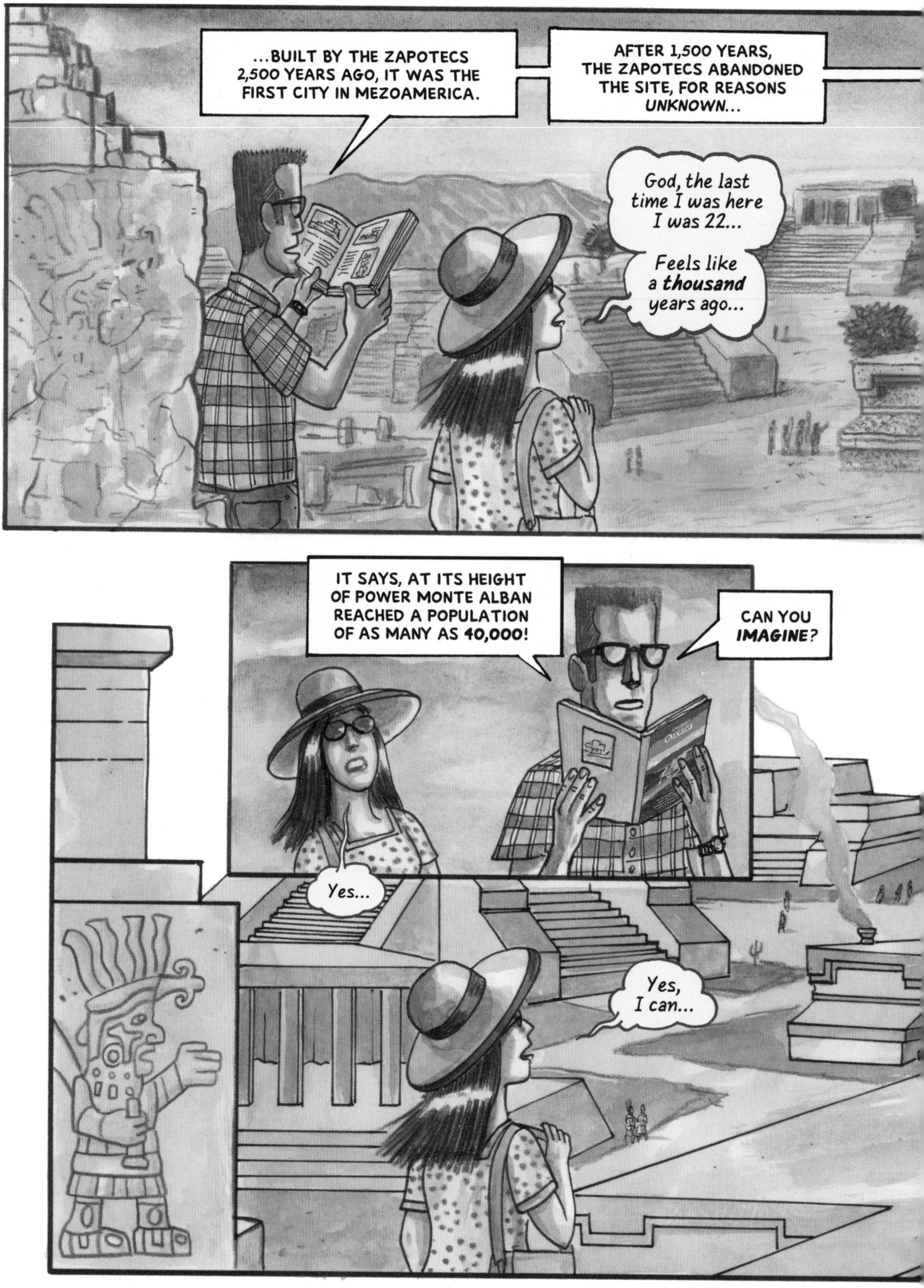
...BUILT BY THE ZAPOTECS 2,500 YEARS AGO, IT WAS THE FIRST CITY IN MEZOAMERICA.
AFTER 1,500 YEARS, THE ZAPOTECS ABANDONED THE SITE, FOR REASONS UNKNOWN...
God, the last time I was here I was 22...
Feels like a **thousand** years ago...
IT SAYS, AT ITS HEIGHT OF POWER MONTE ALBAN REACHED A POPULATION OF AS MANY AS **40,000**!
CAN YOU **IMAGINE**?
Yes...
Yes, I can...

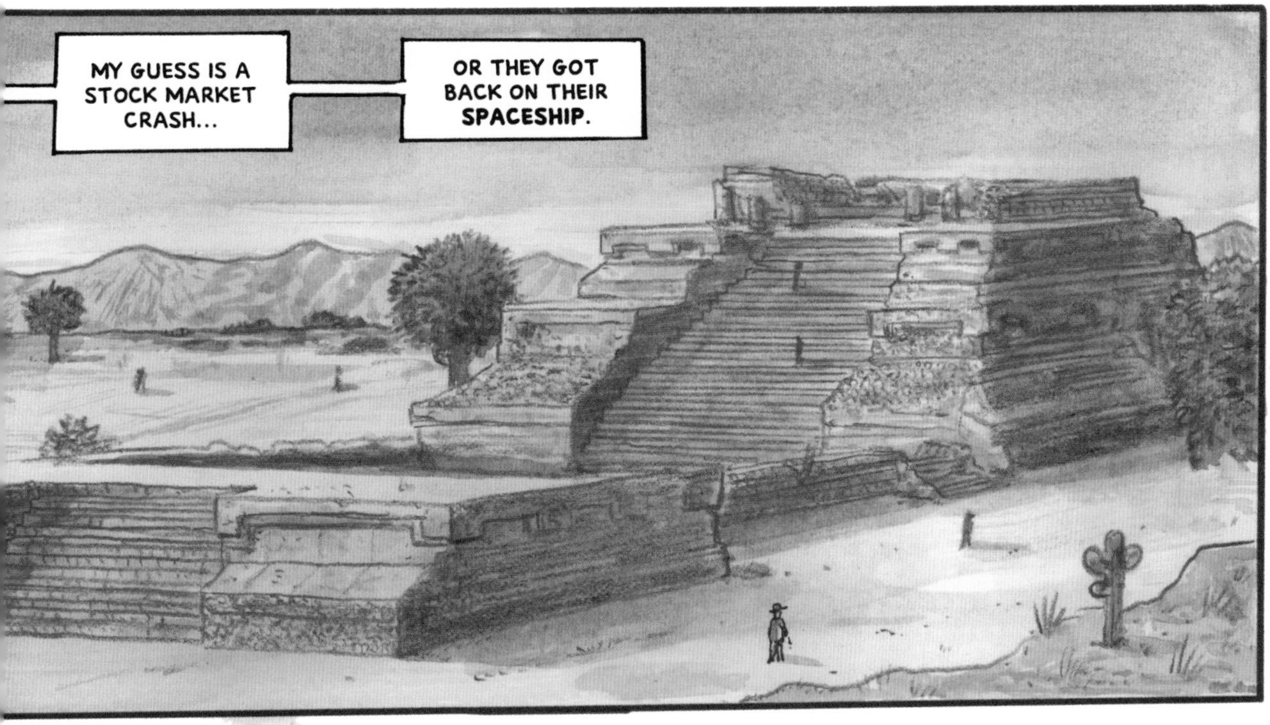
MY GUESS IS A STOCK MARKET CRASH...
OR THEY GOT BACK ON THEIR **SPACESHIP**.

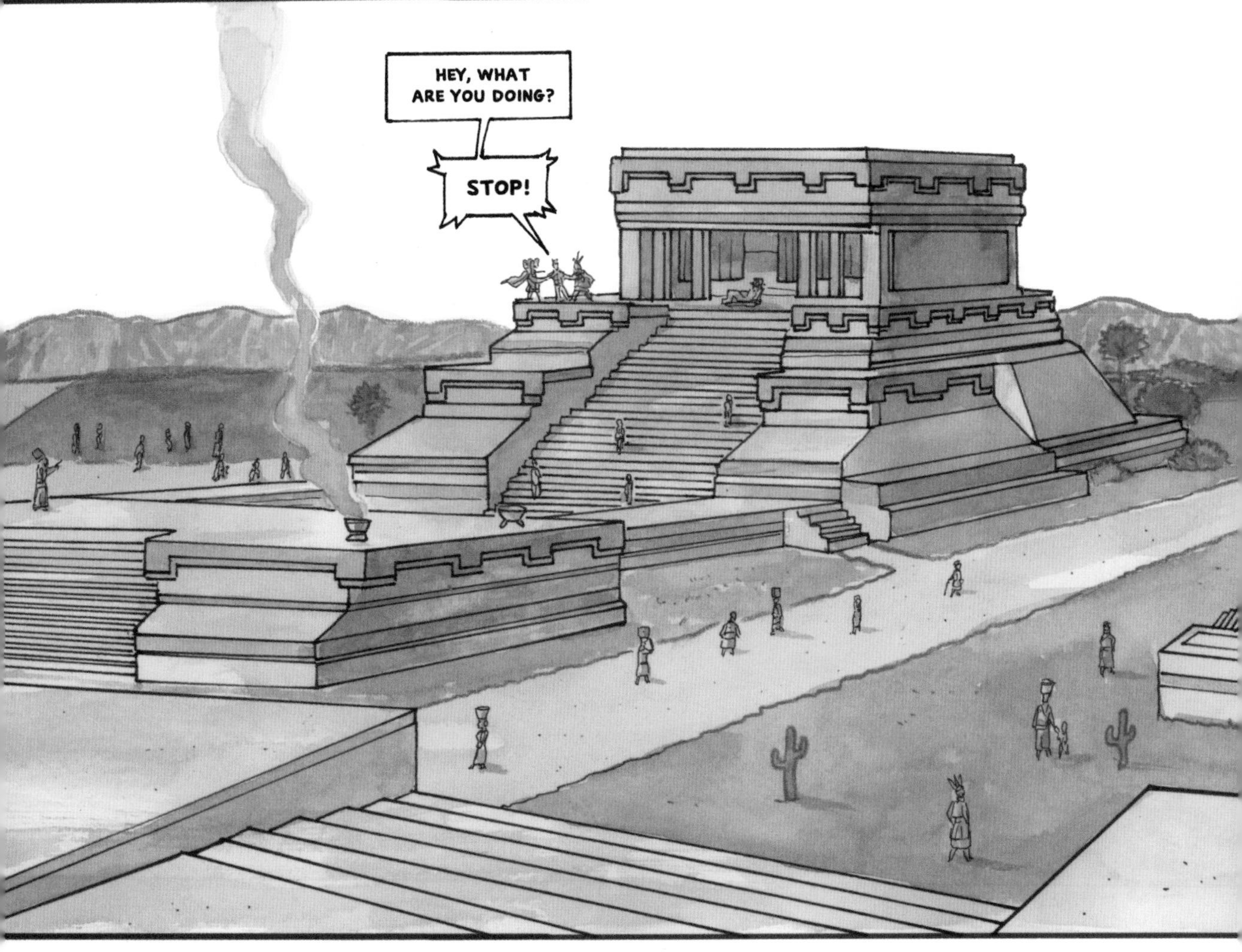
HEY, WHAT ARE YOU DOING?
STOP!

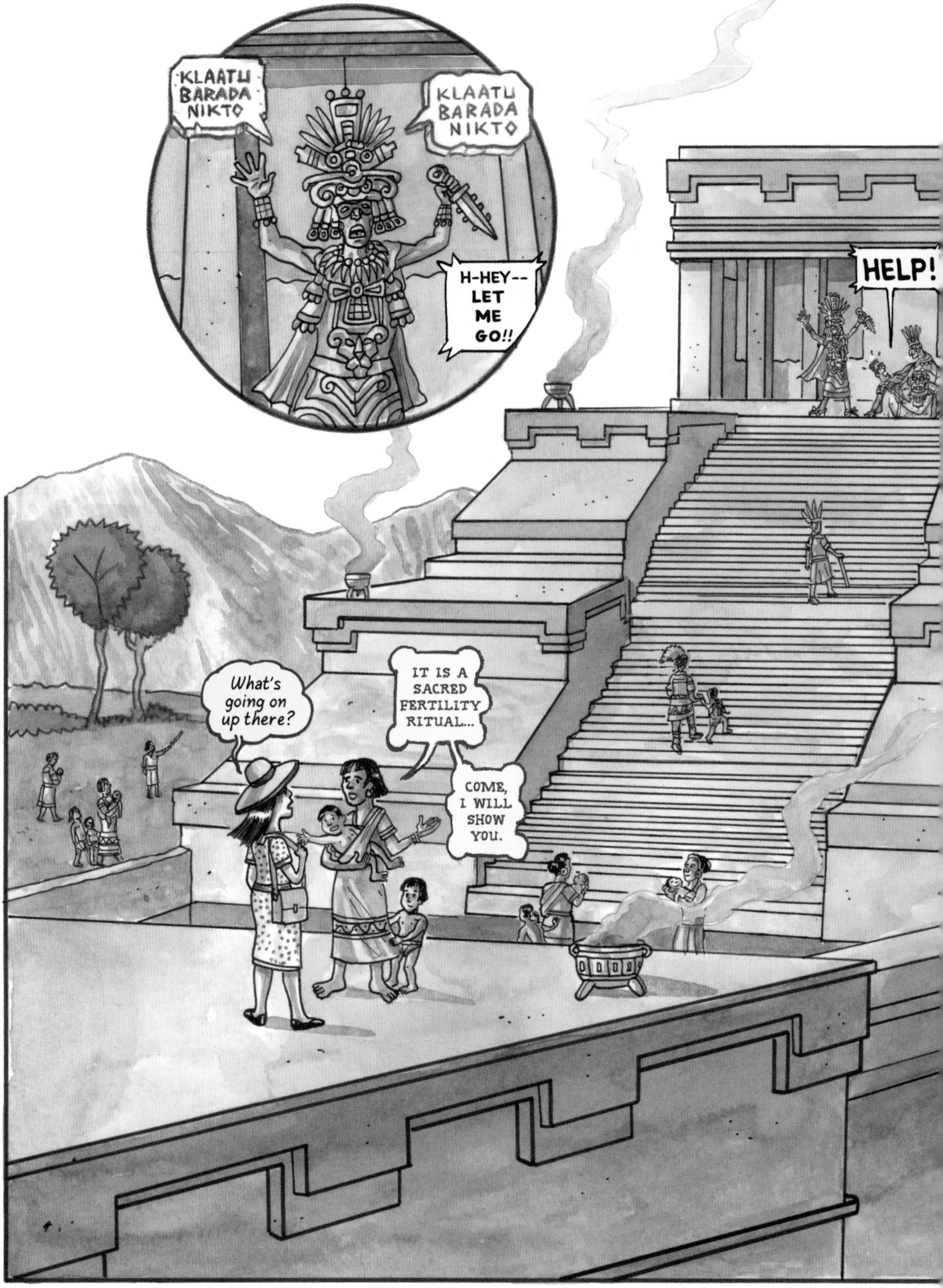
KLAATU BARADA NIKTO
KLAATU BARADA NIKTO
H-HEY-- LET ME GO!!
HELP!
What's going on up there?
IT IS A SACRED FERTILITY RITUAL...
COME, I WILL SHOW YOU.

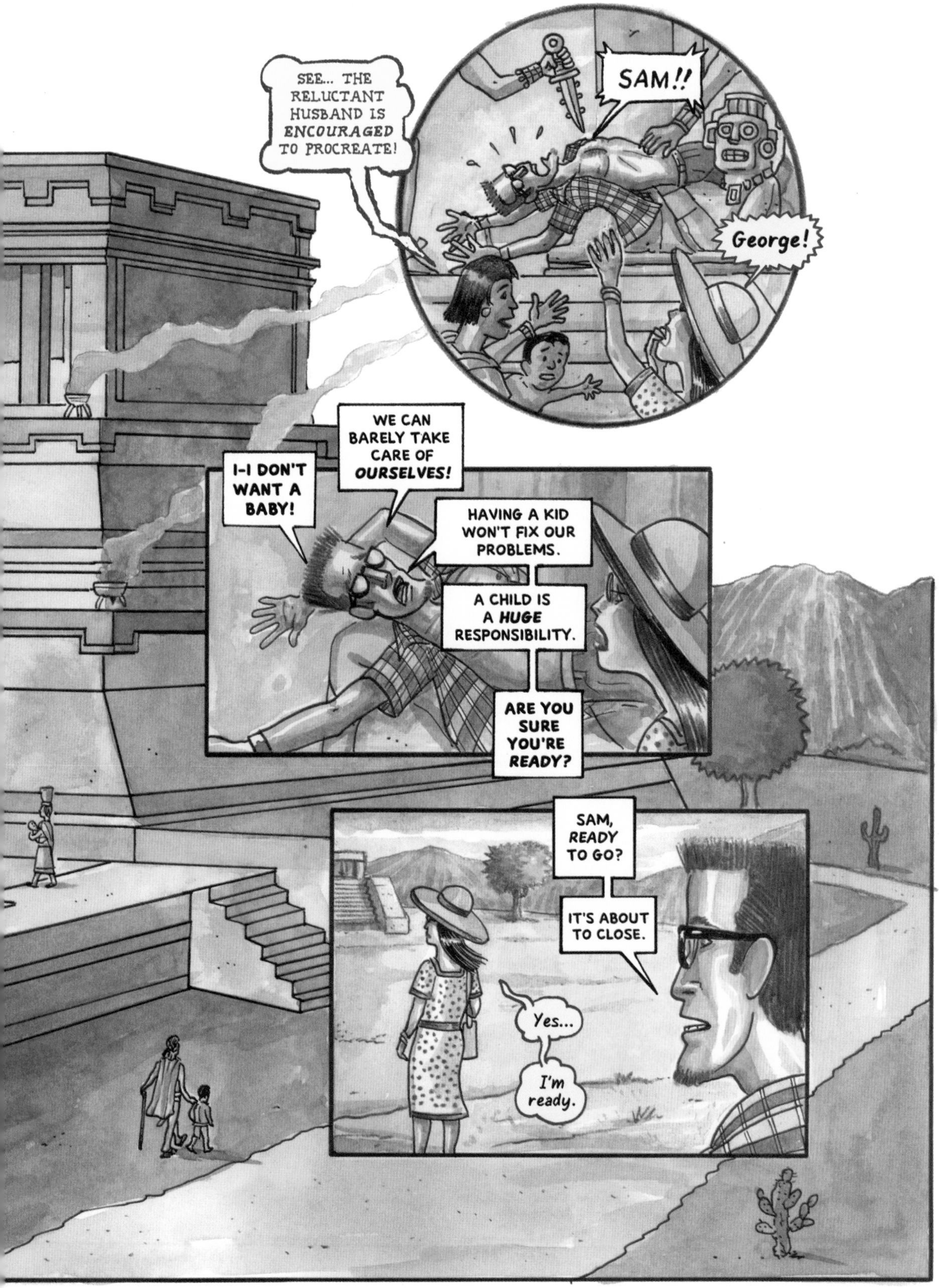
SEE... THE RELUCTANT HUSBAND IS ENCOURAGED TO PROCREATE!
SAM!!
George!
I-I DON'T WANT A BABY!
WE CAN BARELY TAKE CARE OF OURSELVES!
HAVING A KID WON'T FIX OUR PROBLEMS.
A CHILD IS A HUGE RESPONSIBILITY.
ARE YOU SURE YOU'RE READY?
SAM, READY TO GO?
IT'S ABOUT TO CLOSE.
Yes...
I'm ready.

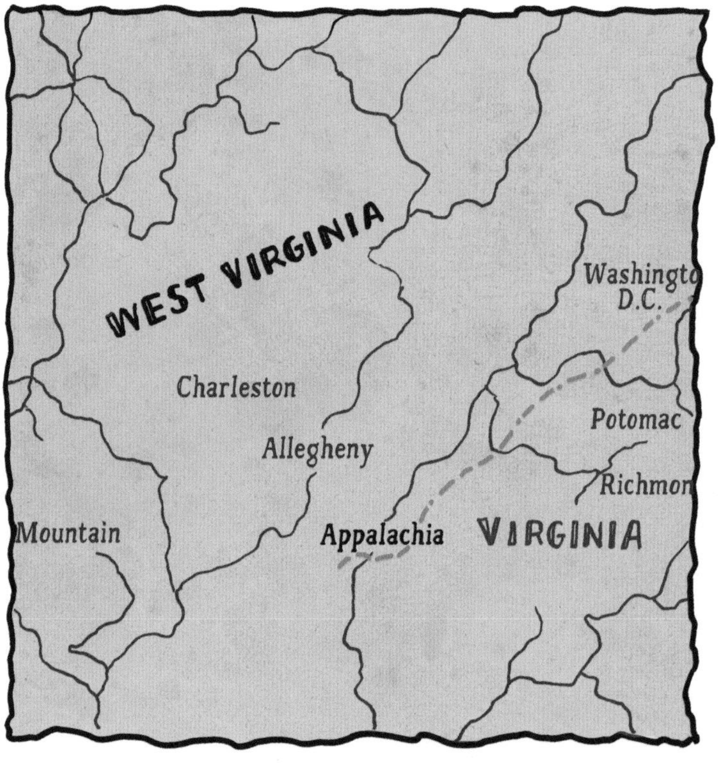
WEST VIRGINIA
Washingto
D.C.
Charleston
Potomac
Allegheny
Richmon
Mountain
Appalachia
VIRGINIA

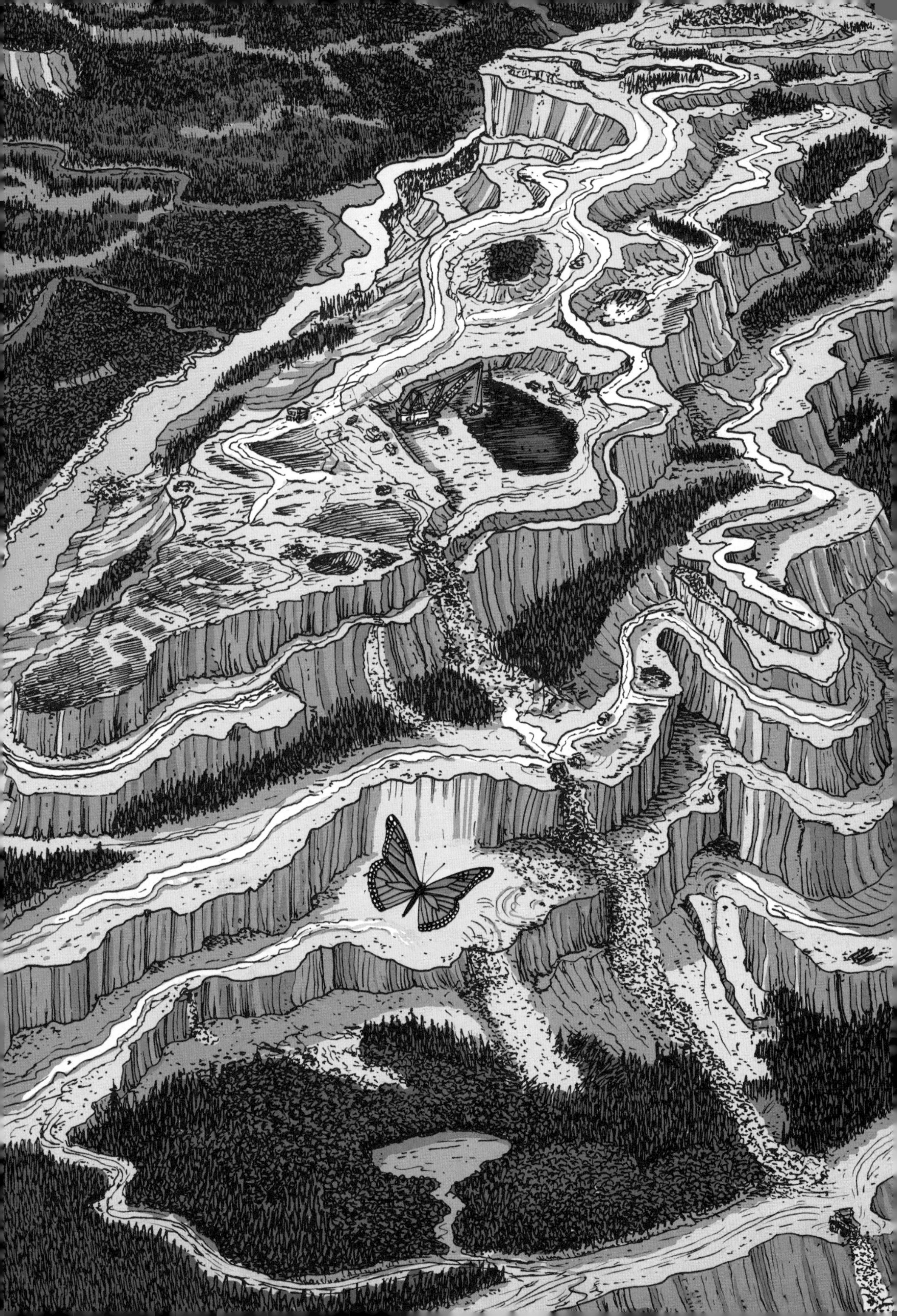

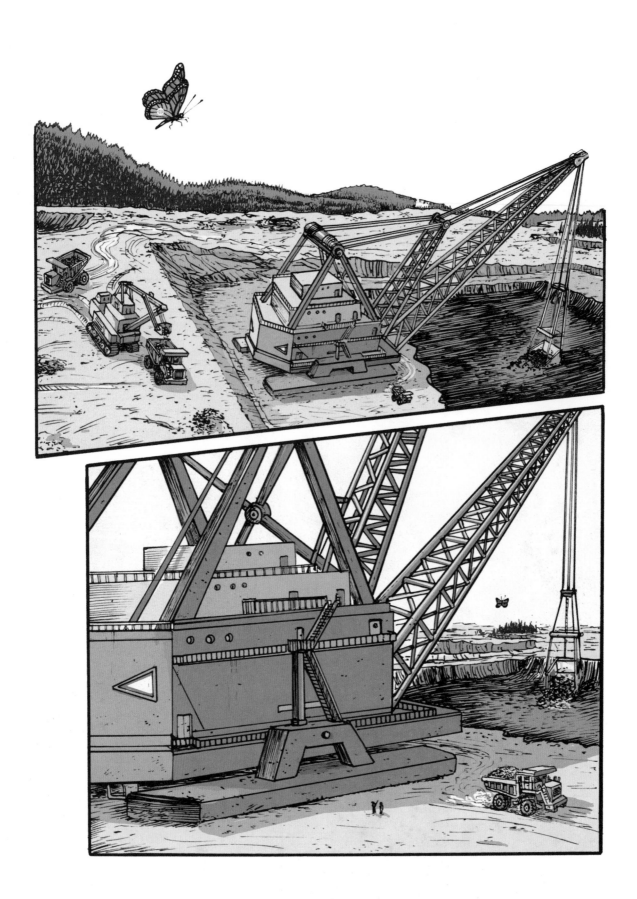

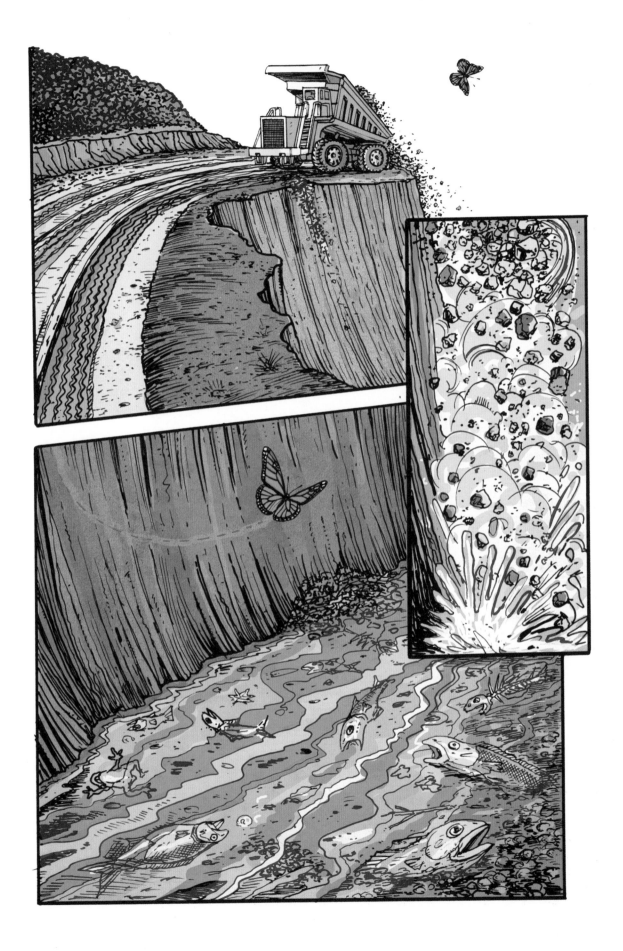

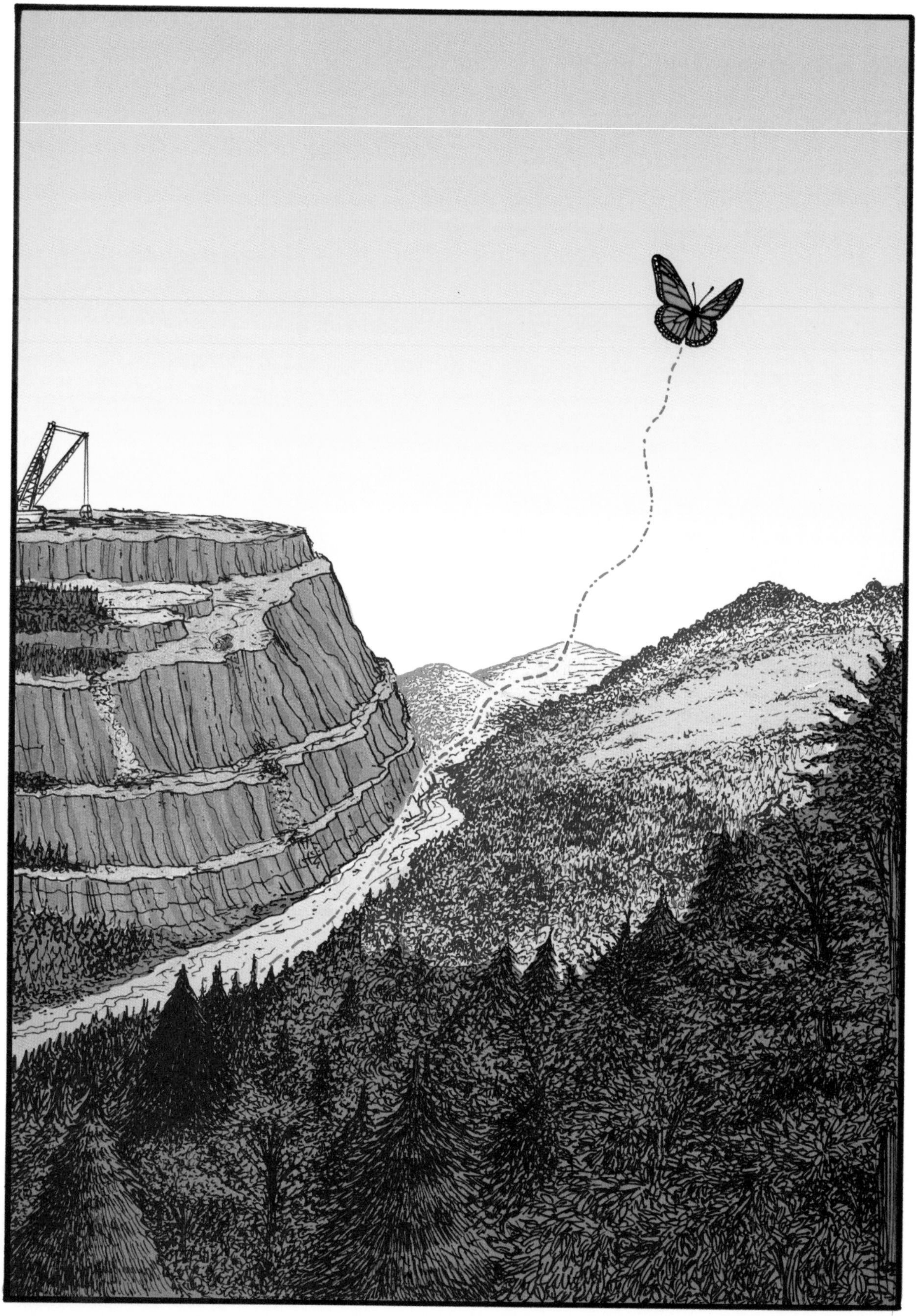

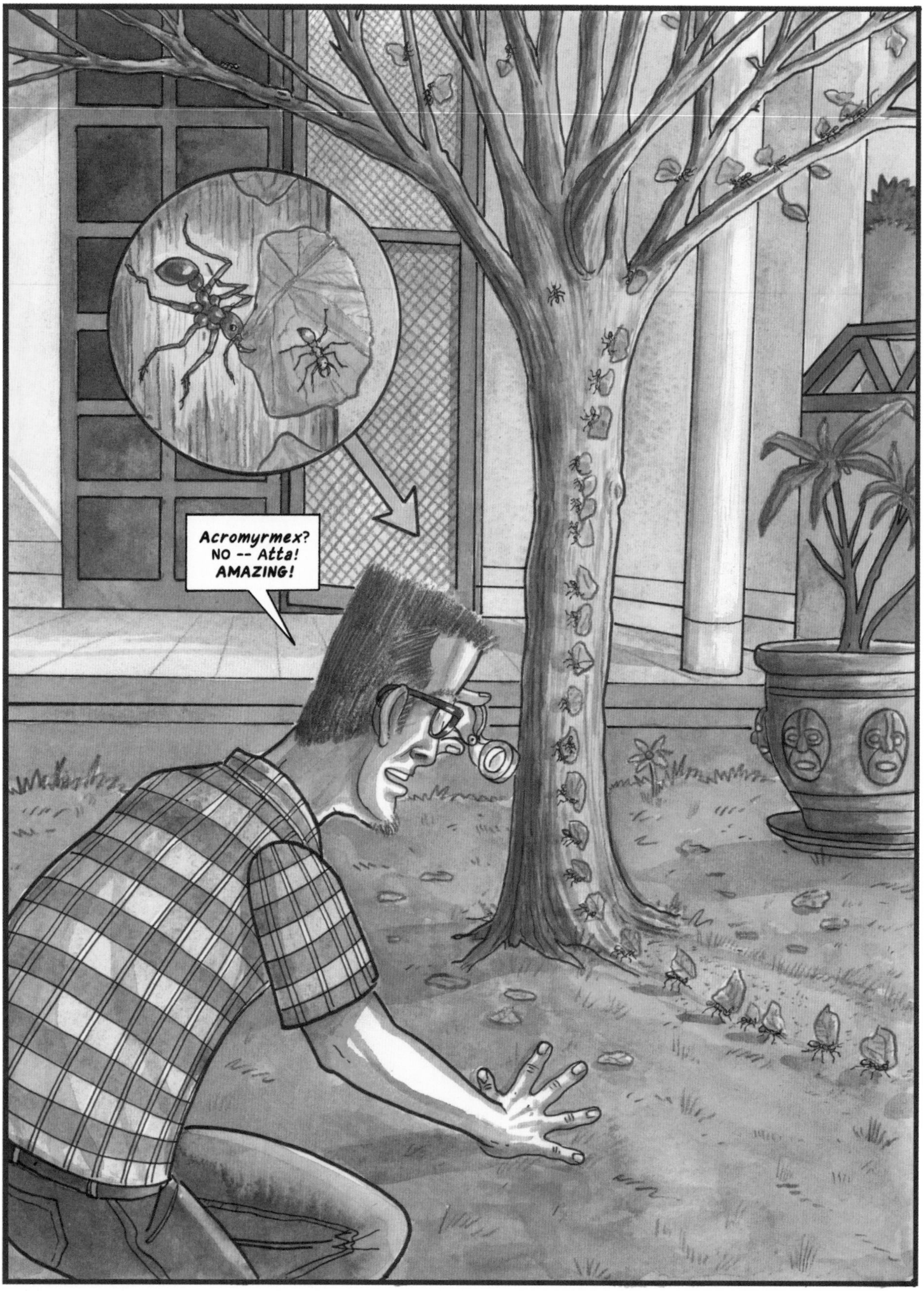
Acromyrmex? NO -- Atta! AMAZING!

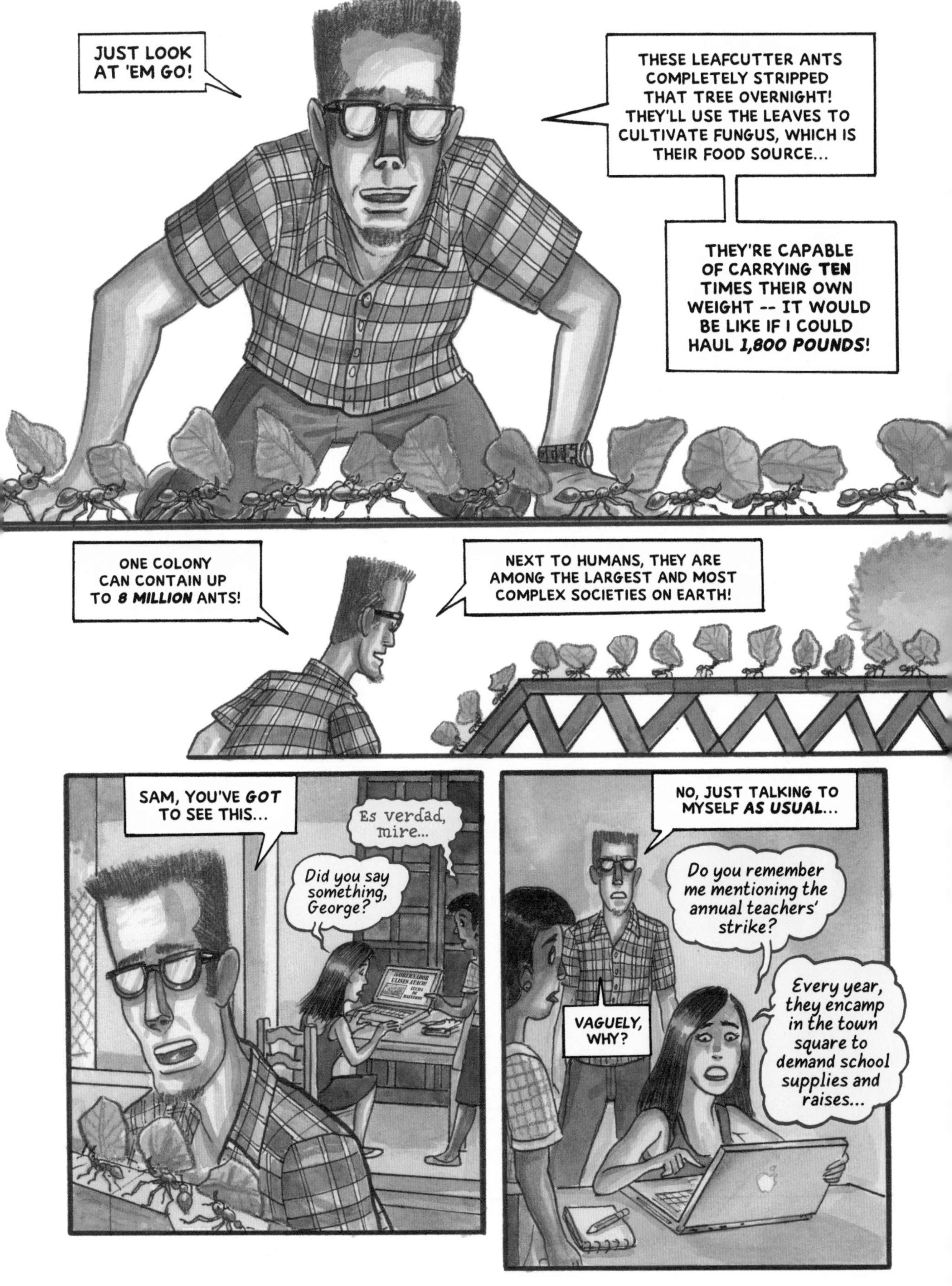
JUST LOOK AT 'EM GO!
THESE LEAFCUTTER ANTS COMPLETELY STRIPPED THAT TREE OVERNIGHT! THEY'LL USE THE LEAVES TO CULTIVATE FUNGUS, WHICH IS THEIR FOOD SOURCE...
THEY'RE CAPABLE OF CARRYING **TEN** TIMES THEIR OWN WEIGHT -- IT WOULD BE LIKE IF I COULD HAUL ***1,800 POUNDS***!
ONE COLONY CAN CONTAIN UP TO ***8 MILLION*** ANTS!
NEXT TO HUMANS, THEY ARE AMONG THE LARGEST AND MOST COMPLEX SOCIETIES ON EARTH!
SAM, YOU'VE **GOT** TO SEE THIS...
Es verdad, mire...
Did you say something, George?
NO, JUST TALKING TO MYSELF ***AS USUAL***...
Do you remember me mentioning the annual teachers' strike?
VAGUELY, WHY?
Every year, they encamp in the town square to demand school supplies and raises...

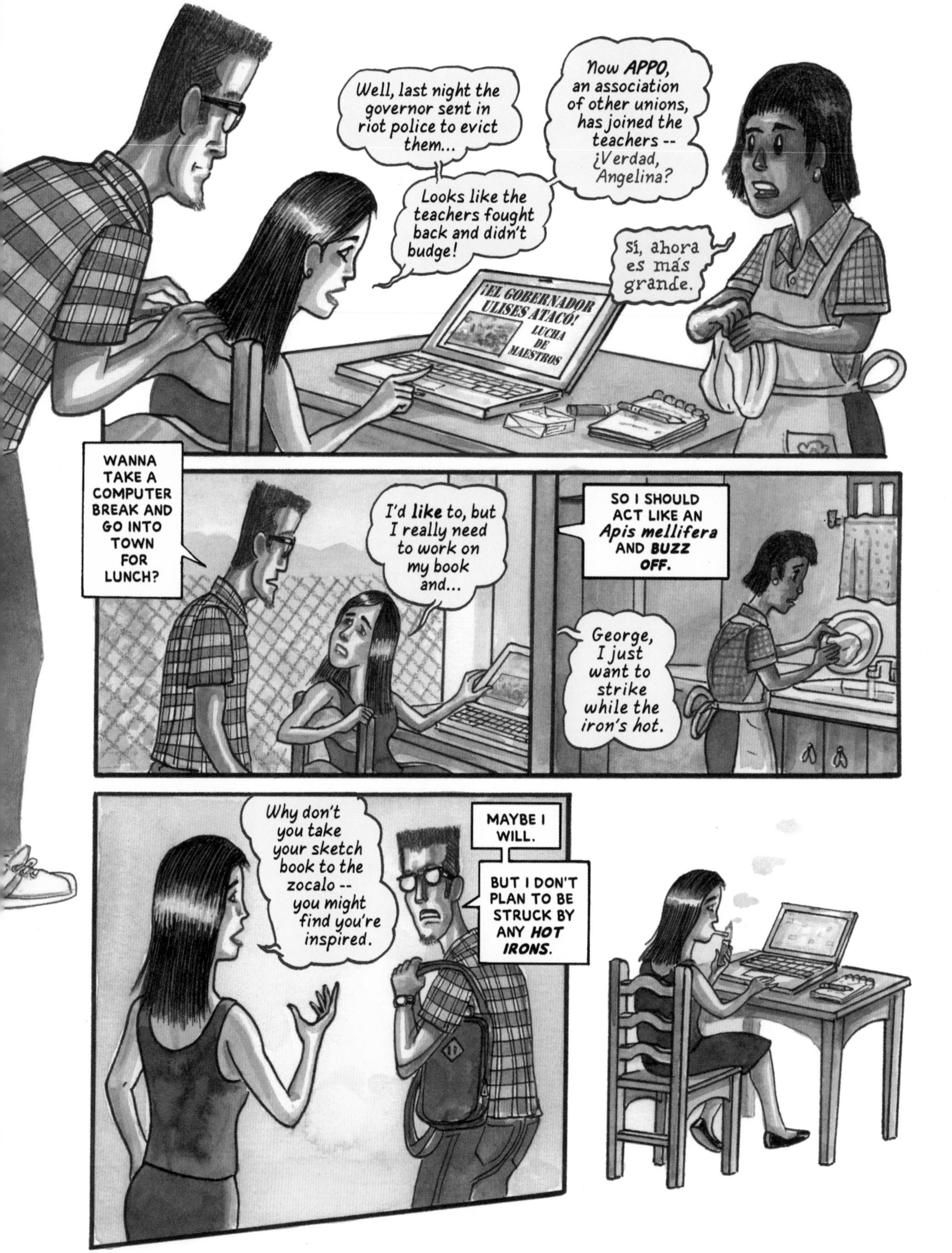

Well, last night the governor sent in riot police to evict them...
Looks like the teachers fought back and didn't budge!
Now APPO, an association of other unions, has joined the teachers -- ¿Verdad, Angelina?
Sí, ahora es más grande.
¡EL GOBERNADOR ULISES ATACÓ! LUCHA DE MAESTROS
WANNA TAKE A COMPUTER BREAK AND GO INTO TOWN FOR LUNCH?
I'd like to, but I really need to work on my book and...
SO I SHOULD ACT LIKE AN Apis mellifera AND BUZZ OFF.
George, I just want to strike while the iron's hot.
Why don't you take your sketch book to the zocalo -- you might find you're inspired.
MAYBE I WILL.
BUT I DON'T PLAN TO BE STRUCK BY ANY HOT IRONS.

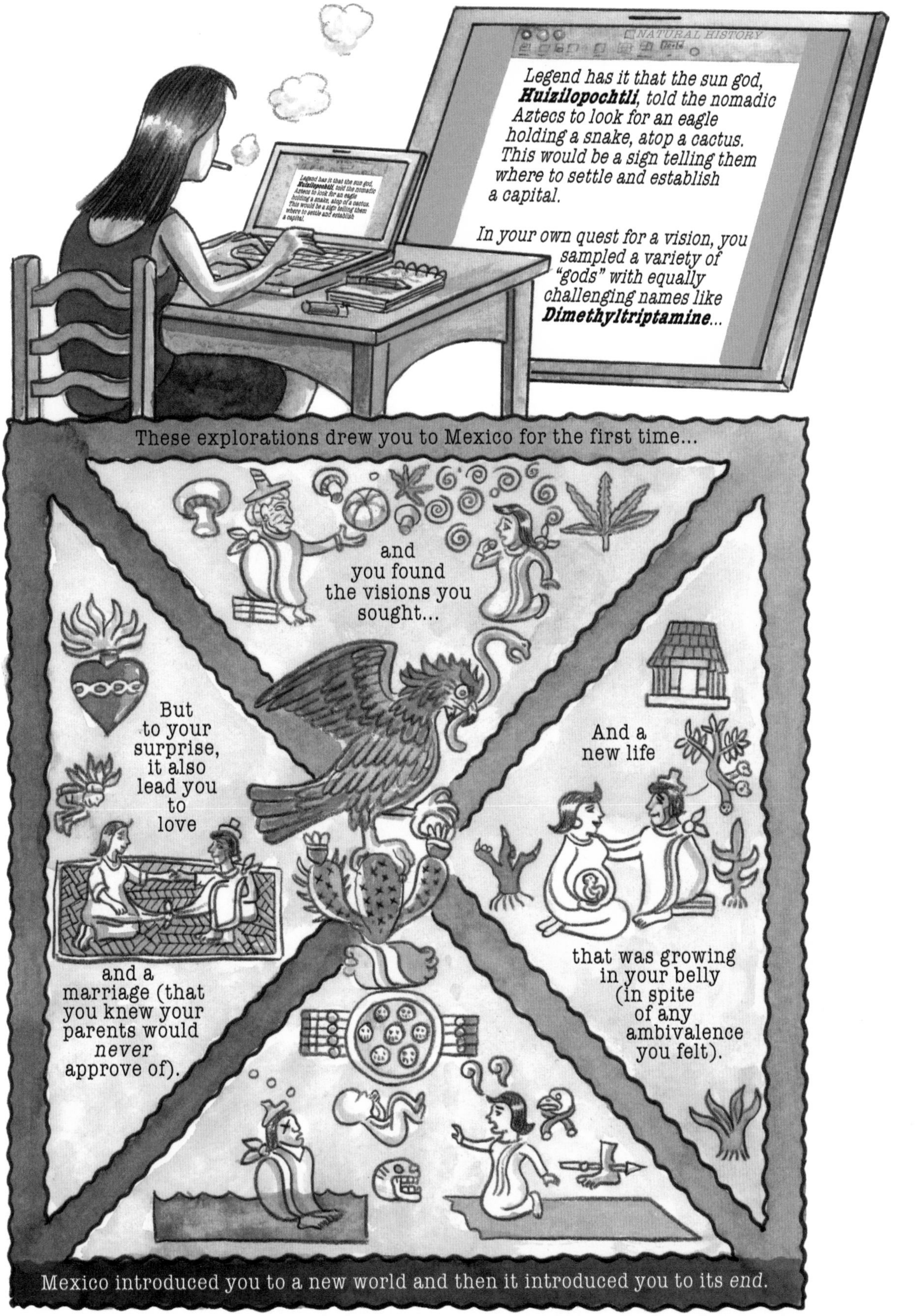
NATURAL HISTORY
Legend has it that the sun god, **Huizilopochtli**, told the nomadic Aztecs to look for an eagle holding a snake, atop a cactus. This would be a sign telling them where to settle and establish a capital.
In your own quest for a vision, you sampled a variety of "gods" with equally challenging names like **Dimethyltriptamine**...
These explorations drew you to Mexico for the first time...
and you found the visions you sought...
And a new life
that was growing in your belly (in spite of any ambivalence you felt).
But to your surprise, it also lead you to love
and a marriage (that you knew your parents would *never* approve of).
Mexico introduced you to a new world and then it introduced you to its *end*.

The civilizations the conquistadors encountered in Mezoamerica were complex societies with a developed knowledge of astronomy, mathematics and architecture. They had created masterpieces of art and a hieroglyphic language to record their history.

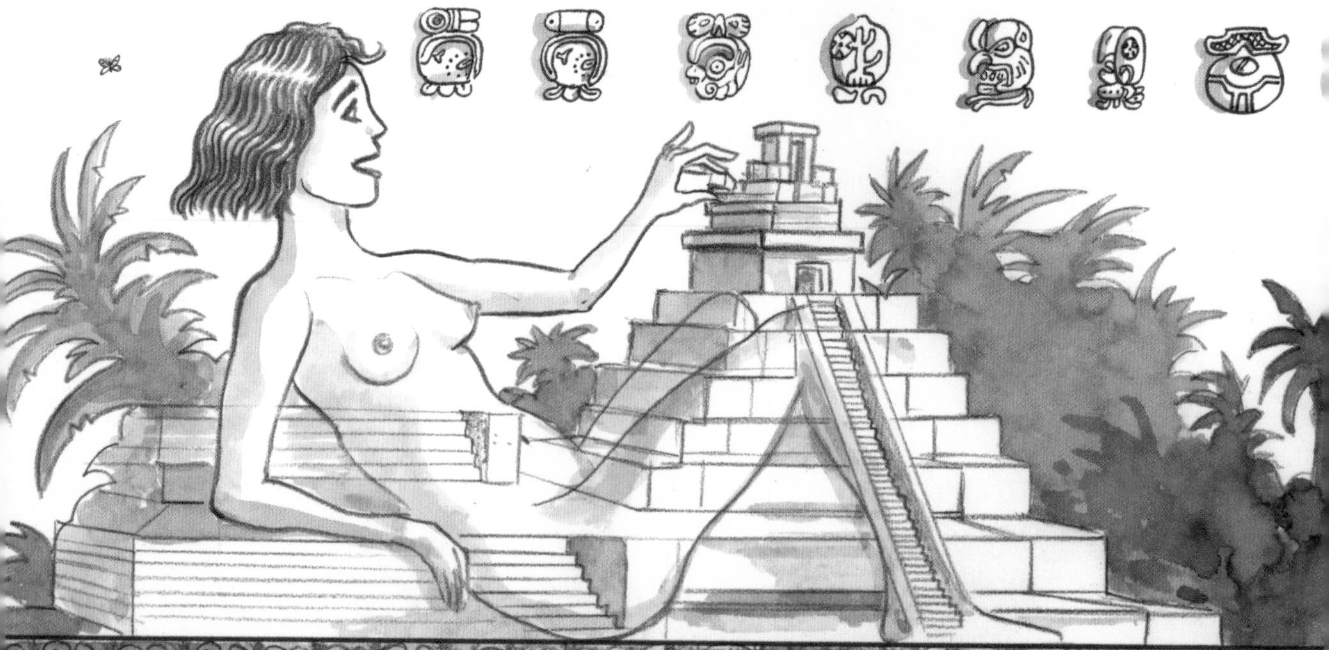

The girl you were in your 20s when you arrived in Mexico had a spirit you'd almost forgotten ever existed. This return to Oaxaca had awoken your former self, but that came with history...

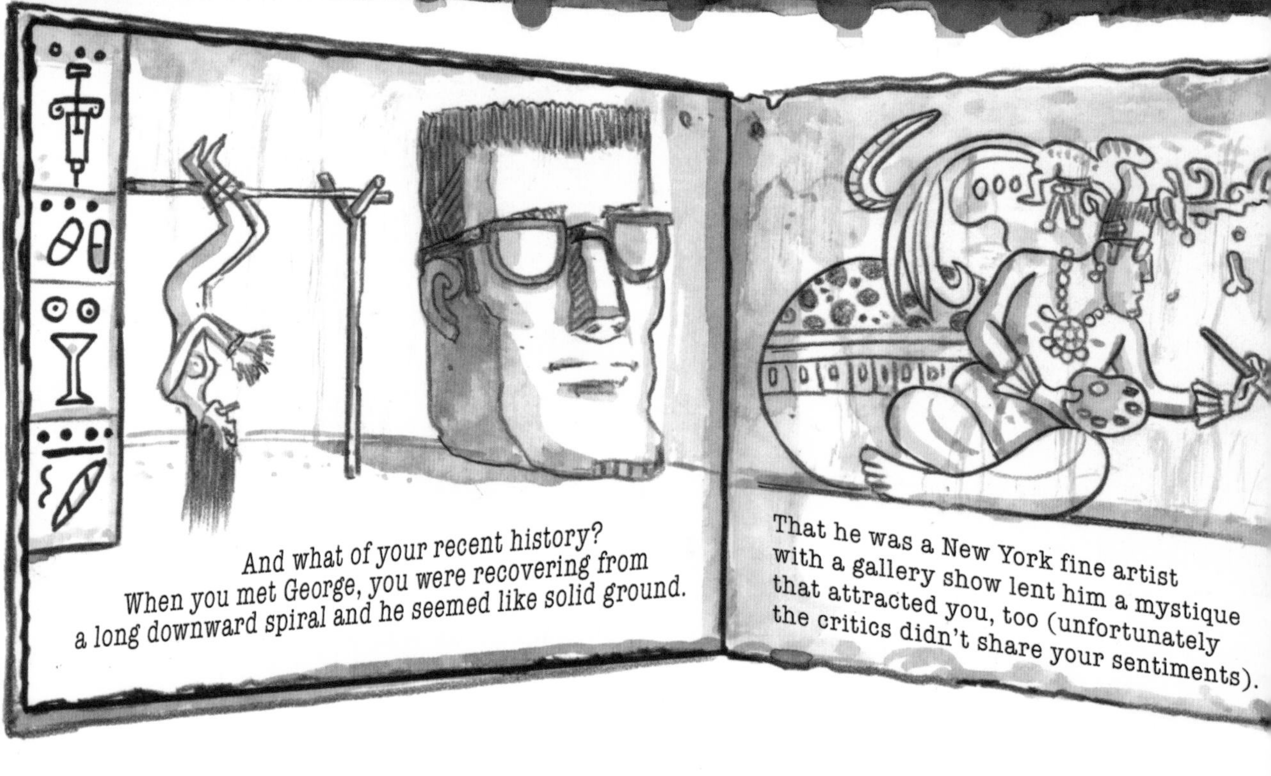
And what of your recent history?
When you met George, you were recovering from a long downward spiral and he seemed like solid ground.
That he was a New York fine artist with a gallery show lent him a mystique that attracted you, too (unfortunately the critics didn't share your sentiments).

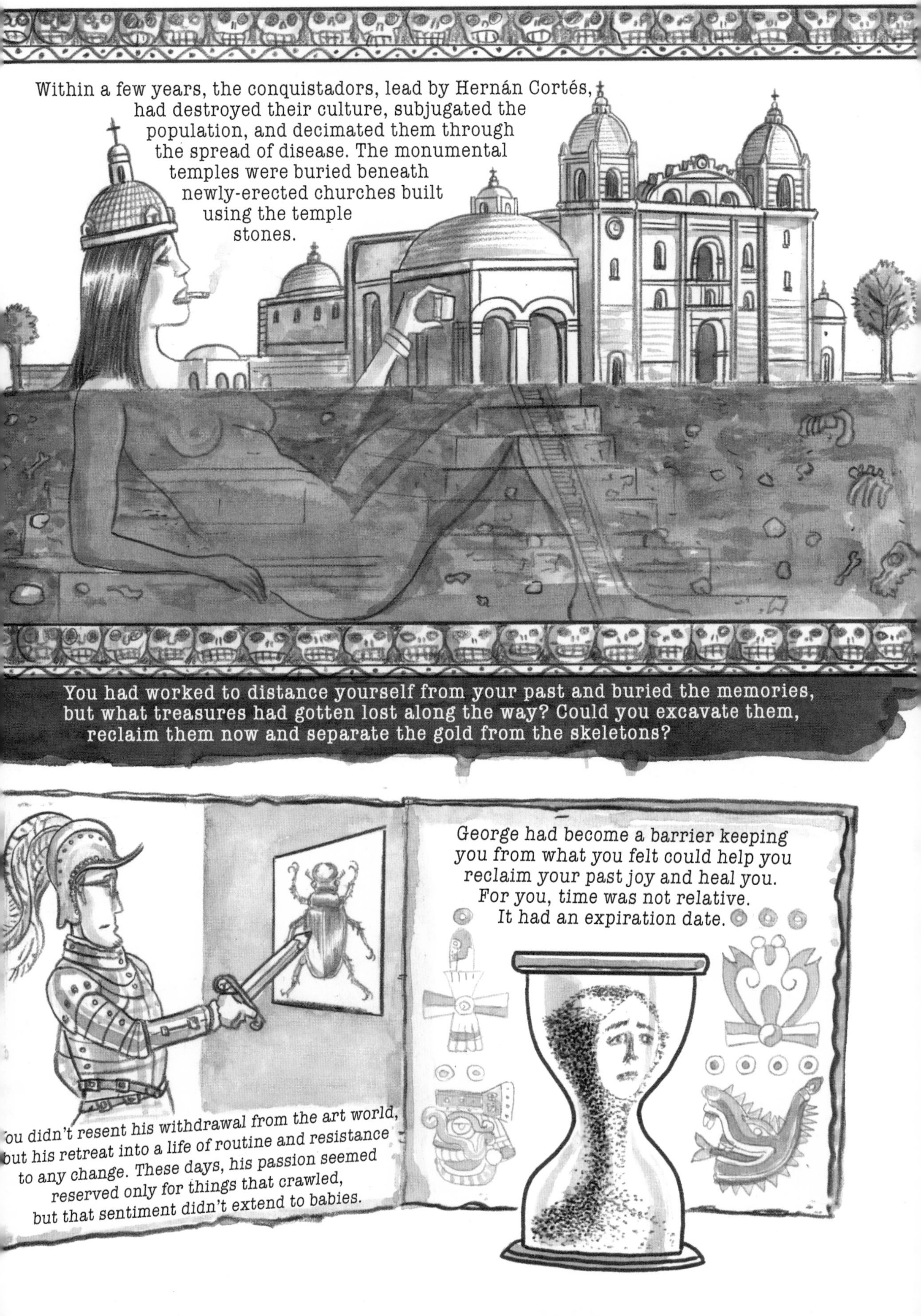

Within a few years, the conquistadors, lead by Hernán Cortés, had destroyed their culture, subjugated the population, and decimated them through the spread of disease. The monumental temples were buried beneath newly-erected churches built using the temple stones.
You had worked to distance yourself from your past and buried the memories, but what treasures had gotten lost along the way? Could you excavate them, reclaim them now and separate the gold from the skeletons?
ou didn't resent his withdrawal from the art world, but his retreat into a life of routine and resistance to any change. These days, his passion seemed reserved only for things that crawled, but that sentiment didn't extend to babies.
George had become a barrier keeping you from what you felt could help you reclaim your past joy and heal you. For you, time was not relative. It had an expiration date.

The Aztec leader, Moctezuma, interpreted the arrival of Cortés as the foretold return of their serpent god, Quetzalcoatl. It was predicted that his return would bring a cosmic end to their world so another could commence. Moctezuma accepted the conquistadors as a foregone conclusion and surrendered to the inevitable.

You longed for a cosmic change of your own, but your marriage felt like **metamorphosis** **in** **reverse.**

It's not that you didn't love George, but he wouldn't give you what you needed to move forward. Could you surrender to things as they were, or would you end one world so another could commence...?

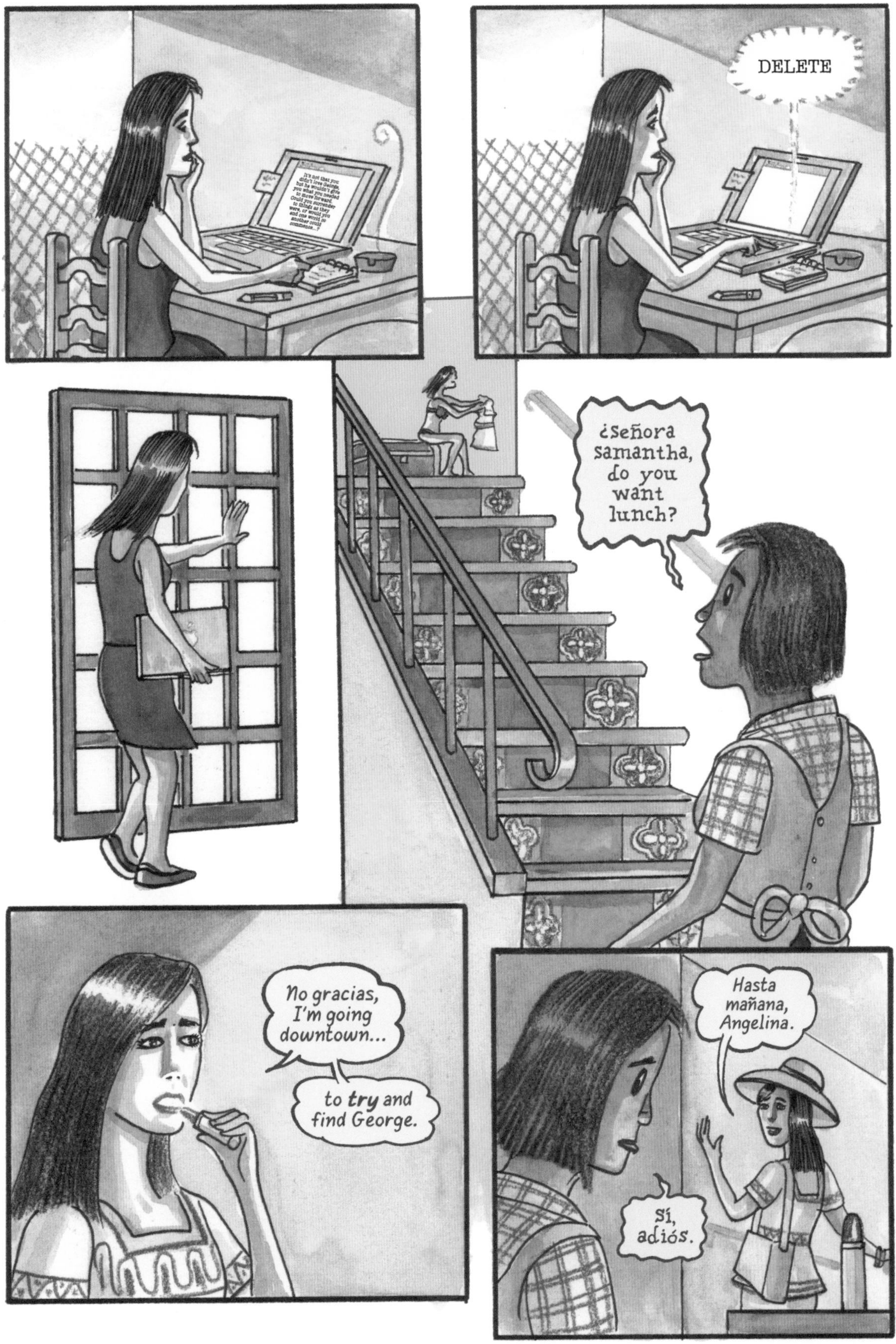
DELETE
¿señora samantha, do you want lunch?
No gracias, I'm going downtown...
to **try** and find George.
Hasta mañana, Angelina.
Sí, adiós.

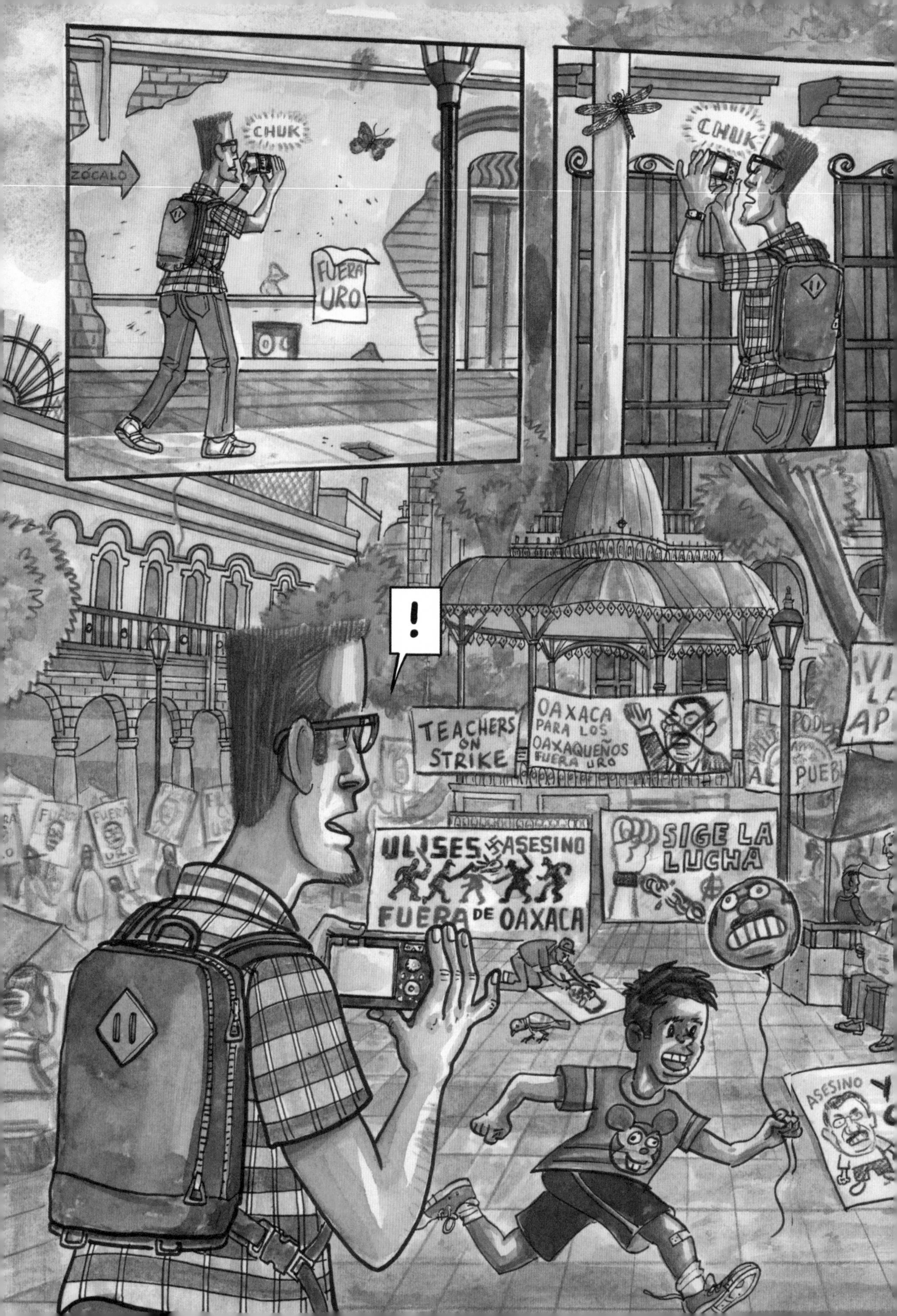
ZÓCALO
CHUK
FUERA URO
CHUK
!
TEACHERS ON STRIKE
OAXACA PARA LOS OAXAQUEÑOS FUERA URO
ULISES ASESINO
FUERA DE OAXACA
SIGE LA LUCHA
ASESINO

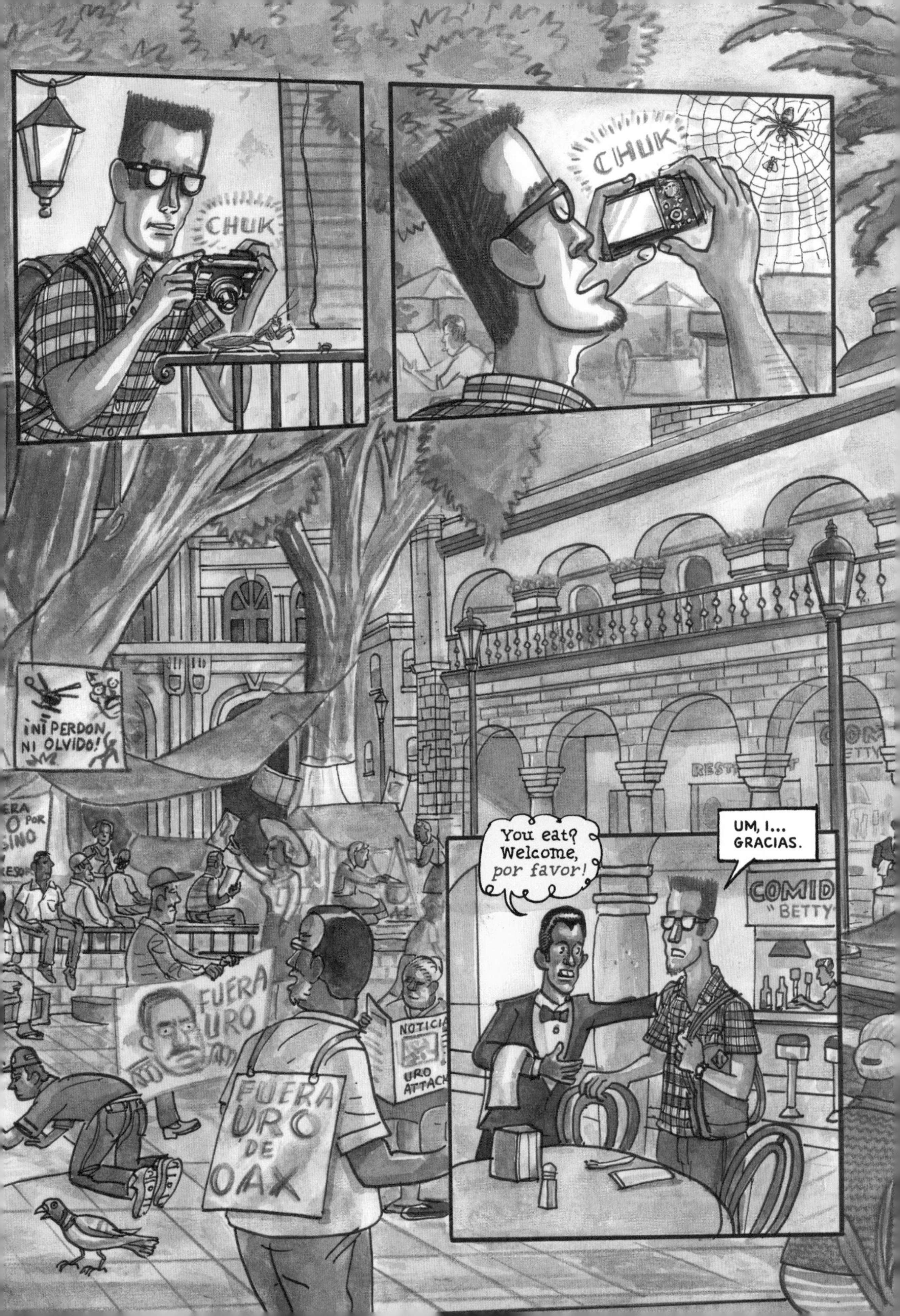

CHUK
CHUK
¡NI PERDON NI OLVIDO!
FUERA URO
FUERA URO DE OAX
You eat? Welcome, *por favor!*
UM, I... GRACIAS.

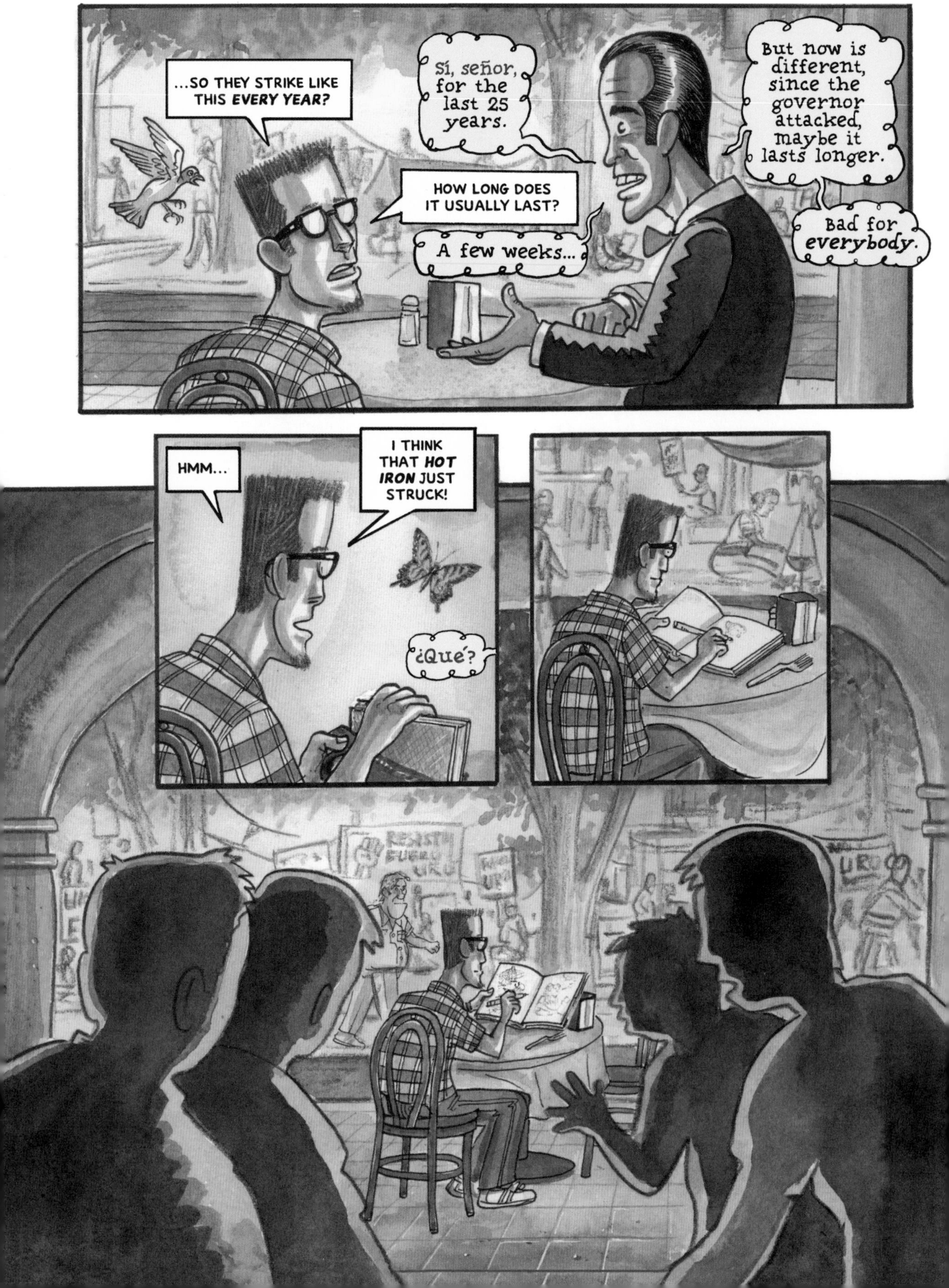
...SO THEY STRIKE LIKE THIS *EVERY YEAR?*
Sí, señor, for the last 25 years.
But now is different, since the governor attacked, maybe it lasts longer.
Bad for *everybody*.
HOW LONG DOES IT USUALLY LAST?
A few weeks...
HMM...
I THINK THAT *HOT IRON* JUST STRUCK!
¿Qué?

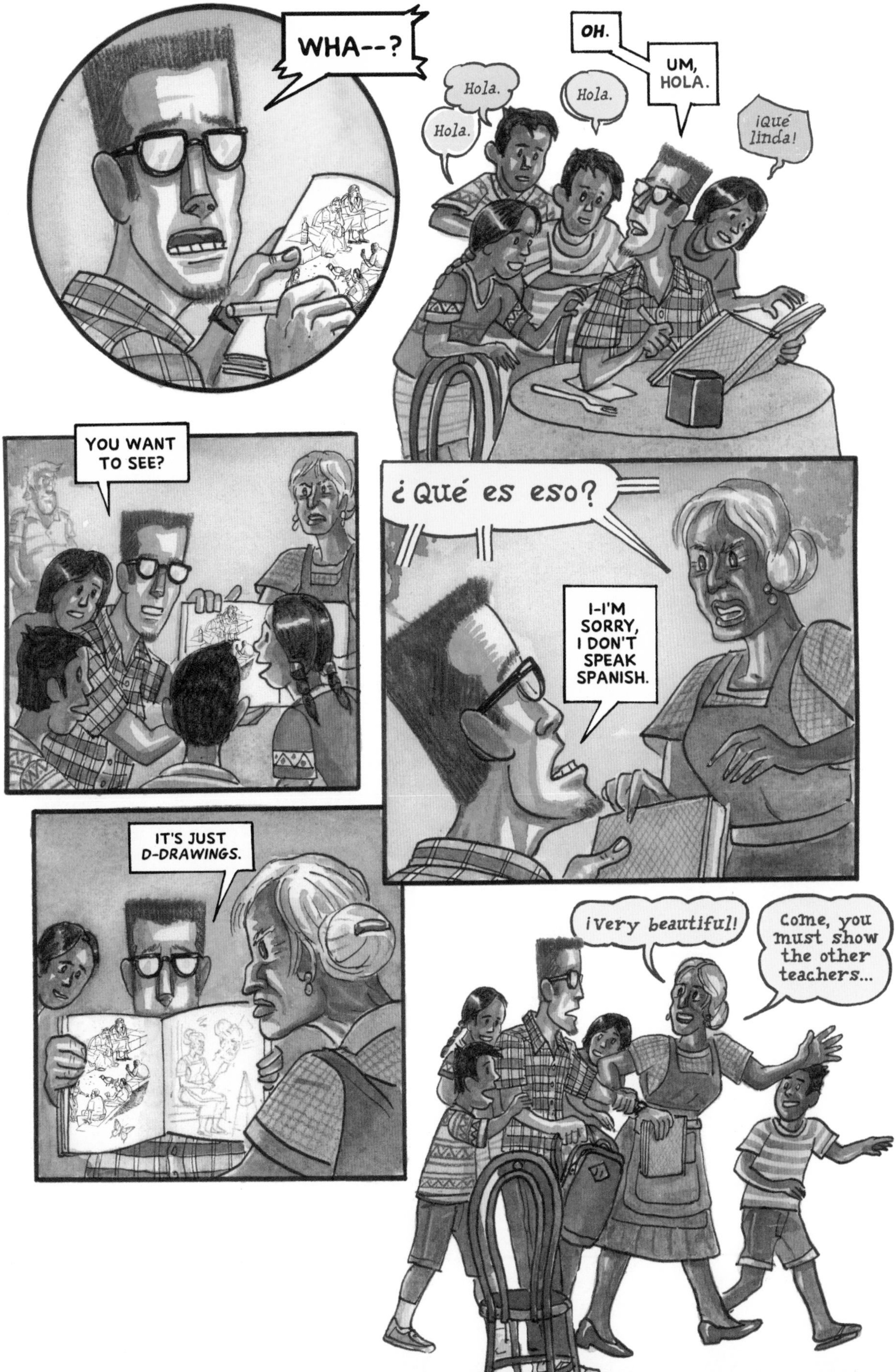
WHA--?
OH.
UM, HOLA.
Hola.
Hola.
Hola.
¡Qué linda!
YOU WANT TO SEE?
¿Qué es eso?
I-I'M SORRY, I DON'T SPEAK SPANISH.
IT'S JUST D-DRAWINGS.
¡Very beautiful!
Come, you must show the other teachers...

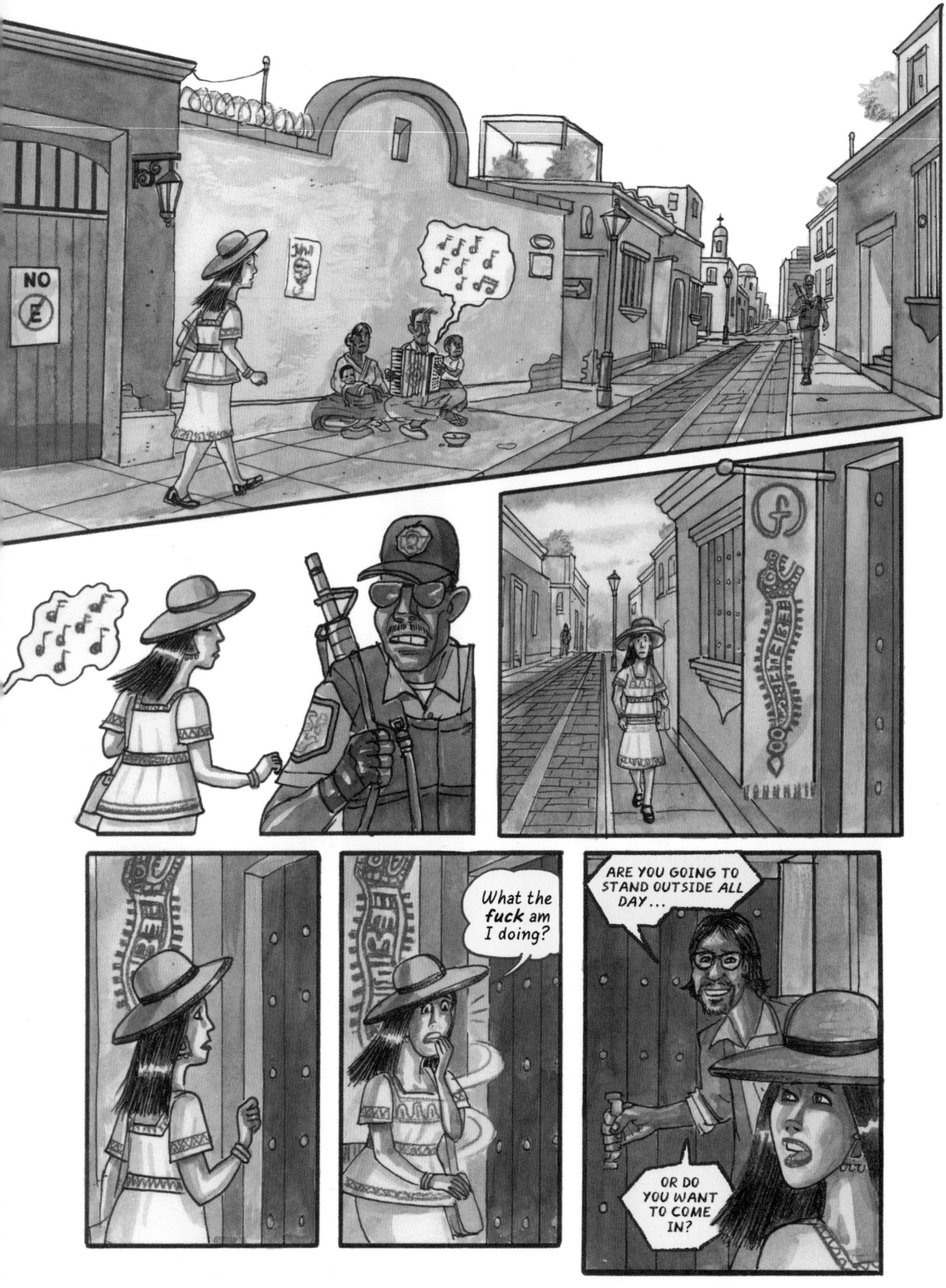
NO
What the **fuck** am I doing?
ARE YOU GOING TO STAND OUTSIDE ALL DAY...
OR DO YOU WANT TO COME IN?

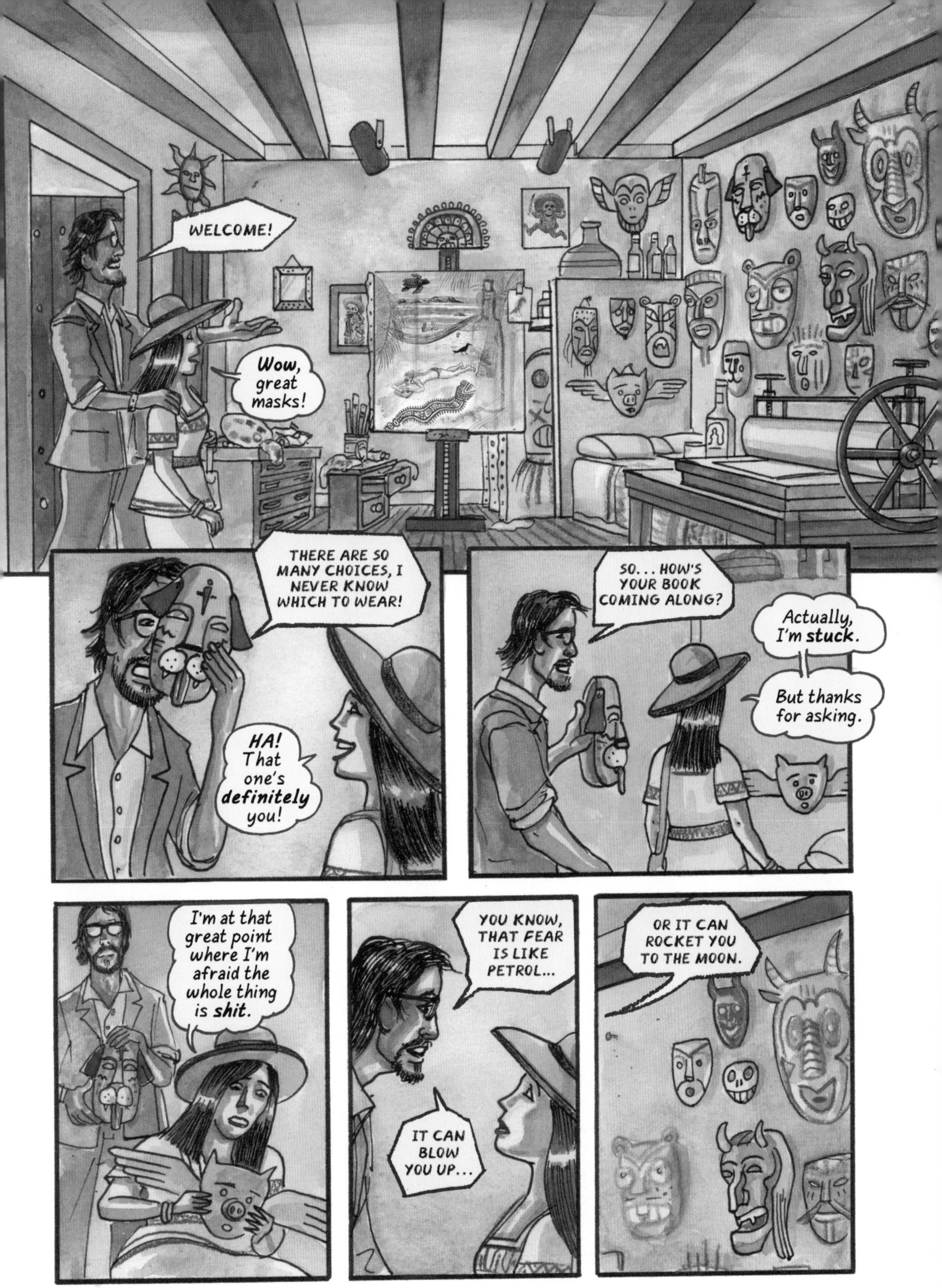
WELCOME!
Wow, great masks!
THERE ARE SO MANY CHOICES, I NEVER KNOW WHICH TO WEAR!
HA! That one's **definitely** you!
SO... HOW'S YOUR BOOK COMING ALONG?
Actually, I'm **stuck**.
But thanks for asking.
I'm at that great point where I'm afraid the whole thing is **shit**.
YOU KNOW, THAT FEAR IS LIKE PETROL...
IT CAN BLOW YOU UP...
OR IT CAN ROCKET YOU TO THE MOON.

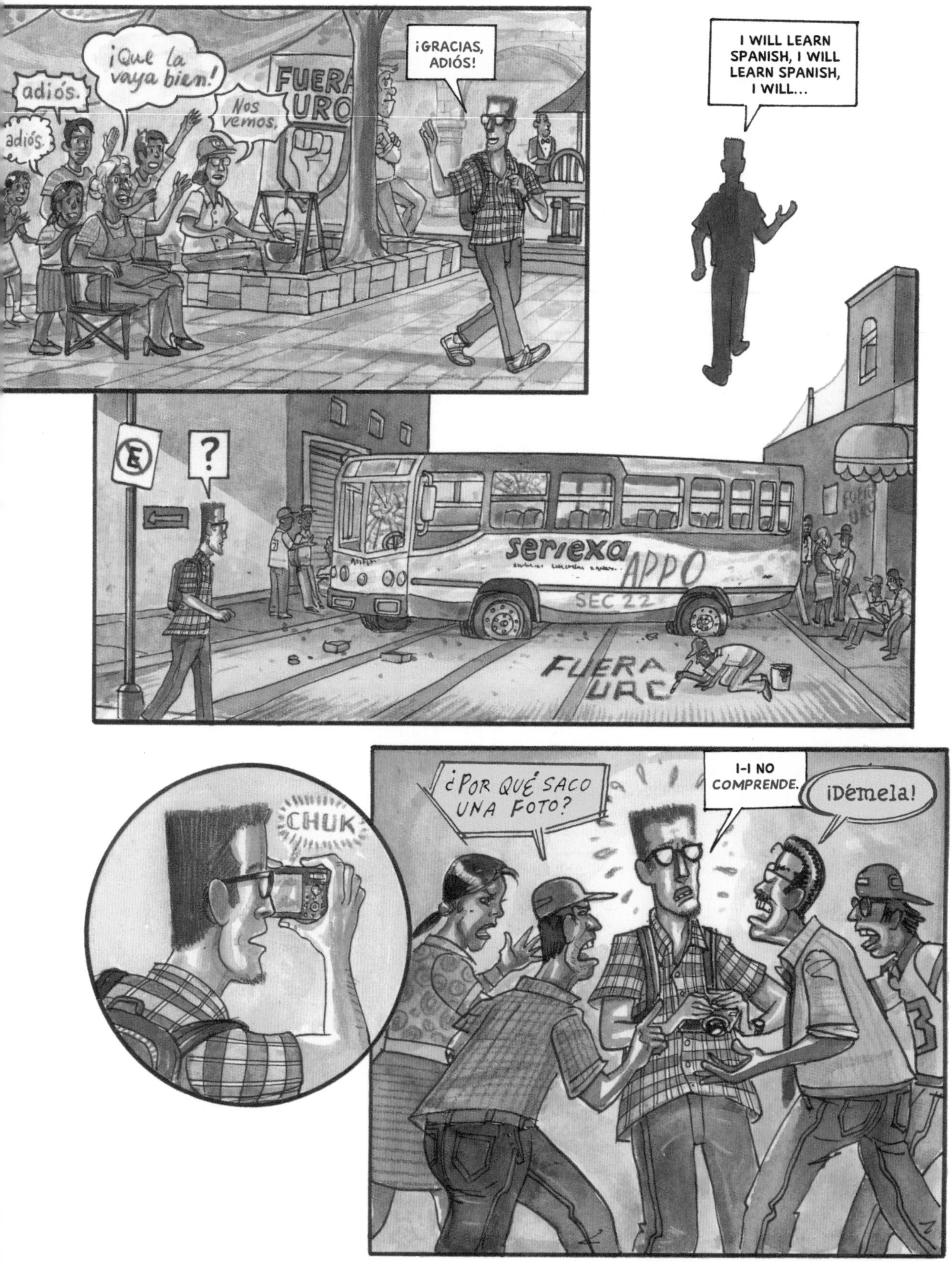

adiós.
adiós.
¡Que la vaya bien!
Nos vemos.
¡GRACIAS, ADIÓS!
I WILL LEARN SPANISH, I WILL LEARN SPANISH, I WILL...
?
seriexa
APPO
SEC 22
FUERA URO
CHUK
¿POR QUÉ SACO UNA FOTO?
I-I NO COMPRENDE.
¡Démela!

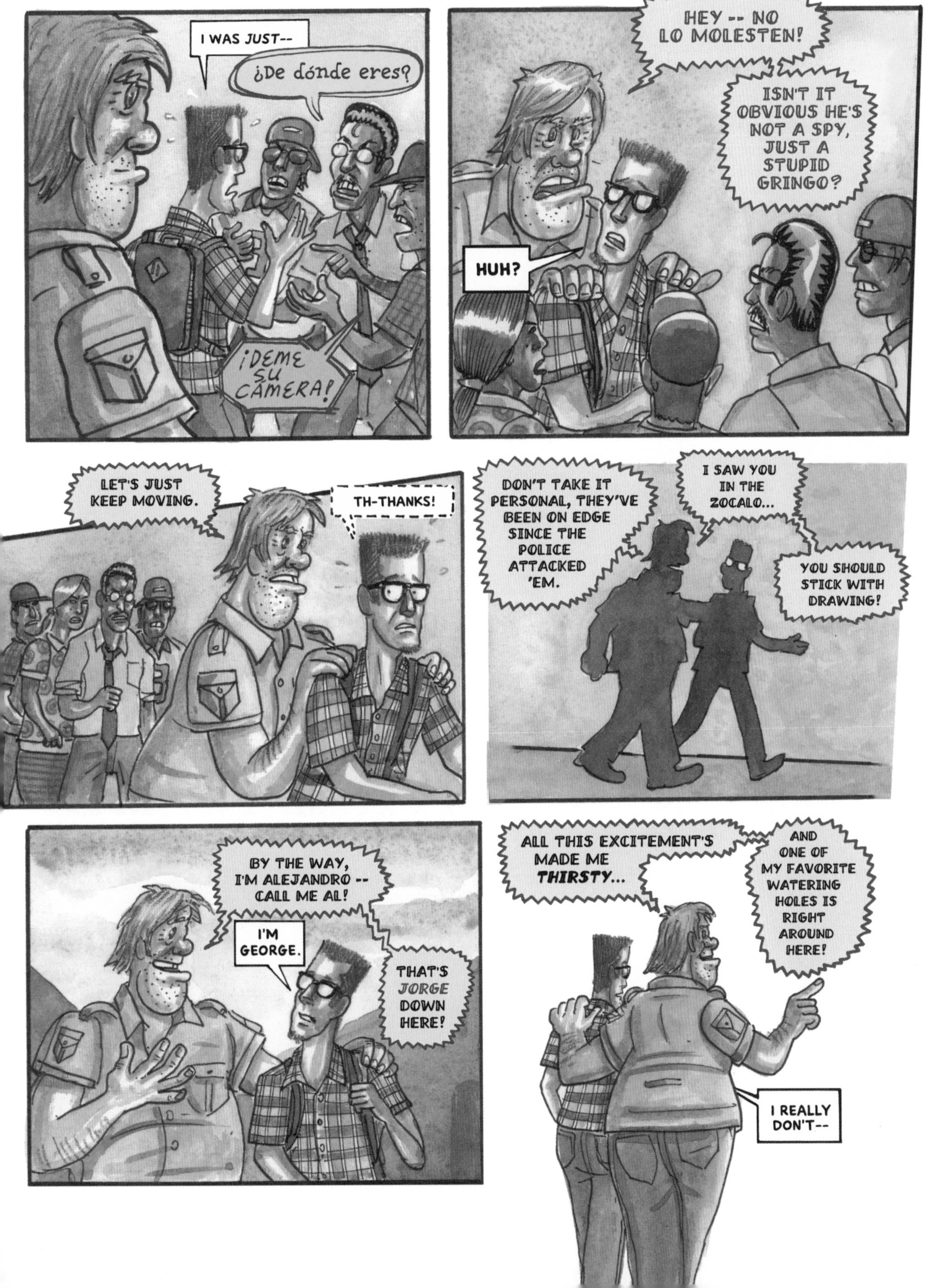

I WAS JUST--
¿De dónde eres?
¡DEME SU CÁMERA!
HEY -- NO LO MOLESTEN!
ISN'T IT OBVIOUS HE'S NOT A SPY, JUST A STUPID GRINGO?
HUH?
LET'S JUST KEEP MOVING.
TH-THANKS!
DON'T TAKE IT PERSONAL, THEY'VE BEEN ON EDGE SINCE THE POLICE ATTACKED 'EM.
I SAW YOU IN THE ZOCALO...
YOU SHOULD STICK WITH DRAWING!
BY THE WAY, I'M ALEJANDRO -- CALL ME AL!
I'M GEORGE.
THAT'S JORGE DOWN HERE!
ALL THIS EXCITEMENT'S MADE ME THIRSTY...
AND ONE OF MY FAVORITE WATERING HOLES IS RIGHT AROUND HERE!
I REALLY DON'T--

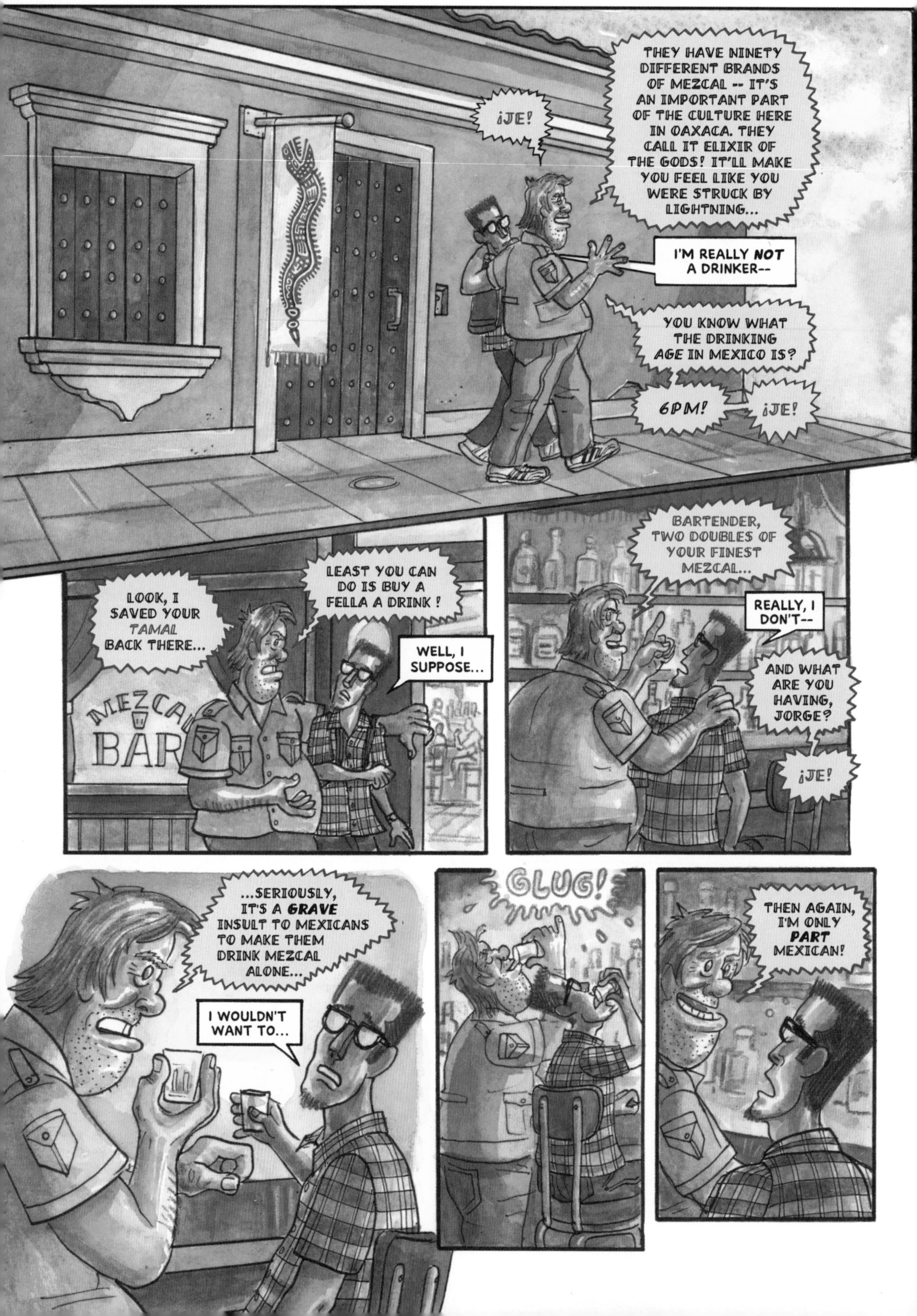
¡JE!
THEY HAVE NINETY DIFFERENT BRANDS OF MEZCAL -- IT'S AN IMPORTANT PART OF THE CULTURE HERE IN OAXACA. THEY CALL IT ELIXIR OF THE GODS! IT'LL MAKE YOU FEEL LIKE YOU WERE STRUCK BY LIGHTNING...
I'M REALLY **NOT** A DRINKER--
YOU KNOW WHAT THE DRINKING *AGE* IN MEXICO IS?
6PM!
¡JE!
LOOK, I SAVED YOUR *TAMAL* BACK THERE...
LEAST YOU CAN DO IS BUY A FELLA A DRINK !
WELL, I SUPPOSE...
MEZCAL BAR
BARTENDER, TWO DOUBLES OF YOUR FINEST MEZCAL...
REALLY, I DON'T--
AND WHAT ARE YOU HAVING, JORGE?
¡JE!
...SERIOUSLY, IT'S A **GRAVE** INSULT TO MEXICANS TO MAKE THEM DRINK MEZCAL ALONE...
I WOULDN'T WANT TO...
GLUG!
THEN AGAIN, I'M ONLY **PART** MEXICAN!

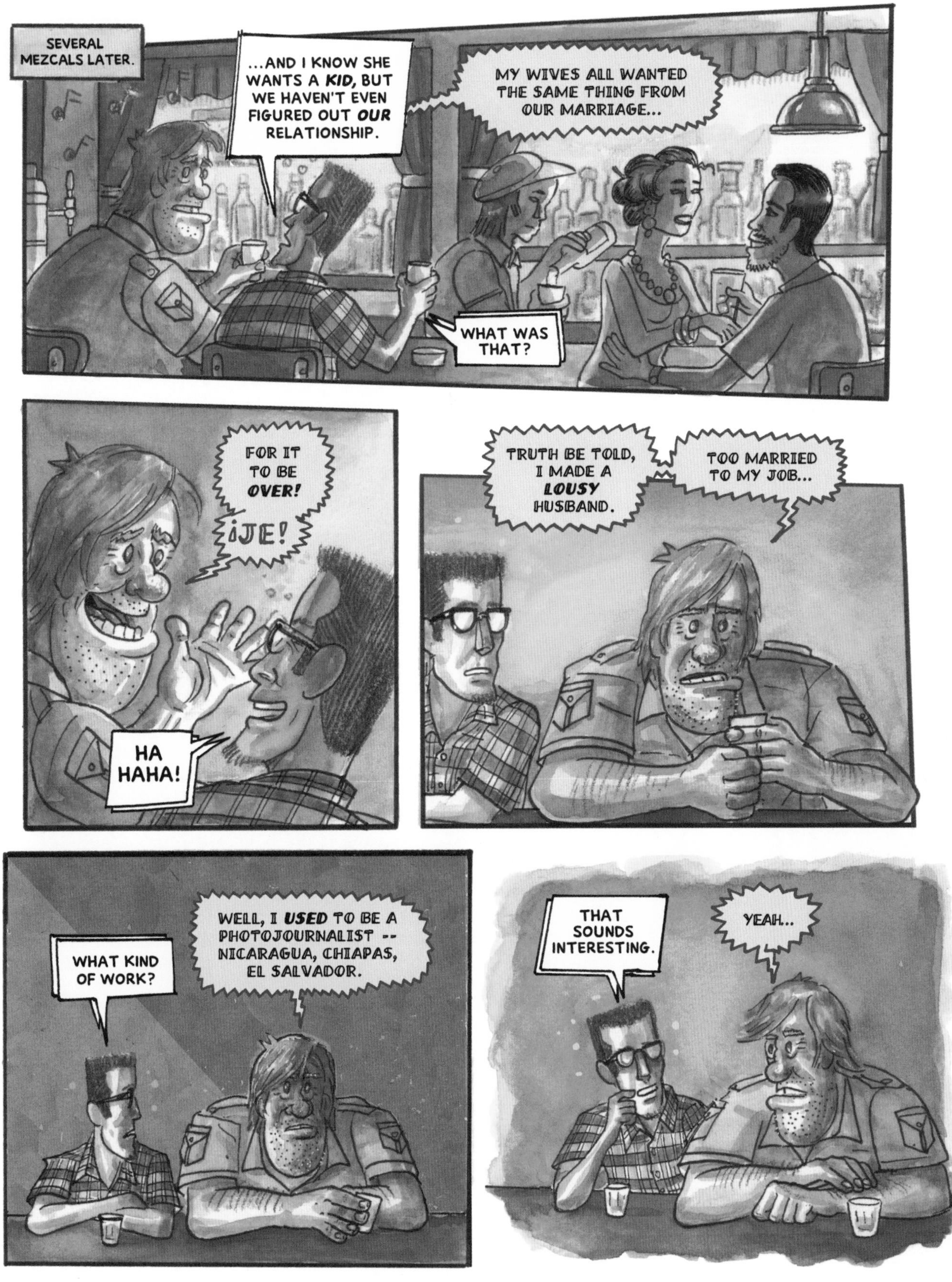
SEVERAL MEZCALS LATER.
...AND I KNOW SHE WANTS A KID, BUT WE HAVEN'T EVEN FIGURED OUT OUR RELATIONSHIP.
MY WIVES ALL WANTED THE SAME THING FROM OUR MARRIAGE...
WHAT WAS THAT?
FOR IT TO BE OVER!
¡JE!
HA HAHA!
TRUTH BE TOLD, I MADE A LOUSY HUSBAND.
TOO MARRIED TO MY JOB...
WHAT KIND OF WORK?
WELL, I USED TO BE A PHOTOJOURNALIST -- NICARAGUA, CHIAPAS, EL SALVADOR.
THAT SOUNDS INTERESTING.
YEAH...

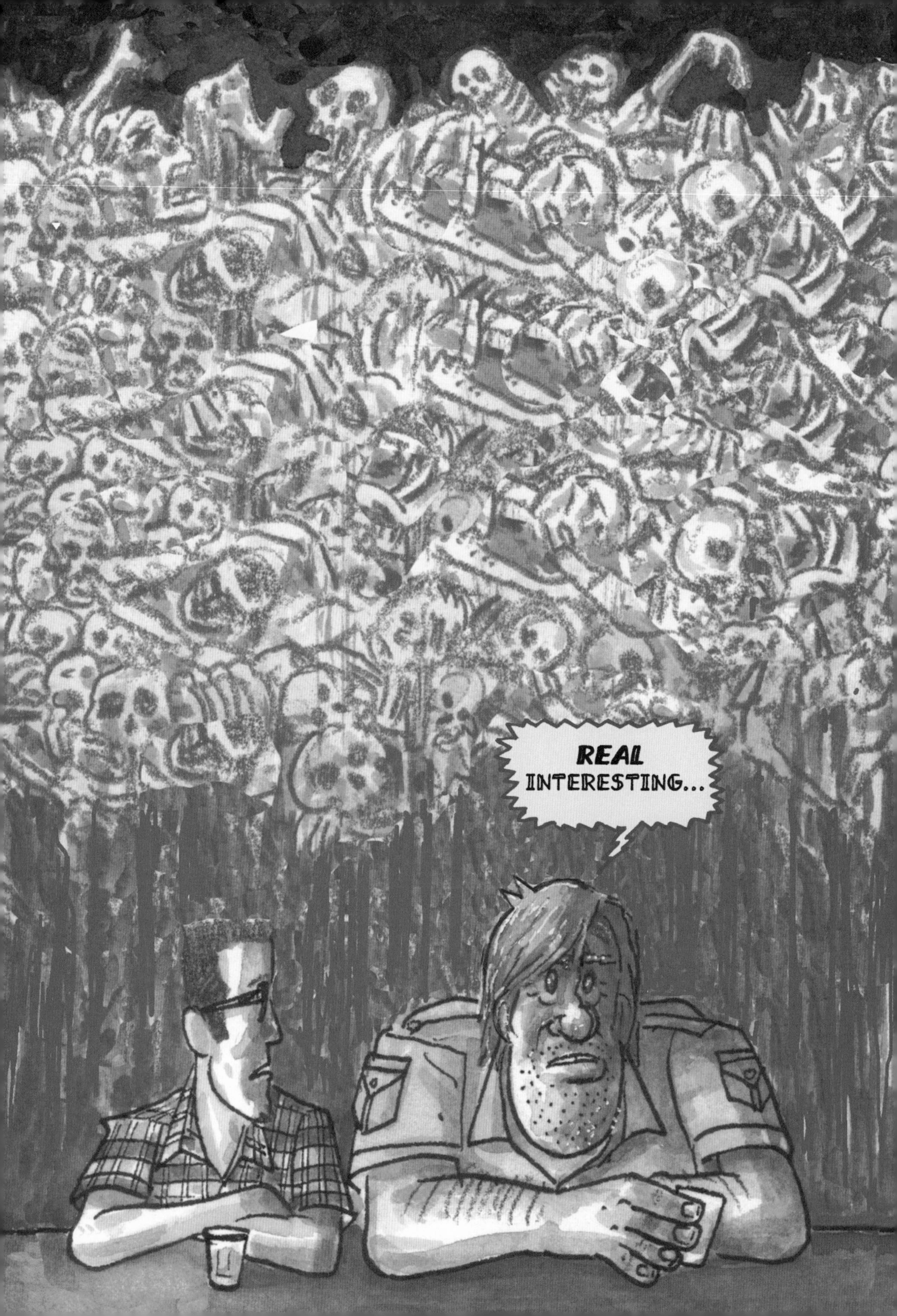
REAL INTERESTING...

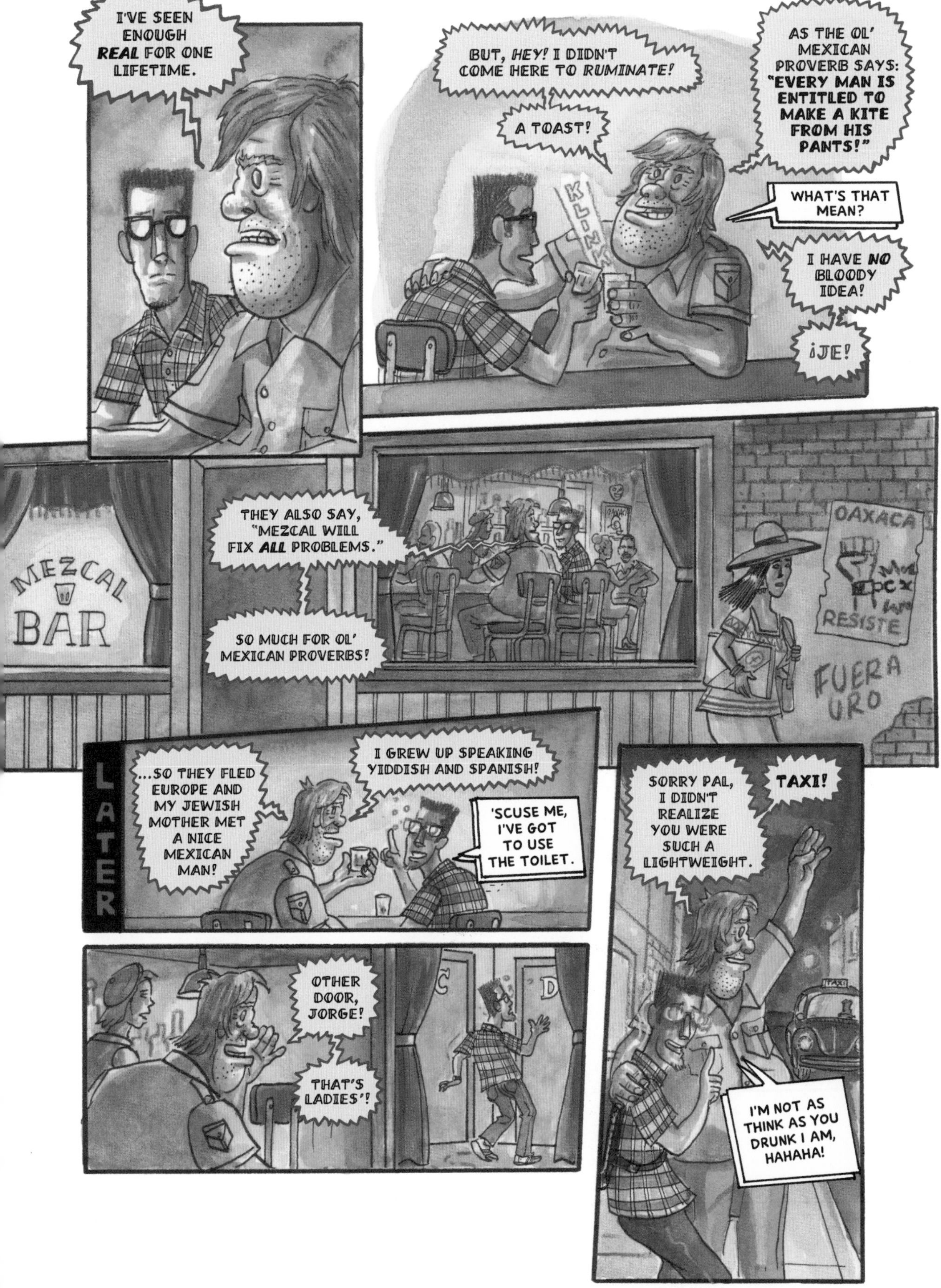

I'VE SEEN ENOUGH REAL FOR ONE LIFETIME.
BUT, HEY! I DIDN'T COME HERE TO RUMINATE!
A TOAST!
KLINK
AS THE OL' MEXICAN PROVERB SAYS: "EVERY MAN IS ENTITLED TO MAKE A KITE FROM HIS PANTS!"
WHAT'S THAT MEAN?
I HAVE NO BLOODY IDEA!
¡JE!
MEZCAL BAR
THEY ALSO SAY, "MEZCAL WILL FIX ALL PROBLEMS."
SO MUCH FOR OL' MEXICAN PROVERBS!
OAXACA
OAXACA
RESISTE
FUERA URO
LATER
...SO THEY FLED EUROPE AND MY JEWISH MOTHER MET A NICE MEXICAN MAN!
I GREW UP SPEAKING YIDDISH AND SPANISH!
'SCUSE ME, I'VE GOT TO USE THE TOILET.
OTHER DOOR, JORGE!
THAT'S LADIES'!
C
D
SORRY PAL, I DIDN'T REALIZE YOU WERE SUCH A LIGHTWEIGHT.
TAXI!
TAXI
I'M NOT AS THINK AS YOU DRUNK I AM, HAHAHA!

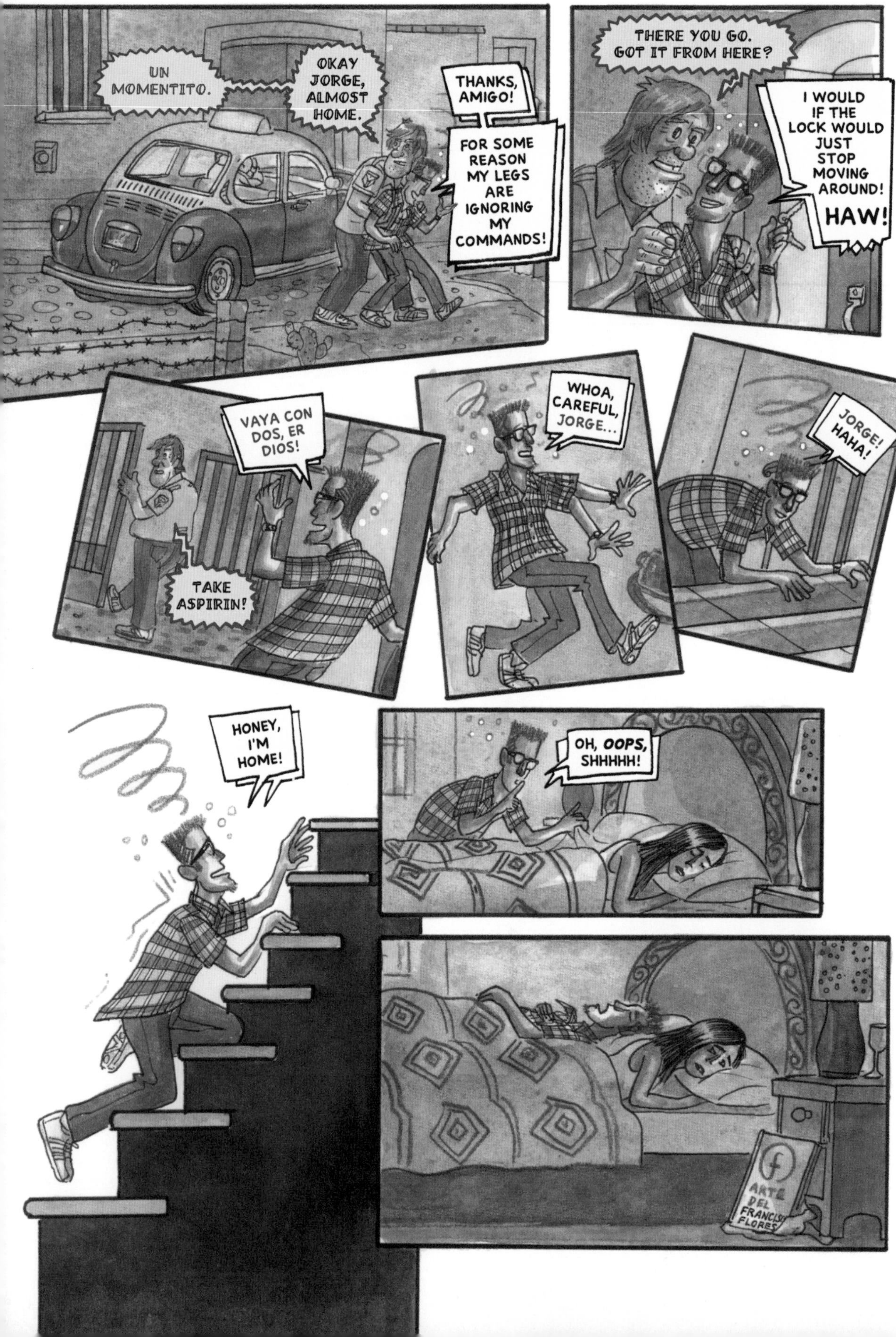
UN MOMENTITO.
OKAY JORGE, ALMOST HOME.
THANKS, AMIGO!
FOR SOME REASON MY LEGS ARE IGNORING MY COMMANDS!
THERE YOU GO. GOT IT FROM HERE?
I WOULD IF THE LOCK WOULD JUST STOP MOVING AROUND!
HAW!
VAYA CON DOS, ER DIOS!
TAKE ASPIRIN!
WHOA, CAREFUL, JORGE...
JORGE! HAHA!
HONEY, I'M HOME!
OH, OOPS, SHHHHH!
ARTE DEL FRANCISCO FLORES

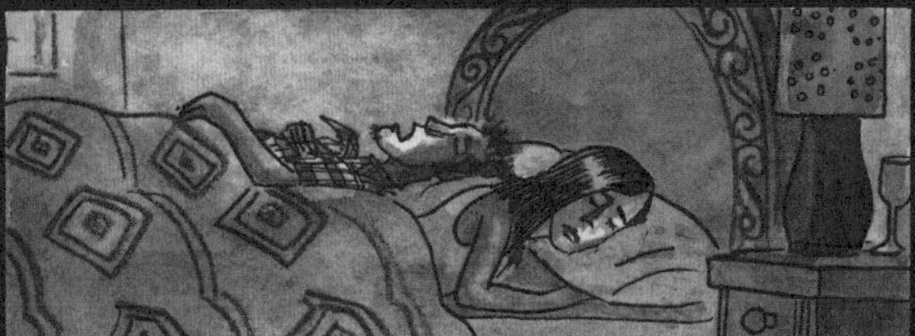
SKIT
SKIT
f
ARTE
DEL
FRANCIS
FLORES

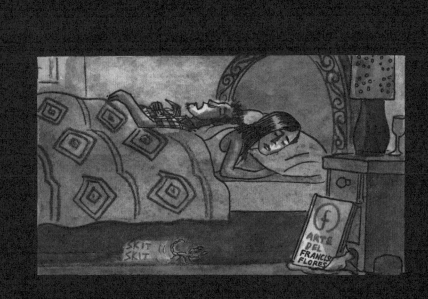

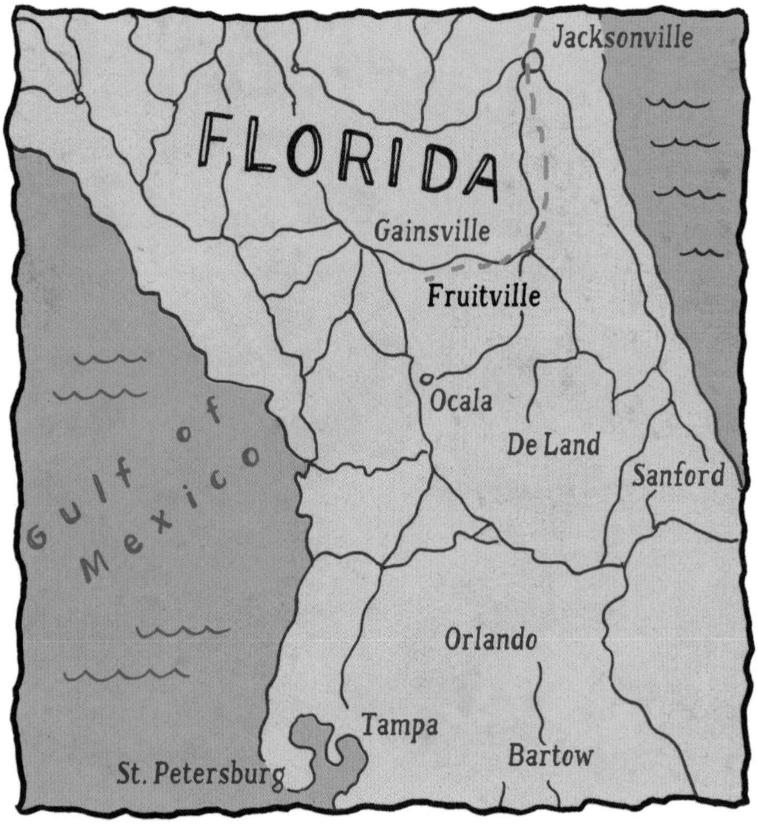

Jacksonville
FLORIDA
Gainsville
Fruitville
Ocala
De Land
Sanford
Gulf of Mexico
Orlando
Tampa
Bartow
St. Petersburg

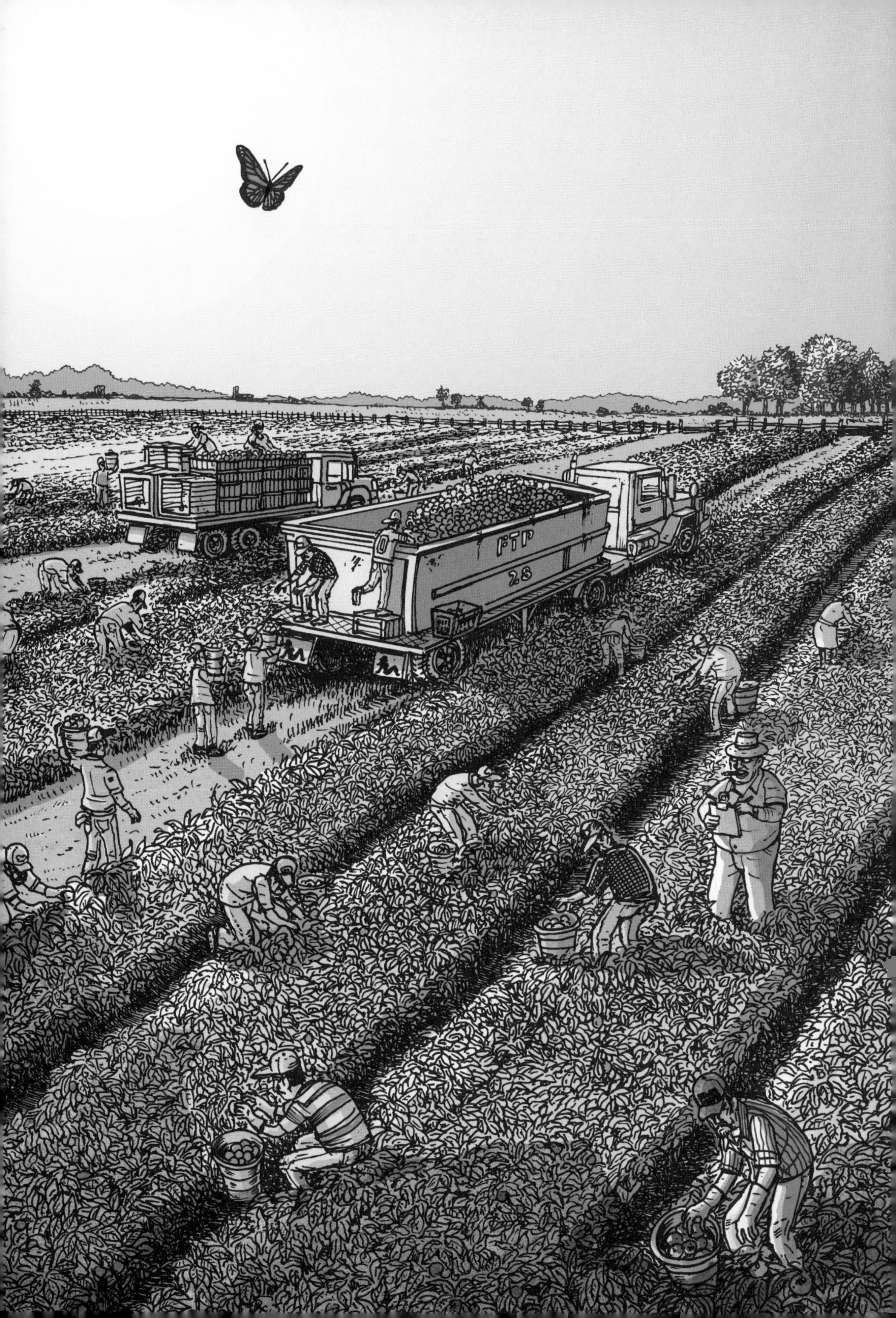
FTP
28

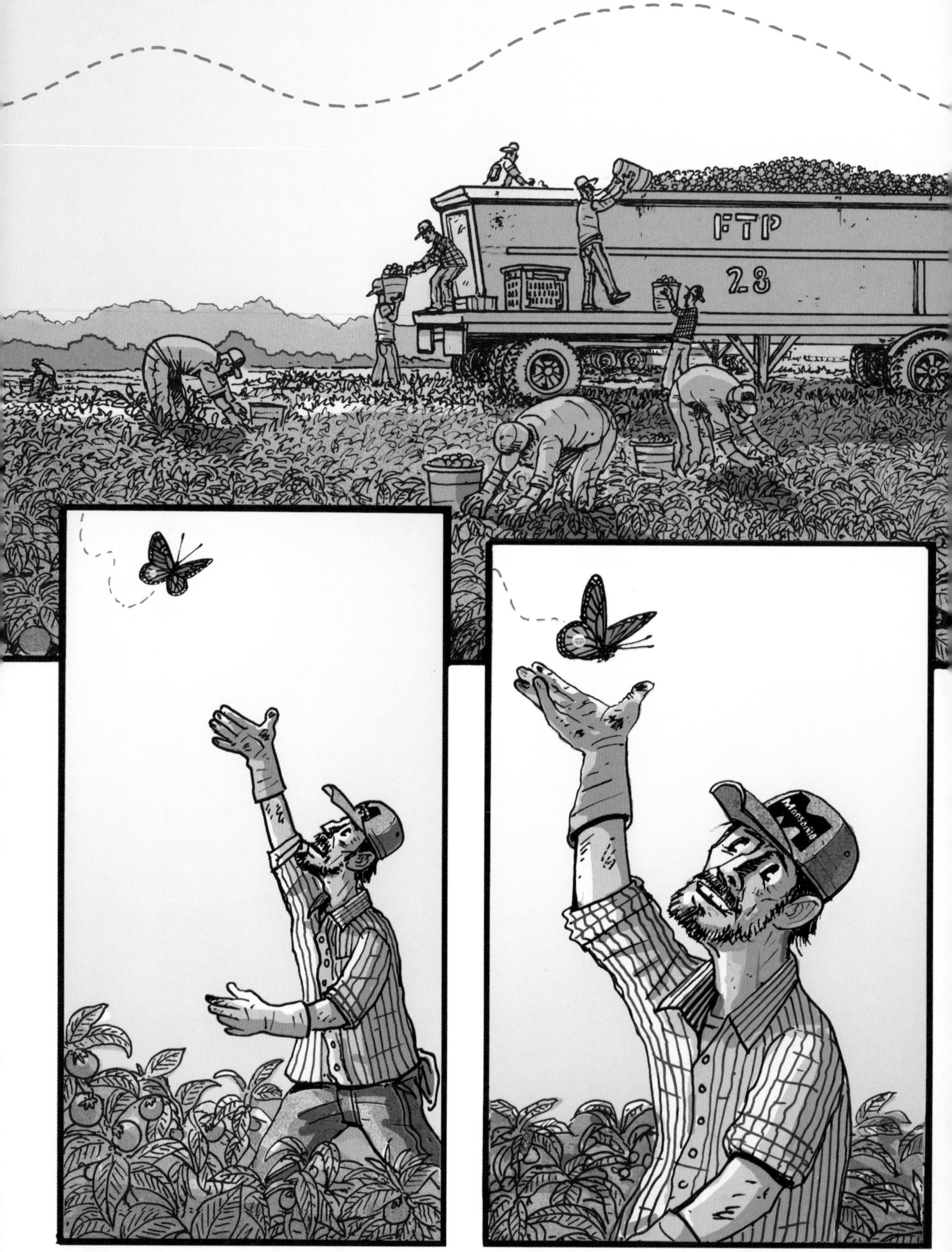
FTP
28
Monsanto

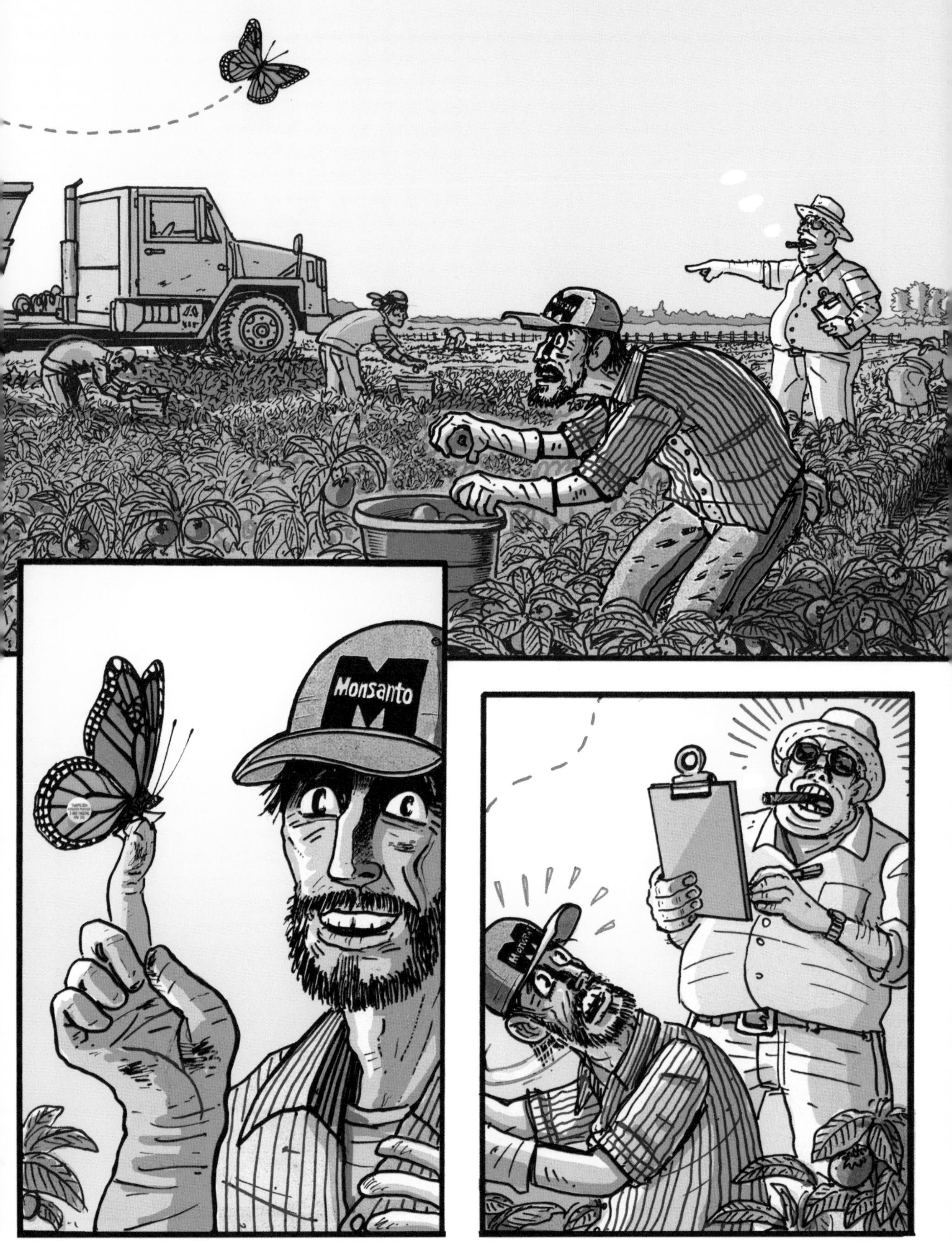
Monsanto

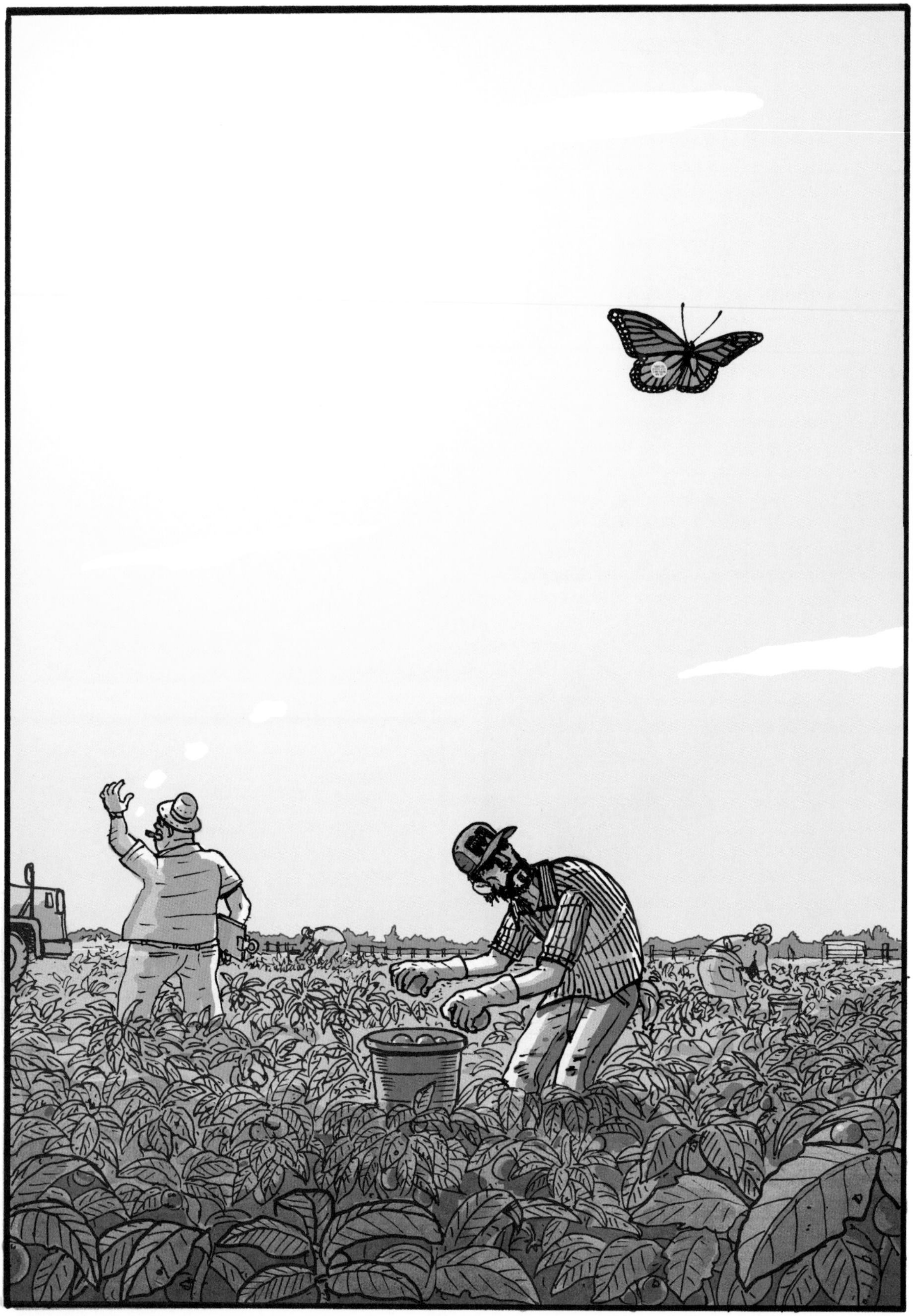

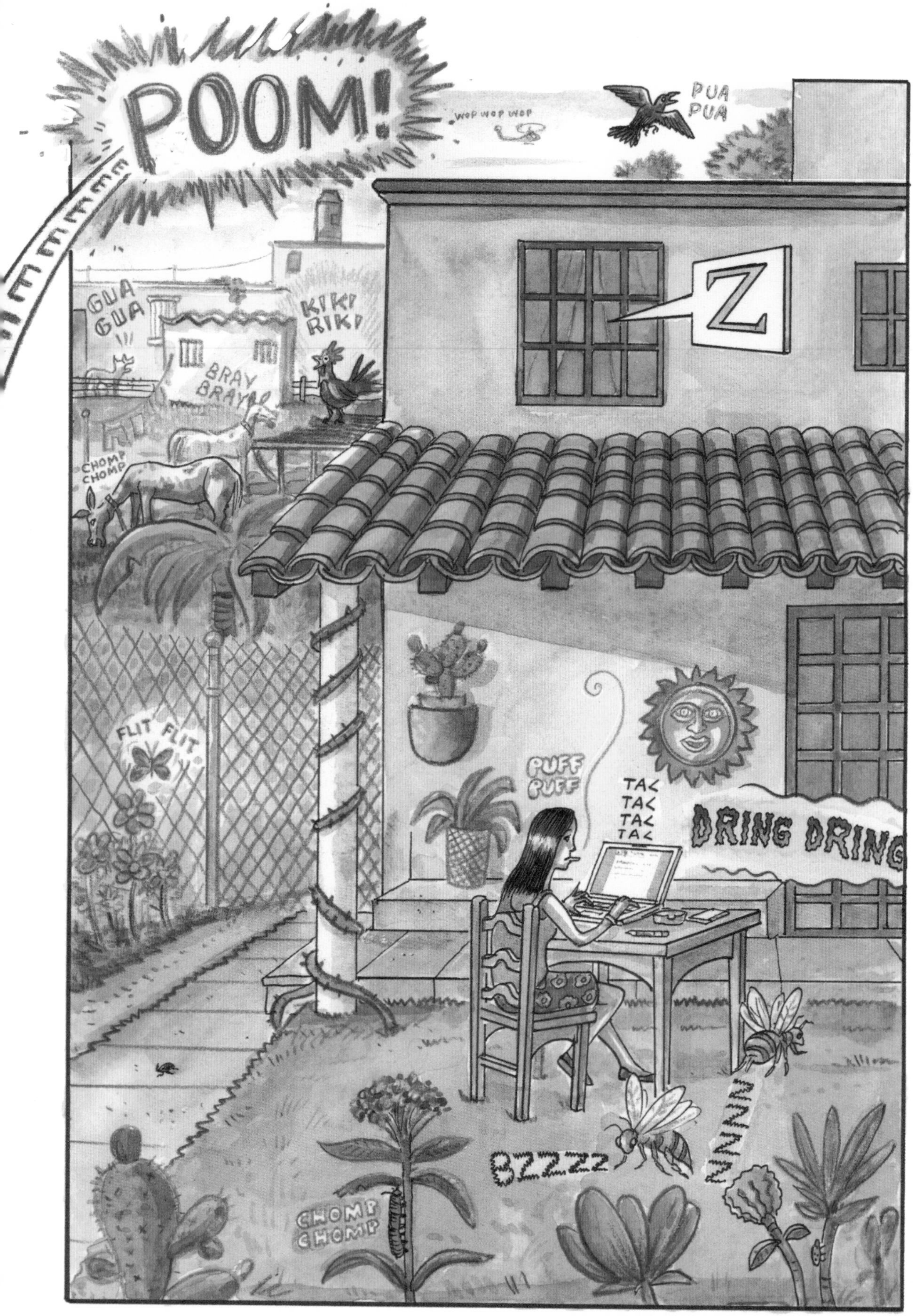
POOM!
WOP WOP WOP
PUA PUA
GUA GUA
KIKI RIKI
BRAY BRAY
Z
CHOMP CHOMP
FLIT FLIT
PUFF PUFF
TAC TAC TAC TAC
DRING DRING
BZZZZ
CHOMP CHOMP

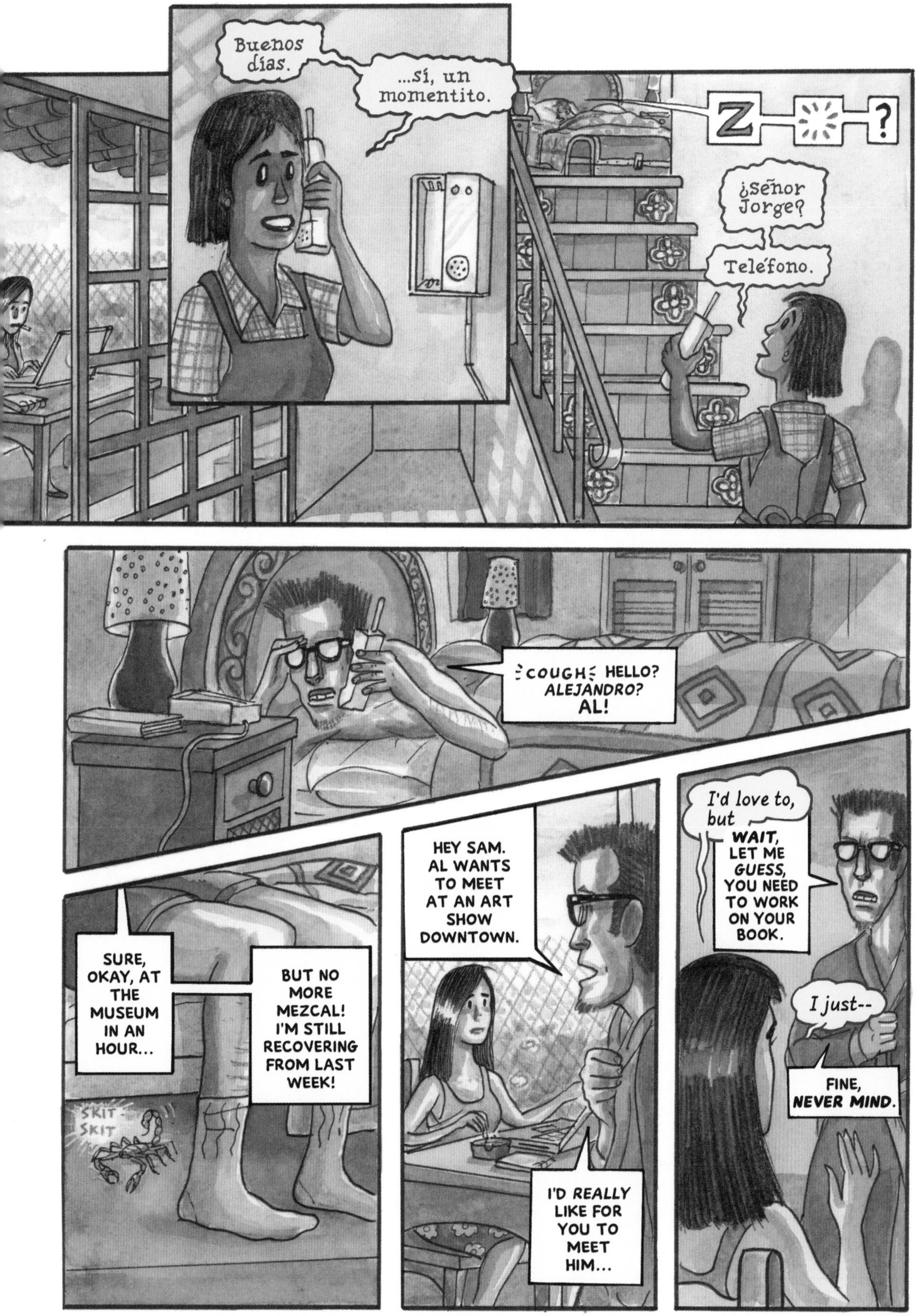
Buenos días.
...sí, un momentito.
Z
?
¿Señor Jorge?
Teléfono.
COUGH HELLO? ALEJANDRO? AL!
SURE, OKAY, AT THE MUSEUM IN AN HOUR...
BUT NO MORE MEZCAL! I'M STILL RECOVERING FROM LAST WEEK!
SKIT-SKIT
HEY SAM. AL WANTS TO MEET AT AN ART SHOW DOWNTOWN.
I'D REALLY LIKE FOR YOU TO MEET HIM...
I'd love to, but
WAIT, LET ME GUESS, YOU NEED TO WORK ON YOUR BOOK.
I just--
FINE, NEVER MIND.

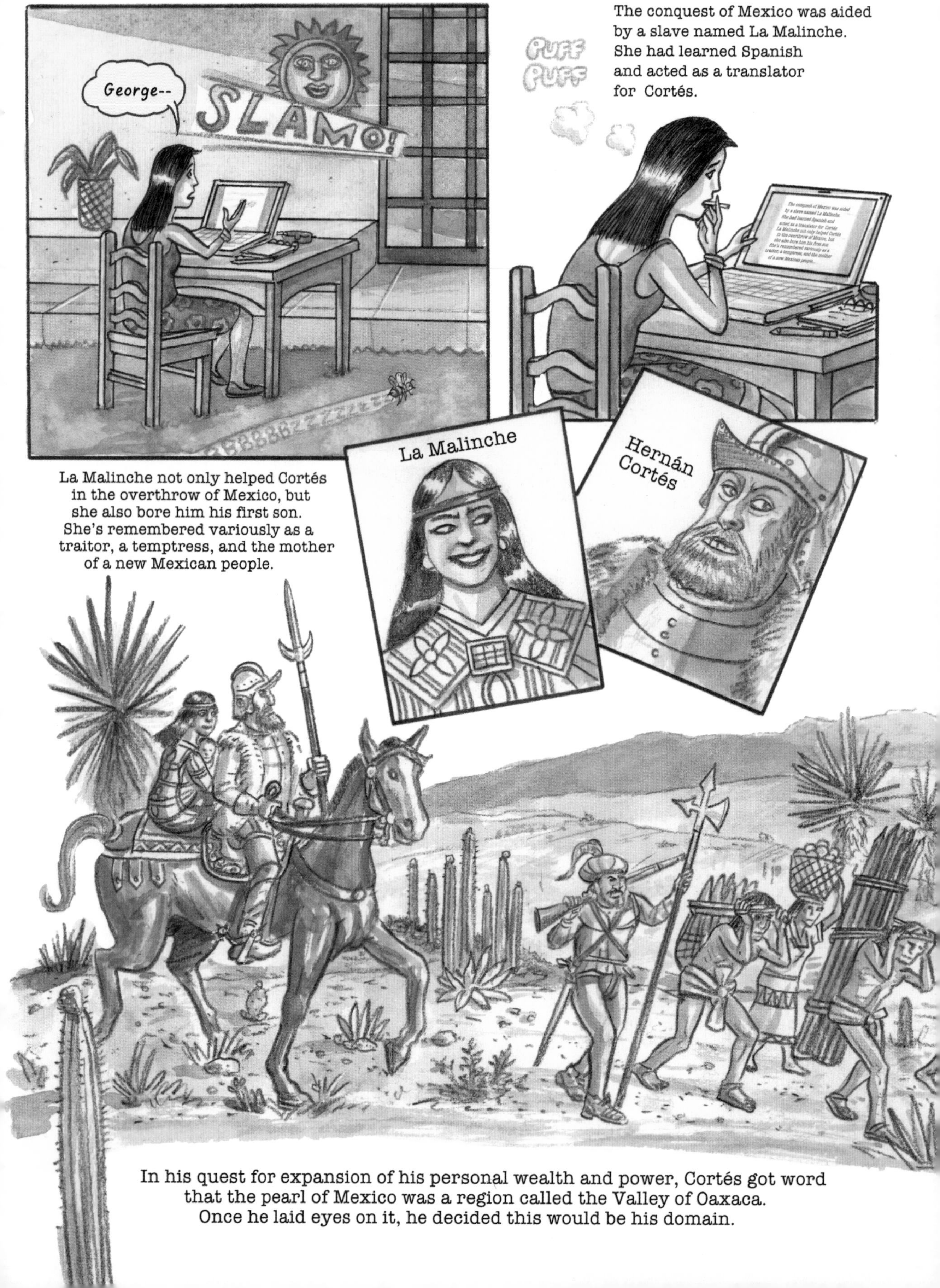
George--
SLAMO!
PUFF
PUFF
The conquest of Mexico was aided by a slave named La Malinche. She had learned Spanish and acted as a translator for Cortés.
La Malinche not only helped Cortés in the overthrow of Mexico, but she also bore him his first son. She's remembered variously as a traitor, a temptress, and the mother of a new Mexican people.
La Malinche
Hernán Cortés
In his quest for expansion of his personal wealth and power, Cortés got word that the pearl of Mexico was a region called the Valley of Oaxaca. Once he laid eyes on it, he decided this would be his domain.

Oaxaca, certainly, was magic. “Magic” was what brought you there in the first place, found in the form of a mushroom called psilocybin. It transported you through time and space and, for better and worse, transformed your perception of reality.

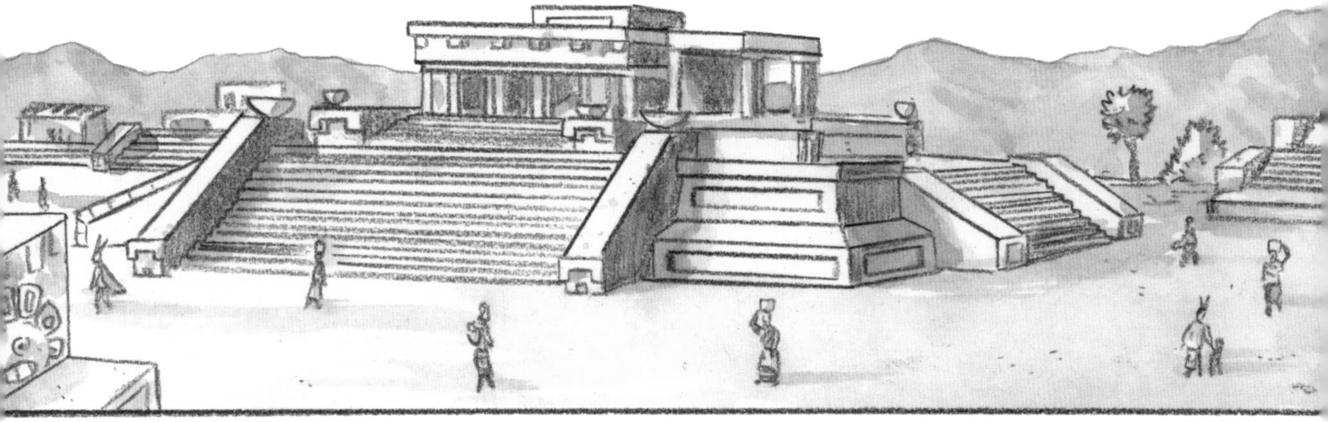

You had left the United States in search of altered states and the guidance you had never found at home. Mexico handed you that in both intangible and literal forms...

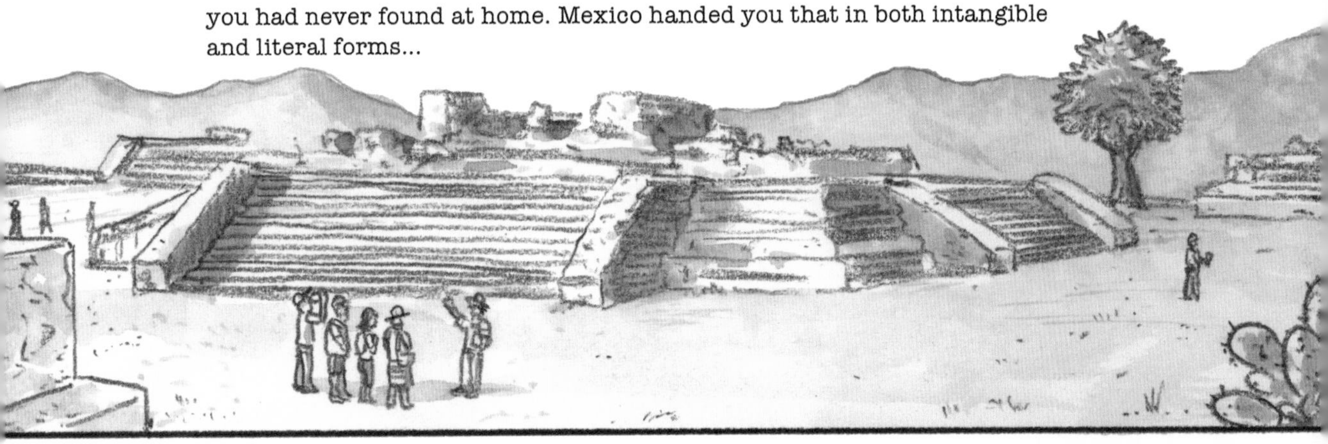

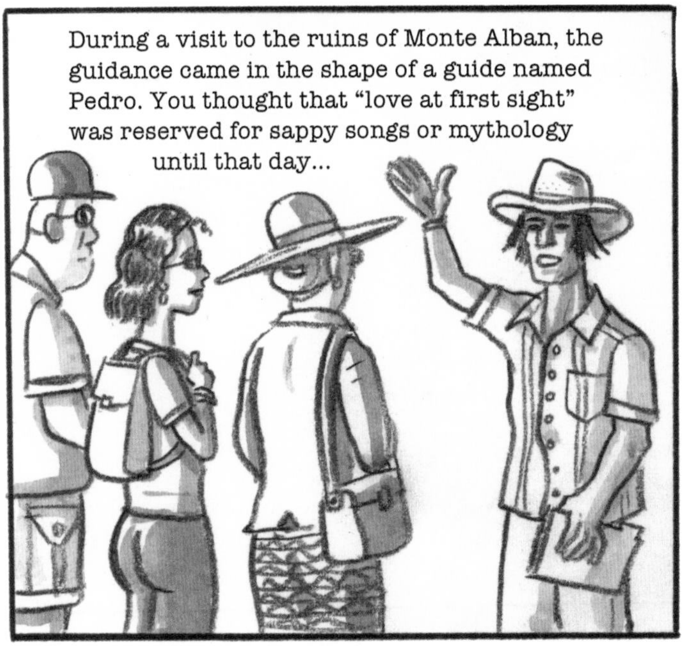
During a visit to the ruins of Monte Alban, the guidance came in the shape of a guide named Pedro. You thought that “love at first sight” was reserved for sappy songs or mythology until that day...

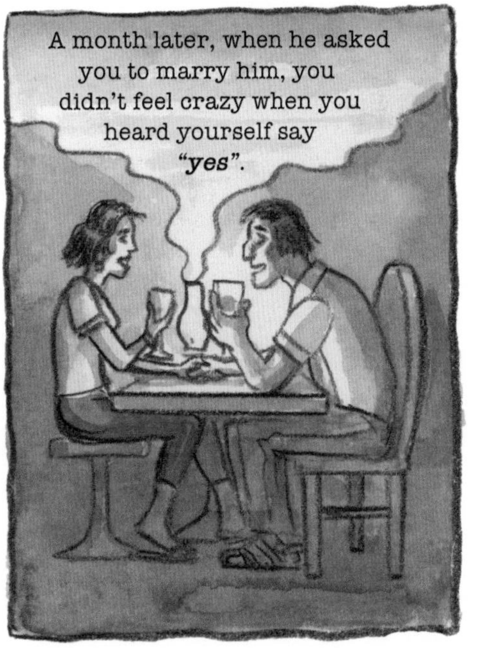
A month later, when he asked you to marry him, you didn’t feel crazy when you heard yourself say “*yes*”.

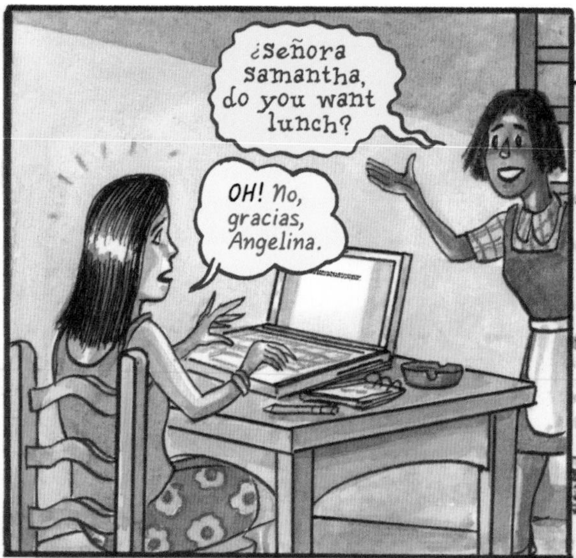
¿Señora samantha, do you want lunch?
OH! No, gracias, Angelina.

Your honeymoon was a glorious road trip across Mexico...

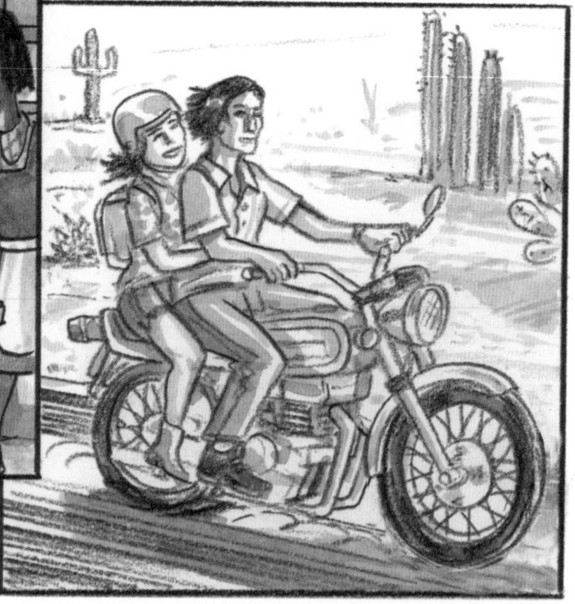

Pedro shared the history of his country while unfolding his own story...

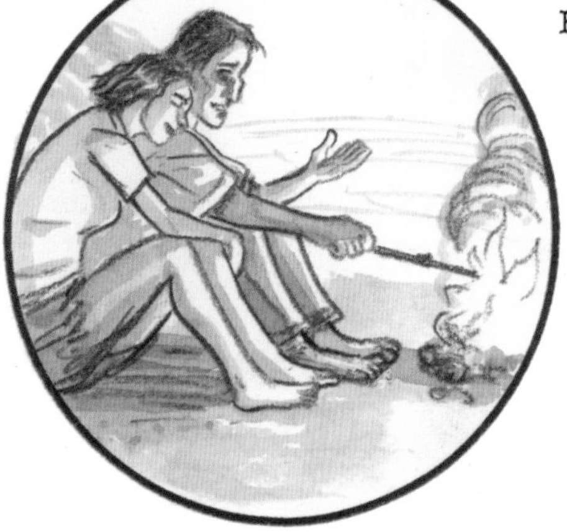

The more he shared, the more you loved him. He made you feel like your history had been reset.

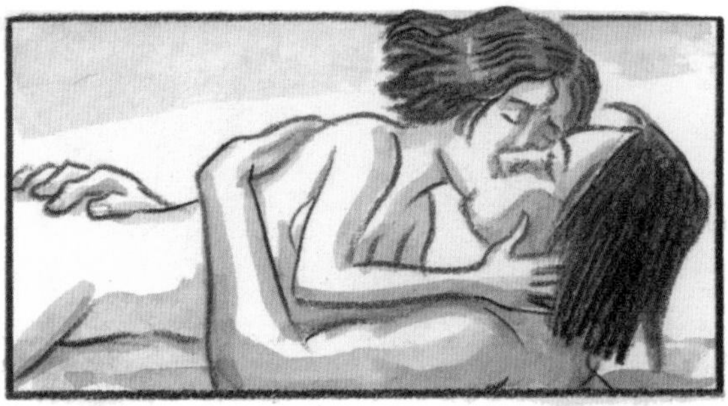

When your biology informed you that a life was forming inside your body, you also felt a new connection to the future...

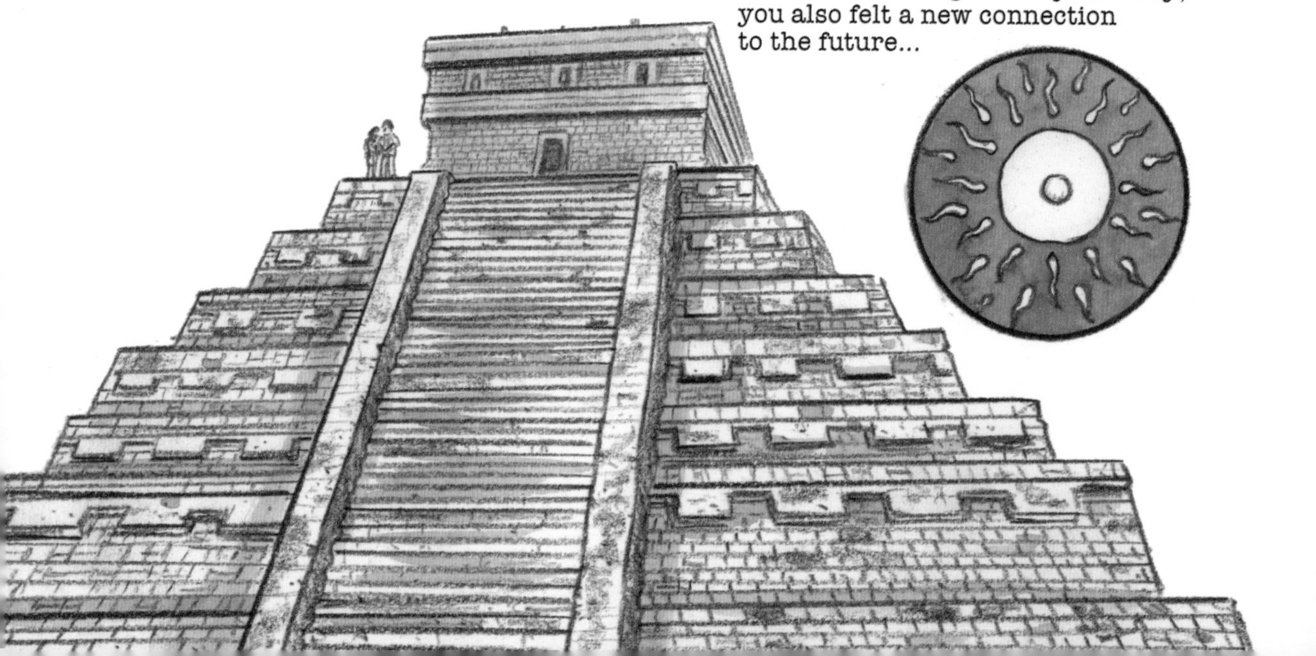

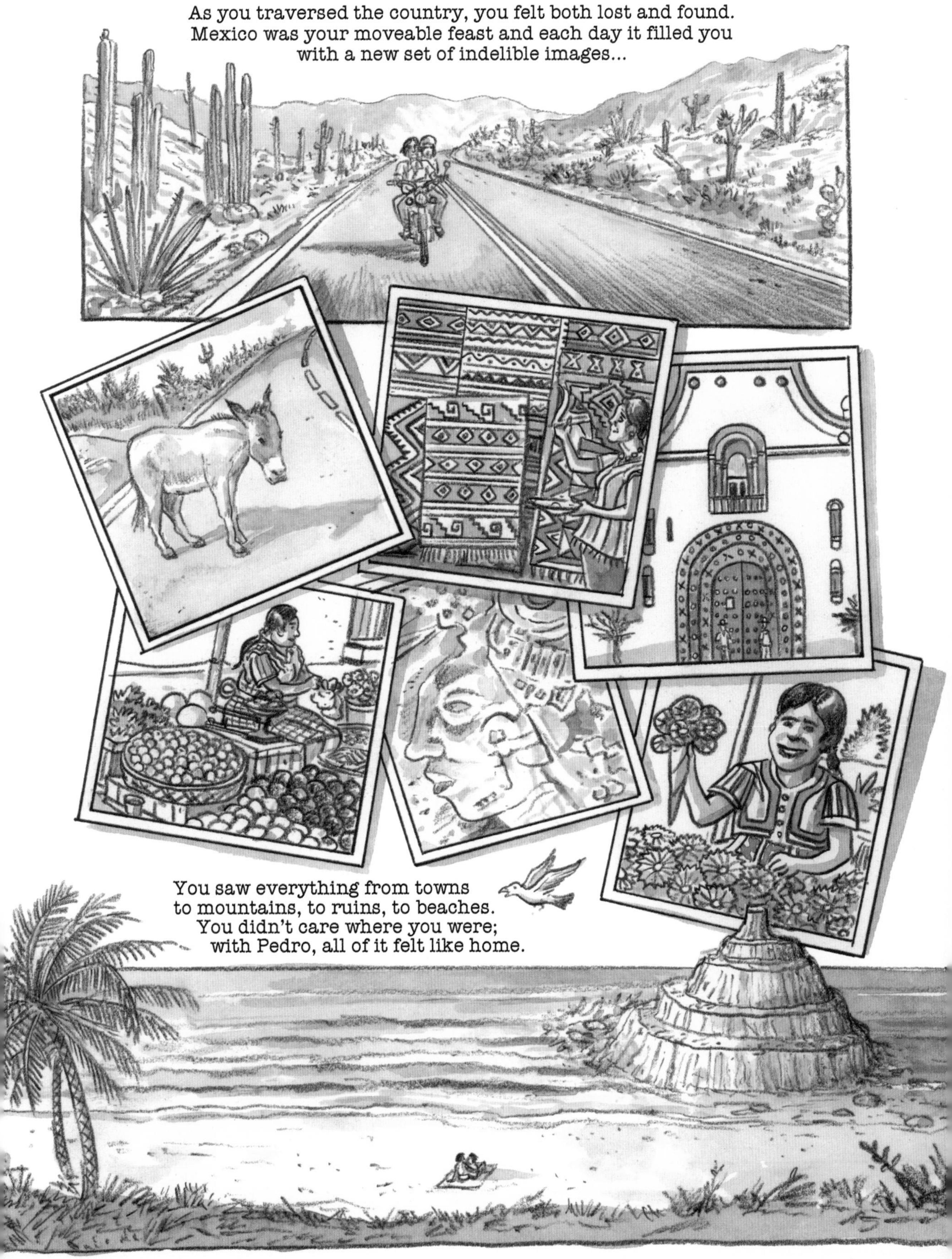
As you traversed the country, you felt both lost and found. Mexico was your moveable feast and each day it filled you with a new set of indelible images...
You saw everything from towns to mountains, to ruins, to beaches. You didn't care where you were; with Pedro, all of it felt like home.

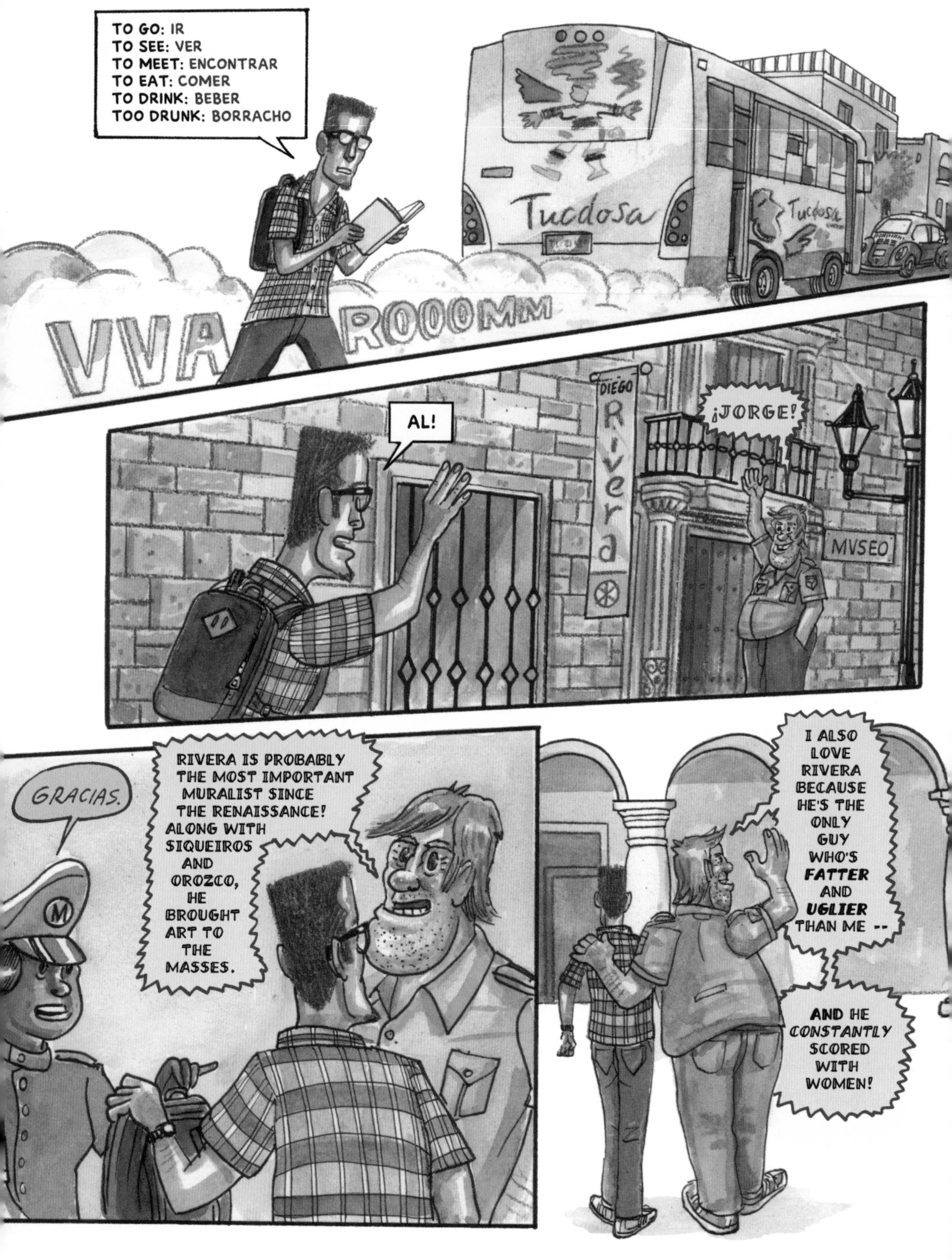

TO GO: IR
TO SEE: VER
TO MEET: ENCONTRAR
TO EAT: COMER
TO DRINK: BEBER
TOO DRUNK: BORRACHO
Tucdosa
Tucdosa
VVA ROOOMM
AL!
¡JORGE!
DIEGO Rivera
MVSEO
GRACIAS.
RIVERA IS PROBABLY THE MOST IMPORTANT MURALIST SINCE THE RENAISSANCE!
ALONG WITH SIQUEIROS AND OROZCO, HE BROUGHT ART TO THE MASSES.
I ALSO LOVE RIVERA BECAUSE HE'S THE ONLY GUY WHO'S **FATTER** AND **UGLIER** THAN ME --
AND HE CONSTANTLY SCORED WITH WOMEN!

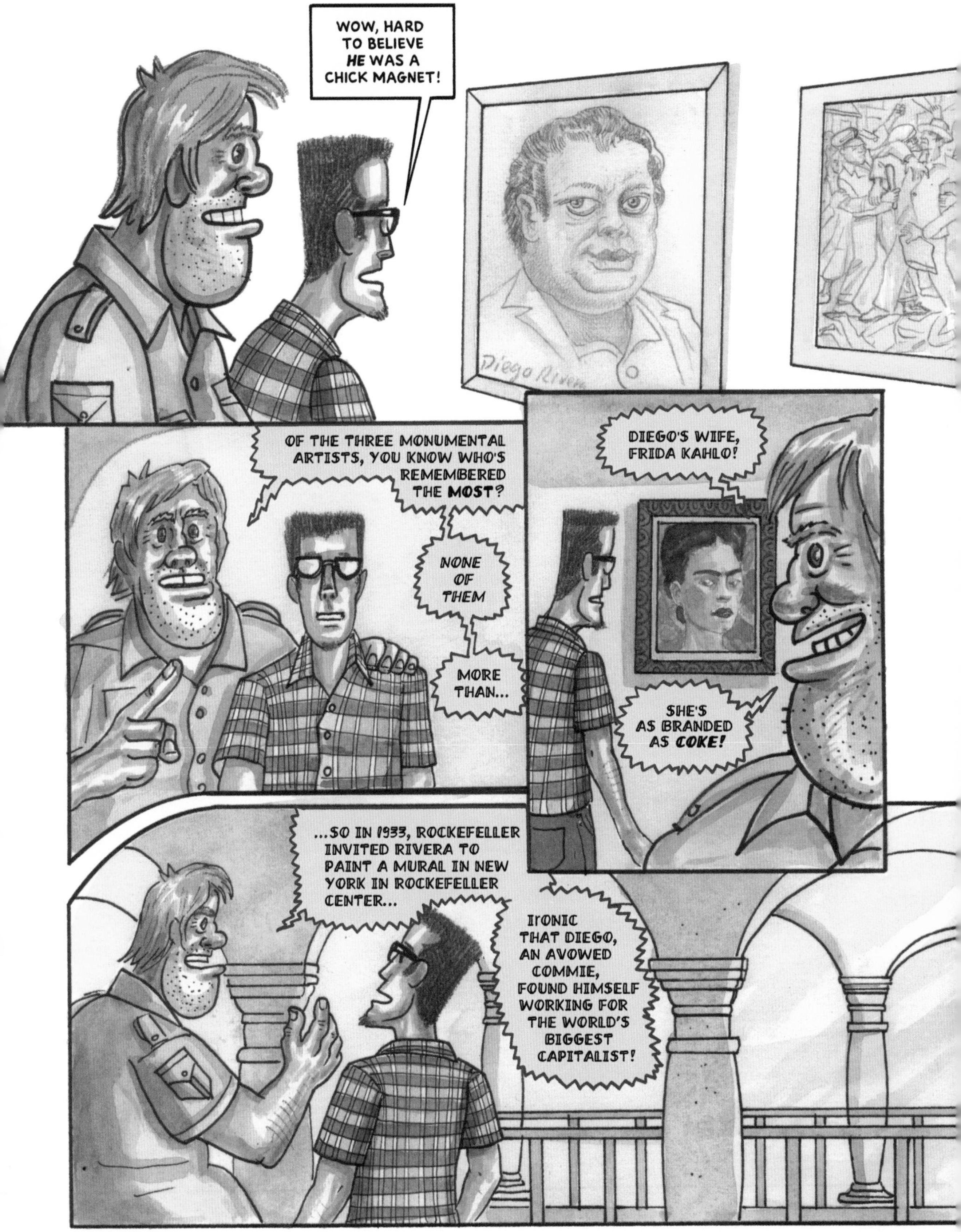
WOW, HARD TO BELIEVE HE WAS A CHICK MAGNET!
Diego Rivera
OF THE THREE MONUMENTAL ARTISTS, YOU KNOW WHO'S REMEMBERED THE MOST?
NONE OF THEM
MORE THAN...
DIEGO'S WIFE, FRIDA KAHLO!
SHE'S AS BRANDED AS COKE!
...SO IN 1933, ROCKEFELLER INVITED RIVERA TO PAINT A MURAL IN NEW YORK IN ROCKEFELLER CENTER...
IRONIC THAT DIEGO, AN AVOWED COMMIE, FOUND HIMSELF WORKING FOR THE WORLD'S BIGGEST CAPITALIST!

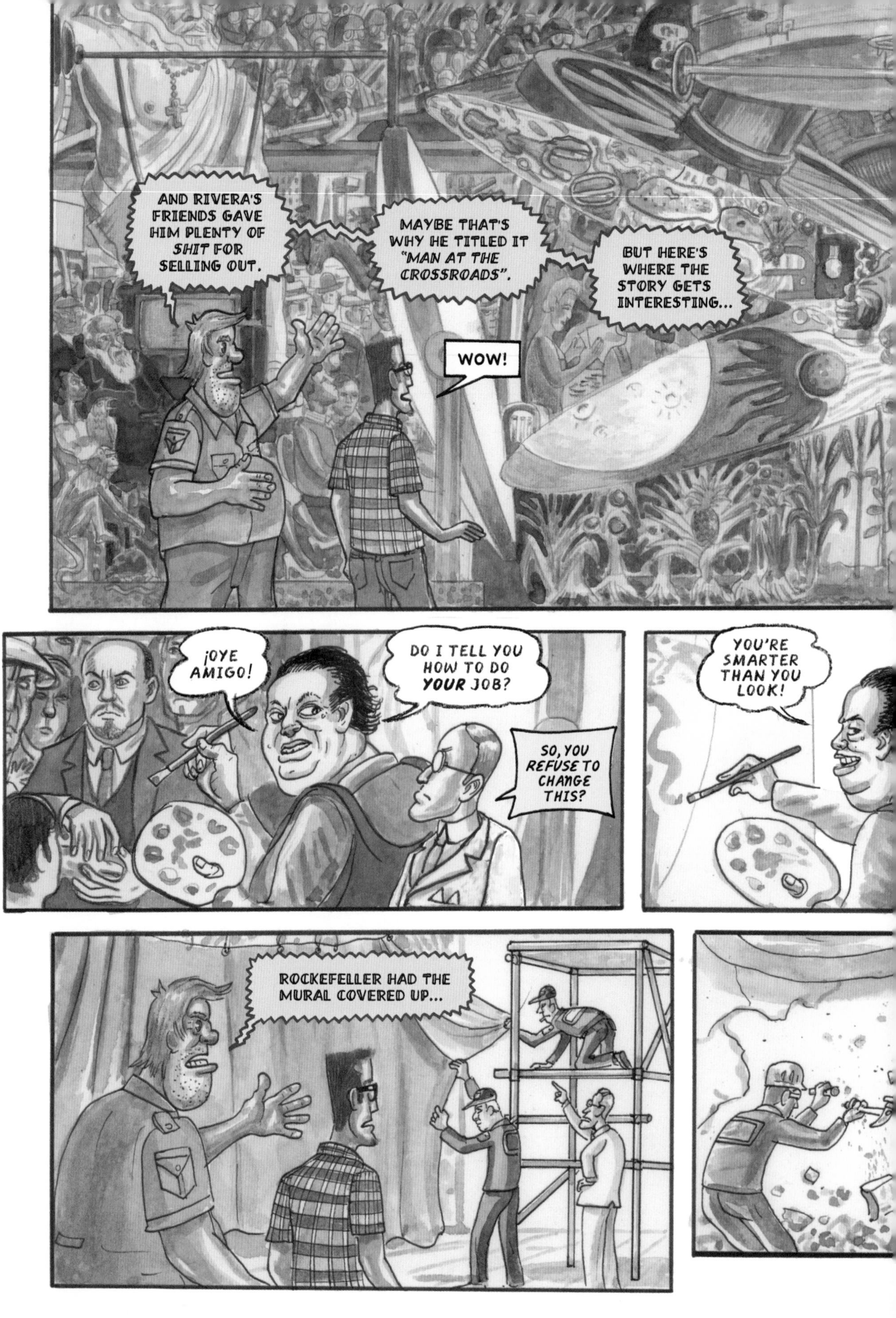
AND RIVERA'S FRIENDS GAVE HIM PLENTY OF *SHIT* FOR SELLING OUT.
MAYBE THAT'S WHY HE TITLED IT *"MAN AT THE CROSSROADS"*.
BUT HERE'S WHERE THE STORY GETS INTERESTING...
WOW!
SO, YOU *REFUSE* TO CHANGE THIS?
¡OYE AMIGO!
DO I TELL YOU HOW TO DO ***YOUR*** JOB?
YOU'RE SMARTER THAN YOU LOOK!
ROCKEFELLER HAD THE MURAL COVERED UP...

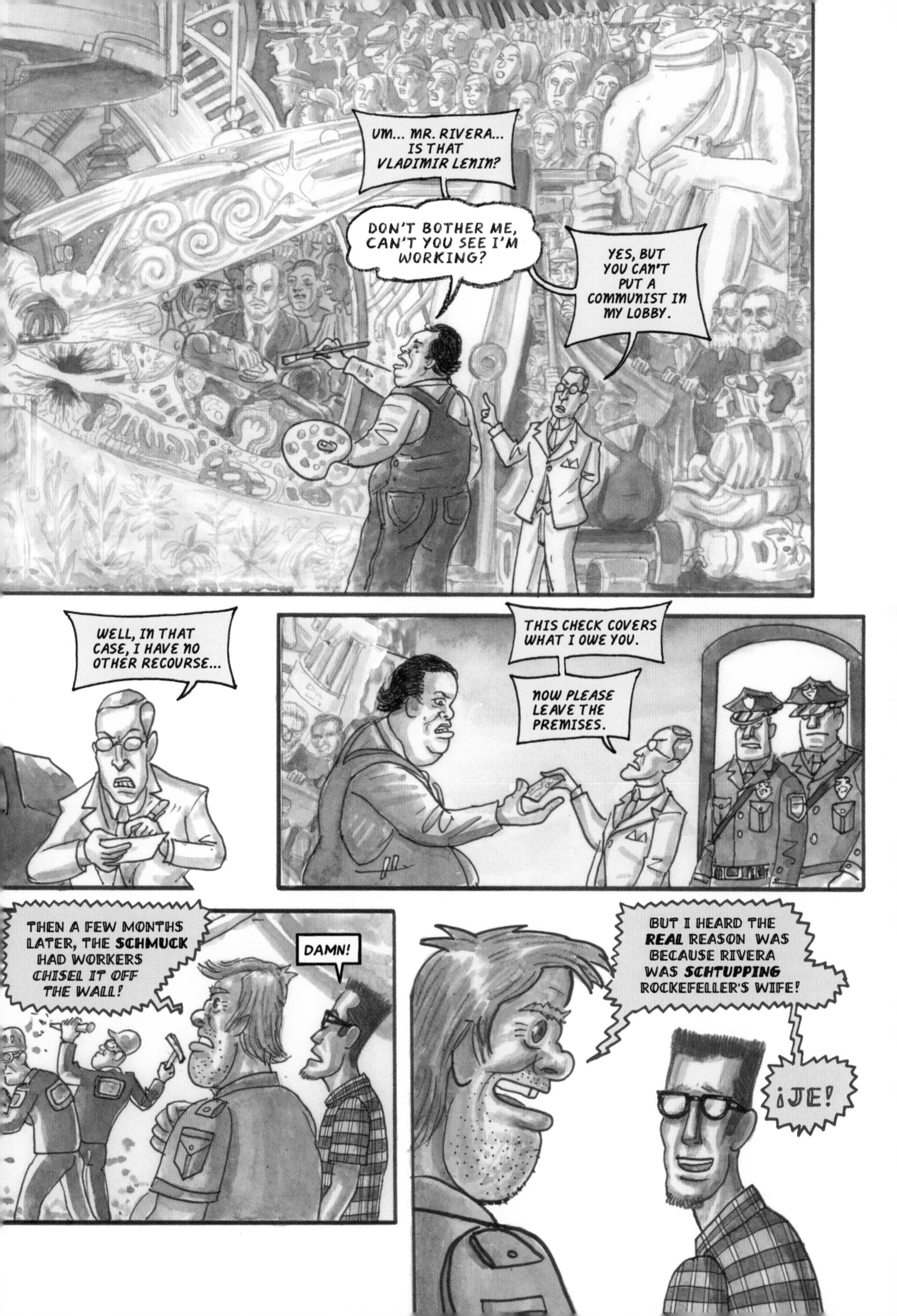
UM... MR. RIVERA... IS THAT VLADIMIR LENIN?
DON'T BOTHER ME, CAN'T YOU SEE I'M WORKING?
YES, BUT YOU CAN'T PUT A COMMUNIST IN MY LOBBY.
WELL, IN THAT CASE, I HAVE NO OTHER RECOURSE...
THIS CHECK COVERS WHAT I OWE YOU.
NOW PLEASE LEAVE THE PREMISES.
THEN A FEW MONTHS LATER, THE SCHMUCK HAD WORKERS CHISEL IT OFF THE WALL!
DAMN!
BUT I HEARD THE REAL REASON WAS BECAUSE RIVERA WAS SCHTUPPING ROCKEFELLER'S WIFE!
¡JE!

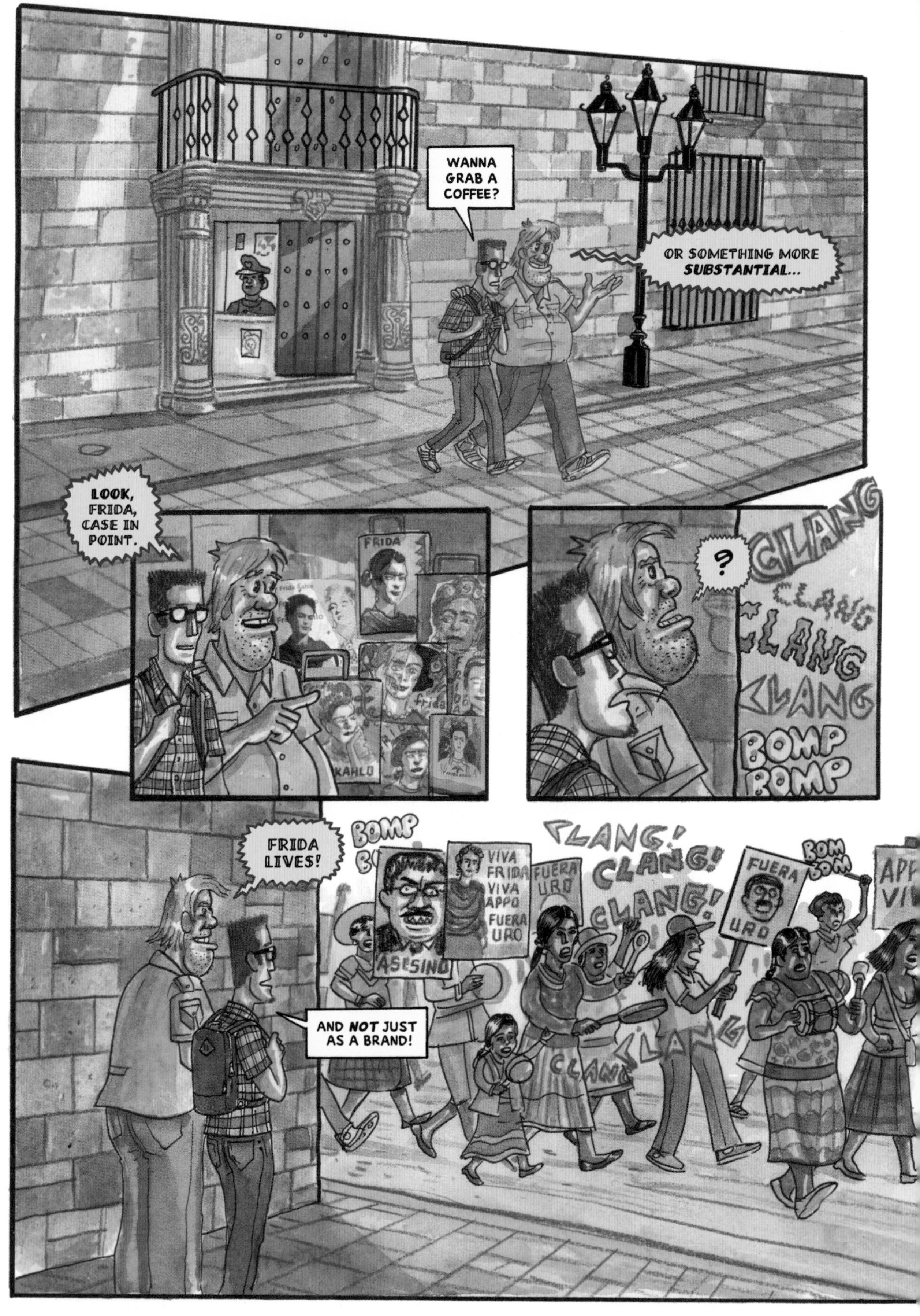
WANNA GRAB A COFFEE?
OR SOMETHING MORE **SUBSTANTIAL**...
LOOK, FRIDA, CASE IN POINT.
FRIDA
KAHLO
?
CLANG
CLANG
CLANG
CLANG
BOMP
BOMP
FRIDA LIVES!
BOMP
VIVA FRIDA VIVA APPO FUERA URO
ASESINO
FUERA URO
CLANG!
CLANG!
CLANG!
FUERA URO
BOM BOM
AND **NOT** JUST AS A BRAND!
CLANG
CLANG

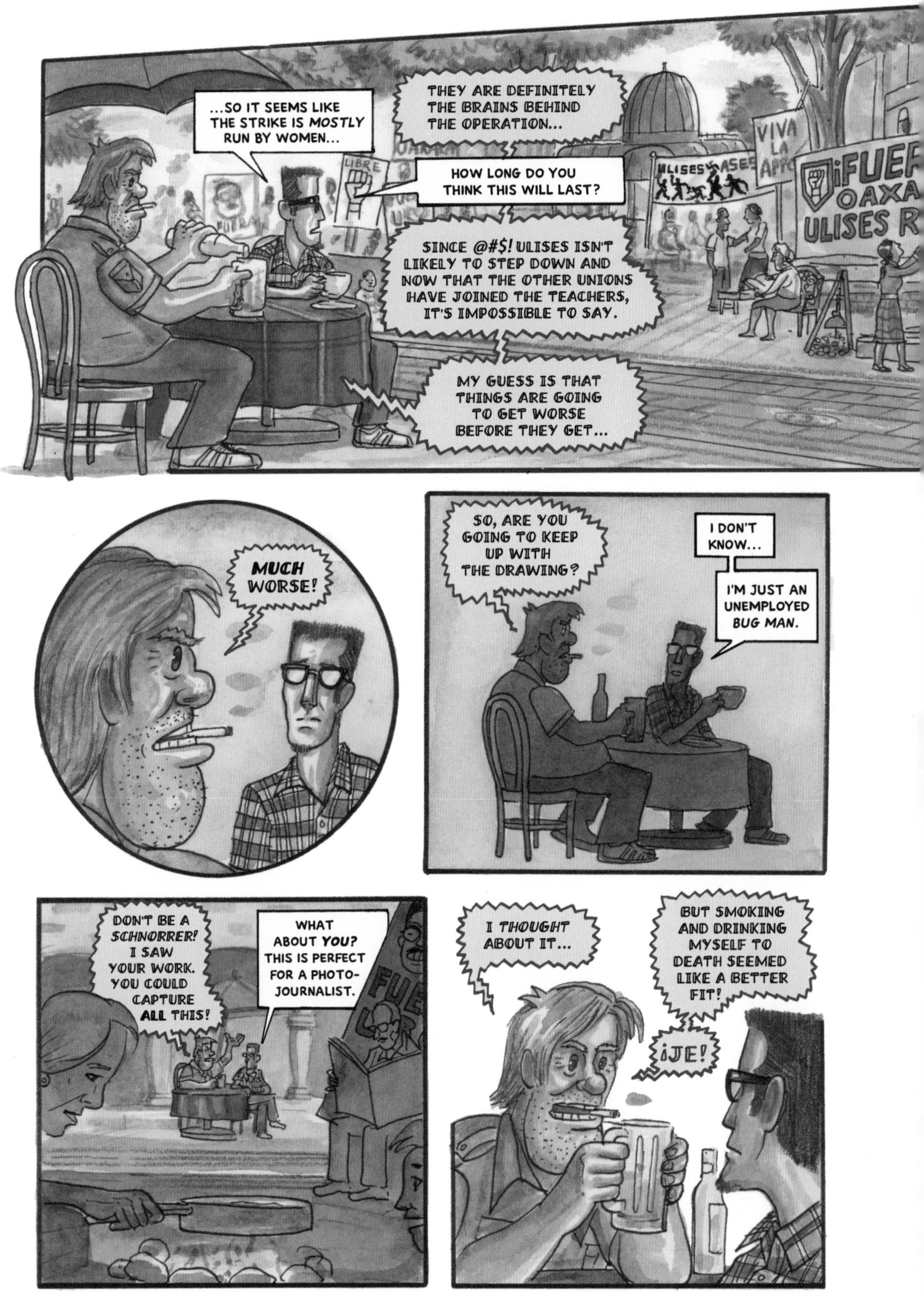
...SO IT SEEMS LIKE THE STRIKE IS MOSTLY RUN BY WOMEN...
THEY ARE DEFINITELY THE BRAINS BEHIND THE OPERATION...
HOW LONG DO YOU THINK THIS WILL LAST?
SINCE @#$! ULISES ISN'T LIKELY TO STEP DOWN AND NOW THAT THE OTHER UNIONS HAVE JOINED THE TEACHERS, IT'S IMPOSSIBLE TO SAY.
MY GUESS IS THAT THINGS ARE GOING TO GET WORSE BEFORE THEY GET...
VIVA LA APPO
¡FUER OAXA ULISES R
MUCH WORSE!
SO, ARE YOU GOING TO KEEP UP WITH THE DRAWING?
I DON'T KNOW...
I'M JUST AN UNEMPLOYED BUG MAN.
DON'T BE A SCHNORRER! I SAW YOUR WORK. YOU COULD CAPTURE ALL THIS!
WHAT ABOUT YOU? THIS IS PERFECT FOR A PHOTO-JOURNALIST.
I THOUGHT ABOUT IT...
BUT SMOKING AND DRINKING MYSELF TO DEATH SEEMED LIKE A BETTER FIT!
¡JE!

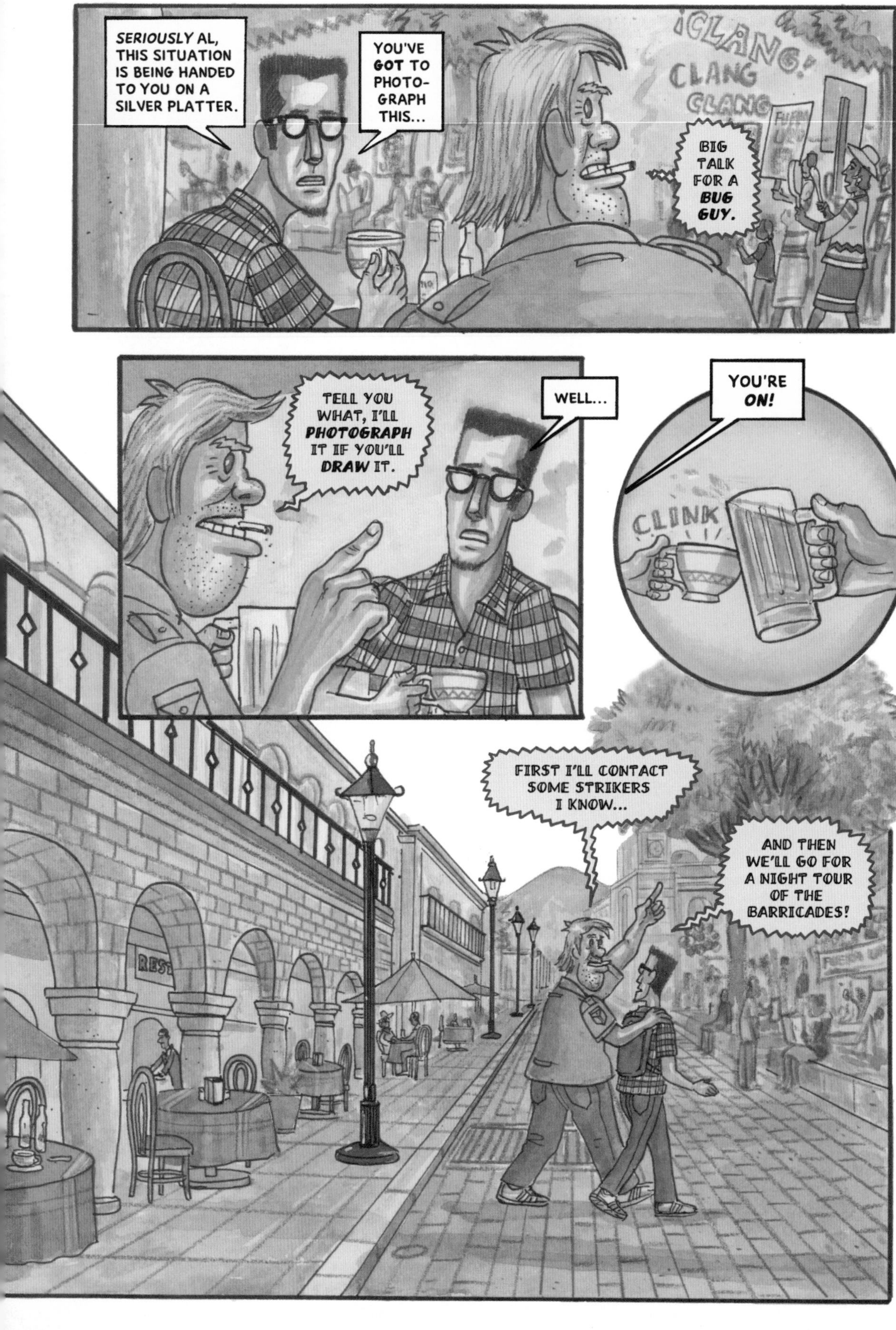
SERIOUSLY AL, THIS SITUATION IS BEING HANDED TO YOU ON A SILVER PLATTER.
YOU'VE GOT TO PHOTOGRAPH THIS...
¡CLANG! CLANG CLANG
BIG TALK FOR A BUG GUY.
TELL YOU WHAT, I'LL PHOTOGRAPH IT IF YOU'LL DRAW IT.
WELL...
YOU'RE ON!
CLINK
FIRST I'LL CONTACT SOME STRIKERS I KNOW...
AND THEN WE'LL GO FOR A NIGHT TOUR OF THE BARRICADES!

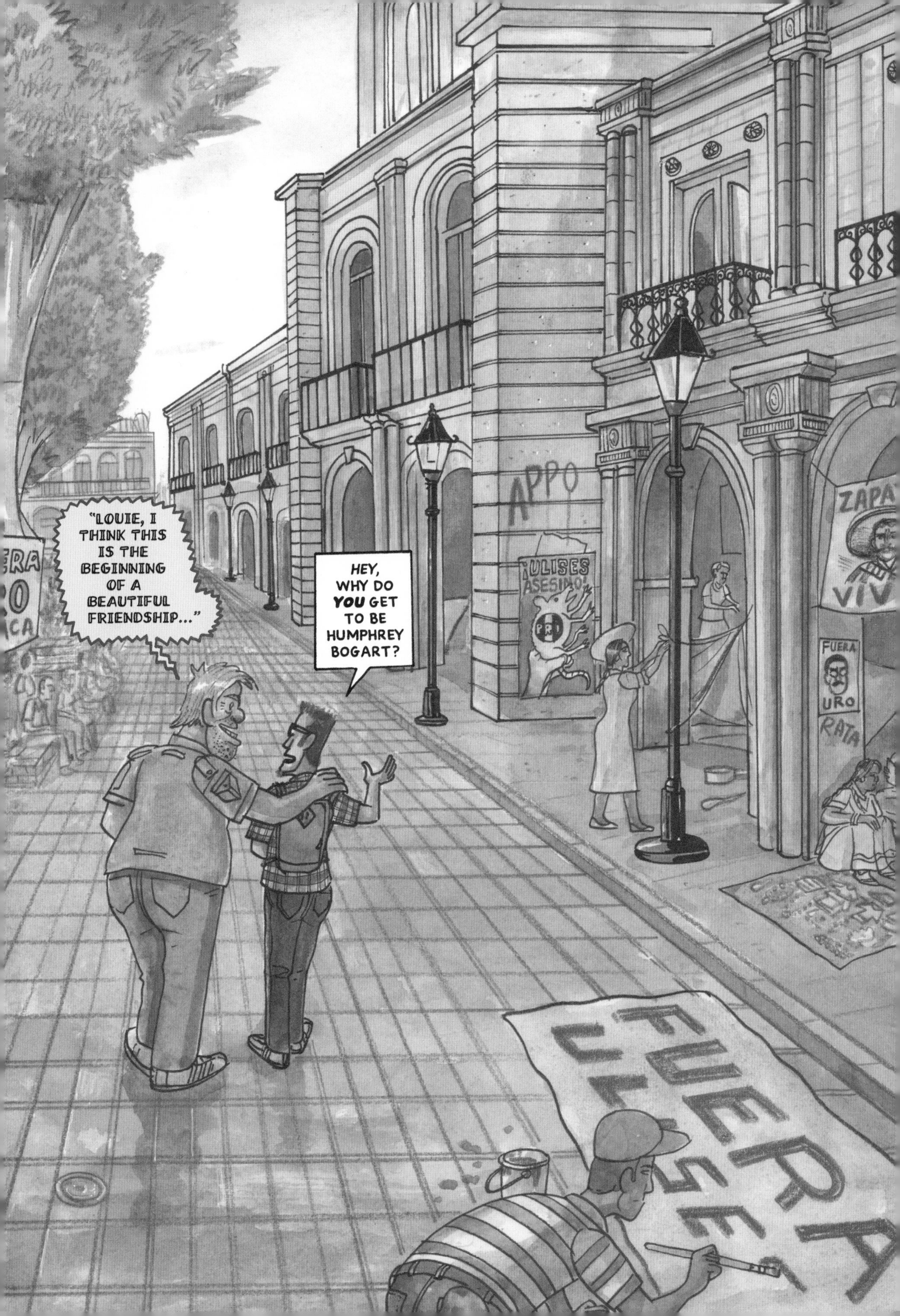
"LOUIE, I THINK THIS IS THE BEGINNING OF A BEAUTIFUL FRIENDSHIP..."
HEY, WHY DO **YOU** GET TO BE HUMPHREY BOGART?
APPO
¡ULISES ASESINO!
PRI
ZAPA
VIV
FUERA
URO
RATA
FUERA ULISES

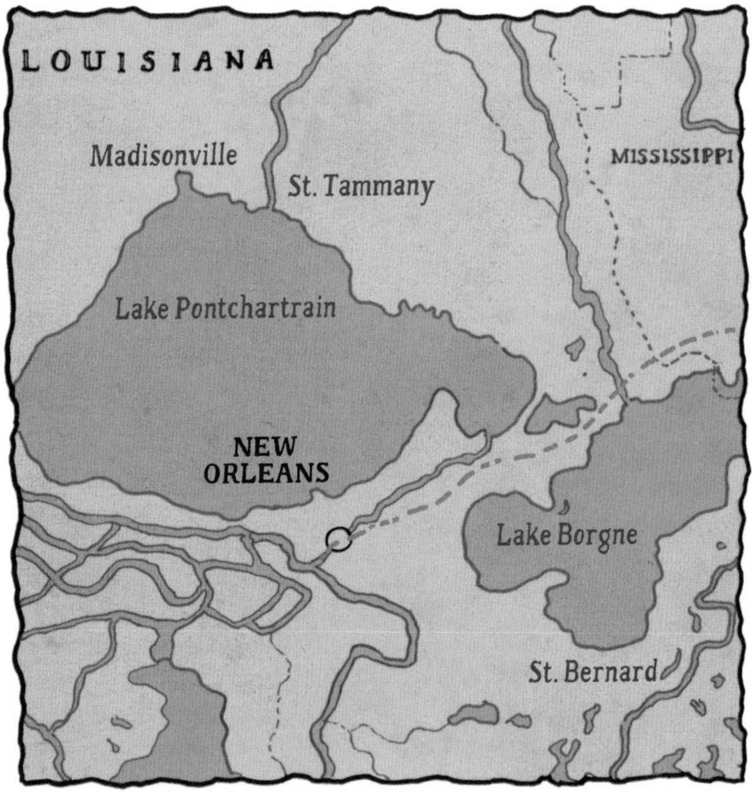
LOUISIANA
Madisonville
St. Tammany
MISSISSIPPI
Lake Pontchartrain
NEW
ORLEANS
Lake Borgne
St. Bernard

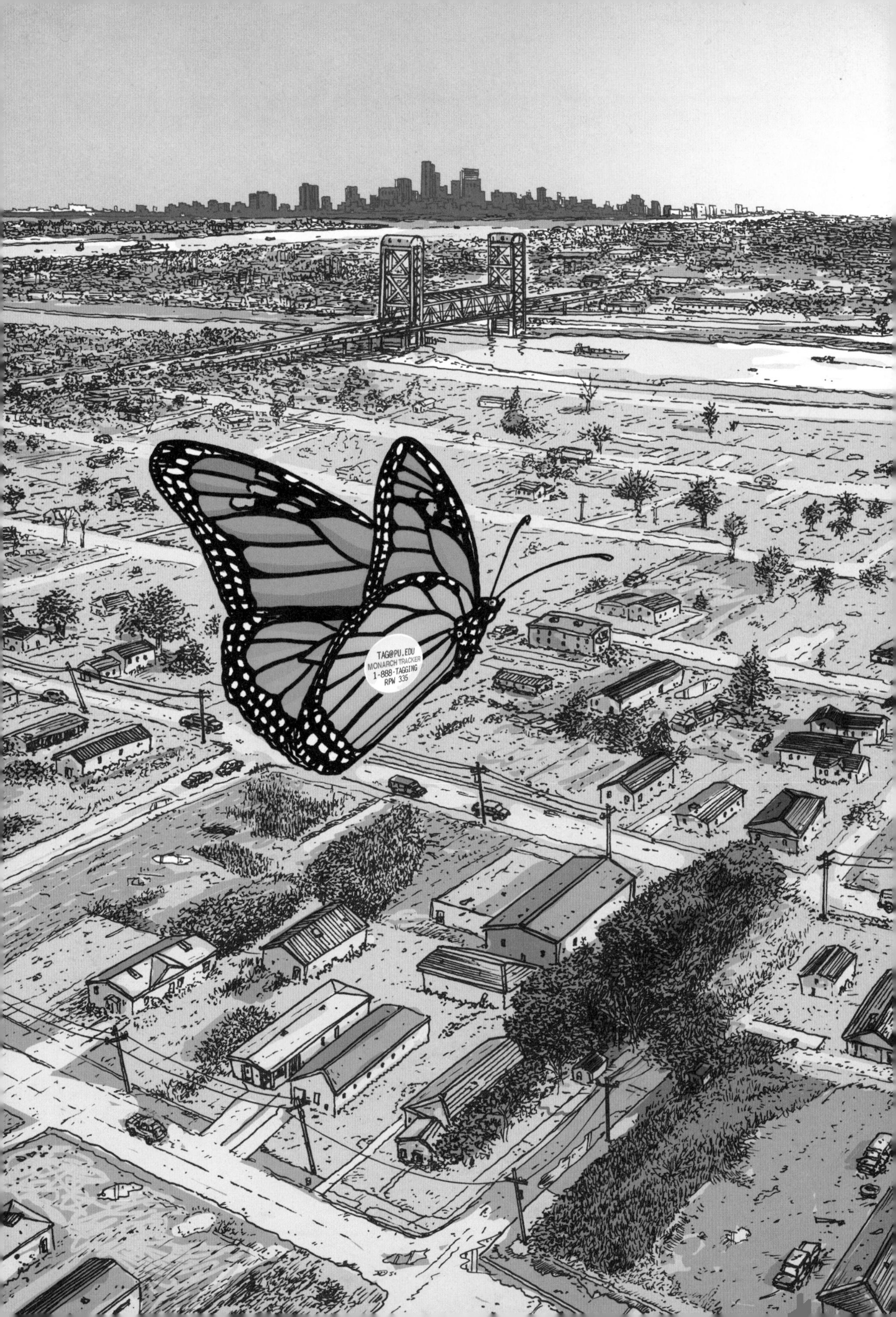
TAG@PU.EDU
MONARCH TRACKER
1-888-TAGGING
RPW 335

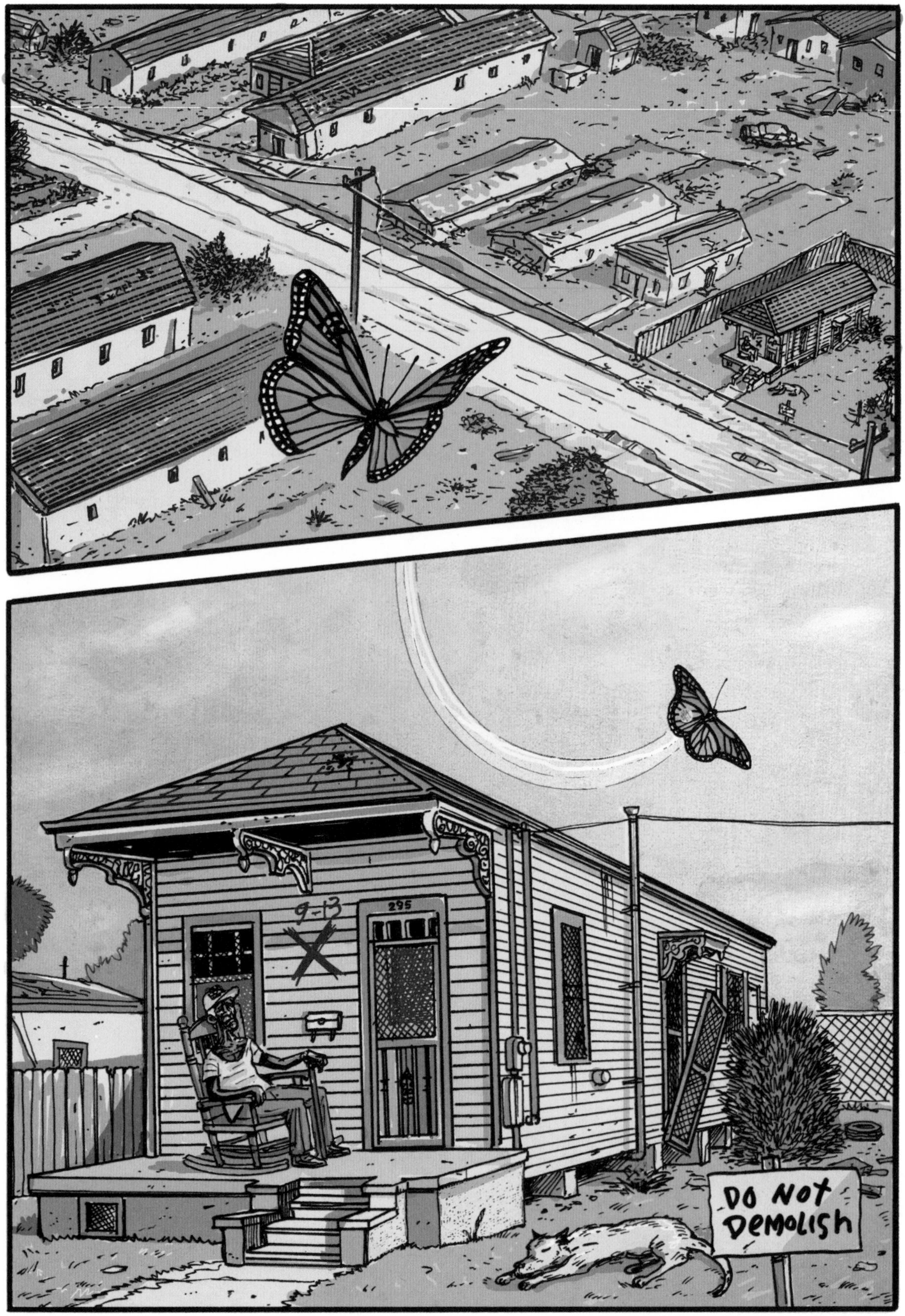
9-13
295
DO NOT
DEMOLISH

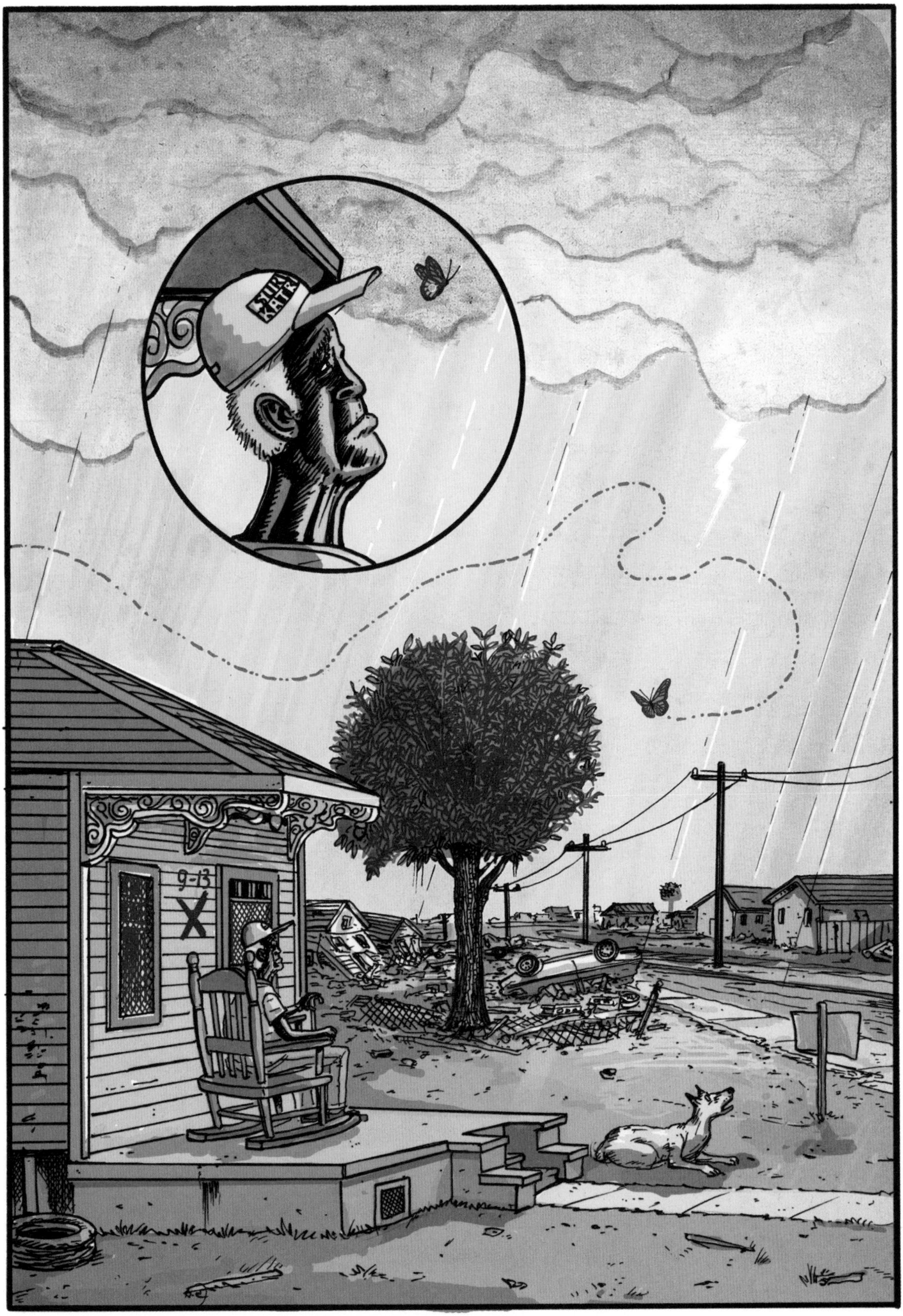
9-13
X

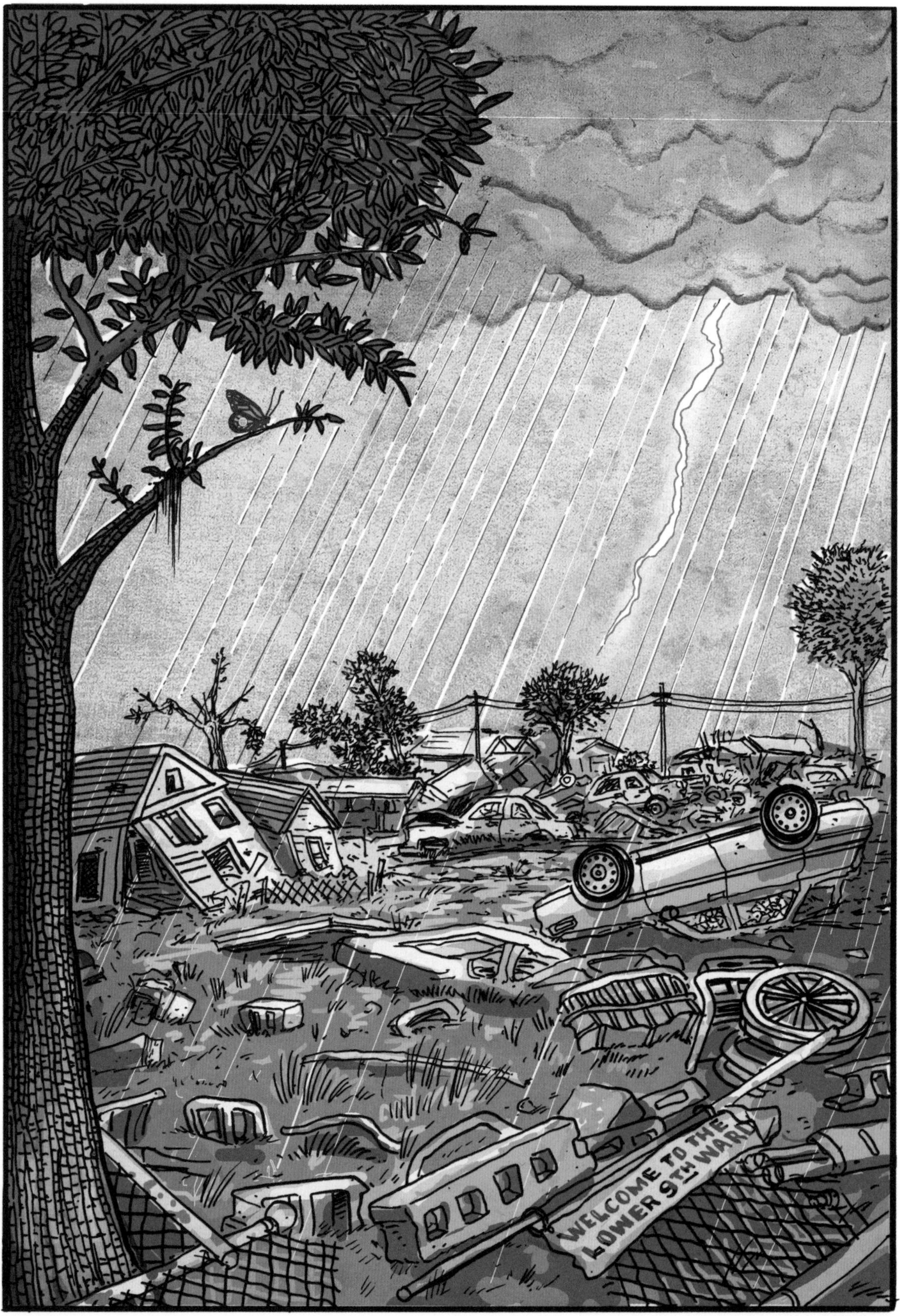
WELCOME TO THE
LOWER 9TH WARD

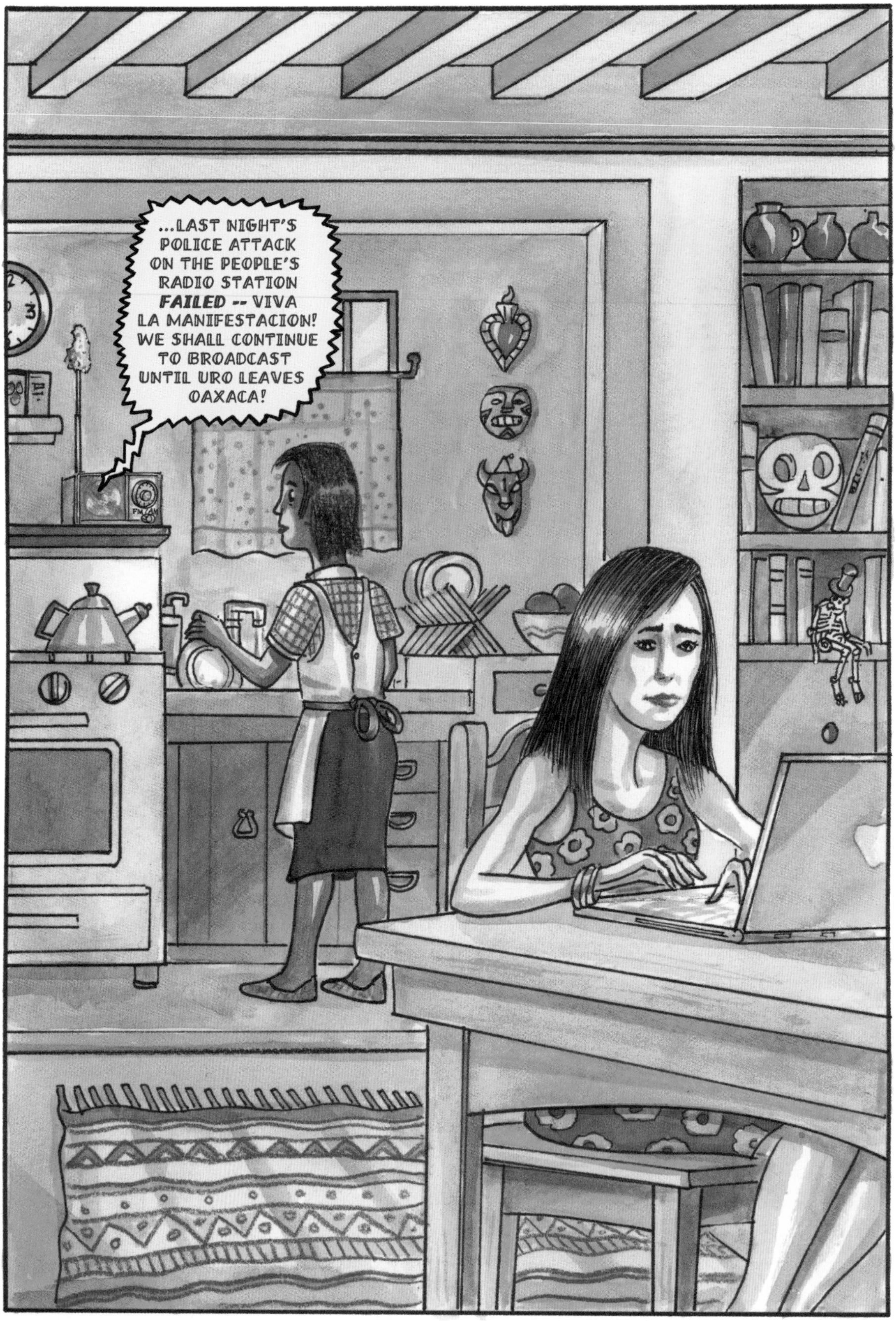
...LAST NIGHT'S POLICE ATTACK ON THE PEOPLE'S RADIO STATION ***FAILED*** -- VIVA LA MANIFESTACION! WE SHALL CONTINUE TO BROADCAST UNTIL URO LEAVES OAXACA!

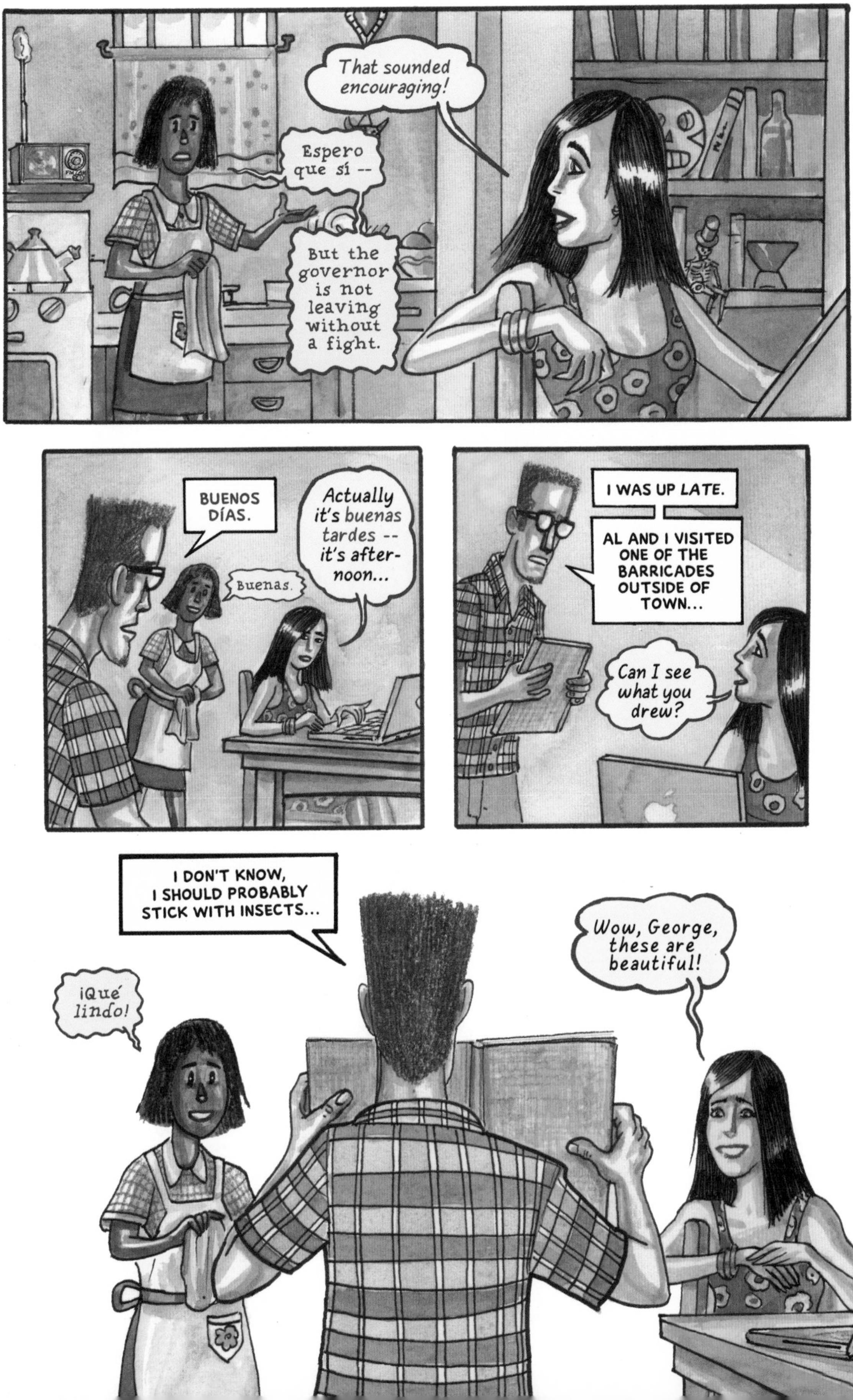
That sounded encouraging!
Espero que sí --
But the governor is not leaving without a fight.
BUENOS DÍAS.
Buenas.
Actually it's buenas tardes -- it's after-noon...
I WAS UP LATE.
AL AND I VISITED ONE OF THE BARRICADES OUTSIDE OF TOWN...
Can I see what you drew?
I DON'T KNOW, I SHOULD PROBABLY STICK WITH INSECTS...
¡Qué lindo!
Wow, George, these are beautiful!

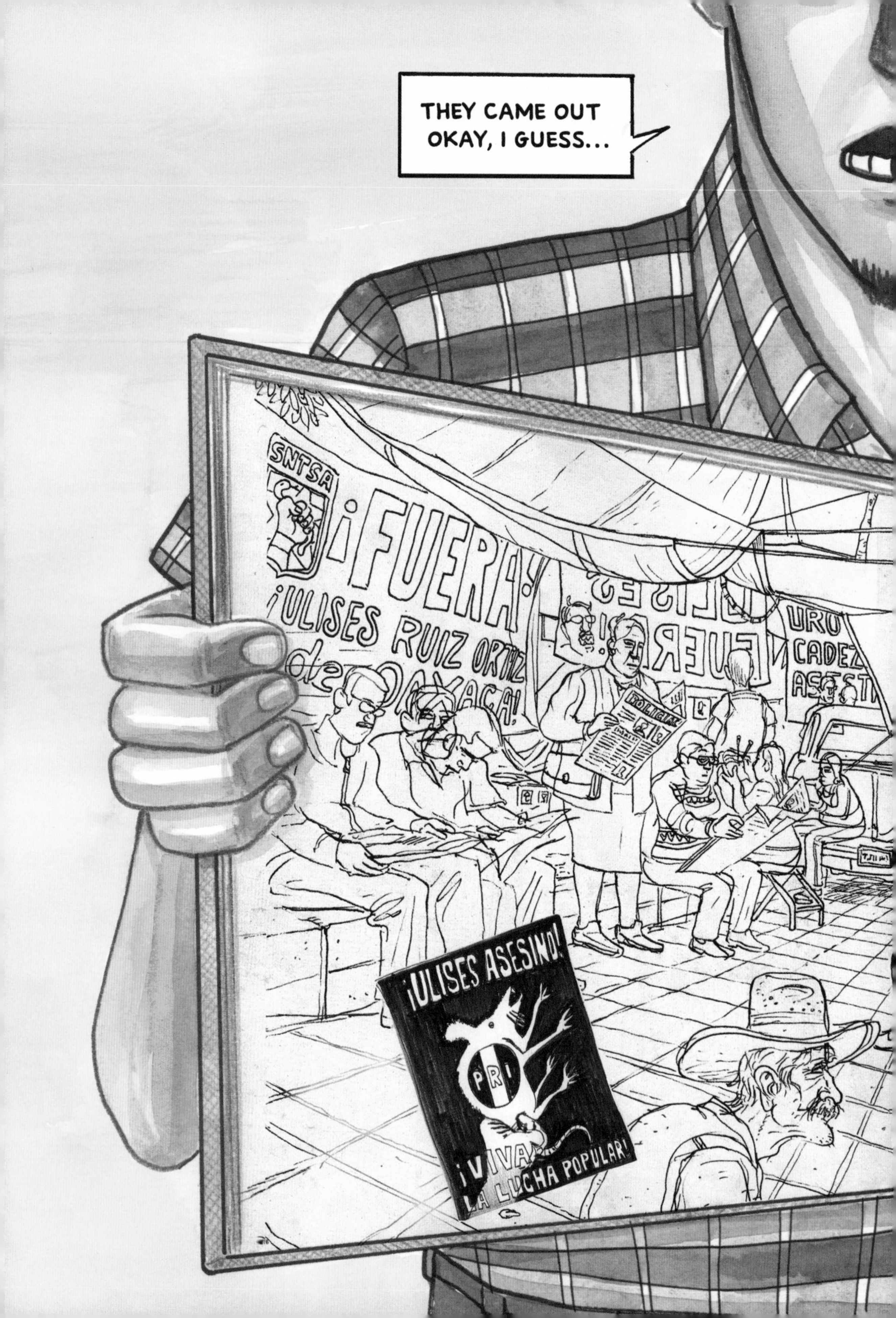
THEY CAME OUT OKAY, I GUESS...
SNTSA
¡FUERA!
¡ULISES RUIZ ORTIZ de OAXACA!
¡ULISES ASESINO!
PRI
¡VIVA LA LUCHA POPULAR!

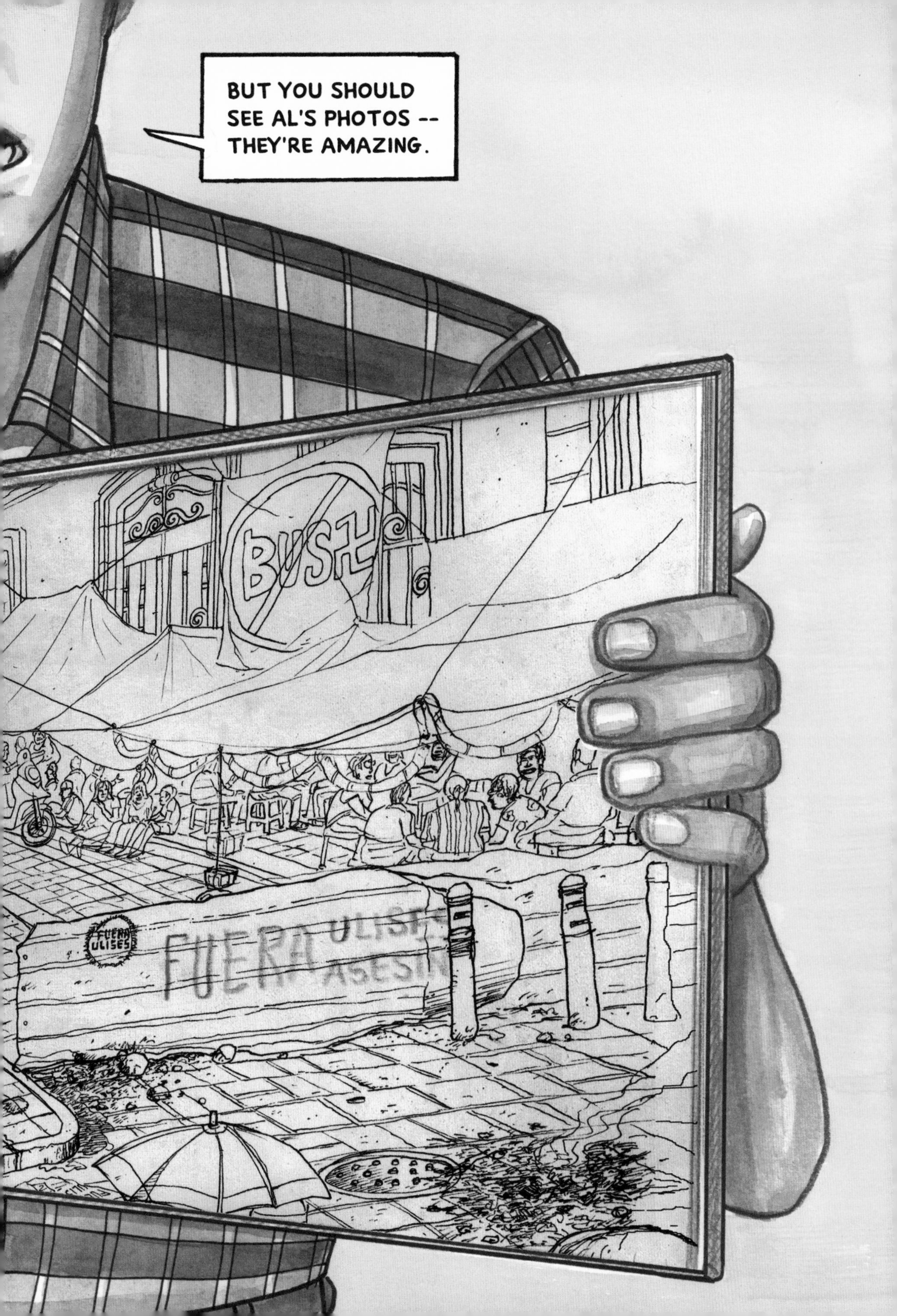
BUT YOU SHOULD SEE AL'S PHOTOS -- THEY'RE AMAZING.
BUSH
FUERA ULISES
FUERA

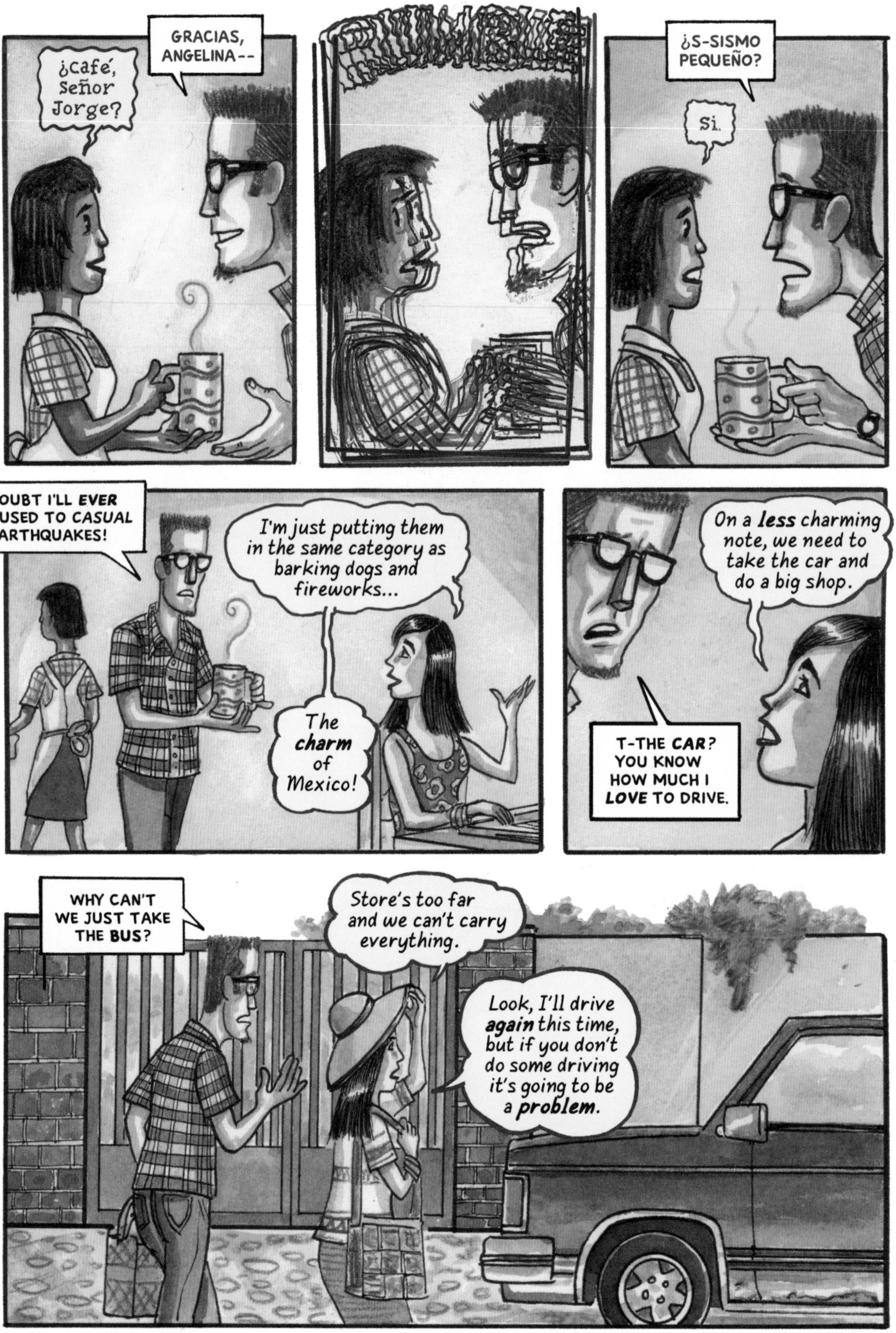
¿Café, Señor Jorge?
GRACIAS, ANGELINA--
¿S-SISMO PEQUEÑO?
Sí.
I DOUBT I'LL EVER GET USED TO CASUAL EARTHQUAKES!
I'm just putting them in the same category as barking dogs and fireworks...
The charm of Mexico!
On a less charming note, we need to take the car and do a big shop.
T-THE CAR? YOU KNOW HOW MUCH I LOVE TO DRIVE.
WHY CAN'T WE JUST TAKE THE BUS?
Store's too far and we can't carry everything.
Look, I'll drive again this time, but if you don't do some driving it's going to be a problem.

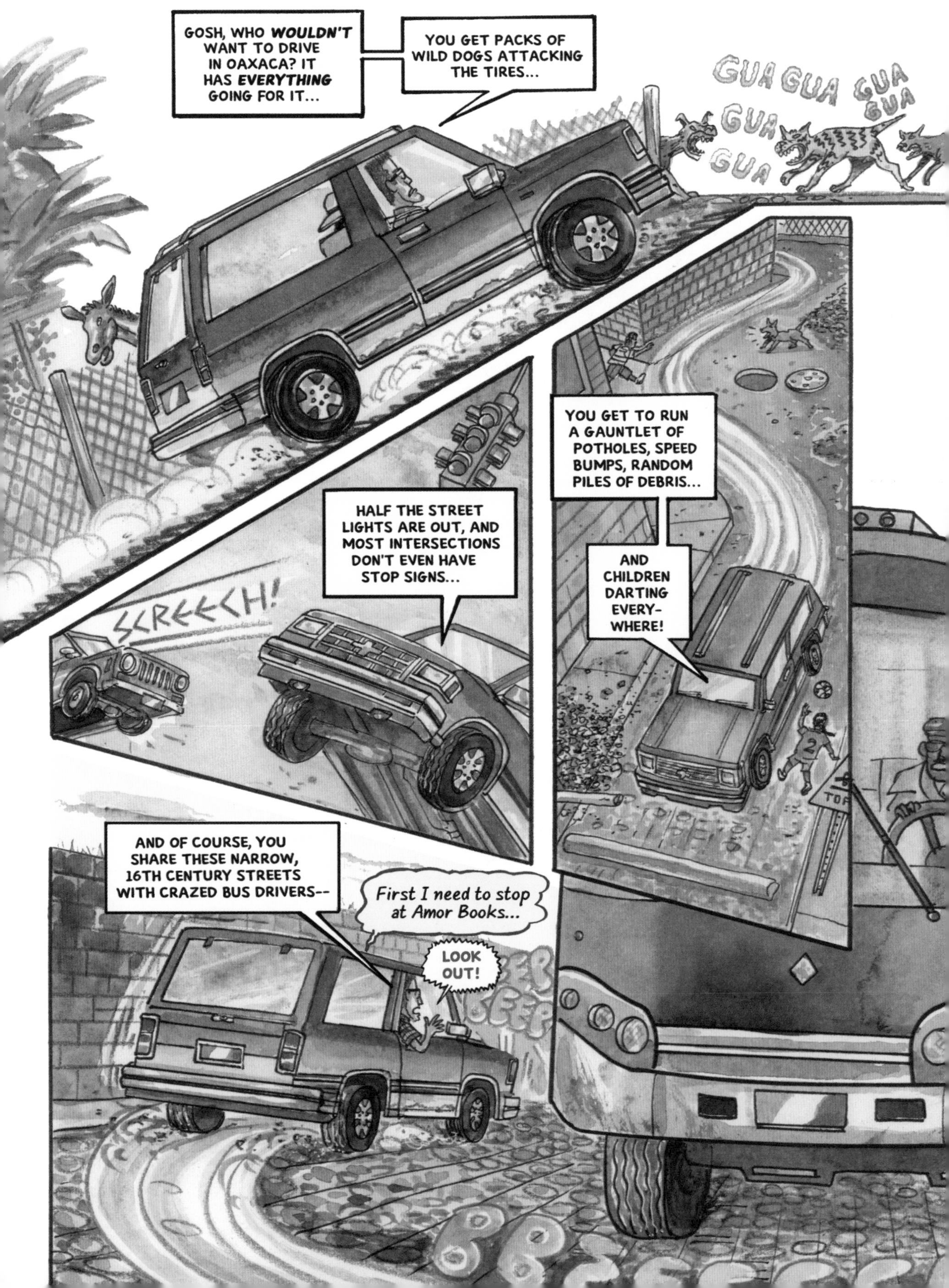

GOSH, WHO **WOULDN'T** WANT TO DRIVE IN OAXACA? IT HAS **EVERYTHING** GOING FOR IT...
YOU GET PACKS OF WILD DOGS ATTACKING THE TIRES...
GUA GUA GUA GUA GUA GUA
YOU GET TO RUN A GAUNTLET OF POTHOLES, SPEED BUMPS, RANDOM PILES OF DEBRIS...
AND CHILDREN DARTING EVERY-WHERE!
HALF THE STREET LIGHTS ARE OUT, AND MOST INTERSECTIONS DON'T EVEN HAVE STOP SIGNS...
SCREECH!
AND OF COURSE, YOU SHARE THESE NARROW, 16TH CENTURY STREETS WITH CRAZED BUS DRIVERS--
First I need to stop at Amor Books...
LOOK OUT!

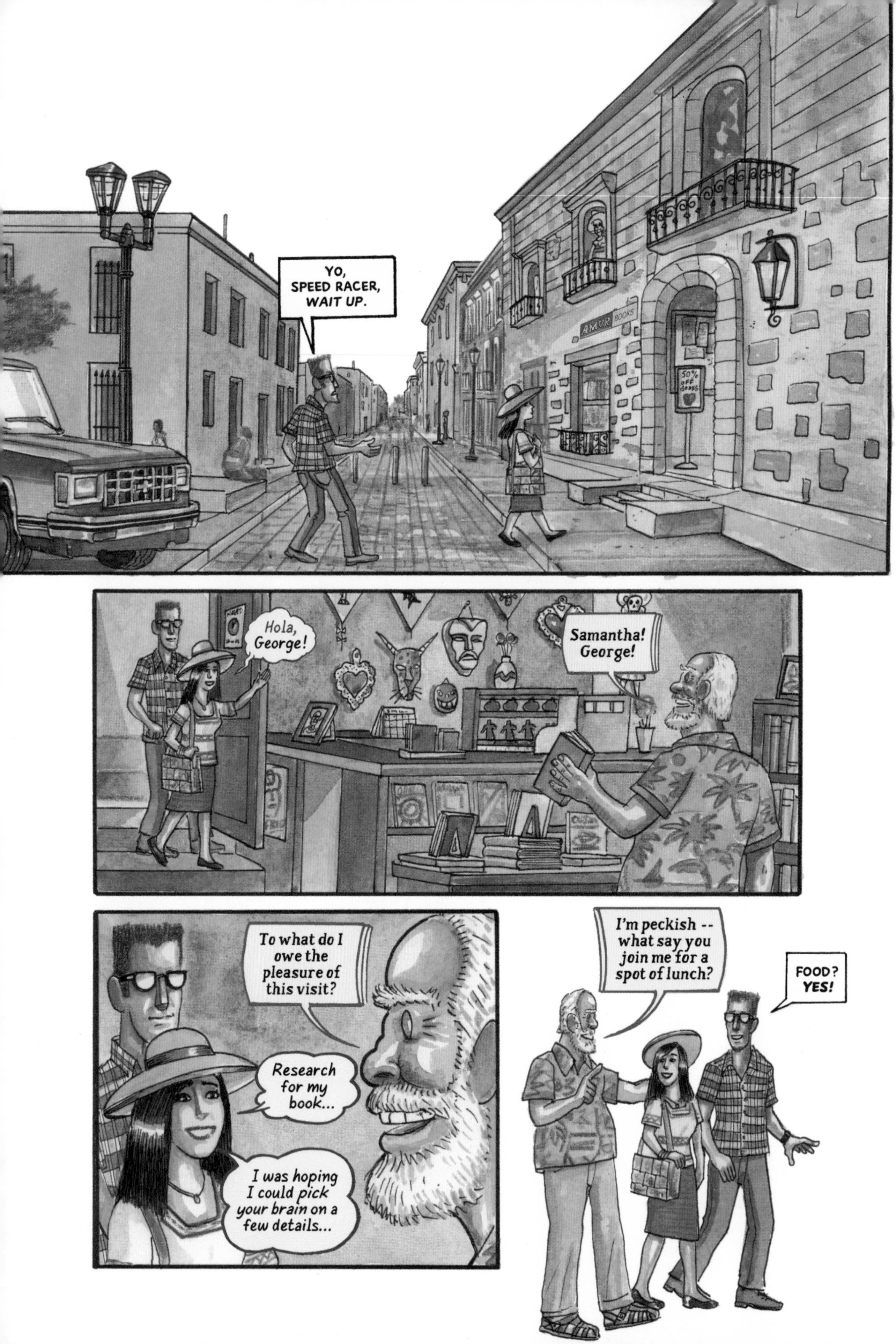
YO, SPEED RACER, WAIT UP.
AMOR BOOKS
50% OFF BOOKS
Hola, George!
Samantha! George!
To what do I owe the pleasure of this visit?
Research for my book...
I was hoping I could *pick* your brain on a few details...
I'm peckish -- what say you join me for a spot of lunch?
FOOD? **YES!**

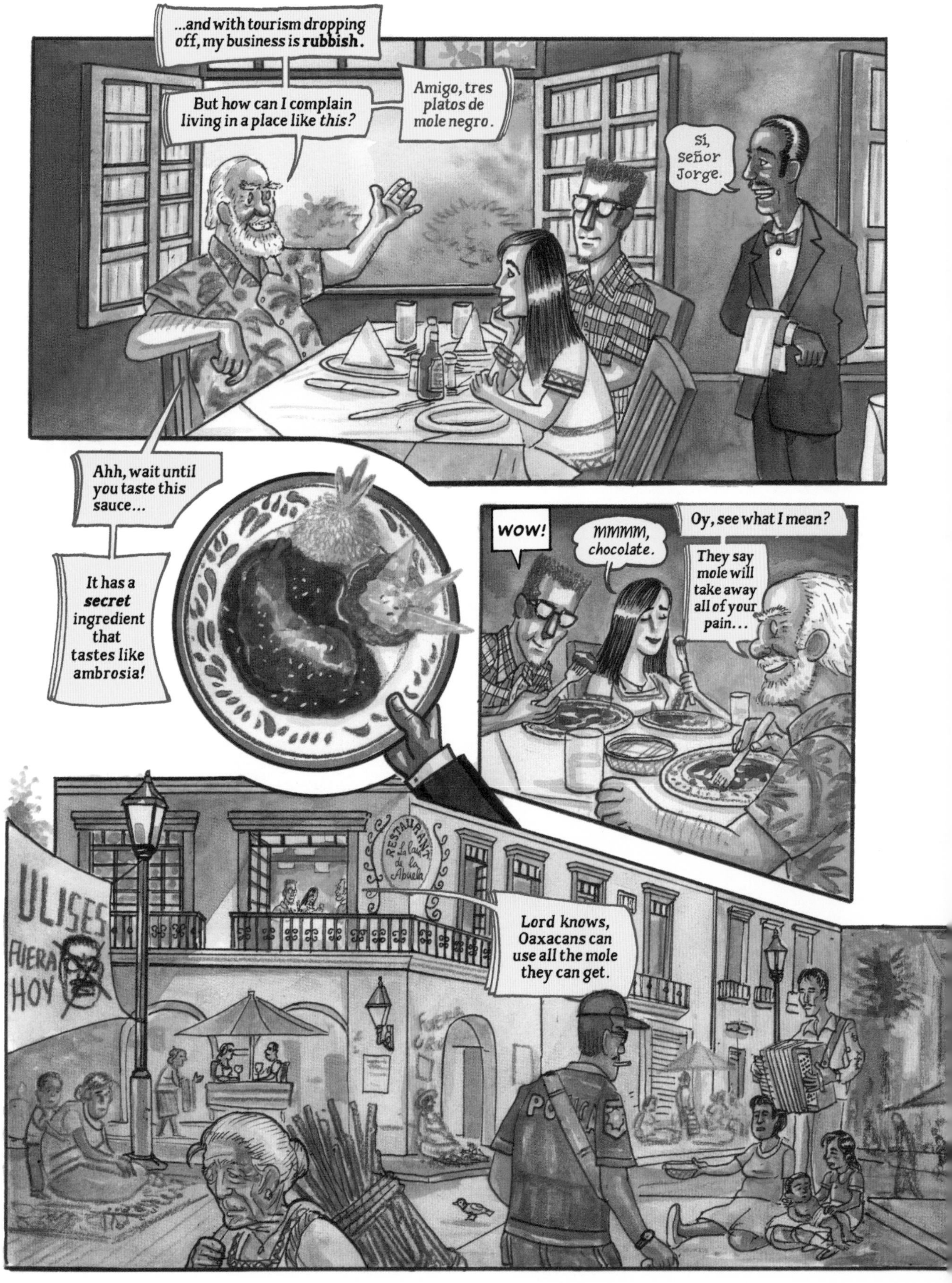
...and with tourism dropping off, my business is **rubbish**.
But how can I complain living in a place like *this?*
Amigo, tres platos de mole negro.
Sí, señor Jorge.
Ahh, wait until you taste this sauce...
It has a ***secret*** ingredient that tastes like ambrosia!
WOW!
mmmm, chocolate.
Oy, see what I mean?
They say mole will take away all of your pain...
RESTAURANT La Casa de la Abuela
ULISES FUERA HOY
Lord knows, Oaxacans can use all the mole they can get.

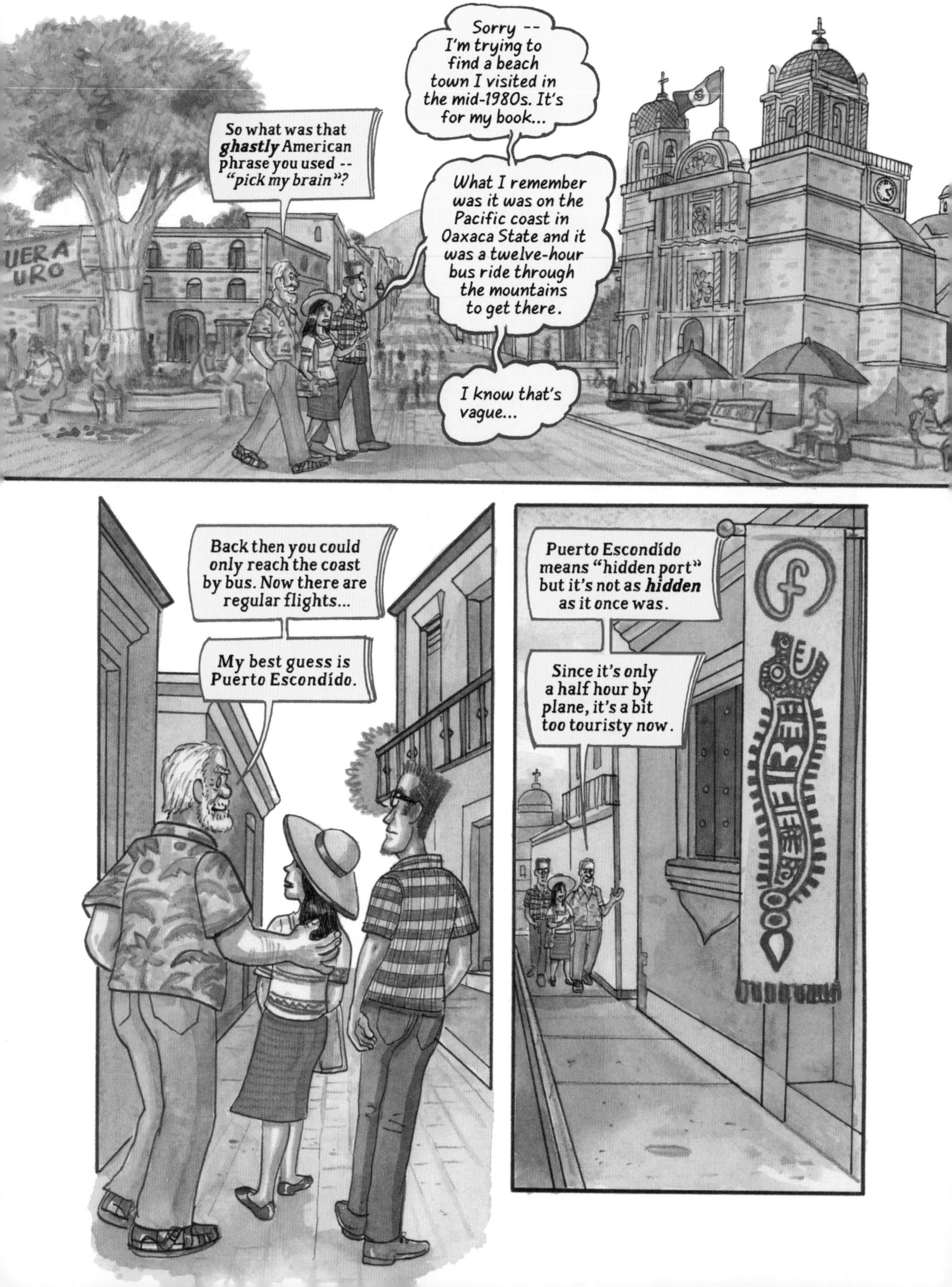

So what was that ***ghastly*** American phrase you used -- "pick my brain"?
Sorry -- I'm trying to find a beach town I visited in the mid-1980s. It's for my book...
What I remember was it was on the Pacific coast in Oaxaca State and it was a twelve-hour bus ride through the mountains to get there.
I know that's vague...
Back then you could only reach the coast by bus. Now there are regular flights...
My best guess is Puerto Escondído.
Puerto Escondído means "hidden port" but it's not as ***hidden*** as it once was.
Since it's only a half hour by plane, it's a bit too touristy now.

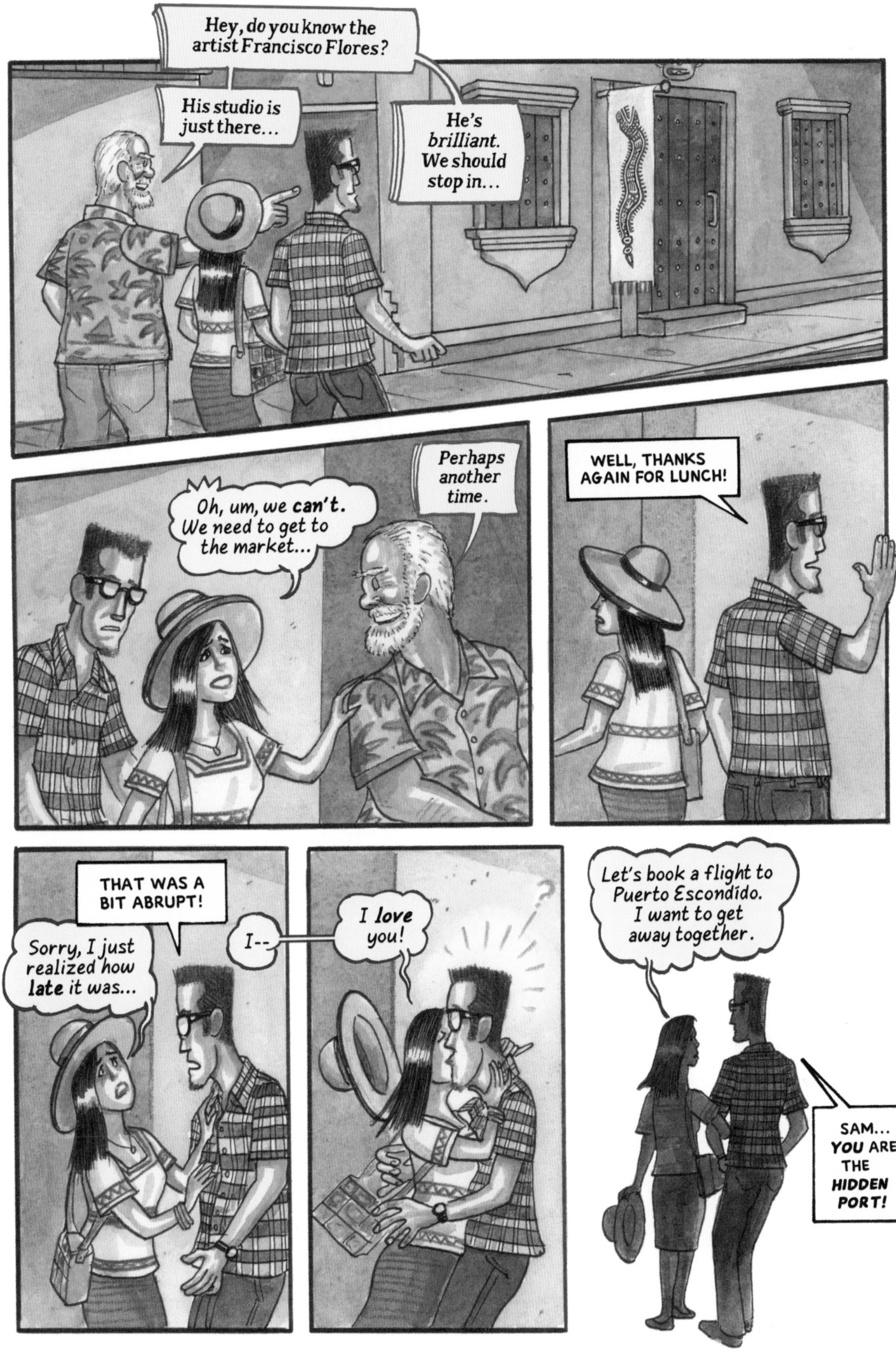
Hey, do you know the artist Francisco Flores?
His studio is just there...
He's brilliant. We should stop in...
Oh, um, we can't. We need to get to the market...
Perhaps another time.
WELL, THANKS AGAIN FOR LUNCH!
THAT WAS A BIT ABRUPT!
Sorry, I just realized how late it was...
I--
I love you!
Let's book a flight to Puerto Escondido. I want to get away together.
SAM... YOU ARE THE HIDDEN PORT!

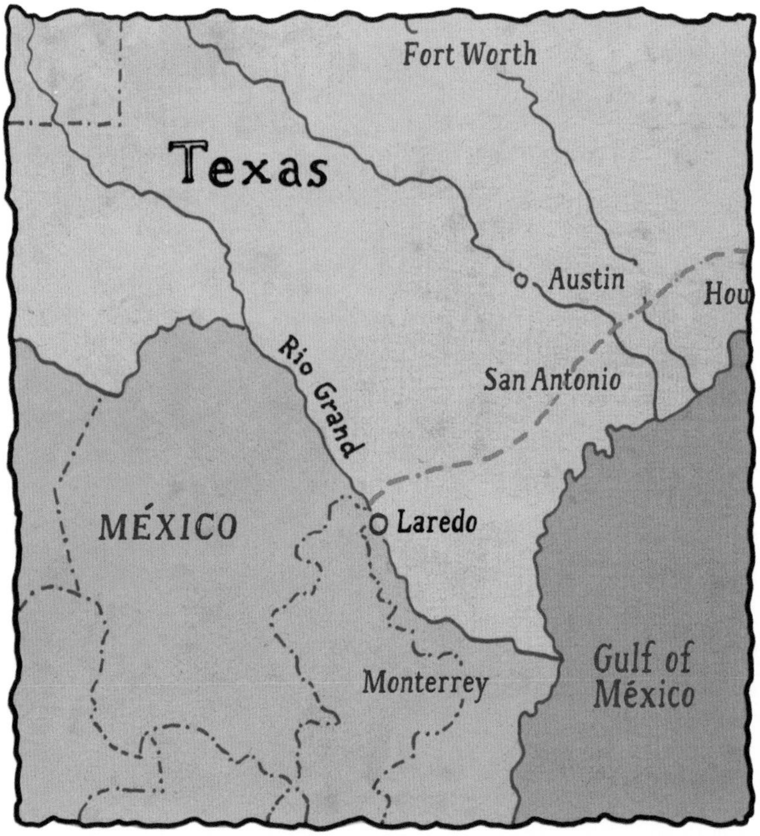
Fort Worth
Texas
Austin
Hou
San Antonio
Rio Grand
Laredo
MÉXICO
Monterrey
Gulf of México

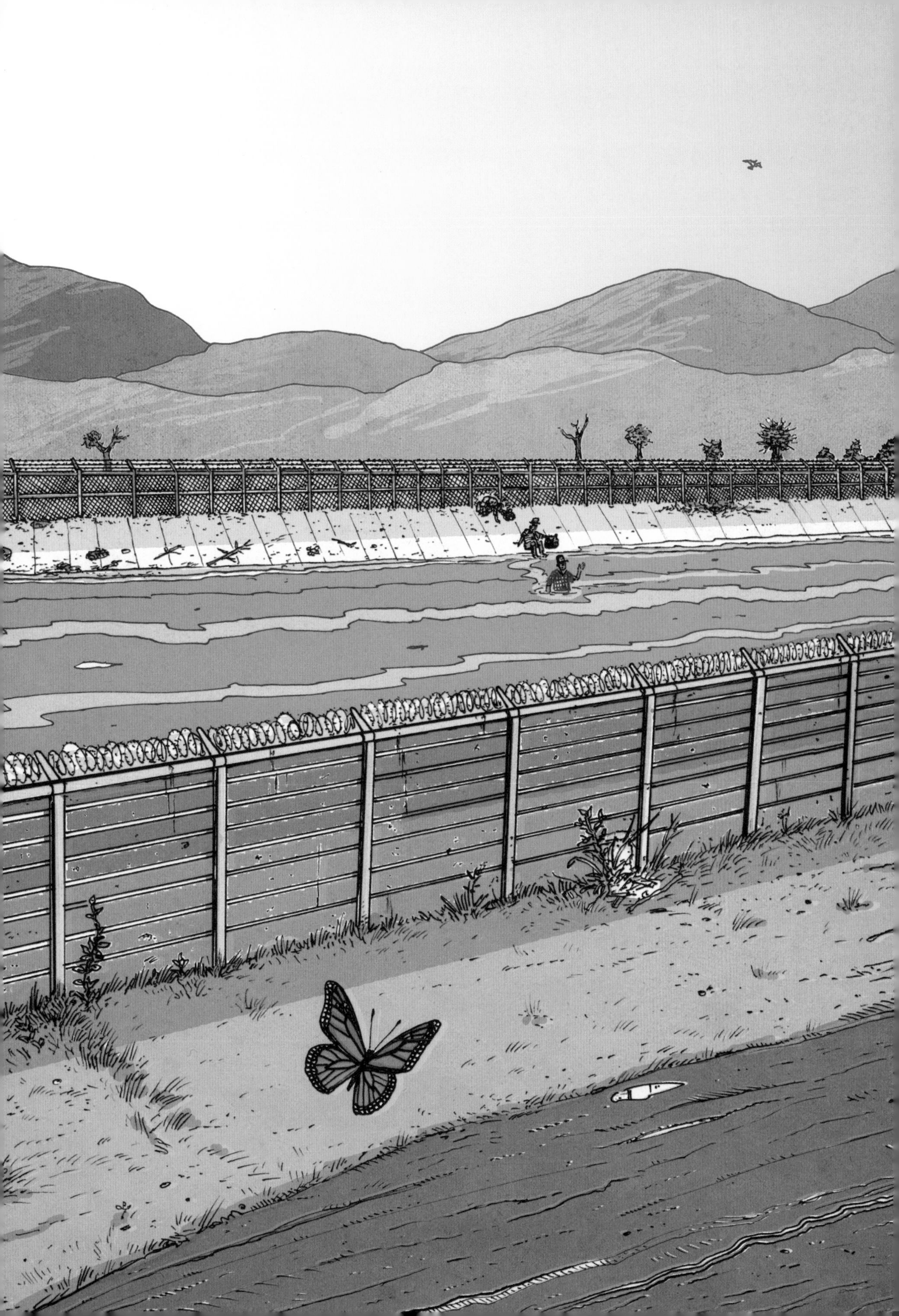

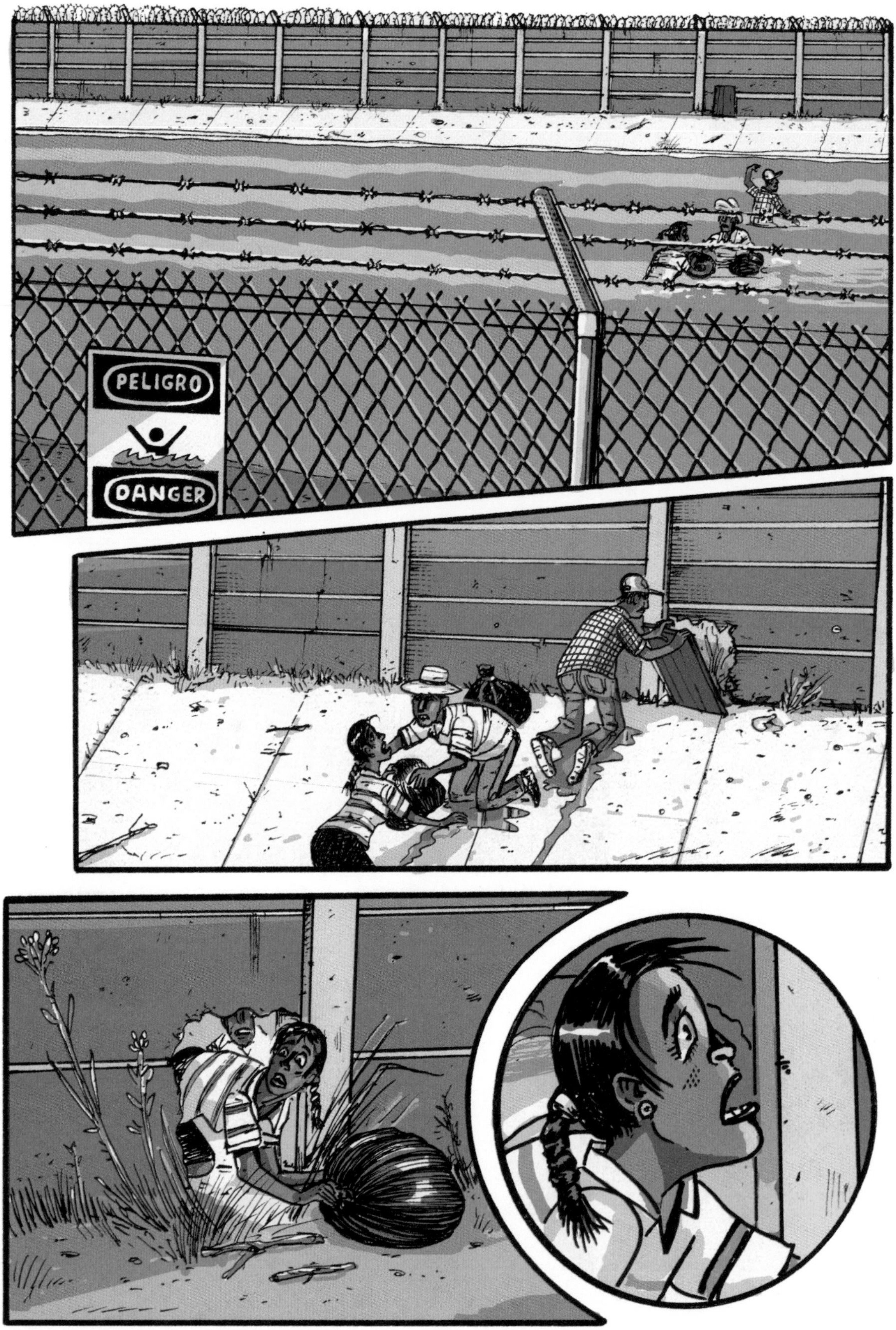

PELIGRO
DANGER

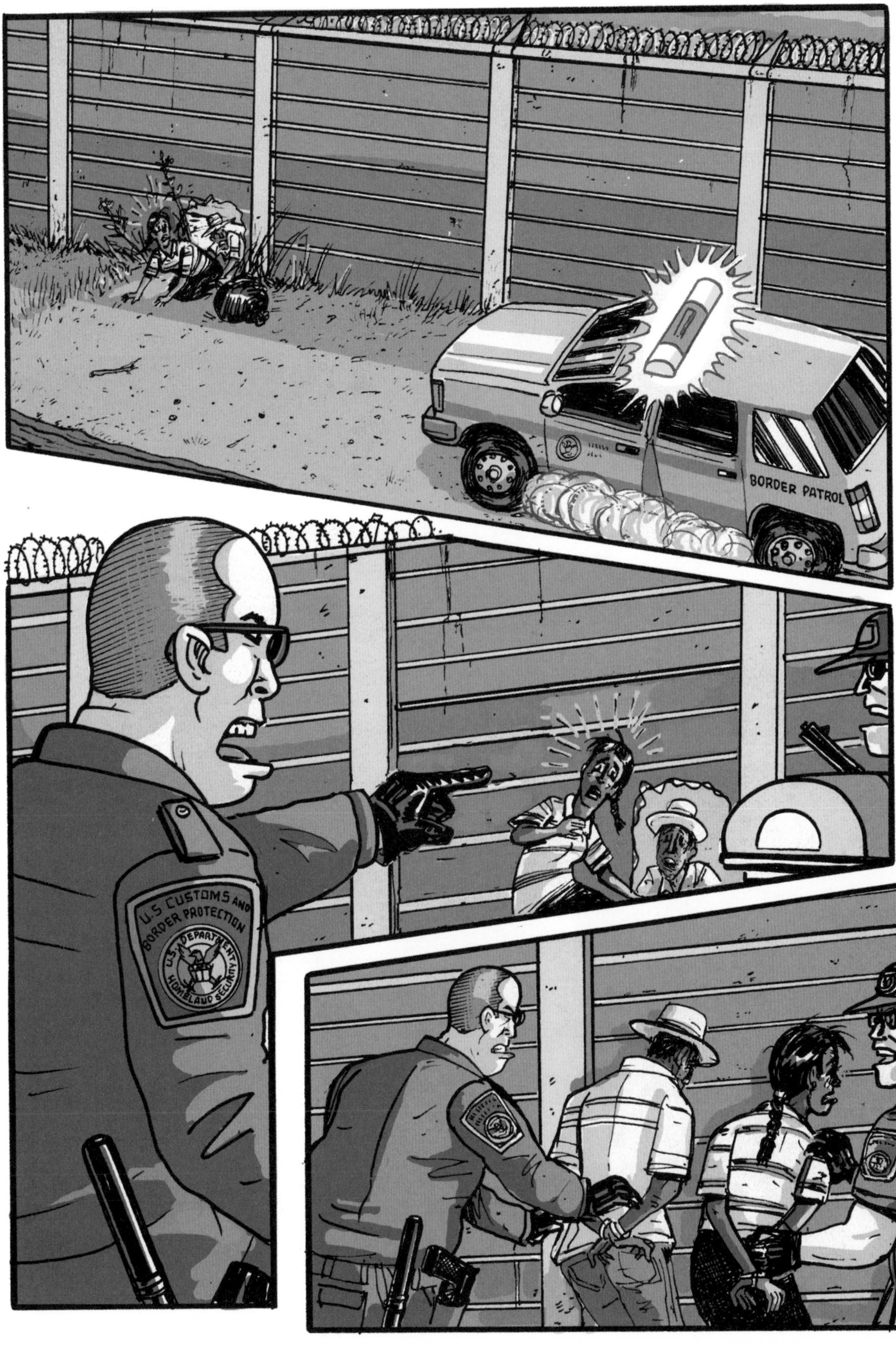
BORDER PATROL
U.S CUSTOMS AND BORDER PROTECTION
U.S. DEPARTMENT HOMELAND SECURITY

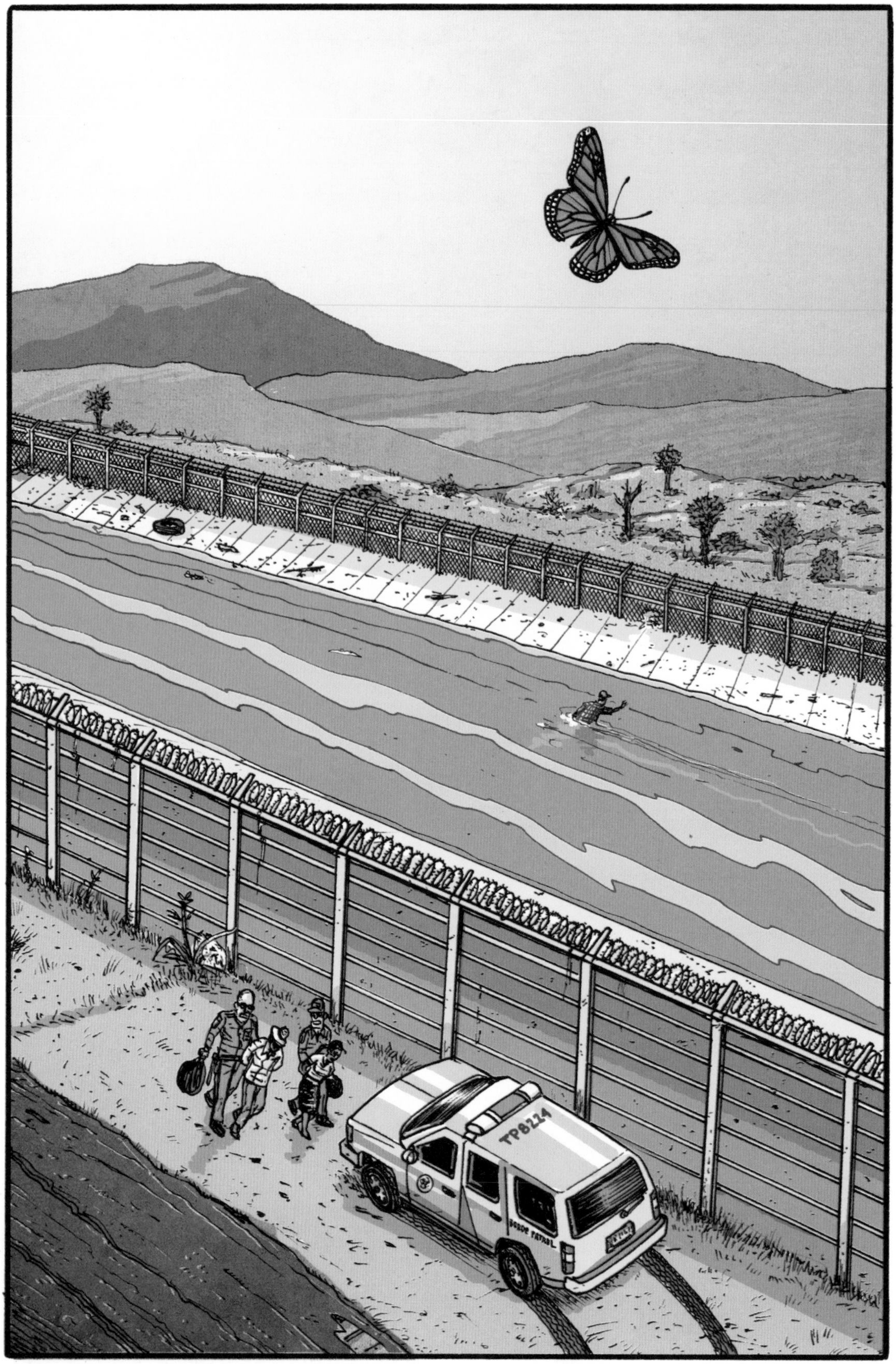

TP8224

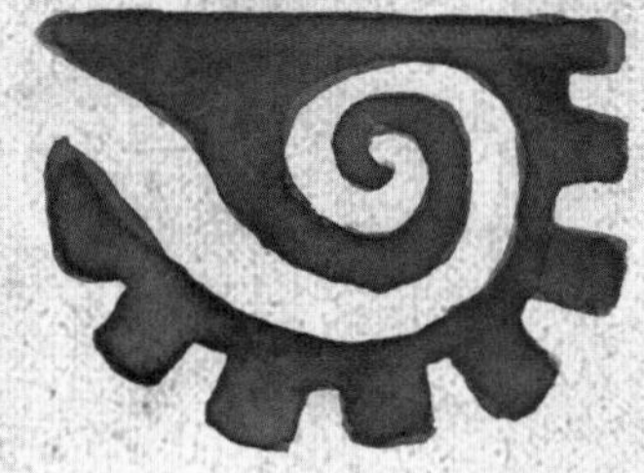

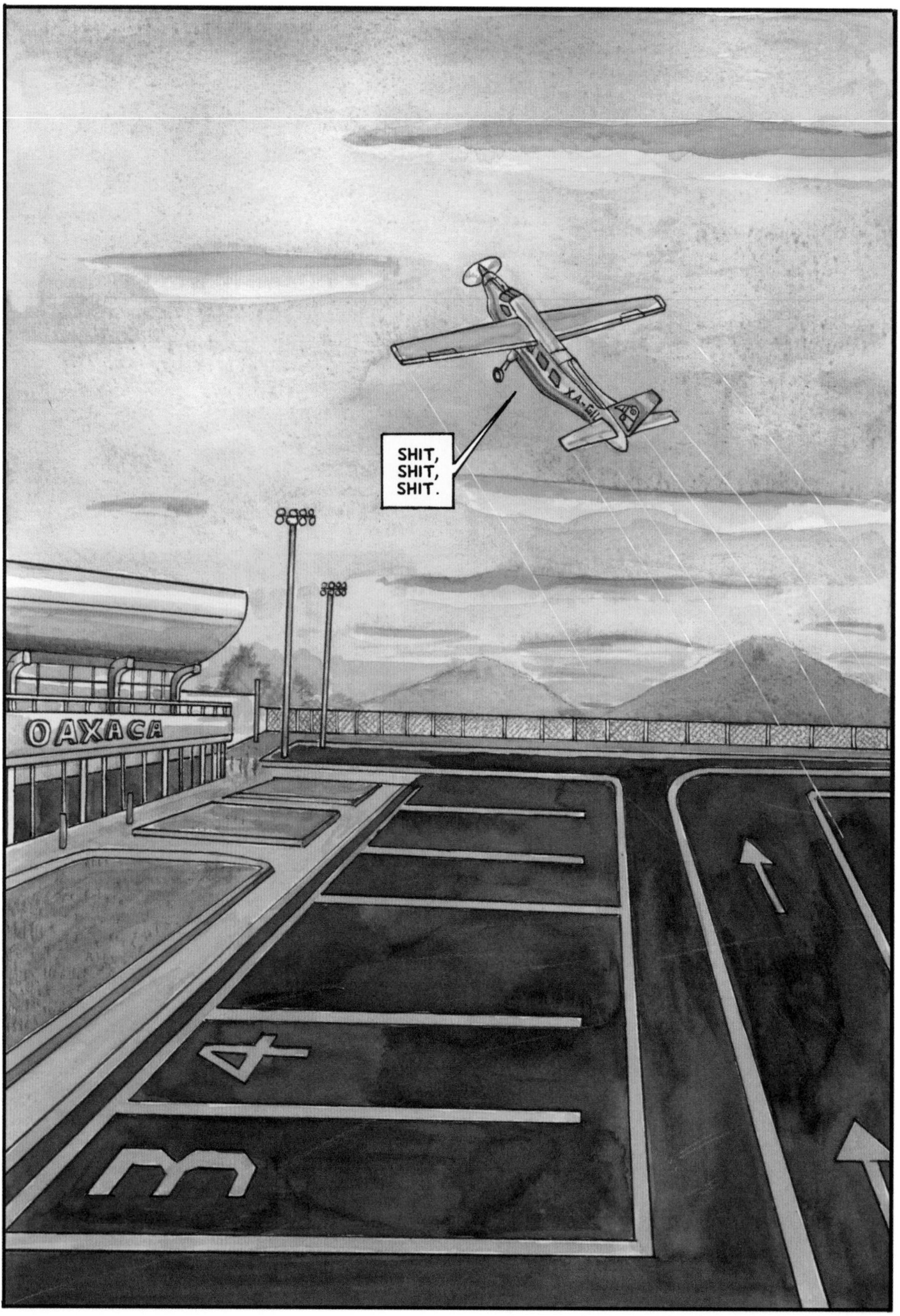
SHIT,
SHIT,
SHIT.
OAXACA
XA-EIL

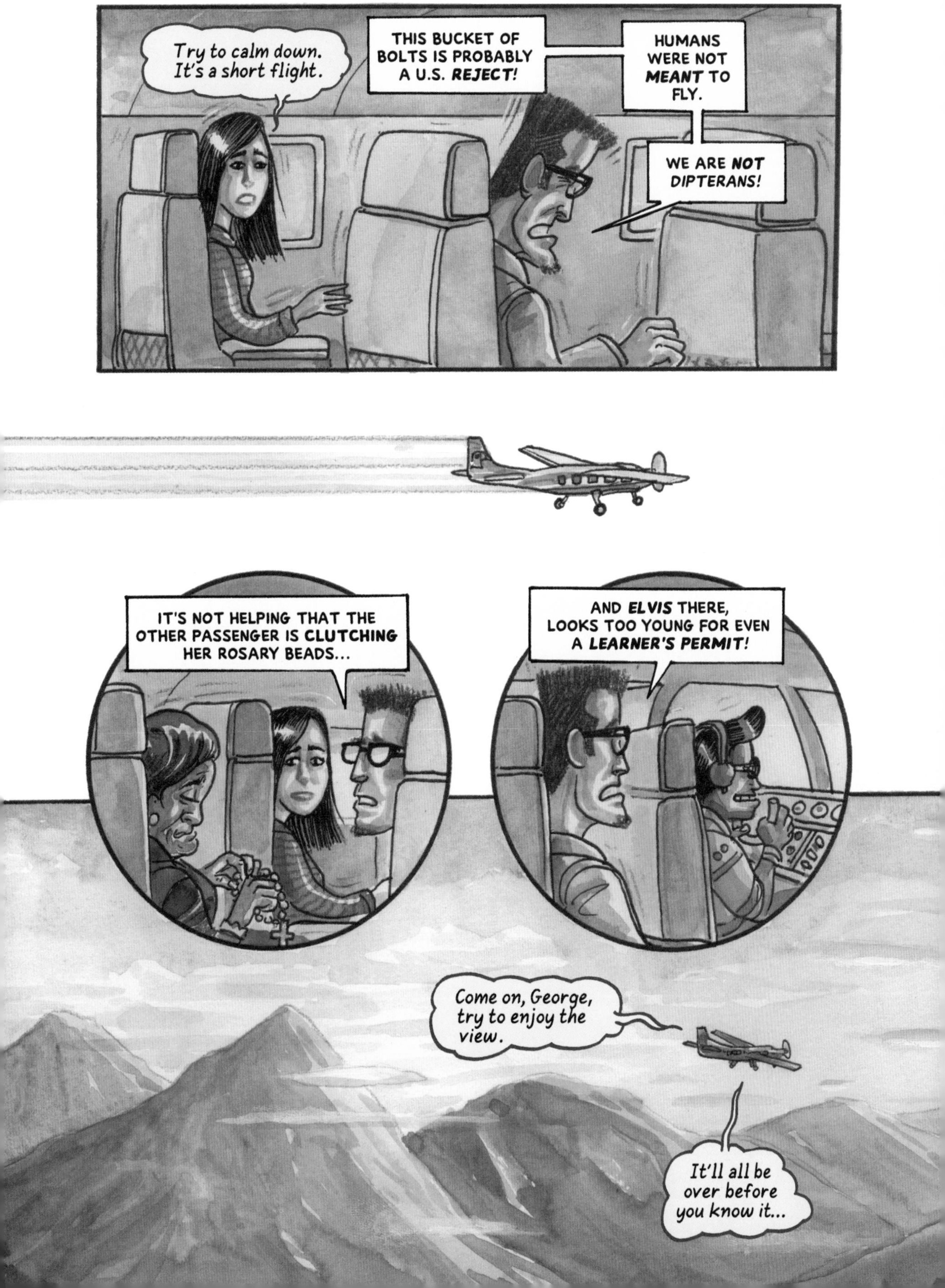
Try to calm down. It's a short flight.
THIS BUCKET OF BOLTS IS PROBABLY A U.S. REJECT!
HUMANS WERE NOT MEANT TO FLY.
WE ARE NOT DIPTERANS!
IT'S NOT HELPING THAT THE OTHER PASSENGER IS CLUTCHING HER ROSARY BEADS...
AND ELVIS THERE, LOOKS TOO YOUNG FOR EVEN A LEARNER'S PERMIT!
Come on, George, try to enjoy the view.
It'll all be over before you know it...

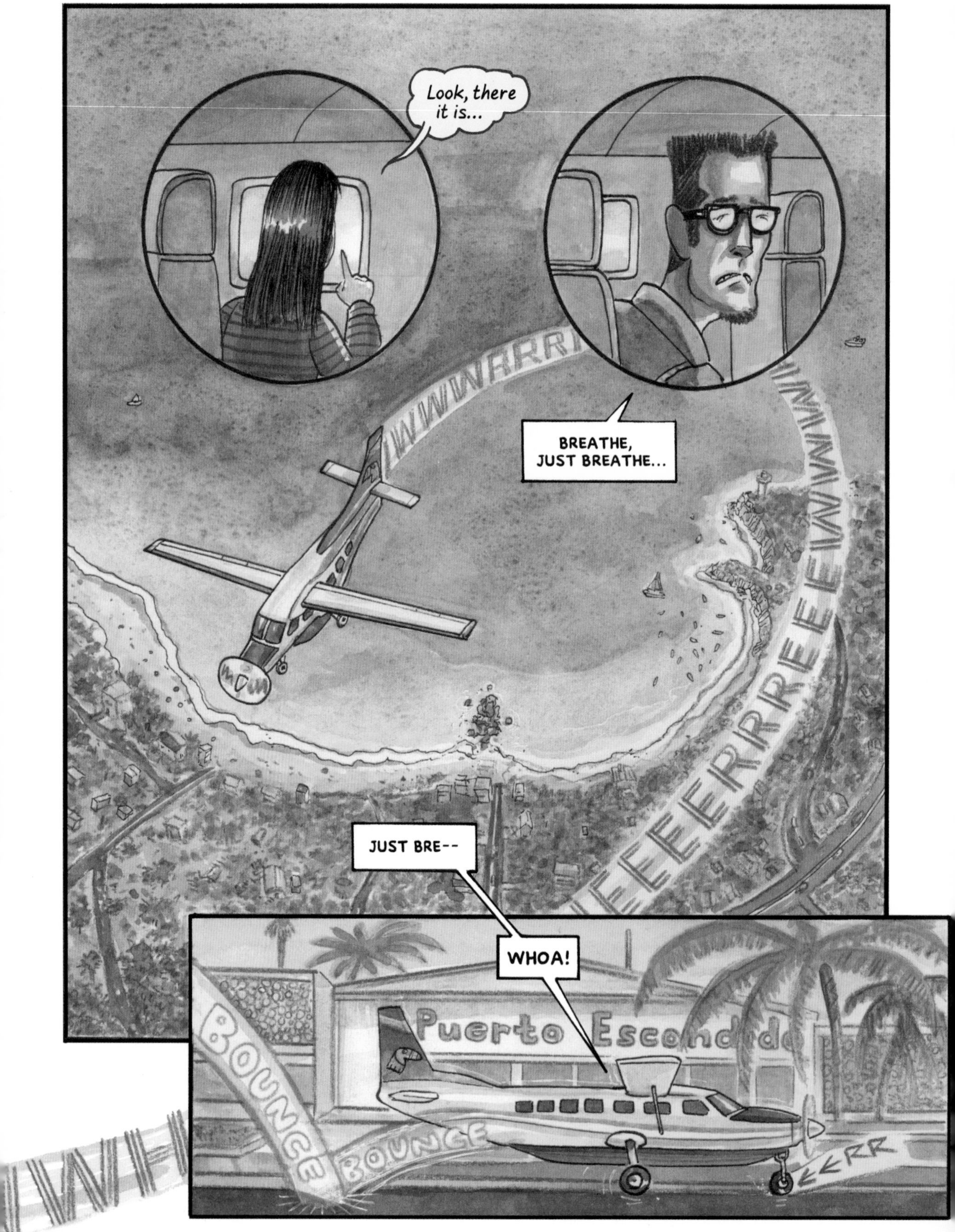

Look, there it is...
BREATHE, JUST BREATHE...
JUST BRE--
WHOA!
BOUNCE
BOUNCE

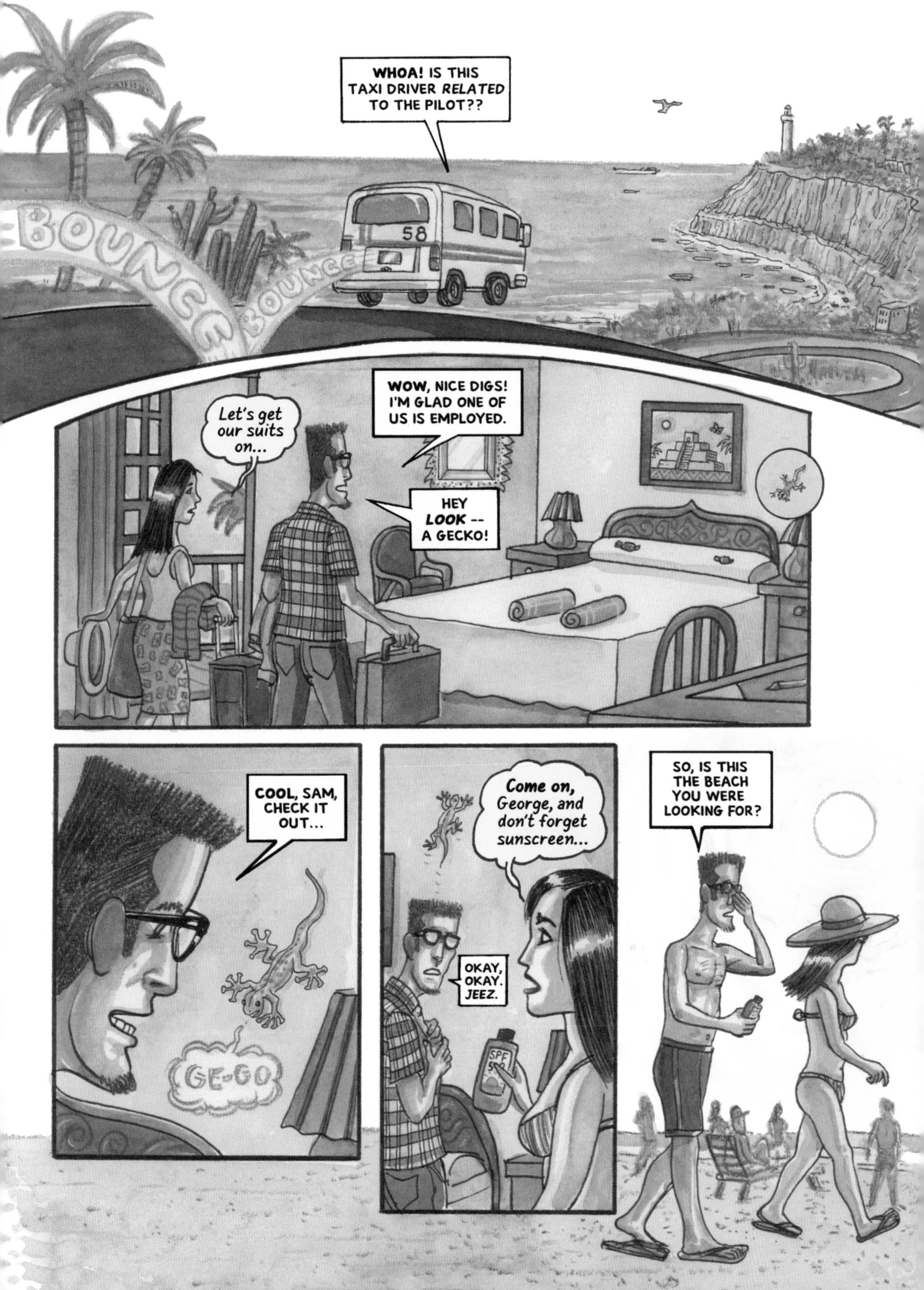
WHOA! IS THIS TAXI DRIVER RELATED TO THE PILOT??
BOUNCE
BOUNCE
BOUNCE
58
Let's get our suits on...
WOW, NICE DIGS! I'M GLAD ONE OF US IS EMPLOYED.
HEY LOOK -- A GECKO!
COOL, SAM, CHECK IT OUT...
GE-GO
Come on, George, and don't forget sunscreen...
OKAY, OKAY. JEEZ.
SPF
SO, IS THIS THE BEACH YOU WERE LOOKING FOR?

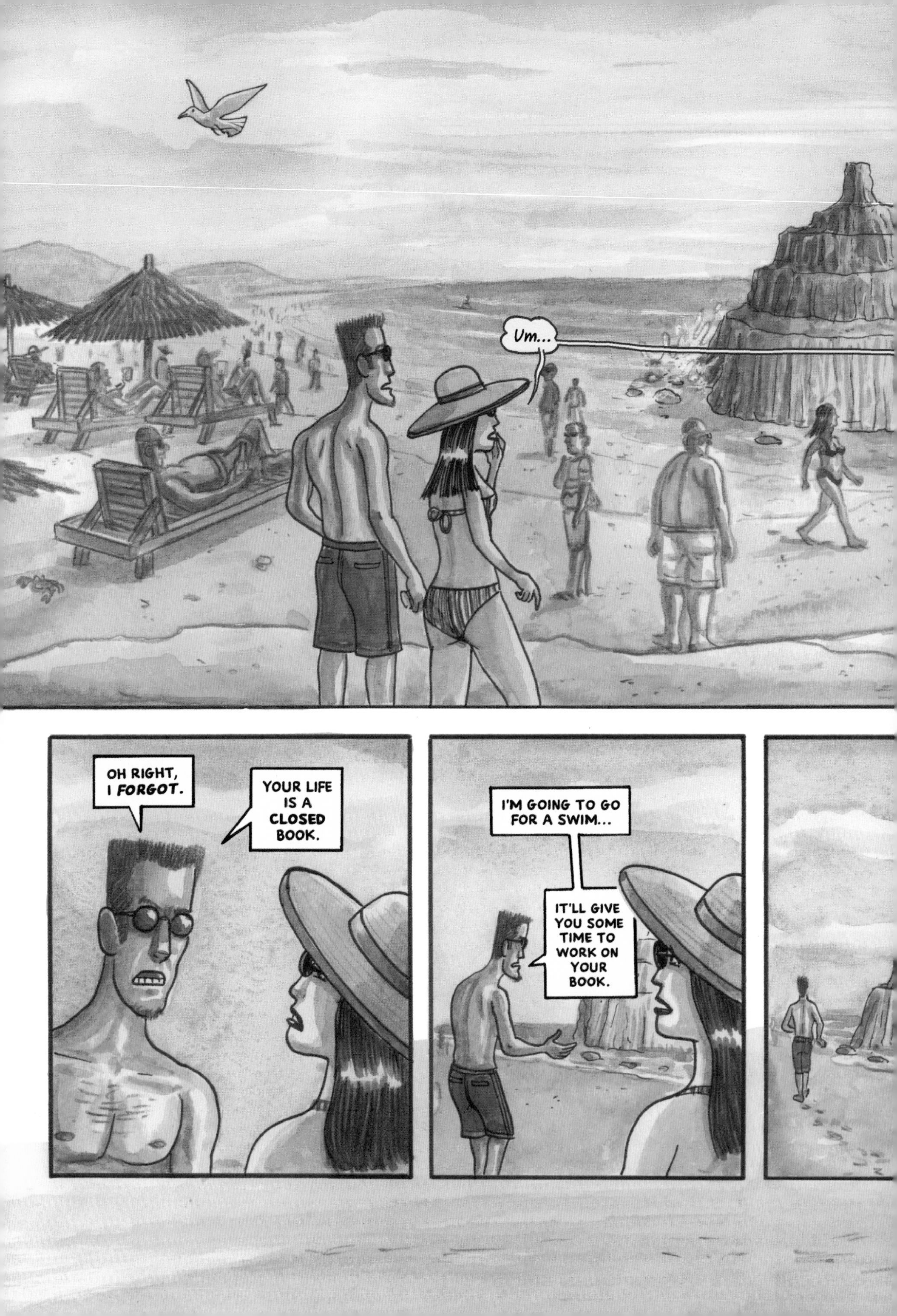

Um...
OH RIGHT, I *FORGOT*.
YOUR LIFE IS A **CLOSED** BOOK.
I'M GOING TO GO FOR A SWIM...
IT'LL GIVE YOU SOME TIME TO WORK ON YOUR BOOK.

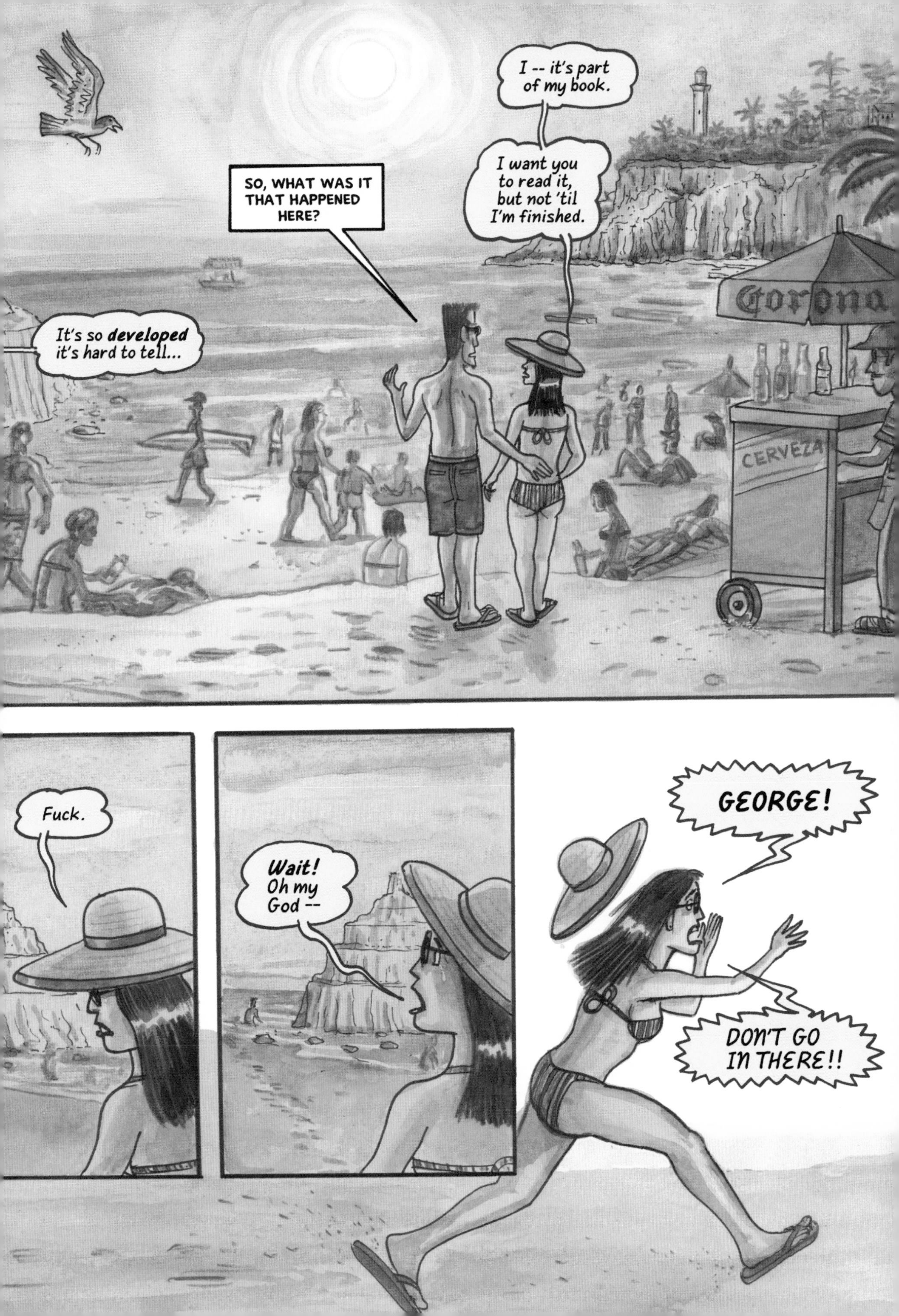
SO, WHAT WAS IT THAT HAPPENED HERE?
I -- it's part of my book.
I want you to read it, but not 'til I'm finished.
It's so **developed** it's hard to tell...
Corona
CERVEZA
Fuck.
Wait! Oh my God --
GEORGE!
DON'T GO IN THERE!!

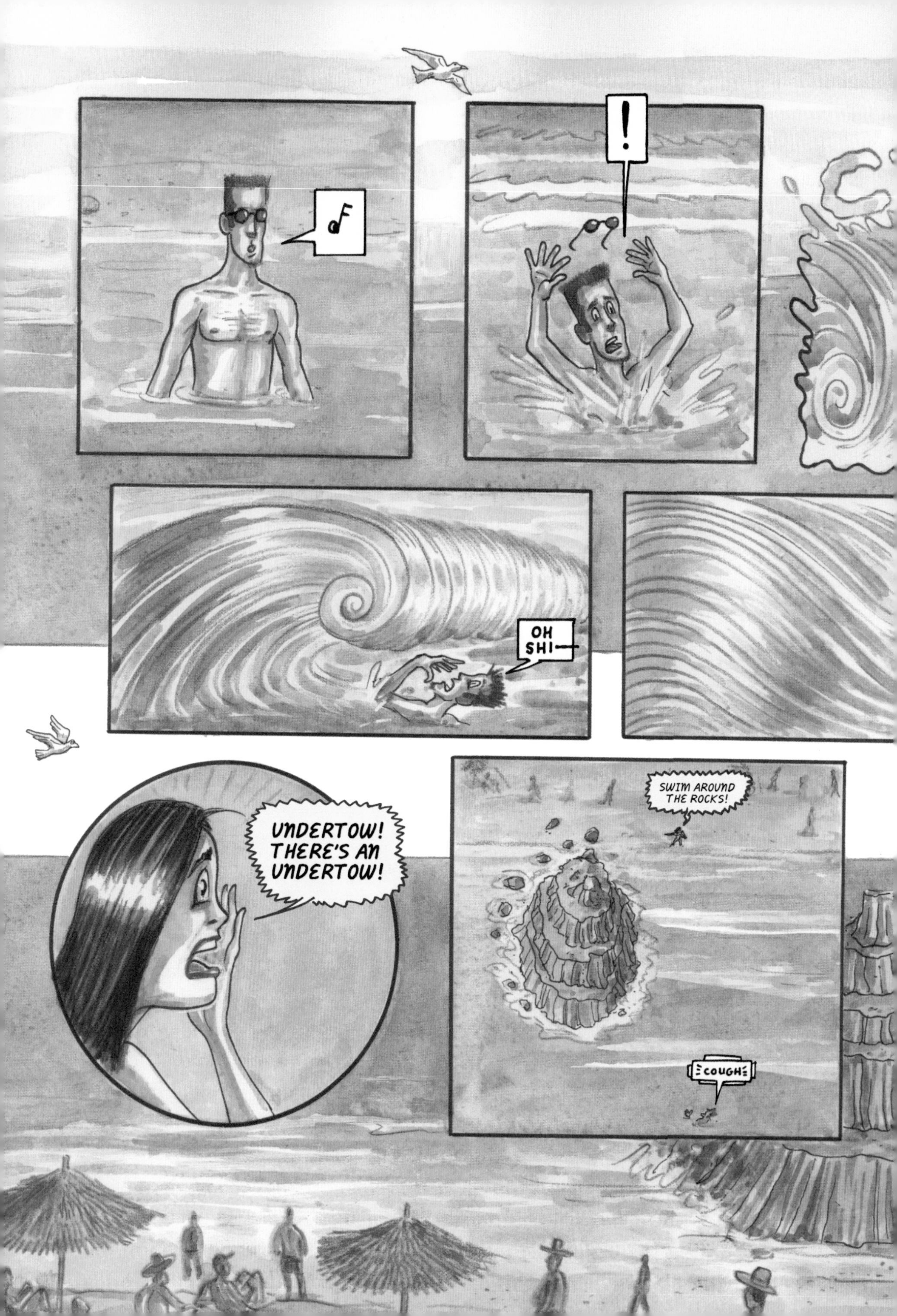
!
OH SHI—
UNDERTOW! THERE'S AN UNDERTOW!
SWIM AROUND THE ROCKS!
COUGH

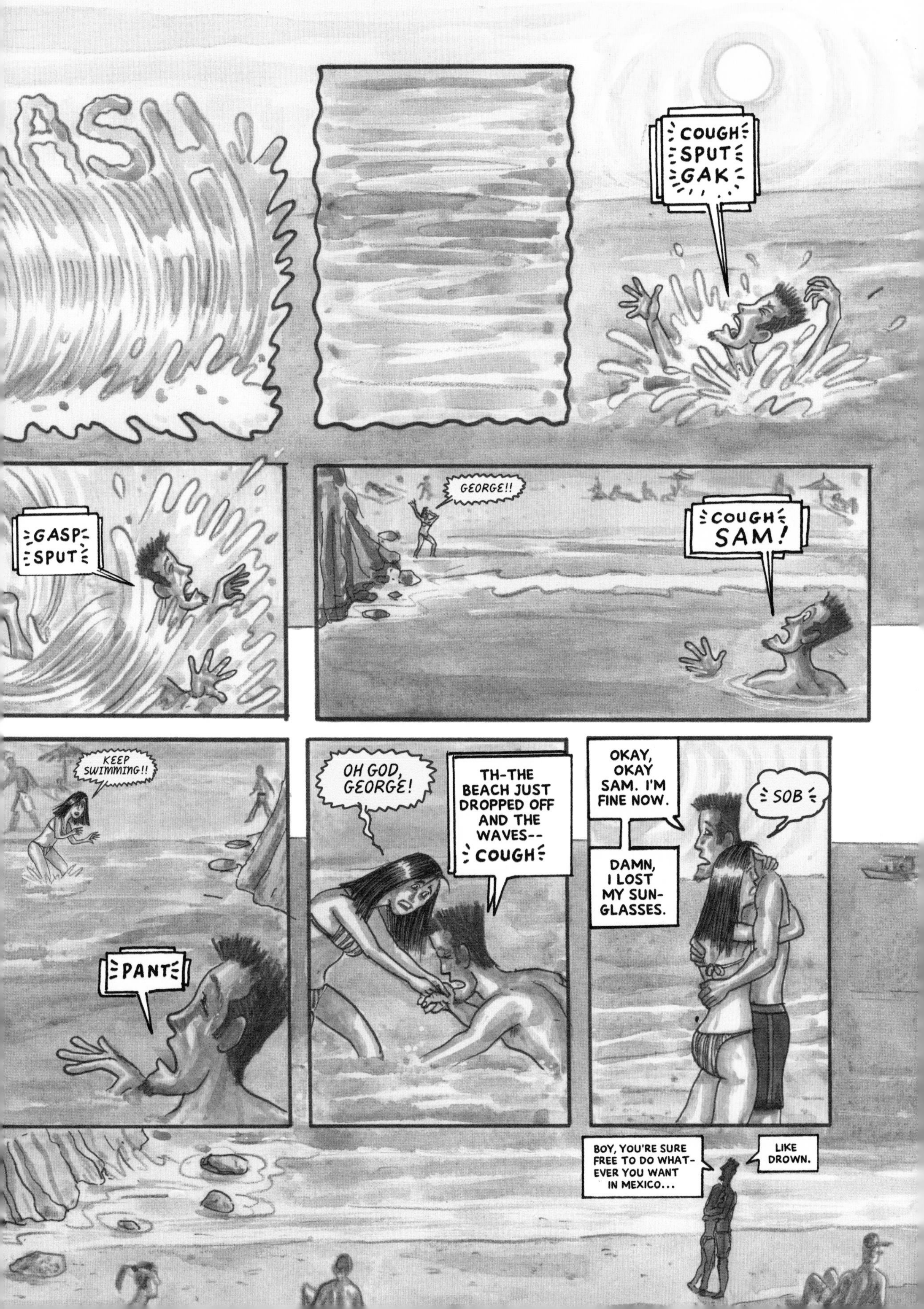
ASH
COUGH SPUT GAK
GASP SPUT
GEORGE!!
COUGH SAM!
KEEP SWIMMING!!
PANT
OH GOD, GEORGE!
TH-THE BEACH JUST DROPPED OFF AND THE WAVES-- COUGH
OKAY, OKAY SAM. I'M FINE NOW.
SOB
DAMN, I LOST MY SUN-GLASSES.
BOY, YOU'RE SURE FREE TO DO WHAT-EVER YOU WANT IN MEXICO...
LIKE DROWN.

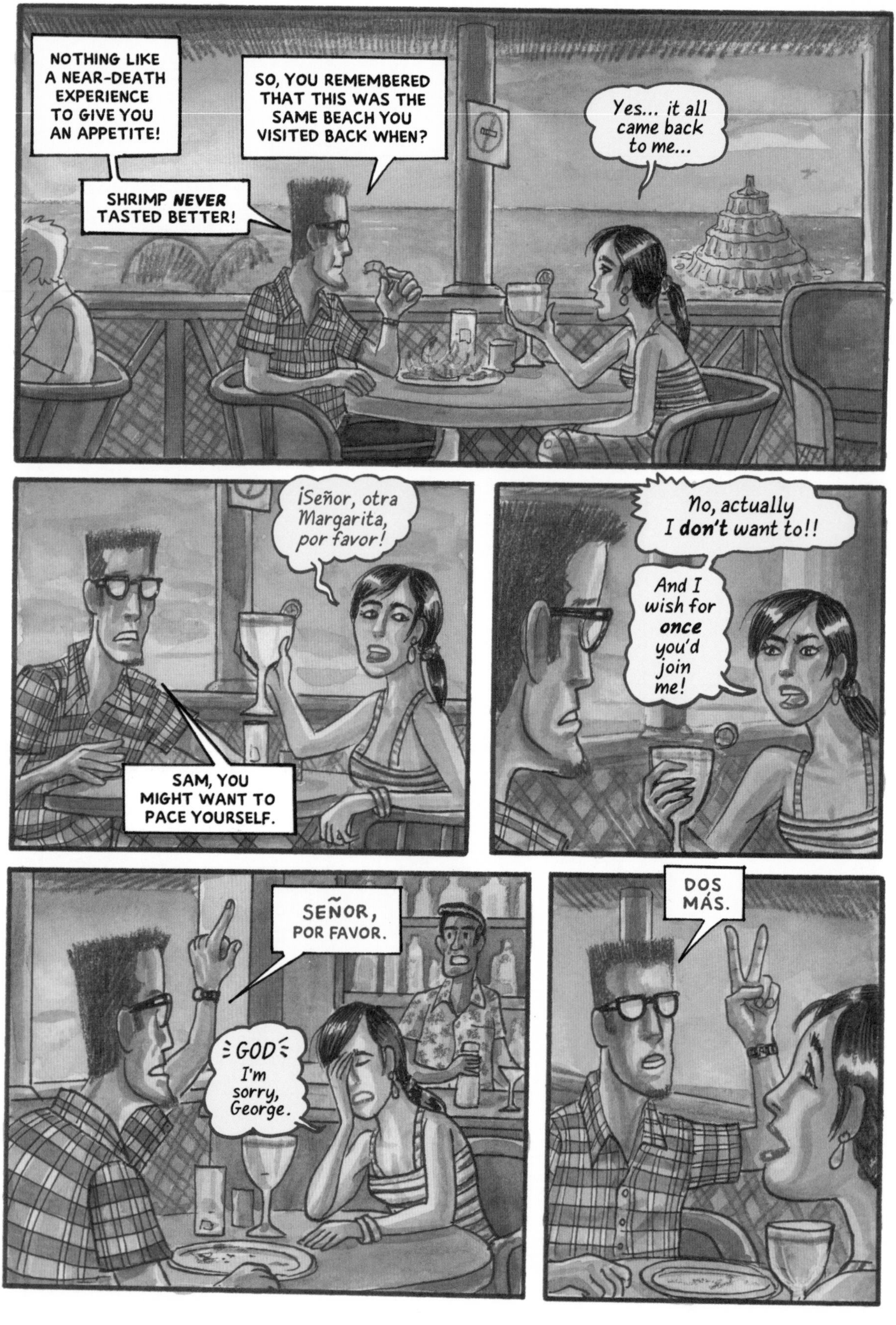
NOTHING LIKE A NEAR-DEATH EXPERIENCE TO GIVE YOU AN APPETITE!
SHRIMP **NEVER** TASTED BETTER!
SO, YOU REMEMBERED THAT THIS WAS THE SAME BEACH YOU VISITED BACK WHEN?
Yes... it all came back to me...
¡Señor, otra Margarita, por favor!
SAM, YOU MIGHT WANT TO PACE YOURSELF.
No, actually I **don't** want to!!
And I wish for **once** you'd join me!
SEÑOR, POR FAVOR.
GOD
I'm sorry, George.
DOS MÁS.

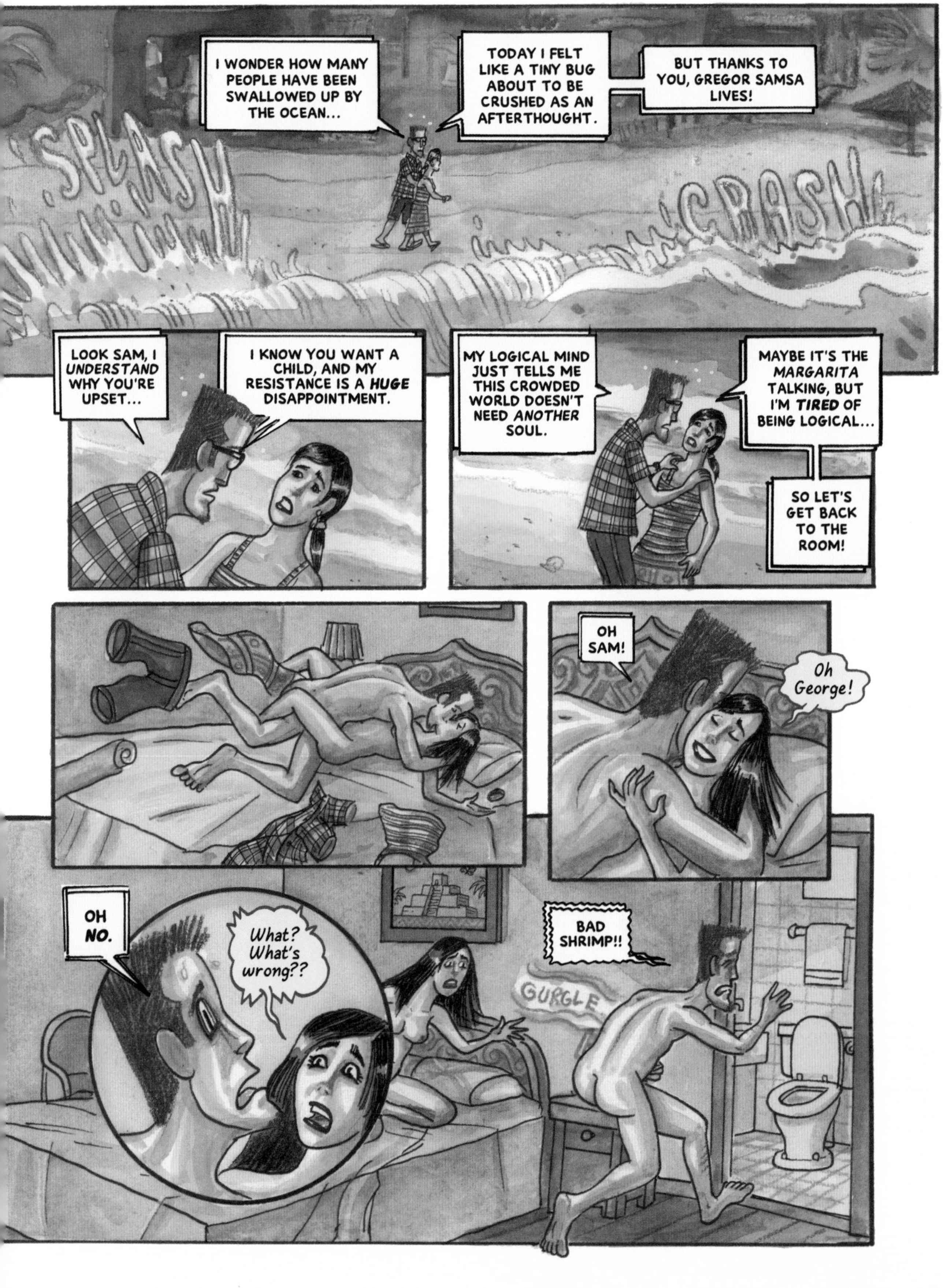
I WONDER HOW MANY PEOPLE HAVE BEEN SWALLOWED UP BY THE OCEAN...
TODAY I FELT LIKE A TINY BUG ABOUT TO BE CRUSHED AS AN AFTERTHOUGHT.
BUT THANKS TO YOU, GREGOR SAMSA LIVES!
SPLASH
CRASH
LOOK SAM, I *UNDERSTAND* WHY YOU'RE UPSET...
I KNOW YOU WANT A CHILD, AND MY RESISTANCE IS A ***HUGE*** DISAPPOINTMENT.
MY LOGICAL MIND JUST TELLS ME THIS CROWDED WORLD DOESN'T NEED *ANOTHER* SOUL.
MAYBE IT'S THE *MARGARITA* TALKING, BUT I'M ***TIRED*** OF BEING LOGICAL...
SO LET'S GET BACK TO THE ROOM!
OH SAM!
Oh George!
OH **NO.**
What? What's wrong??
BAD SHRIMP!!
GURGLE

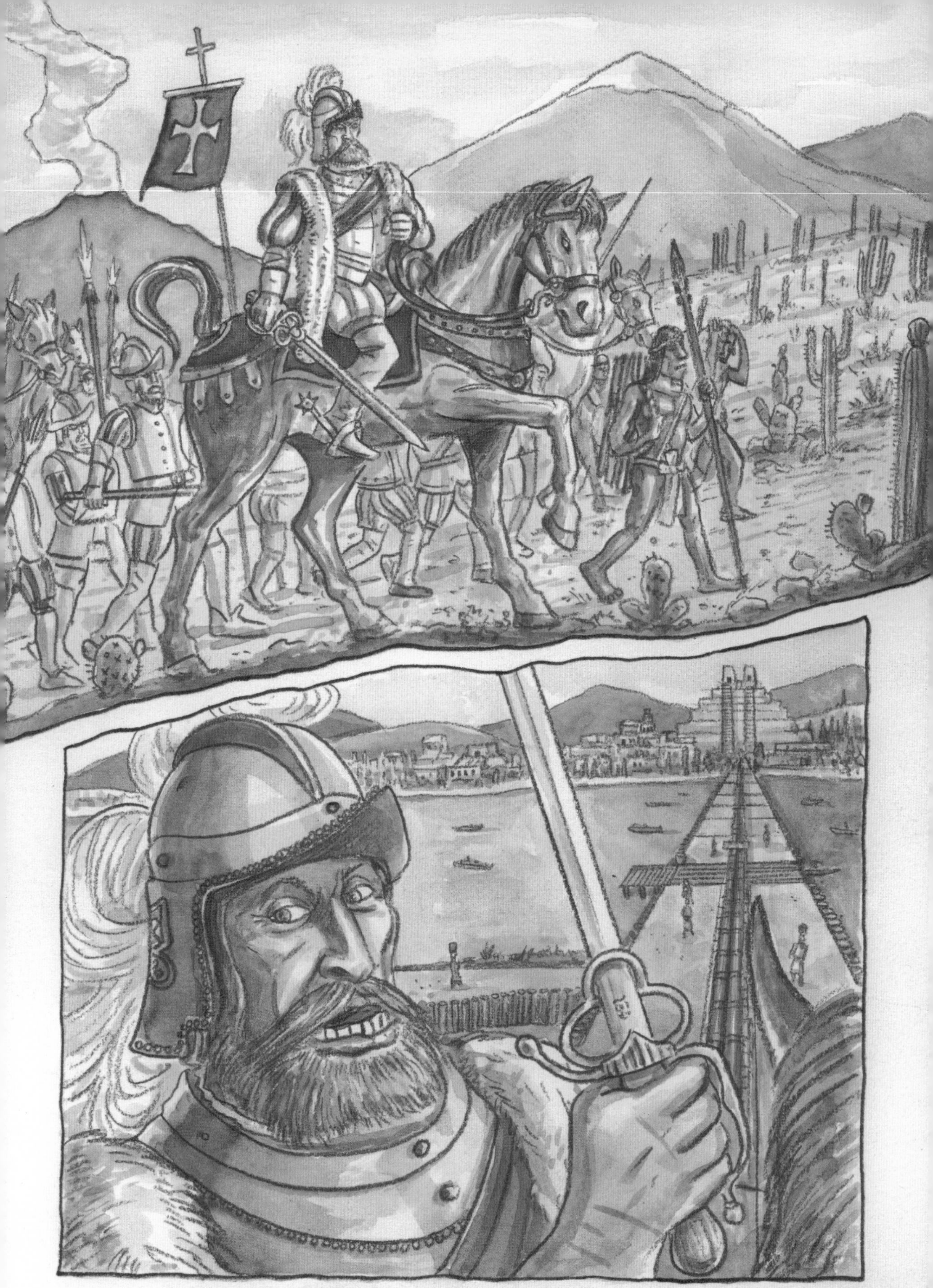

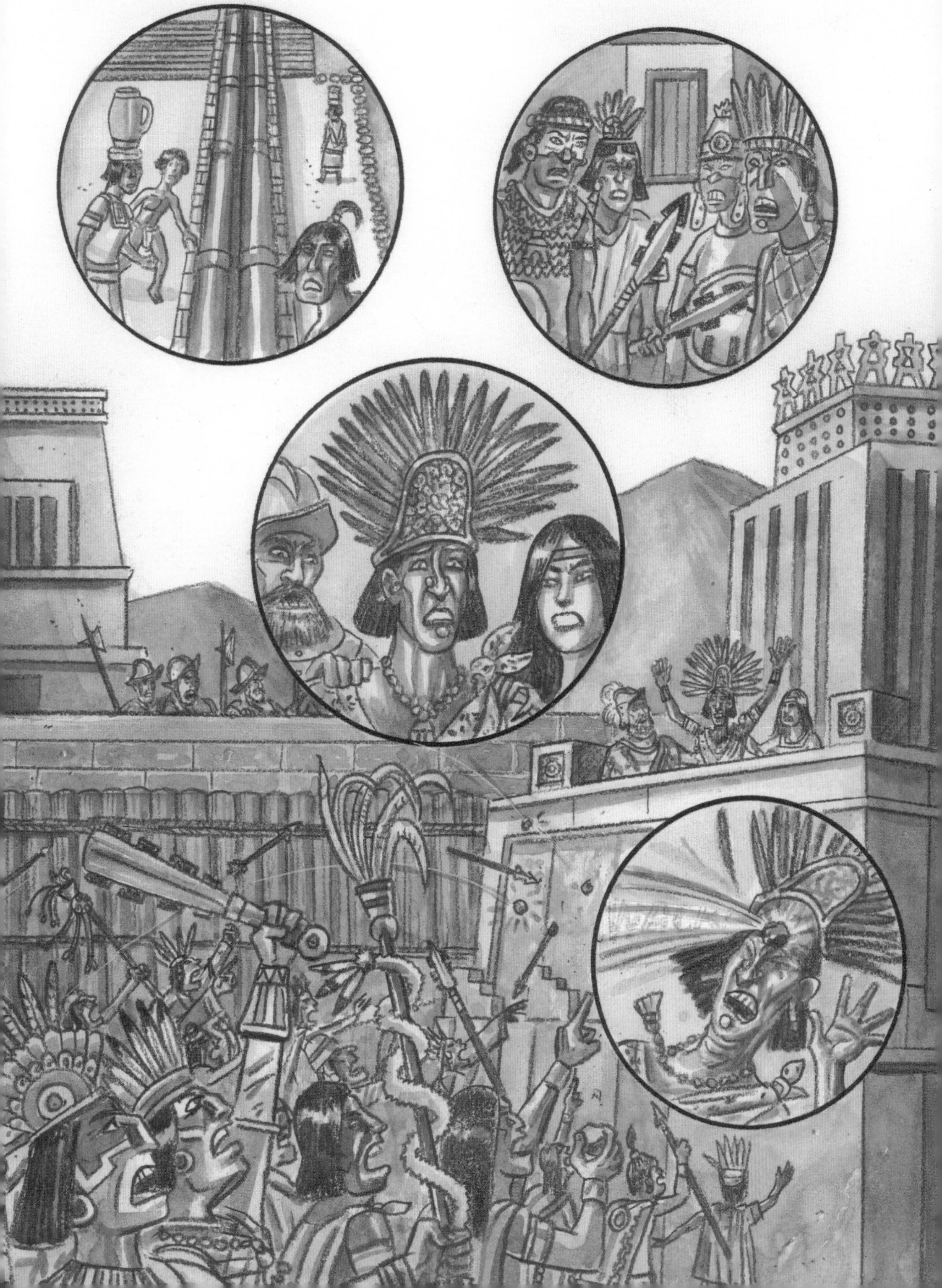

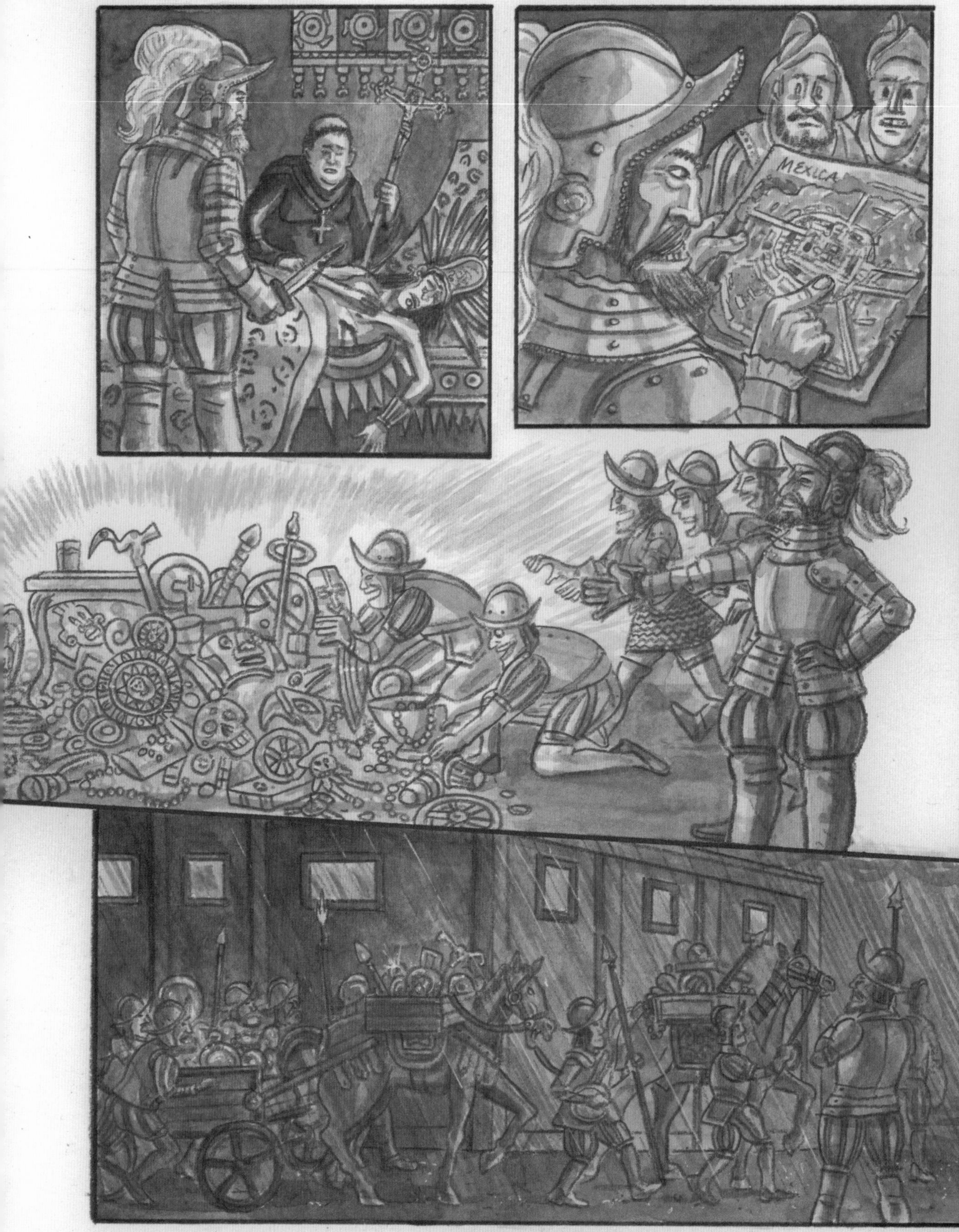
MEXICA

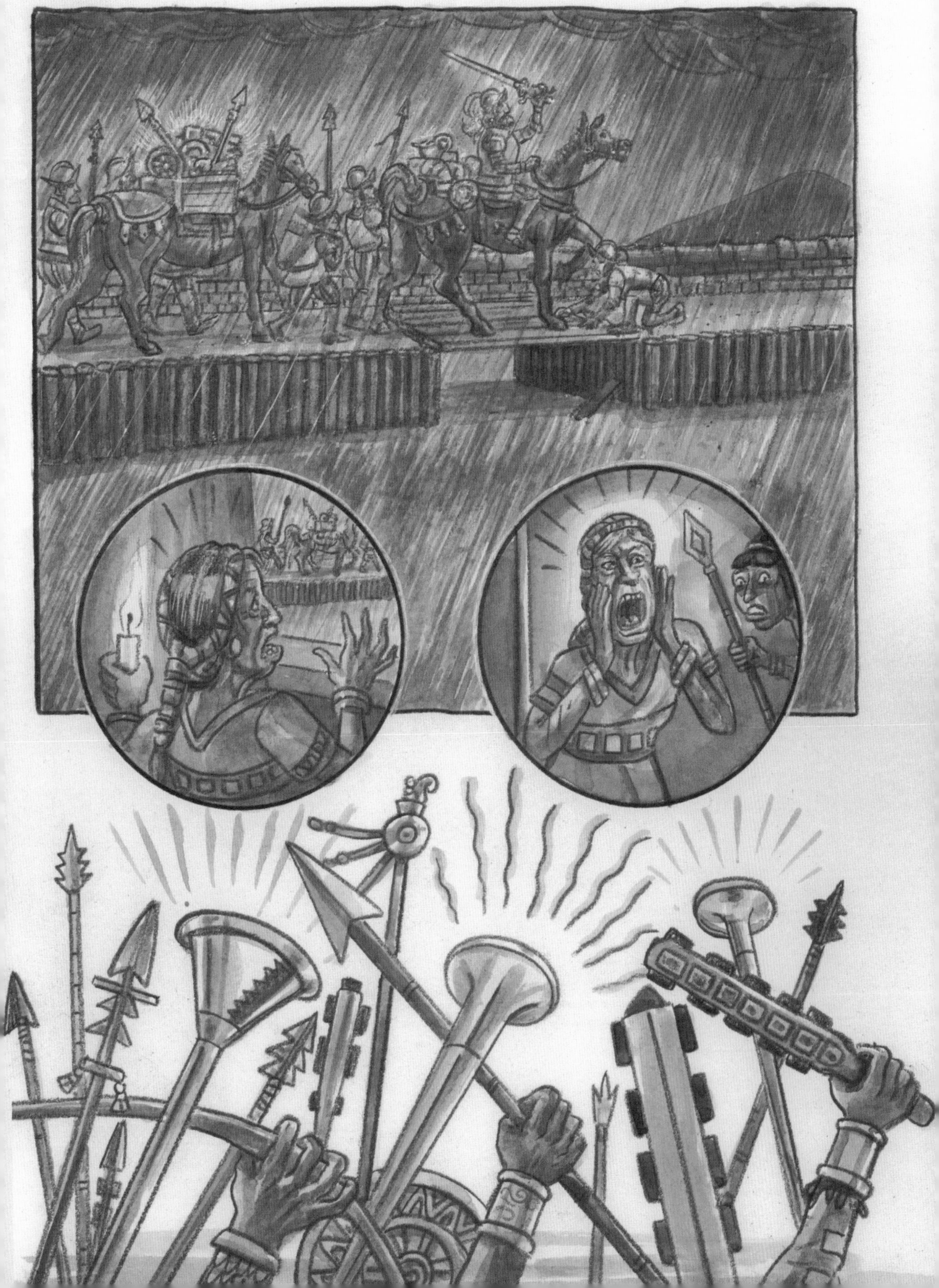

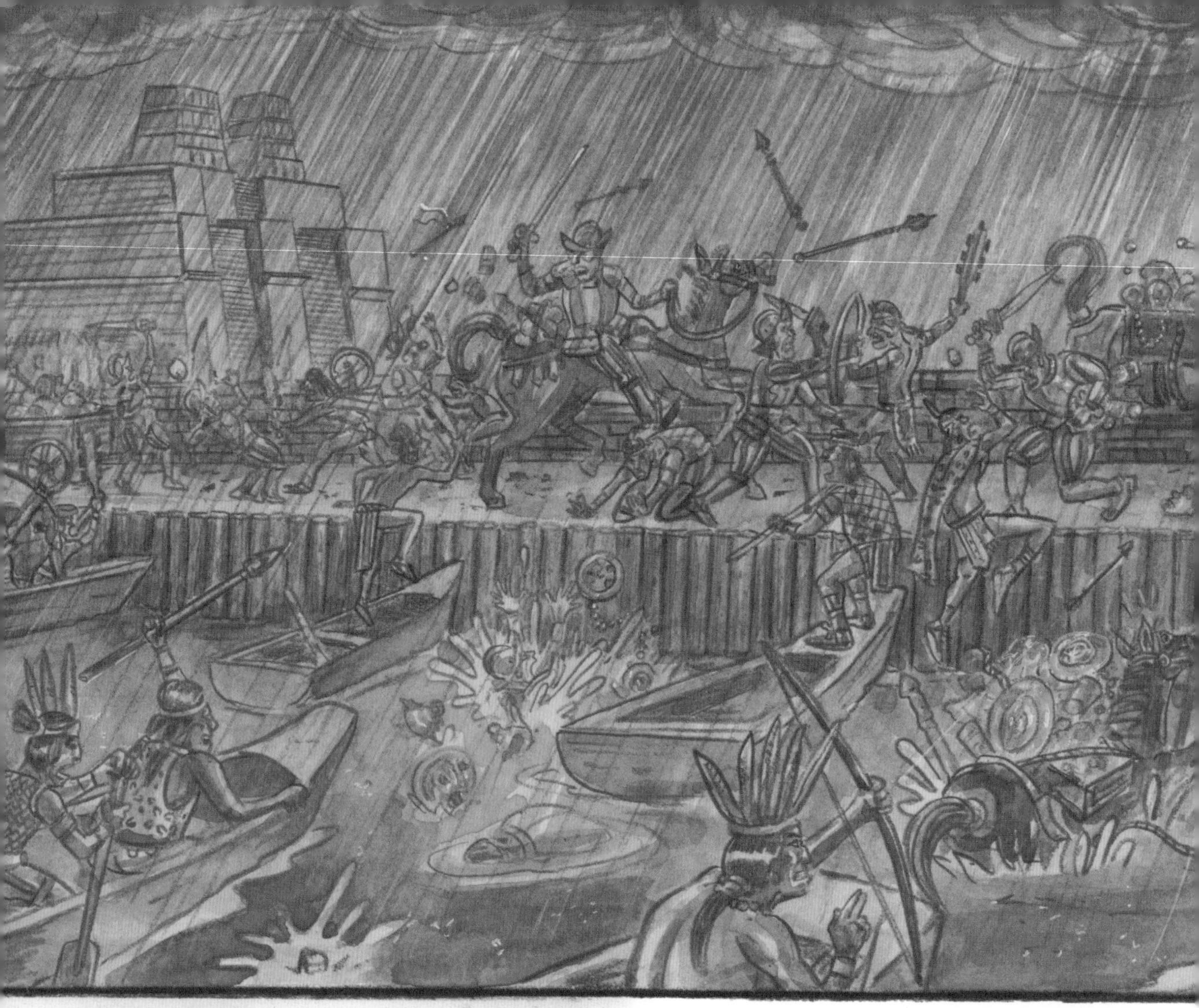

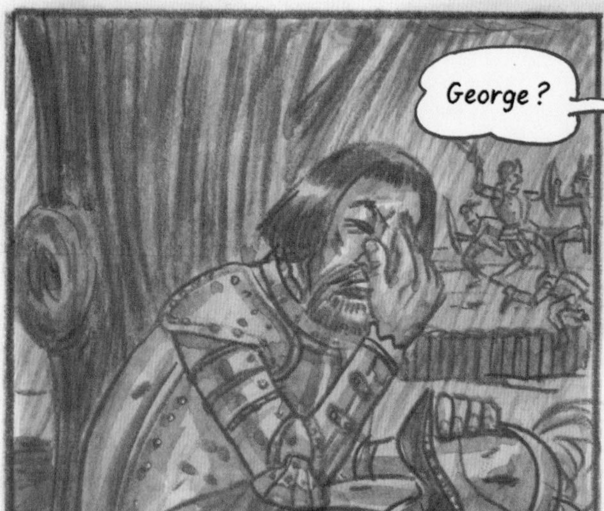
George ?

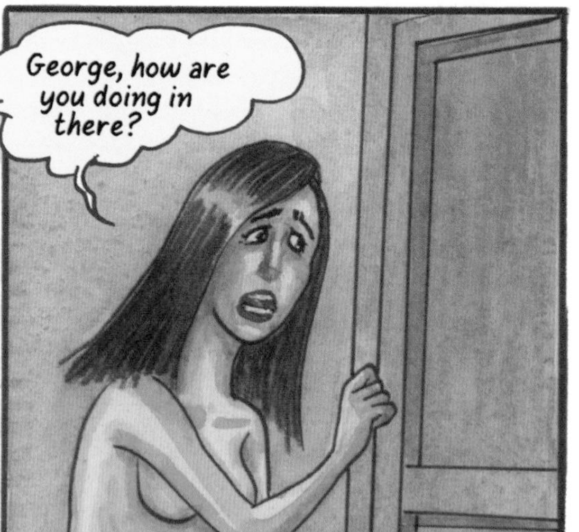
George, how are you doing in there?

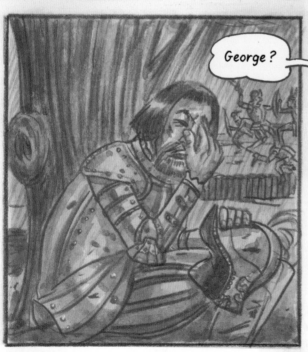

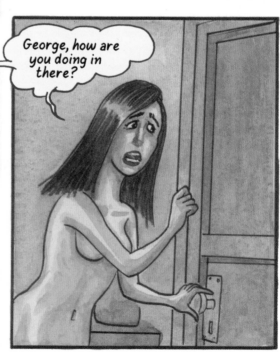

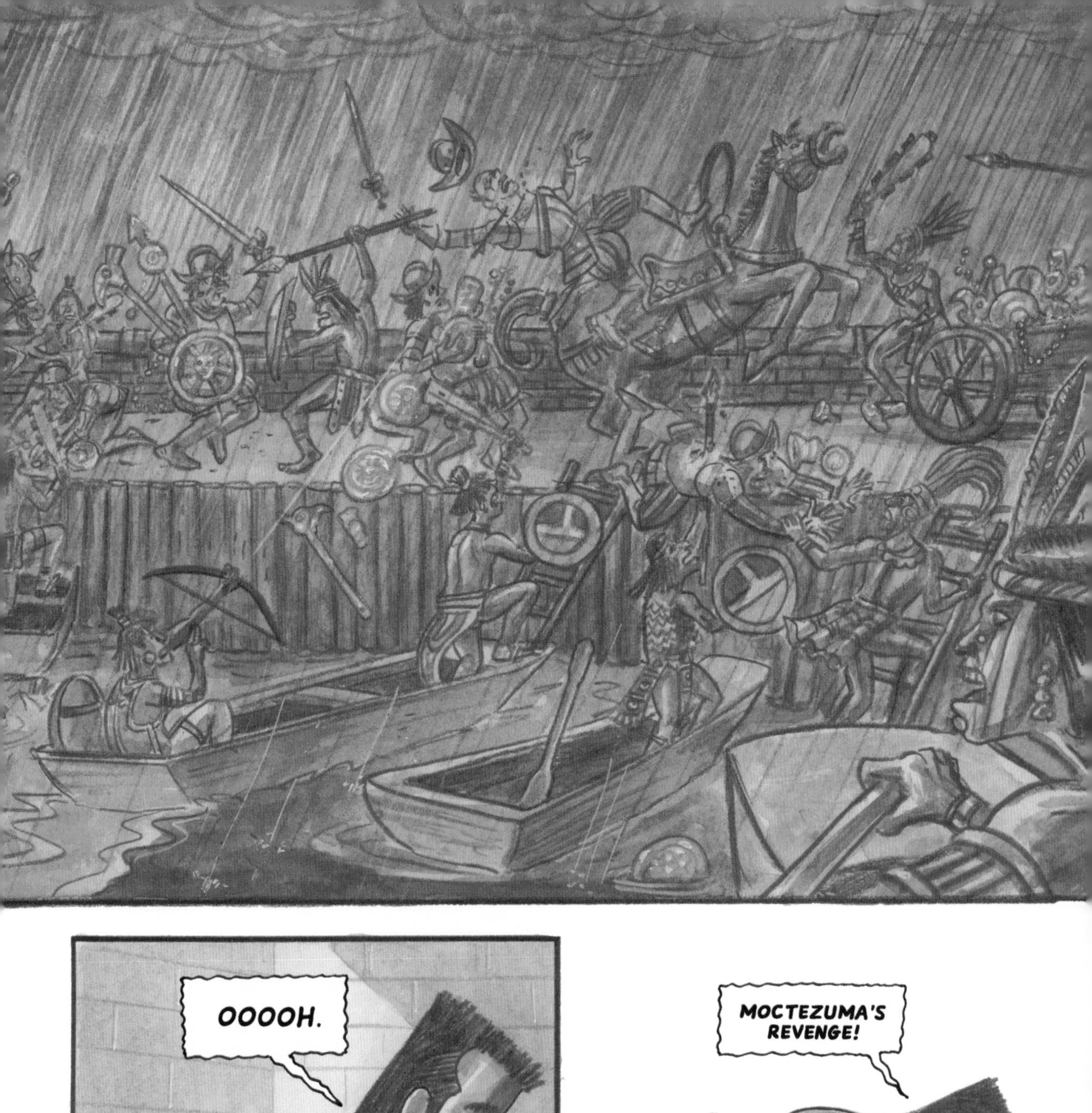

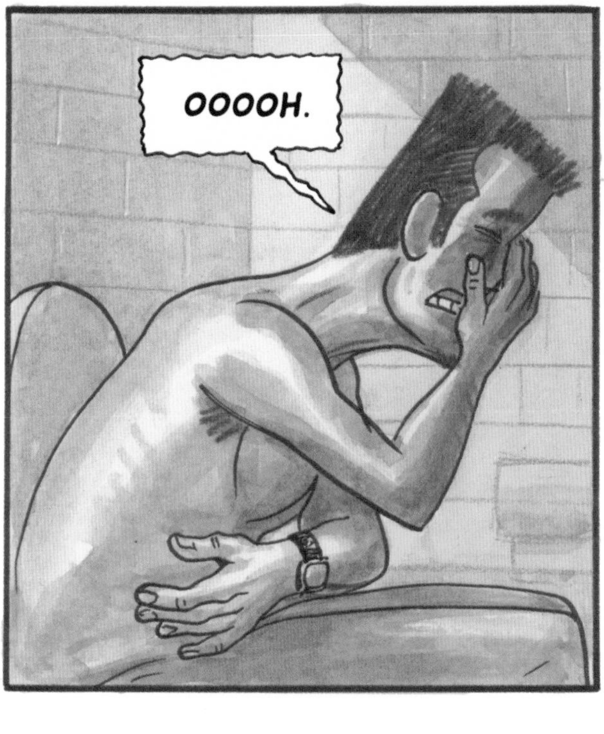
OOOOH.

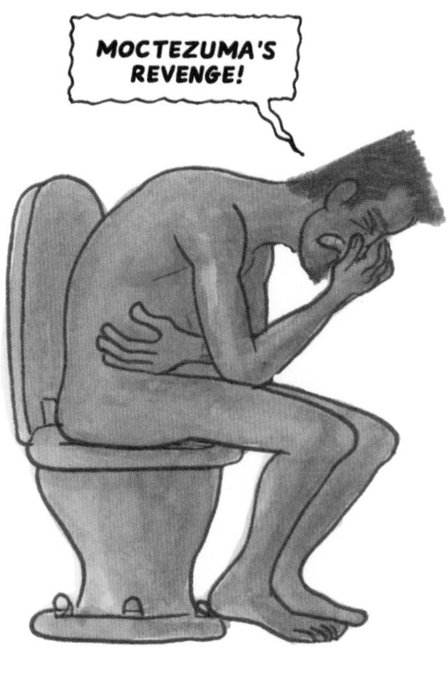
MOCTEZUMA'S REVENGE!

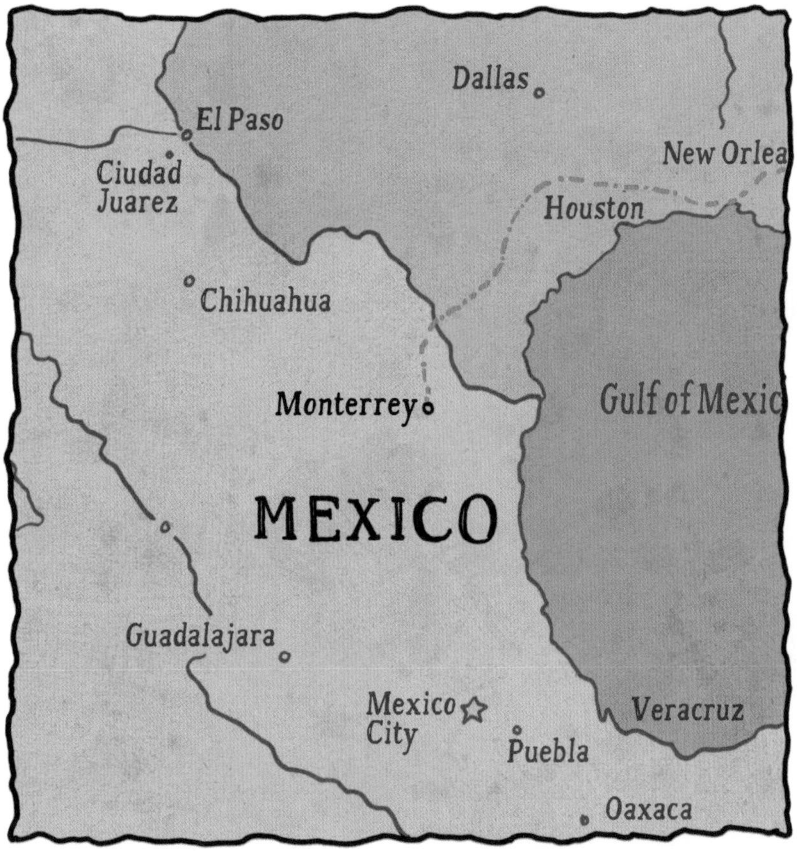
Dallas
El Paso
New Orlea
Ciudad
Juarez
Houston
Chihuahua
Monterrey
Gulf of Mexic
MEXICO
Guadalajara
Mexico
City
Veracruz
Puebla
Oaxaca

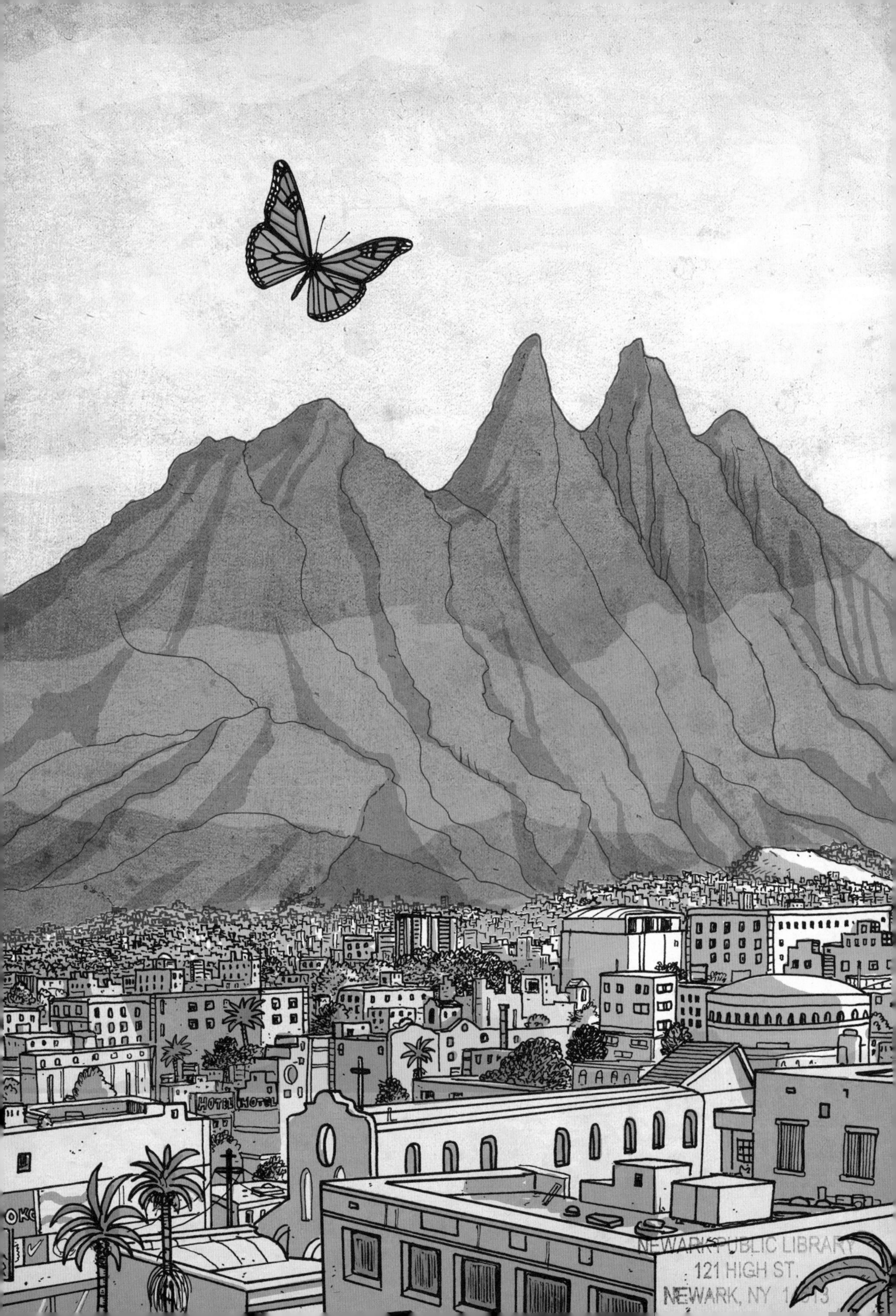
HOTEL
HOTEL

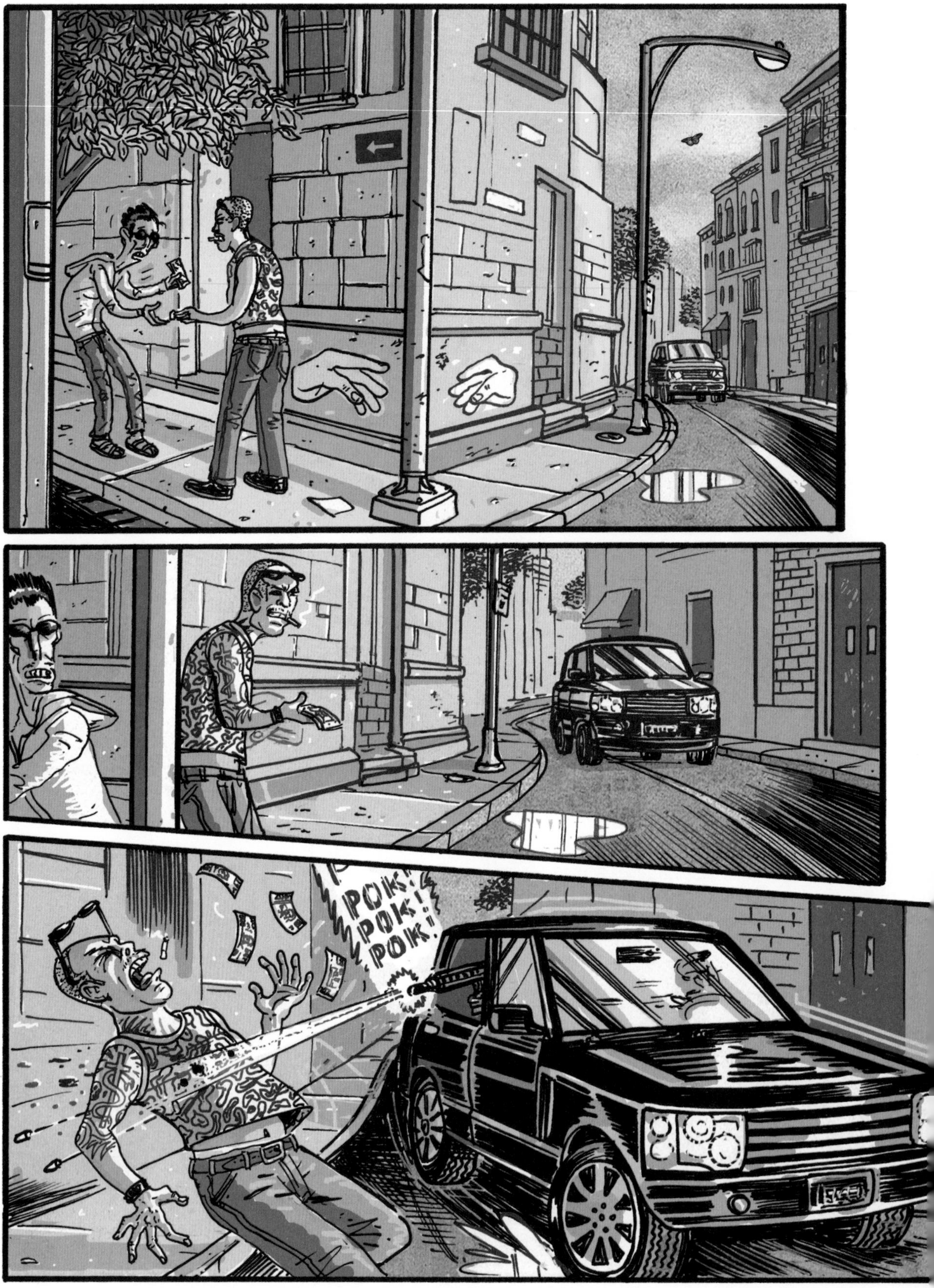
POK! POK! POK!

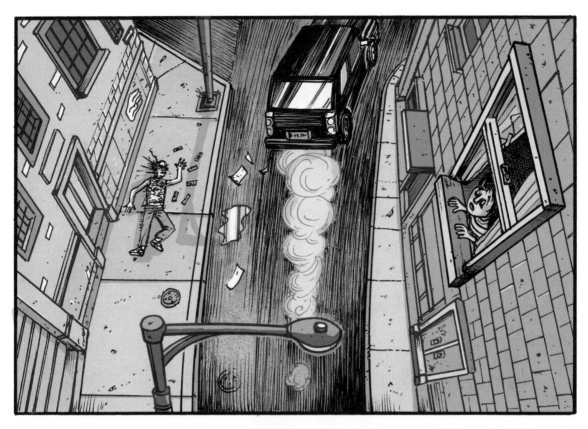

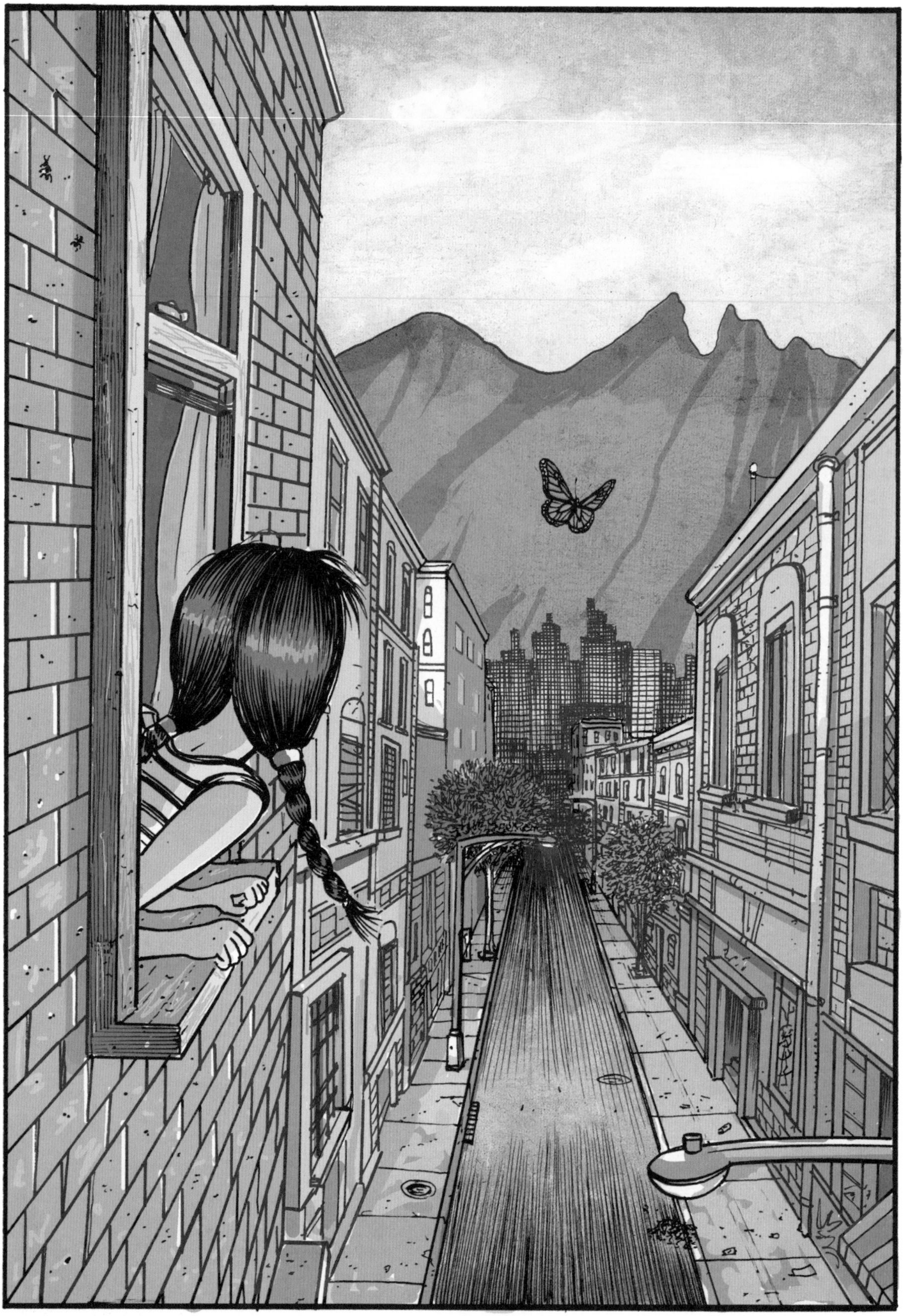

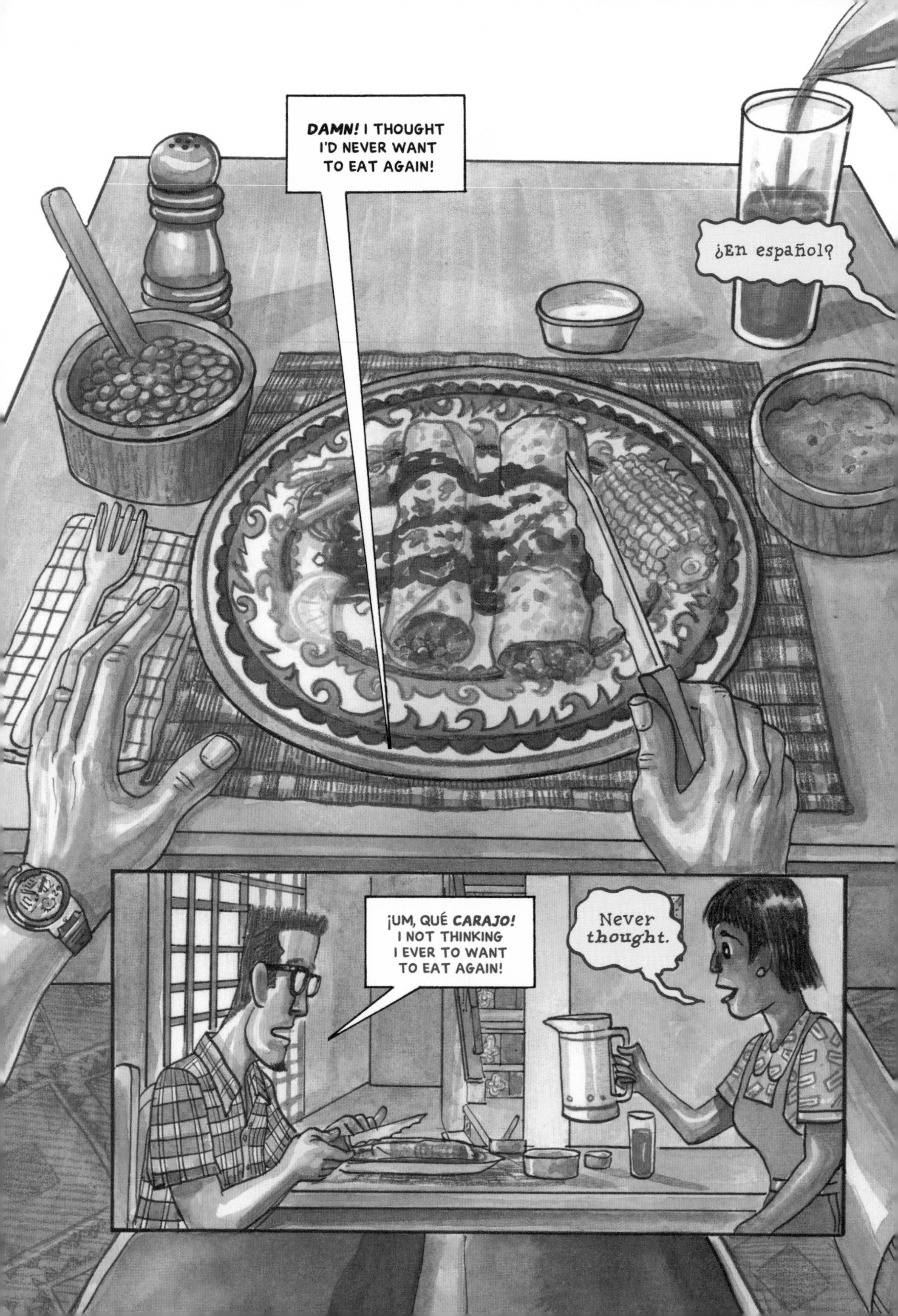
DAMN! I THOUGHT I'D NEVER WANT TO EAT AGAIN!
¿En español?
¡UM, QUÉ CARAJO! I NOT THINKING I EVER TO WANT TO EAT AGAIN!
Never thought.

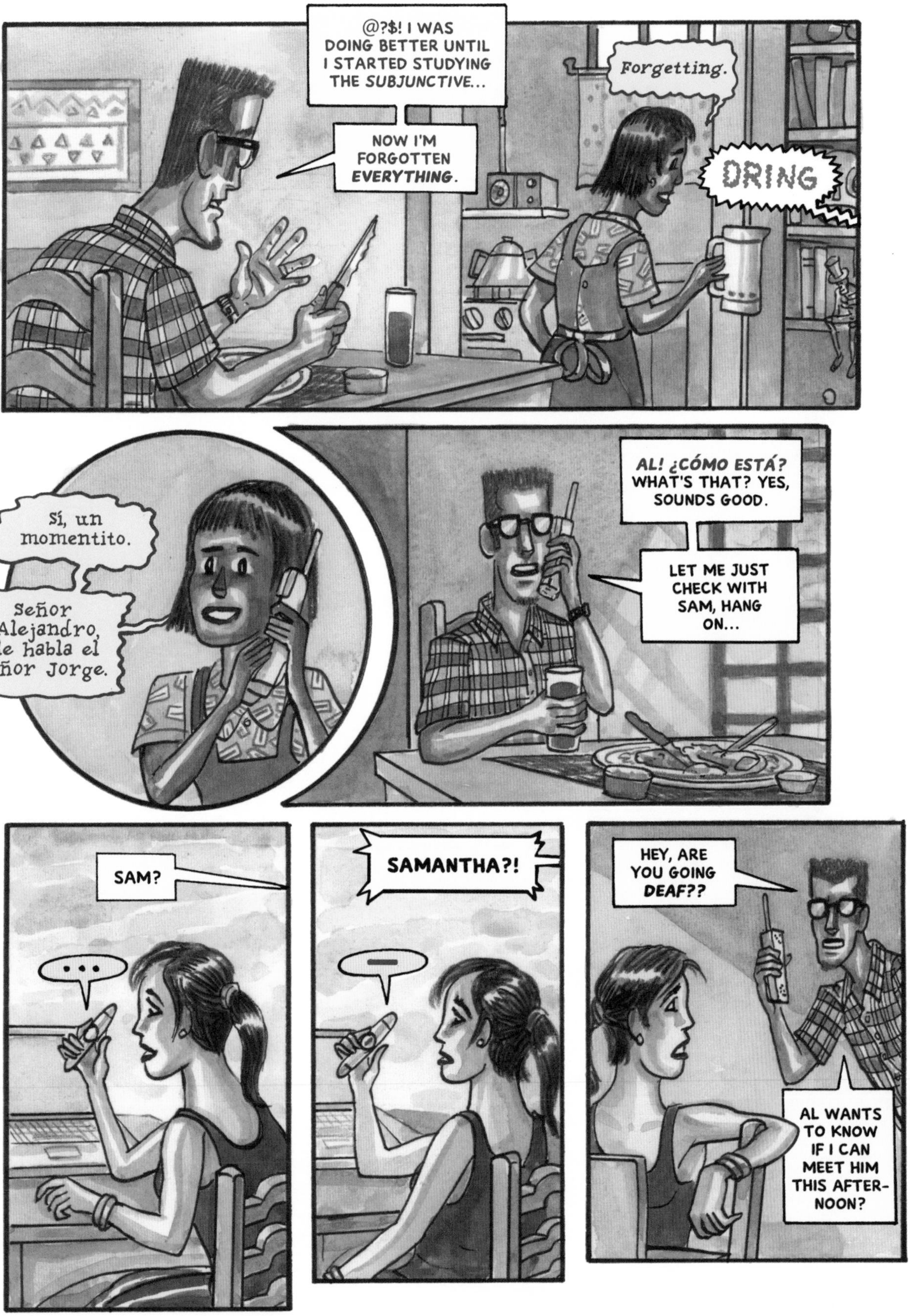

@?$! I WAS DOING BETTER UNTIL I STARTED STUDYING THE *SUBJUNCTIVE*...
NOW I'M FORGOTTEN *EVERYTHING*.
Forgetting.
DRING
Sí, un momentito.
Señor Alejandro, le habla el señor Jorge.
AL! ¿CÓMO ESTÁ? WHAT'S THAT? YES, SOUNDS GOOD.
LET ME JUST CHECK WITH SAM, HANG ON...
SAM?
...
SAMANTHA?!
—
HEY, ARE YOU GOING *DEAF??*
AL WANTS TO KNOW IF I CAN MEET HIM THIS AFTER-NOON?

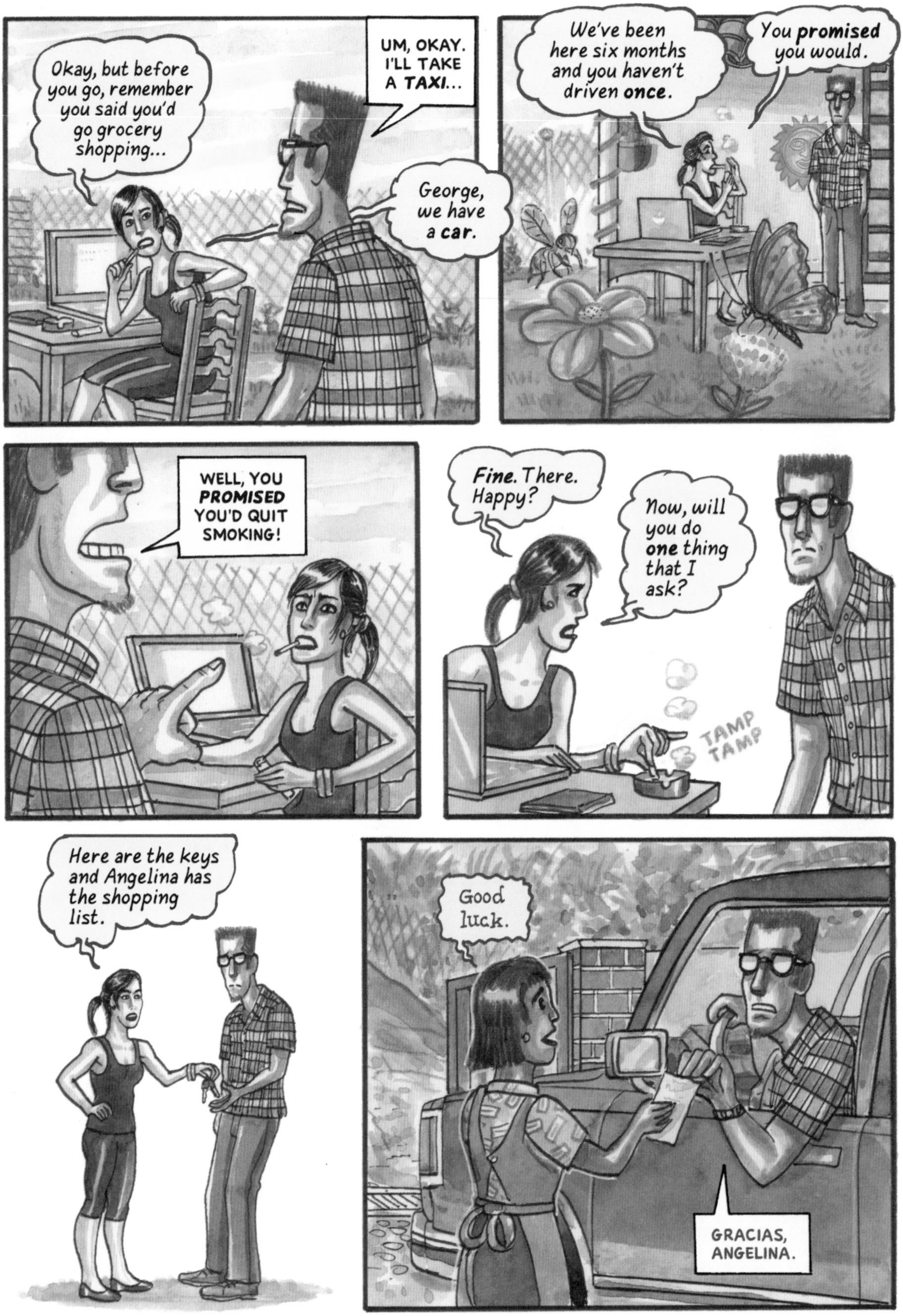
Okay, but before you go, remember you said you'd go grocery shopping...
UM, OKAY. I'LL TAKE A **TAXI**...
George, we have a **car**.
We've been here six months and you haven't driven **once**.
You **promised** you would.
WELL, YOU **PROMISED** YOU'D QUIT SMOKING!
Fine. There. Happy?
Now, will you do **one** thing that I ask?
TAMP TAMP
Here are the keys and Angelina has the shopping list.
Good luck.
GRACIAS, ANGELINA.

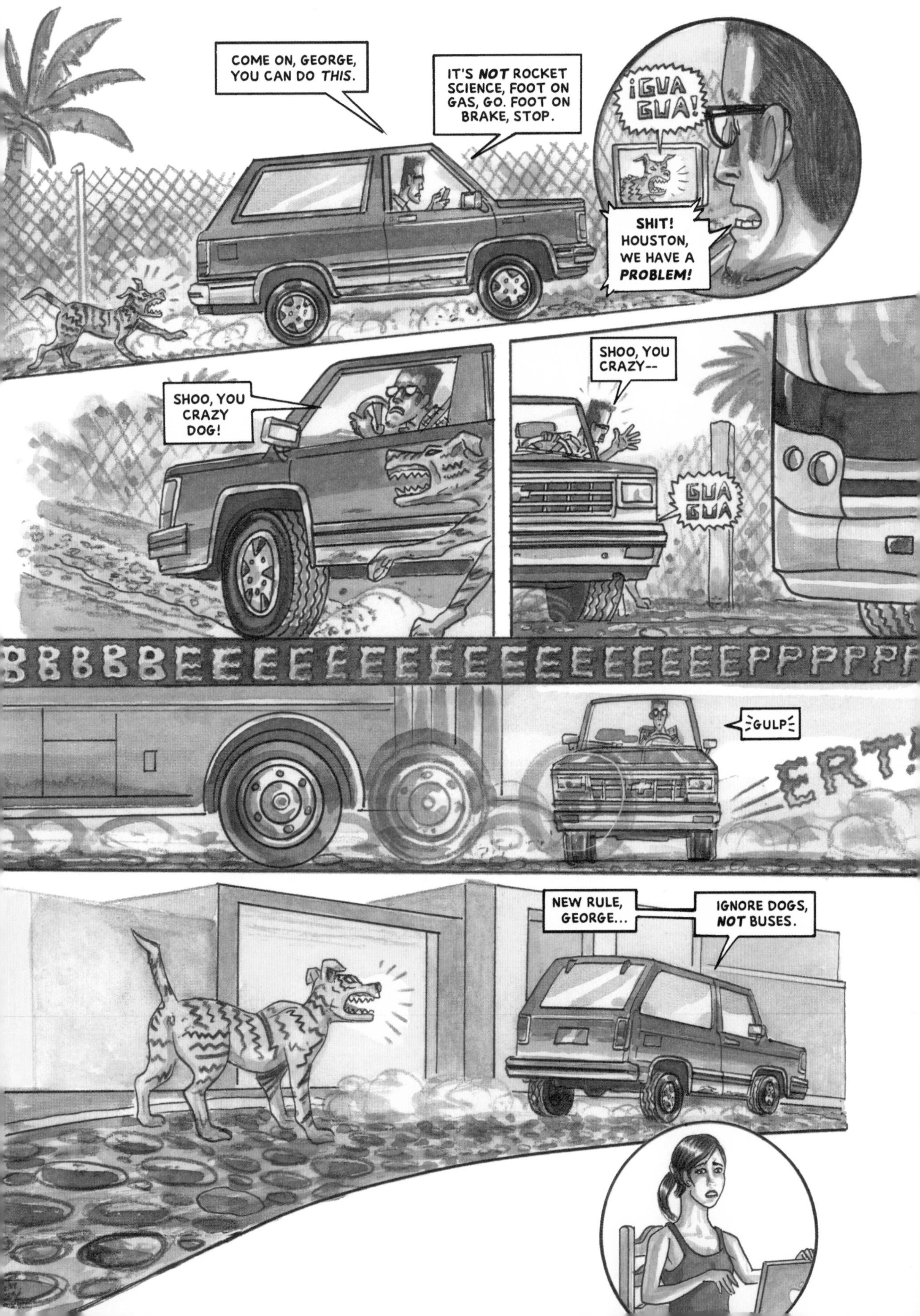
COME ON, GEORGE, YOU CAN DO *THIS*.
IT'S ***NOT*** ROCKET SCIENCE, FOOT ON GAS, GO. FOOT ON BRAKE, STOP.
¡GUA GUA!
SHIT! HOUSTON, WE HAVE A *PROBLEM!*
SHOO, YOU CRAZY DOG!
SHOO, YOU CRAZY--
GUA GUA
BBBBBEEEEEEEEEEEEEEEEEEEPPPPPP
GULP
ERT!
NEW RULE, GEORGE...
IGNORE DOGS, ***NOT*** BUSES.

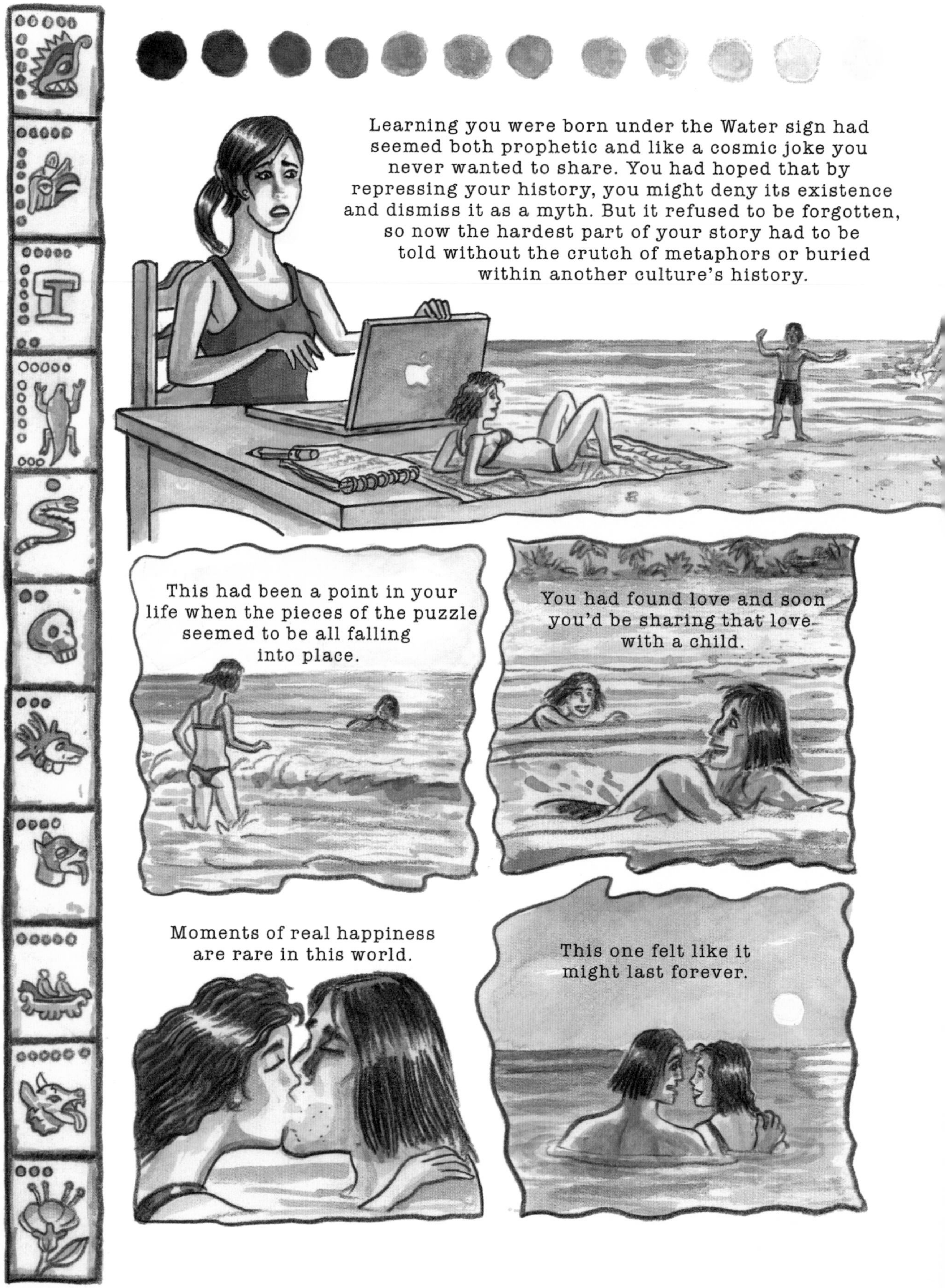
Learning you were born under the Water sign had seemed both prophetic and like a cosmic joke you never wanted to share. You had hoped that by repressing your history, you might deny its existence and dismiss it as a myth. But it refused to be forgotten, so now the hardest part of your story had to be told without the crutch of metaphors or buried within another culture's history.
This had been a point in your life when the pieces of the puzzle seemed to be all falling into place.
You had found love and soon you'd be sharing that love with a child.
Moments of real happiness are rare in this world.
This one felt like it might last forever.

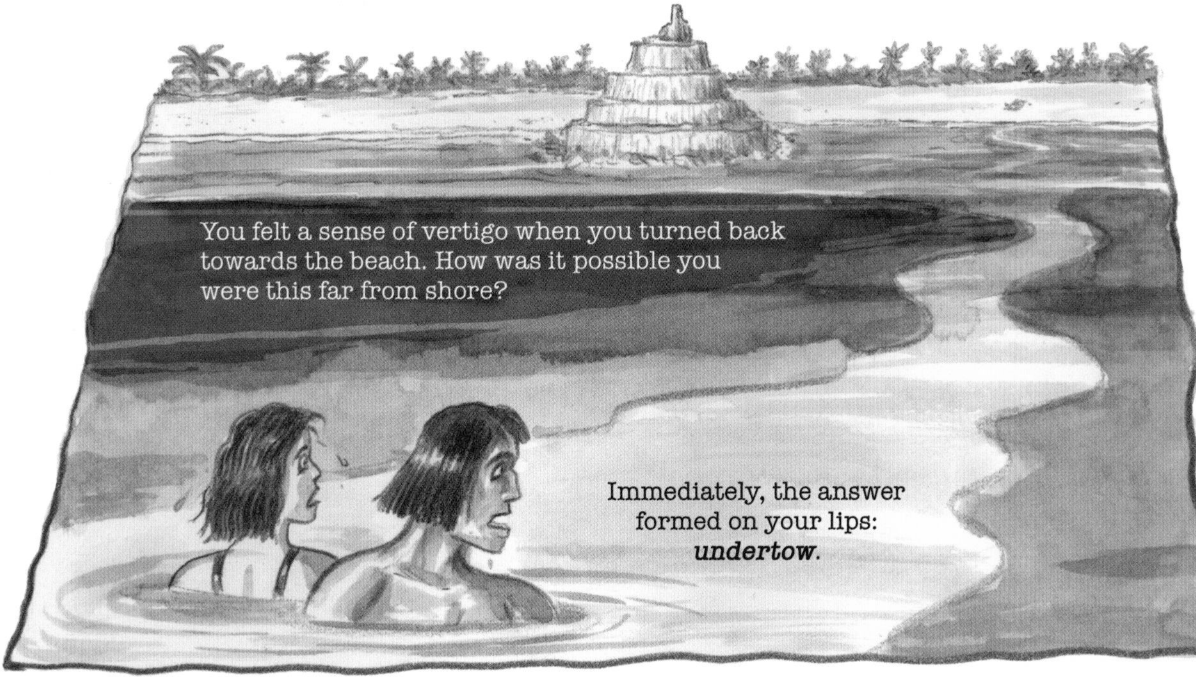
You felt a sense of vertigo when you turned back towards the beach. How was it possible you were this far from shore?
Immediately, the answer formed on your lips: ***undertow.***

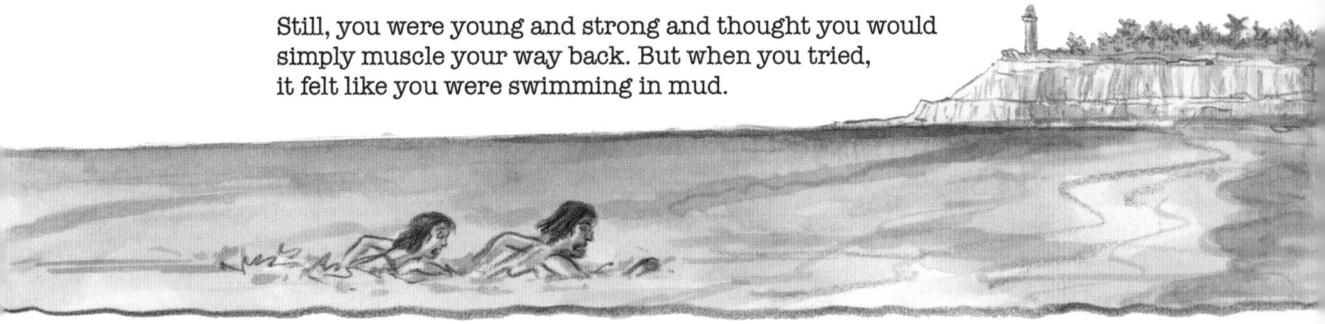
Still, you were young and strong and thought you would simply muscle your way back. But when you tried, it felt like you were swimming in mud.

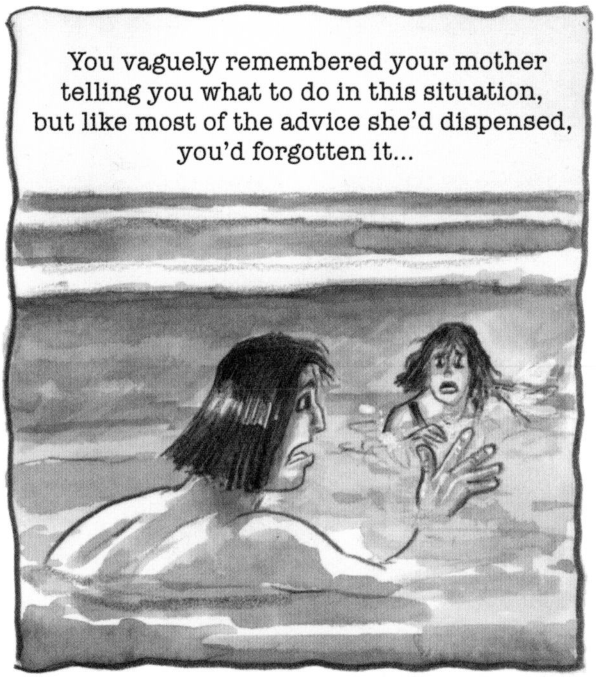
You vaguely remembered your mother telling you what to do in this situation, but like most of the advice she'd dispensed, you'd forgotten it...

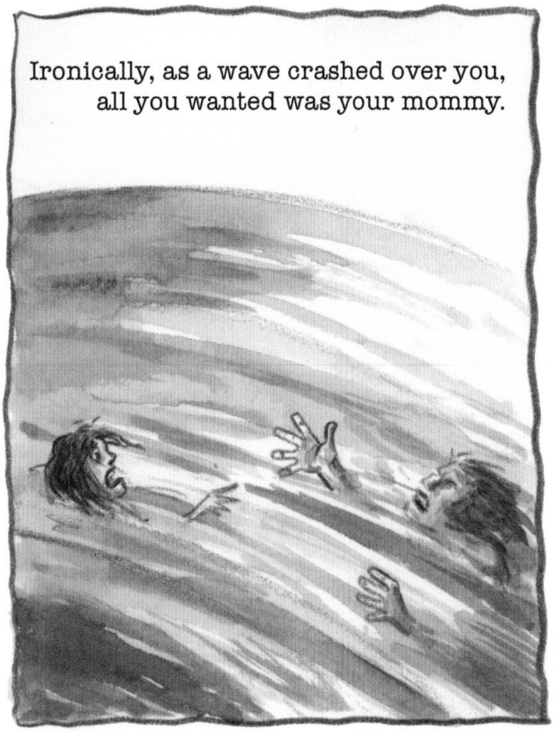
Ironically, as a wave crashed over you, all you wanted was your mommy.

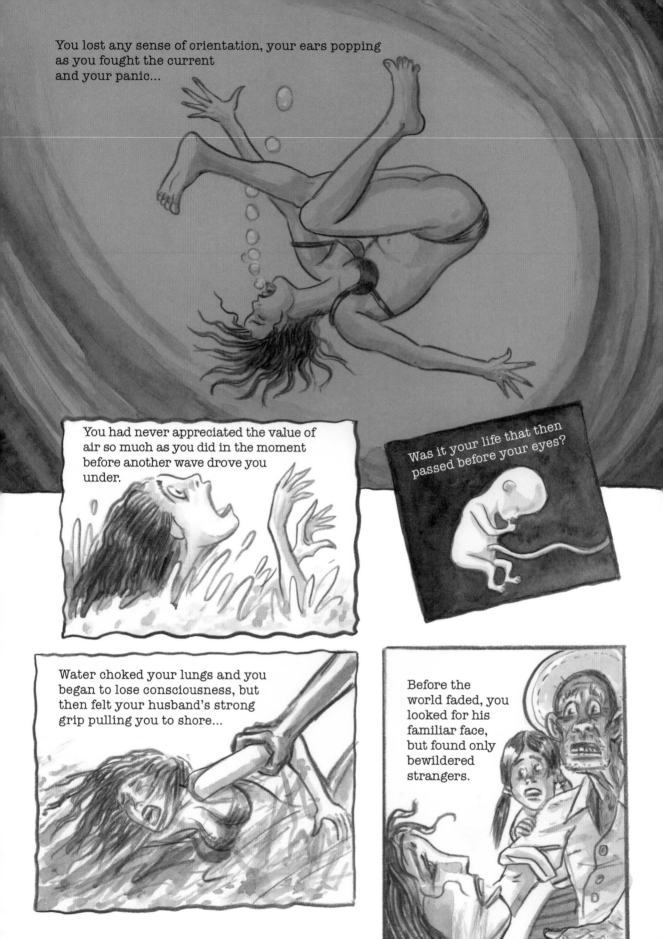

You lost any sense of orientation, your ears popping as you fought the current and your panic...

You had never appreciated the value of air so much as you did in the moment before another wave drove you under.

Was it your life that then passed before your eyes?

Water choked your lungs and you began to lose consciousness, but then felt your husband's strong grip pulling you to shore...

Before the world faded, you looked for his familiar face, but found only bewildered strangers.

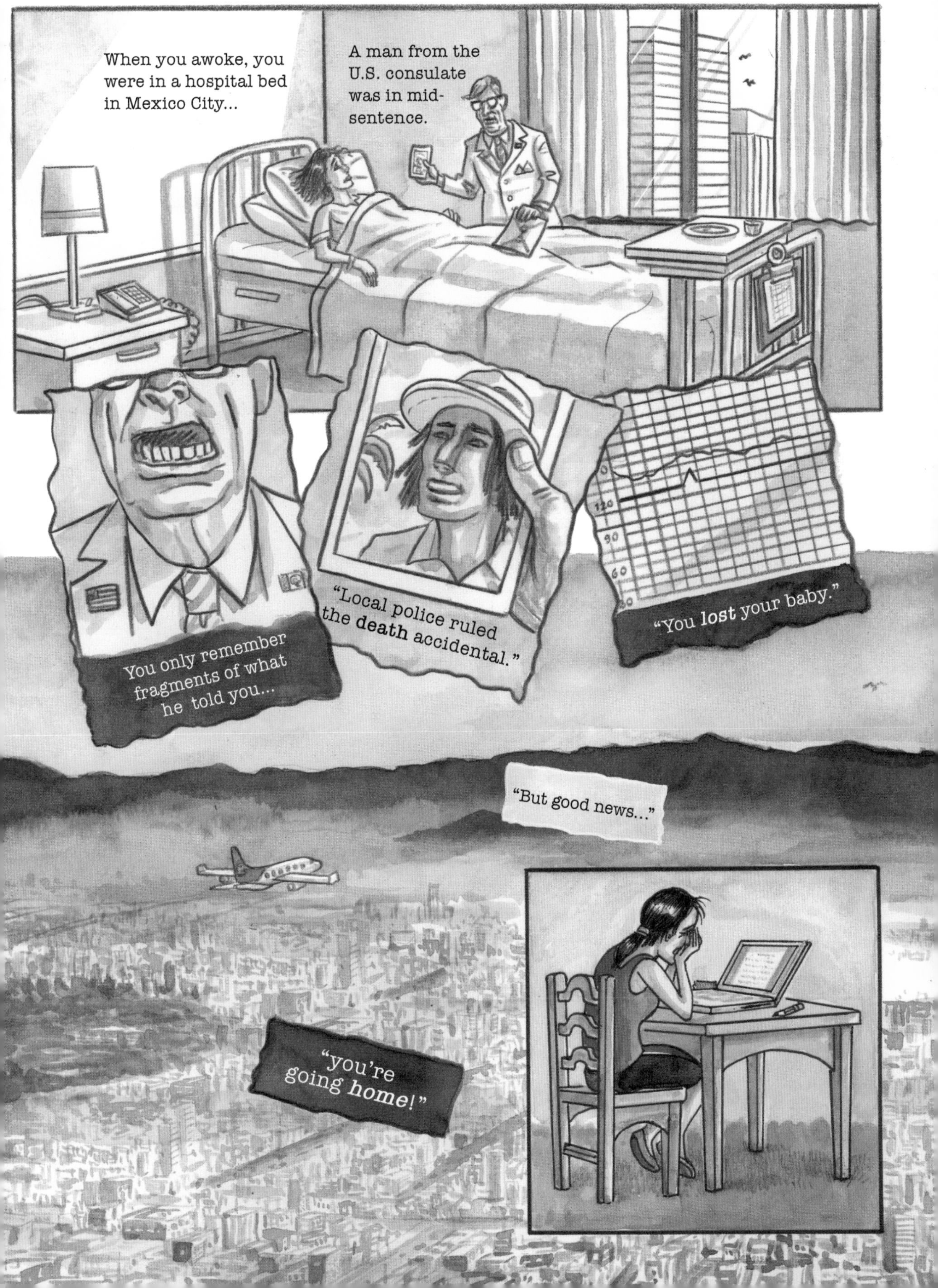
When you awoke, you were in a hospital bed in Mexico City...
A man from the U.S. consulate was in mid-sentence.
You only remember fragments of what he told you...
"Local police ruled the death accidental."
"You lost your baby."
"But good news..."
"you're going home!"

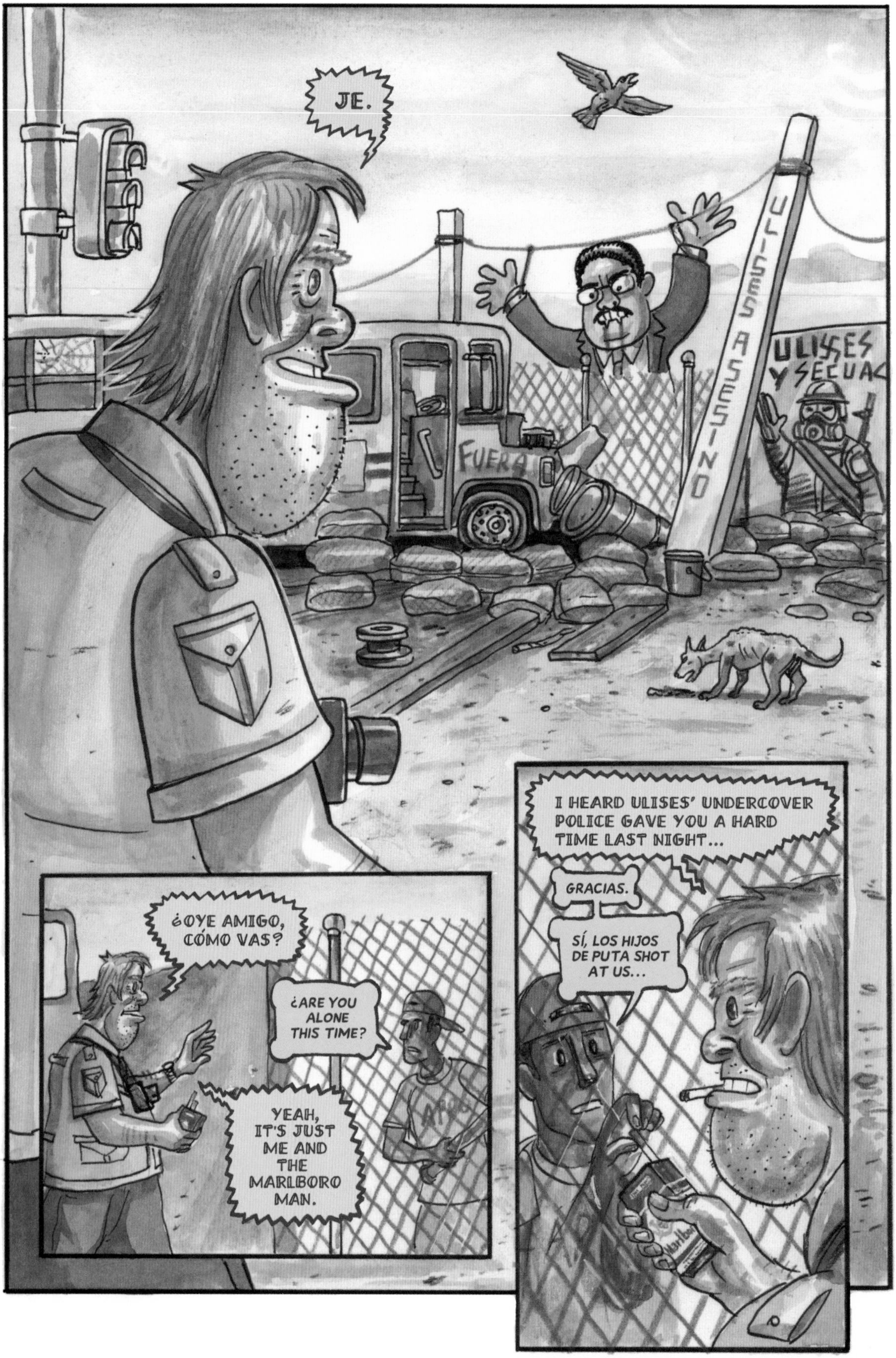
JE.
ULISES ASESINO
ULISSES Y SECUAC
FUERA
¿OYE AMIGO, CÓMO VAS?
¿ARE YOU ALONE THIS TIME?
YEAH, IT'S JUST ME AND THE MARLBORO MAN.
I HEARD ULISES' UNDERCOVER POLICE GAVE YOU A HARD TIME LAST NIGHT...
GRACIAS.
SÍ, LOS HIJOS DE PUTA SHOT AT US...

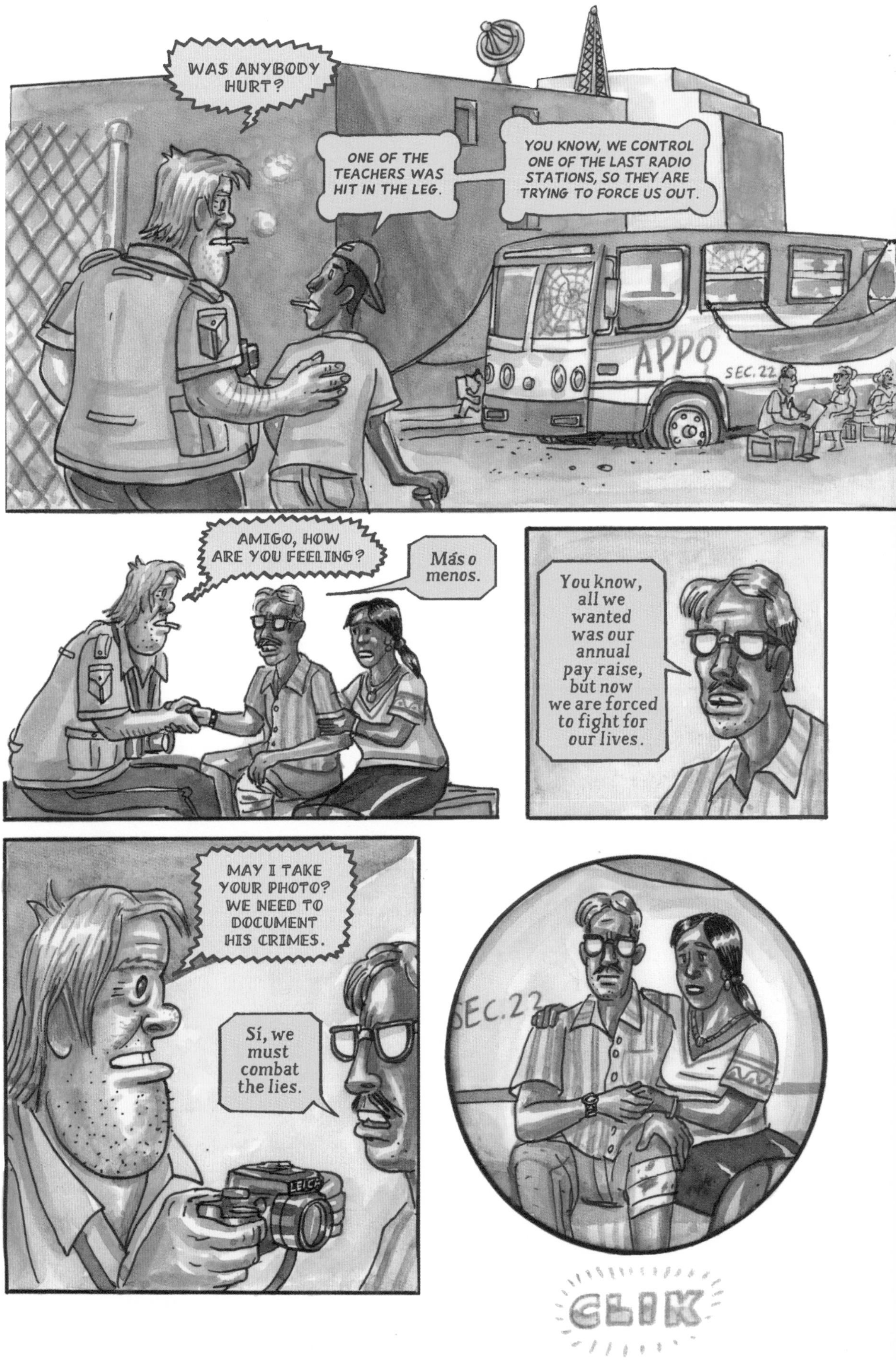

WAS ANYBODY HURT?
ONE OF THE TEACHERS WAS HIT IN THE LEG.
YOU KNOW, WE CONTROL ONE OF THE LAST RADIO STATIONS, SO THEY ARE TRYING TO FORCE US OUT.
APPO
SEC. 22
AMIGO, HOW ARE YOU FEELING?
Más o menos.
You know, all we wanted was our annual pay raise, but now we are forced to fight for our lives.
MAY I TAKE YOUR PHOTO? WE NEED TO DOCUMENT HIS CRIMES.
Sí, we must combat the lies.
LEICA
SEC. 22
CLIK

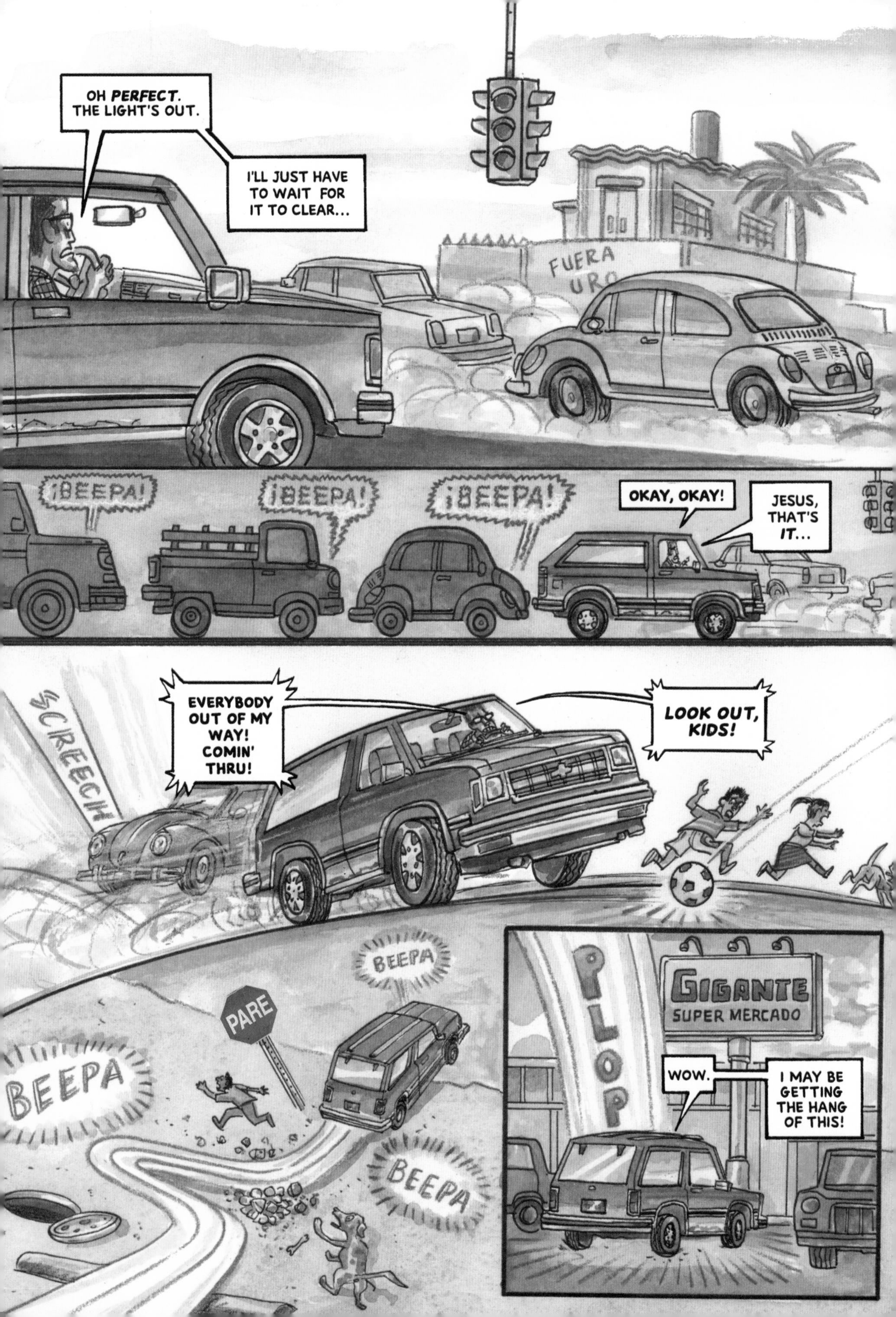

OH PERFECT. THE LIGHT'S OUT.
I'LL JUST HAVE TO WAIT FOR IT TO CLEAR...
FUERA URO
¡BEEPA!
¡BEEPA!
¡BEEPA!
OKAY, OKAY!
JESUS, THAT'S IT...
SCREECH
EVERYBODY OUT OF MY WAY! COMIN' THRU!
LOOK OUT, KIDS!
BEEPA
PARE
BEEPA
BEEPA
PLOP
GIGANTE SUPER MERCADO
WOW.
I MAY BE GETTING THE HANG OF THIS!

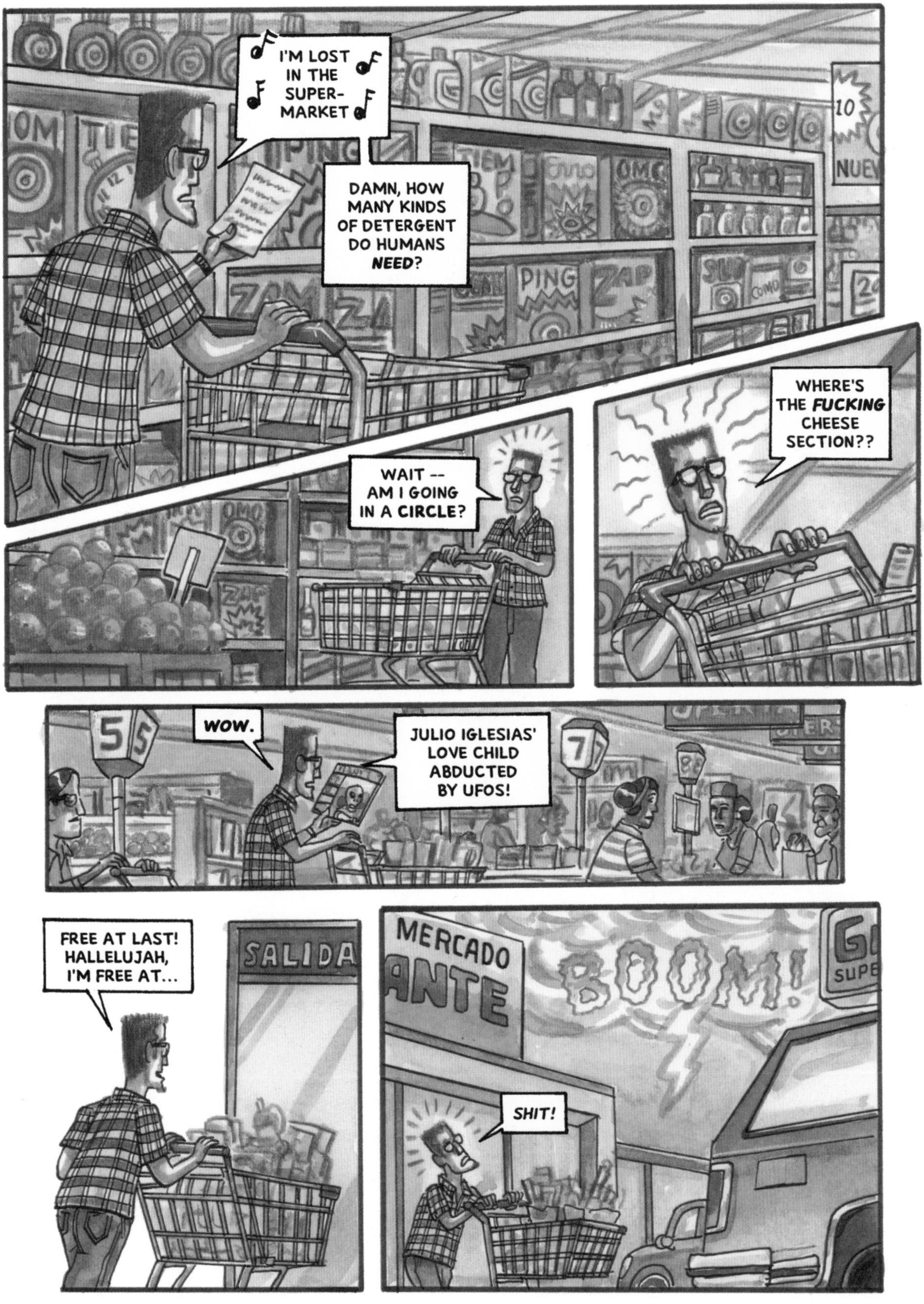
I'M LOST IN THE SUPER-MARKET
DAMN, HOW MANY KINDS OF DETERGENT DO HUMANS *NEED*?
WAIT -- AM I GOING IN A CIRCLE?
WHERE'S THE *FUCKING* CHEESE SECTION??
WOW.
JULIO IGLESIAS' LOVE CHILD ABDUCTED BY UFOS!
FREE AT LAST! HALLELUJAH, I'M FREE AT...
SALIDA
MERCADO
ANTE
BOOM!
SHIT!

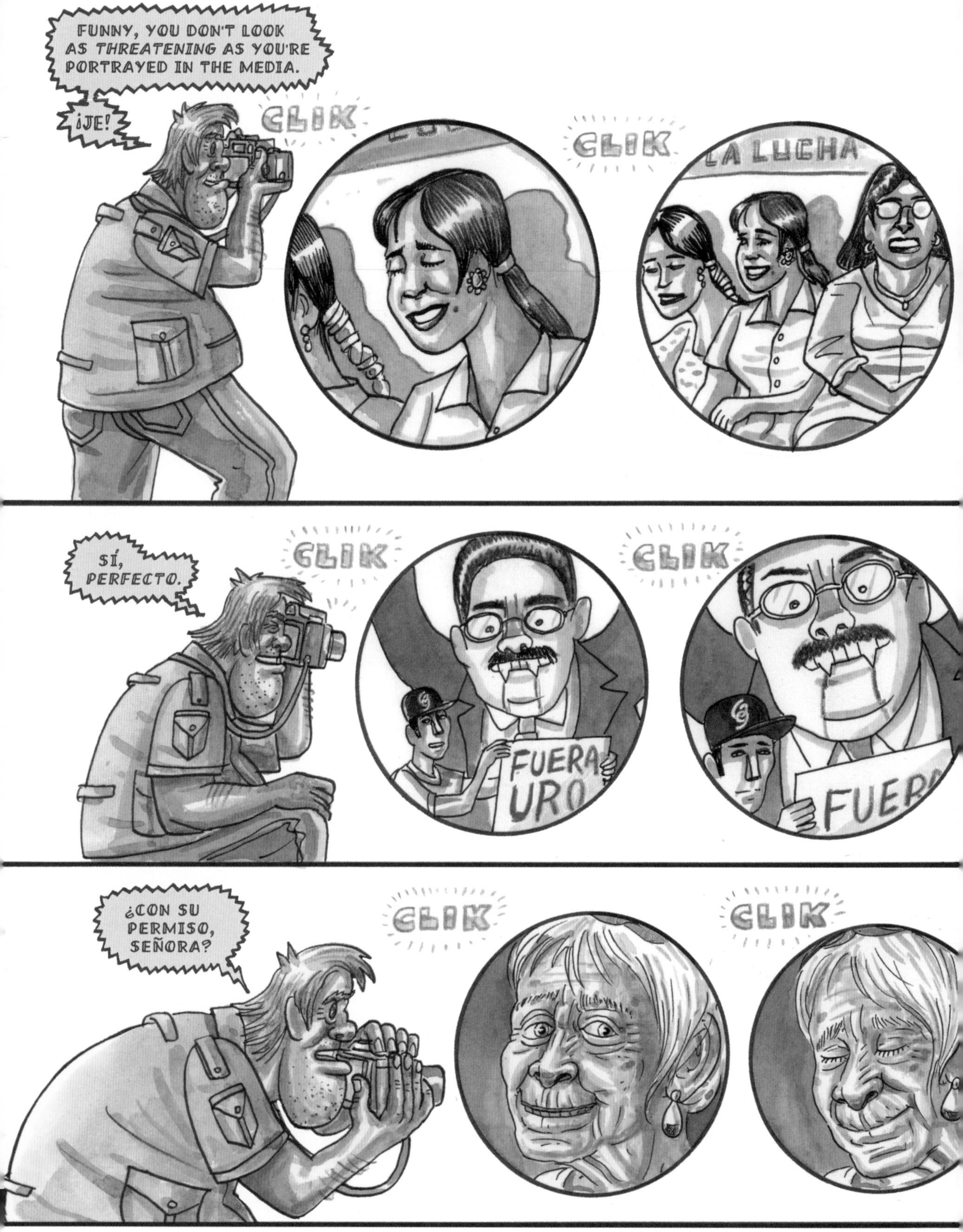

FUNNY, YOU DON'T LOOK AS *THREATENING* AS YOU'RE PORTRAYED IN THE MEDIA.
¡JE!
CLIK
CLIK
LA LUCHA
SÍ, PERFECTO.
CLIK
FUERA URO
CLIK
FUERA
¿CON SU PERMISO, SEÑORA?
CLIK
CLIK

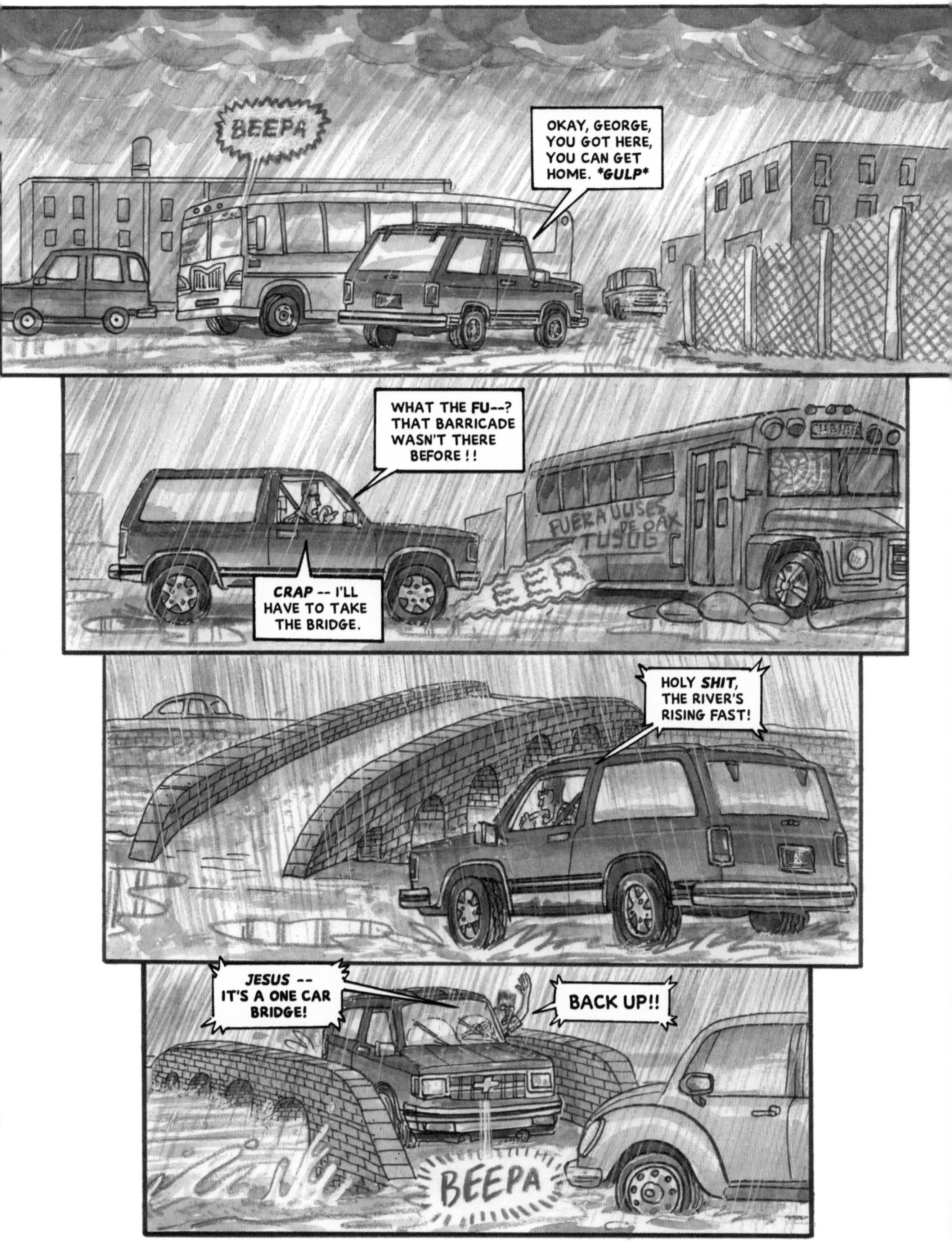
BEEPA
OKAY, GEORGE, YOU GOT HERE, YOU CAN GET HOME. *GULP*
WHAT THE FU--? THAT BARRICADE WASN'T THERE BEFORE!!
CRAP -- I'LL HAVE TO TAKE THE BRIDGE.
HOLY SHIT, THE RIVER'S RISING FAST!
JESUS -- IT'S A ONE CAR BRIDGE!
BACK UP!!
BEEPA

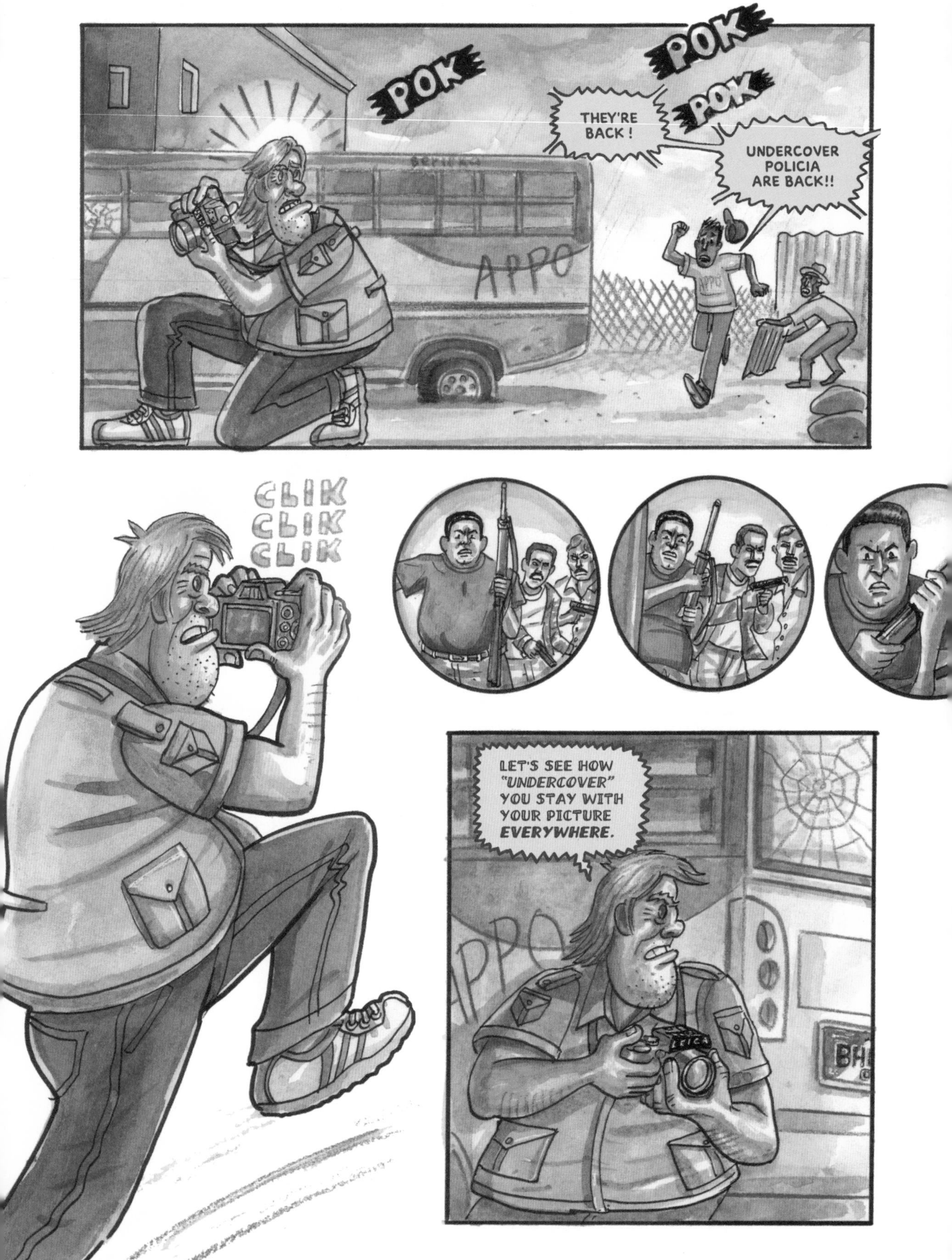
POK
POK
POK
THEY'RE BACK !
UNDERCOVER POLICIA ARE BACK!!
APPO
CLIK CLIK CLIK
LET'S SEE HOW "UNDERCOVER" YOU STAY WITH YOUR PICTURE EVERYWHERE.

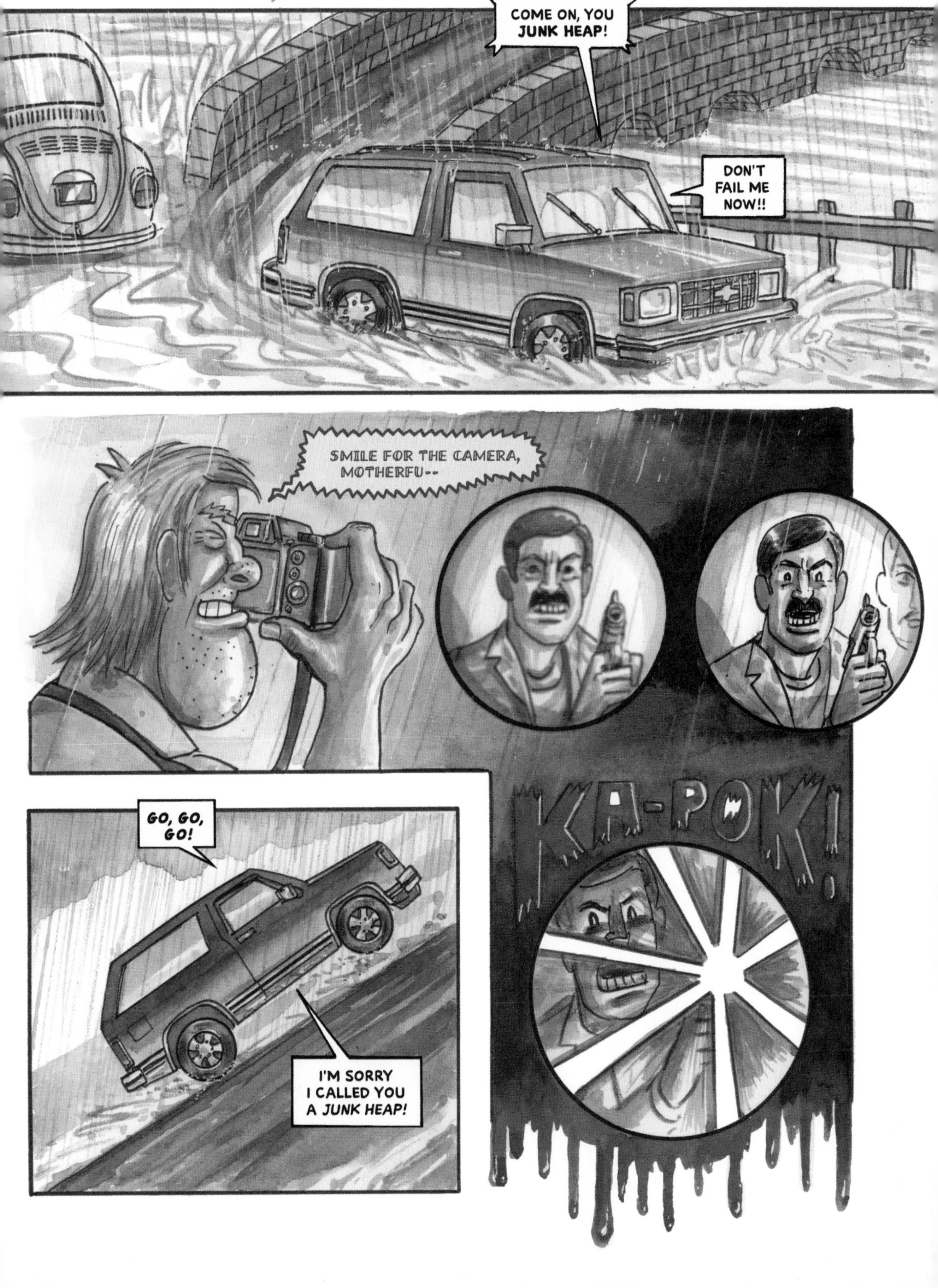

COME ON, YOU JUNK HEAP!
DON'T FAIL ME NOW!!
SMILE FOR THE CAMERA, MOTHERFU--
GO, GO, GO!
I'M SORRY I CALLED YOU A JUNK HEAP!
KA-POK!

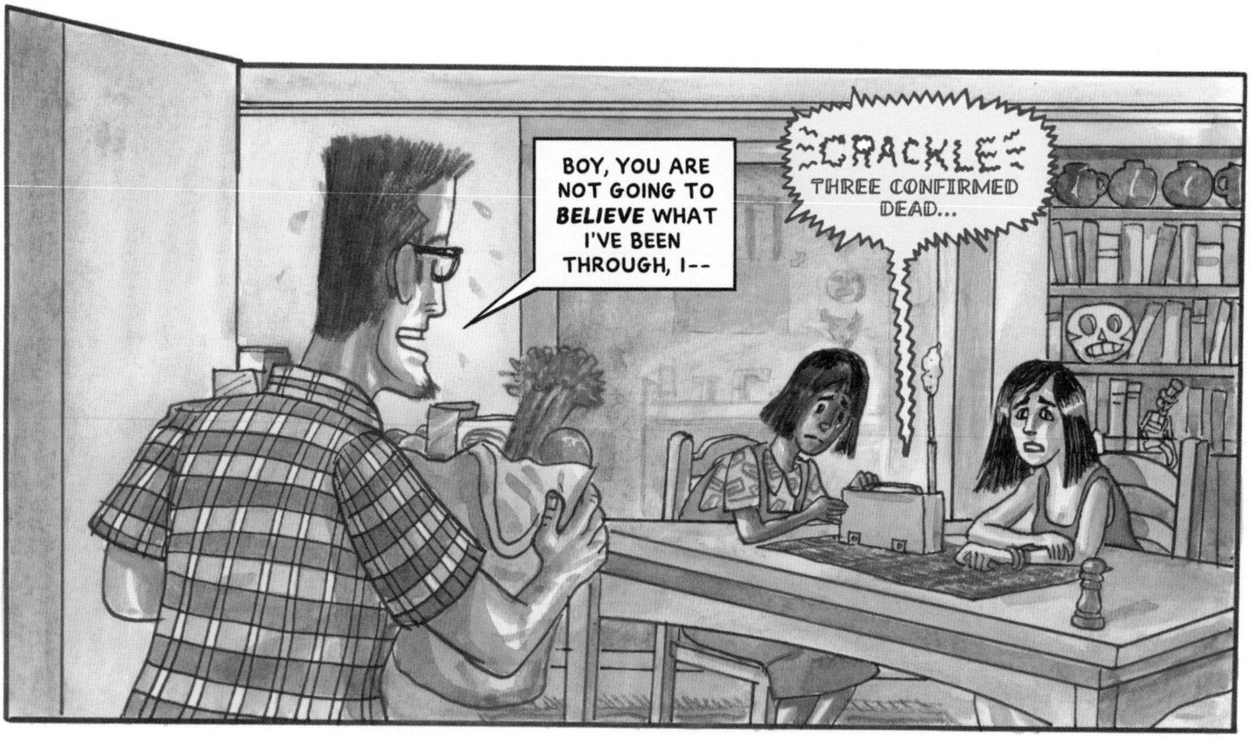
BOY, YOU ARE NOT GOING TO **BELIEVE** WHAT I'VE BEEN THROUGH, I--
CRACKLE THREE CONFIRMED DEAD...

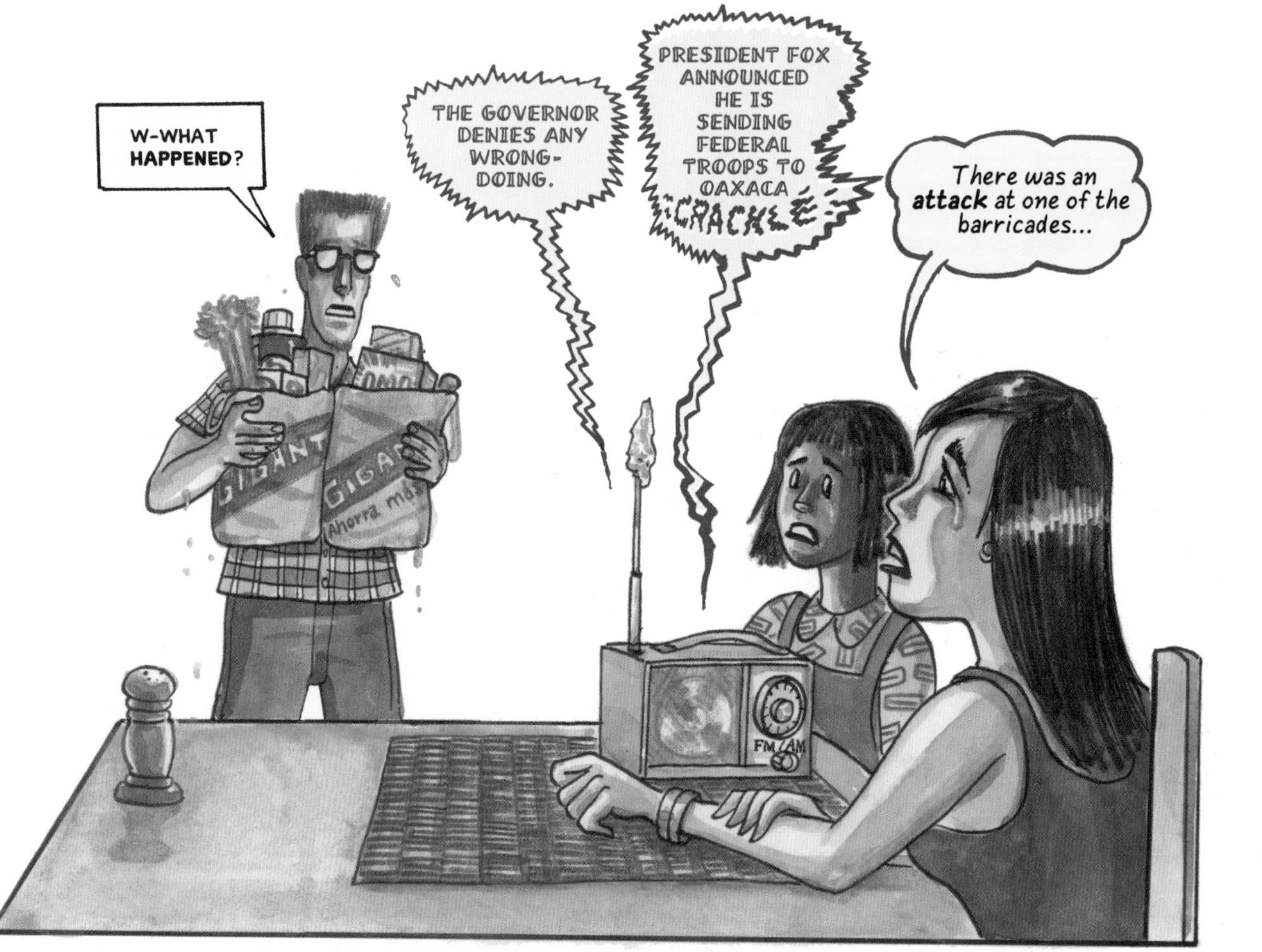
W-WHAT **HAPPENED**?
THE GOVERNOR DENIES ANY WRONG-DOING.
PRESIDENT FOX ANNOUNCED HE IS SENDING FEDERAL TROOPS TO OAXACA CRACKLE
There was an **attack** at one of the barricades...
GIGANT
GIGANT
Ahorra más
FM/AM

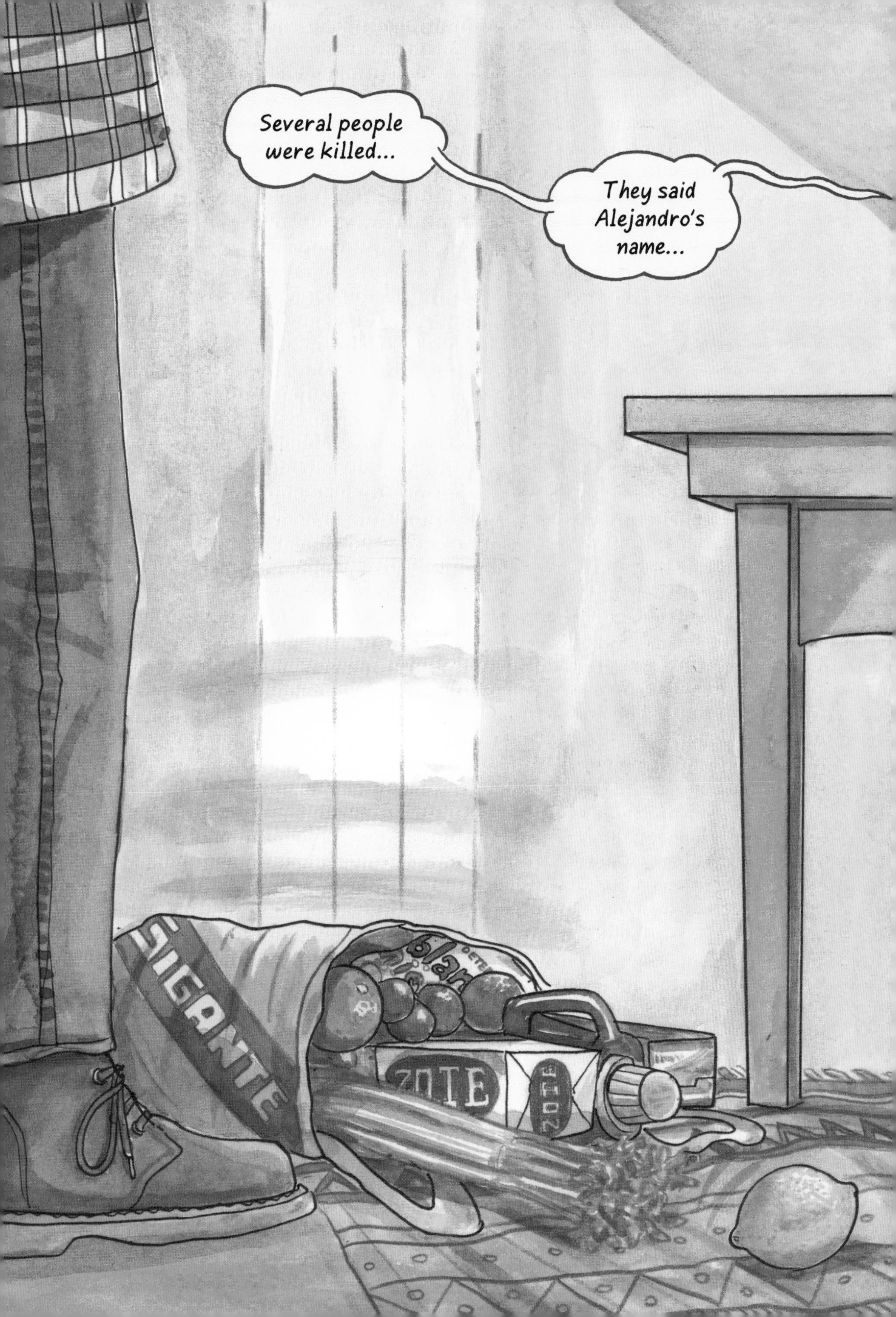
Several people were killed...
They said Alejandro's name...
ZOTE

Monterrey

Gulf
of
Mexico

Zacatecas

Guanajuato

San Miguel
de Allende

Morelia

☆ Mexico City   Veracruz

Puebla

Taxco

PACIFIC
OCEAN

Acapulco   Oaxaca

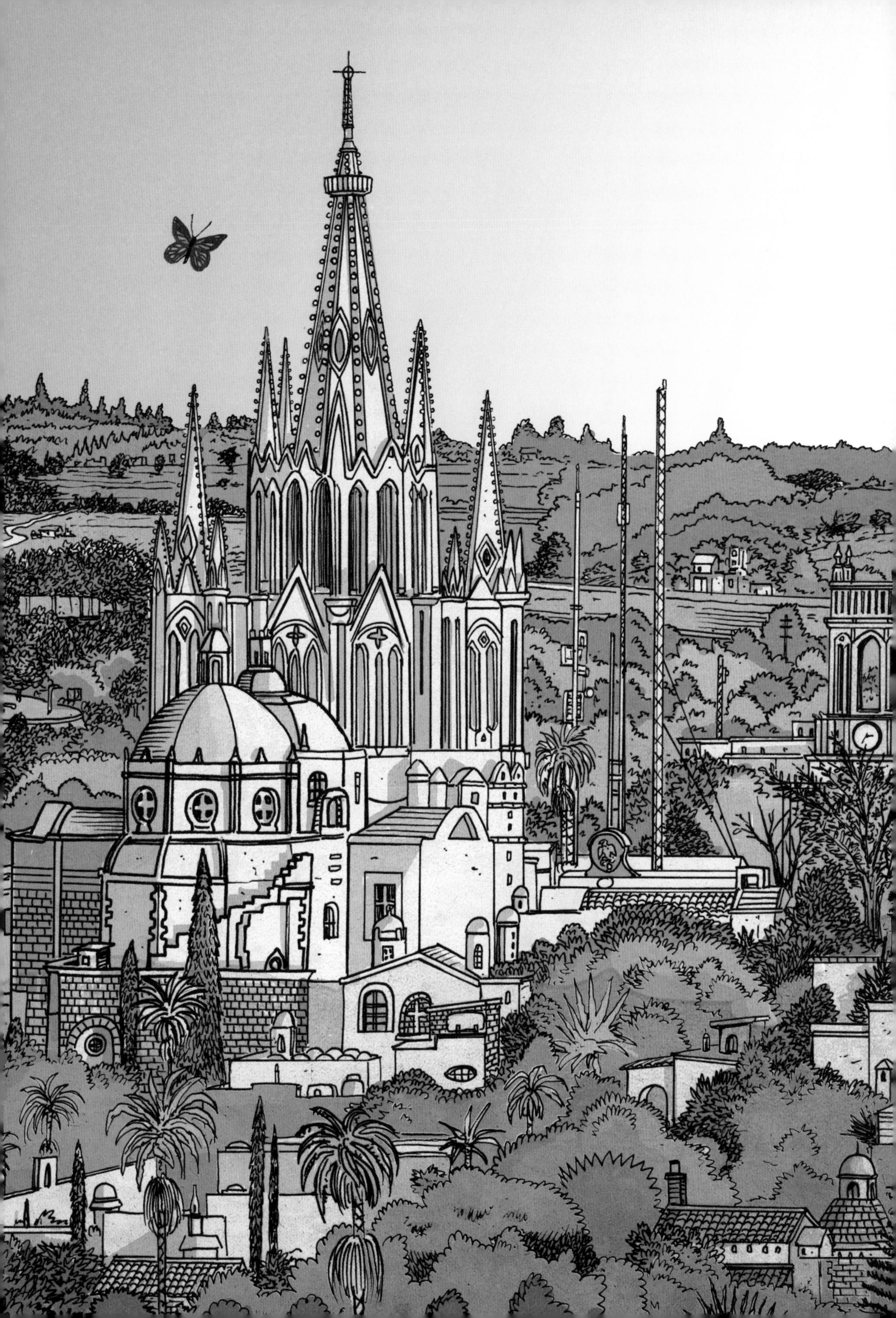

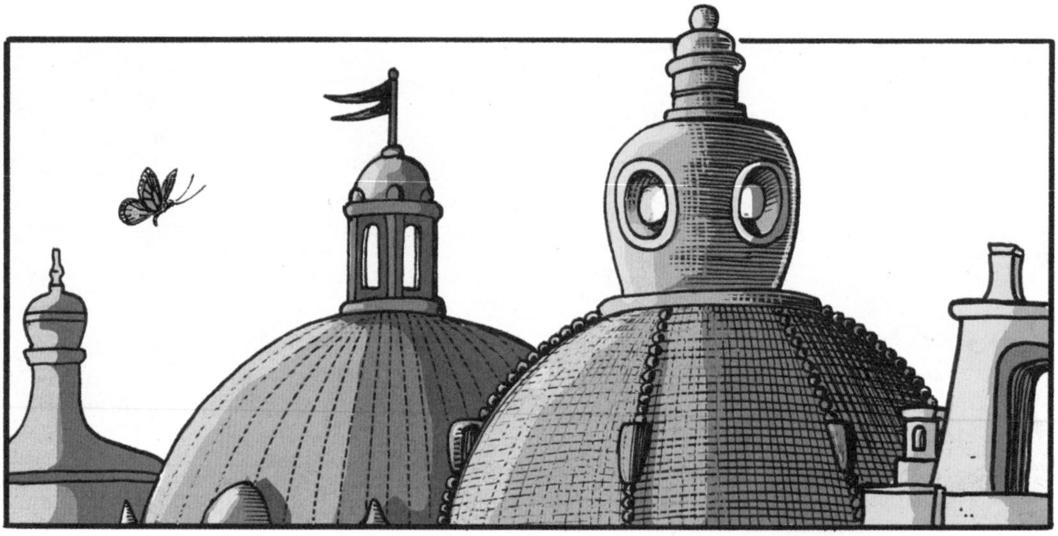

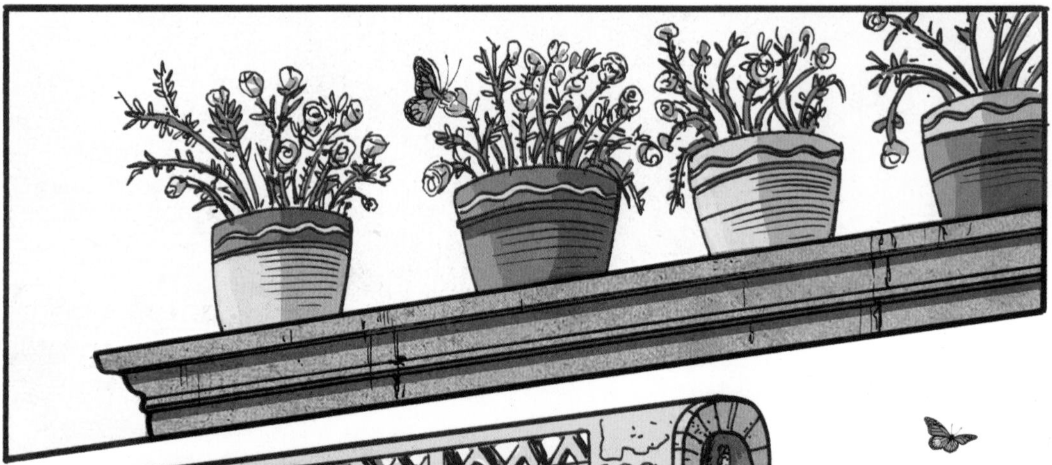

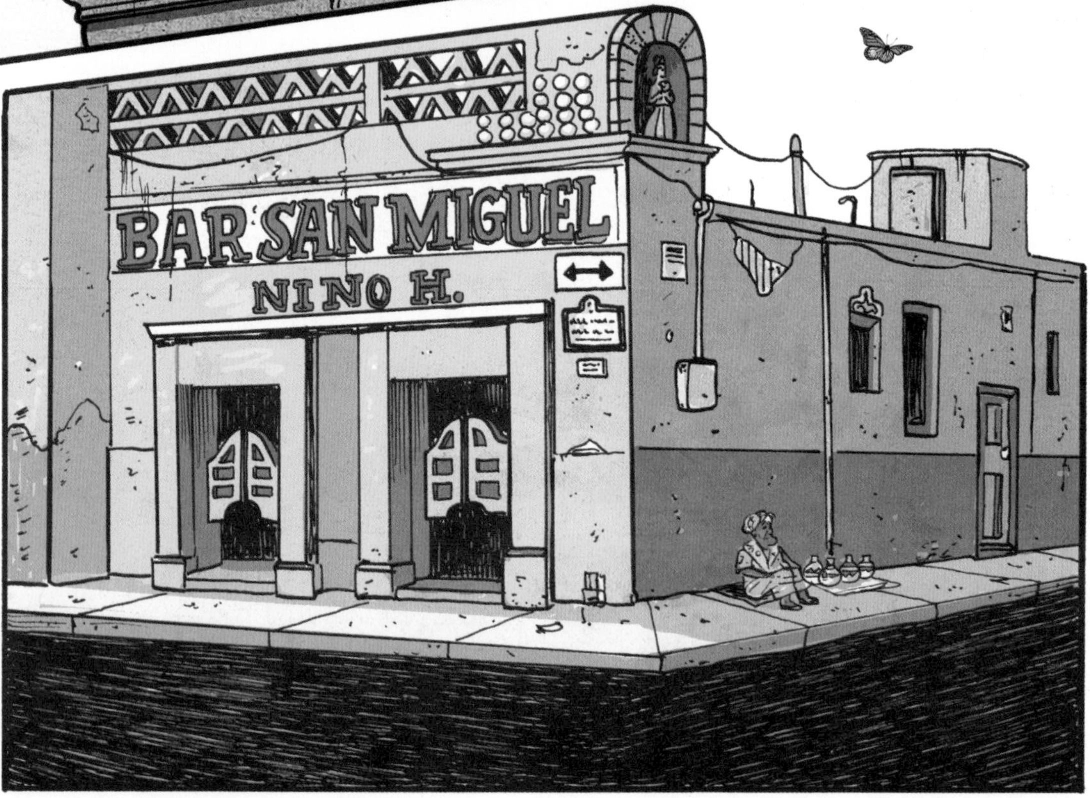
BAR SAN MIGUEL
NINO H.

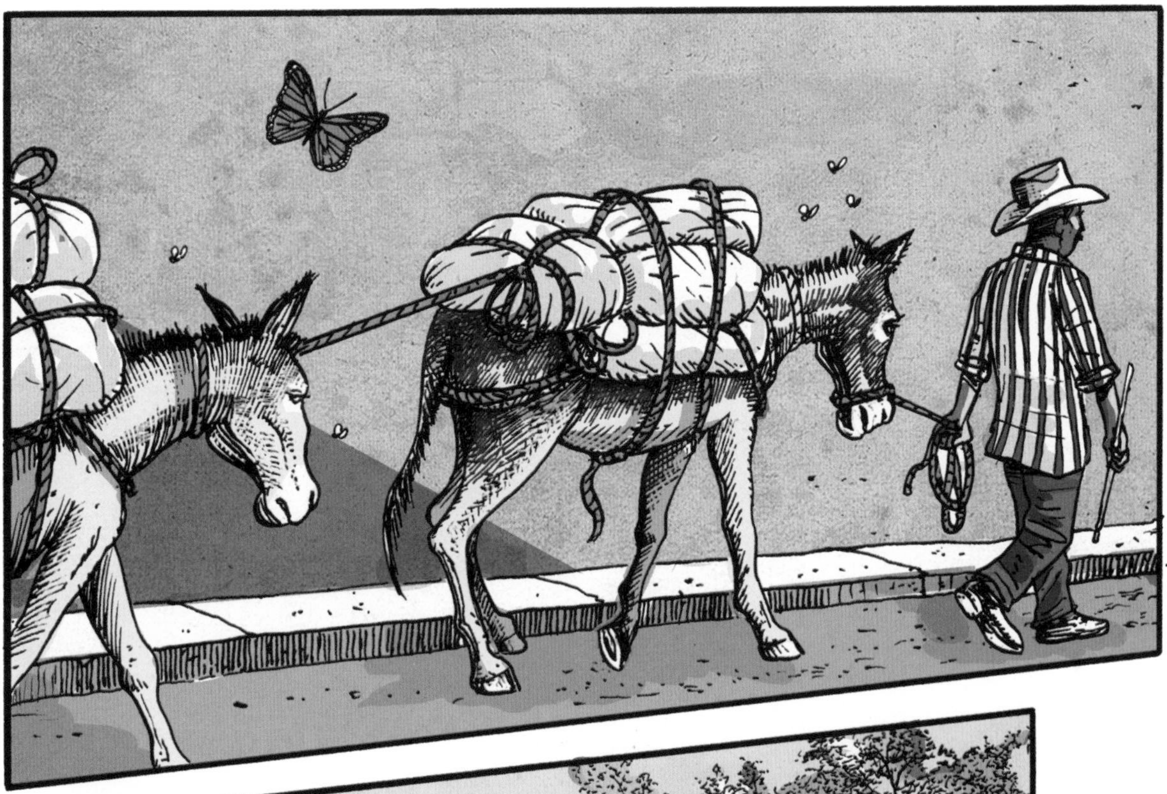
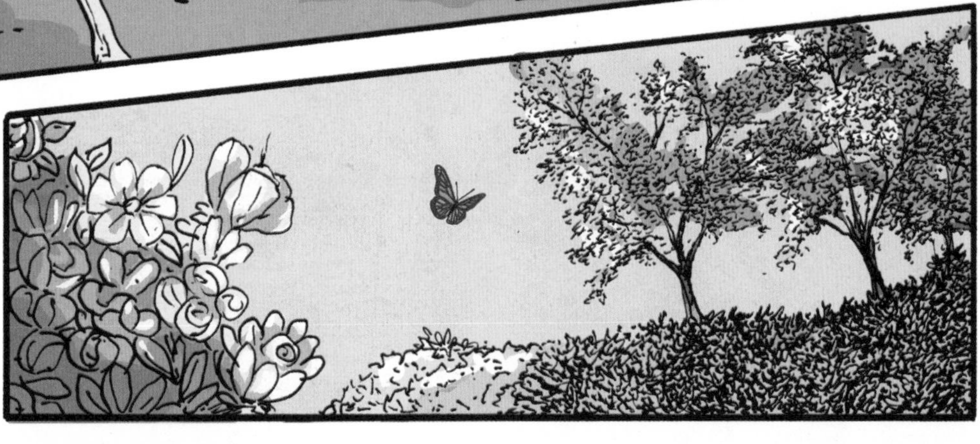
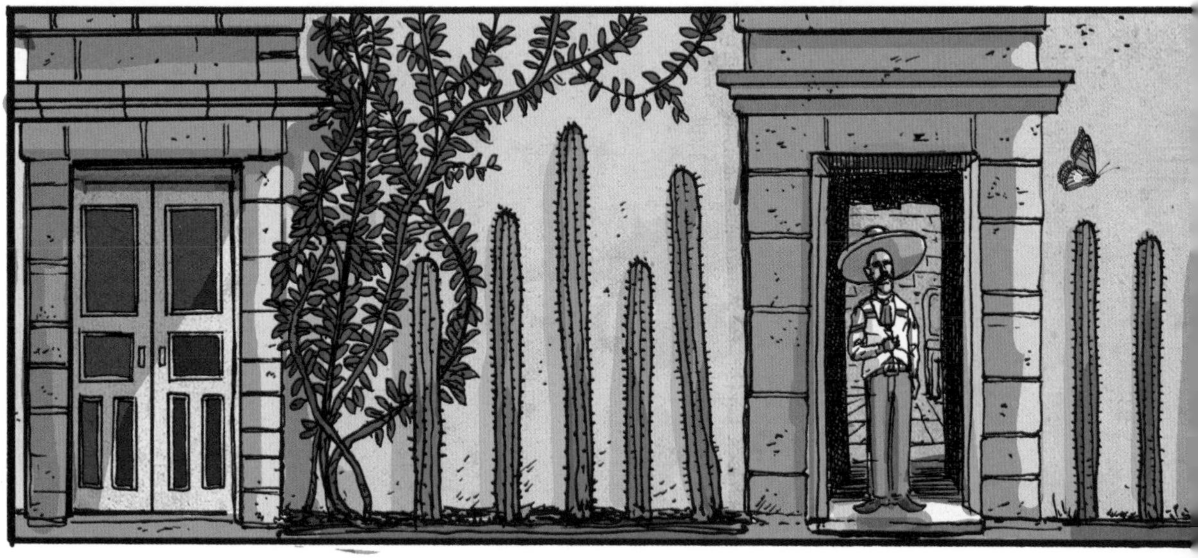

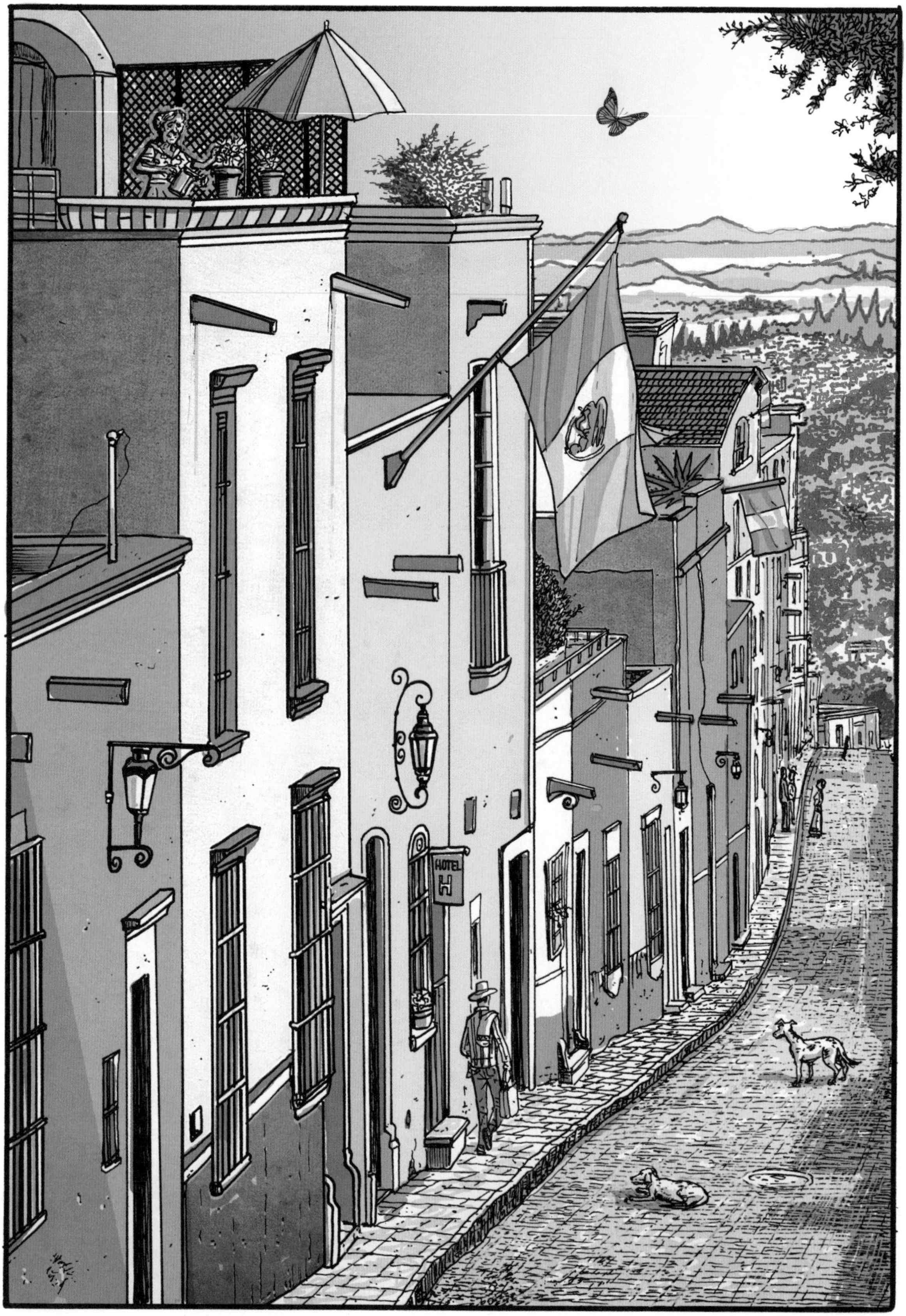
HOTEL
H

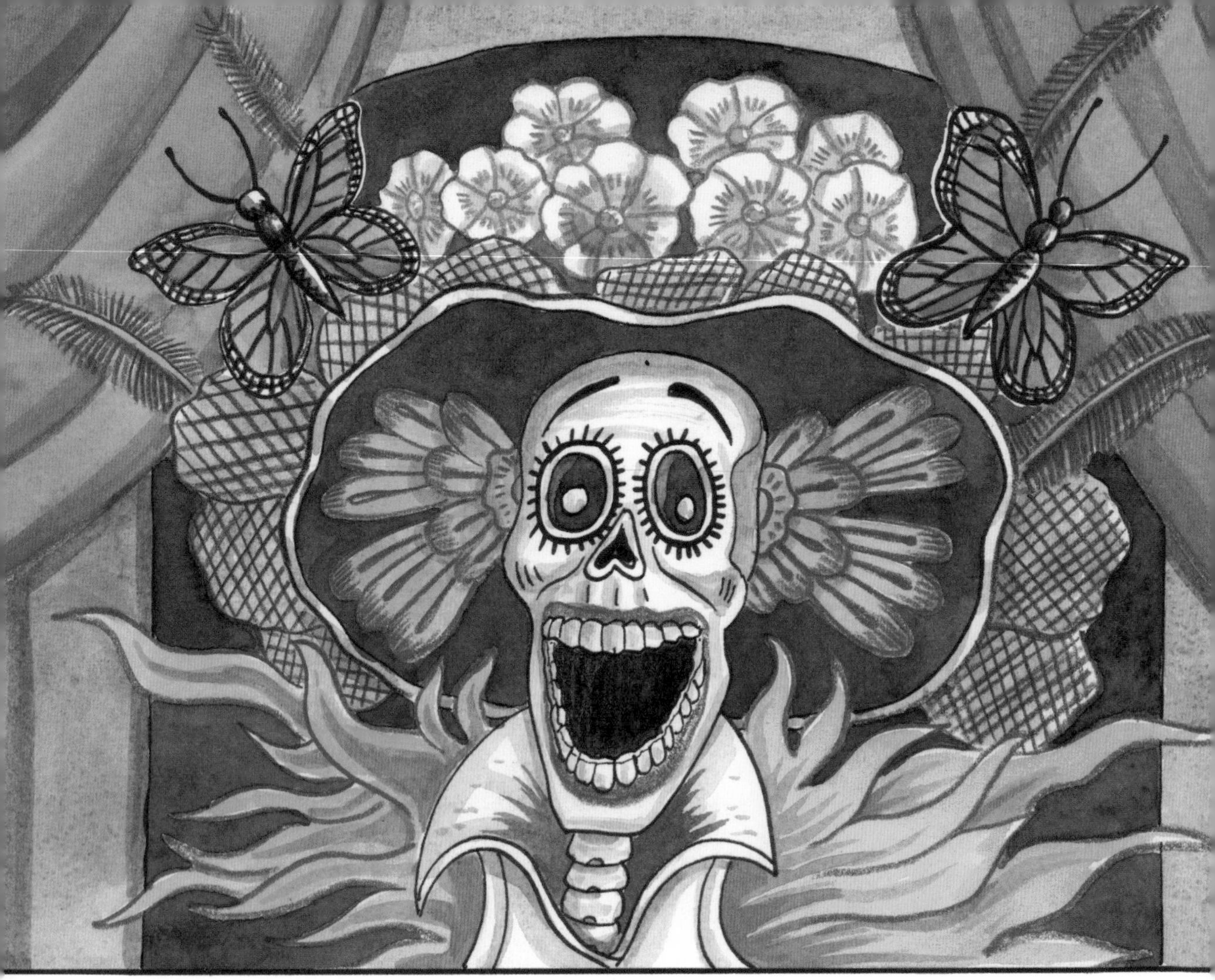

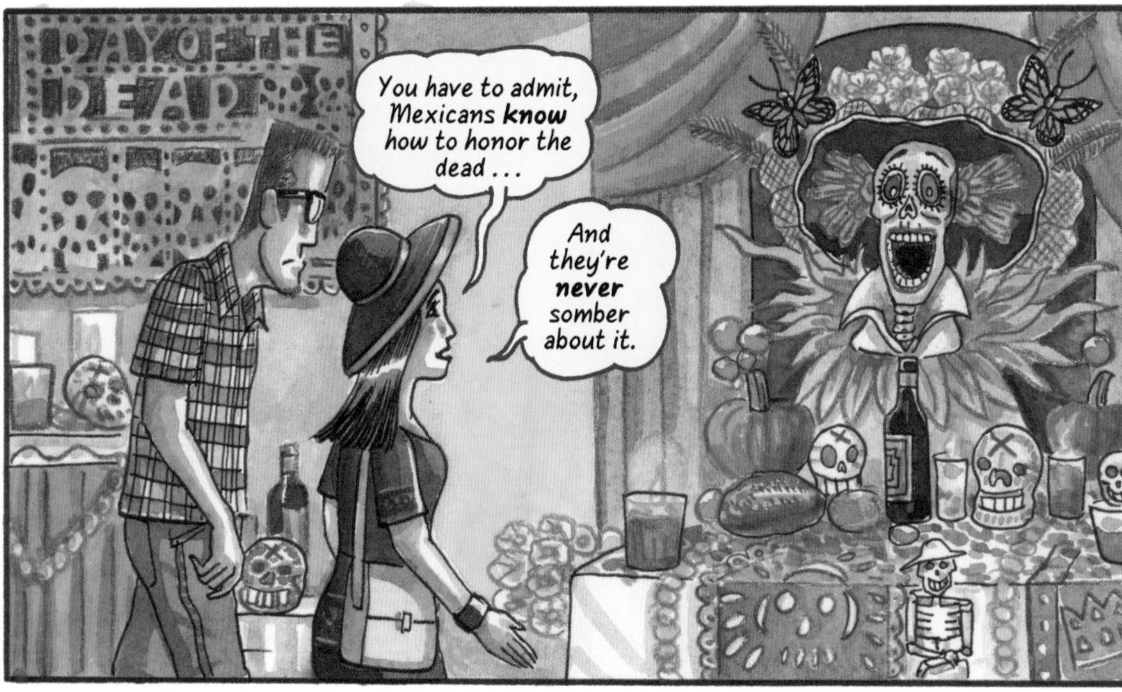

DAY OF THE DEAD
You have to admit, Mexicans **know** how to honor the dead . . .
And they're **never** somber about it.

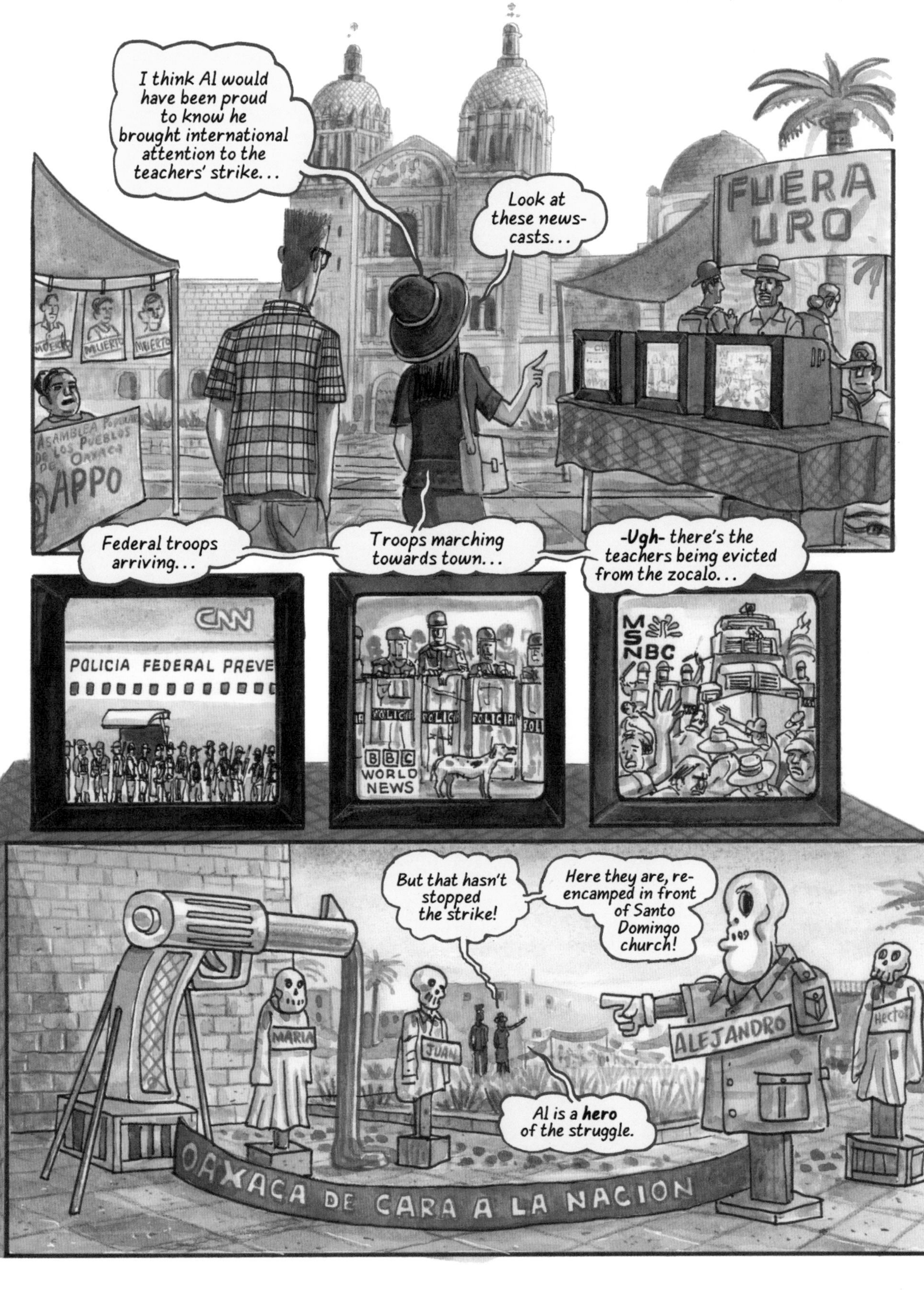
I think Al would have been proud to know he brought international attention to the teachers' strike...
Look at these news-casts...
FUERA URO
ASAMBLEA POPULAR DE LOS PUEBLOS DE OAXACA
APPO
Federal troops arriving...
Troops marching towards town...
-**Ugh**- there's the teachers being evicted from the zocalo...
CNN
POLICIA FEDERAL PREVE
BBC WORLD NEWS
MSNBC
But that hasn't stopped the strike!
Here they are, re-encamped in front of Santo Domingo church!
Al is a **hero** of the struggle.
MARIA
JUAN
ALEJANDRO
HECTOR
OAXACA DE CARA A LA NACION

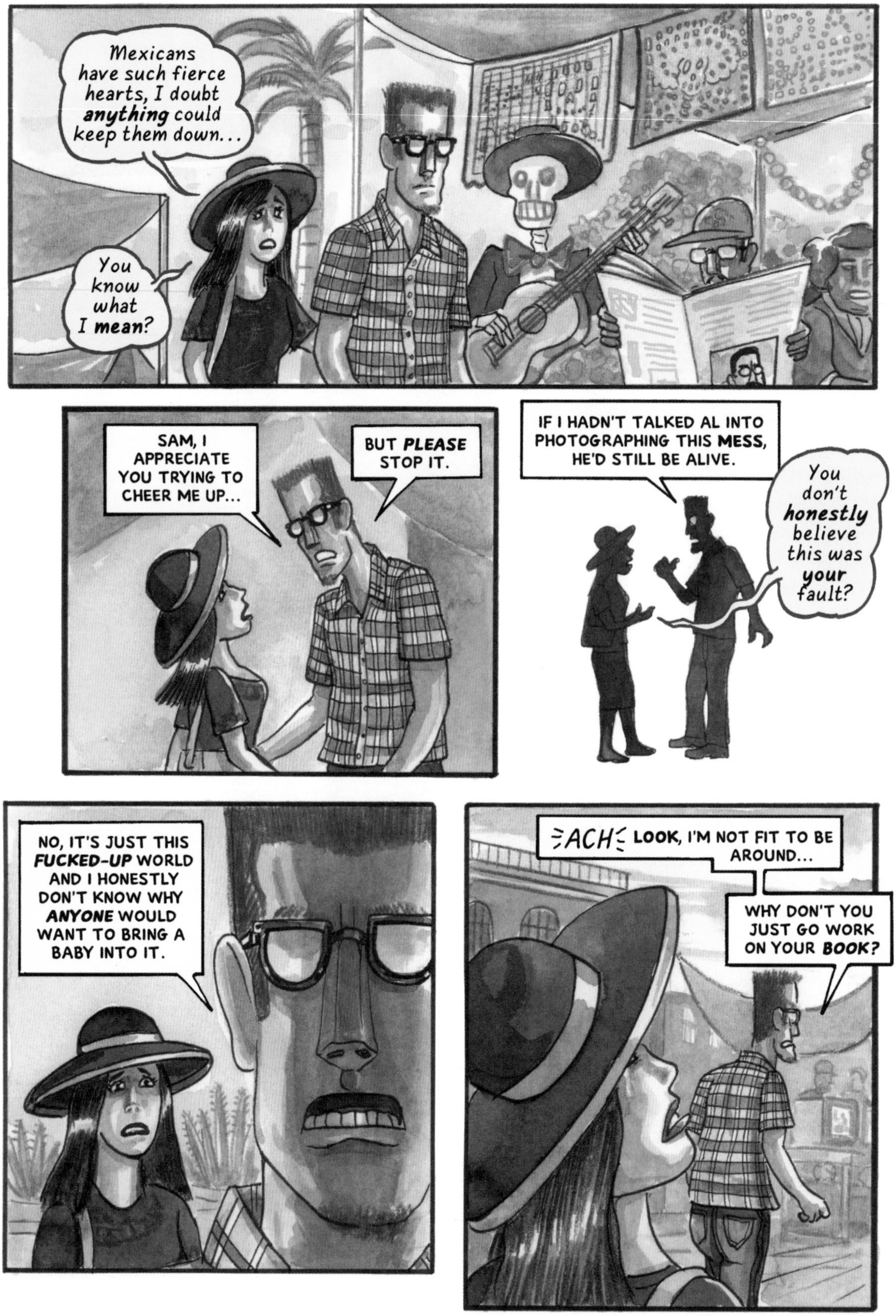
Mexicans have such fierce hearts, I doubt **anything** could keep them down...
You know what I **mean**?
SAM, I APPRECIATE YOU TRYING TO CHEER ME UP...
BUT ***PLEASE*** STOP IT.
IF I HADN'T TALKED AL INTO PHOTOGRAPHING THIS **MESS**, HE'D STILL BE ALIVE.
You don't **honestly** believe this was **your** fault?
NO, IT'S JUST THIS ***FUCKED-UP*** WORLD AND I HONESTLY DON'T KNOW WHY ***ANYONE*** WOULD WANT TO BRING A BABY INTO IT.
ACH **LOOK**, I'M NOT FIT TO BE AROUND...
WHY DON'T YOU JUST GO WORK ON YOUR ***BOOK***?

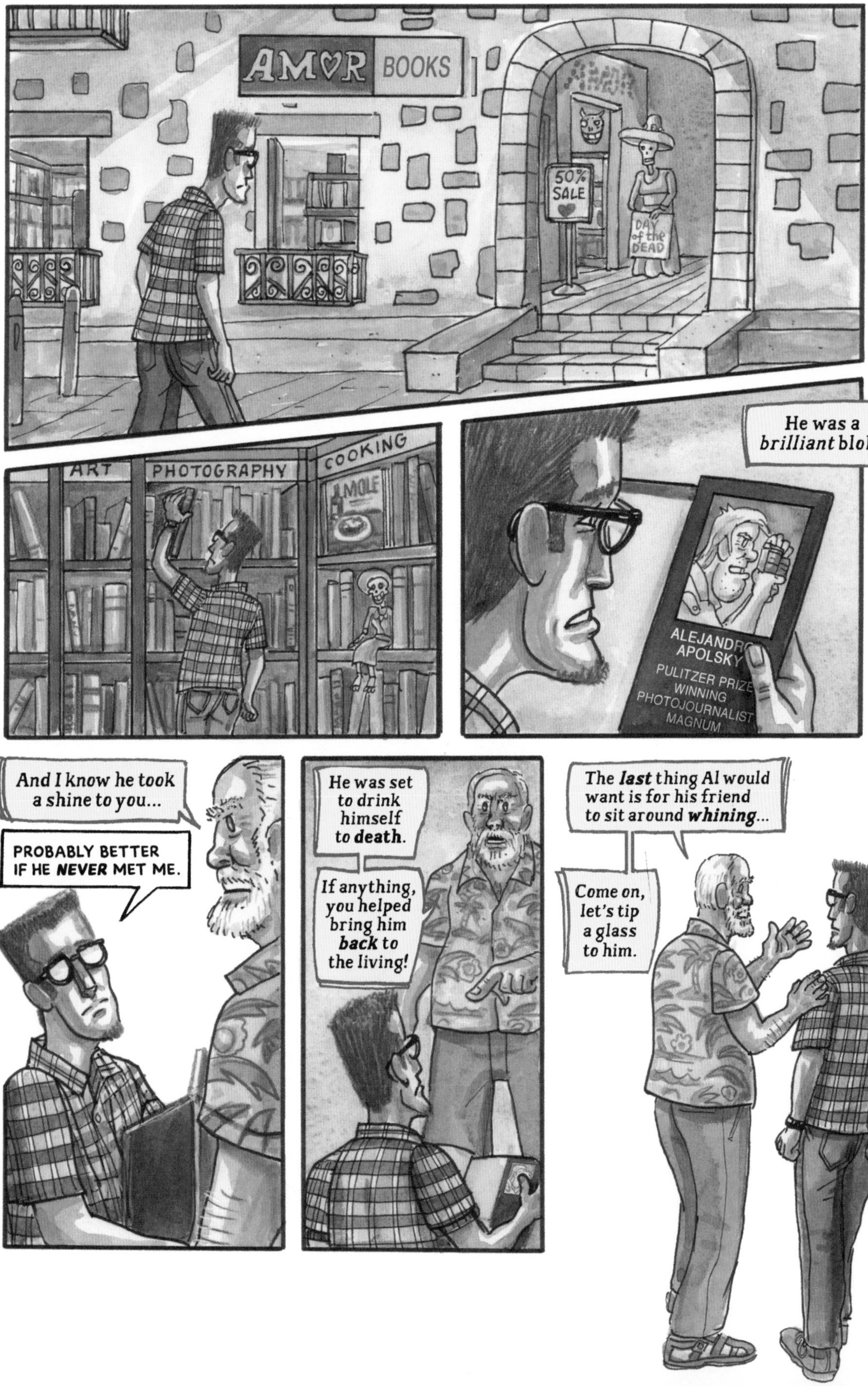

AMOR BOOKS
50% SALE
DAY of the DEAD
ART
PHOTOGRAPHY
COOKING
MOLE
He was a *brilliant* bloke...
ALEJANDRO APOLSKY
PULITZER PRIZE WINNING PHOTOJOURNALIST
MAGNUM
And I know he took a shine to you...
PROBABLY BETTER IF HE ***NEVER*** MET ME.
He was set to drink himself to **death**.
If anything, you helped bring him ***back*** to the living!
The ***last*** thing Al would want is for his friend to sit around ***whining***...
Come on, let's tip a glass to him.

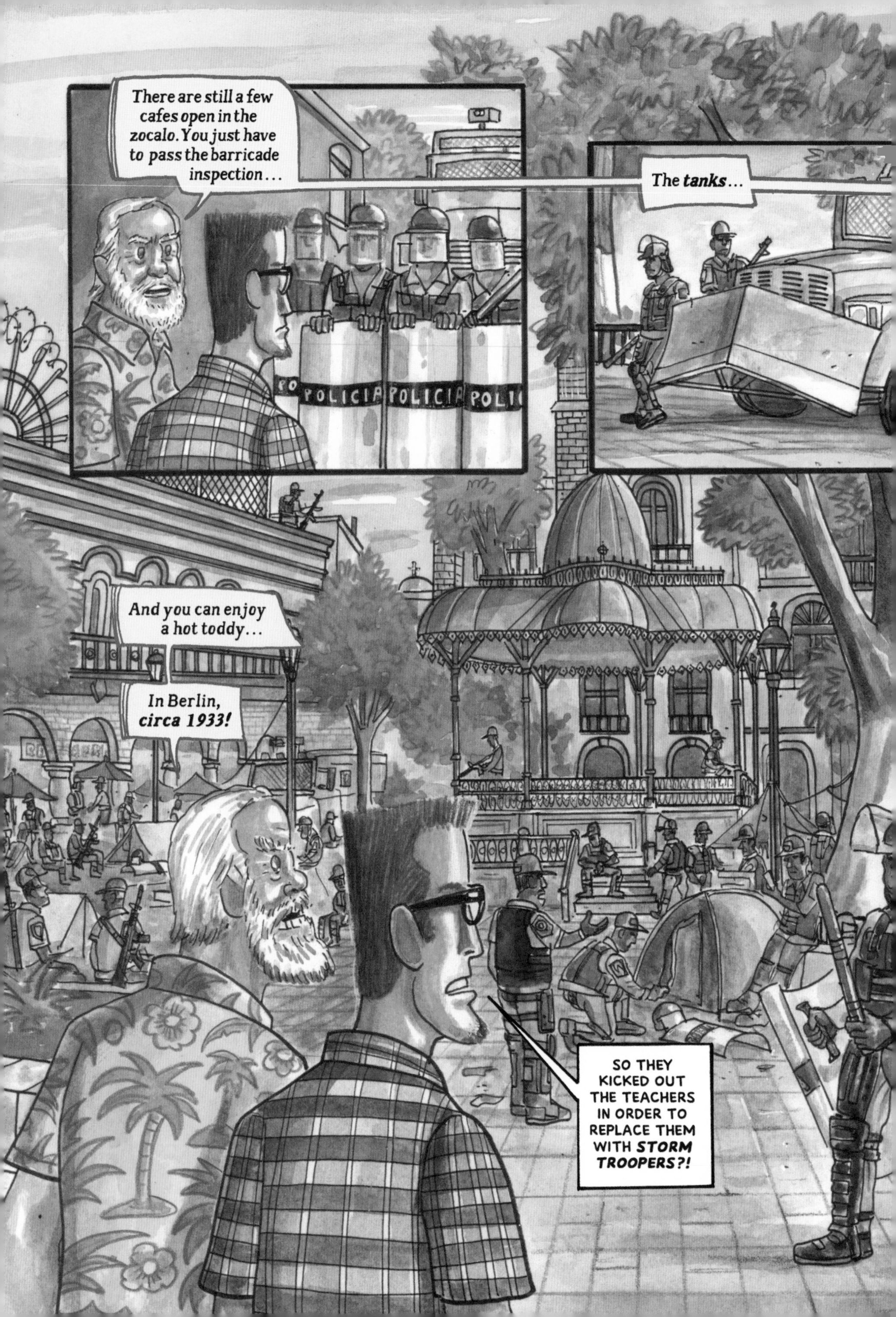
There are still a few cafes open in the zocalo. You just have to pass the barricade inspection...
POLICIA POLICIA POLI
The tanks...
And you can enjoy a hot toddy...
In Berlin, circa 1933!
SO THEY KICKED OUT THE TEACHERS IN ORDER TO REPLACE THEM WITH STORM TROOPERS?!

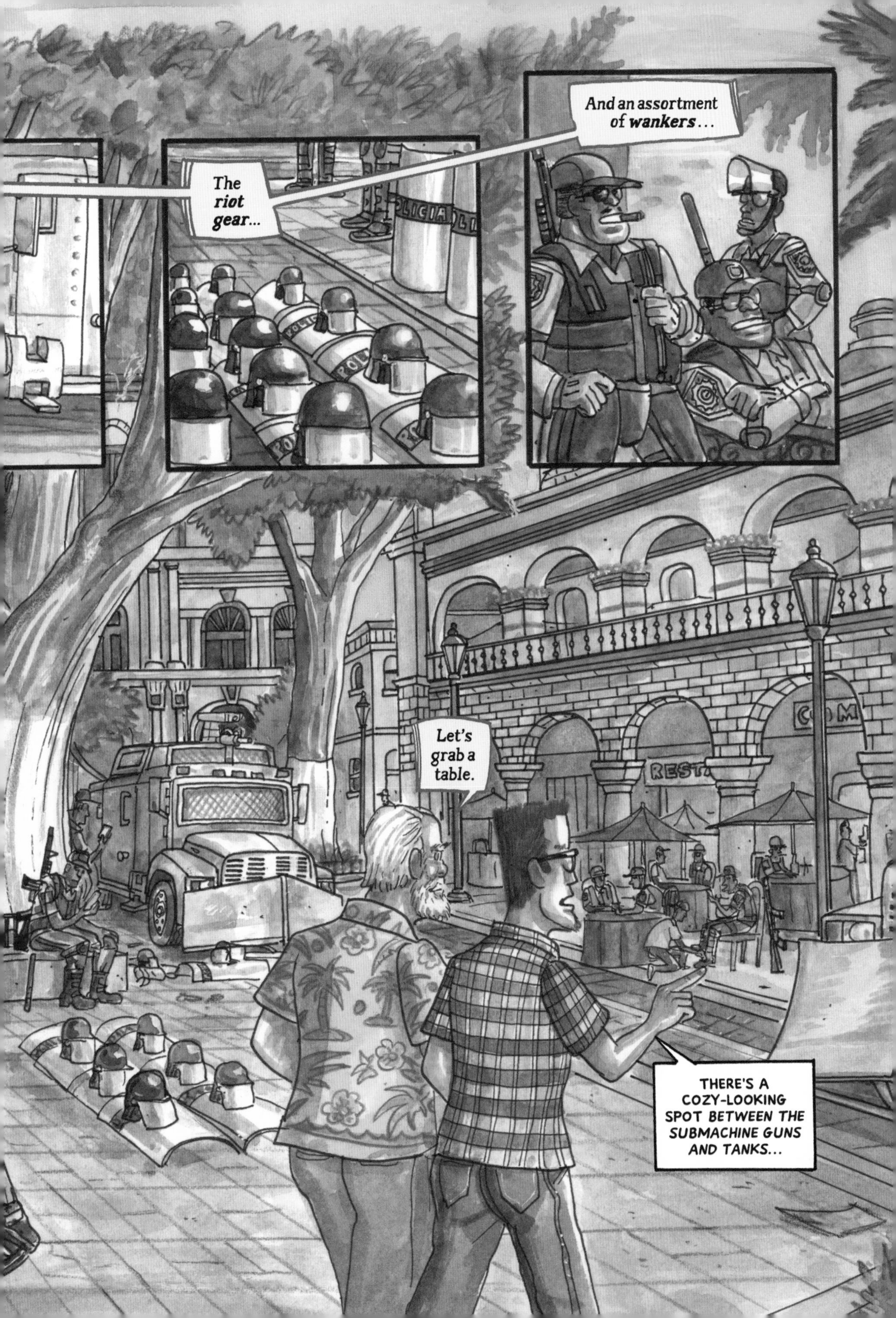
The *riot* *gear*...
And an assortment of ***wankers***...
POLICIA
Let's grab a table.
RESTA
COM
THERE'S A COZY-LOOKING SPOT BETWEEN THE SUBMACHINE GUNS AND TANKS...

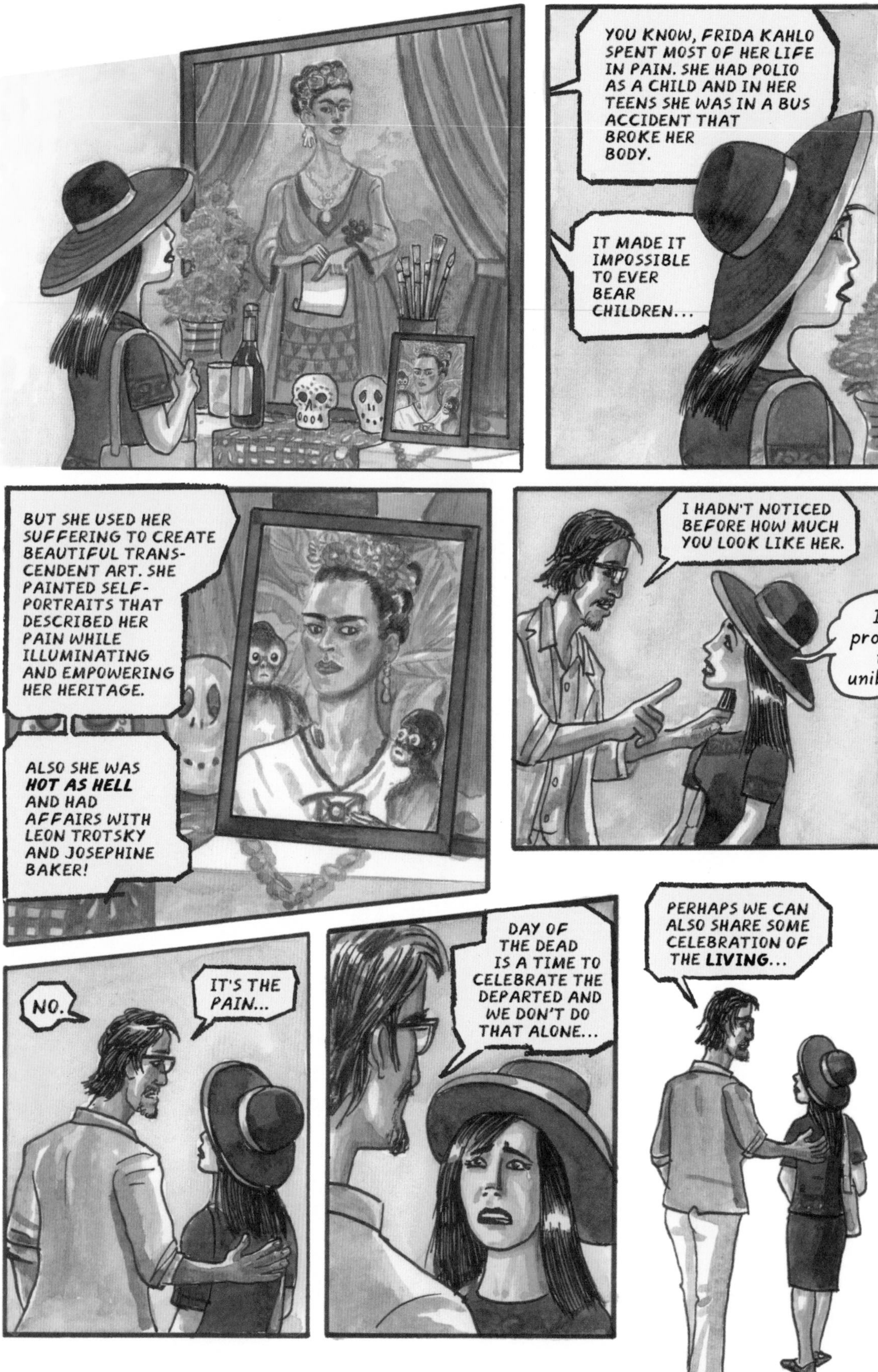

YOU KNOW, FRIDA KAHLO SPENT MOST OF HER LIFE IN PAIN. SHE HAD POLIO AS A CHILD AND IN HER TEENS SHE WAS IN A BUS ACCIDENT THAT BROKE HER BODY.
IT MADE IT IMPOSSIBLE TO EVER BEAR CHILDREN...
BUT SHE USED HER SUFFERING TO CREATE BEAUTIFUL TRANSCENDENT ART. SHE PAINTED SELF-PORTRAITS THAT DESCRIBED HER PAIN WHILE ILLUMINATING AND EMPOWERING HER HERITAGE.
ALSO SHE WAS **HOT AS HELL** AND HAD AFFAIRS WITH LEON TROTSKY AND JOSEPHINE BAKER!
I HADN'T NOTICED BEFORE HOW MUCH YOU LOOK LIKE HER.
It's probably the unibrow...
NO.
IT'S THE PAIN...
DAY OF THE DEAD IS A TIME TO CELEBRATE THE DEPARTED AND WE DON'T DO THAT ALONE...
PERHAPS WE CAN ALSO SHARE SOME CELEBRATION OF THE **LIVING**...

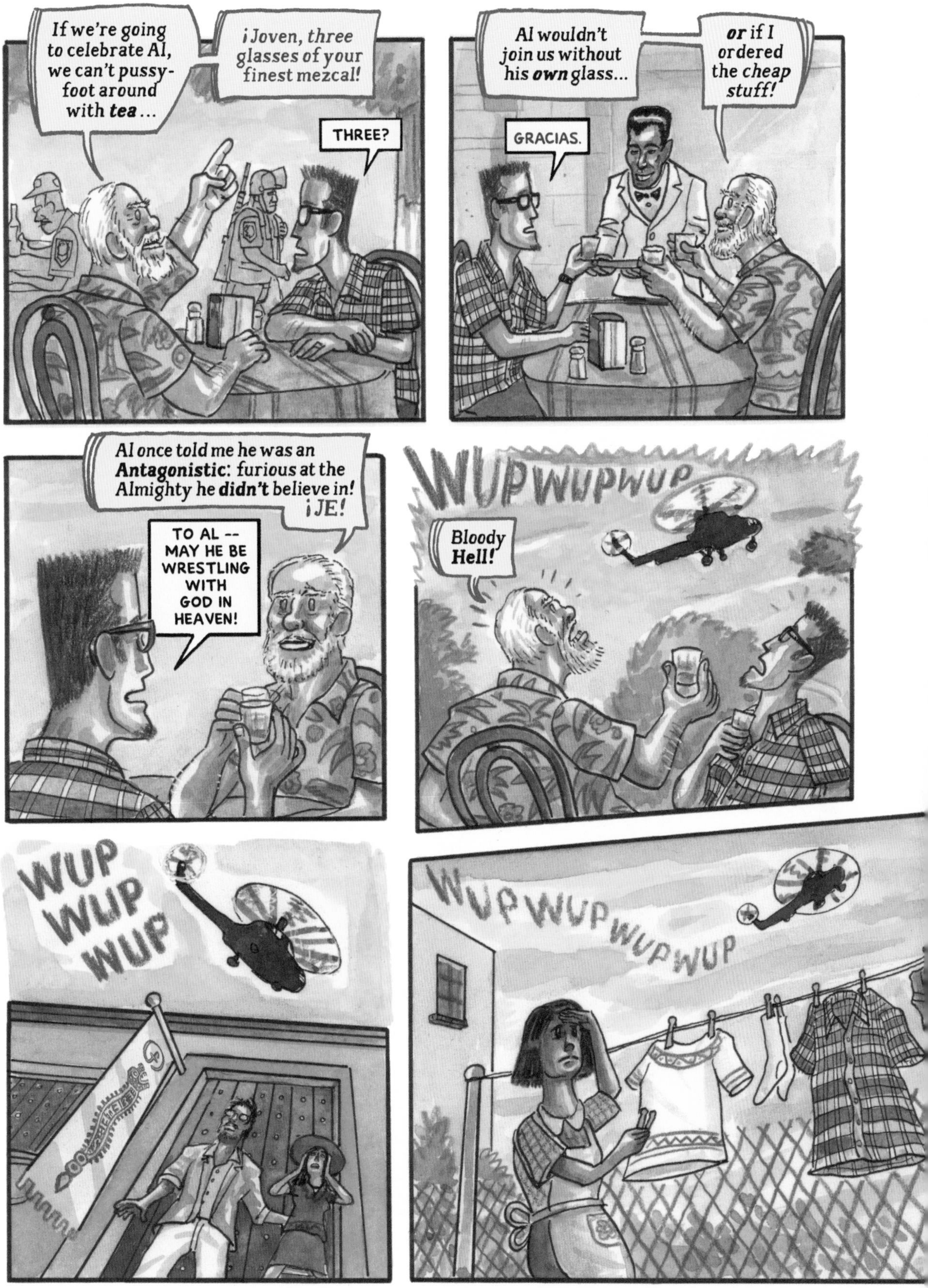

If we're going to celebrate Al, we can't pussy-foot around with *tea* ...
¡Joven, *three* glasses of your finest mezcal!
THREE?
Al wouldn't join us without his ***own*** glass...
or if I ordered the *cheap* stuff!
GRACIAS.
Al once told me he was an **Antagonistic**: furious at the Almighty he **didn't** believe in! ¡JE!
TO AL -- MAY HE BE WRESTLING WITH GOD IN HEAVEN!
WUPWUPWUPWUP
Bloody **Hell!**
WUP WUP WUP
WUPWUPWUPWUPWUP

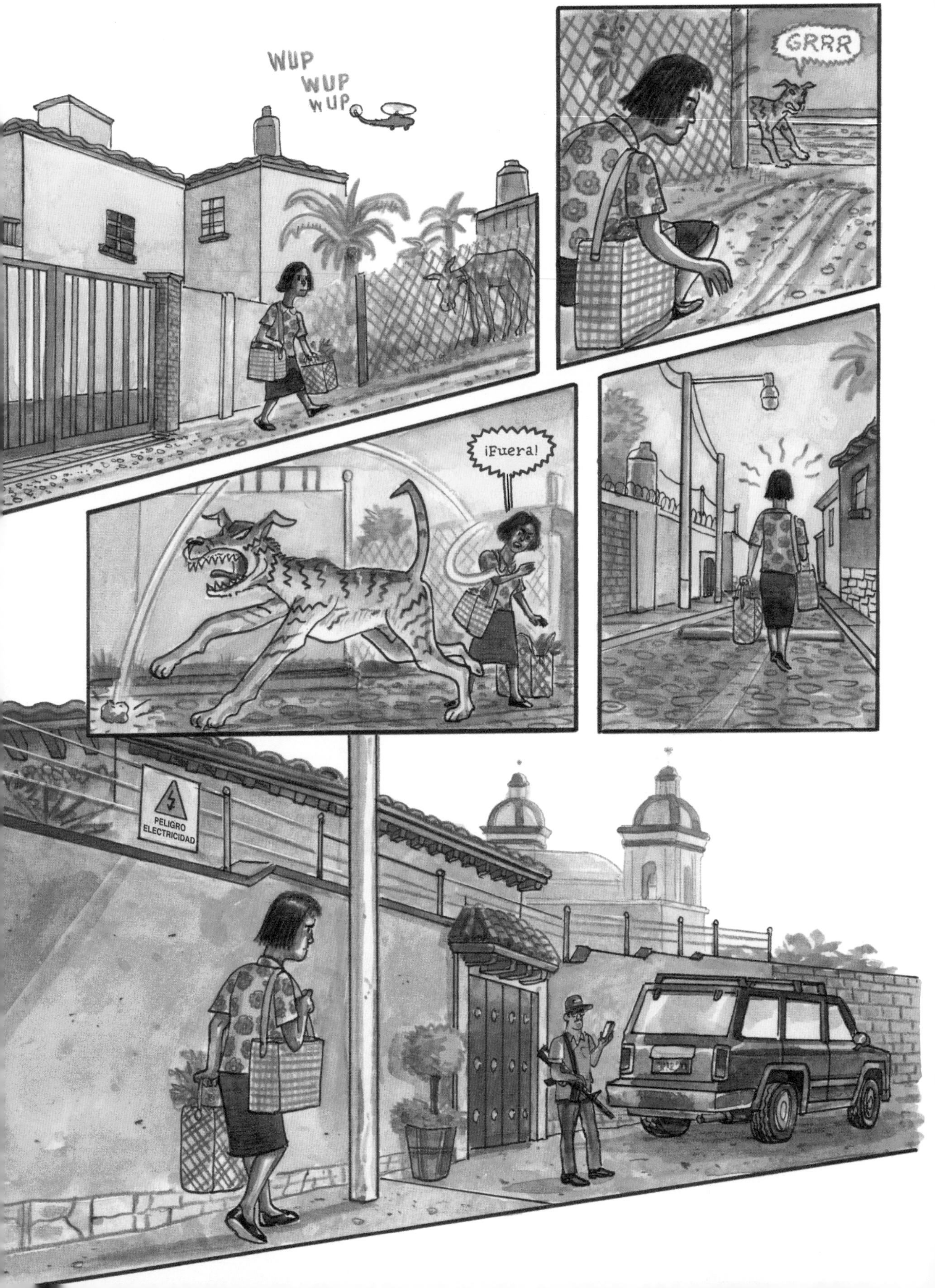

WUP
WUP
WUP
GRRR
¡Fuera!
PELIGRO ELECTRICIDAD

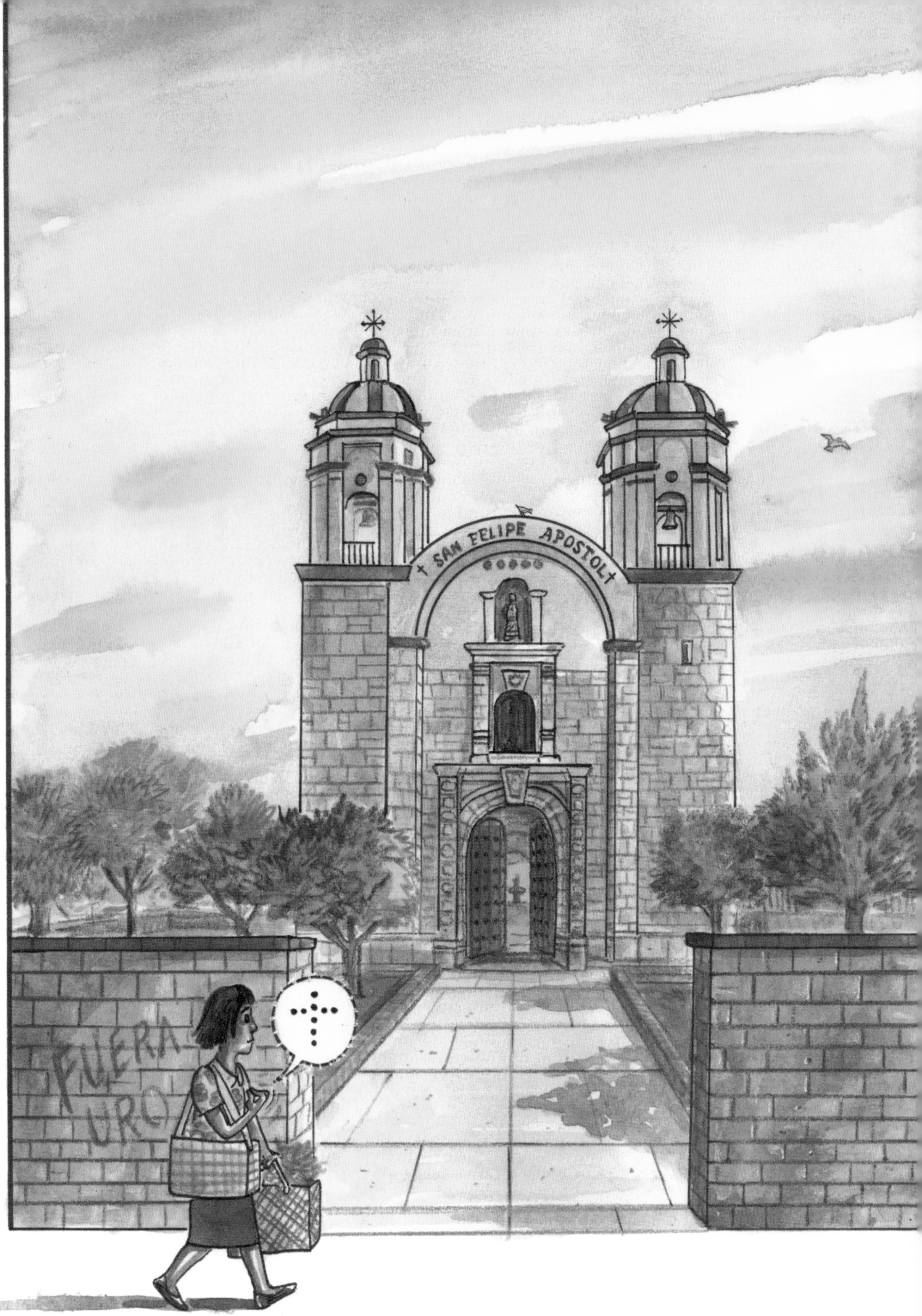

SAN FELIPE APOSTOL
FUERA URO

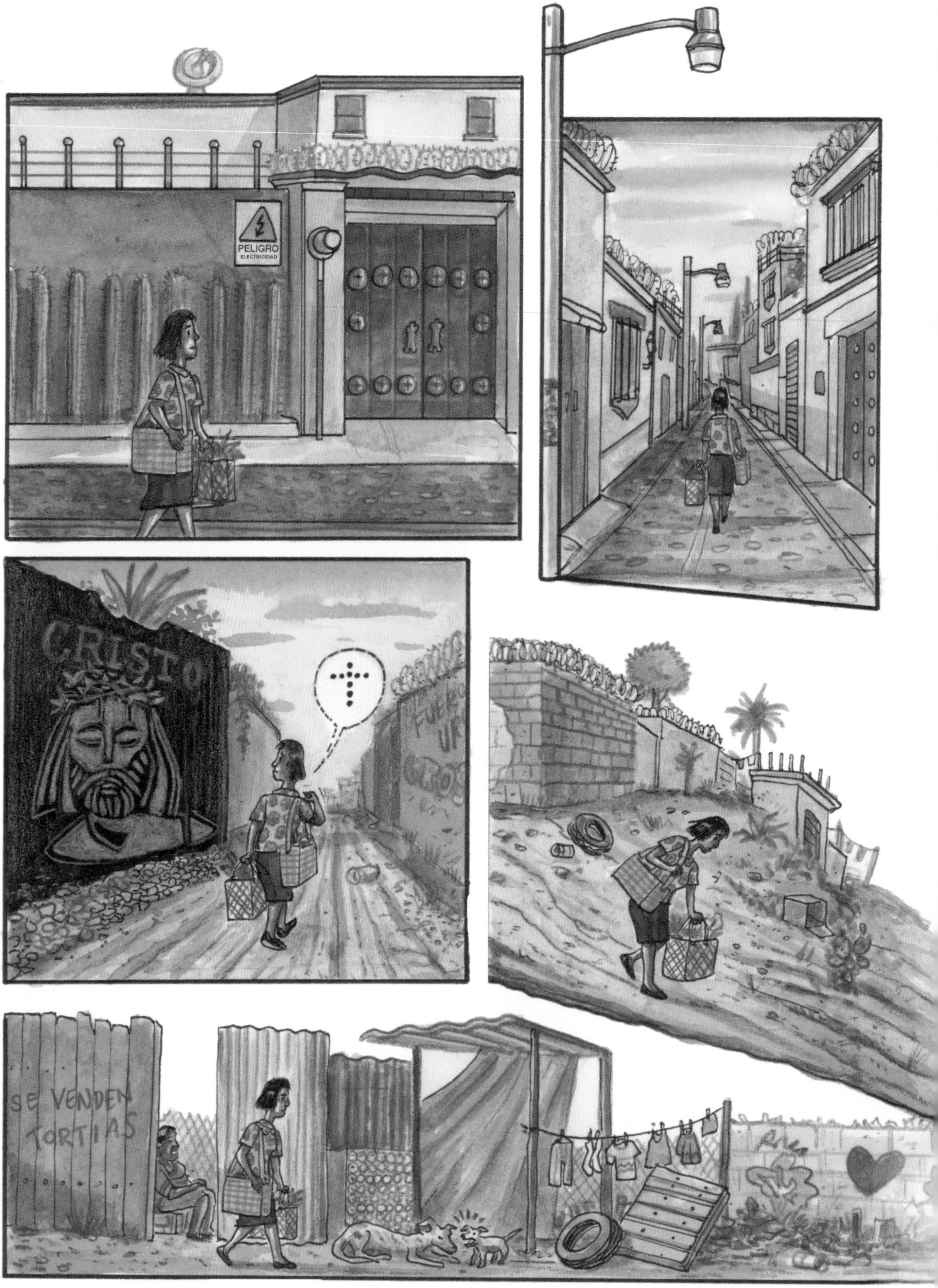
PELIGRO
ELECTRICIDAD
CRISTO
SE VENDEN TORTIAS

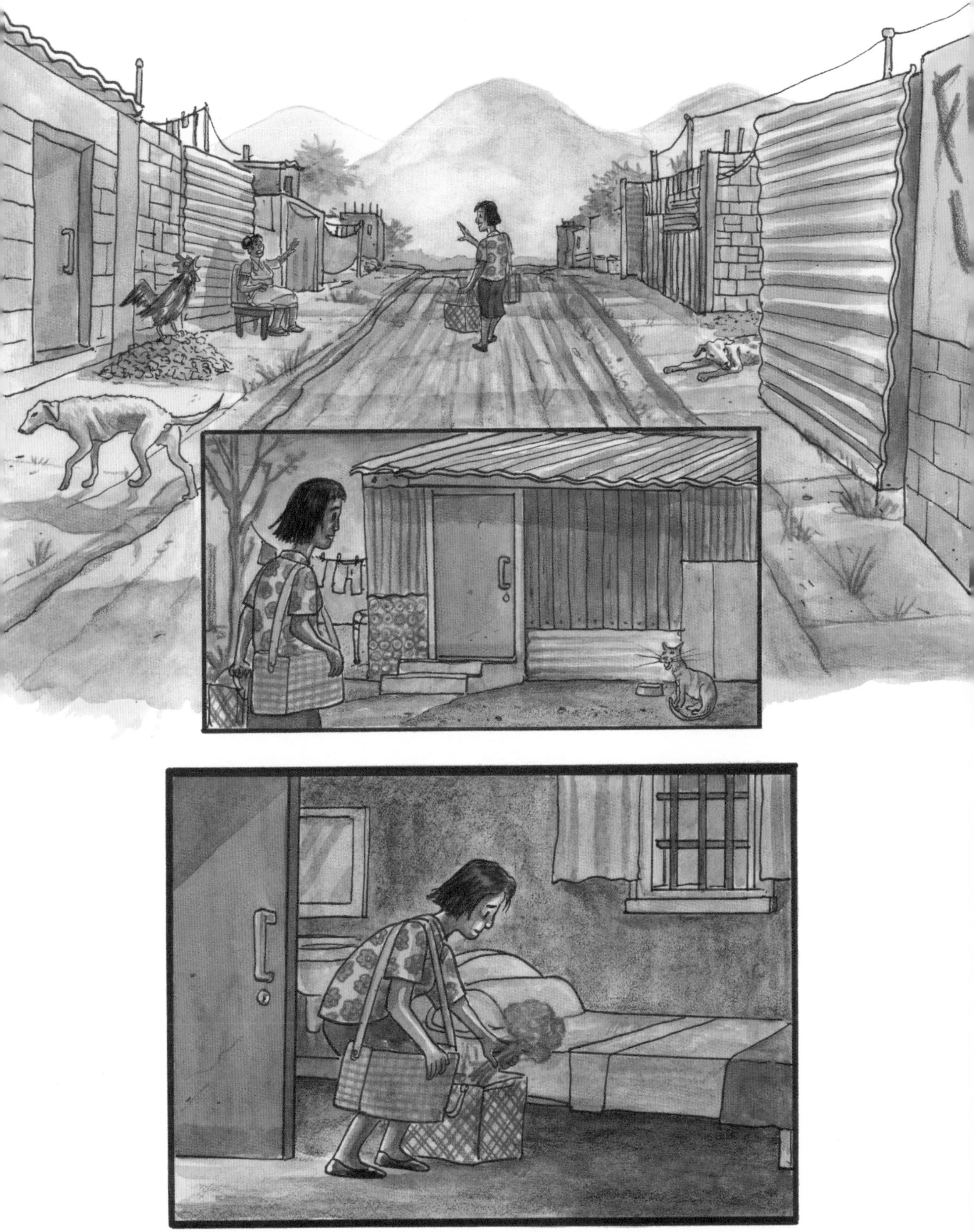

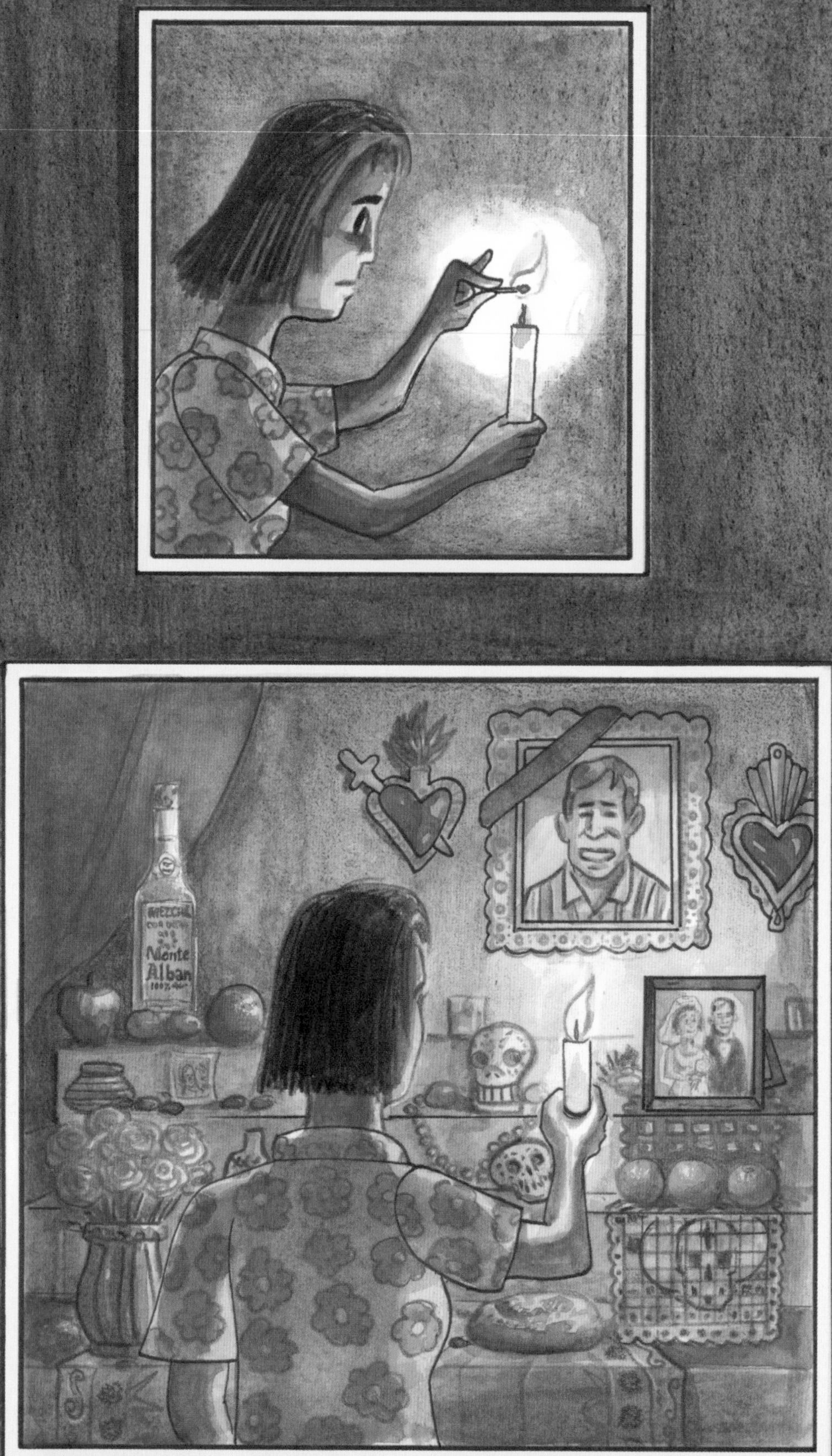
Monte Alban

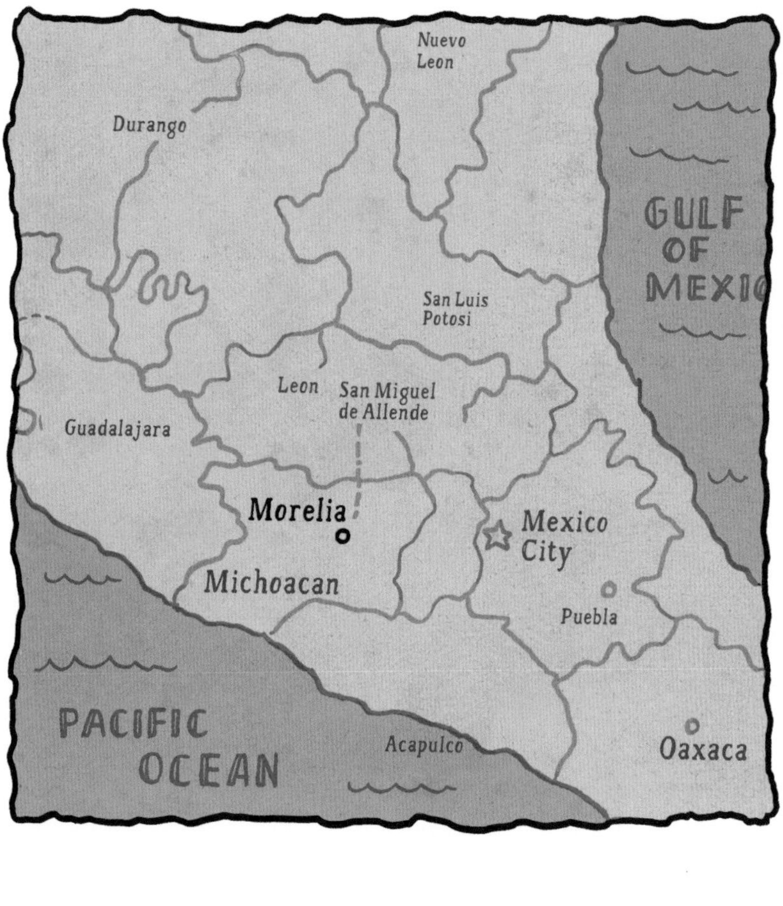

Nuevo Leon
Durango
GULF OF MEXIC
San Luis Potosi
Leon
San Miguel de Allende
Guadalajara
Morelia
Mexico City
Michoacan
Puebla
PACIFIC OCEAN
Acapulco
Oaxaca

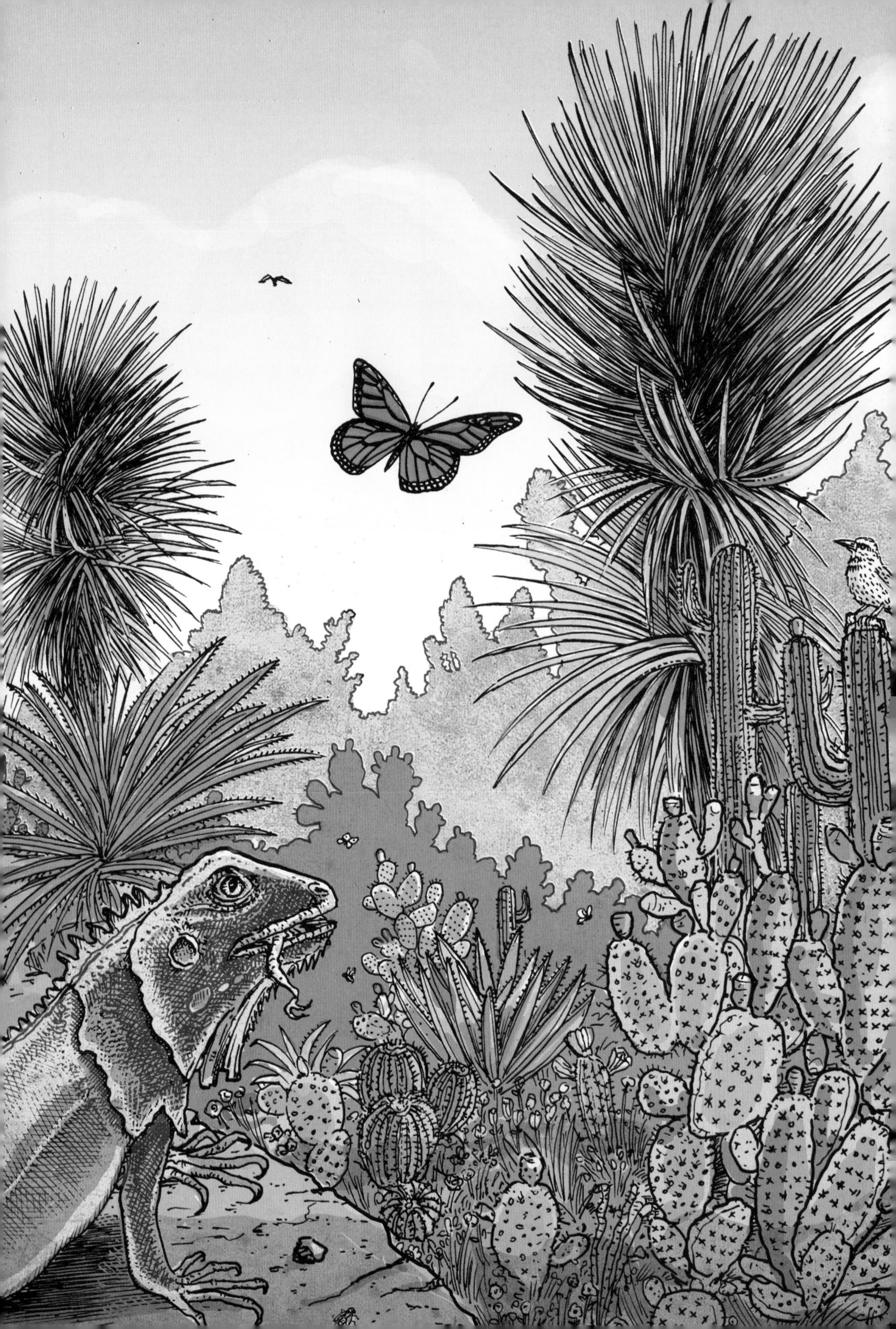

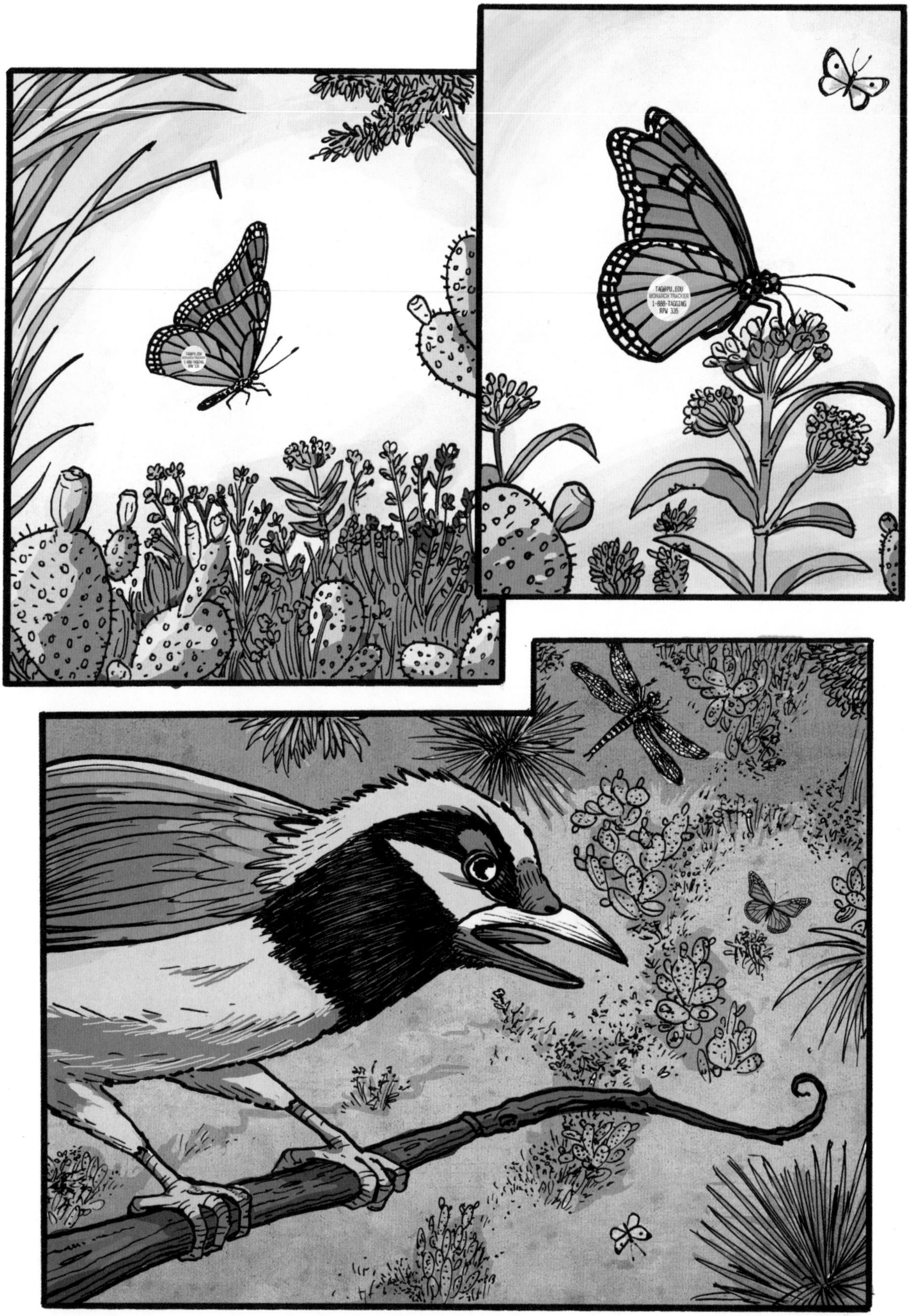
TAG@PU.EDU
MONARCH TRACKER
1-888-TAGGING
RPW 335

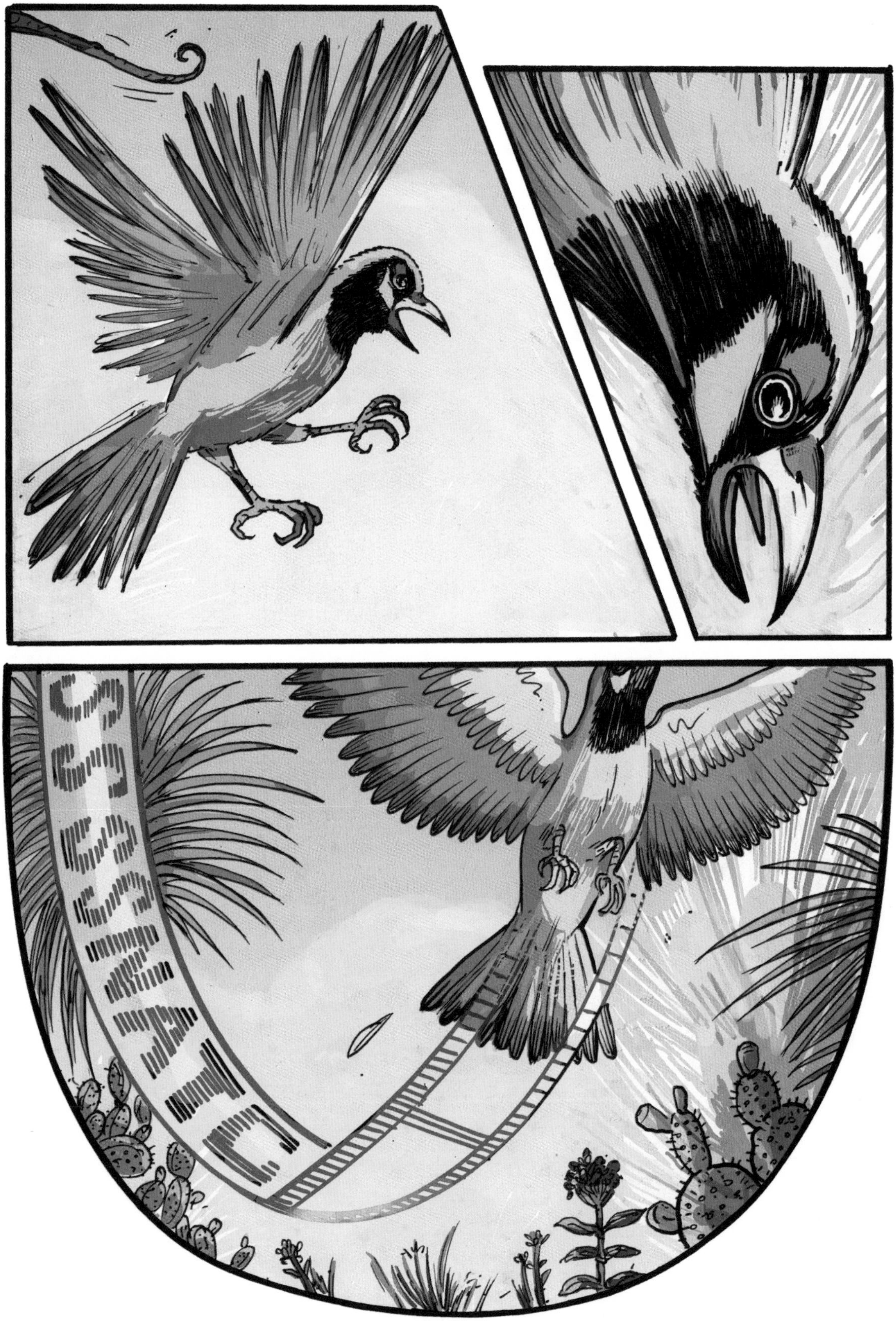

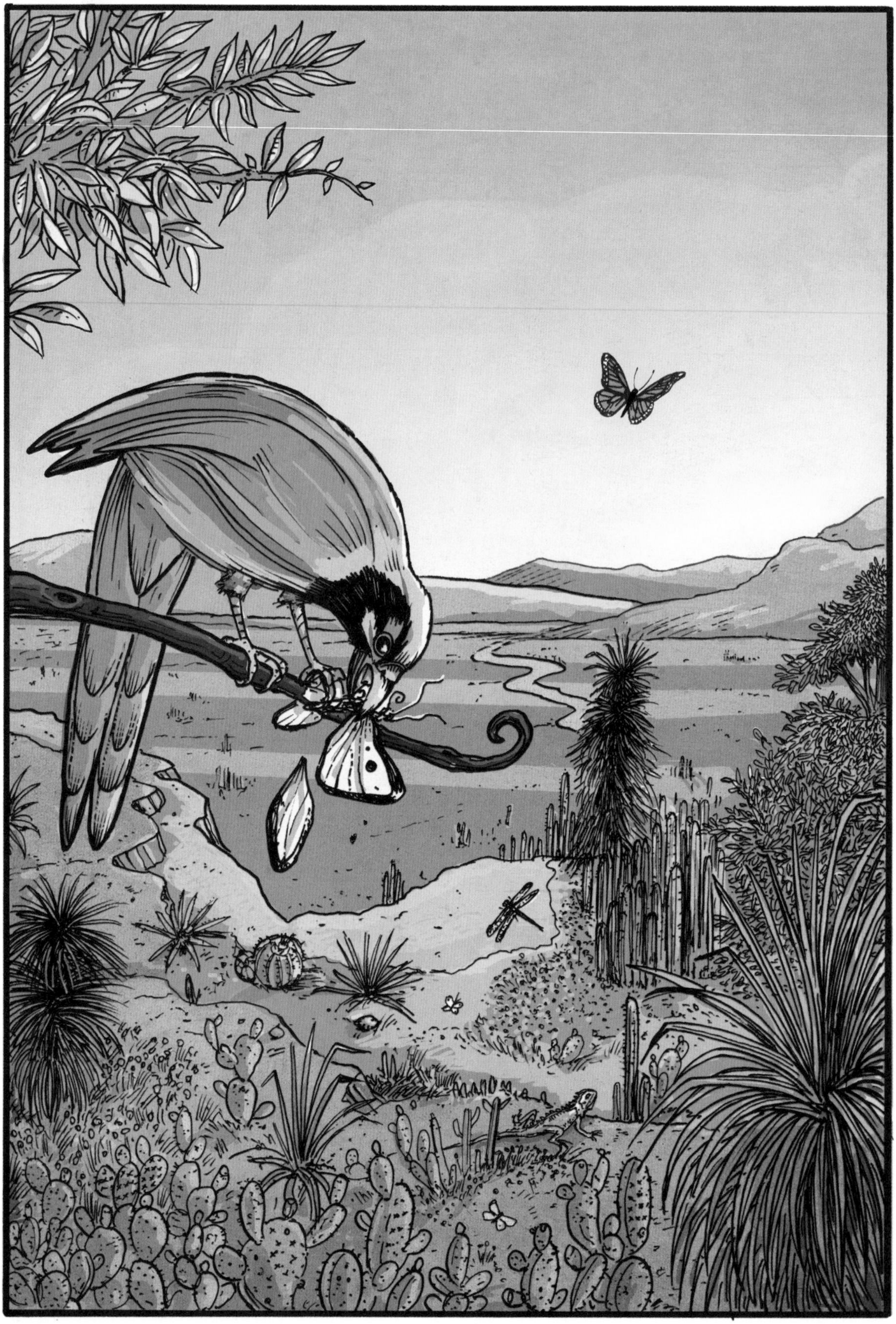

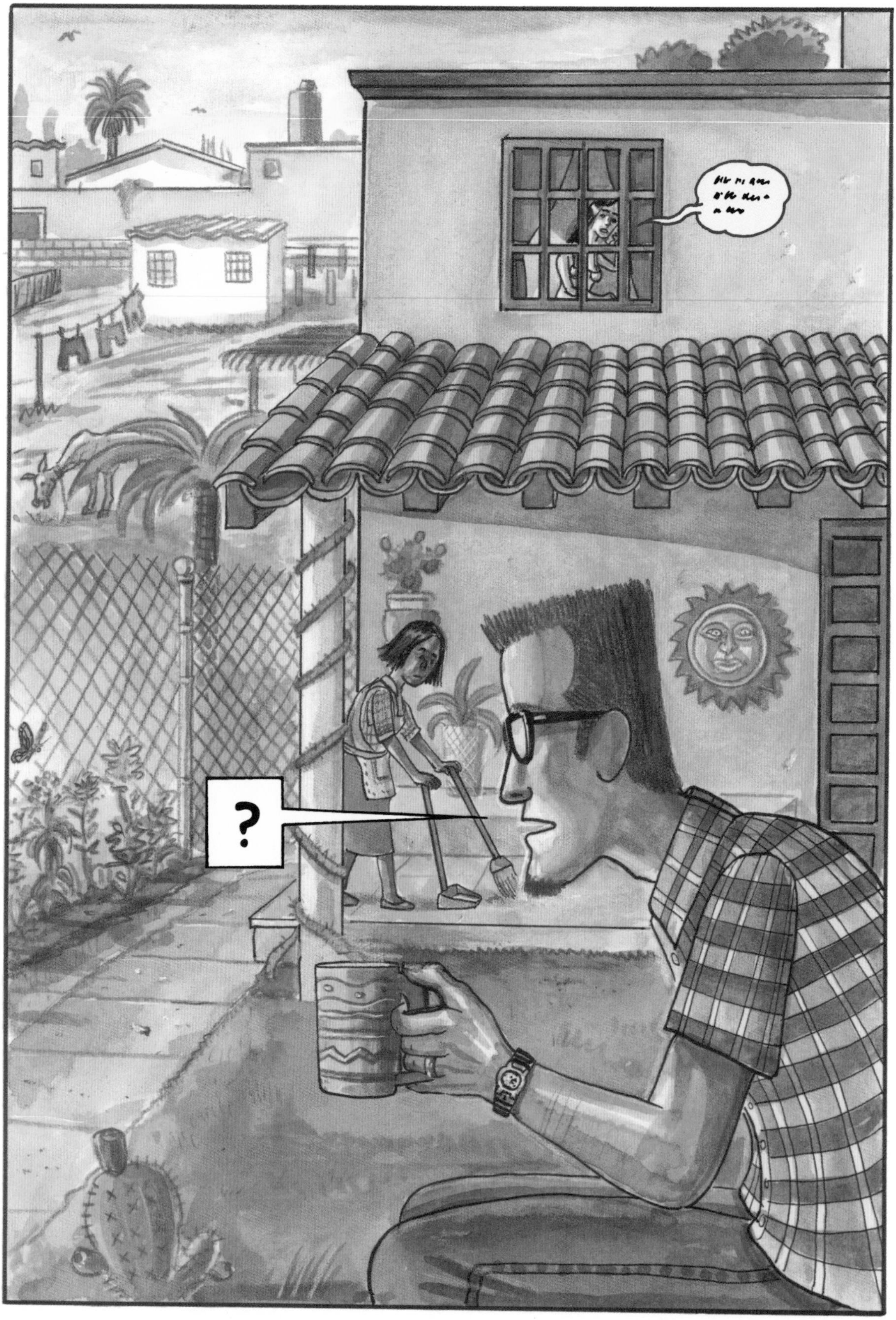
?

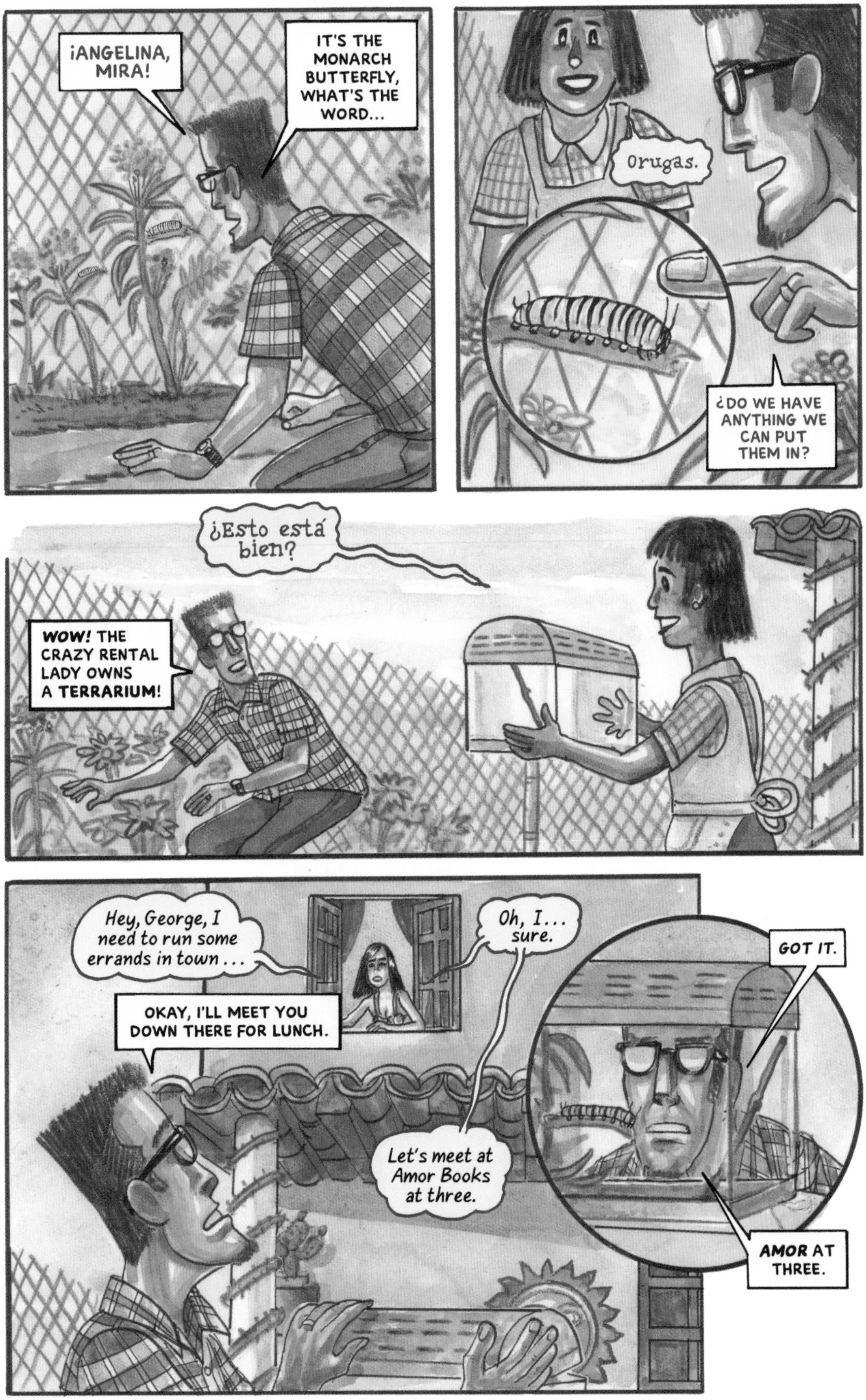
¡ANGELINA, MIRA!
IT'S THE MONARCH BUTTERFLY, WHAT'S THE WORD...
Orugas.
¿DO WE HAVE ANYTHING WE CAN PUT THEM IN?
¿Esto está bien?
WOW! THE CRAZY RENTAL LADY OWNS A TERRARIUM!
Hey, George, I need to run some errands in town . . .
Oh, I... sure.
OKAY, I'LL MEET YOU DOWN THERE FOR LUNCH.
Let's meet at Amor Books at three.
GOT IT.
AMOR AT THREE.

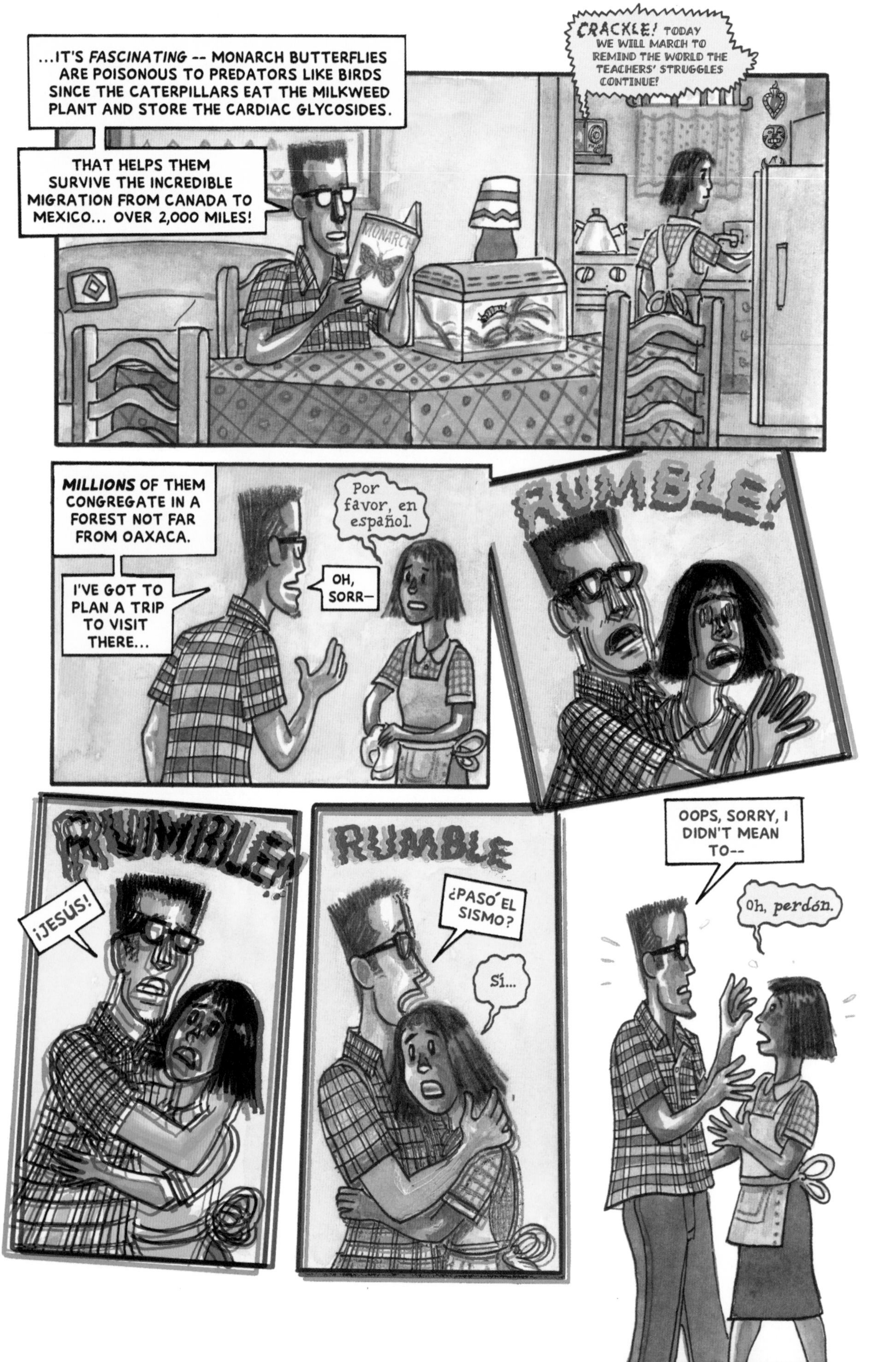
...IT'S *FASCINATING* -- MONARCH BUTTERFLIES ARE POISONOUS TO PREDATORS LIKE BIRDS SINCE THE CATERPILLARS EAT THE MILKWEED PLANT AND STORE THE CARDIAC GLYCOSIDES.
THAT HELPS THEM SURVIVE THE INCREDIBLE MIGRATION FROM CANADA TO MEXICO... OVER 2,000 MILES!
MONARCH
CRACKLE! TODAY WE WILL MARCH TO REMIND THE WORLD THE TEACHERS' STRUGGLES CONTINUE!
MILLIONS OF THEM CONGREGATE IN A FOREST NOT FAR FROM OAXACA.
I'VE GOT TO PLAN A TRIP TO VISIT THERE...
Por favor, en español.
OH, SORR—
RUMBLE!
RUMBLE!
¡JESÚS!
RUMBLE
¿PASÓ EL SISMO?
SÍ...
OOPS, SORRY, I DIDN'T MEAN TO--
Oh, perdón.

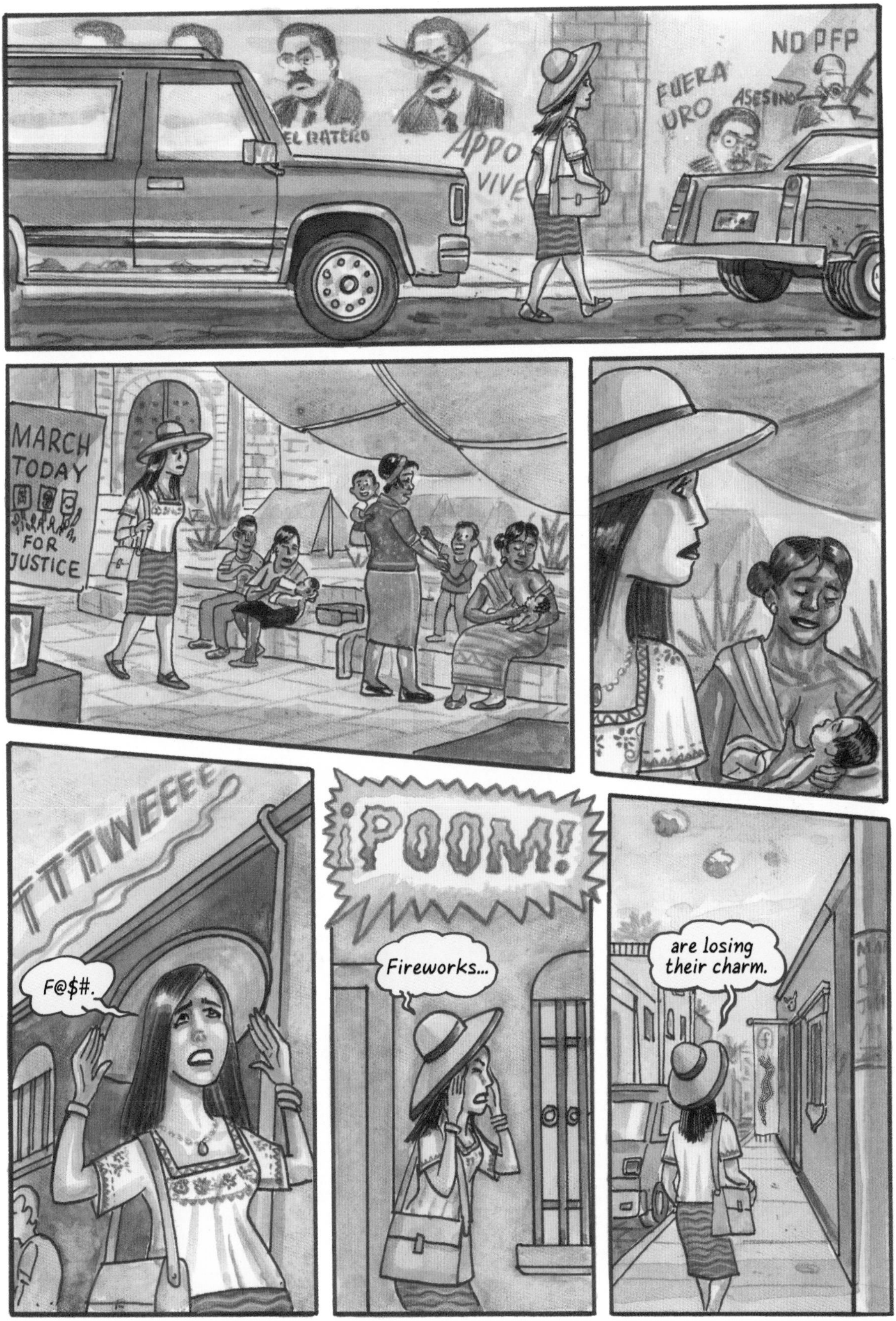
EL RATERO
APPO VIVE
FUERA URO
ASESINO
NO PFP
MARCH TODAY
FOR JUSTICE
TTTTWEEEEE
F@$#.
¡POOM!
Fireworks...
are losing their charm.

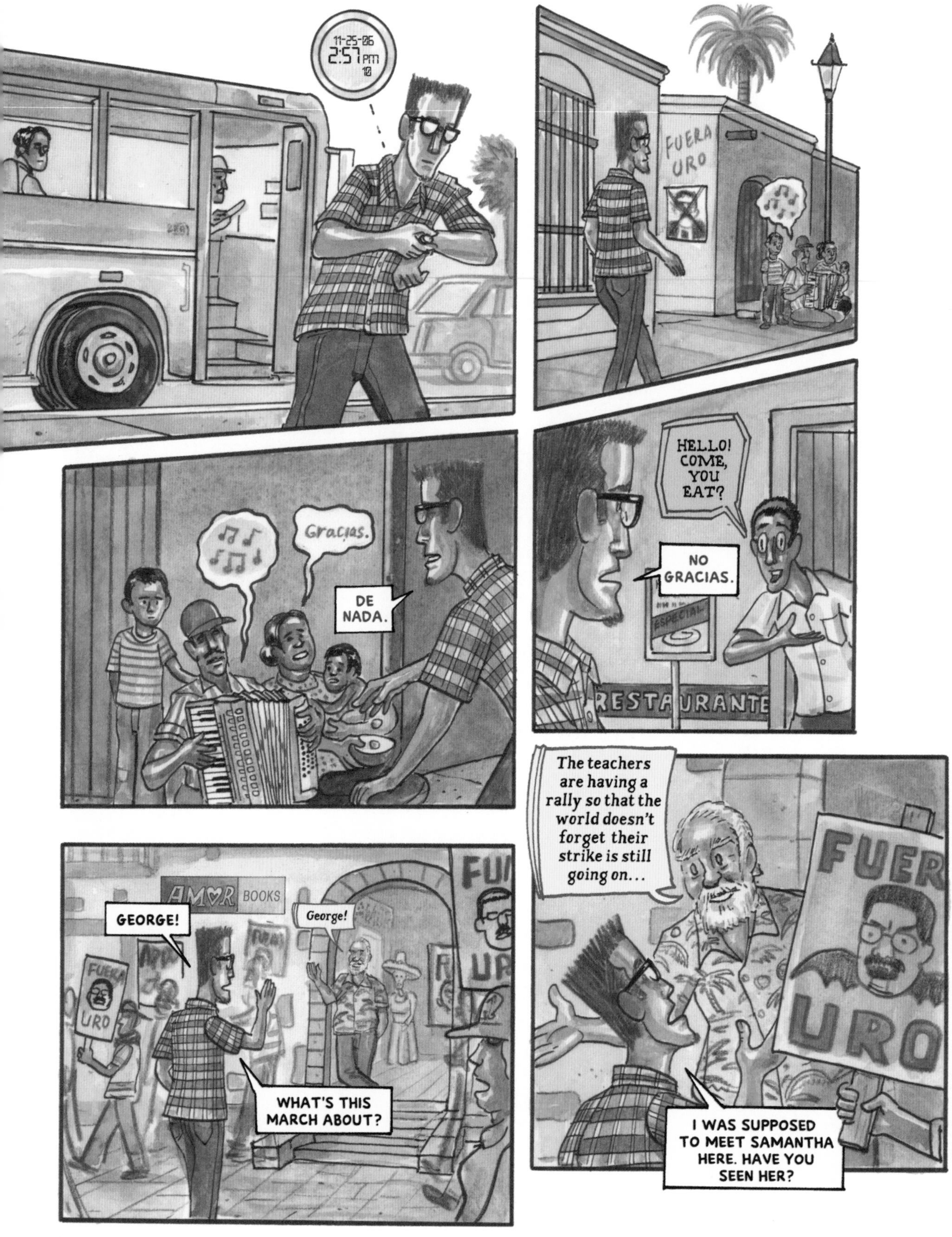
11-25-06
2:57 pm
10
FUERA
URO
Gracias.
DE NADA.
HELLO! COME, YOU EAT?
NO GRACIAS.
ESPECIAL
RESTAURANTE
AMOR BOOKS
GEORGE!
George!
FUERA
URO
WHAT'S THIS MARCH ABOUT?
The teachers are having a rally so that the world doesn't forget their strike is still going on...
FUER
URO
I WAS SUPPOSED TO MEET SAMANTHA HERE. HAVE YOU SEEN HER?

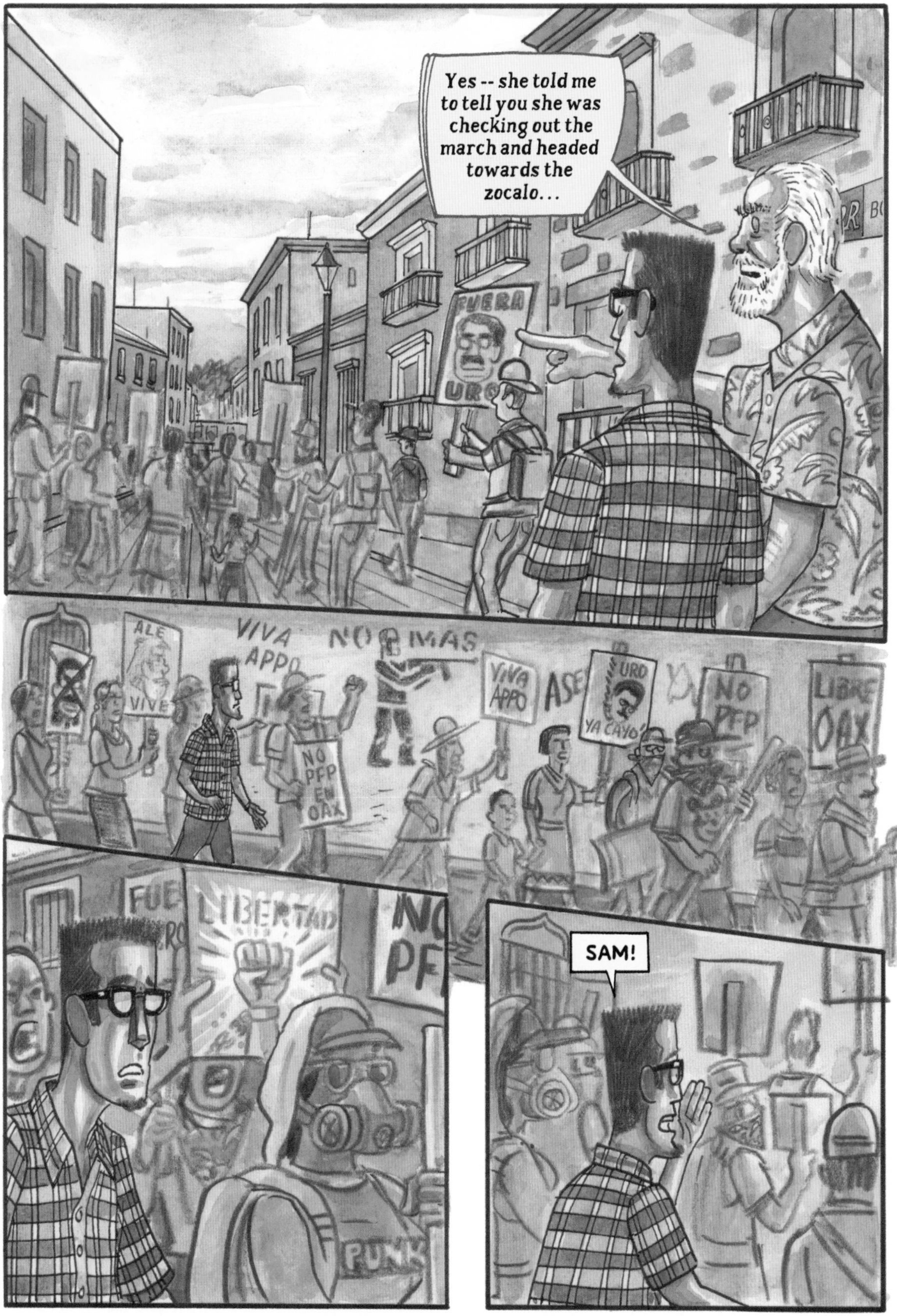
Yes -- she told me to tell you she was checking out the march and headed towards the zocalo...
FUERA
URO
VIVA APPO
NO MAS
VIVA APPO
URO YA CAYO
NO PFP
LIBRE OAX
NO PFP EN OAX
LIBERTAD
PUNK
SAM!

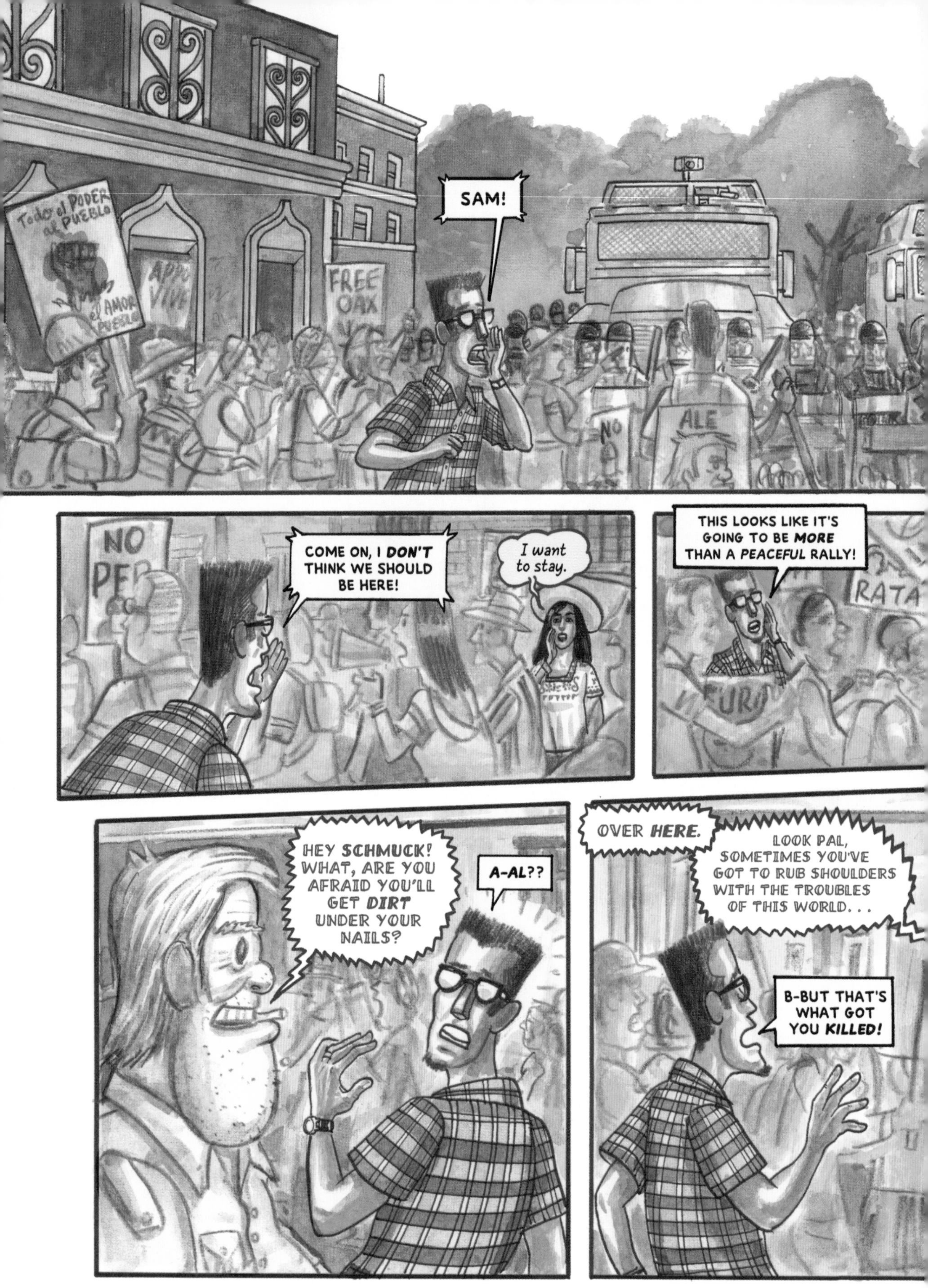
Todo el PODER al PUEBLO
el AMOR PUEBLO
APPO VIVE
FREE OAX
SAM!
NO
ALE
NO PEP
COME ON, I **DON'T** THINK WE SHOULD BE HERE!
I want to stay.
THIS LOOKS LIKE IT'S GOING TO BE **MORE** THAN A *PEACEFUL* RALLY!
RATA
HEY **SCHMUCK!** WHAT, ARE YOU AFRAID YOU'LL GET ***DIRT*** UNDER YOUR NAILS?
A-AL??
OVER ***HERE.***
LOOK PAL, SOMETIMES YOU'VE GOT TO RUB SHOULDERS WITH THE TROUBLES OF THIS WORLD. . .
B-BUT THAT'S WHAT GOT YOU ***KILLED!***

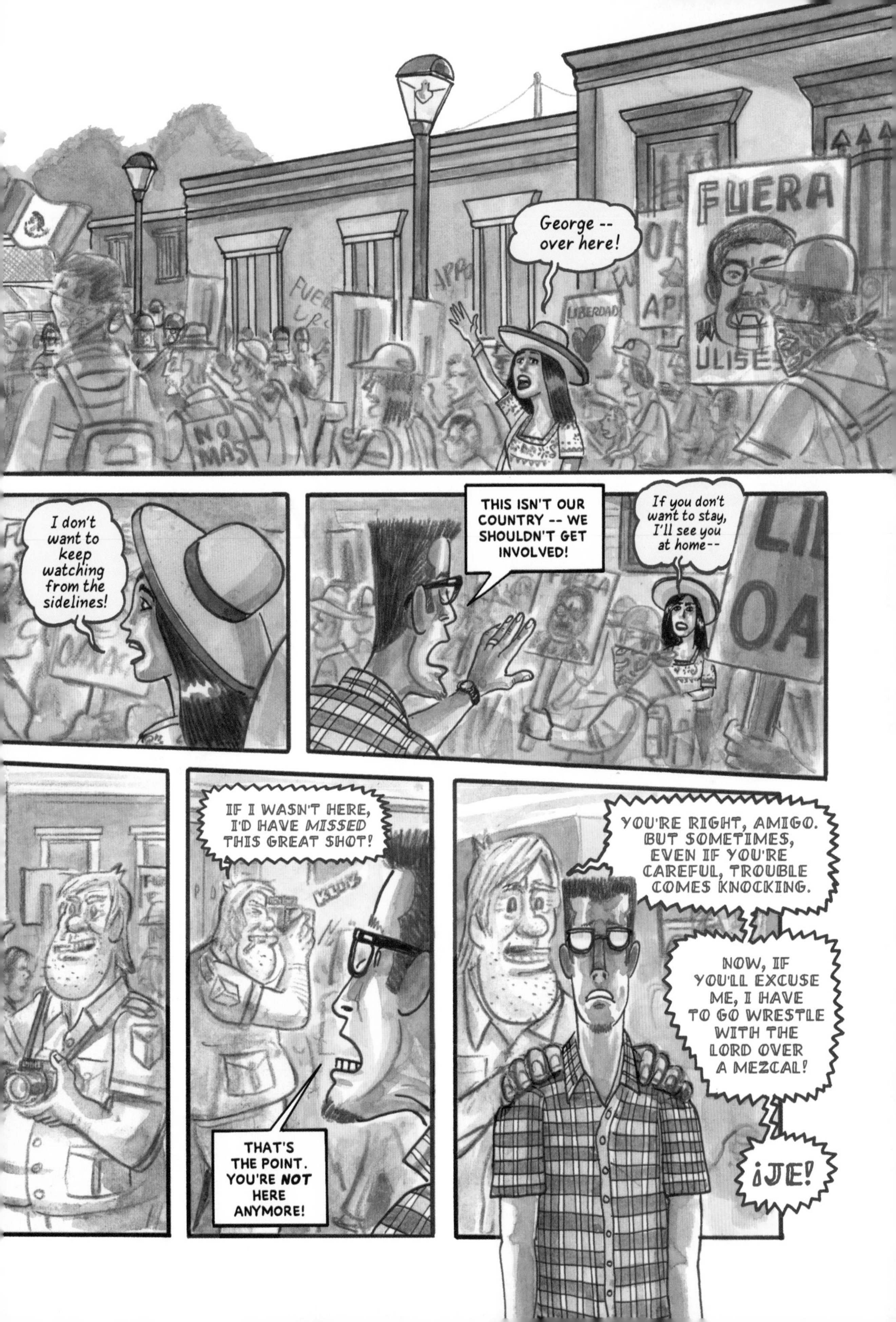

FUERA
OA
APP
ULISE
LIBERDAD
NO MAS
George -- over here!
I don't want to keep watching from the sidelines!
THIS ISN'T OUR COUNTRY -- WE SHOULDN'T GET INVOLVED!
If you don't want to stay, I'll see you at home--
IF I WASN'T HERE, I'D HAVE MISSED THIS GREAT SHOT!
THAT'S THE POINT. YOU'RE NOT HERE ANYMORE!
YOU'RE RIGHT, AMIGO. BUT SOMETIMES, EVEN IF YOU'RE CAREFUL, TROUBLE COMES KNOCKING.
NOW, IF YOU'LL EXCUSE ME, I HAVE TO GO WRESTLE WITH THE LORD OVER A MEZCAL!
¡JE!

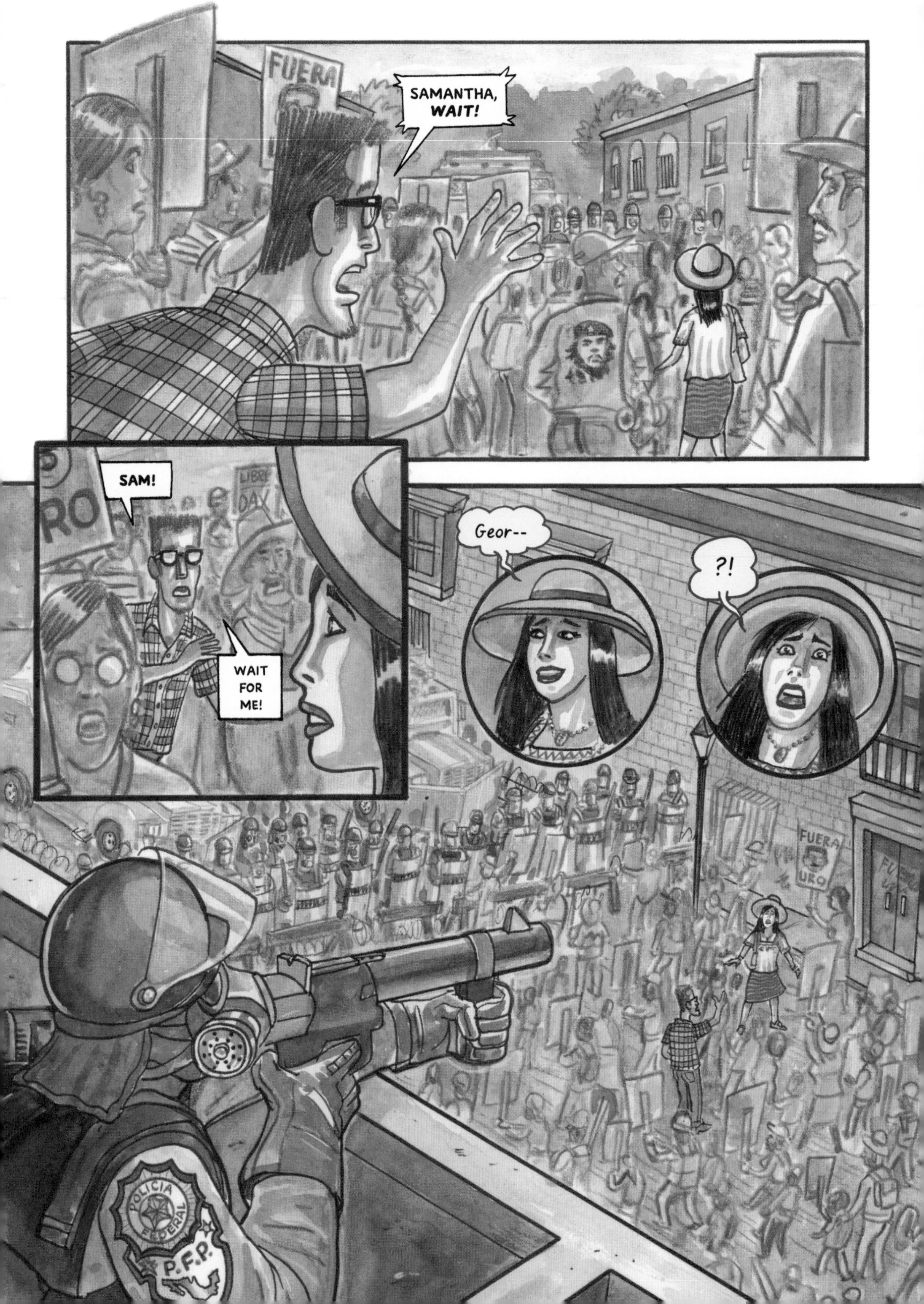
FUERA
SAMANTHA, WAIT!
SAM!
WAIT FOR ME!
Geor--
?!
FUERA URO
POLICIA FEDERAL
P.F.P.

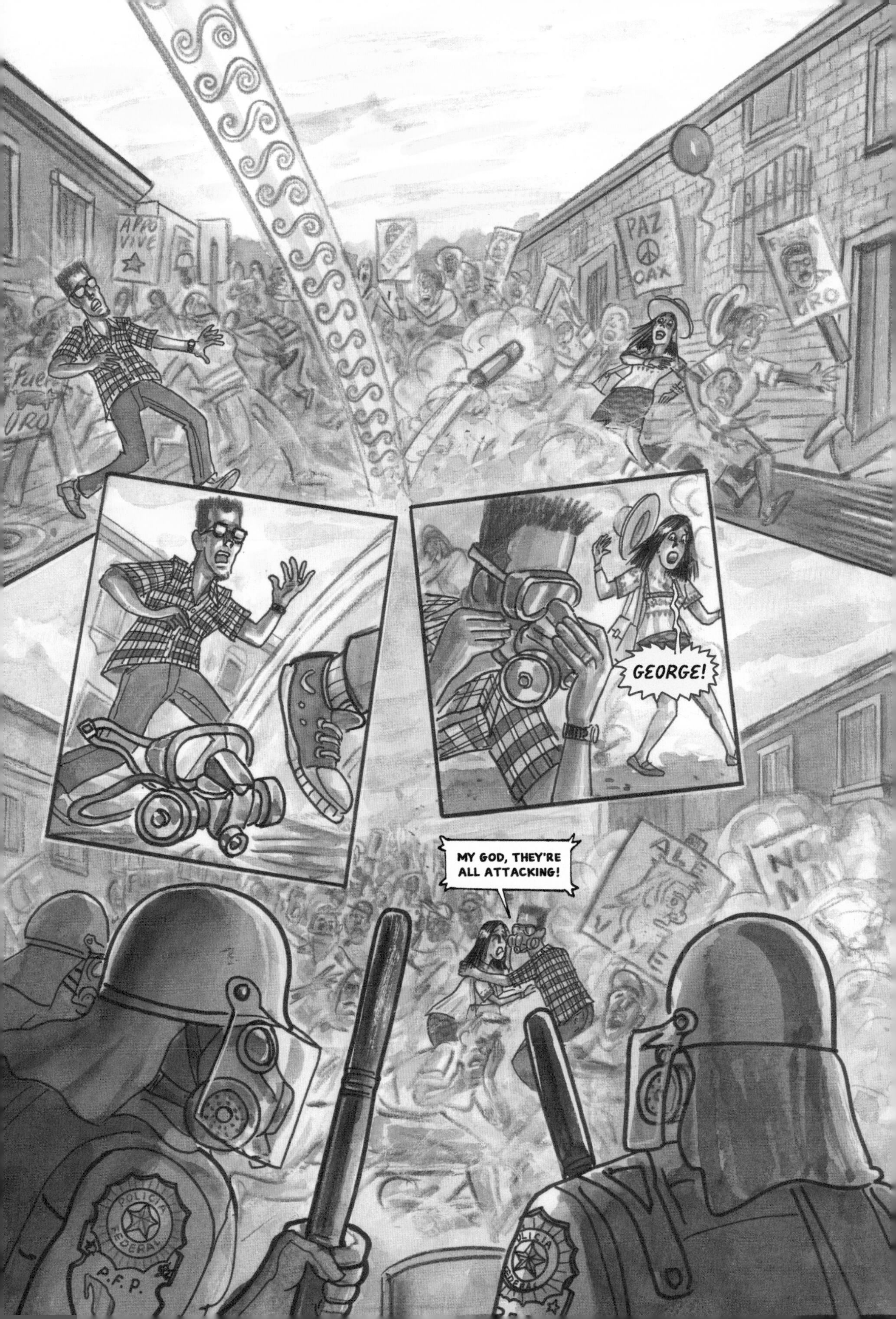
APPO
VIVE
PAZ
OAX
GEORGE!
MY GOD, THEY'RE ALL ATTACKING!
POLICIA FEDERAL
P.F.P.

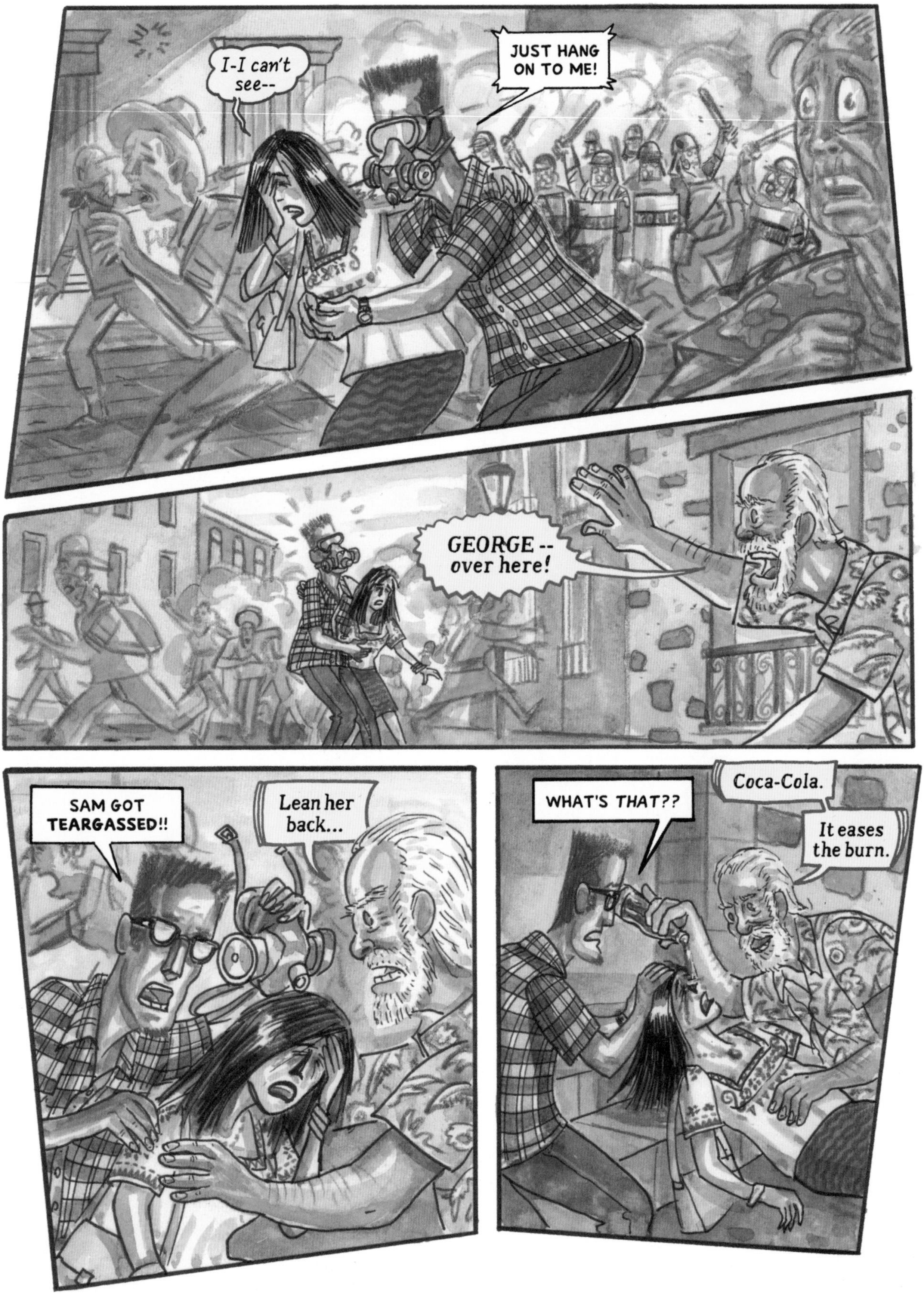

I-I can't see--
JUST HANG ON TO ME!
GEORGE -- over here!
SAM GOT TEARGASSED!!
Lean her back...
WHAT'S THAT??
Coca-Cola.
It eases the burn.

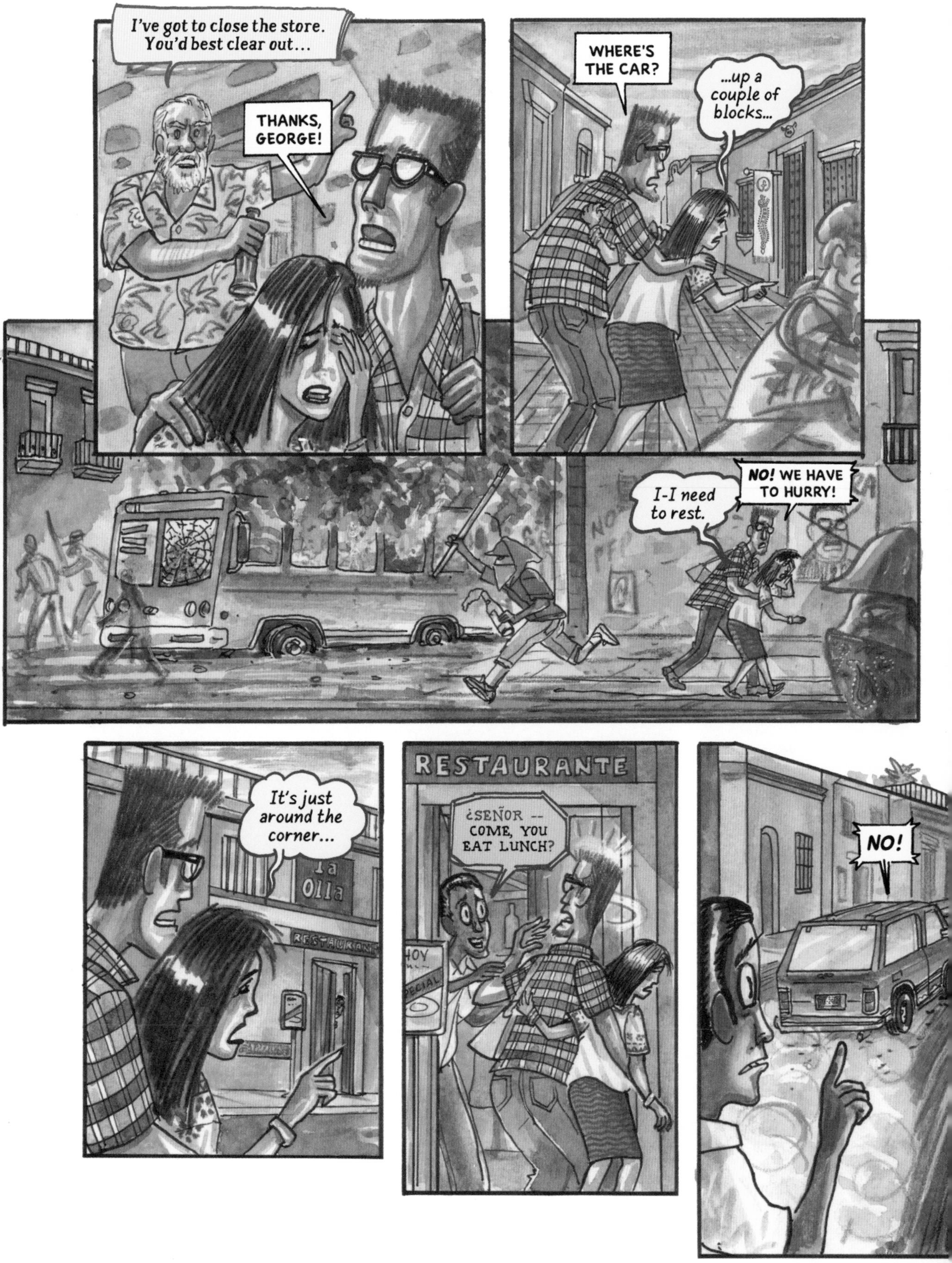
I've got to close the store. You'd best clear out...
THANKS, GEORGE!
WHERE'S THE CAR?
...up a couple of blocks...
I-I need to rest.
NO! WE HAVE TO HURRY!
It's just around the corner...
La Olla
RESTAURANTE
¿SEÑOR -- COME, YOU EAT LUNCH?
NO!

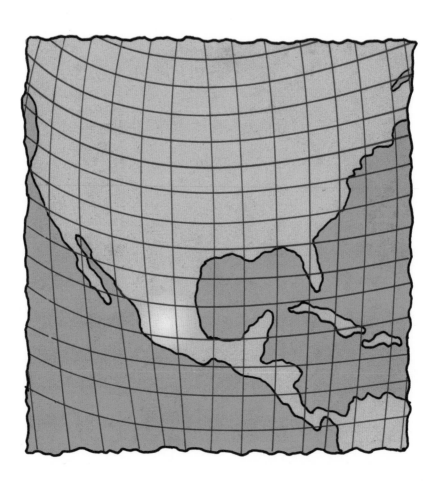

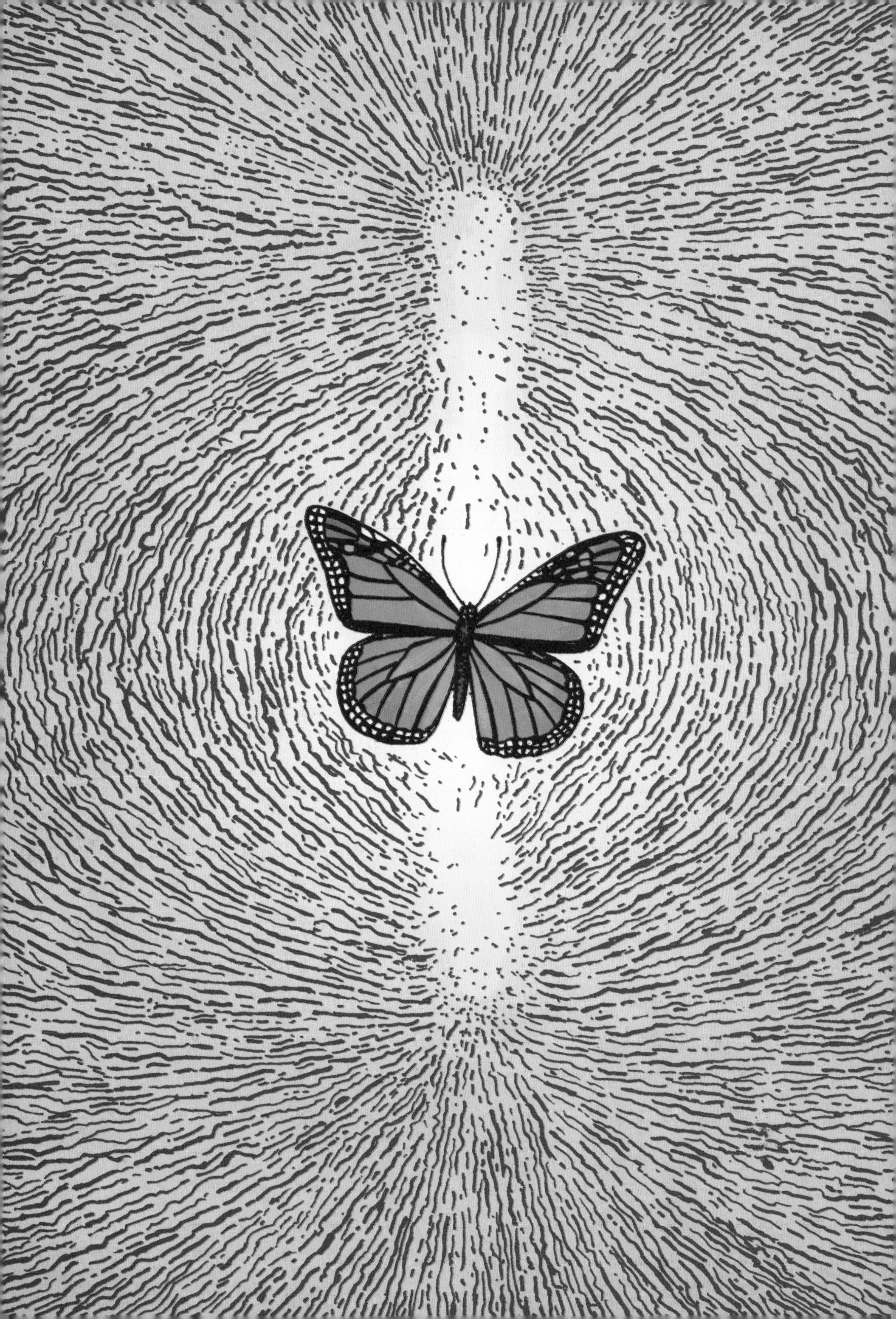

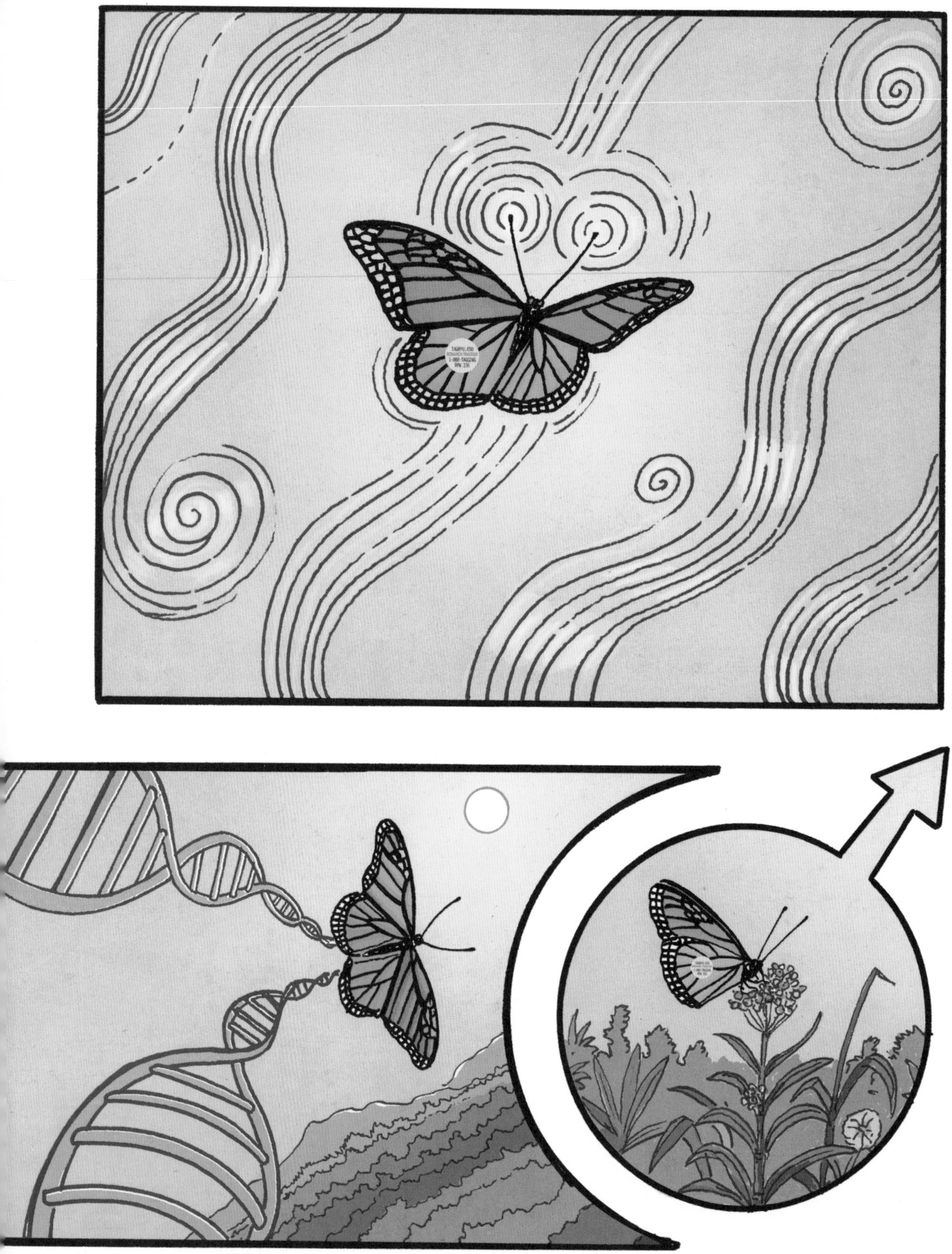
MONARCH TRACKER
1-888-TAGGING

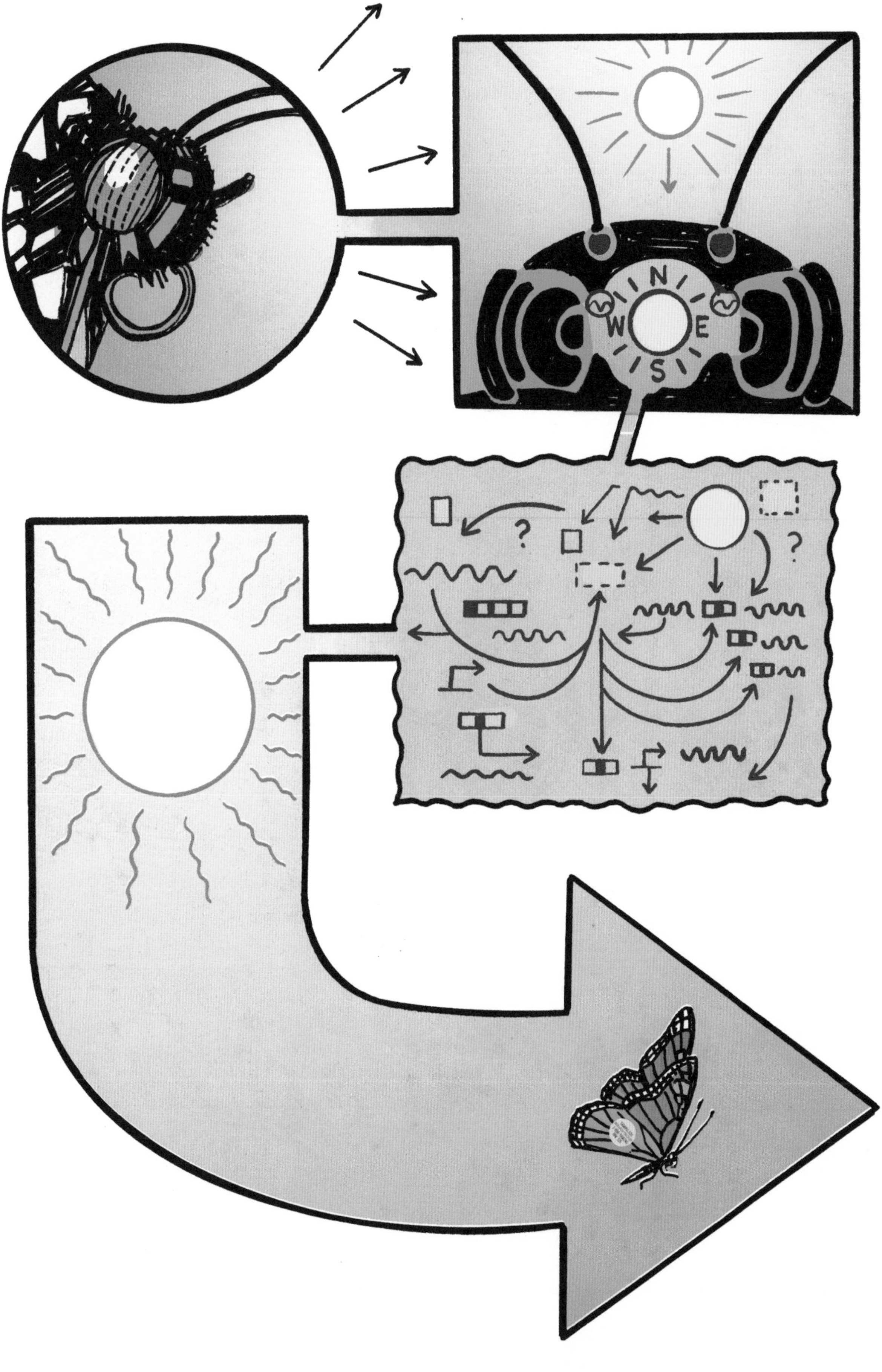
N
W
E
S
?
?

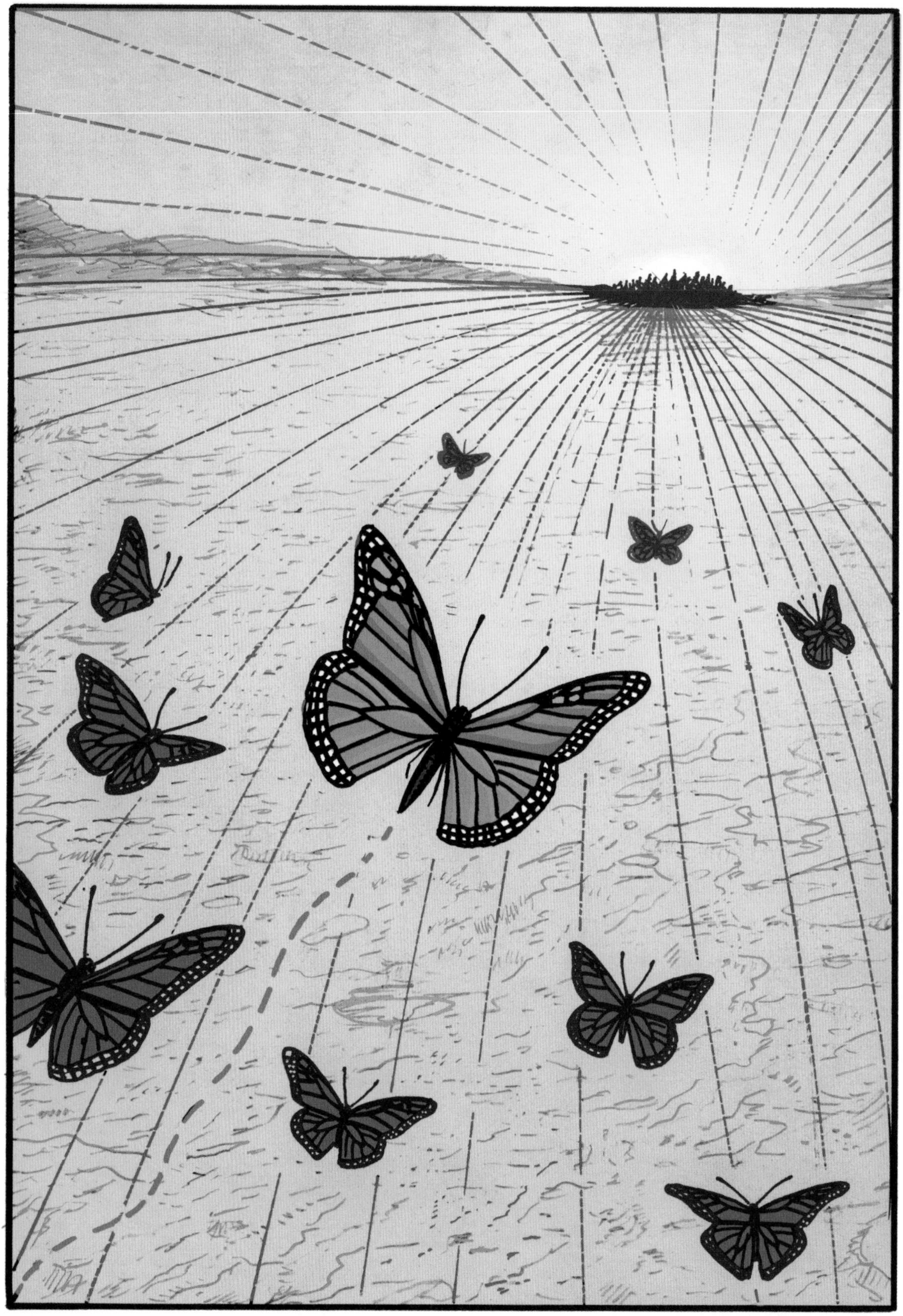

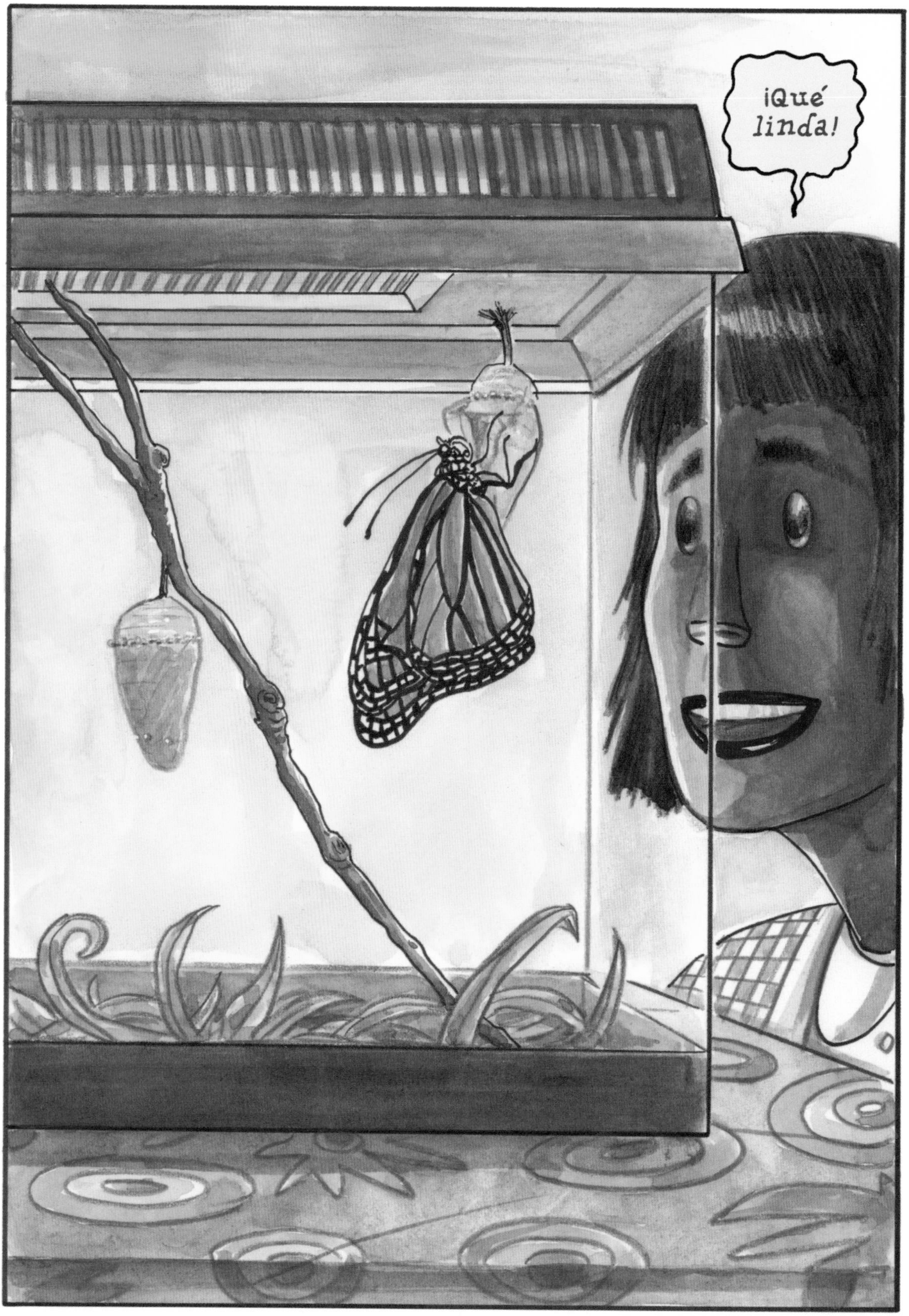
¡Qué linda!

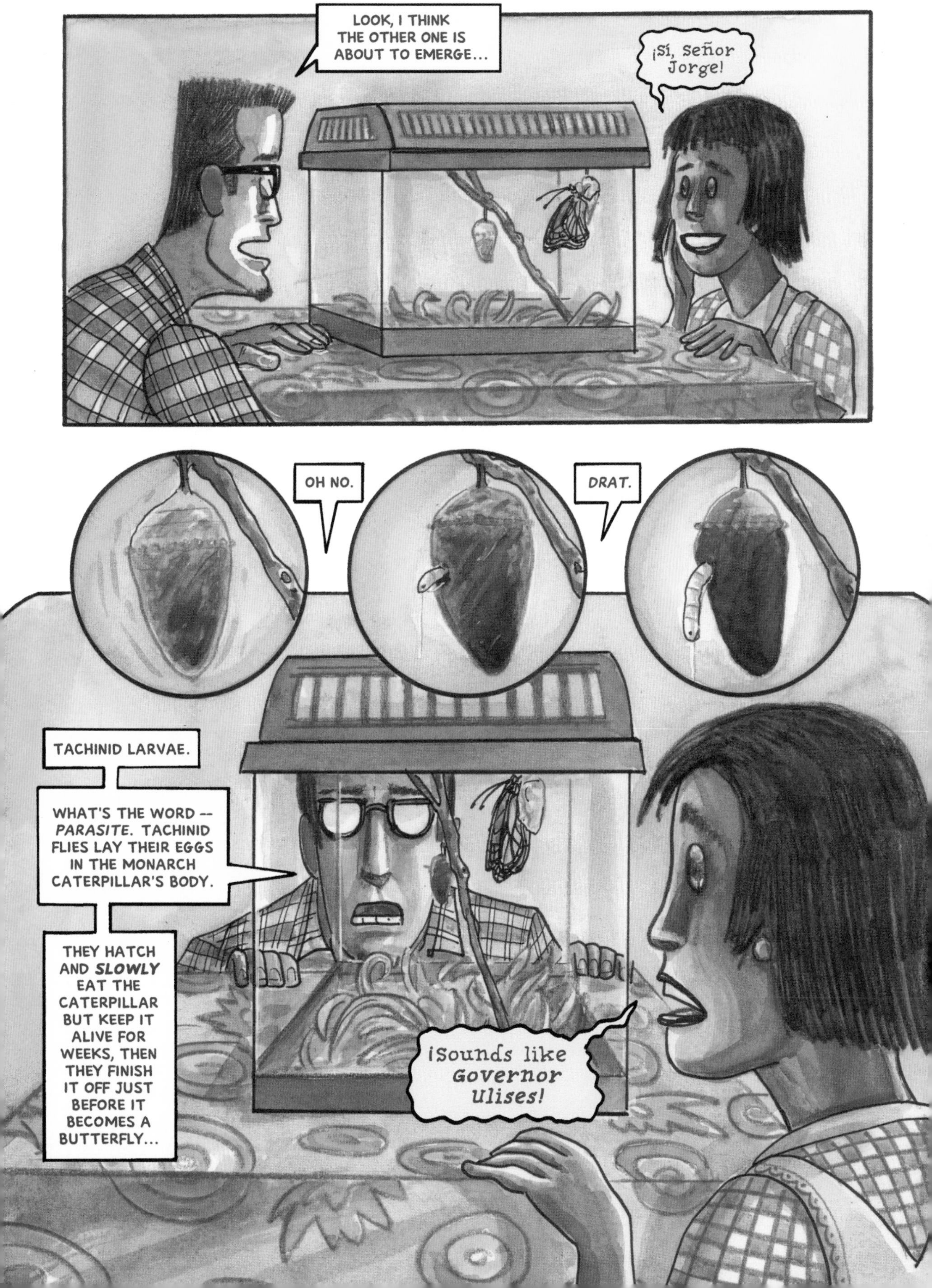
LOOK, I THINK THE OTHER ONE IS ABOUT TO EMERGE...
¡Sí, Señor Jorge!
OH NO.
DRAT.
TACHINID LARVAE.
WHAT'S THE WORD -- *PARASITE*. TACHINID FLIES LAY THEIR EGGS IN THE MONARCH CATERPILLAR'S BODY.
THEY HATCH AND ***SLOWLY*** EAT THE CATERPILLAR BUT KEEP IT ALIVE FOR WEEKS, THEN THEY FINISH IT OFF JUST BEFORE IT BECOMES A BUTTERFLY...
¡Sounds like ***Governor Ulises!***

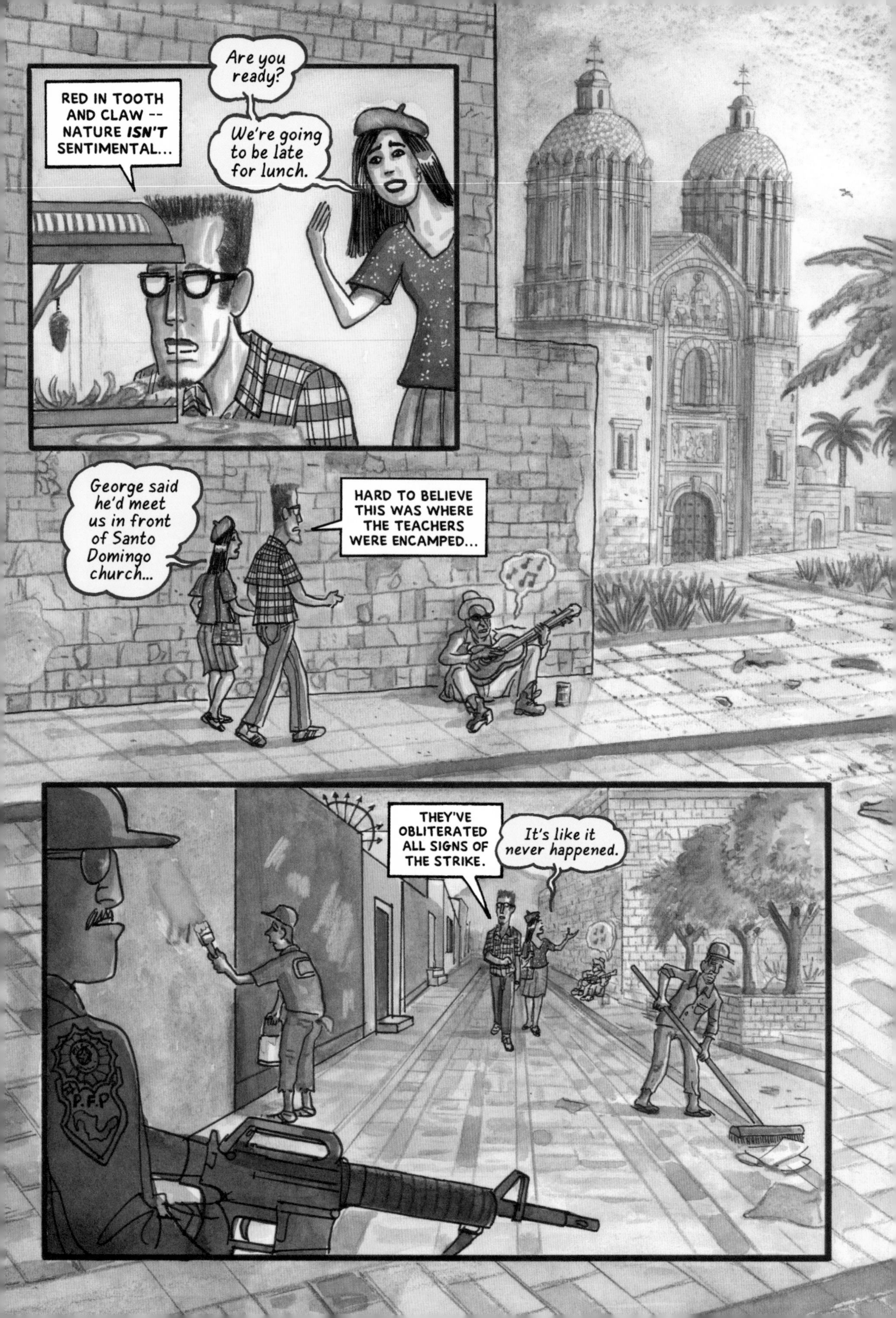
RED IN TOOTH AND CLAW -- NATURE *ISN'T* SENTIMENTAL...
Are you ready?
We're going to be late for lunch.
George said he'd meet us in front of Santo Domingo church...
HARD TO BELIEVE THIS WAS WHERE THE TEACHERS WERE ENCAMPED...
THEY'VE OBLITERATED ALL SIGNS OF THE STRIKE.
It's like it never happened.
P.F.P

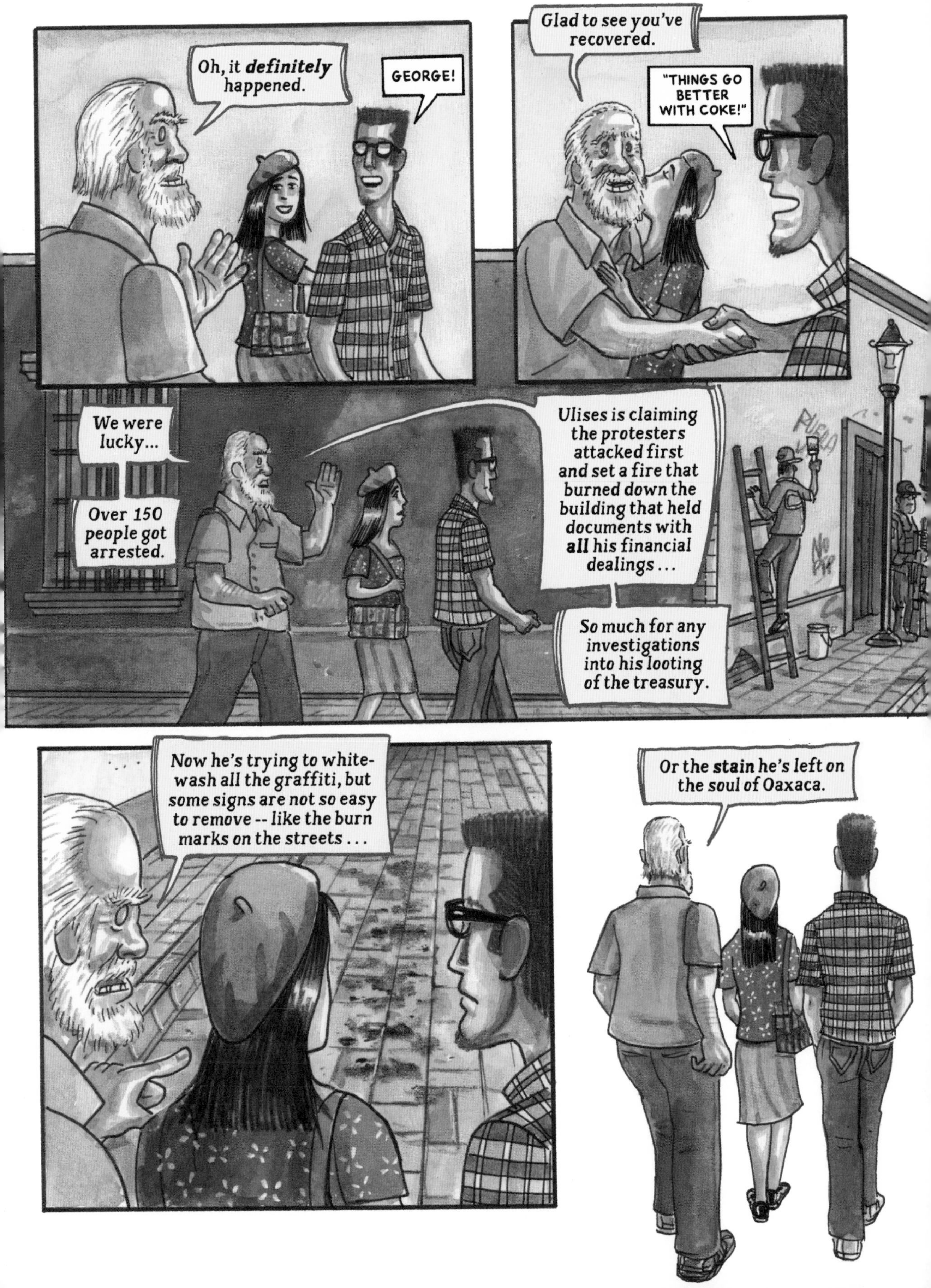

Oh, it *definitely* happened.
GEORGE!
Glad to see you've recovered.
"THINGS GO BETTER WITH COKE!"
We were lucky...
Over 150 people got arrested.
Ulises is claiming the protesters attacked first and set a fire that burned down the building that held documents with **all** his financial dealings...
So much for any investigations into his looting of the treasury.
Now he's trying to white-wash all the graffiti, but some signs are not so easy to remove -- like the burn marks on the streets...
Or the **stain** he's left on the soul of Oaxaca.

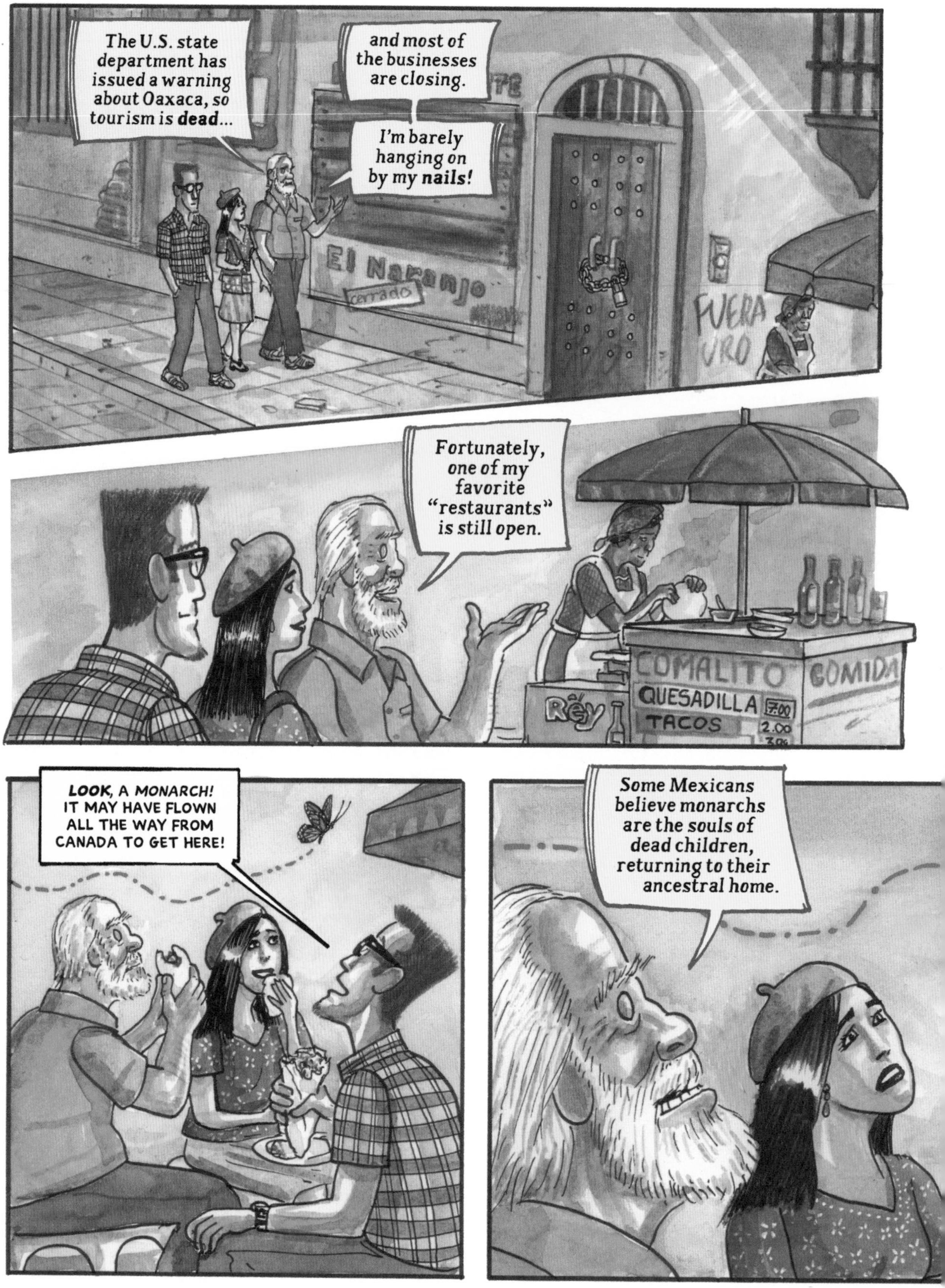
The U.S. state department has issued a warning about Oaxaca, so tourism is **dead**...
and most of the businesses are closing.
I'm barely hanging on by my **nails**!
El Naranjo
cerrado
FUERA URO
Fortunately, one of my favorite "restaurants" is still open.
COMALITO
COMIDA
QUESADILLA 7.00
TACOS 2.00
Rey
LOOK, A *MONARCH*! IT MAY HAVE FLOWN ALL THE WAY FROM CANADA TO GET HERE!
Some Mexicans believe monarchs are the souls of dead children, returning to their ancestral home.

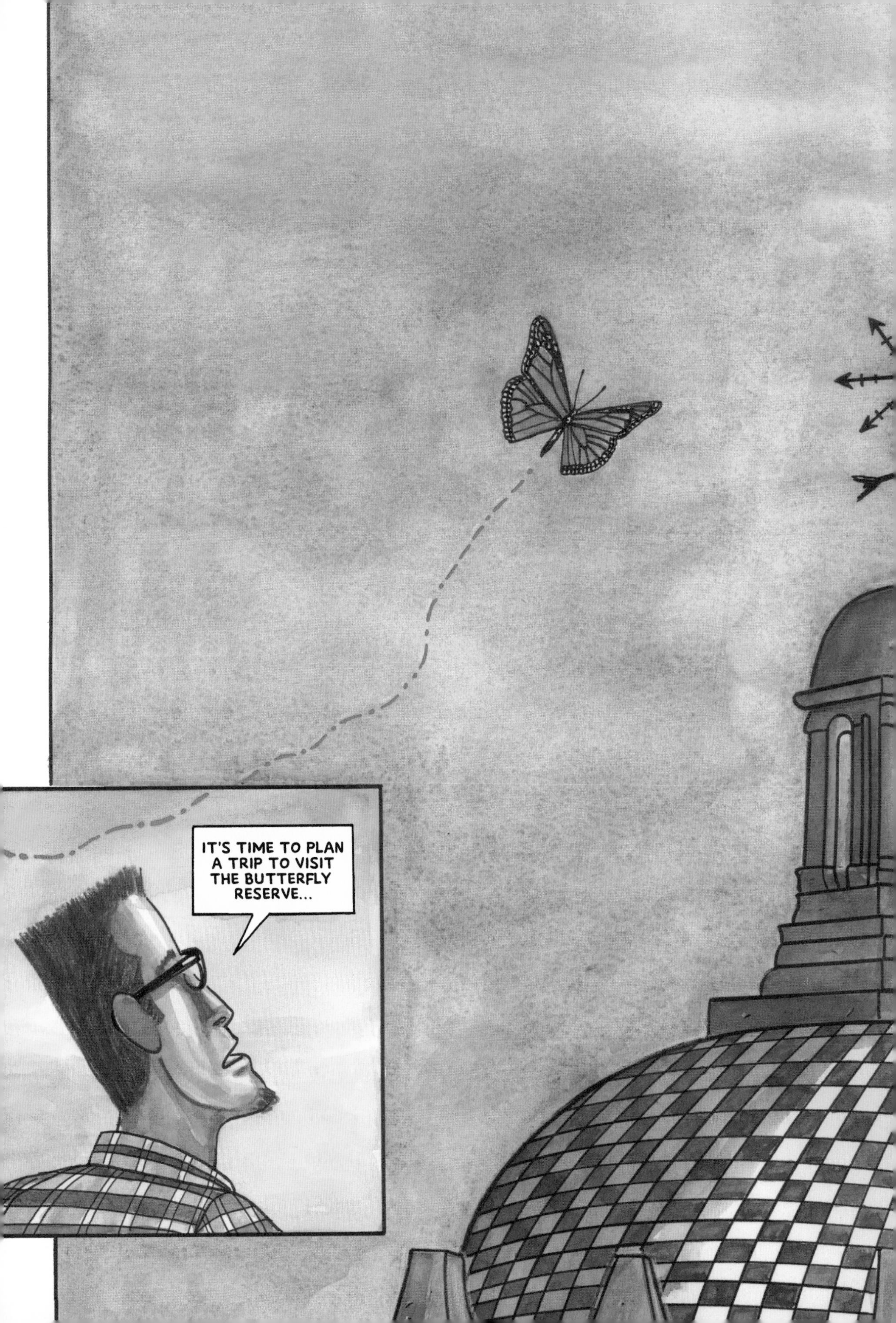
IT'S TIME TO PLAN A TRIP TO VISIT THE BUTTERFLY RESERVE...

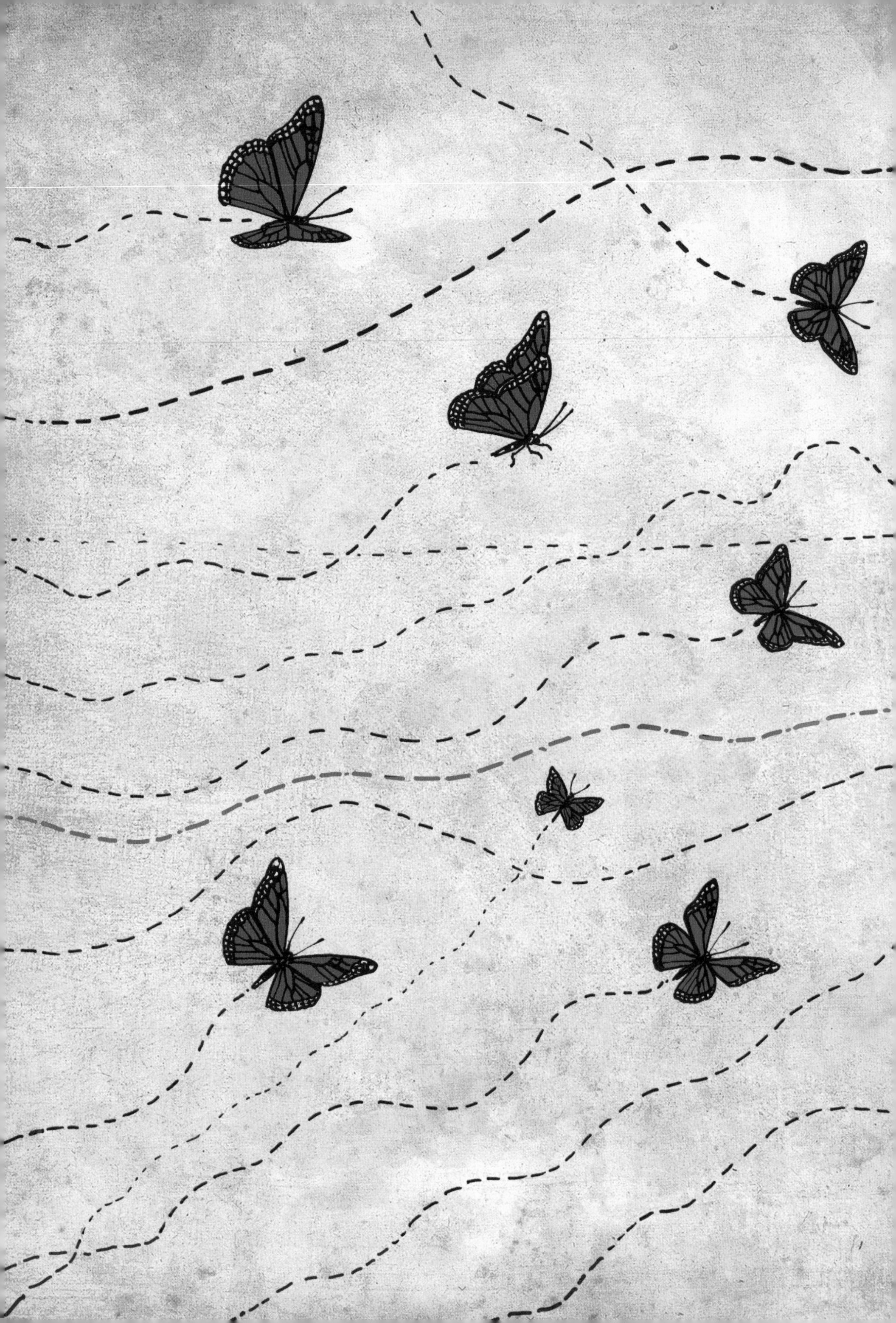

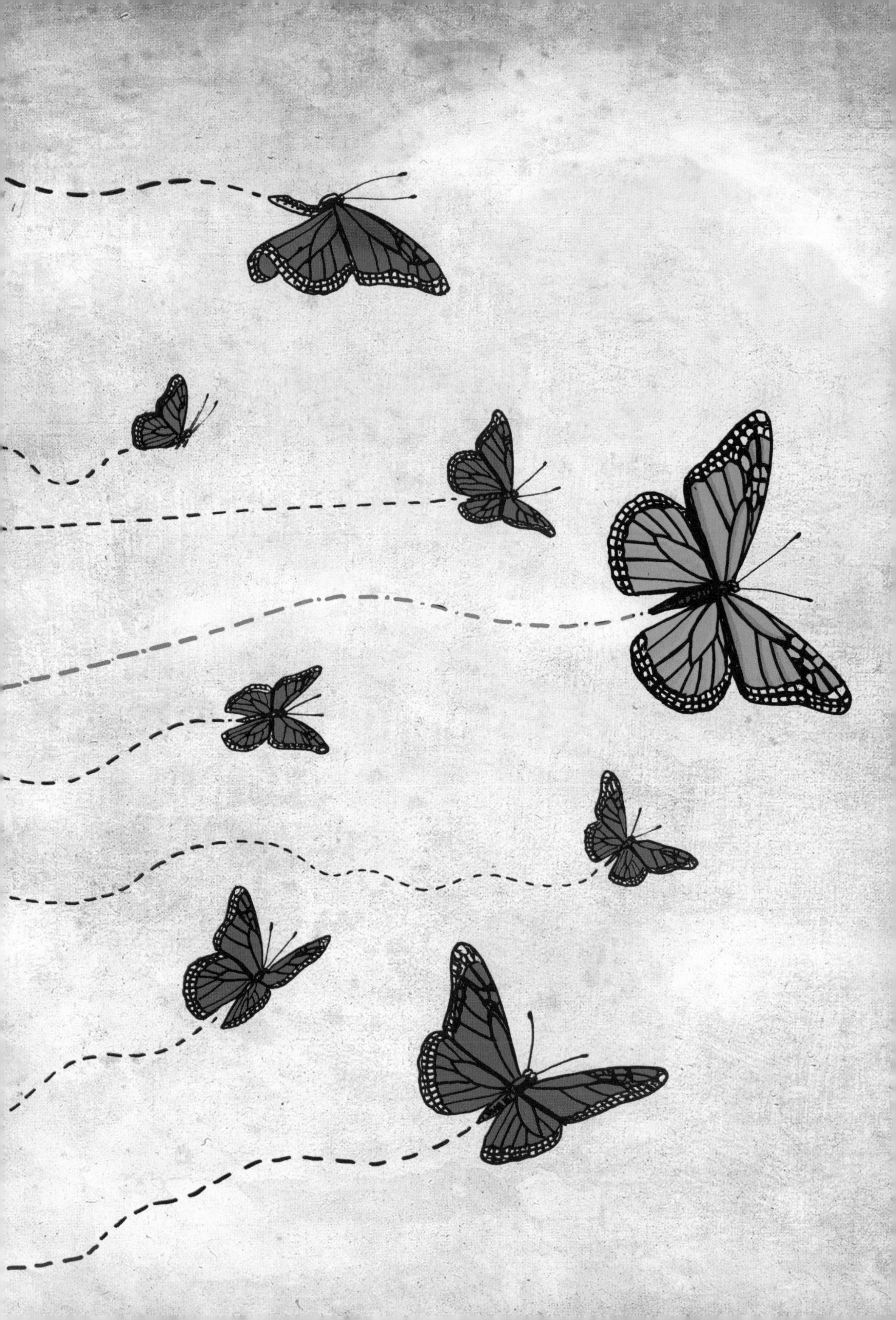

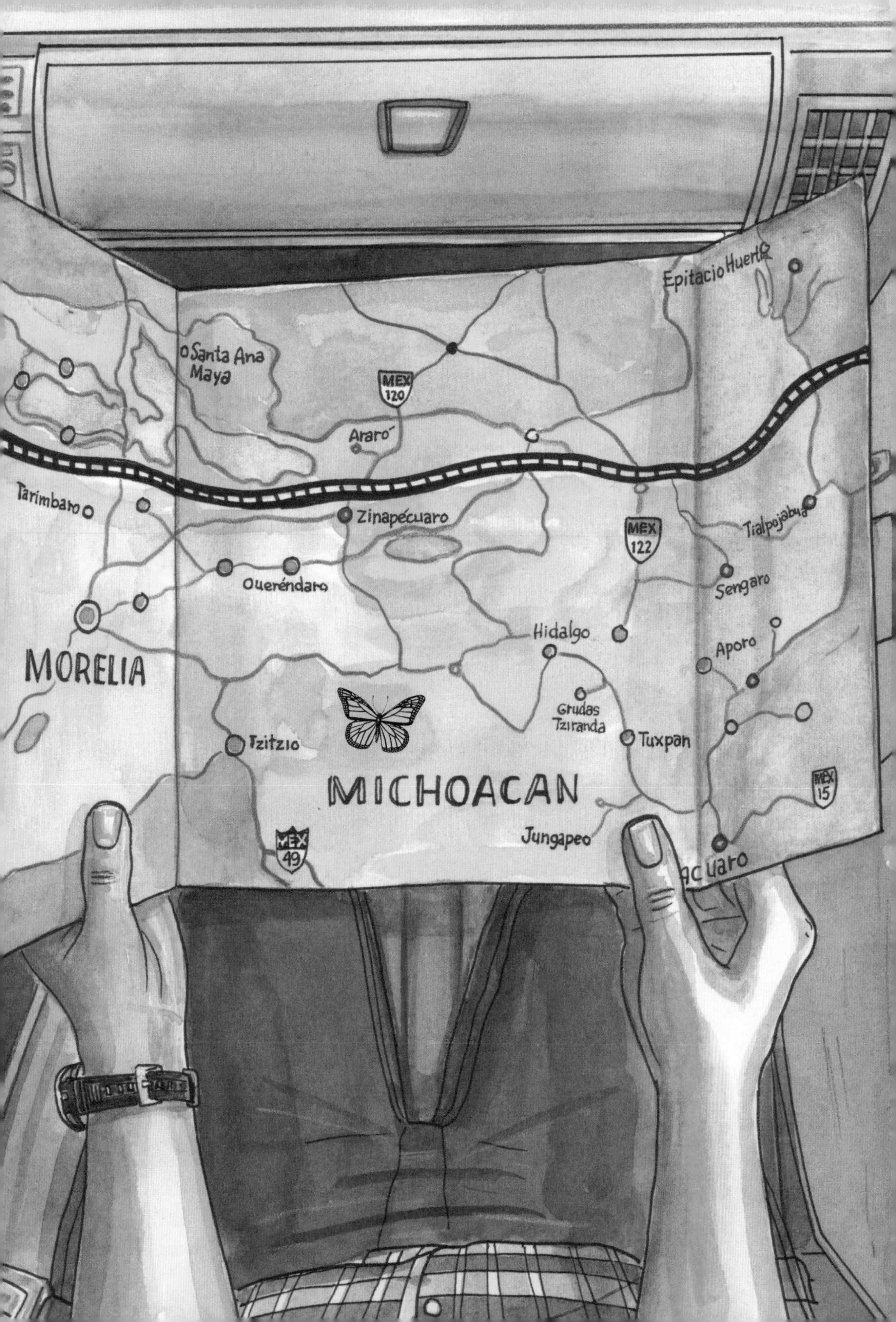
Epitacio Huert
Santa Ana Maya
MEX 120
Araró
Tarimbaro
Zinapécuaro
MEX 122
Tialpujahua
Oueréndaro
Sengaro
Hidalgo
Aporo
MORELIA
Grudas Tziranda
Tzitzio
Tuxpan
MICHOACAN
MEX 15
Jungapeo
MEX 49
acuaro

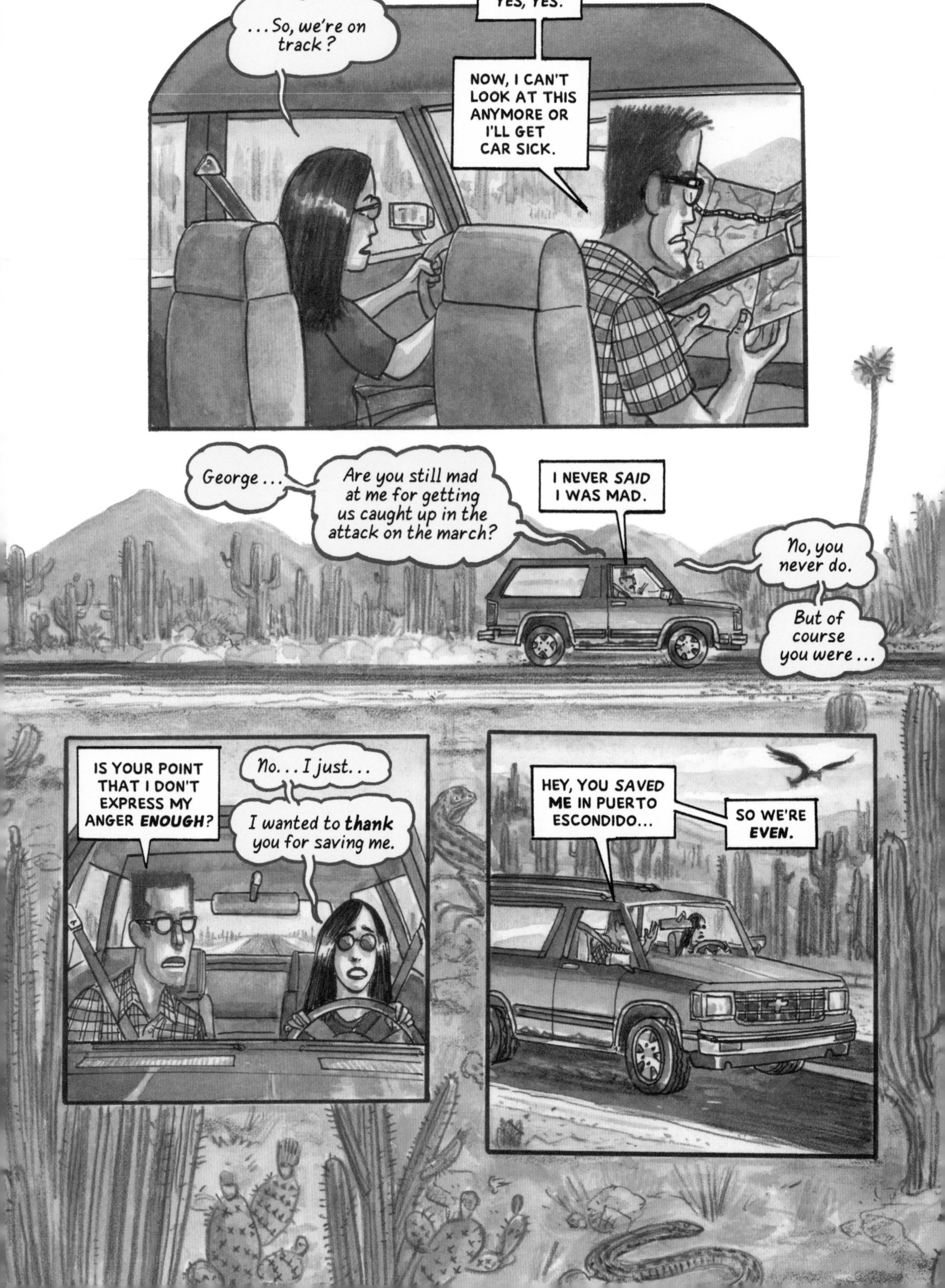

...So, we're on track?
YES, YES.
NOW, I CAN'T LOOK AT THIS ANYMORE OR I'LL GET CAR SICK.
George...
Are you still mad at me for getting us caught up in the attack on the march?
I NEVER SAID I WAS MAD.
No, you never do.
But of course you were...
IS YOUR POINT THAT I DON'T EXPRESS MY ANGER ENOUGH?
No... I just...
I wanted to thank you for saving me.
HEY, YOU SAVED ME IN PUERTO ESCONDIDO...
SO WE'RE EVEN.

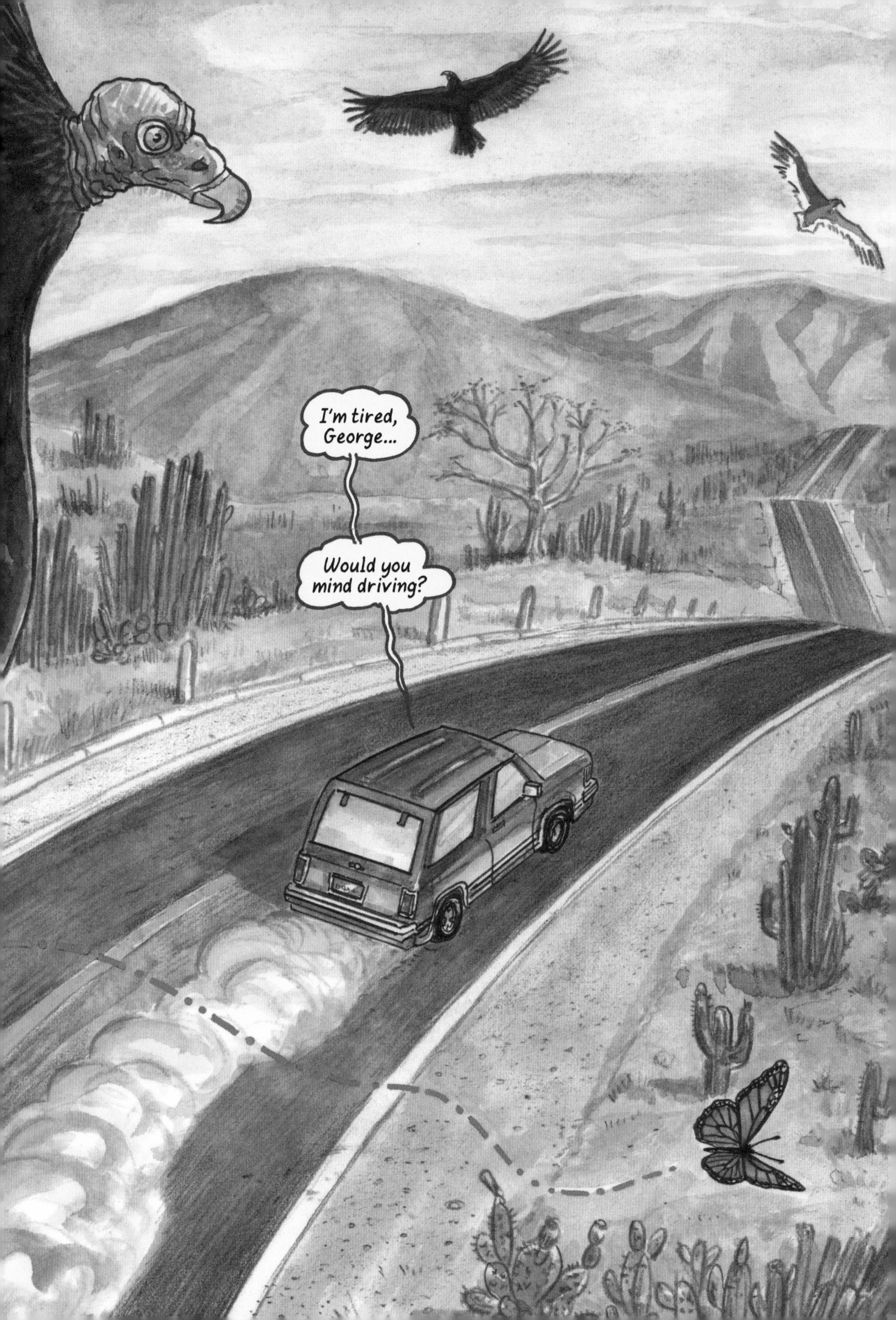
I'm tired, George...
Would you mind driving?

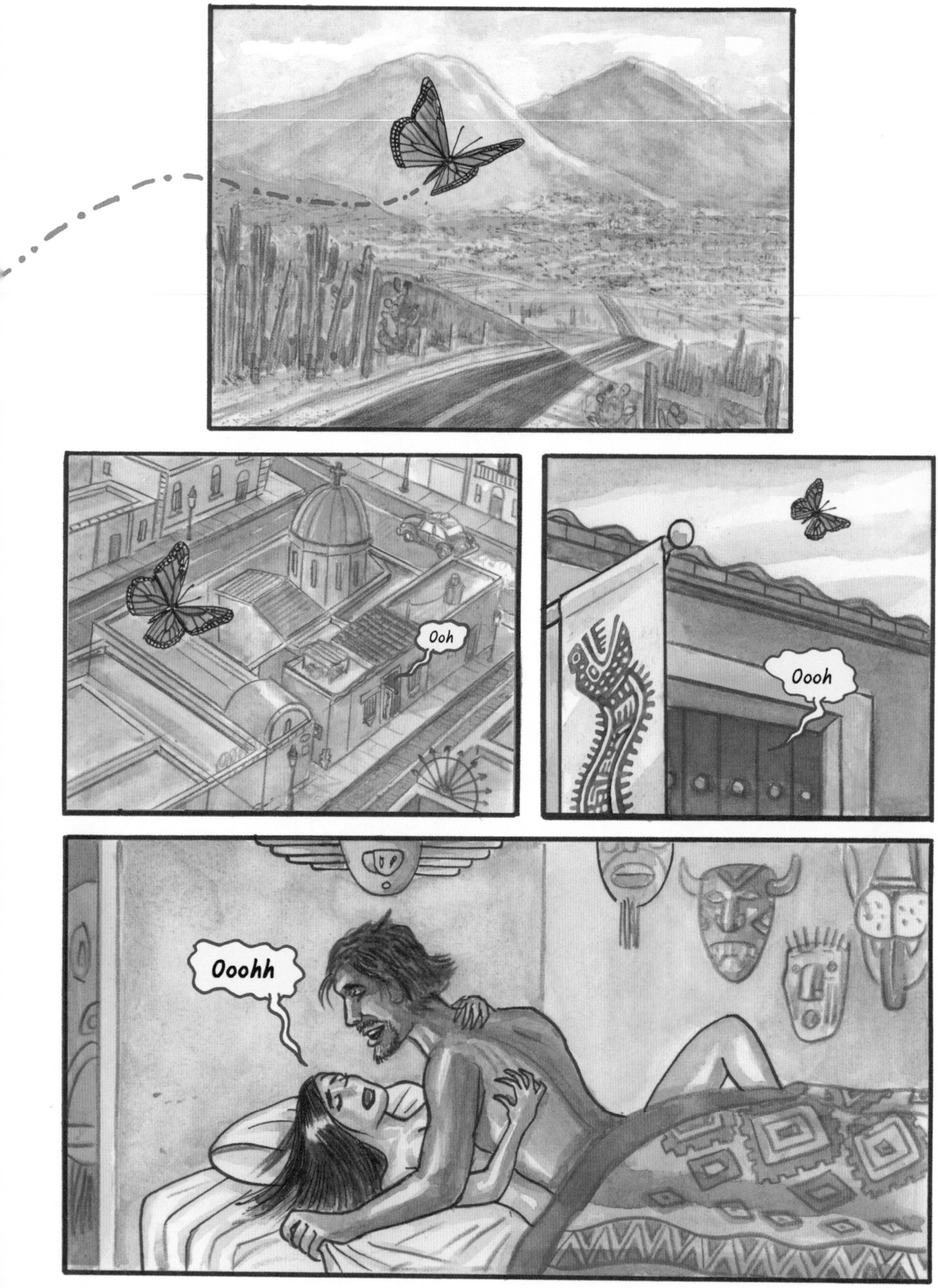
Ooh
Oooh
Ooohh

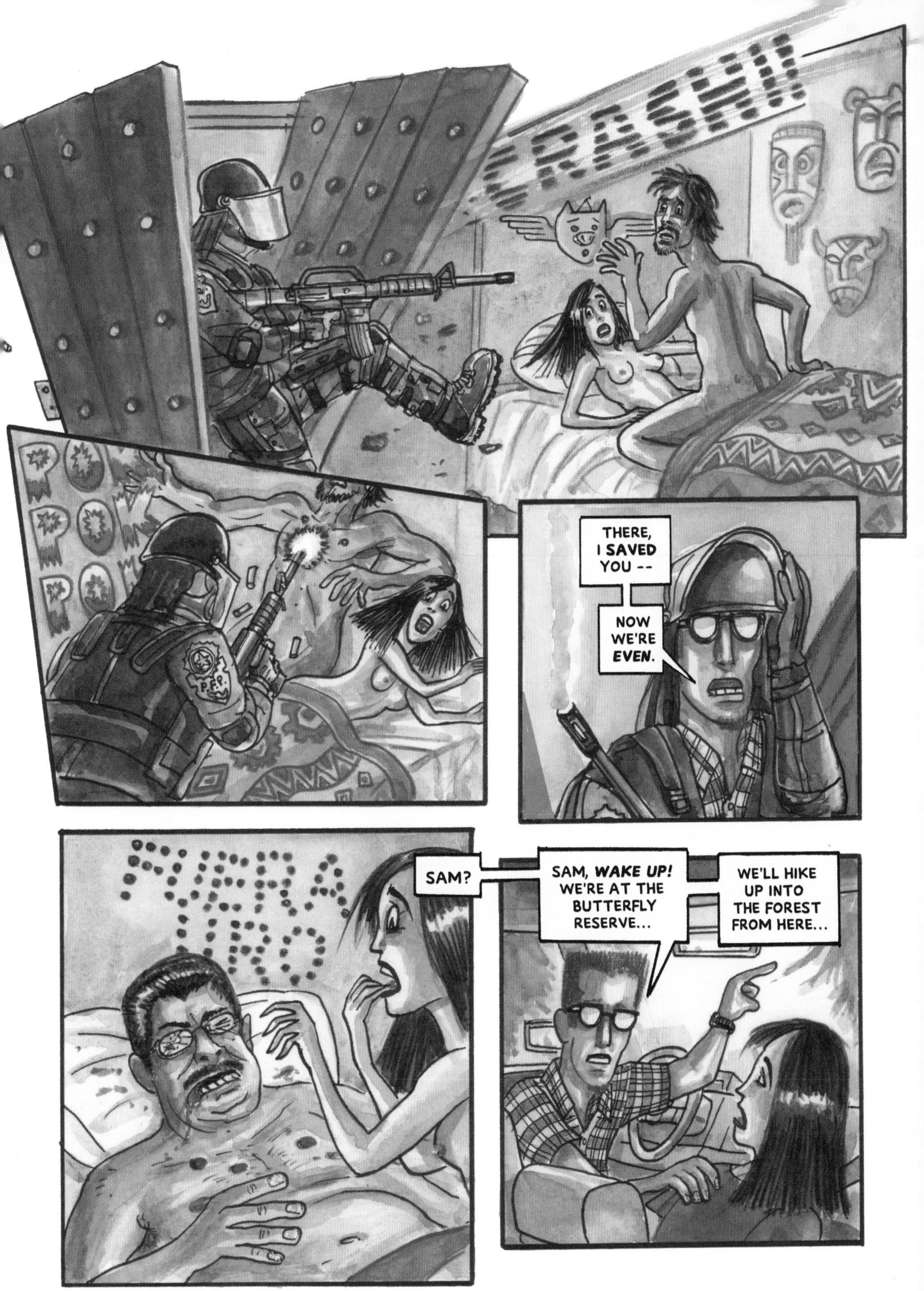
CRASH!!
THERE, I SAVED YOU --
NOW WE'RE EVEN.
SAM?
SAM, WAKE UP! WE'RE AT THE BUTTERFLY RESERVE...
WE'LL HIKE UP INTO THE FOREST FROM HERE...

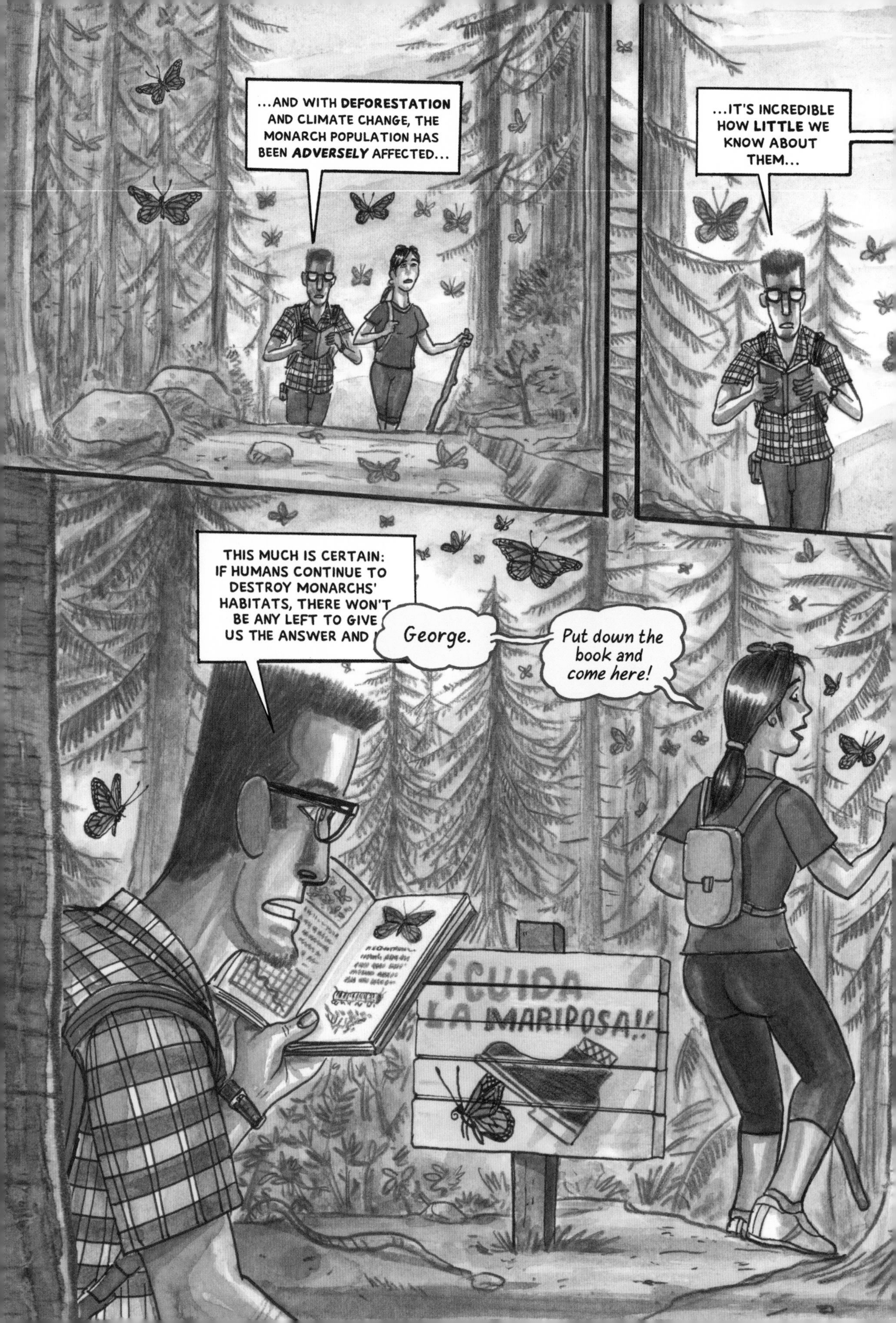
...AND WITH DEFORESTATION AND CLIMATE CHANGE, THE MONARCH POPULATION HAS BEEN ADVERSELY AFFECTED...
...IT'S INCREDIBLE HOW LITTLE WE KNOW ABOUT THEM...
THIS MUCH IS CERTAIN: IF HUMANS CONTINUE TO DESTROY MONARCHS' HABITATS, THERE WON'T BE ANY LEFT TO GIVE US THE ANSWER AND
George.
Put down the book and come here!
¡CUIDA LA MARIPOSA!

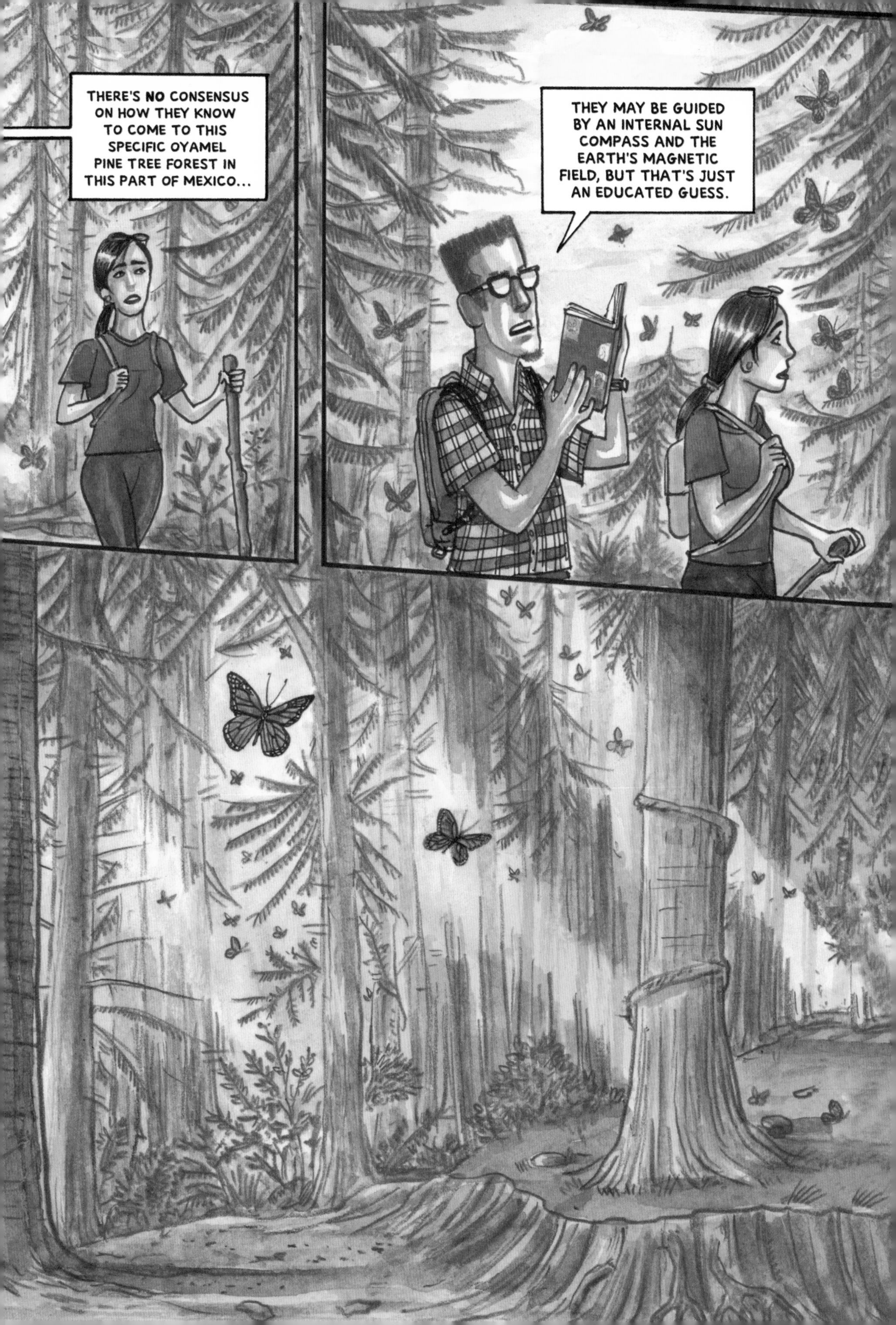
THERE'S NO CONSENSUS ON HOW THEY KNOW TO COME TO THIS SPECIFIC OYAMEL PINE TREE FOREST IN THIS PART OF MEXICO...
THEY MAY BE GUIDED BY AN INTERNAL SUN COMPASS AND THE EARTH'S MAGNETIC FIELD, BUT THAT'S JUST AN EDUCATED GUESS.

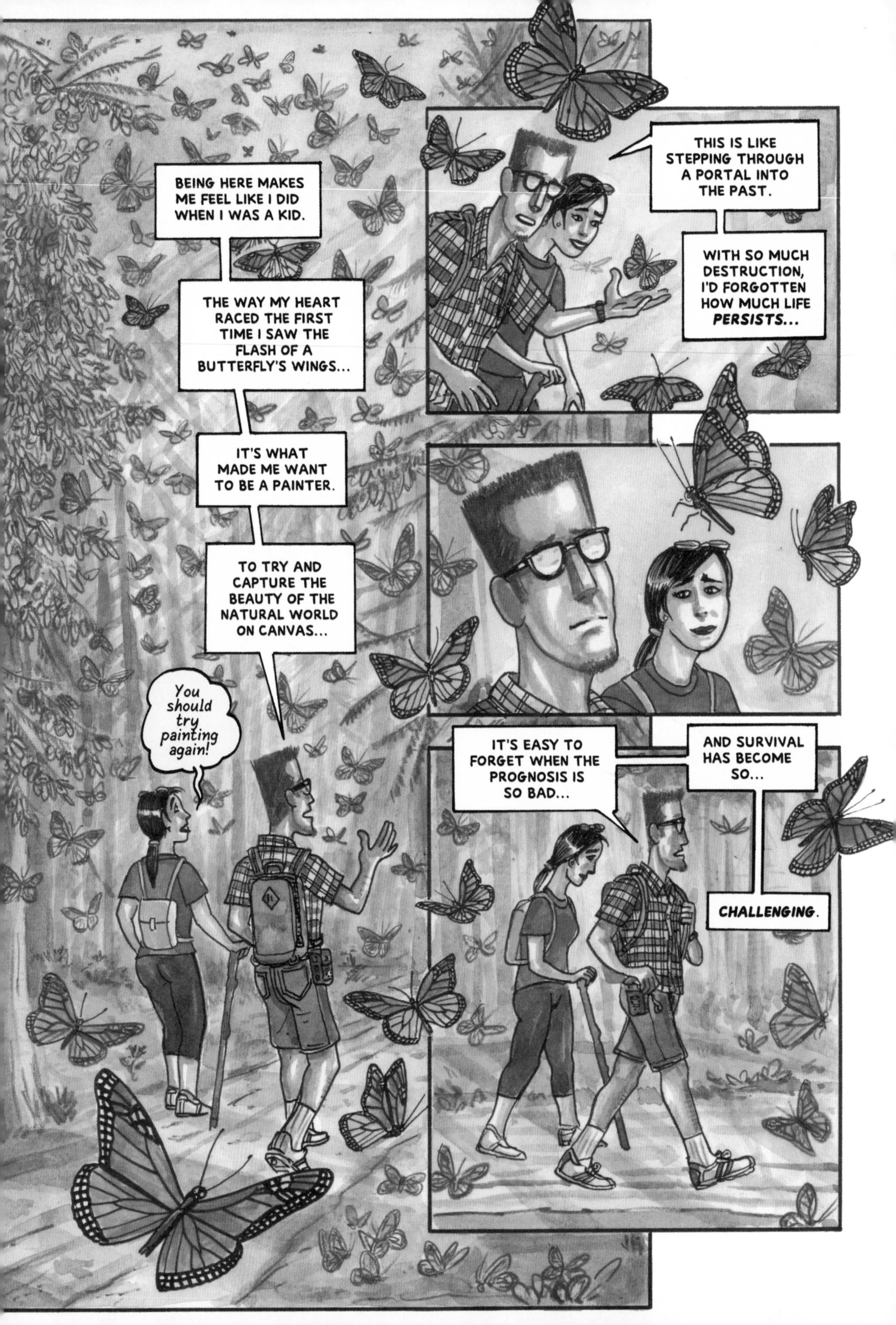
BEING HERE MAKES ME FEEL LIKE I DID WHEN I WAS A KID.
THE WAY MY HEART RACED THE FIRST TIME I SAW THE FLASH OF A BUTTERFLY'S WINGS...
IT'S WHAT MADE ME WANT TO BE A PAINTER.
TO TRY AND CAPTURE THE BEAUTY OF THE NATURAL WORLD ON CANVAS...
You should try painting again!
THIS IS LIKE STEPPING THROUGH A PORTAL INTO THE PAST.
WITH SO MUCH DESTRUCTION, I'D FORGOTTEN HOW MUCH LIFE *PERSISTS*...
IT'S EASY TO FORGET WHEN THE PROGNOSIS IS SO BAD...
AND SURVIVAL HAS BECOME SO...
CHALLENGING.

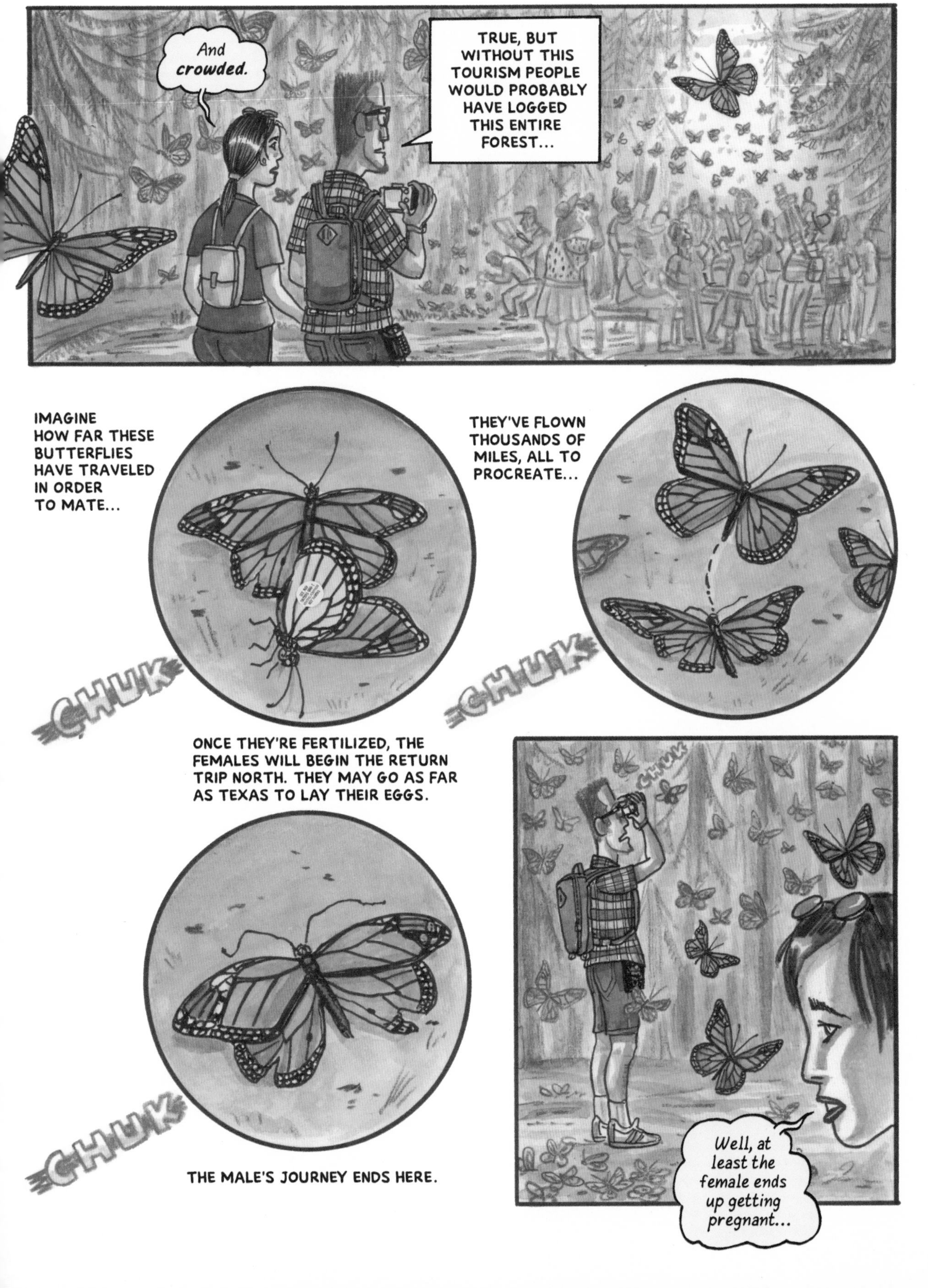
And *crowded.*
TRUE, BUT WITHOUT THIS TOURISM PEOPLE WOULD PROBABLY HAVE LOGGED THIS ENTIRE FOREST...
IMAGINE HOW FAR THESE BUTTERFLIES HAVE TRAVELED IN ORDER TO MATE...
CHUK
THEY'VE FLOWN THOUSANDS OF MILES, ALL TO PROCREATE...
CHUK
ONCE THEY'RE FERTILIZED, THE FEMALES WILL BEGIN THE RETURN TRIP NORTH. THEY MAY GO AS FAR AS TEXAS TO LAY THEIR EGGS.
CHUK
THE MALE'S JOURNEY ENDS HERE.
CHUK
Well, at least the female ends up getting pregnant...

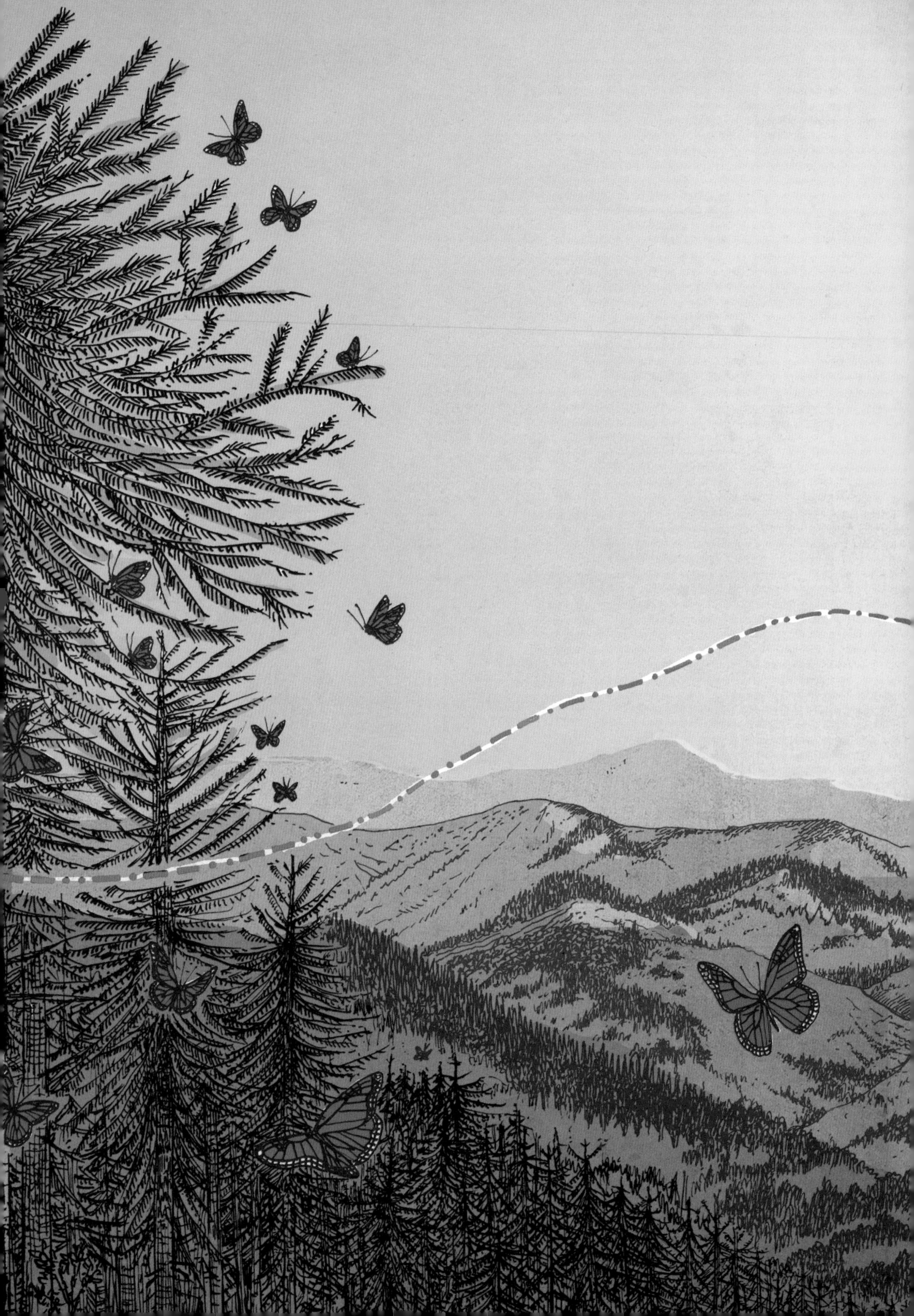

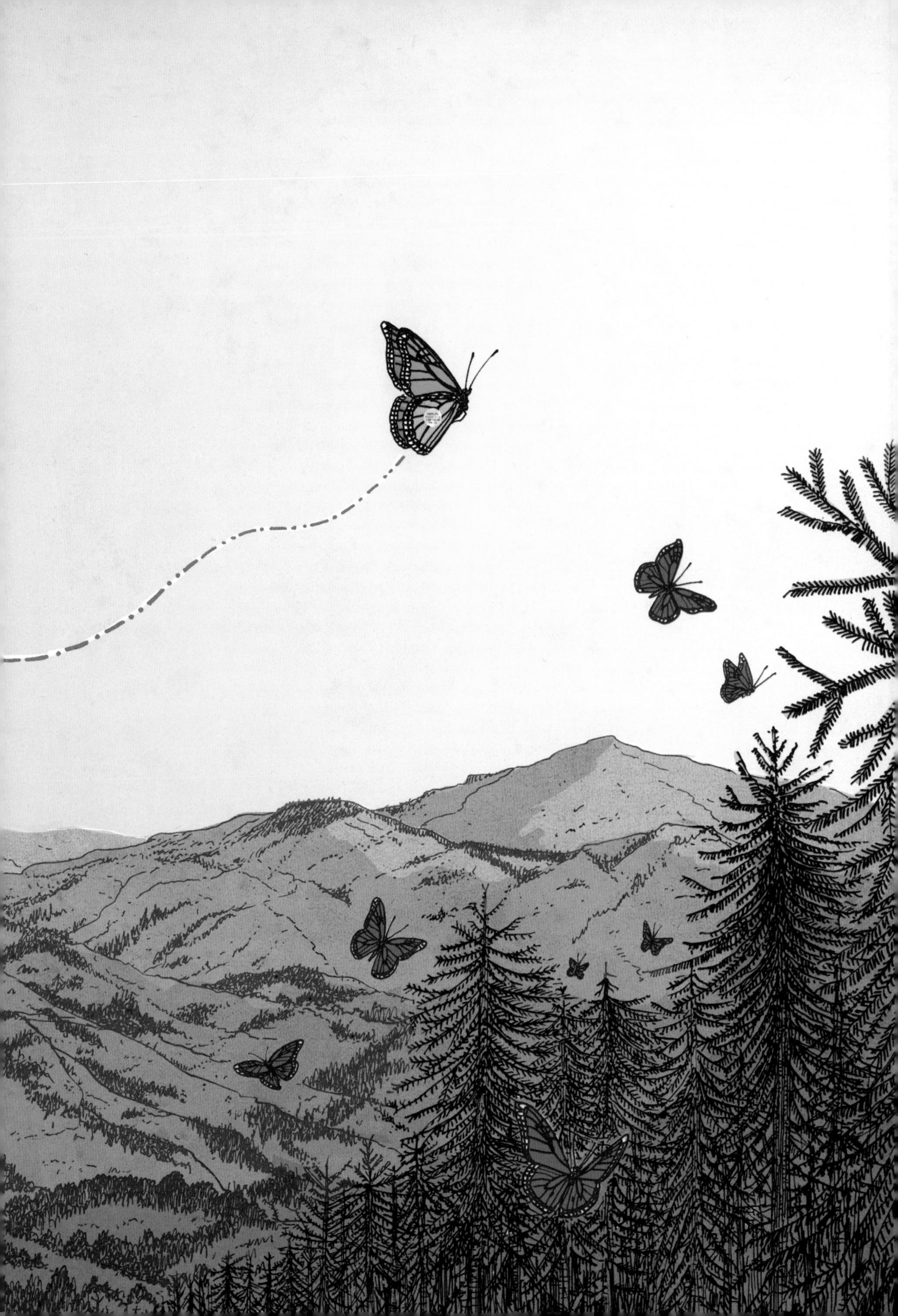

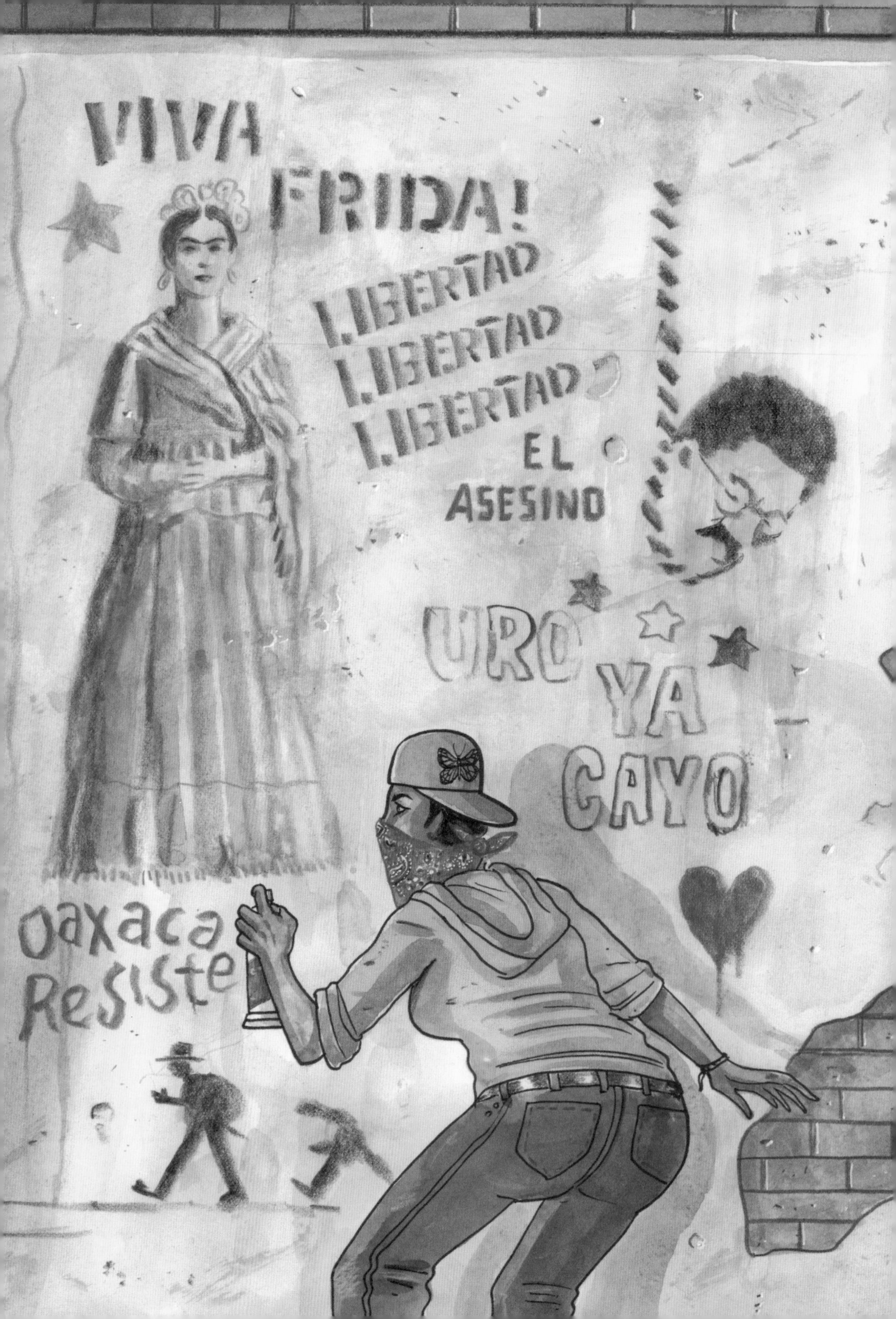
VIVA
FRIDA!
LIBERTAD
LIBERTAD
LIBERTAD
EL
ASESINO
URO
YA
CAYO
Oaxaca
Resiste

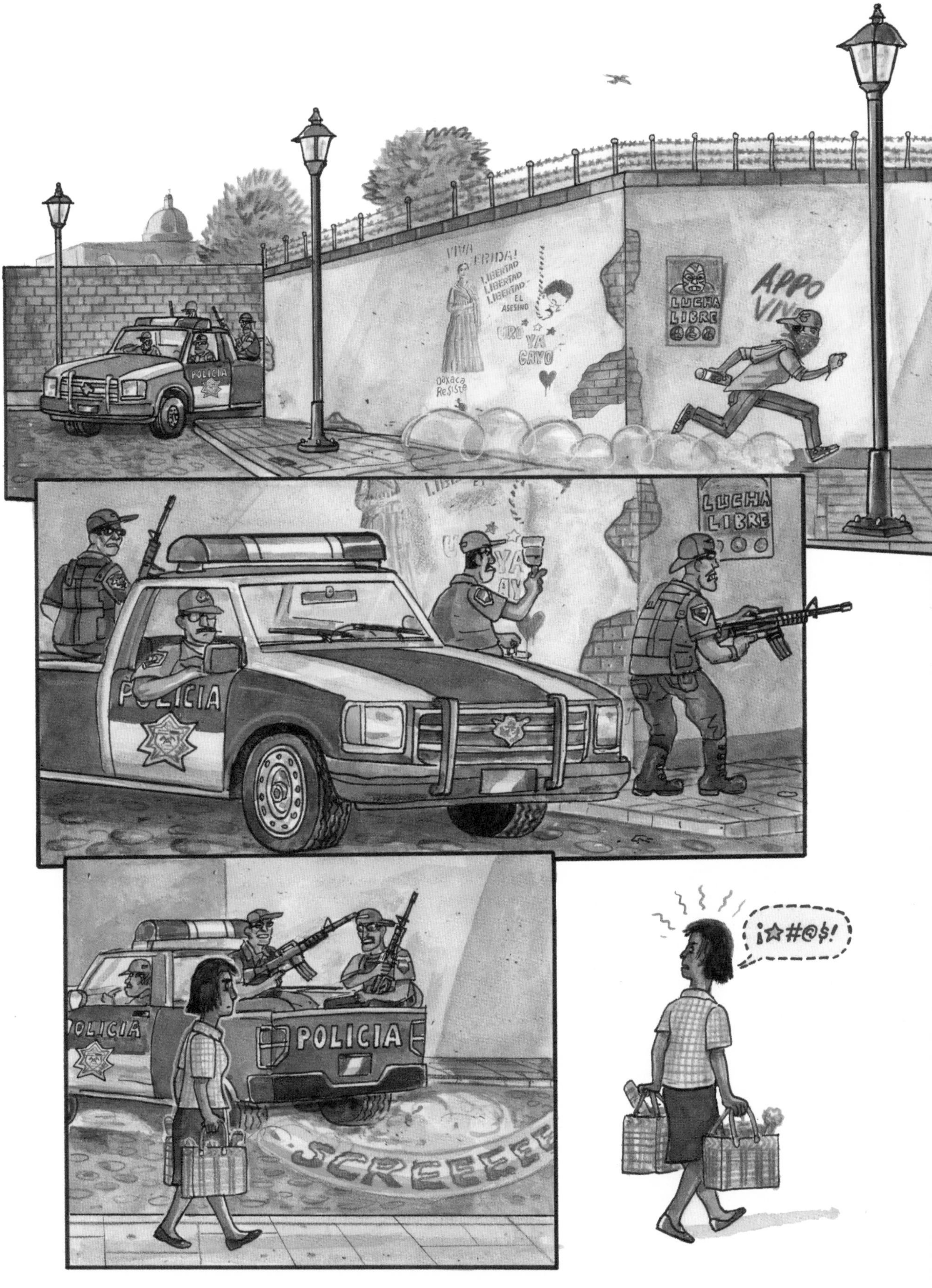

VIVA FRIDA!
LIBERTAD
LIBERTAD
LIBERTAD
EL ASESINO
YA CAYO
Oaxaca Resiste
LUCHA LIBRE
APPO VIV
POLICIA
LUCHA LIBRE
POLICIA
POLICIA
POLICIA
SCREEEEE
¡☆#@$!

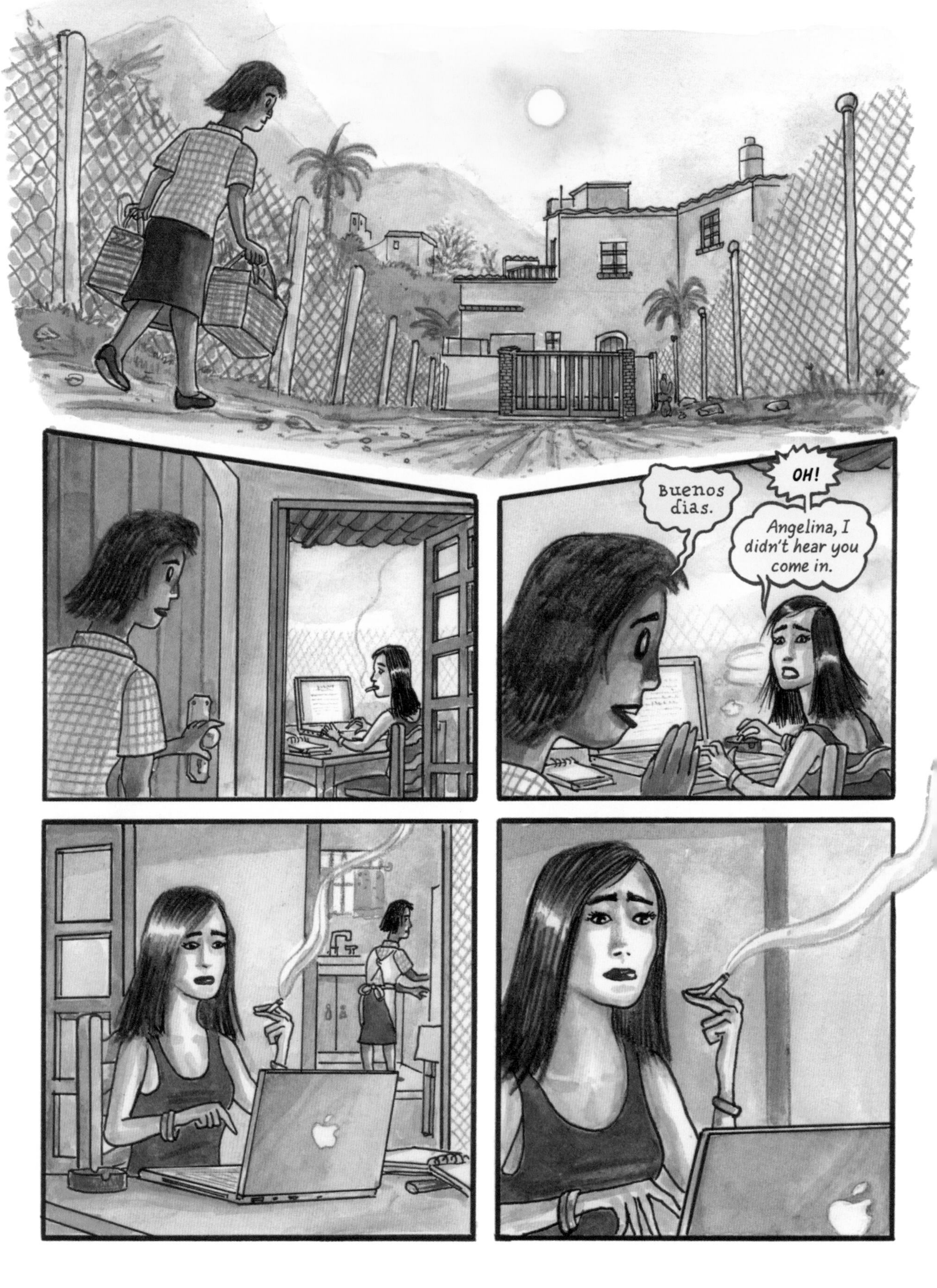
Buenos dias.
OH!
Angelina, I didn't hear you come in.

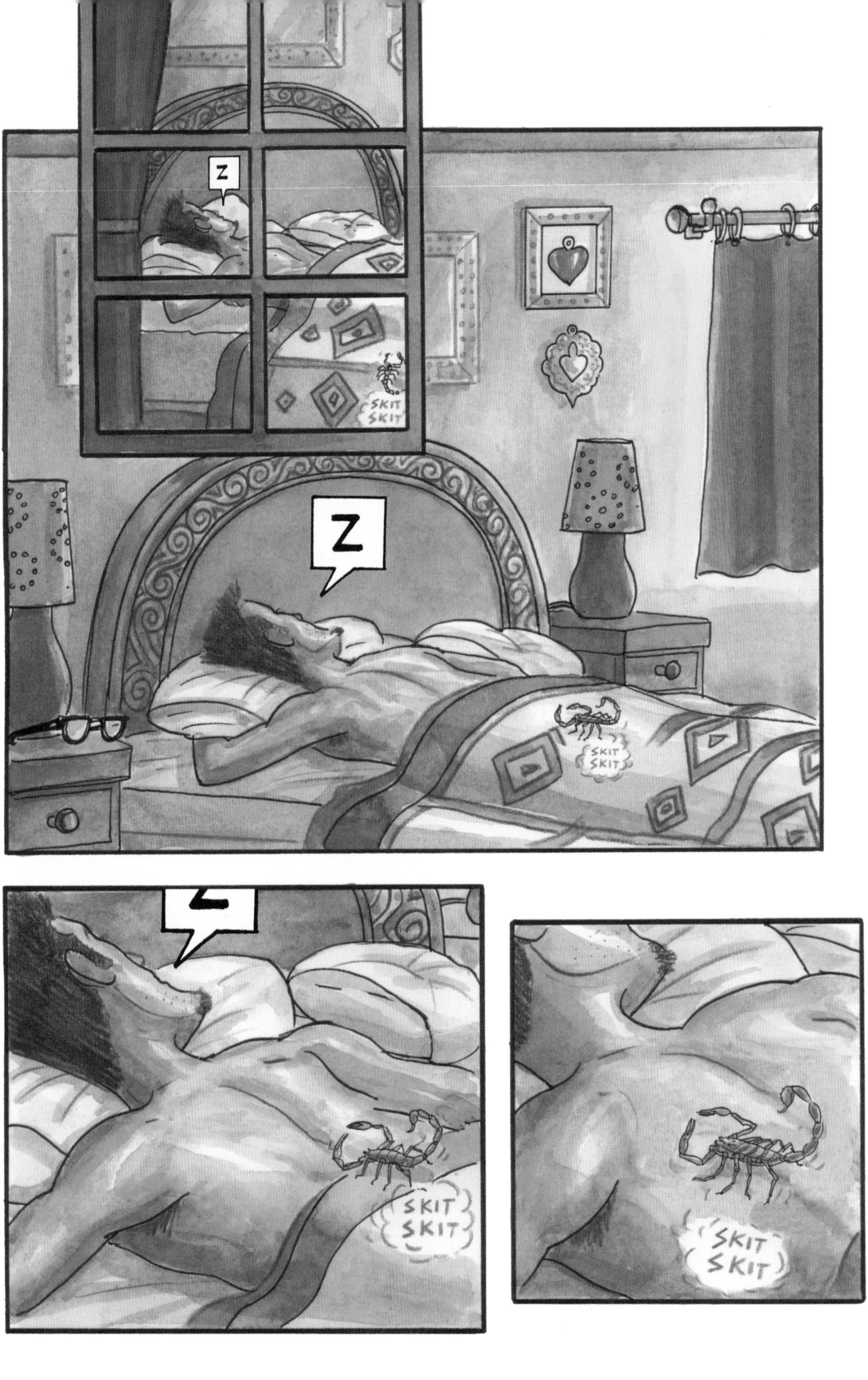
Z
SKIT SKIT
Z
SKIT SKIT
SKIT SKIT
SKIT SKIT

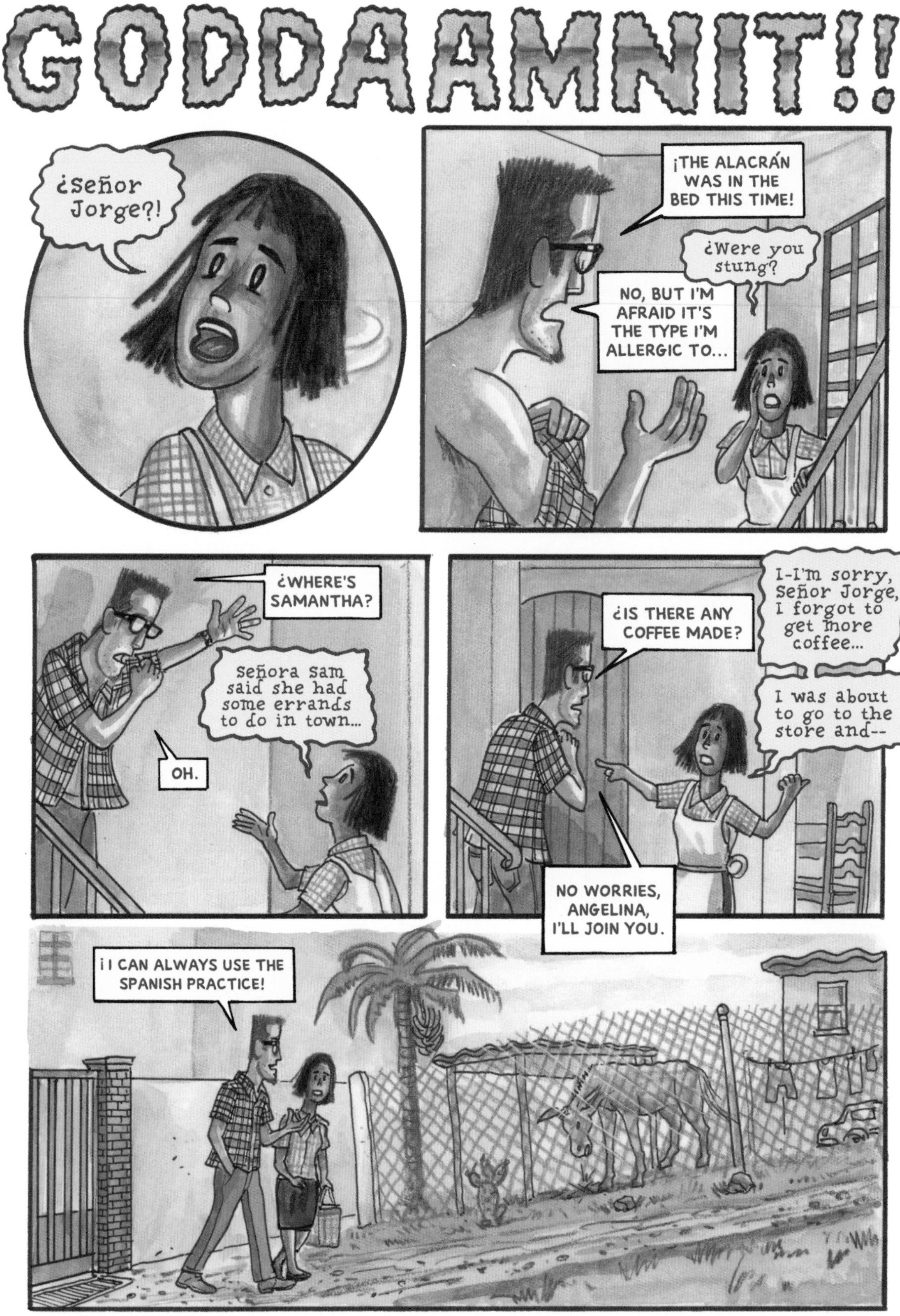
GODDAMNIT!!
¿Señor Jorge?!
¡THE ALACRÁN WAS IN THE BED THIS TIME!
¿Were you stung?
NO, BUT I'M AFRAID IT'S THE TYPE I'M ALLERGIC TO...
¿WHERE'S SAMANTHA?
Señora Sam said she had some errands to do in town...
OH.
¿IS THERE ANY COFFEE MADE?
I-I'm sorry, Señor Jorge, I forgot to get more coffee...
I was about to go to the store and--
NO WORRIES, ANGELINA, I'LL JOIN YOU.
¡I CAN ALWAYS USE THE SPANISH PRACTICE!

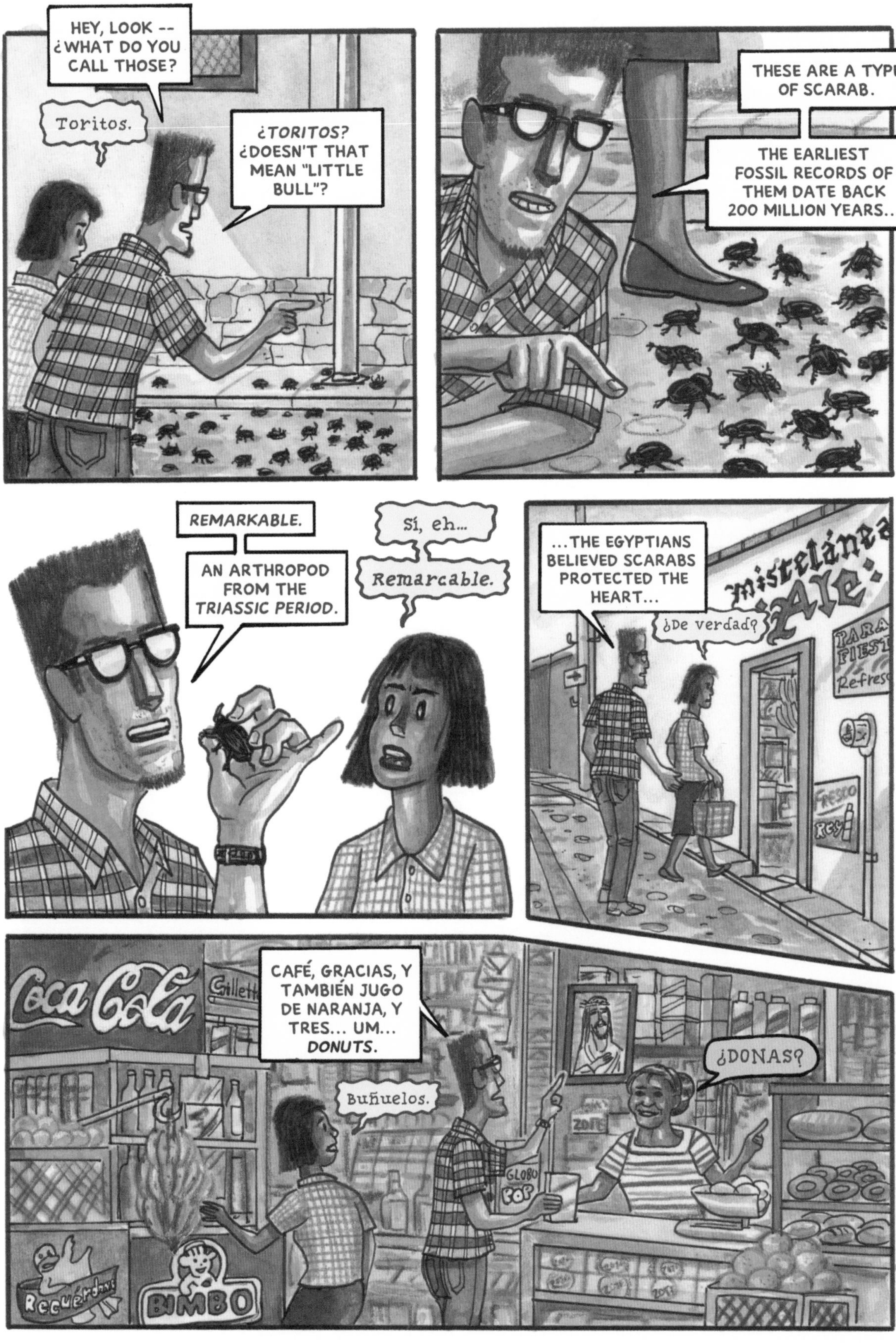

HEY, LOOK -- ¿WHAT DO YOU CALL THOSE?
Toritos.
¿TORITOS? ¿DOESN'T THAT MEAN "LITTLE BULL"?
THESE ARE A TYPE OF SCARAB.
THE EARLIEST FOSSIL RECORDS OF THEM DATE BACK 200 MILLION YEARS...
REMARKABLE.
AN ARTHROPOD FROM THE TRIASSIC PERIOD.
Sí, eh...
Remarcable.
...THE EGYPTIANS BELIEVED SCARABS PROTECTED THE HEART...
¿De verdad?
Miscelánea ¡Ale!
CAFÉ, GRACIAS, Y TAMBIÉN JUGO DE NARANJA, Y TRES... UM... DONUTS.
Buñuelos.
¿DONAS?
Coca-Cola
BIMBO

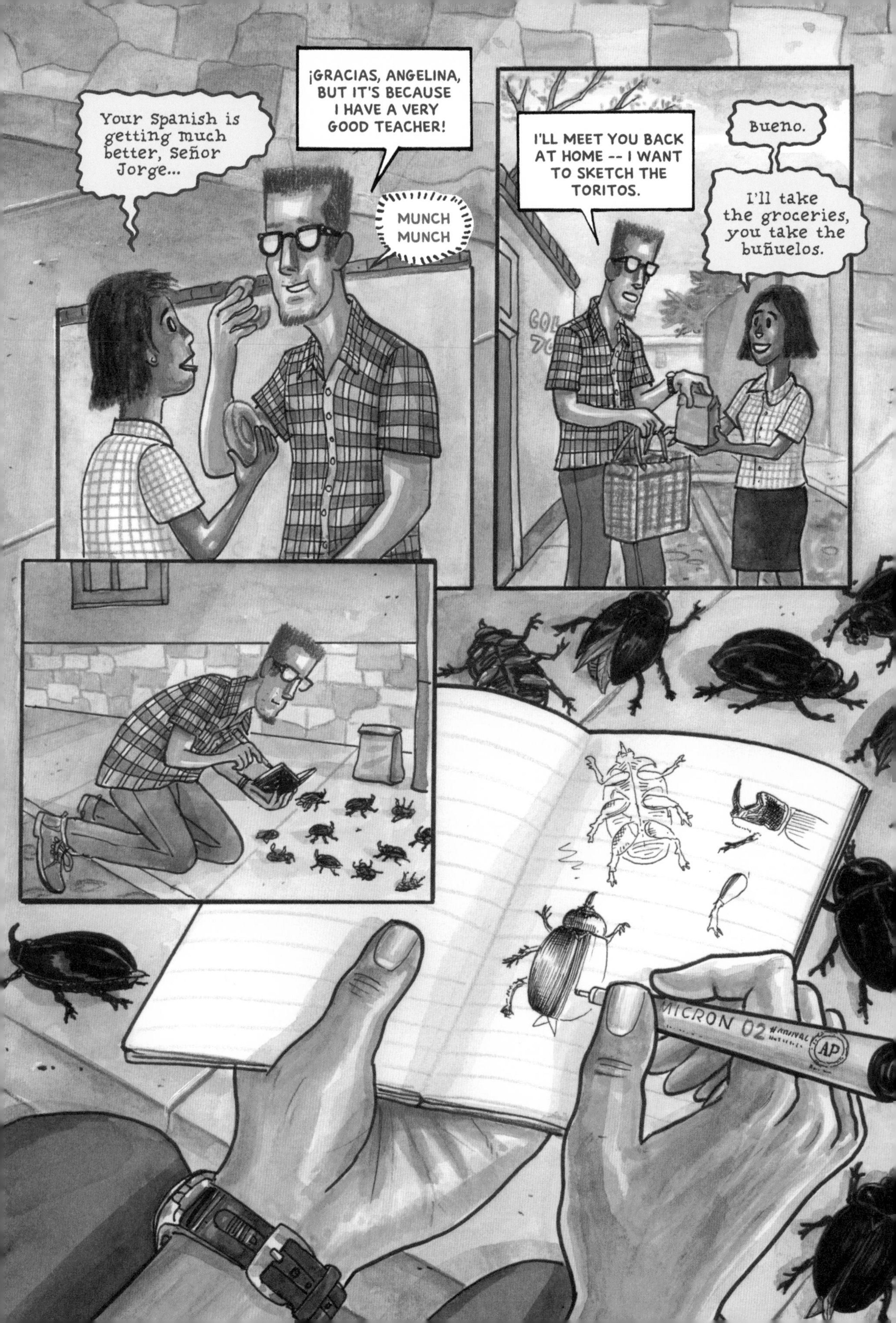
Your Spanish is getting much better, Señor Jorge...
¡GRACIAS, ANGELINA, BUT IT'S BECAUSE I HAVE A VERY GOOD TEACHER!
MUNCH MUNCH
I'LL MEET YOU BACK AT HOME -- I WANT TO SKETCH THE TORITOS.
Bueno.
I'll take the groceries, you take the buñuelos.
MICRON 02

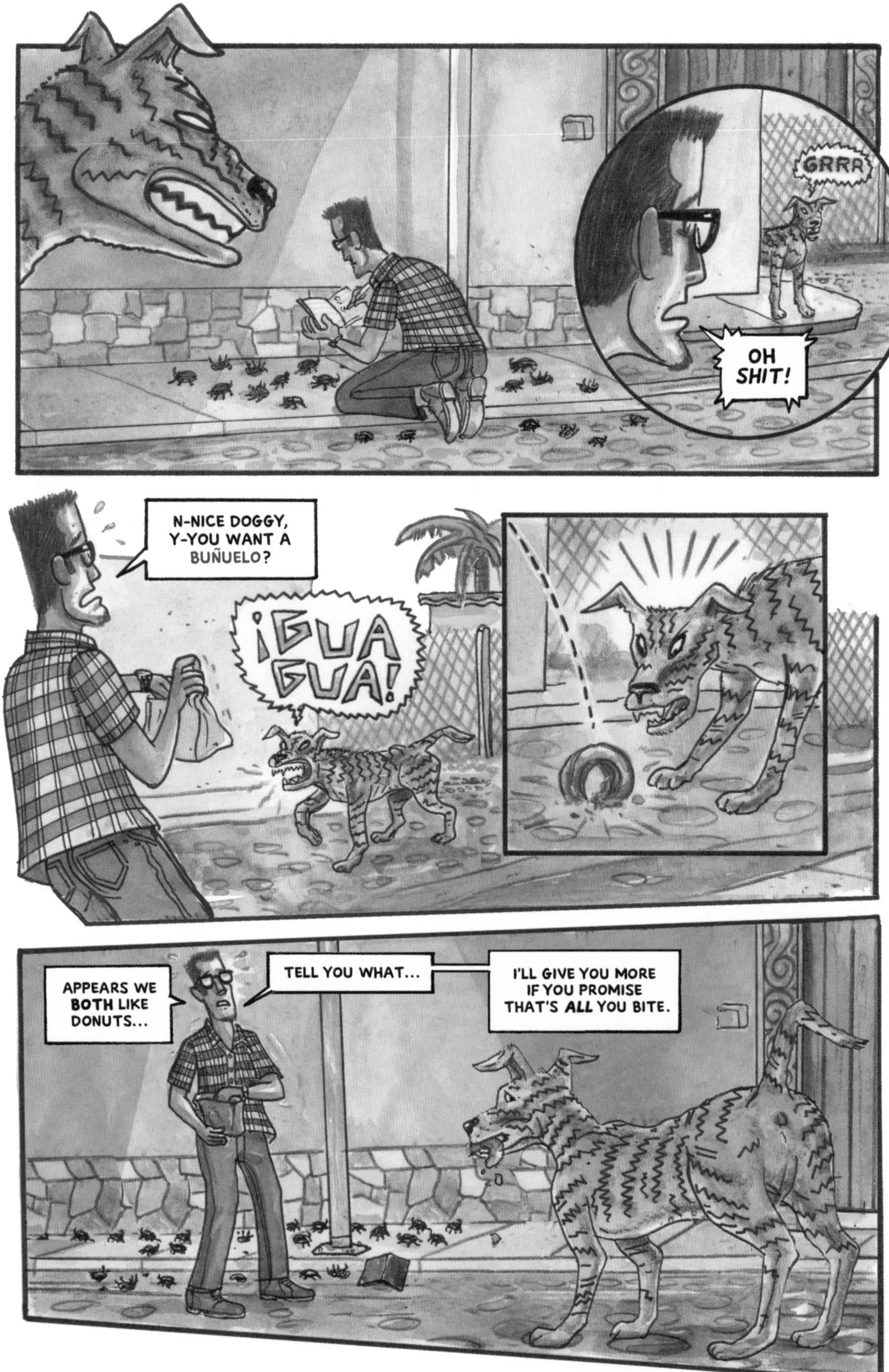
GRRR
OH SHIT!
N-NICE DOGGY, Y-YOU WANT A BUÑUELO?
¡GUA GUA!
APPEARS WE BOTH LIKE DONUTS...
TELL YOU WHAT...
I'LL GIVE YOU MORE IF YOU PROMISE THAT'S ALL YOU BITE.

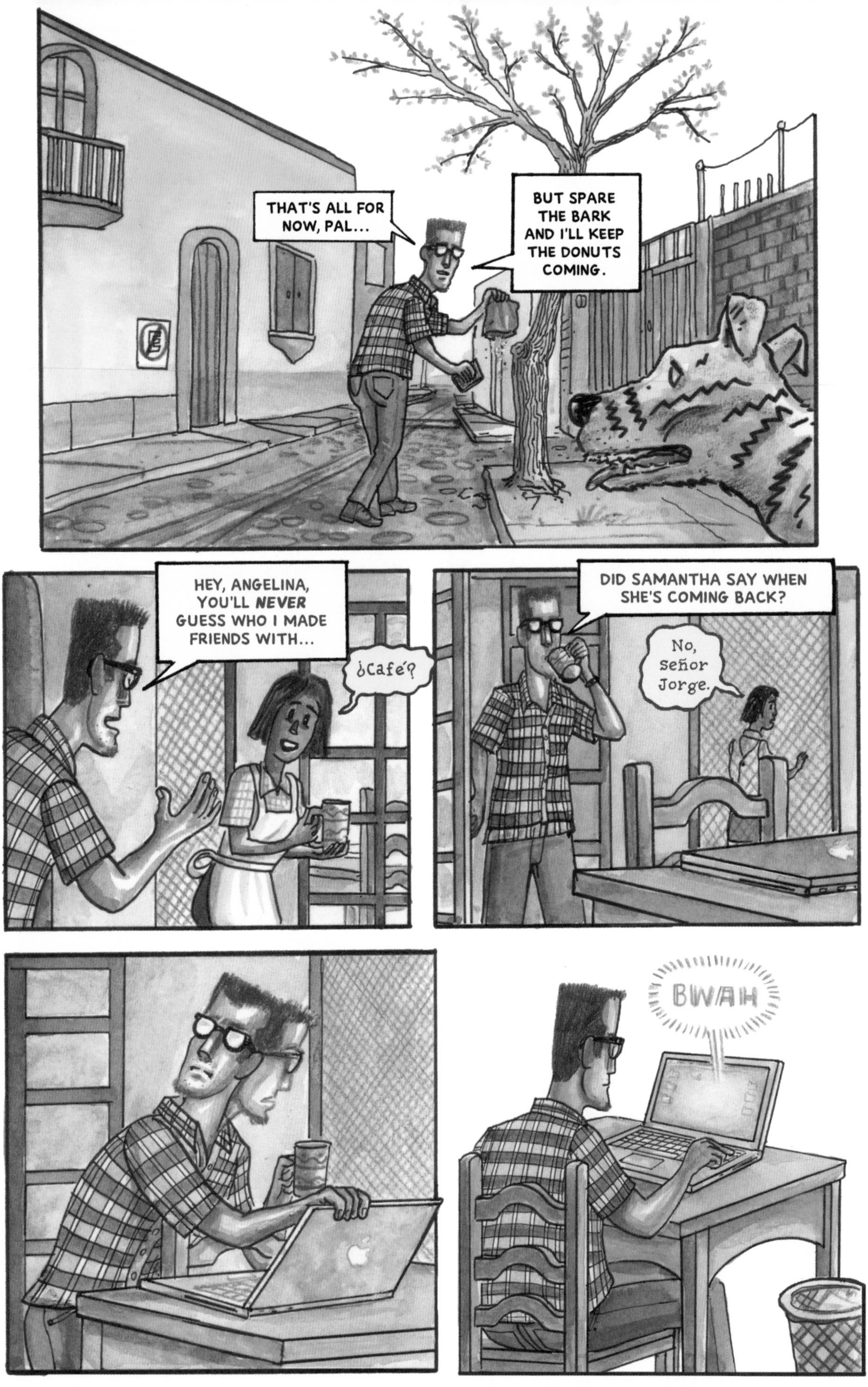
THAT'S ALL FOR NOW, PAL...
BUT SPARE THE BARK AND I'LL KEEP THE DONUTS COMING.
HEY, ANGELINA, YOU'LL *NEVER* GUESS WHO I MADE FRIENDS WITH...
¿Café?
DID SAMANTHA SAY WHEN SHE'S COMING BACK?
No, señor Jorge.
BWAH

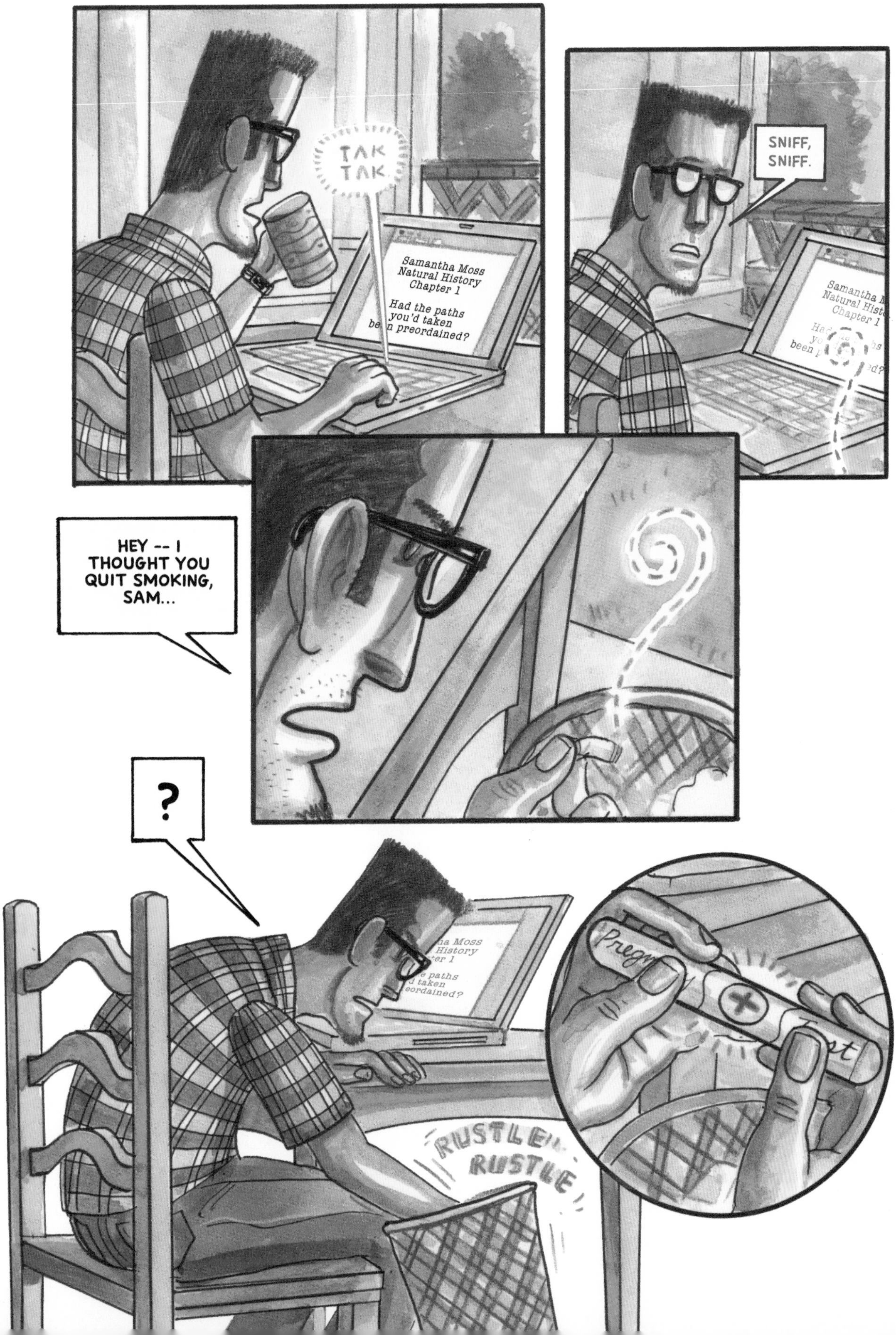

TAK TAK.
Samantha Moss
Natural History
Chapter 1
Had the paths you'd taken been preordained?
SNIFF, SNIFF.
HEY -- I THOUGHT YOU QUIT SMOKING, SAM...
?
RUSTLE RUSTLE

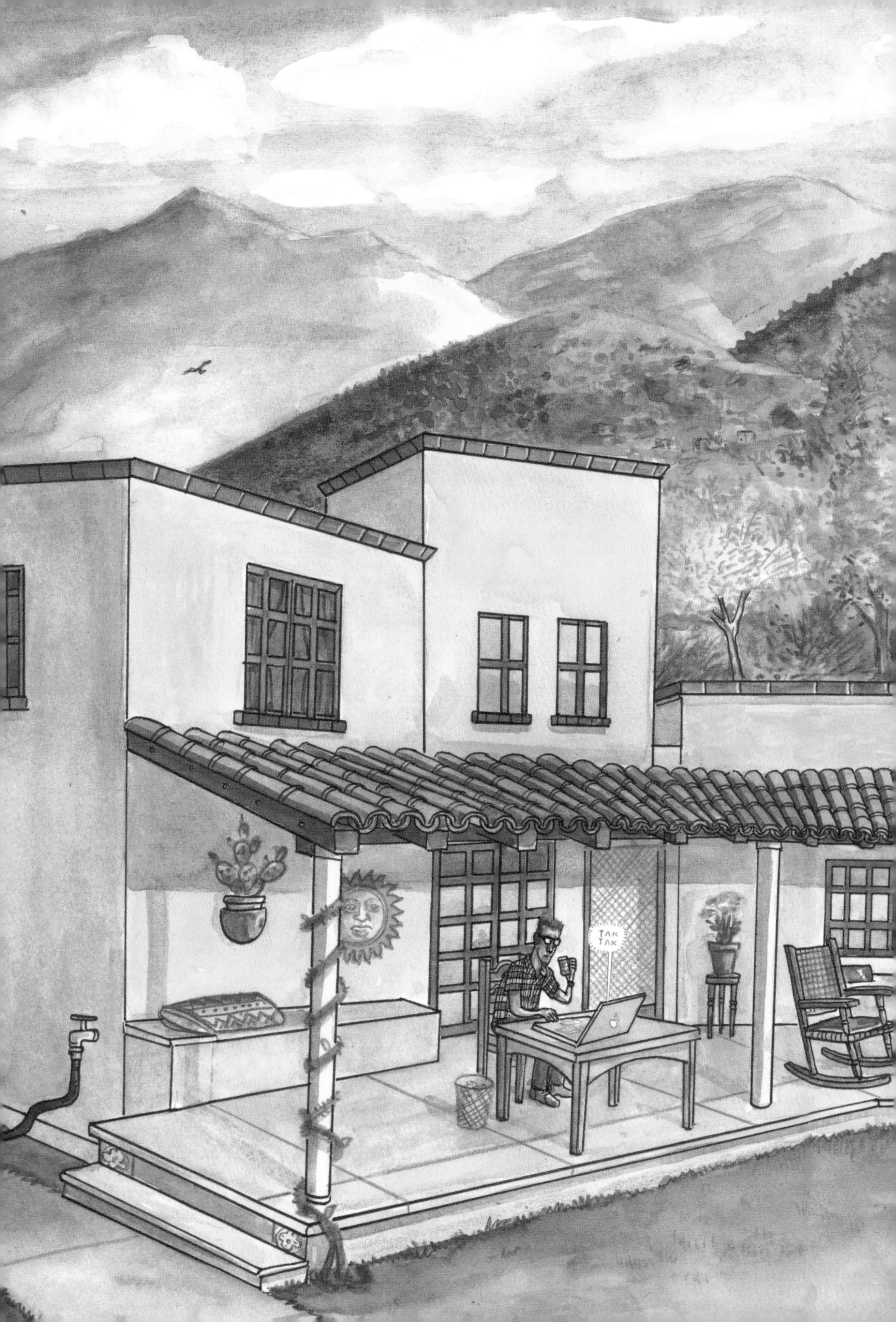
TAK TAK

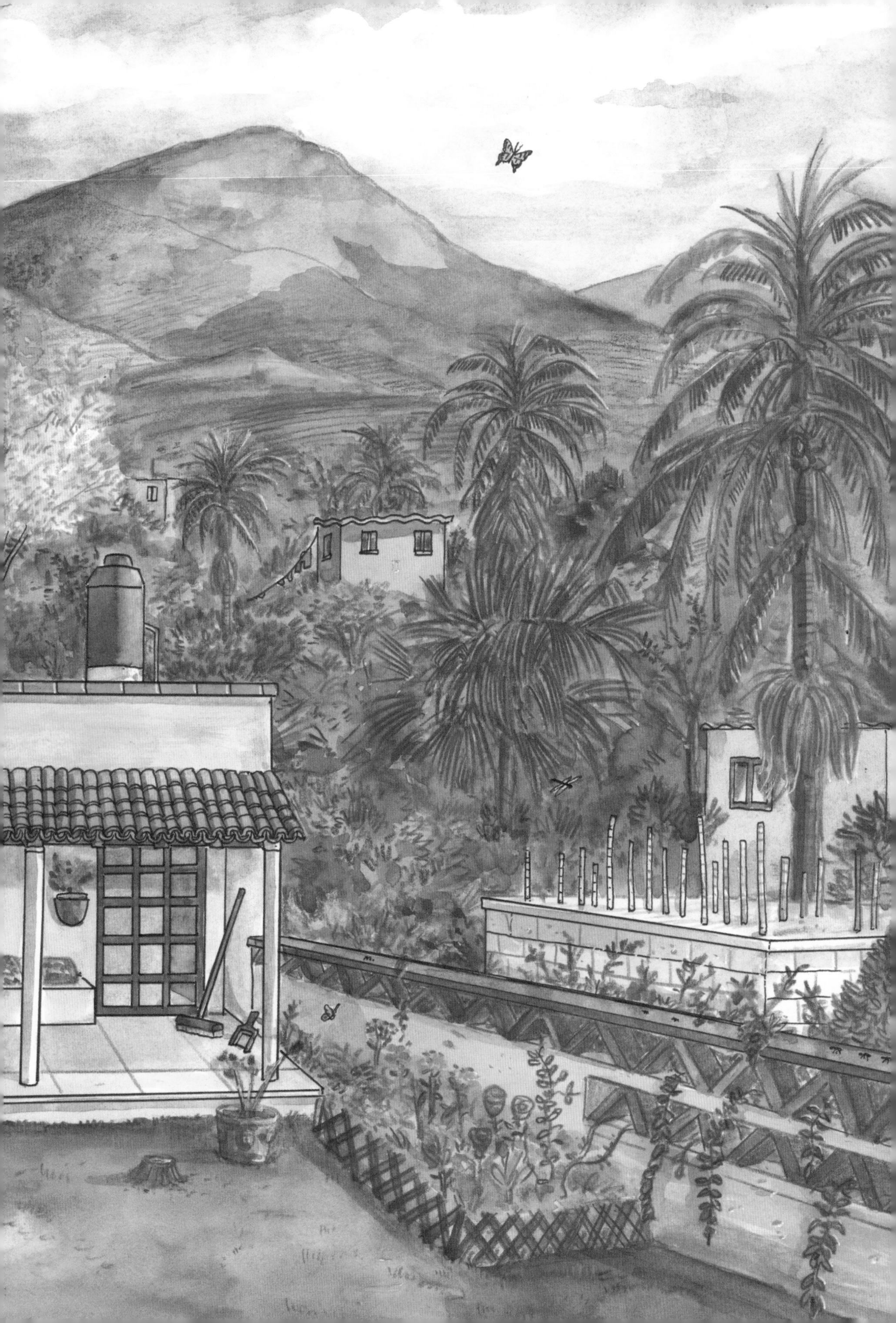

YOU HAVE GONE TOO FAR.
PLEASE TURN AROUND...

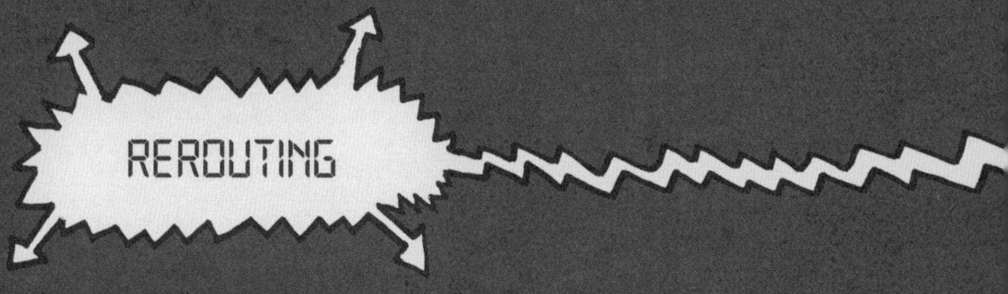
REROUTING

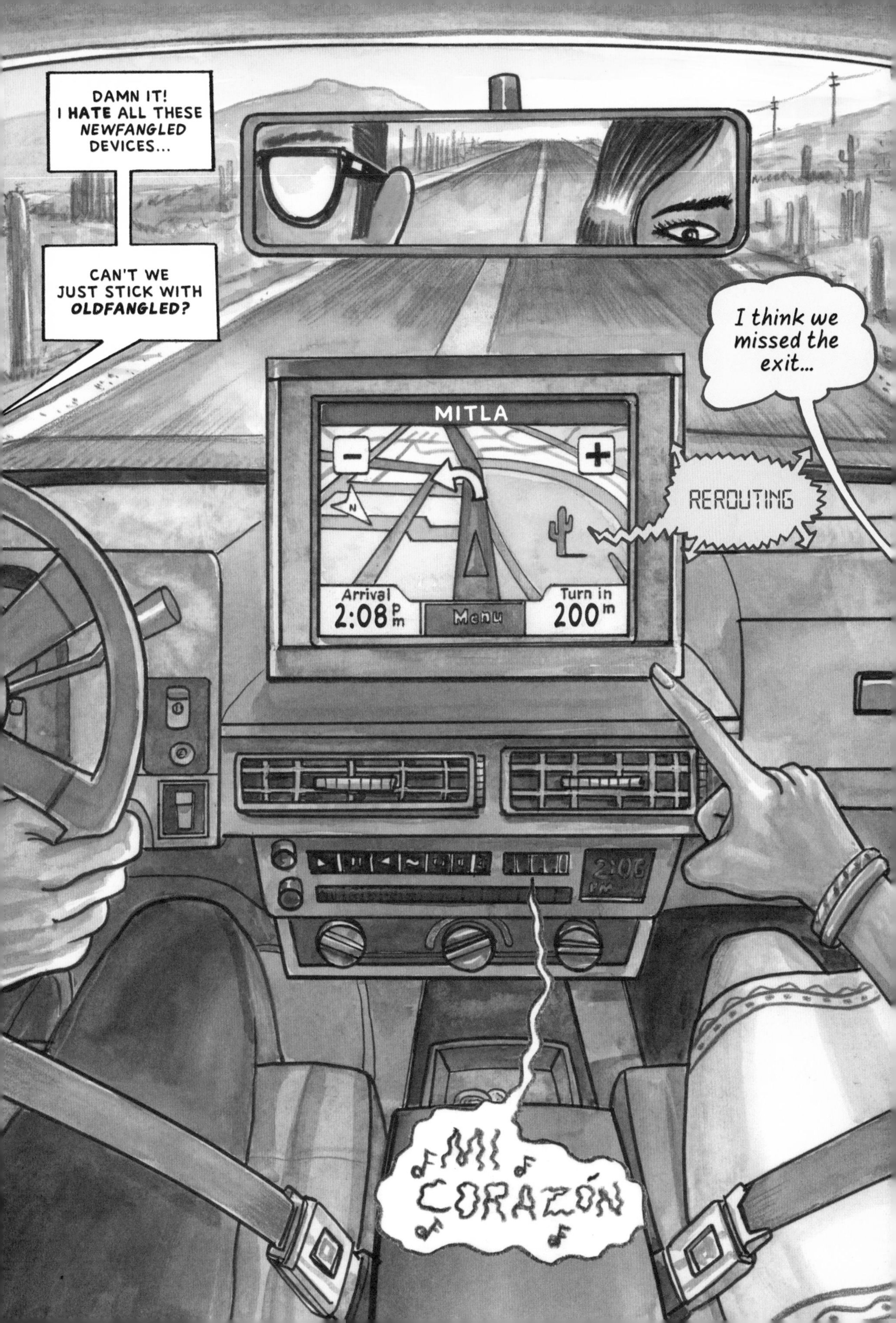
DAMN IT! I HATE ALL THESE NEWFANGLED DEVICES...
CAN'T WE JUST STICK WITH OLDFANGLED?
I think we missed the exit...
MITLA
Arrival 2:08 pm
Menu
Turn in 200m
REROUTING
MI CORAZÓN

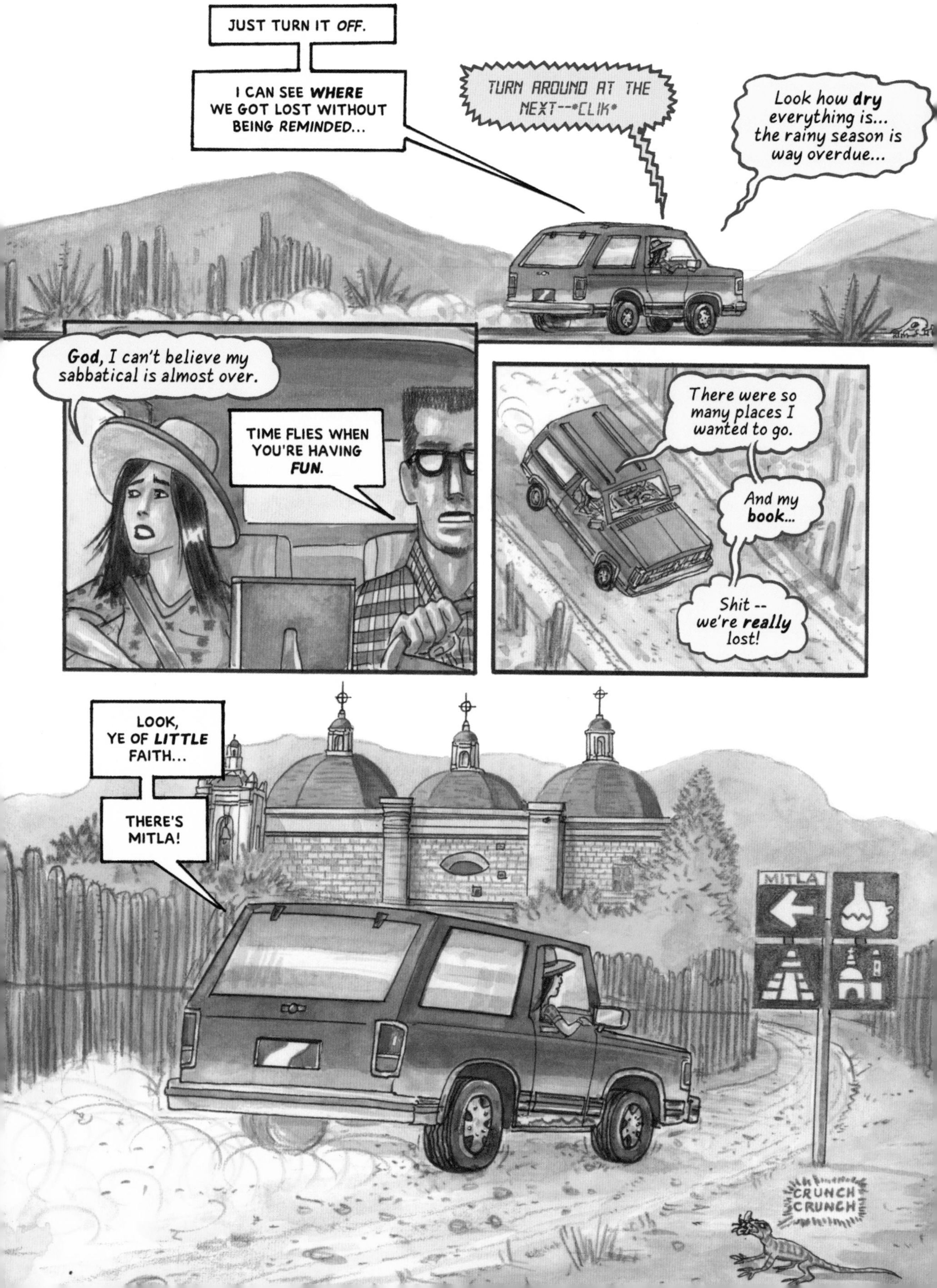

JUST TURN IT *OFF*.
I CAN SEE **WHERE** WE GOT LOST WITHOUT BEING REMINDED...
TURN AROUND AT THE NEXT--*CLIK*
Look how **dry** everything is... the rainy season is way overdue...
God, I can't believe my sabbatical is almost over.
TIME FLIES WHEN YOU'RE HAVING ***FUN***.
There were so many places I wanted to go.
And my **book**...
Shit -- we're **really** lost!
LOOK, YE OF ***LITTLE*** FAITH...
THERE'S MITLA!
MITLA
CRUNCH CRUNCH

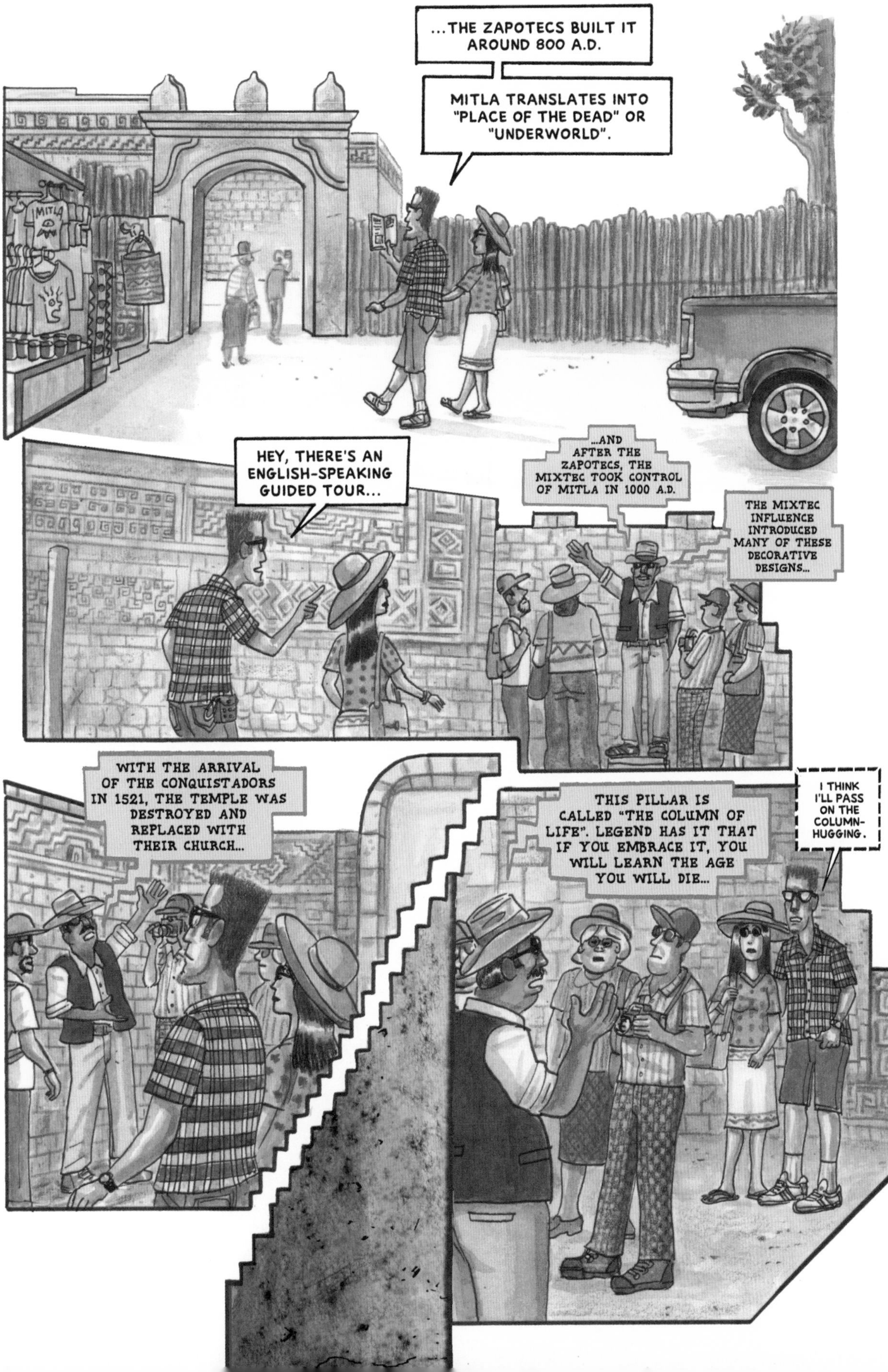
...THE ZAPOTECS BUILT IT AROUND 800 A.D.
MITLA TRANSLATES INTO "PLACE OF THE DEAD" OR "UNDERWORLD".
MITLA
HEY, THERE'S AN ENGLISH-SPEAKING GUIDED TOUR...
...AND AFTER THE ZAPOTECS, THE MIXTEC TOOK CONTROL OF MITLA IN 1000 A.D.
THE MIXTEC INFLUENCE INTRODUCED MANY OF THESE DECORATIVE DESIGNS...
WITH THE ARRIVAL OF THE CONQUISTADORS IN 1521, THE TEMPLE WAS DESTROYED AND REPLACED WITH THEIR CHURCH...
THIS PILLAR IS CALLED "THE COLUMN OF LIFE". LEGEND HAS IT THAT IF YOU EMBRACE IT, YOU WILL LEARN THE AGE YOU WILL DIE...
I THINK I'LL PASS ON THE COLUMN-HUGGING.

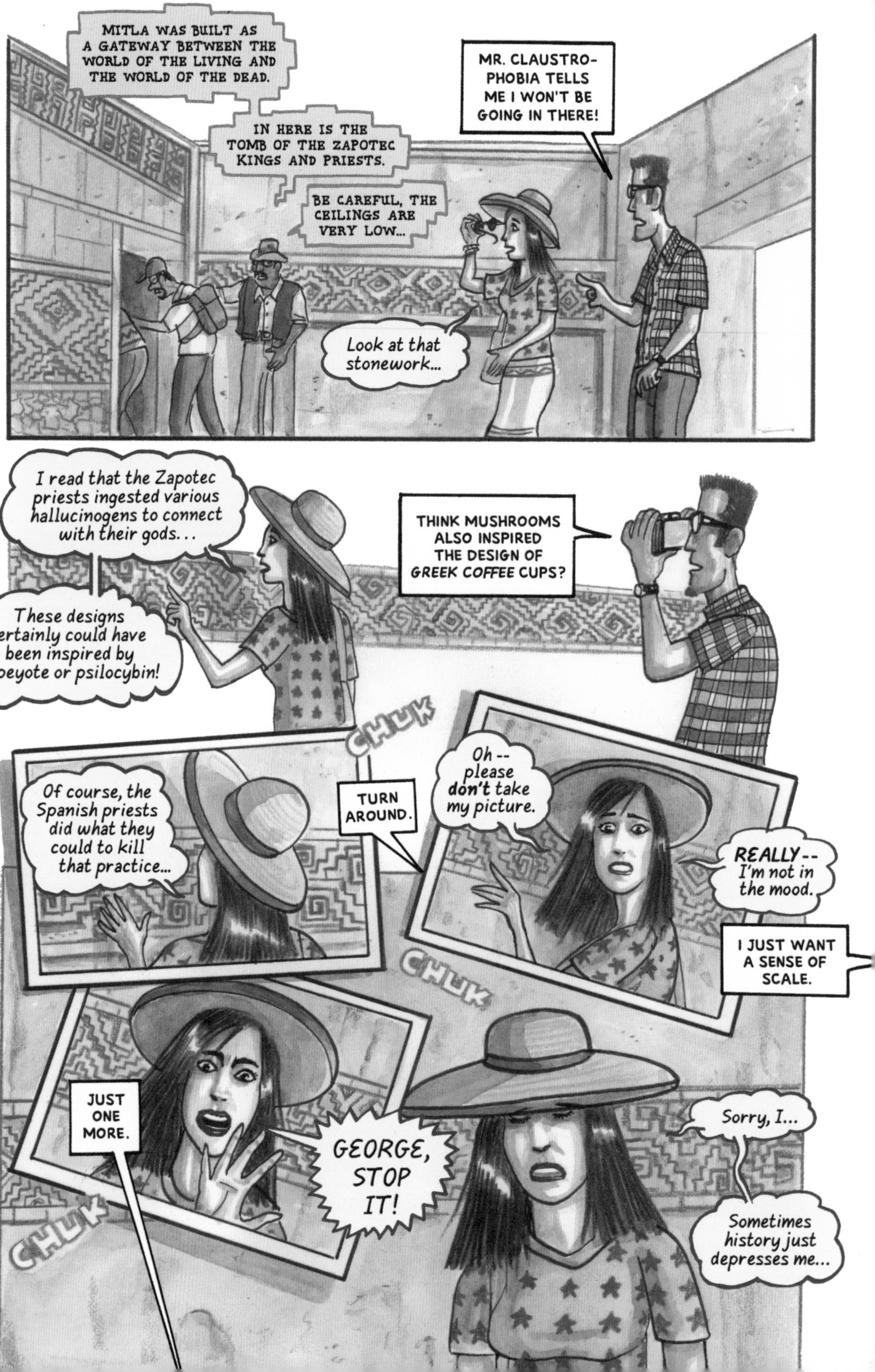
MITLA WAS BUILT AS A GATEWAY BETWEEN THE WORLD OF THE LIVING AND THE WORLD OF THE DEAD.
IN HERE IS THE TOMB OF THE ZAPOTEC KINGS AND PRIESTS.
BE CAREFUL, THE CEILINGS ARE VERY LOW...
MR. CLAUSTRO-PHOBIA TELLS ME I WON'T BE GOING IN THERE!
Look at that stonework...
I read that the Zapotec priests ingested various hallucinogens to connect with their gods. . .
These designs certainly could have been inspired by peyote or psilocybin!
THINK MUSHROOMS ALSO INSPIRED THE DESIGN OF GREEK COFFEE CUPS?
CHUK
Of course, the Spanish priests did what they could to kill that practice...
TURN AROUND.
Oh -- please **don't** take my picture.
REALLY -- I'm not in the mood.
CHUK
I JUST WANT A SENSE OF SCALE.
JUST ONE MORE.
GEORGE, STOP IT!
CHUK
Sorry, I...
Sometimes history just depresses me...

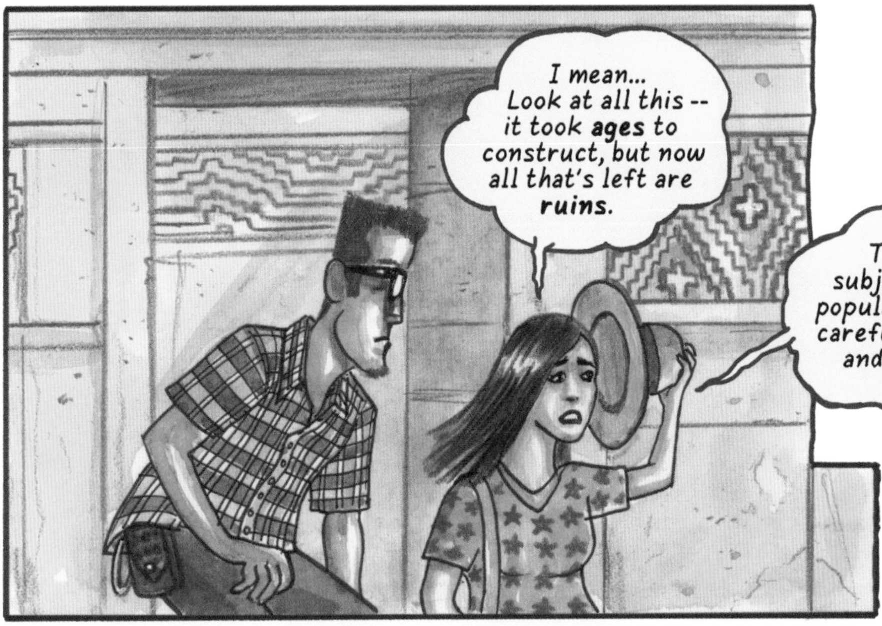
I mean... Look at all this -- it took **ages** to construct, but now all that's left are **ruins**.
The conquistadors subjugated or killed the population, then took their carefully recorded history and ***burned*** the books.

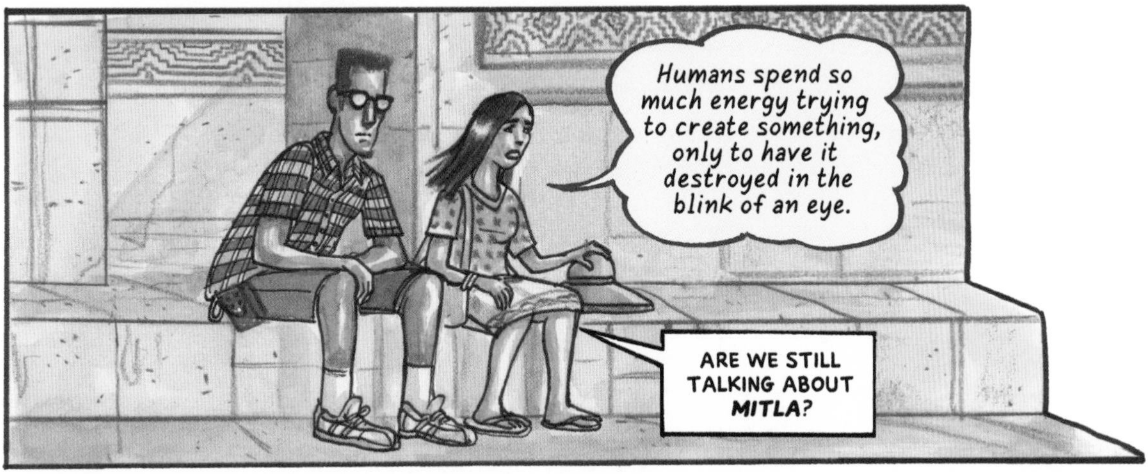
Humans spend so much energy trying to create something, only to have it destroyed in the blink of an eye.
ARE WE STILL TALKING ABOUT ***MITLA***?

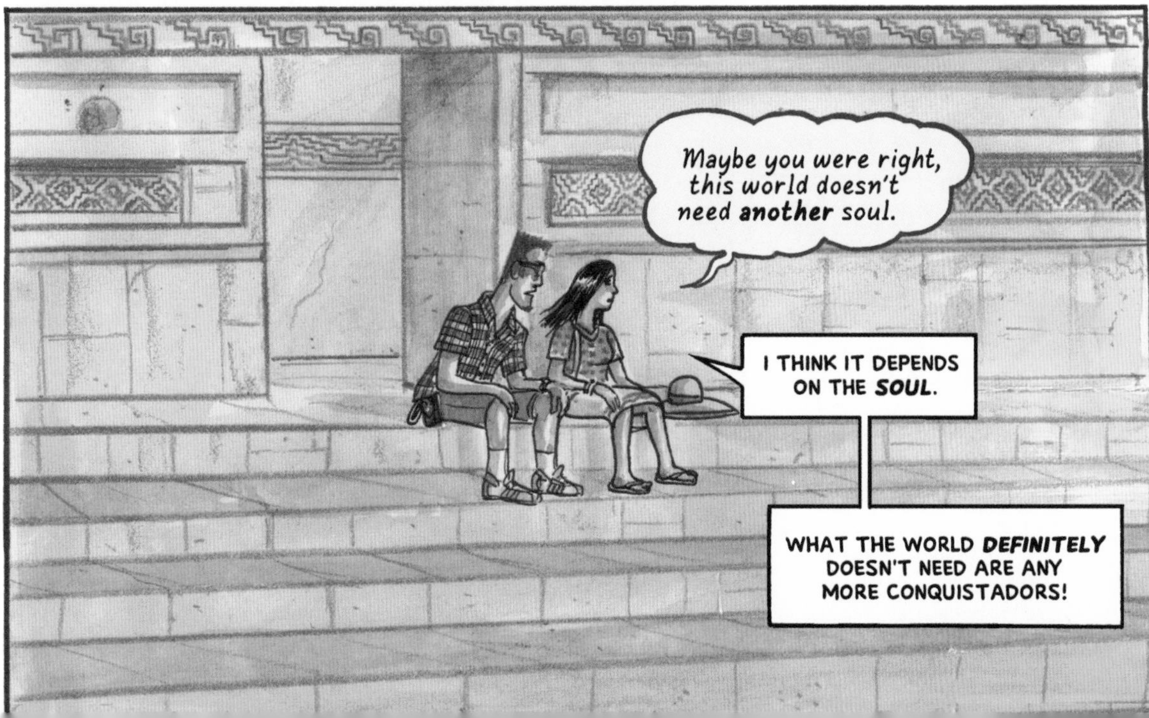
Maybe you were right, this world doesn't need **another** soul.
I THINK IT DEPENDS ON THE ***SOUL***.
WHAT THE WORLD ***DEFINITELY*** DOESN'T NEED ARE ANY MORE CONQUISTADORS!

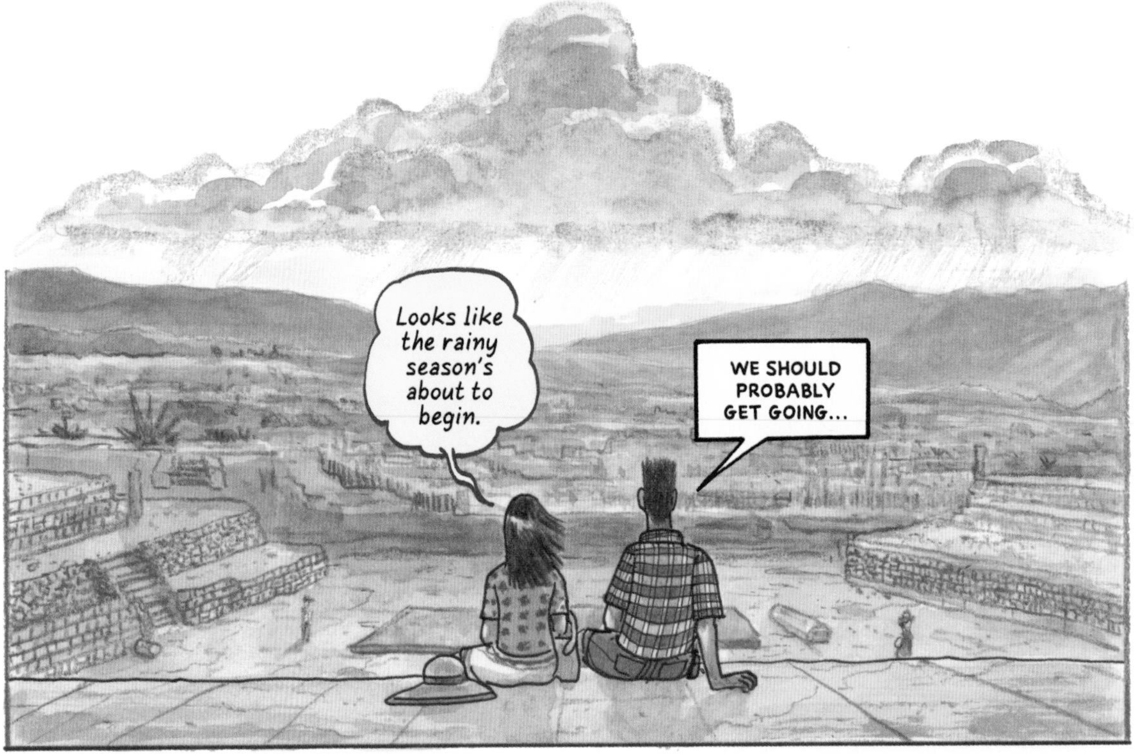
Looks like the rainy season's about to begin.
WE SHOULD PROBABLY GET GOING...

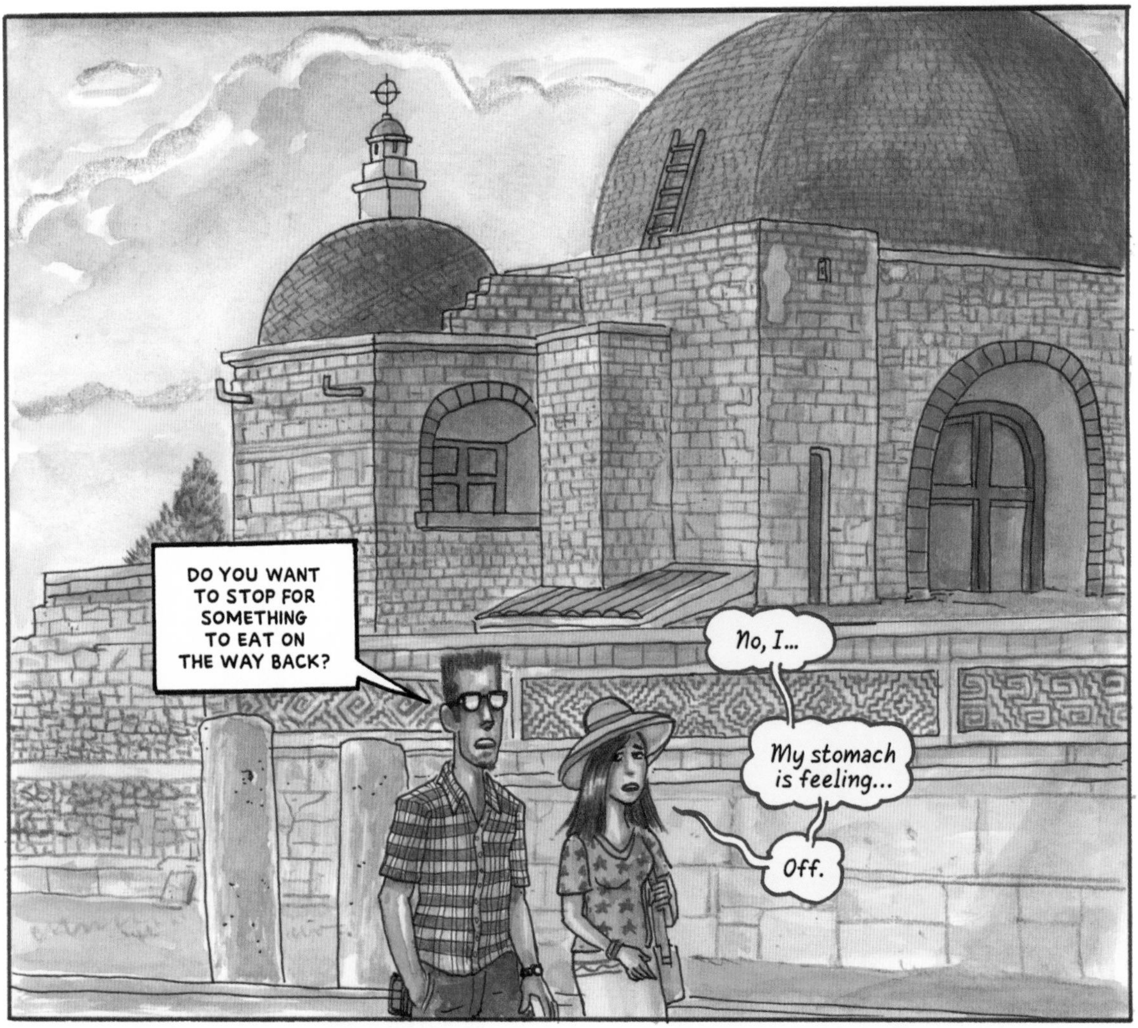
DO YOU WANT TO STOP FOR SOMETHING TO EAT ON THE WAY BACK?
No, I...
My stomach is feeling...
Off.

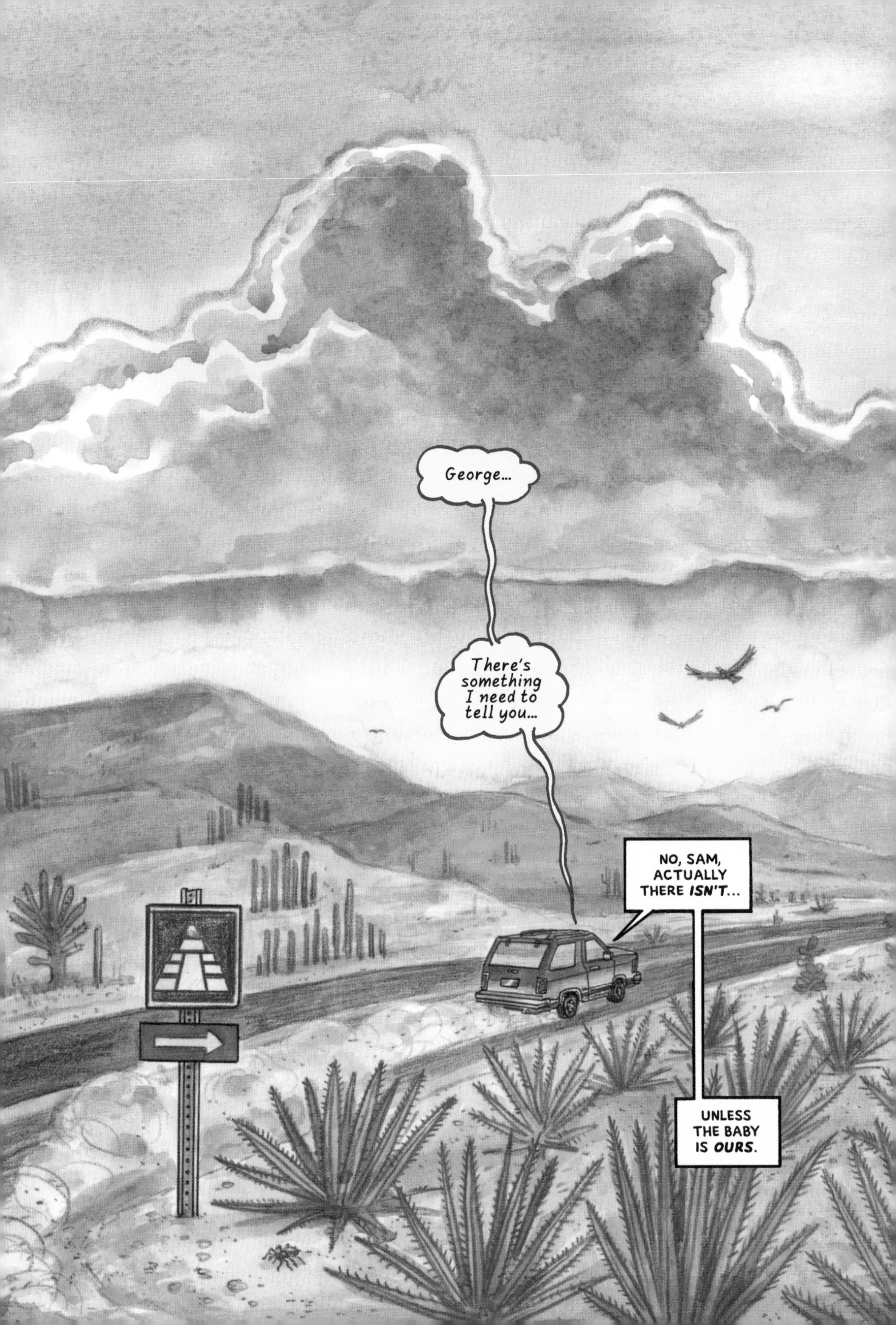

George...
There's something I need to tell you...
NO, SAM, ACTUALLY THERE *ISN'T*...
UNLESS THE BABY IS *OURS*.

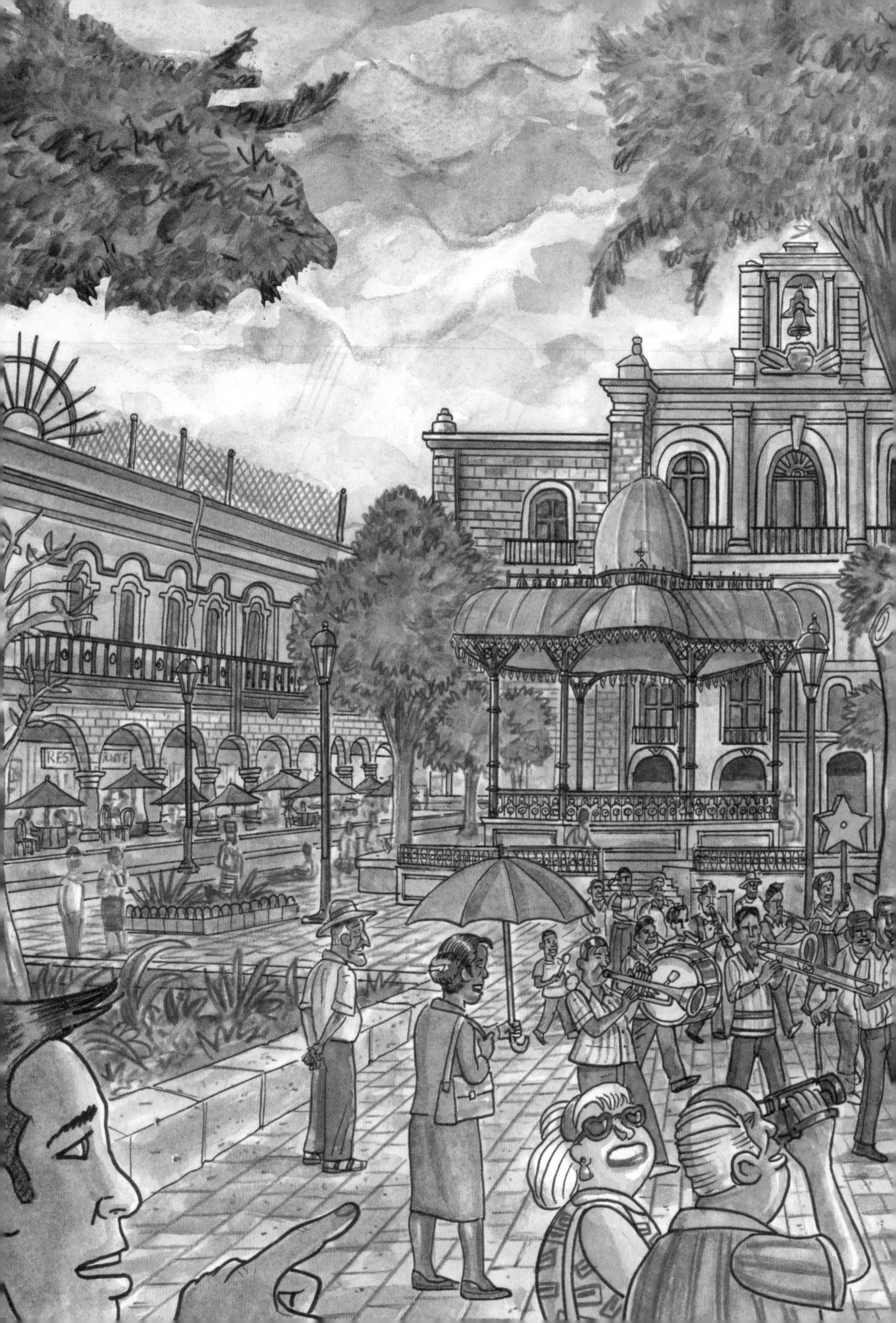
REST

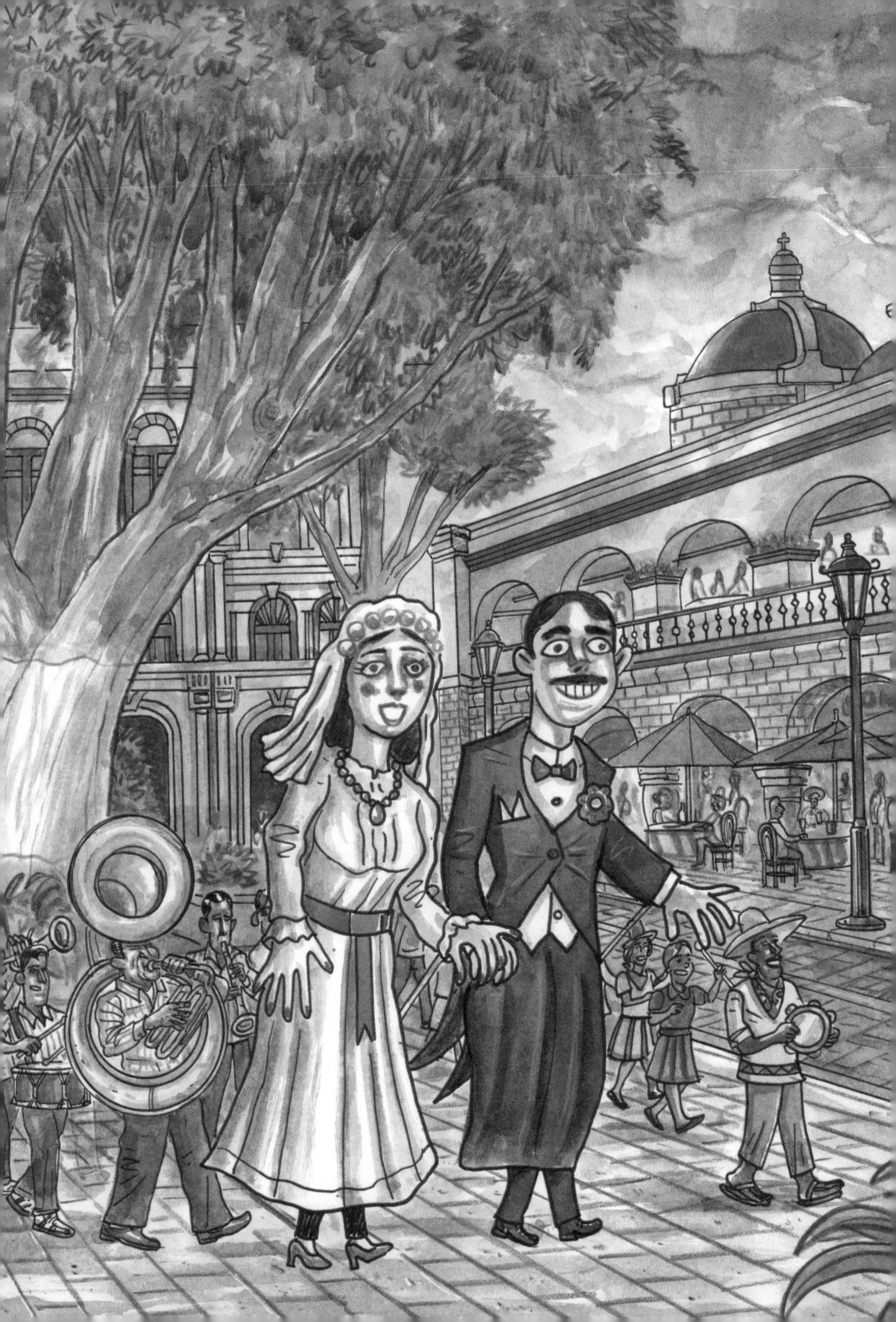

BEEEEEPAA

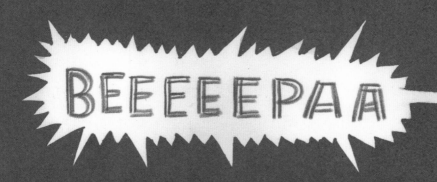

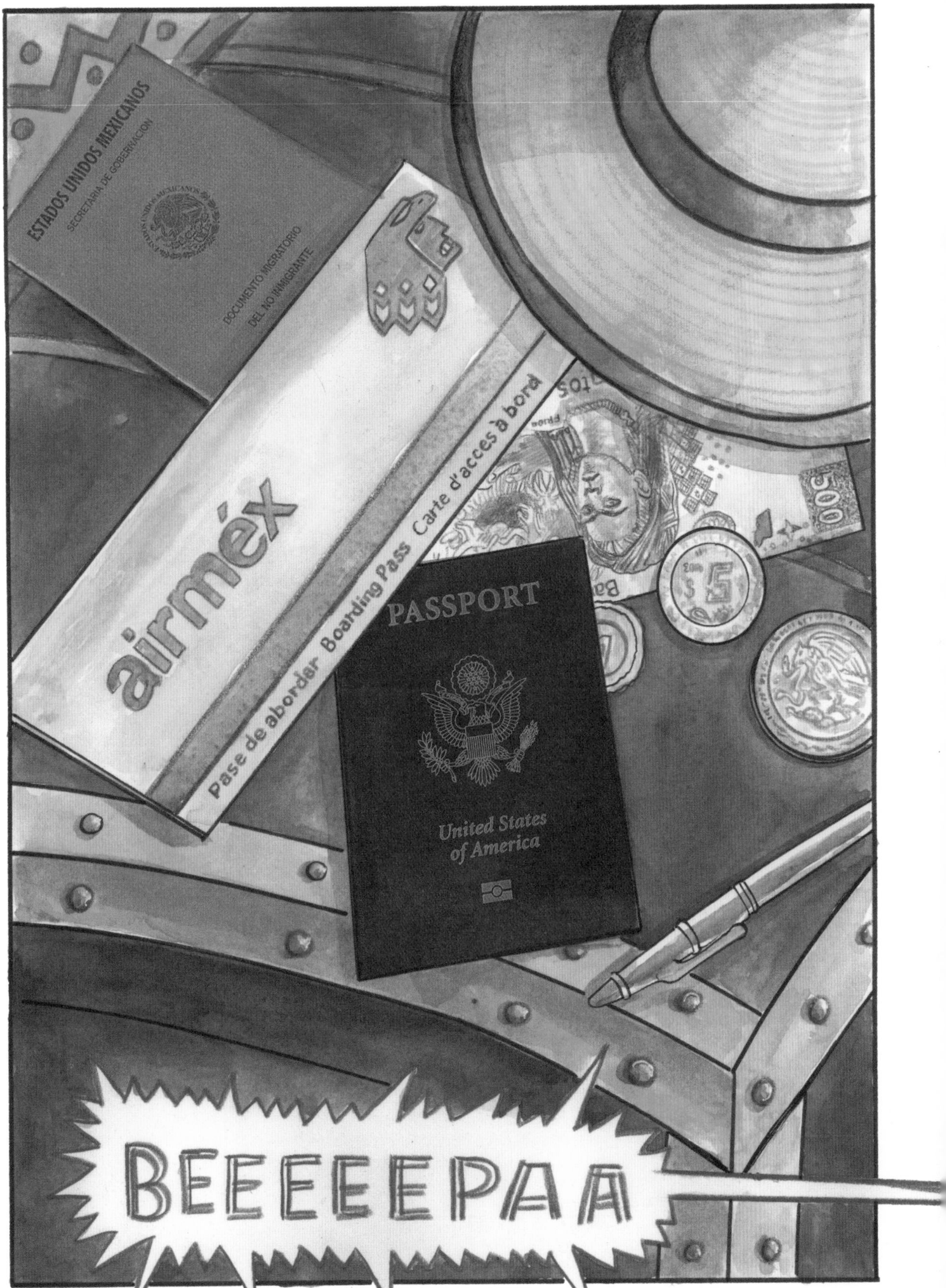
ESTADOS UNIDOS MEXICANOS
SECRETARIA DE GOBERNACION
DOCUMENTO MIGRATORIO
DEL NO INMIGRANTE
airméx
Pase de abordar Boarding Pass Carte d'acces à bord
PASSPORT
United States
of America
BEEEEEPAA

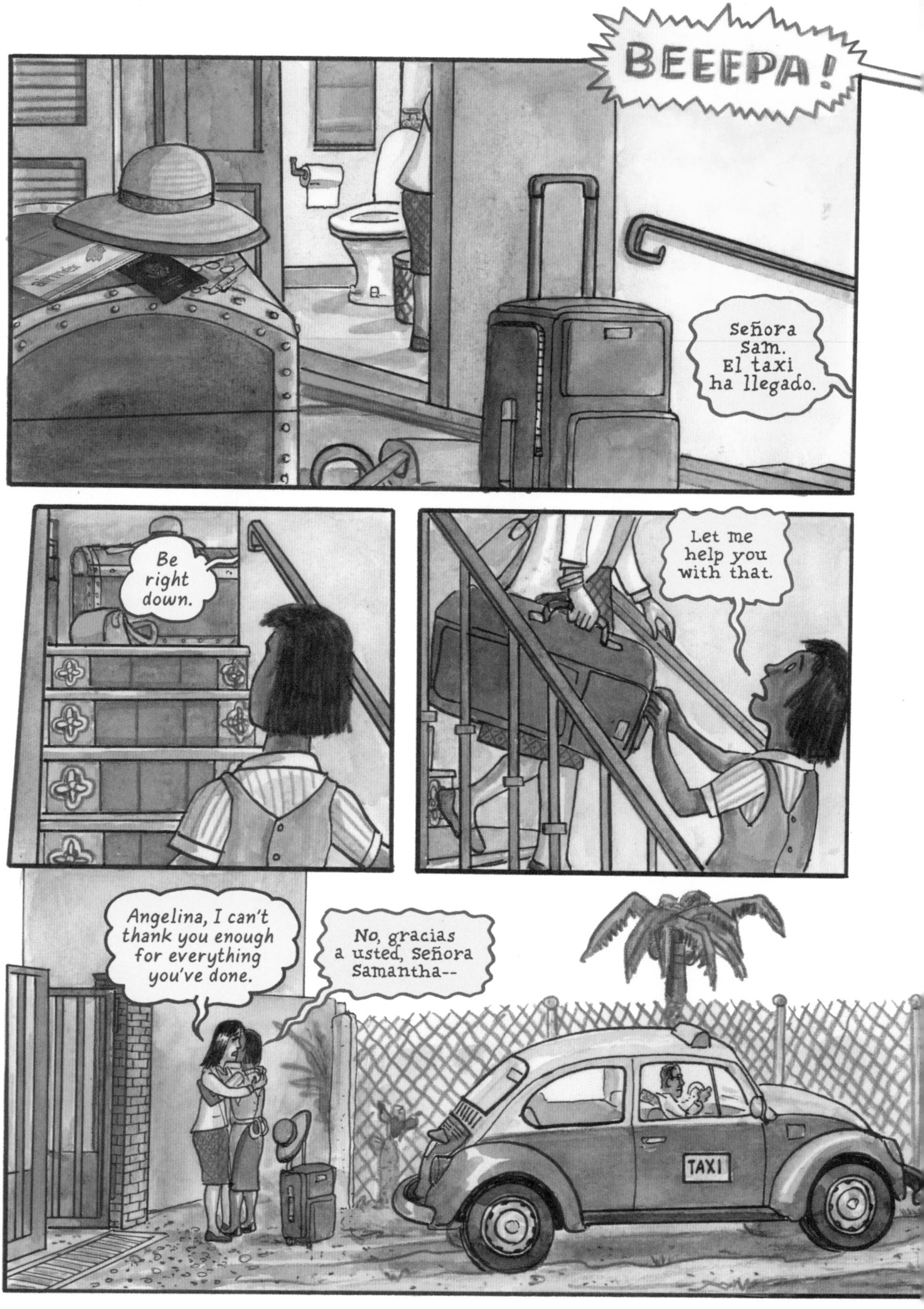

BEEEPA!
Señora Sam. El taxi ha llegado.
Be right down.
Let me help you with that.
Angelina, I can't thank you enough for everything you've done.
No, gracias a usted, Señora Samantha--
TAXI

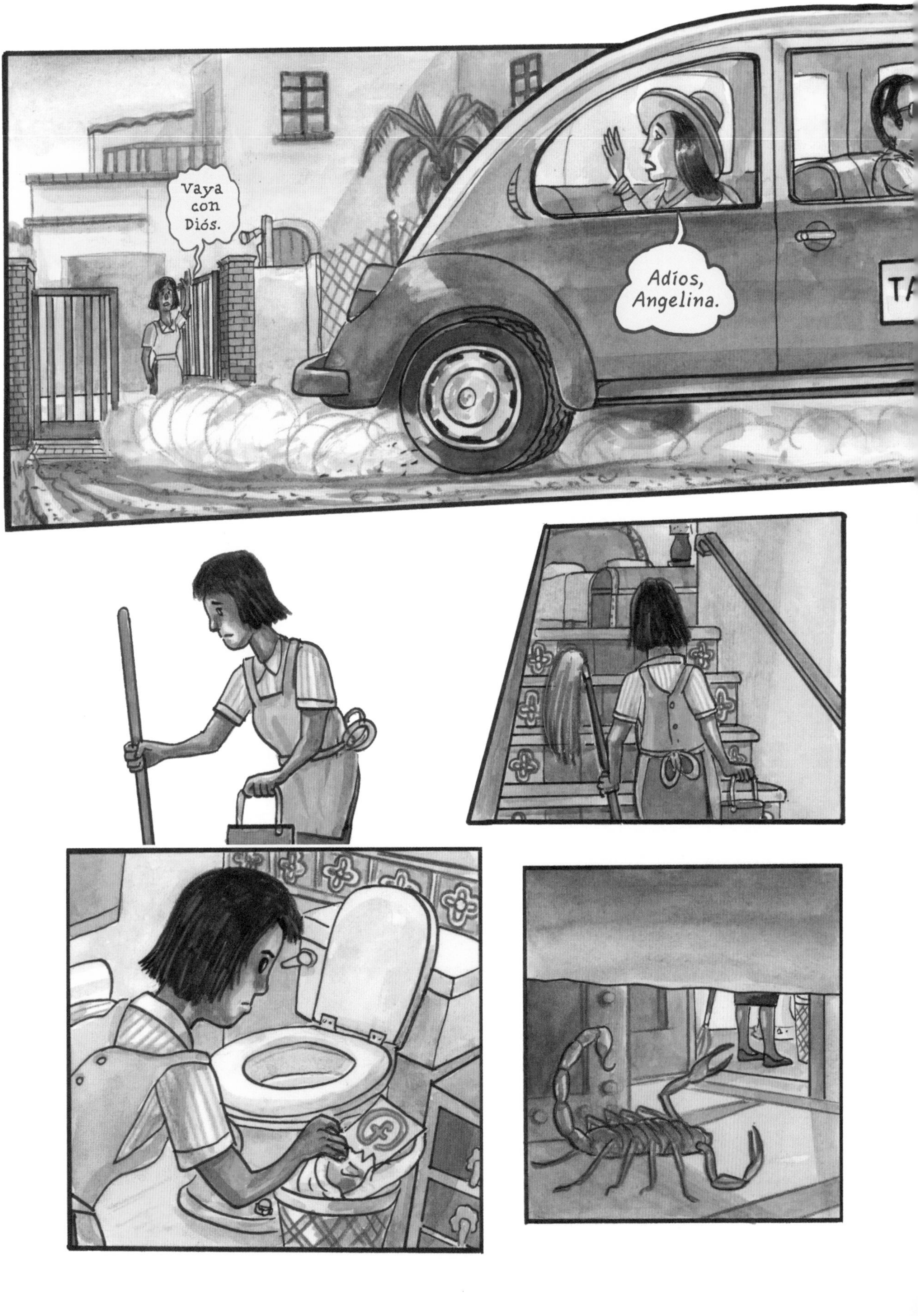
Vaya con Diós.
Adíos, Angelina.

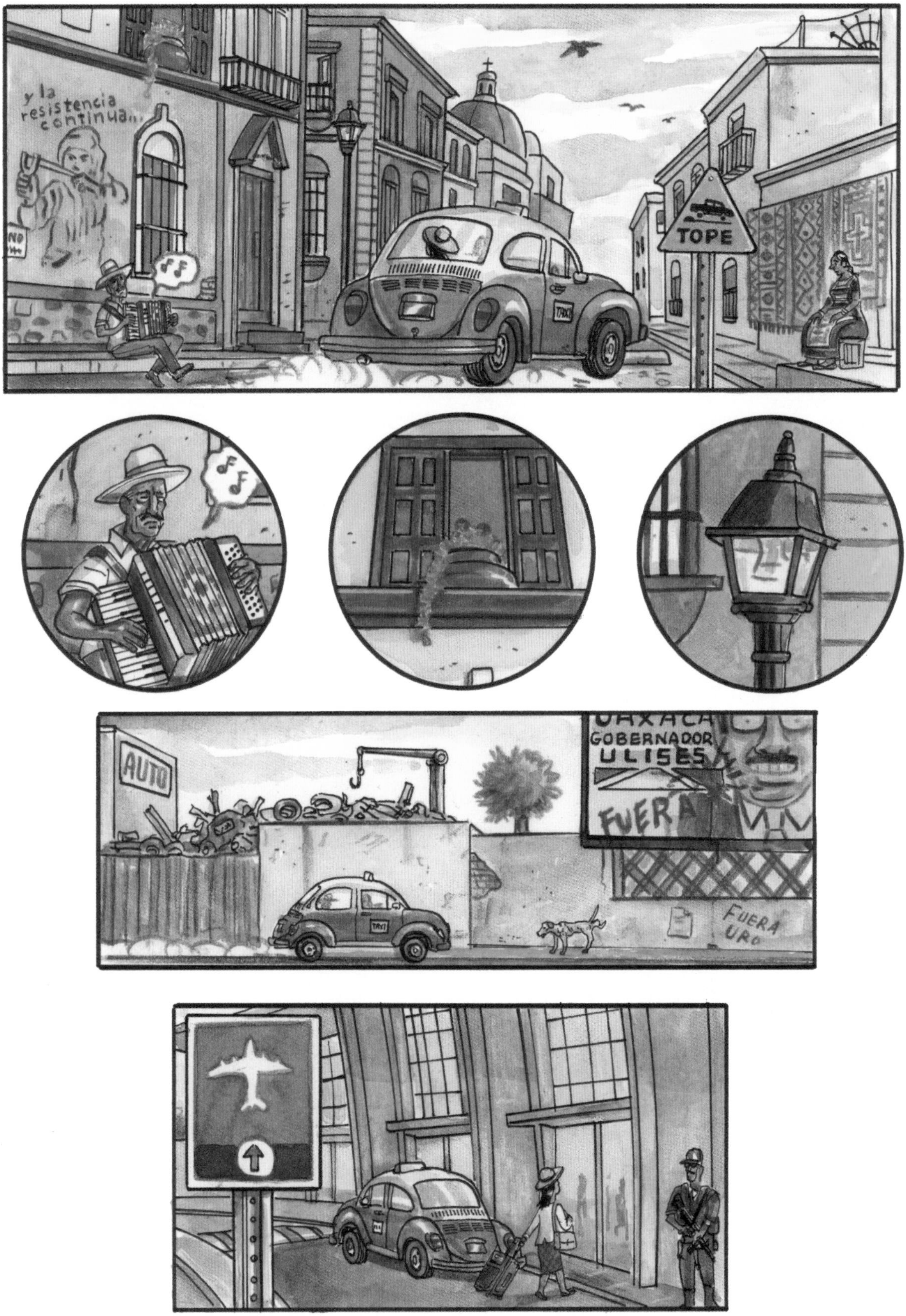

y la resistencia continua...
TOPE
TAXI
AUTO
GOBERNADOR
ULISES
FUERA
FUERA URO

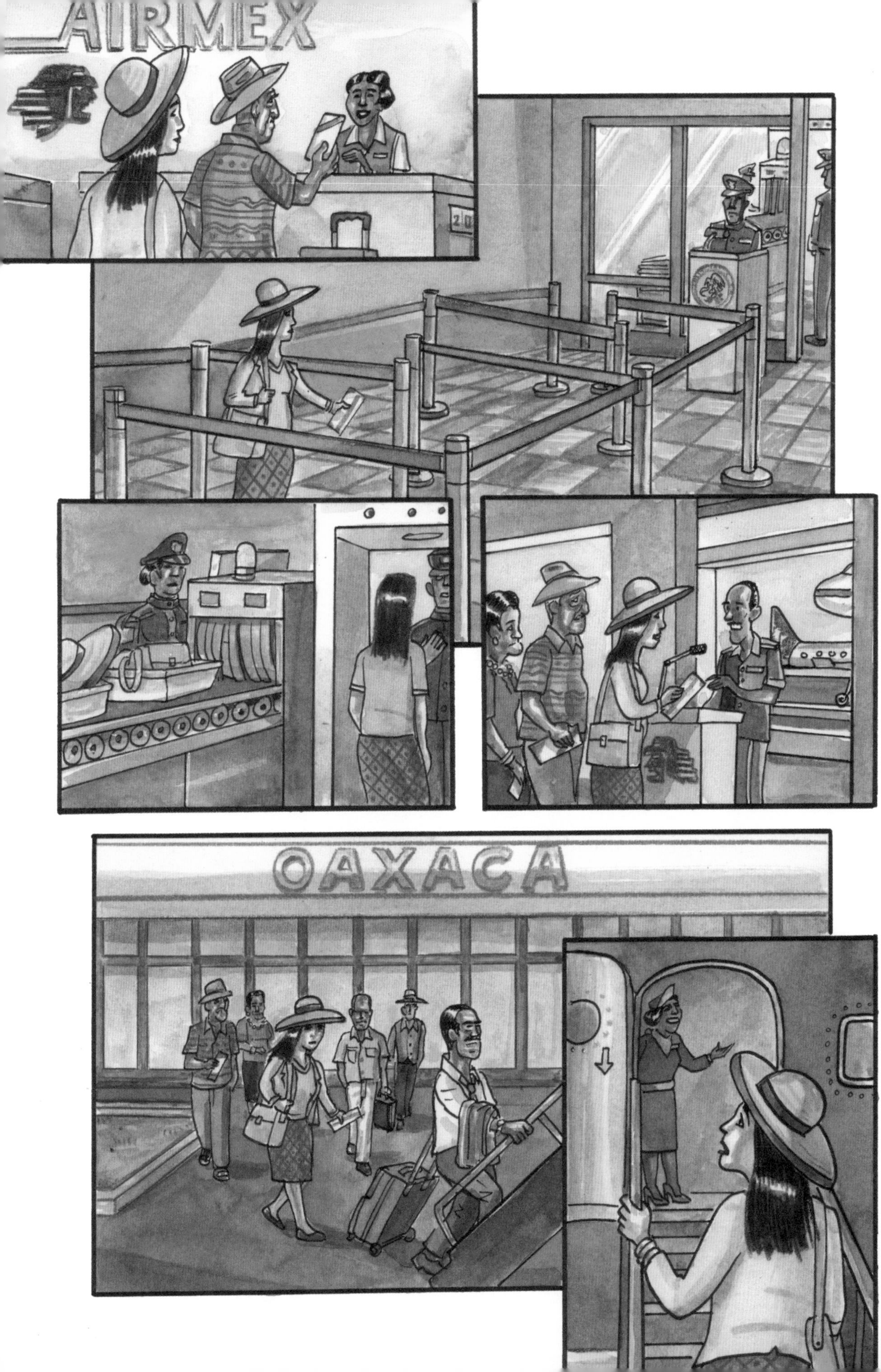
AIRMEX
OAXACA

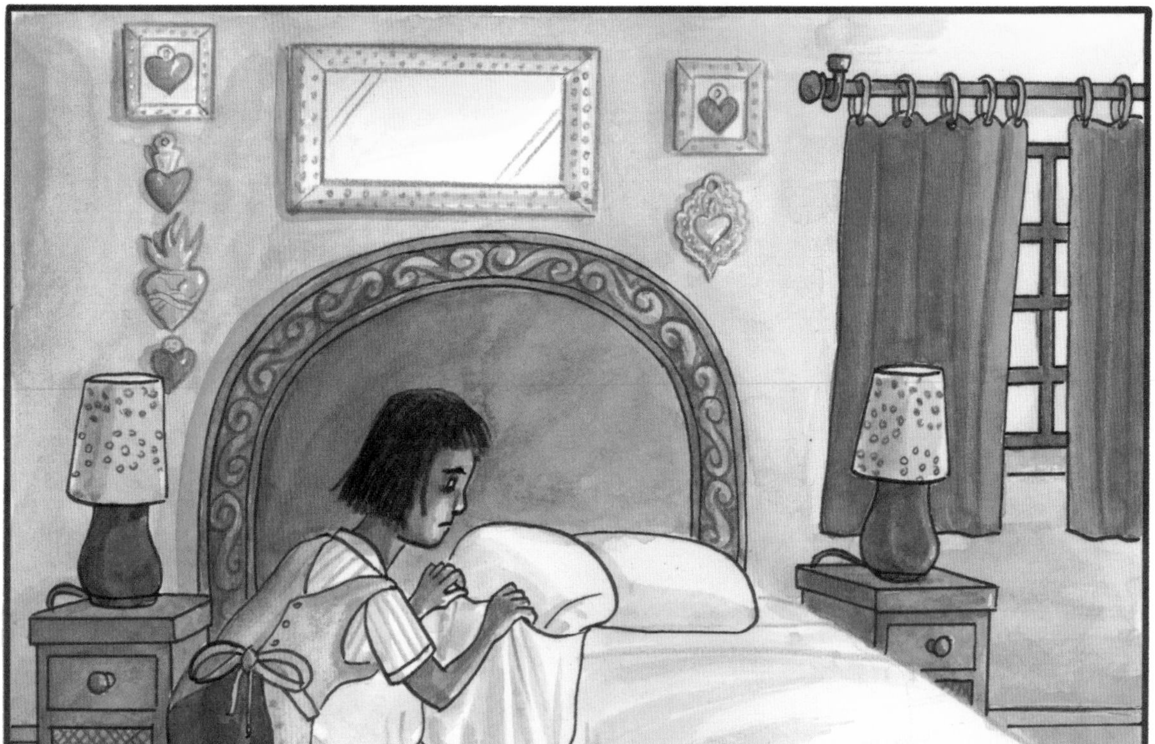
SKIT
SKIT

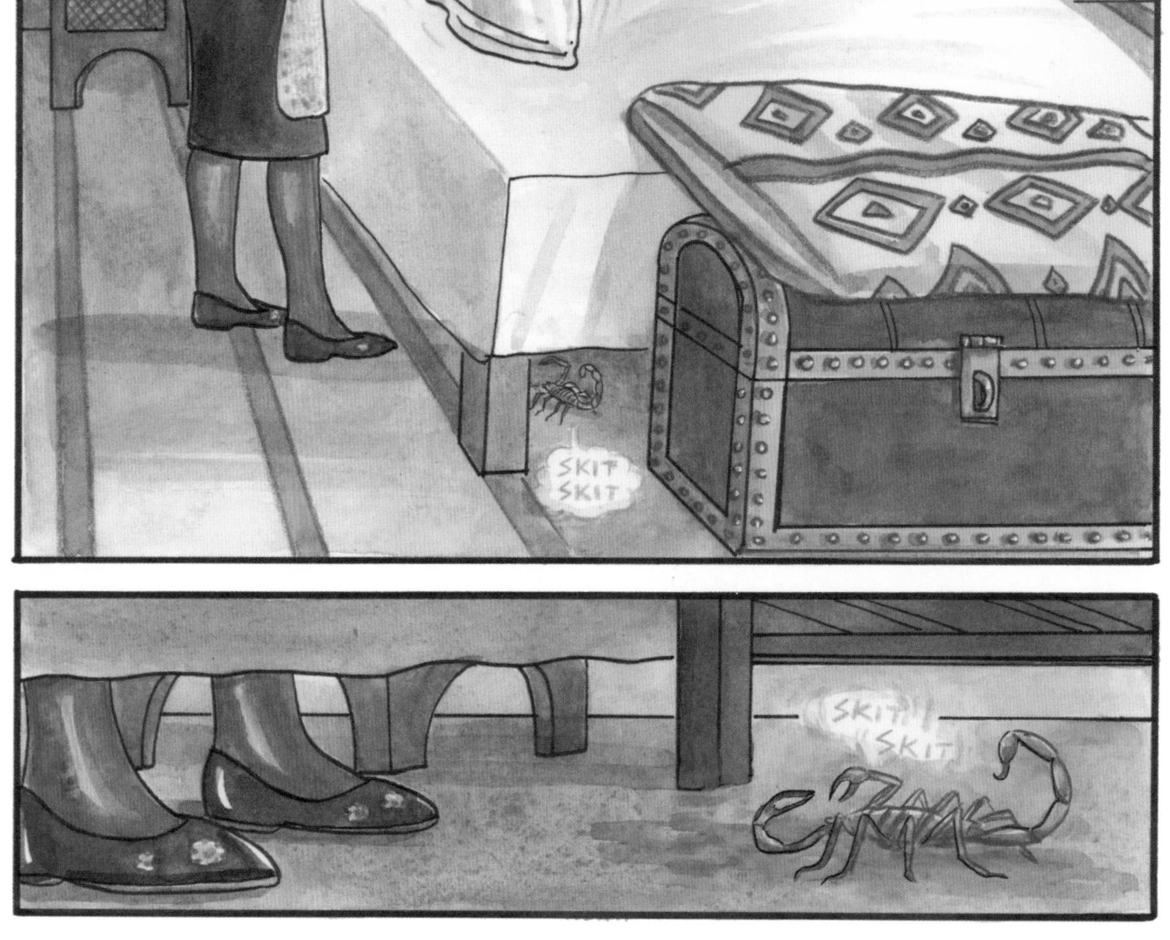
SKIT
SKIT

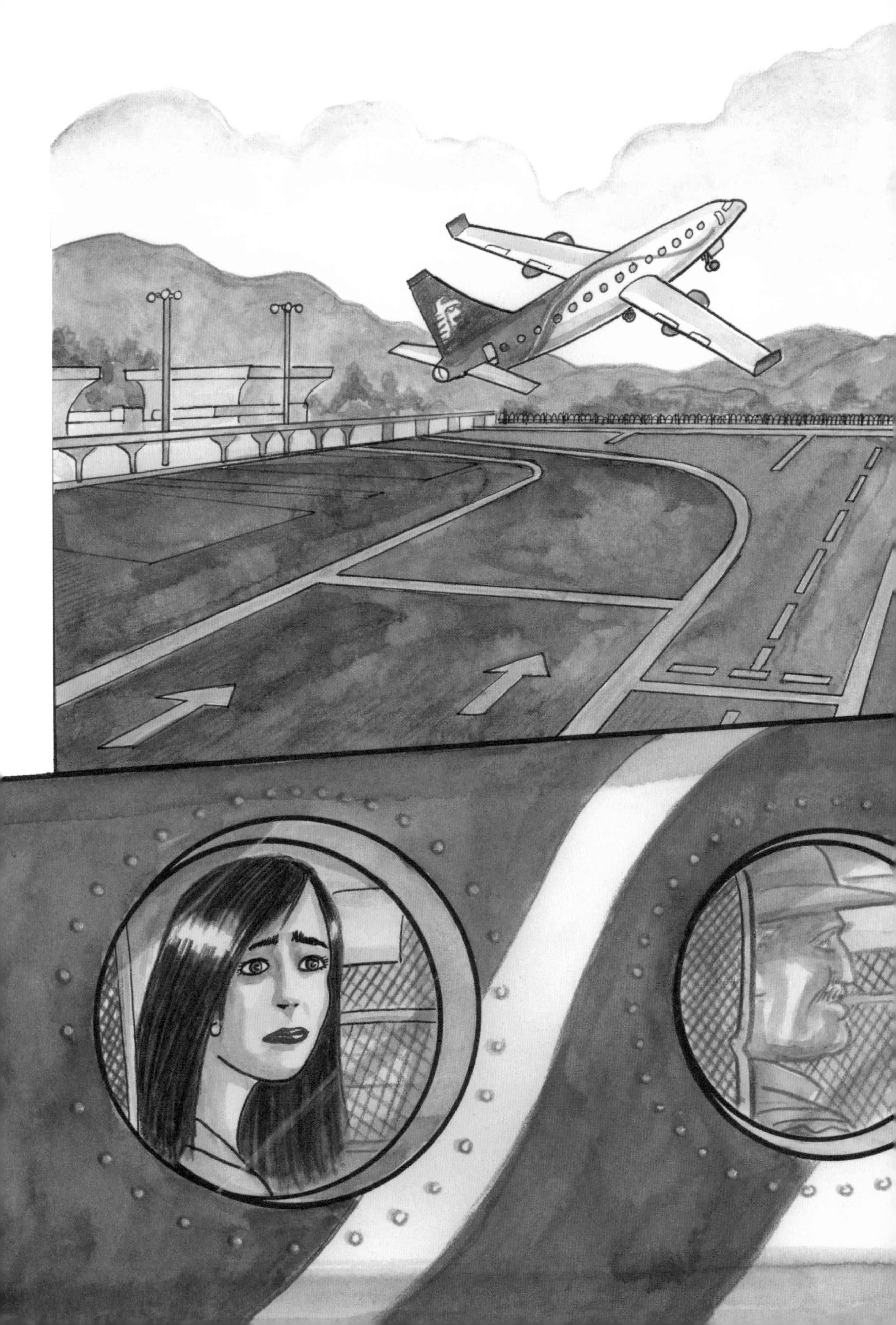

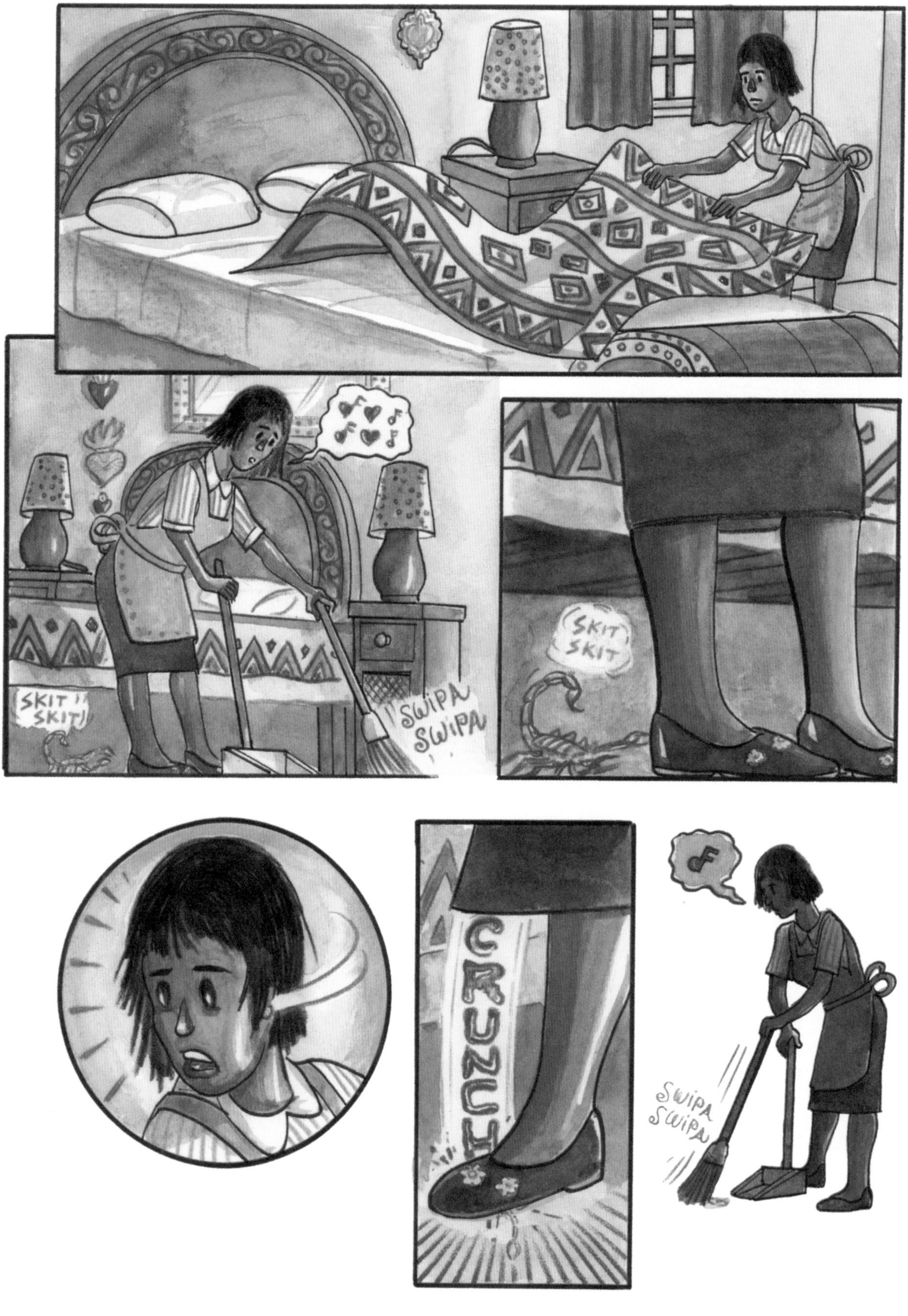
SKIT SKIT
SWIPA SWIPA
SKIT SKIT
CRUNCH
SWIPA SWIPA

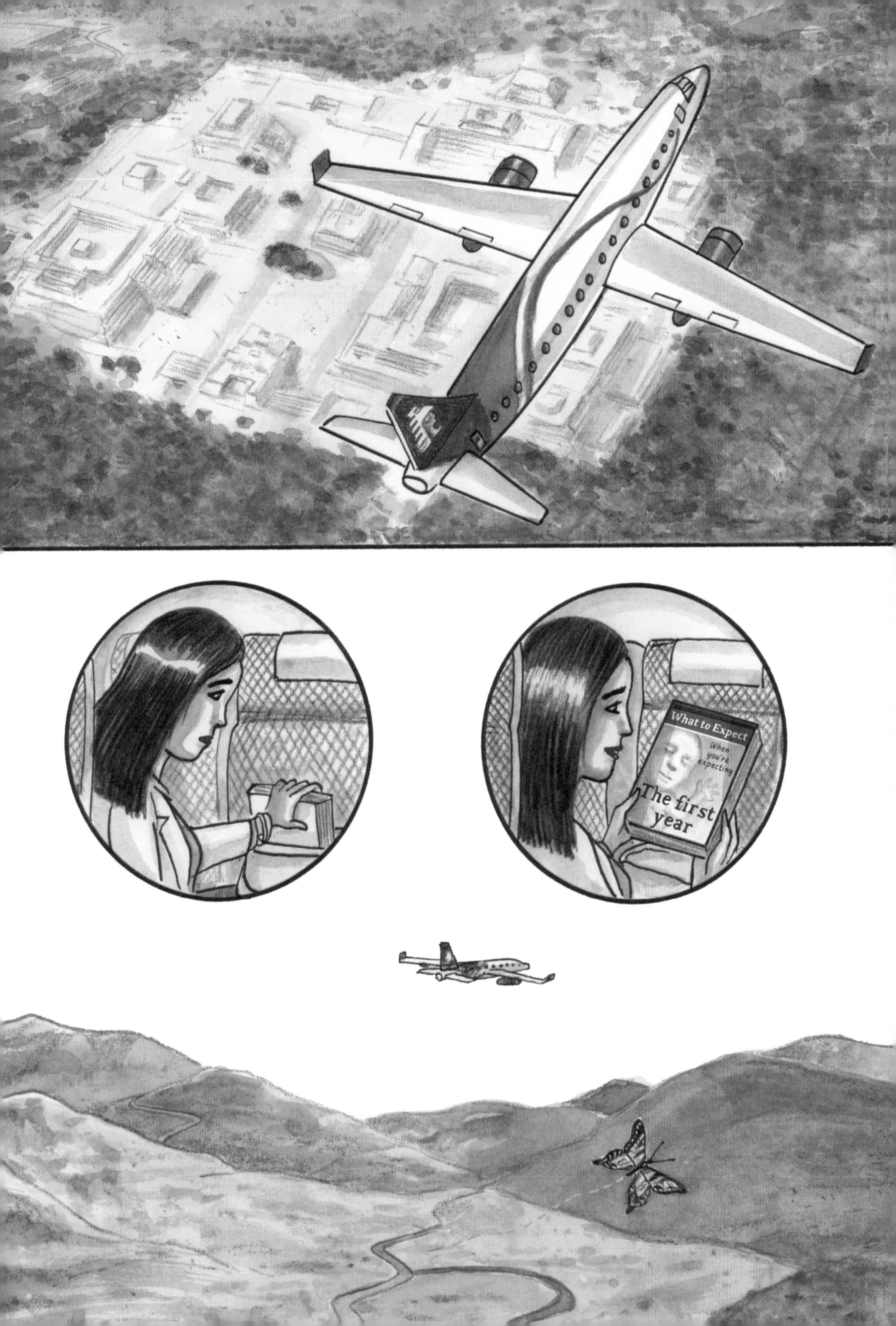
What to Expect
When you're expecting
The first year

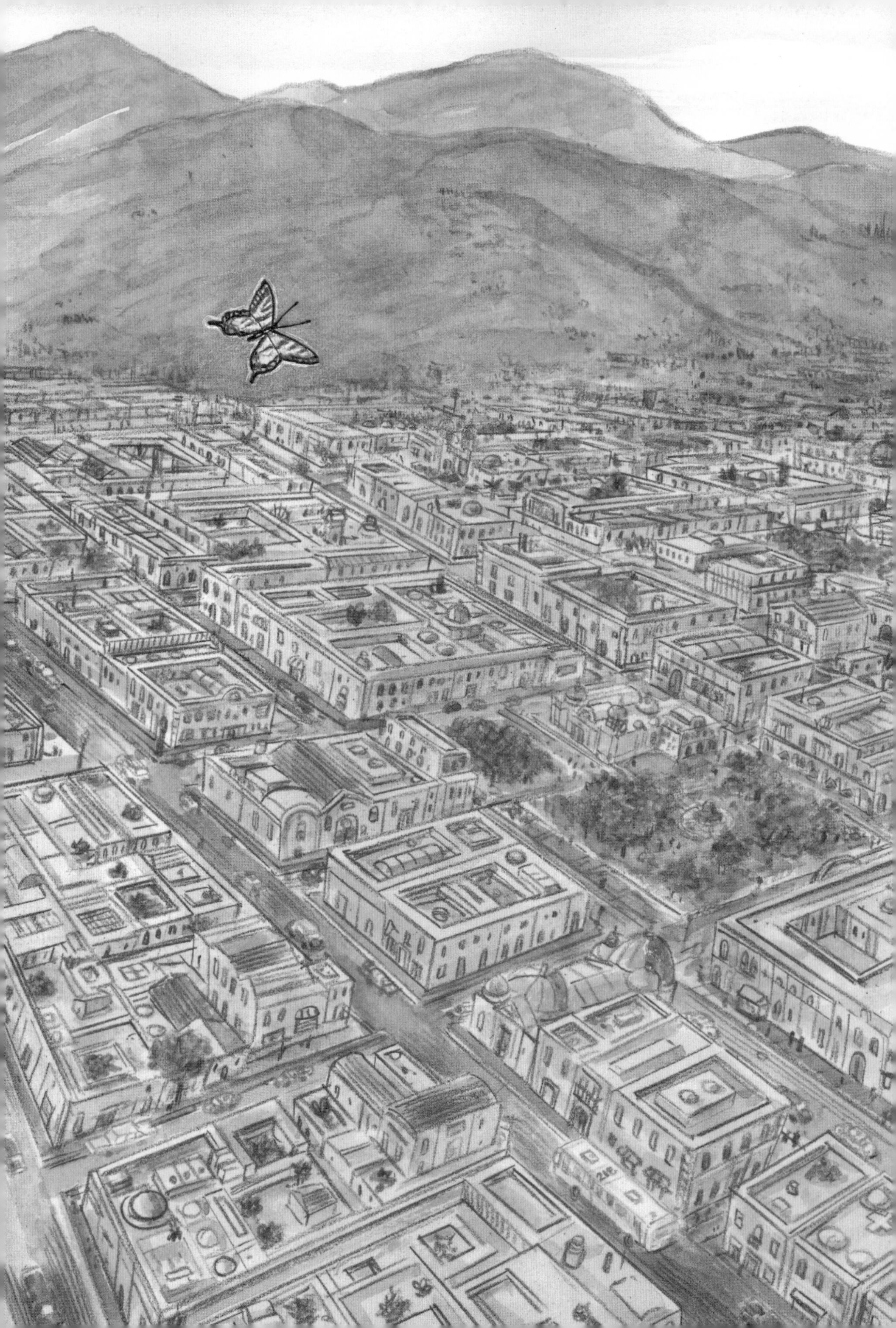

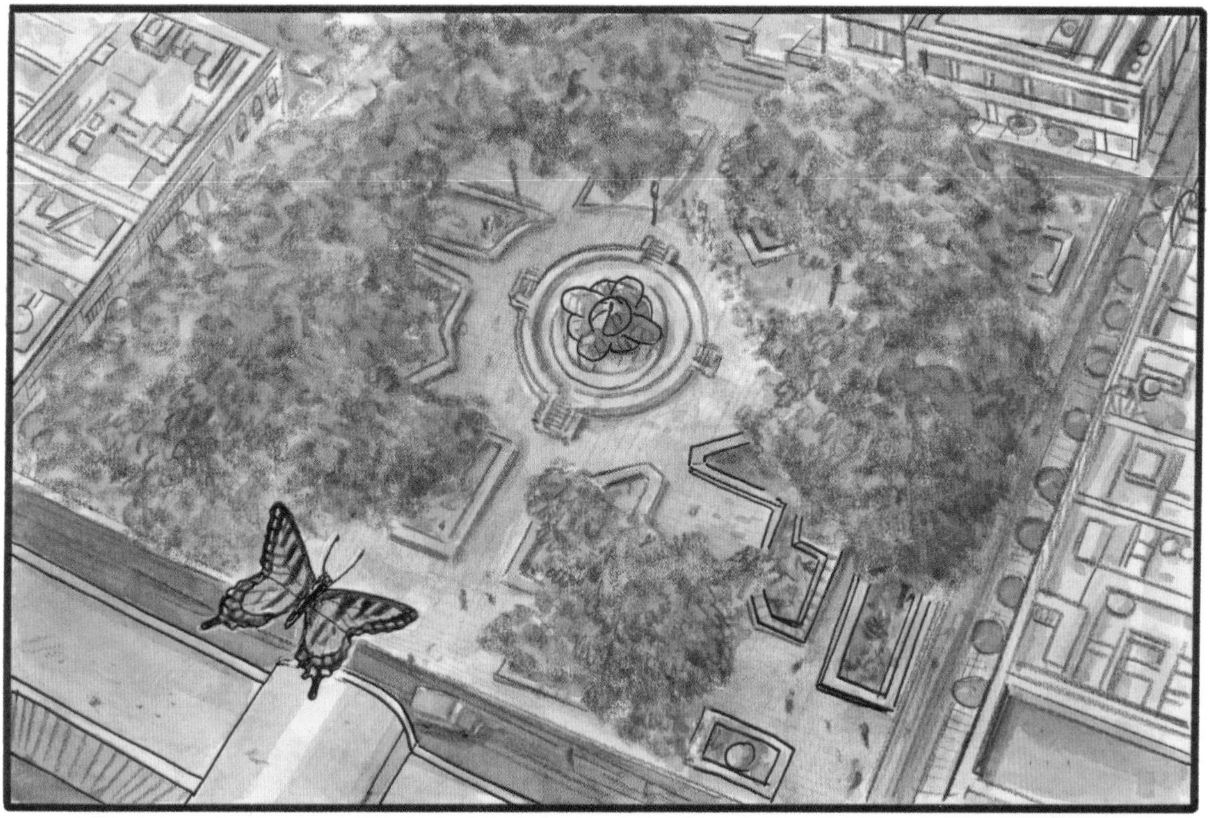

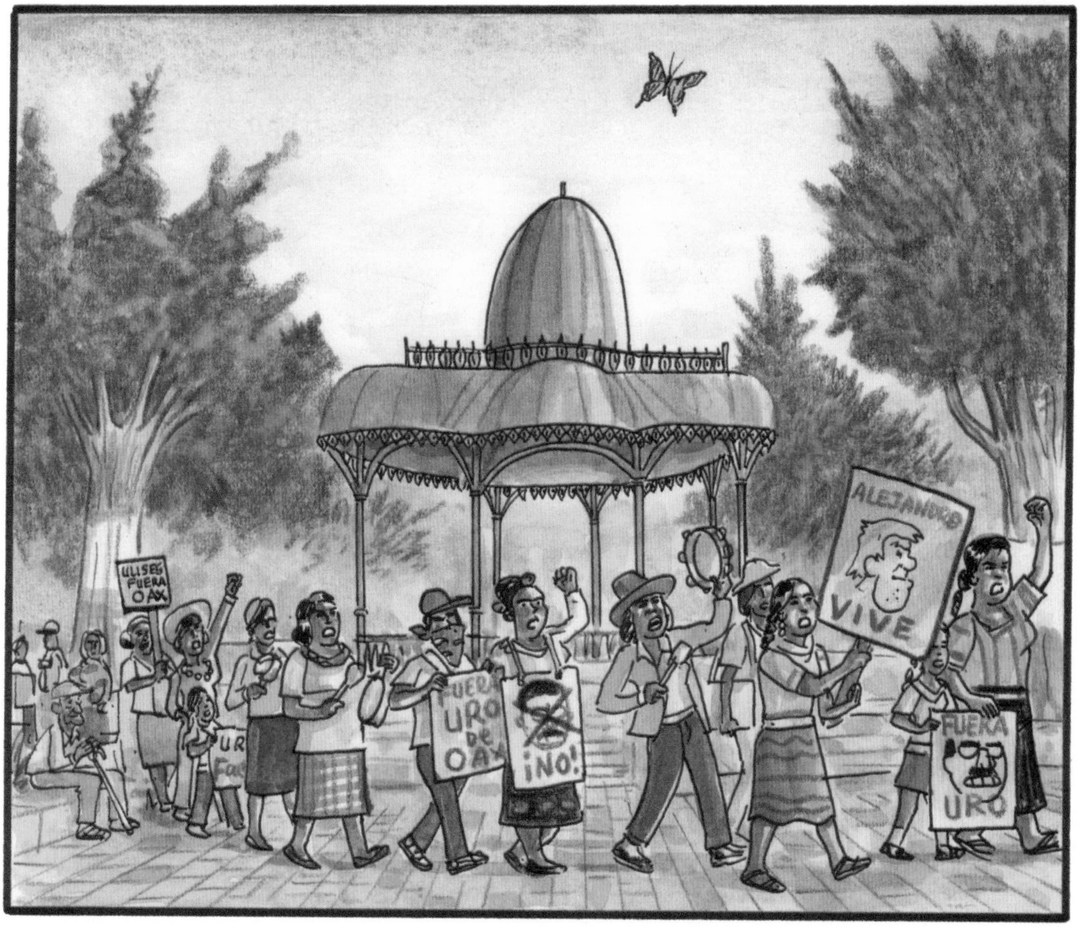

ULISES FUERA OAX
FUERA URO DE OA
¡NO!
ALEJANDRO VIVE
FUERA URO

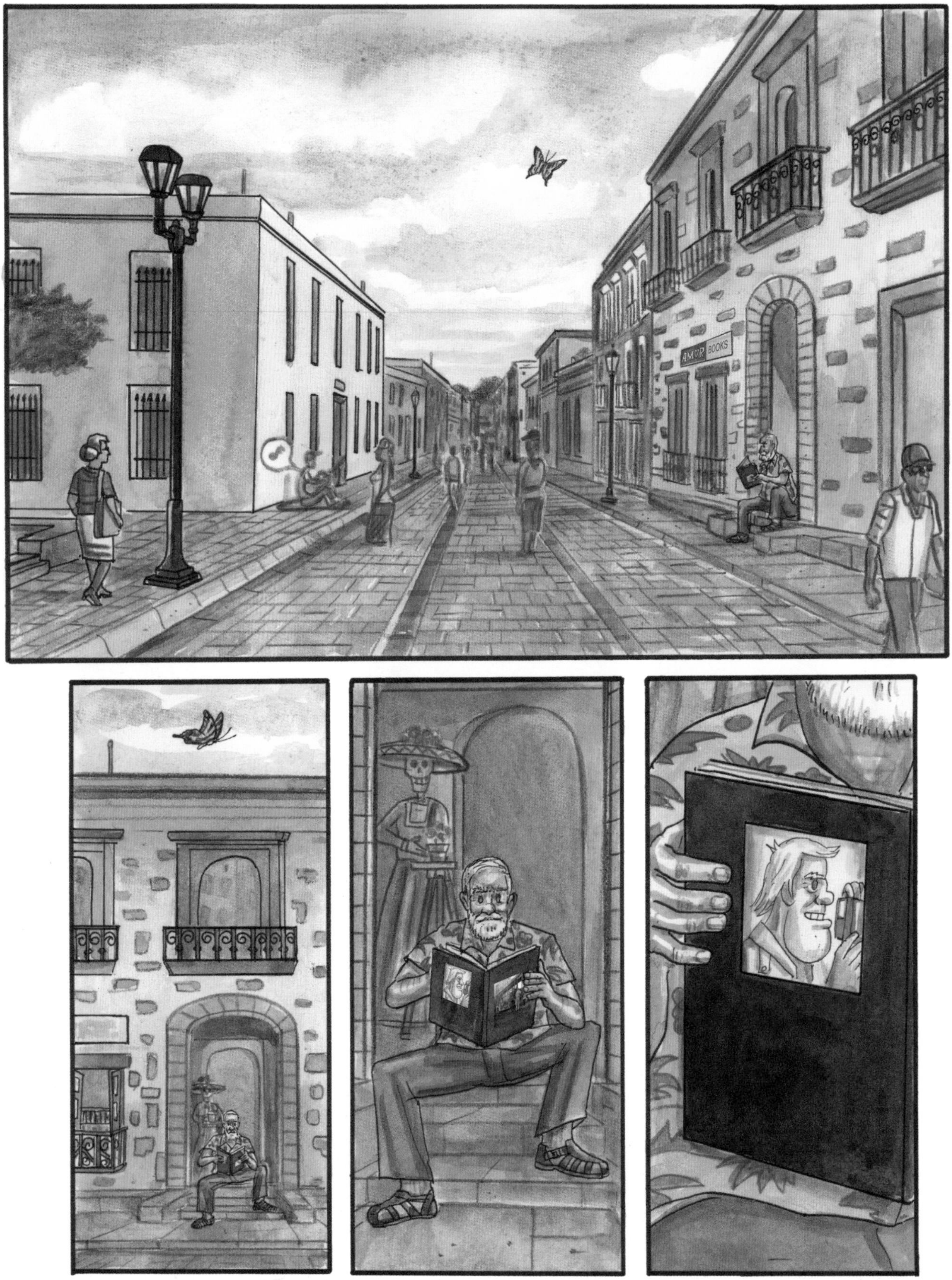
AM♡R BOOKS

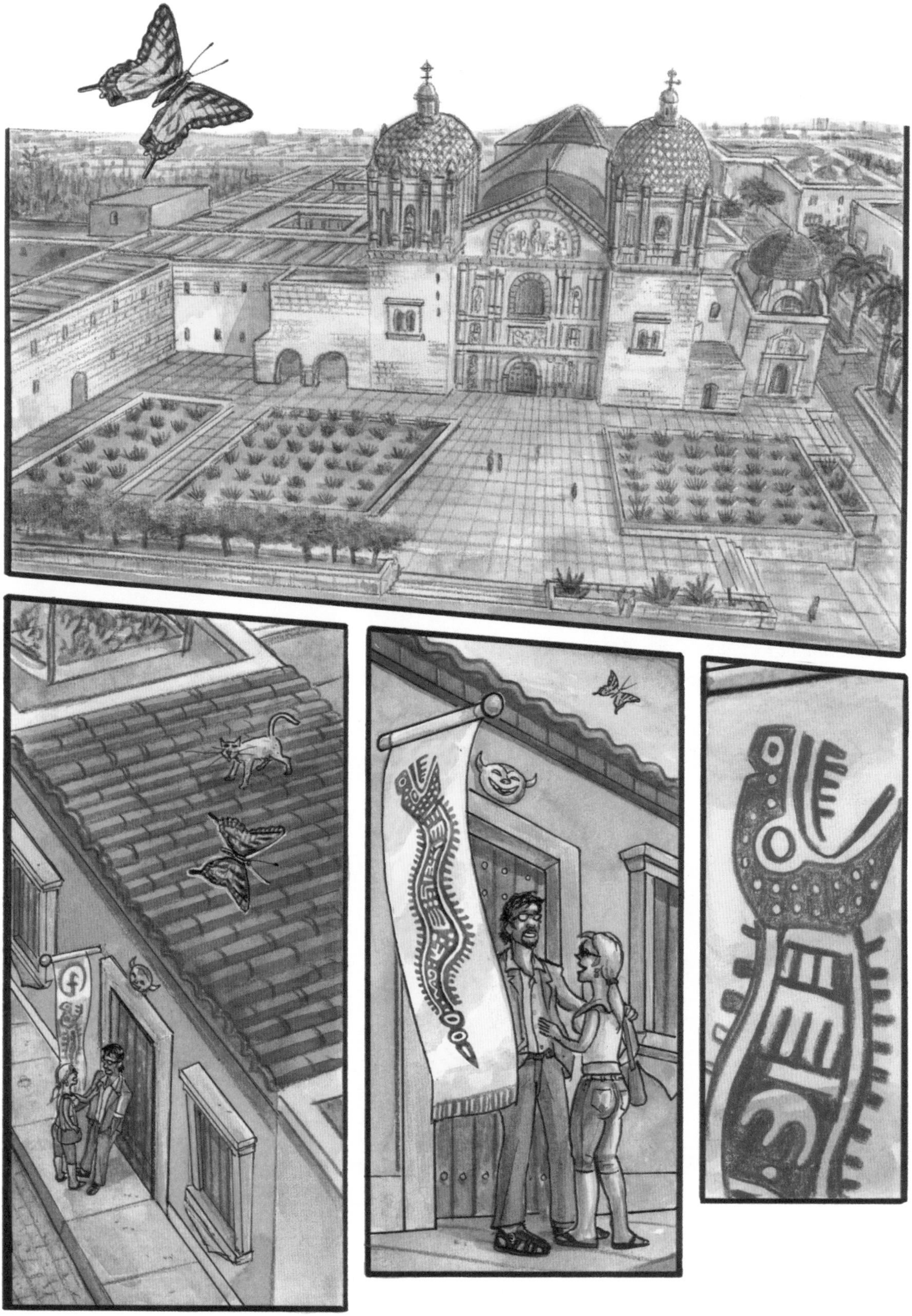

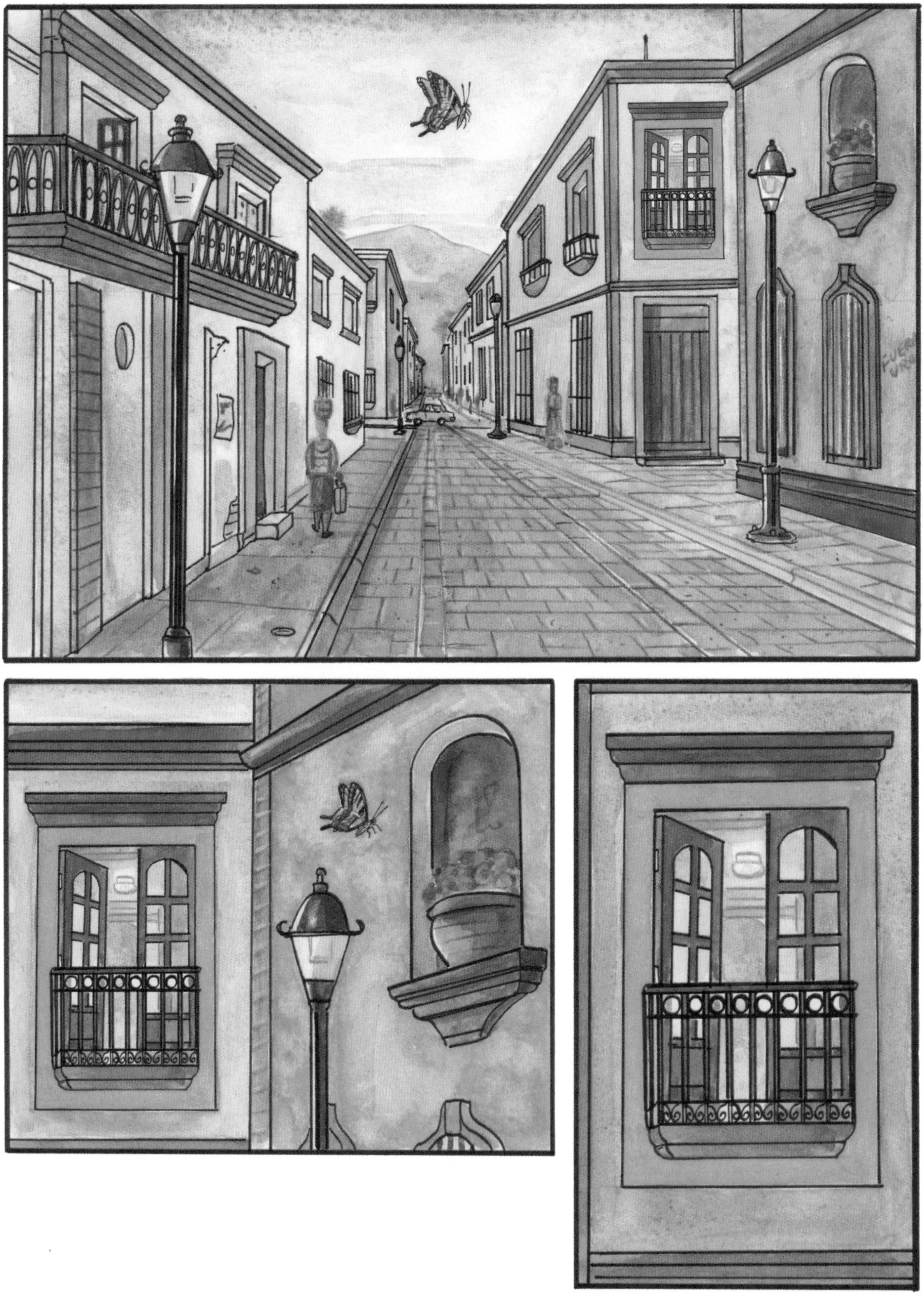

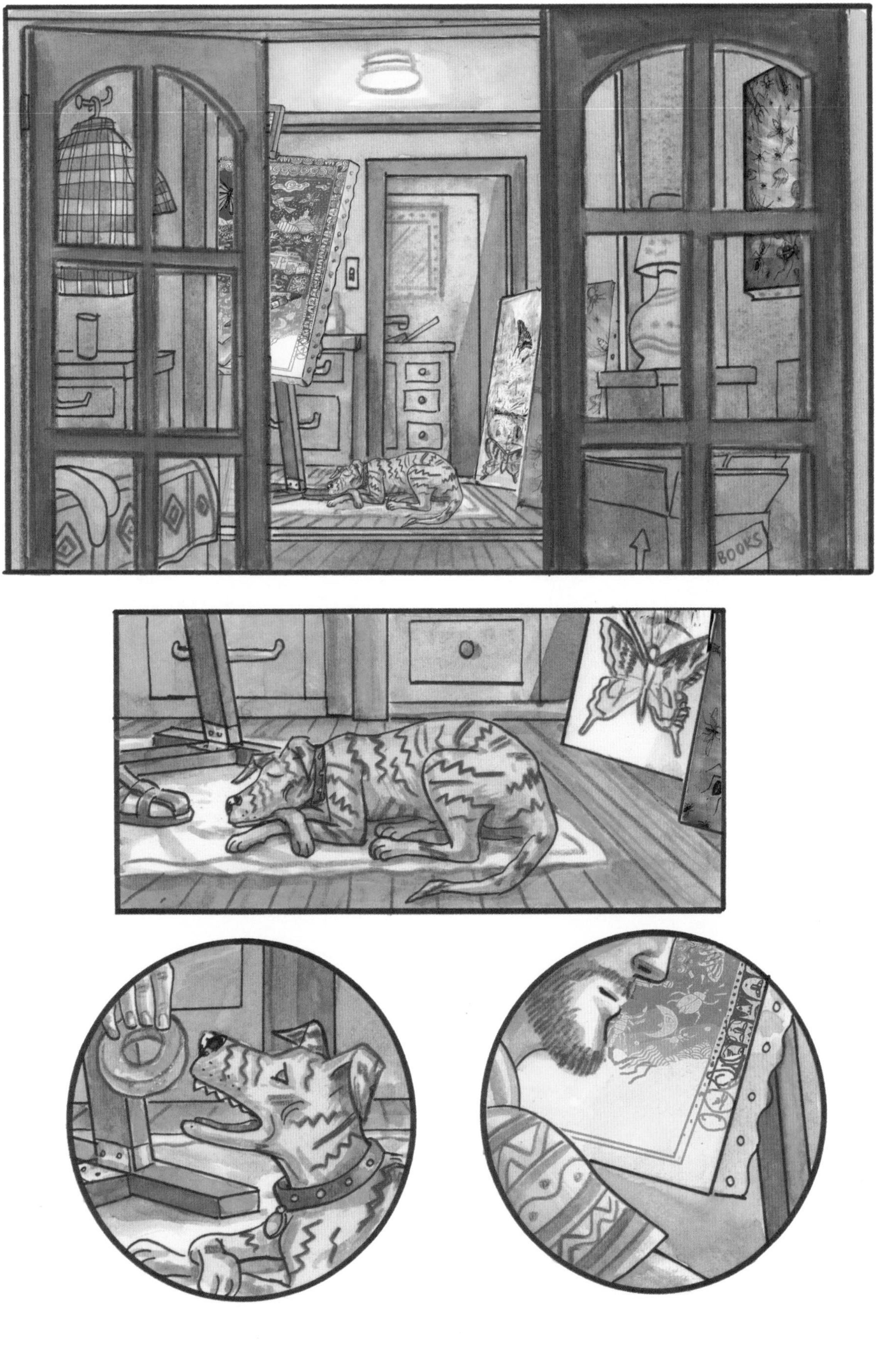
BOOKS

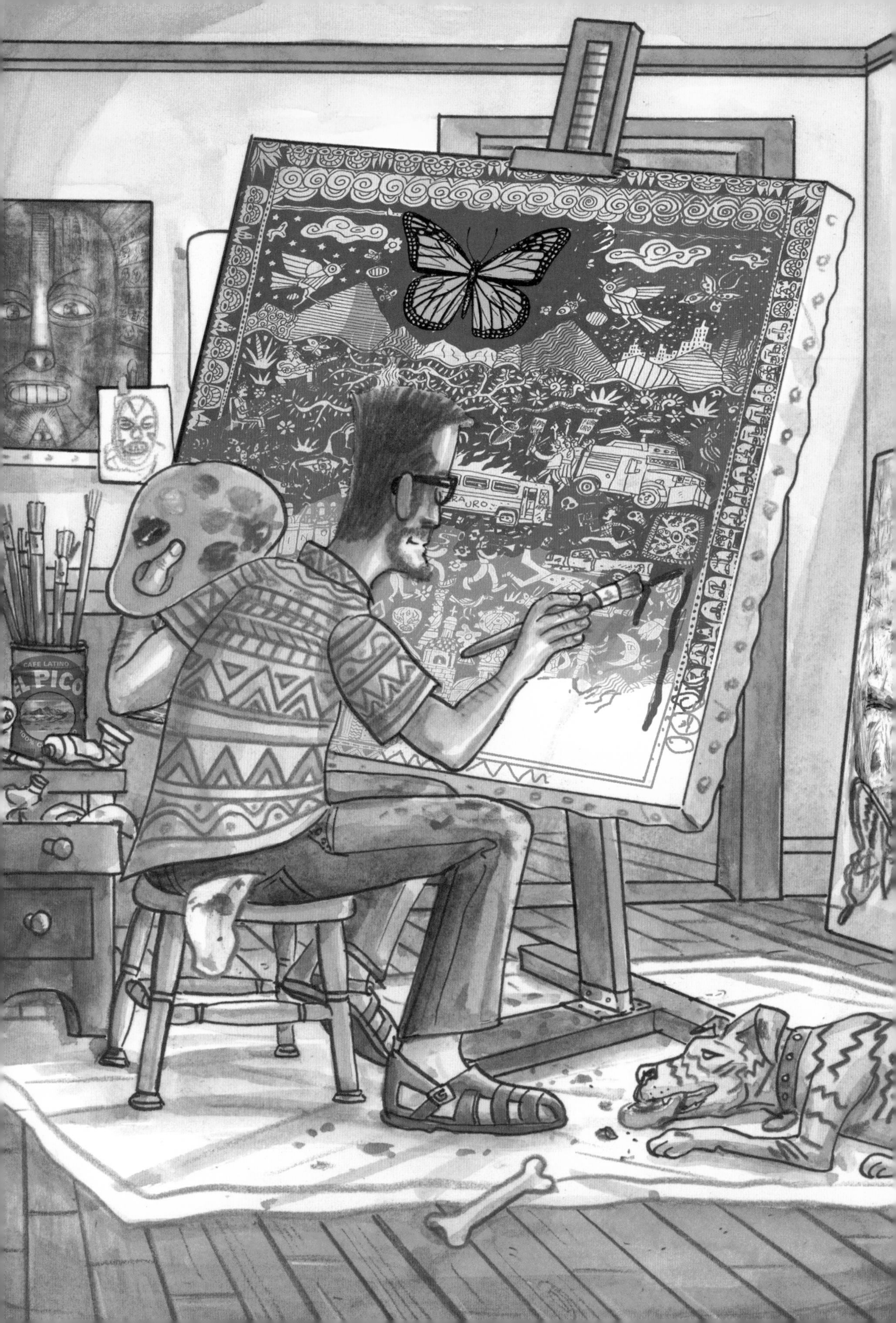
CAFE LATINO
EL PICO

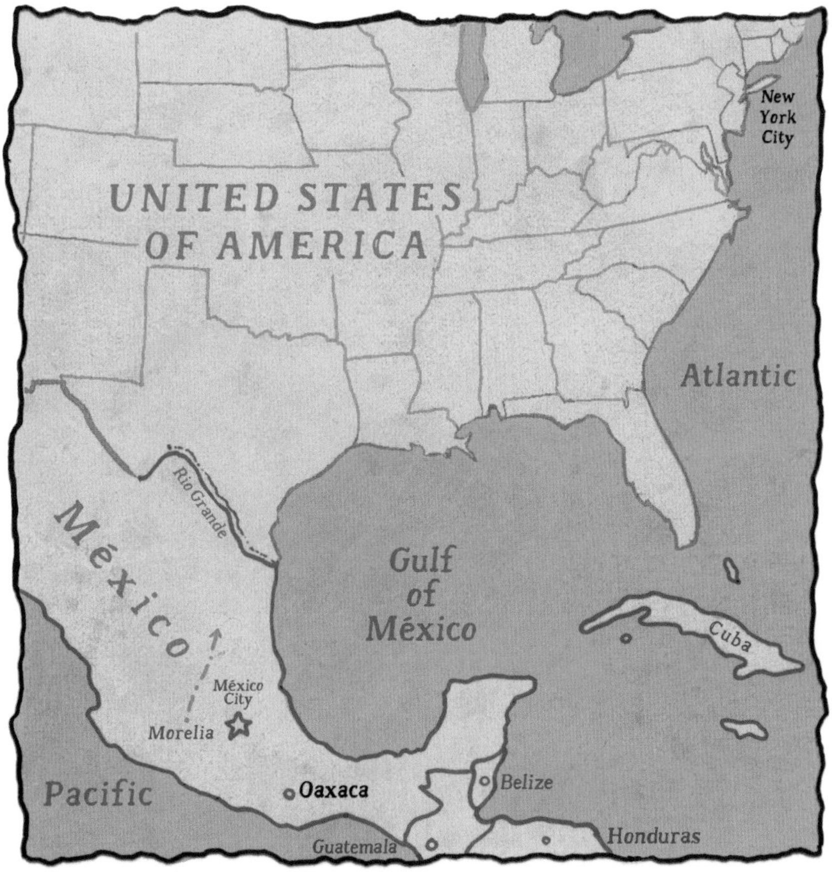
New York City
UNITED STATES OF AMERICA
Atlantic
Rio Grande
México
Gulf of México
Cuba
México City
Morelia
Pacific
Oaxaca
Belize
Guatemala
Honduras

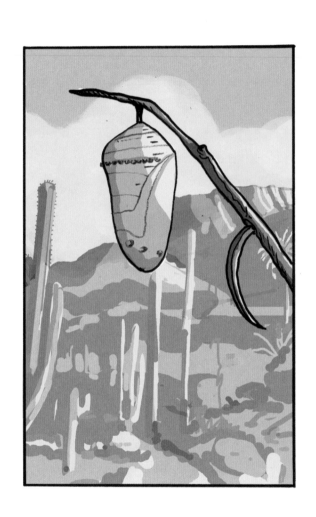

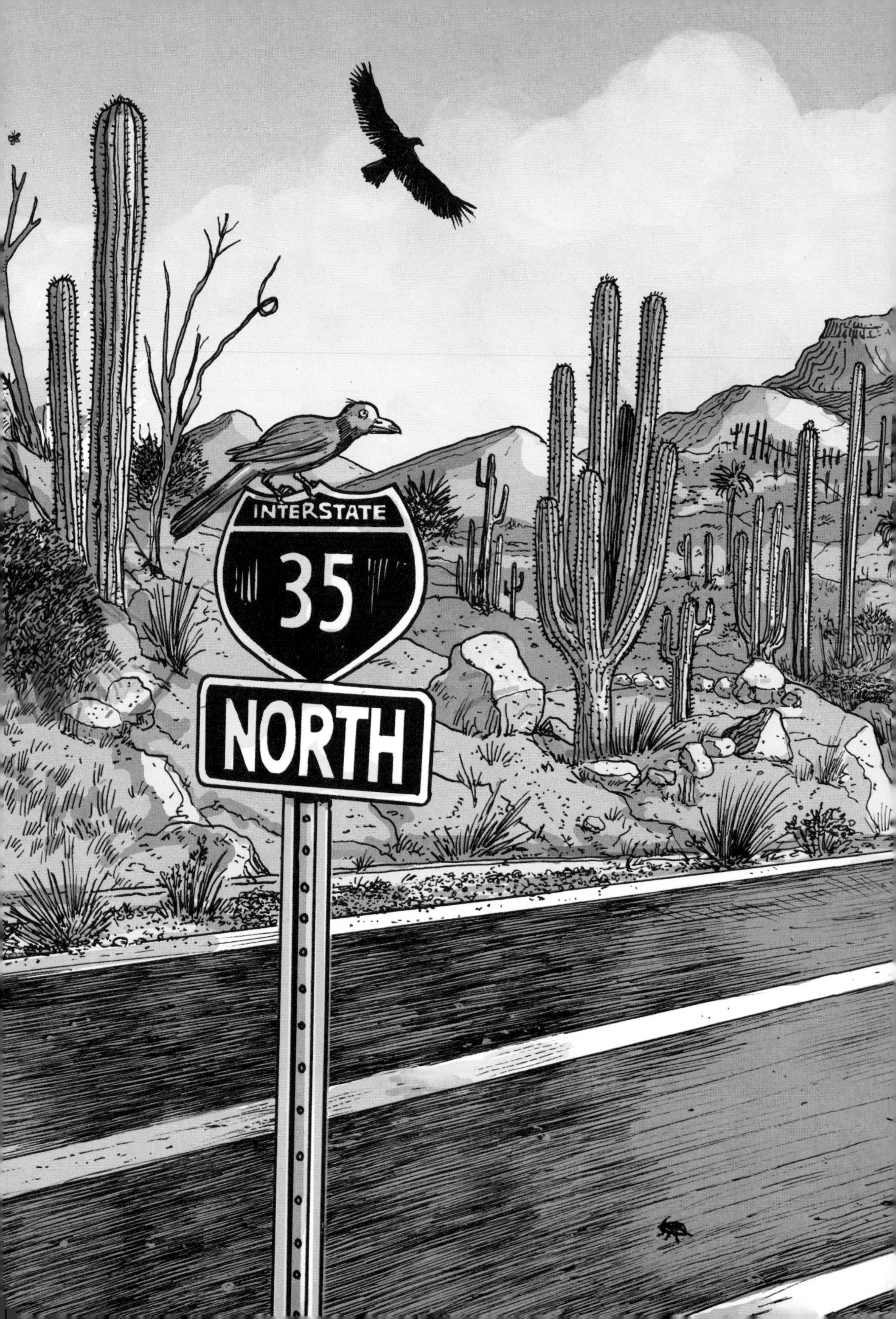
INTERSTATE
35
NORTH

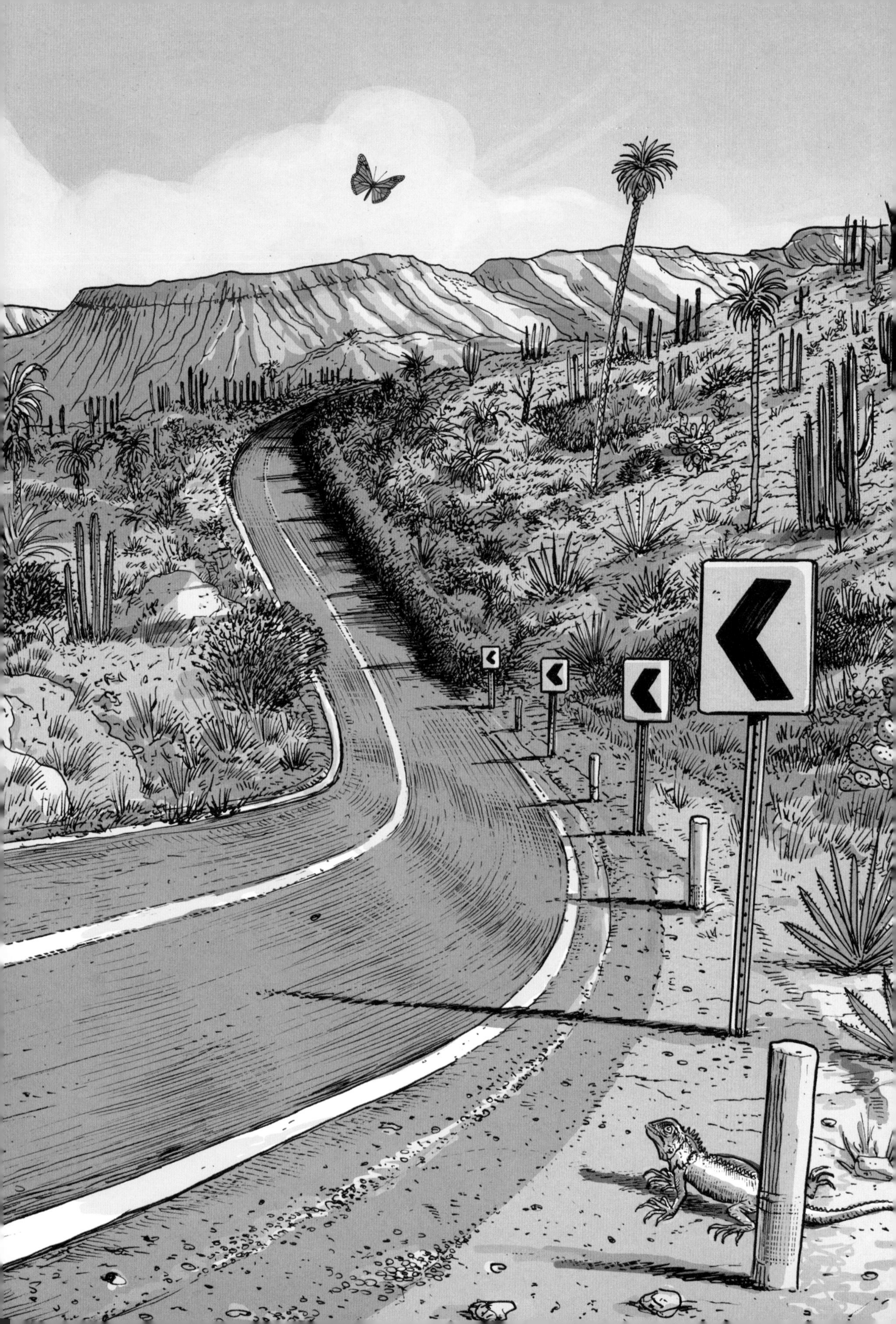

Afterwords

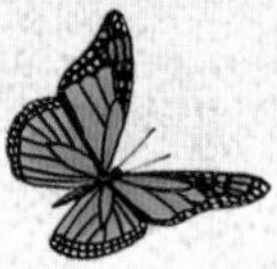

Though *Ruins* is a work of fiction, many aspects of it are inspired by events that occurred during the two years my wife, my daughter and I spent living in Oaxaca from 2006 to 2008.

In 2006, then Governor Ulises Ruíz Ortiz ordered the police to attack the striking teachers in the early morning hours of June 14th. Over the next several months, police clashed with strikers, and a number of union members were wounded or killed. The strike became an international event on October 27th when US journalist Brad Will was killed by undercover police.

The strike was ultimately crushed on November 25th 2006 when federal troops attacked marchers and dismantled the teachers' encampment. Roughly 150 people were incarcerated without trial and some languished in jail for years.

In the end, the governor remained in office for his full six-year term, leaving a trail of corruption and bloodshed as he exited without prosecution. Nonetheless, Oaxaca has survived and flourished under conquistadors past and present, and remains the pearl of Mexico.

To avoid disappointment, should you travel to Oaxaca, note that the VW bug taxi doesn't exist there. For that, you'll have to visit Mexico City. I just found them far more interesting to draw than the Nissan taxis that are prevalent in Oaxaca. Also on the subject of taxis, the last New York City checker cab was retired in 1999.

Hopefully, the artistic license I've taken in *Ruins* won't be revoked.

To serve my story, I've attenuated the monarch migration. Their actual journey from Canada to Mexico (2,000 to 3,000 miles) begins in the fall and lasts a few months. A remarkable aspect of their lifecycle is that while most generations live 3 or 4 weeks, the generation that makes this arduous migration can live up to 9 months. In recent years, the monarch population has been gravely diminished as their habitats disappear. Though the prognosis is dire, there are action steps to be taken, many of which can easily be found through websites like monarchwatch.org.

On another insect note, they say that if you eat the chapulines (fried grasshoppers), you will always return to Oaxaca. I did, and have fulfilled that promise year after year. I highly recommend a visit to that gorgeous, friendly town. Eating the chapulines... well, that's your call.

Ruins is the product of many years of gestation and another several years of applying pencil and pen and ink and watercolor to paper, as well as a bit of computer pixie dust.

I was helped on this journey by many friends along the way.

My greatest appreciation goes to my wife, Betty Russell, and my daughter, Emily, who saw me through the many stages of development and the endless hours ensconced in my studio. I'd also like to thank the following for their invaluable editorial suggestions and enthusiasm: Leslie Schnur, Scott Cunningham, Jim Rasenberger, Emily Russell, Henry Wangeman, Barrett Klein, Kate Kuper, Mercedes Lopez-Zschaemisch, Tony Stonier, Philip Dolin, Molly Bernstein, Ryan Inzana, Ruth Lingford, Deirdre Barrett, Karen Green, Holly Kuper, Rocky Maffit, Seth Tobocman, Judy Hanson, John Thomas, Diego Rabasa, Eduardo Rabasa and Serge Ewenczyk.

For their kind, quotable words: Jules Feiffer, John Vaillant, Mark Moffett and Stephen Buchmann.

For bringing the book to print and helping it migrate into your hands: Emma Hayley, Sam Humphrey, Dan Lockwood and Kate McLauchlan at SelfMadeHero, and the fine people at Abrams ComicArts.

Immense gratitude to the individuals who assisted in the arduous production: Kat Fajardo, Veronica Agarwal, Hilary Allison, Minah Kim and Noah Levy.

And to my many friends in Oaxaca, among them Marietta Bernstorff and Tony Turok, the Olguin family, Fernanda Cuellar and Reynaldo Perez, Peter Graham and Lili Wright, Judith Zur, Sergio Navarrete, Miriam and Luis Shein, Jane and Thorny Robison and Steve Lafler to name but a few.

Author photo by Holly Kuper

Peter Kuper's illustrations and comics have appeared in publications around the world, including *MAD Magazine*, where he has written and illustrated "Spy vs Spy" every issue since 1997. He is the co-founder of *World War 3 Illustrated*, a political comix magazine, and has produced over two dozen books, including *Diario de Oaxaca, The System, Sticks and Stones, Drawn to New York*, and adaptations of many of Franz Kafka's works, including *The Metamorphosis*.
He has been teaching courses in comics at The School of Visual Arts in Manhattan for over 25 years and is a visiting professor at Harvard University.
He lives in New York City with his wife, his daughter and a small black dog.

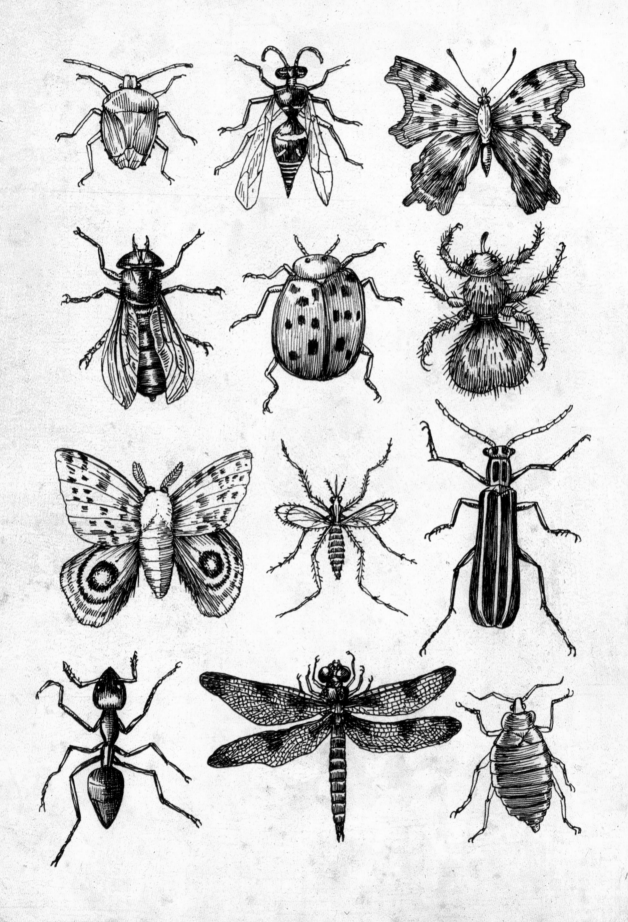